BARRON'S

ACT®

17TH EDITION

George Ehrenhaft, Ed.D.
Former English Department Chairman
Mamaroneck High School, Mamaroneck, New York

Robert L. Lehrman, M.A.
Former Science Department Supervisor
Roslyn High School, Roslyn, New York

Allan Mundsack, M.A.
Professor Emeritus of Mathematics
Los Angeles Pierce College, Los Angeles, California

Fred Obrecht, M.A.
Professor of English
Los Angeles Pierce College, Los Angeles, California

All inquiries should be addressed to:
Barron's Educational Series, Inc.
250 Wireless Boulevard
Hauppauge, New York 11788
www.barronseduc.com

ISBN: 978-1-4380-0097-8 (book)
ISBN: 978-1-4380-7234-0 (book/CD-ROM package)

ISSN: 1942-3942 (book)
ISSN: 1942-4019 (book/CD-ROM package)

PRINTED IN THE UNITED STATES OF AMERICA

9 8 7 6 5 4 3 2 1

Contents

PART 1: PREPARING FOR THE ACT

PART 2: DIAGNOSTIC EXAMINATION

PART 3: TAKING THE ACT

PART 1

PREPARING FOR THE ACT

Introduction

- An Overview of the ACT
- The Four Subject Tests (Plus One That's Optional)
- Boosting Your Scores
- What to Study and What Not to Study
- What Your Test Scores Mean

THE ACT

The ACT is a test required for admission to many colleges. It takes just under 3 hours to complete and consists of multiple-choice questions in English, math, reading, and science. In addition, for students applying to colleges that require or recommend it, the ACT offers an optional writing test consisting of an essay to be written in 30 minutes.

SUBJECT	NUMBER OF QUESTIONS	LENGTH
English	75	45 minutes
Mathematics	60	60 minutes
Reading	40	35 minutes
Science Reasoning	40	35 minutes
Writing (optional)	1 essay	30 minutes

Performance on the ACT is one of the important pieces of information that college admissions people weigh when they decide whether to accept an applicant. Because the ACT is taken by students all over the country, colleges use the scores to compare the achievement and ability of applicants from a great variety of secondary schools. In effect, the exam serves as a common standard for predicting students' success in college courses.

The Optional ACT Writing Test

When registering for the ACT, also register for the ACT Writing Test if it is required or recommended by any colleges to which you are planning to apply. If in doubt, check with the colleges or consult the Writing Test Option on the ACT web site (*www.act.org*) for the names of colleges that do and do not expect you to take the Writing Test. Some colleges will accept the score even though they don't require it. If your list of colleges is still tentative, it makes sense to register for the test. By doing so, you'll pay a higher fee, but you'll also fulfill an admissions requirement for a college that you may apply to in the future. What's more, you'll save the time and expense of retaking the entire ACT in order to write the essay.

Primary Focus of the ACT

To answer most of the questions, you must solve problems, draw conclusions, make inferences, and think analytically. Colleges prefer students who can figure out answers rather than those whose main strength is simply the ability to memorize and recall information.

Remember: The ACT emphasizes *thinking* skills.

PARTS OF THE ACT

English Test

The English Test measures your understanding of the skills needed to write well. In particular, it tests:

Usage and Mechanics		
Punctuation		10 questions
Grammar and Usage		12 questions
Sentence Structure		18 questions
	Total	40
Rhetorical Skills		
Writing Strategy		12 questions
Organization		11 questions
Style		12 questions
	Total	35

Satisfactory performance on the English Test tells a college that you know the conventions of standard grammatical English and that you can punctuate and write complete, carefully structured sentences. The test further assesses your understanding of rhetoric, that is, whether you can tell when a piece of writing is unified, well organized, and consistent in style.

On the English Test you are given five prose passages, each about 325 words. Portions of the passage are underlined and numbered. Most of the questions ask you to decide whether the underlined sections are correct, and, if not, which of four alternative choices is the most appropriate substitute. An item may contain an error in punctuation, sentence structure, or some other aspect of grammar and usage. If all the underlined sections are correct, the choice "NO CHANGE" is the right answer. The remaining questions on the English Test, which ask you to judge the quality of expression, unity, clarity, or overall effectiveness of the writing, refer to passages in their entirety or to selected portions of the text.

For the English Test, the ACT reports a total score in addition to two subscores:

Subscore 1. *Usage/Mechanics*
Subscore 2. *Rhetorical Skills*

If you take the Writing Test, you'll receive an additional score that combines the results of both the English and Writing Tests. This combined English/Writing Test score is a separate number that has no effect on your scores on either the English or Writing Test. Colleges are likely to consider all these scores in their admissions process. Then, they'll use them again to place you in an appropriate English course during your freshman year.

Mathematics Test

The Mathematics Test measures knowledge and understanding of mathematics, in particular:

Pre-Algebra	14 questions
Elementary Algebra	10 questions
Intermediate Algebra	9 questions
Coordinate Geometry	9 questions
Plane Geometry	14 questions
Trigonometry	4 questions

Each of the 60 items presents a mathematical problem to be solved by using algebra, geometry, or trigonometry. This is not a test of your ability to memorize elaborate formulas or perform extensive computations. Accuracy and knowledge of basic formulas are important, but what counts the most are your mathematical reasoning skills.

For each problem, you must pick one of five alternative solutions, one of which may be "None of the above." About half the items on the test are application items that require you to perform a sequence of operations. Another eight items require you to analyze the sequence of operations and conditions of the problem. The remaining problems test your basic mathematical proficiency.

Certain kinds of calculators may be used for the Mathematics Test. If you bring a calculator, be sure you know how to use it. Install fresh batteries so it won't expire during the exam. For more details, turn to "Use of Calculators," page 165, or refer to "ACT's calculator policy" on the ACT web site.

The ACT reports your total score on the Mathematics Test in addition to three subscores:

Subscore 1. *Pre-Algebra/Elementary Algebra*

Subscore 2. *Intermediate Algebra/Coordinate Geometry*

Subscore 3. *Plane Geometry/Trigonometry*

Bring a calculator that you are familiar with to use on the exam.

Subscores reveal your strengths and weaknesses and are often used by college advisors to place you appropriately in college math courses.

Reading Test

The Reading Test measures your ability to understand materials similar to those you'll read in various college courses. The test consists of four passages, each about 750 words, drawn from four different areas of knowledge:

Prose Fiction: novels and short stories	10 questions
Social Studies: anthropology, archaeology, business, economics, education, geography, history, political science, psychology, and sociology	10 questions
Humanities: architecture, art, dance, ethics, film, language, literary criticism, music, philosophy, radio, television, and theater	10 questions
Natural Science: anatomy, astronomy, biology, botany, chemistry, ecology, geology, medicine, meteorology, microbiology, natural history, physiology, physics, technology, and zoology	10 questions

Reading passages are excerpts from books, articles, periodicals, and other publications. Because each passage contains whatever information you need for answering the questions, no additional background or knowledge is required.

To answer the questions correctly, you'll need—among other things—to

- draw inferences from the passages
- find and perceive implications
- determine main ideas
- see cause-effect relationships
- interpret the meaning of words and ideas in the context
- identify the author's intent and method of presentation
- analyze the sequence of events
- identify the significance of selected details
- separate fact from opinion
- evaluate the validity of ideas

In short, to answer all the questions correctly, you need to understand the content and purpose of each passage.

For the Reading Test, the ACT reports a total score as well as two subscores:

Subscore 1. *Arts/Literature*, which measures your performance on the prose fiction and humanities passages.

Subscore 2. *Social Studies/Sciences*, which indicates how well you read the social sciences and natural sciences passages.

A significant difference between subscores could be useful to both you and your college advisor in making decisions about courses and programs of study. A higher subscore in one area, for example, could indicate that your interests and talents lean in a particular direction.

Science Reasoning Test

You don't need to be a scientific genius to do well on the Science Reasoning Test. Why? Because the test doesn't ask you to recall masses of facts that you may have learned in science courses. Rather, it tests your ability to *think* like a scientist. On the test you must answer questions about seven sets of scientific information presented in three formats:

Data Representation: graphs, tables, other schematics	15 questions
Research Summaries: several related experiments	18 questions
Conflicting Viewpoints: alternative interpretations of several related hypotheses or views that are inconsistent with each other	7 questions

TIP

The science reasoning test does not call for any specific information learned in science classes.

The sets of information come from biology, chemistry, physics, and the physical sciences, including earth science, meteorology, astronomy, and space science. Three of the seven groups of questions are presented as graphs, charts, tables, or scientific drawings similar to those found in science journals and texts.

The key word in this test is *reasoning*. About half the questions ask you to determine the accuracy and validity of conclusions and hypotheses based on the information presented. Several other questions require you to generalize from given data by drawing conclusions or making predictions. The remaining questions check your understanding of the information itself. Simple arithmetic or algebra may be necessary to answer some of the questions. Calculators are not permitted on the Science Reasoning Test.

There are no subscores on this test. The ACT reports only the total score based on 40 questions.

Writing Test

The Writing Test is meant to test your ability to plan and compose a clear, concise, and persuasive essay in a relatively short time—30 minutes, to be precise.

In addition, it provides colleges with useful information about how well you can 1) think, 2) organize ideas, 3) express yourself, and 4) use standard English.

- You demonstrate your ability to *think* by writing an essay that reveals a grasp of the assigned topic and the use of relevant ideas and examples to support your point of view. In that sense, the essay offers you an opportunity to present a side of you that is different from the one you have shown in the English section of the ACT.
- Your ability to *organize* can be made clear by the arrangement of material in your essay. Good writers avoid a random sequence. Rather, they plan a succession of ideas that will best convey their thoughts and create the desired effect on their audience.
- You make evident how well you *express yourself* by using the best words in the best order. Having good ideas is not enough. Clearly and confidently articulating those ideas to a reader confirms that you know what you are talking about.
- By writing correctly and using *standard English*, you show a mastery of the language that can take you far in college and beyond.

Choosing a Test Date

Most students take the ACT during the spring of the junior year or at the beginning of the senior year. The date you choose works neither for nor against you in the eyes of college admissions officials.

TIP

For test dates, visit the official ACT web site: *www.act.org*.

If you take the ACT as a junior . . .	If you take the ACT as a senior . . .
1. You'll get a clearer picture of your prospects for admission to the colleges you may be considering. As a result, you can make more realistic college plans.	**1.** You are likely to earn higher scores, because you will have had more courses and more experience.
2. You'll have more opportunities to retake the ACT.* Hoping to improve scores, students often use the time between exams to prepare themselves more thoroughly.	**2.** You will have the opportunity to retake the ACT but with less preparation time between examination dates.
3. You'll have one less thing to worry about during the hectic college application season early in your senior year.	**3.** By taking the September ACT, you can use the score for most early-decision applications, usually due by November 1st. (Note, however, that the September exam is not given in United States territories, Puerto Rico, or Canada.)

*By taking the April, June, or December exam, you can apply for Test Information Release (TIR). For an $18 fee, ACT will send you a complete copy of the test you took along with your answers and an answer key. If you took the Writing Test, you'll also receive a copy of the essay question, a scoring rubric, and the scores assigned by two readers. A photocopy of your actual essay will be added to your TIR for an additional fee.

Your TIR will show you the questions you missed—useful information for preparing to retake the ACT. Also, it's eye-opening to re-read the Writing Test essay you wrote several weeks earlier. In effect, it's like reading it for the first time and you're apt to make surprising discoveries about its strengths and weaknesses.

Ultimately, the date you take the ACT may depend on your college application deadlines. Although most colleges leave the decision to the applicant, some require that you take the ACT at a particular time.

Registering for the ACT

The ACT is given several times a year. The exact dates, times, and testing sites are listed on the ACT web site (*www.act.org*) and in the ACT Register by Mail packet distributed in the college counseling or guidance offices of most high schools.

In light of recent changes in test security protocols, be sure to check the official ACT web site for the most up-to-date information on the documentation you need to register for the test and bring with you on test day.

The registration deadline is typically one month before the exam. Late registration is available any time until about two weeks prior to the test date.

The ACT provides for students with disabilities and for those requiring non-Saturday testing. Provisions can also be made for homebound or confined students and junior high/middle school students. For details and for information about fee waivers and state-funded vouchers, check the ACT Register by Mail packet or the ACT web site, which also offers answers to almost any question under "FAQs" or via a link called "Ask a Question."

TIP 

Since fees can and do change from time to time, it's best to check the official ACT web site for the most current information.

Preparing to Boost Your Score

This book will help you to do your best on the ACT. It guides you step by step through a program of preparation. Ideally, you should have weeks or months to prepare. The more time, the better, but even if your test date is just around the corner, the book contains enough descriptive material, practical test-taking hints, and sample questions to make it worth your while to spend at least a few hours perusing it. In fact, except for starting high school all over again, working methodically through the pages of this book is the best thing you can do to prepare for the ACT.

Each part has a distinct function and purpose:

- **Preparing for the ACT**—Introduces the components of the exam and gets you started
- **Diagnostic Exam**—Helps you assess the present state of your knowledge and skills
- **Taking the ACT**—Prepares you for the multiple-choice tests in English, Math, Reading, and Science Reasoning, and for composing the essay on the ACT Writing Test
- **Model Exams**—Systematically evaluates your growth and progress, using sample examinations to be taken under simulated testing conditions

For the most thorough preparation, start at the beginning of the book and slowly work your way to the end. You'll find much to read, study, and ultimately, master.

In the English section you may need to apply rules of grammar that you learned long ago but have since faded from memory. In math you'll encounter problems the likes of which you may not have seen since freshman year. The reading test will challenge your comprehension of four passages and ask you to infer meaning by reading between the lines. Finally, the science section will pose questions different from any you may have faced before. Unlike the SAT, the ACT is largely a "curriculum-based" test. That is, it focuses on what is typically taught in schools. Therefore, studying *can* and *will* improve your performance.

Here are some of the book's features that students find most useful:

1. Profile of your present academic strengths and weaknesses	Start with the Diagnostic Exam in Part 2. Record the results on the charts at the end of the test. At a glance, you'll know what you do well and what you should concentrate on as you get ready for the ACT.
2. Read the descriptions of what you are expected to know	Each of the four subject areas in Part 3 begins with a complete description of the test in that subject. Preparation is more purposeful when you know what you are preparing for.
3. Adopt a long-range preparation plan	In addition, each subject chapter contains several practical, long-range ideas for sharpening your test-taking skills. See the 6-month and 2- to 3-month study plans explained on pages 12–15.
4. Review skills needed for the English and Mathematics Tests	The English and Math chapters in Part 3 contain review sections to be used for studying and for handy reference while you work on sample questions.
5. Read, read, read	Read high-quality newspaper columnists, op-ed pieces, and editorials, as well as prestigious publications like the *Atlantic* and the *New Yorker.* Reading GAP catalogs, cereal boxes, and *The National Enquirer* won't help.
6. Complete practice exercises using ACT-type questions	Each of the subject chapters offers numerous sample questions with suggestions for finding the right answers. Since all answers are fully explained, you learn as you go.
7. Use the specific recommended techniques for answering ACT questions	In each subject chapter, you'll find test-taking hints for answering questions in that subject. The use of trustworthy test-taking tactics can boost your ACT scores.
8. Practice essay writing	Read Chapter 5, especially the student-written sample essays and critiques. Write an essay at least once a week on suggested topics. If you run out of topics, write on the old ones again. Get used to writing an essay in 30 minutes. Use the unique self-evaluation guide to score the essays that you write for practice.
9. Take model exams under simulated test conditions	Turn to Part 4 and take Model Exam A. Follow the test directions and pace yourself through each of the four sections. As you answer the questions, apply the tactics you learned in this book.
10. Check your growth and progress	When you complete each model exam, check your answers and evaluate your work, using the special performance evaluation chart provided. After further study, take another model exam. Again, check the results to bring your self-assessment up to date.

For each model exam, set aside at least 3 hours, or 3½ hours if you take the Writing Test. By taking all the exams, you'll learn to pace yourself and get to know what to expect on test day.

TIP 

Build ACT preparation time into your daily routine—especially during the weeks before taking the ACT.

Evaluating Your Performance

After taking the diagnostic exam or any of the model exams, use the following four steps—or five steps if you took the Writing Test—to evaluate your performance:

1. **Check your answers.** Use the answer key provided after each exam. Return to each question you missed and try it again. Chances are good that you'll get it right the second time around. To be fair, however, don't count it as a correct answer when you calculate your test score.
2. **Read all the answer explanations**. Don't skip explanations for questions you got right because they often contain helpful insights into shorter or different methods of answering questions. For each question you got wrong, be sure you understand why you made an error. That will help you avoid making a similar mistake in the future.
3. **Calculate your overall test score.** Following each exam you'll find instructions for figuring out your test score. The process will yield several different kinds of scores including raw scores, scale scores, and the composite score—all explained later in this chapter. *Note*: For the Writing Test, you'll get a separate score, not included in determining your overall ACT score.
4. **Rate your performance.** Use the chart below, which shows ranges of raw scores—that is, the number of correct answers on each of the four tests.

Rate Your Performance

Rating	English	Mathematics	Reading	Science Reasoning
Excellent	66–75	54–60	35–40	36–40
Very good	54–65	44–53	29–34	29–35
Above average	45–53	30–43	24–28	20–28
Below average	36–44	21–29	19–23	14–19
Weak	25–35	14–20	14–18	9–13
Poor	0–24	0–13	0–13	0–8

If you get more than 88 to 90 percent of the questions right, your ACT performance rating will be "excellent." Right answers on roughly 72 to 87 percent of the questions yields a "very good" rating. And you'll earn an "above average" rating for correctly answering 60–70 percent of the questions in English, reading, and science, and 50–71 percent of the questions in math.

To boost your score in any area, find the appropriate sections to study in Part 3 of this book. Also, identify the types of questions you got wrong. If you find that you consistently missed certain types, review the relevant sections of Part 3.

5. **Evaluate your essay**. The Writing Test can be scored by using the self-evaluation chart found at the end of each exam. Scores on the essay range from 1 (low) to 6 (high). Evaluating your own essay requires a perspective that is often difficult to achieve immediately after completing the work. It would be advantageous to let the essay cool for a day or more. Then go back to it and examine it with a fresh pair of eyes. An alternative is to let someone else do it—a teacher, counselor, parent, or a trusted friend. Turn to pages 433–434 for more information on how to score essays.
6. To calculate your combined English/Writing Test score, use the table following each of the Essay Self-Assessments in this book.

TEST TAKING: A GUIDE TO HIGH SCORES

All the studying in the world won't mean a thing on test day unless you know how to take the test. Knowing the basics of test taking offers you the chance to score high on the ACT or any other standardized test. Much of what you need to know is common sense. Anyone who has passed through high school knows, for example, that you should answer the question being asked, not a similar question or the one you think ought to be asked. Another common-sense tactic is to check regularly that the numbers on the answer sheet correspond with the numbers of the questions. If you put the answer to #9 in the space for #10, every subsequent answer will be in the wrong place. Don't laugh; it's been done!

As the ACT approaches, students sometimes feel apprehensive. They wonder how they'll perform, and they worry about disappointing themselves and others who may be counting on them. It's normal to feel a bit uneasy about an approaching exam. In fact, some degree of tension can help your performance. With your adrenaline pumping, you can push harder toward the peak of your ability and perhaps turn in the performance of your life. If you're basically a fretter, you obviously have to prepare harder to take the ACT than someone who is blessed with a positive attitude. In the long run, however, some anxiety may work in your favor. In contrast, superconfident test takers need to be wary of stumbling over their attitude.

TIP 

Odd numbered questions have A, B, C, D, E as answer choices. Even questions have F, G, H, J, K.

Many things must be done to reach the most advantageous frame of mind for taking the ACT, the first of which is being well prepared.

Getting Ready for Test Day

Since the ACT concentrates on four subjects found in all schools, most students are well prepared for the exam by the time they reach eleventh or twelfth grade. If you haven't taken a math course recently, however, or if you don't remember your basic English usage, reviewing the appropriate sections of this book will help. However, studying specifically for the Reading Test or the Science Reasoning Test may not be very fruitful. In fact, it's hard to know exactly what material would be worth studying. It would be smart, however, to devote considerable time to taking the practice tests in this book.

Overall familiarity with the ACT not only reduces test anxiety but enhances performance. Self-assurance, the feeling that you will do well, helps too, but be wary of over-confidence. Regardless of how ready you think you are, remember that it's impossible to be too well prepared for the ACT.

Beyond that, being prepared depends partly on knowing what to expect when you open your exam booklet and start to work. For example, you can count on finding a specific set of test directions that do not vary from one exam to the next. Read the directions carefully while taking practice exams, and follow them to the letter. Once you've taken a few exams, the directions are likely to become second nature.

A top priority: Know what to expect when the proctor says "Start!"

Since each section of the ACT is timed literally to the second, pacing is critical. By taking practice exams, you can adjust the rate at which you answer questions. With experience you can learn to set a comfortable pace, neither too fast nor too slow. Then, on test day you'll have one less thing to worry about.

You have a surprisingly large amount of control over the score you'll earn on the ACT. Some control will grow out of the concentration and practice you devote to the lessons in this book. Still more control, though, will develop from your mastery of common sense test-taking tactics. While high scores on college entrance tests come from knowing your material, they also come from knowing yourself and knowing which techniques work best for you. When you take the Reading Test, for example, which should you read first, the passage or the questions? Should you read slowly or quickly? On the English Test, which types of questions do you always get right? Which kind do you stumble over? Are the diagrams on the Science Reasoning Test more comprehensible to you than the charts? Do you coast through algebra problems but get bogged down in trigonometry? The more you know about your personal test-taking style, the better you'll do.

A STUDY PLAN FOR THE ACT

With six or more months to go until test day . . .

- **Pat yourself on the back for having the foresight to start now.** By starting early you're already miles ahead of 90 percent of other test-takers.

- **Schedule a certain number of hours per week—as many as you can afford—for ACT prep.** Logically, the more you study, the higher your ACT score will be. Start with an hour a day four times a week, but be prepared to add hours and days as the exam nears. Every month lengthen each of your study sessions by 15 minutes. After two hours, studying efficiency declines. Rather than fight brain fatigue, add a fifth day to your weekly schedule.

  Build specific hours of ACT study into your routine. In effect, post a DO NOT DISTURB sign that informs friends, family, or whoever that during certain hours each day for the two months prior to the ACT you won't blog, respond to texts, or answer Facebook messages.

- **Write out your study timetable each week.**
  Putting it on paper improves the odds that you'll stick to it.

- **Decide when your brain works best and reserve that time for ACT studying.**
  Make the most of your peak hours. If you're a morning person, set your alarm for an early wake-up. As a night owl—a common trait among teenagers—go to work when the rest of the population goes to bed.

- **Find a quiet, distraction-free place to study.**
  Nothing beats quiet isolation for focusing the mind and being productive. If you must, go to the library, find a park bench, a 24-hour diner, or any other place where you can concentrate.

- **Memorize the ACT's format: a sequence of four tests, the length of each, the number and types of questions, and the optional Writing Test.**
  Test-takers who know what to expect study more efficiently and do better on the exam.

- **Take the Diagnostic Exam under timed, simulated test conditions.**
  Set aside three uninterrupted hours—three and a half if you plan to take the Writing Test. Sit down with a couple of pencils (with erasers), scrap paper, a calculator that works, and a clock or timer. For your convenience, cut the answer sheet out of the book. Don't work on any test for more than the allotted time or start a new test prematurely. Take a ten-minute break before going to work on the Writing Test.

- **After taking the Diagnostic or other tests for practice, check your answers and determine your scores.**
  Read answer explanations for *all* questions, whether you got them right or wrong. Raw scores enable you to target areas for future studying, especially in English and math, which, unlike reading and science, contain specific content that you should know.

- **Focus your study sessions on one subject at a time.**
  Bursts of intense studying in one area pay greater dividends than a scatter-shot approach.

- **While studying, take a five-minute break every 30–40 minutes.**
  A brain needs a chance to rest and recharge.

Sample 4-Day/Week Study Timetable

WEEK 1

Day 1 1 hour ENGLISH	Day 2 1 hour MATH	Day 3 1 Hour READING	Day 4 1 Hour SCIENCE REASONING
Read material on Sentence Structure *Do Warm-Up Drill(s) and Practice Exercises* *Check answers* *Review material related to wrong answers (if time permits)*	*Read material on Prime and Composite Numbers, Prime Factorization, Proper and Improper Fractions, and Mixed Numbers* *Do Warm-Up Drill(s) and Practice Exercises* *Check answers* *Review material related to wrong answers (if time permits)*	*Read material on Test-Taking Tactics* *Practice different tactics on two different reading passages* *Analyze results to see which works better*	*Read material on types of passages on the ACT and on Test Strategies* *Read material on Research Summaries Questions* *Answer Sample Questions* *Do Warm-Up Drill and check answers* *Review material and return to the passage to review incorrect answers (if time permits)*

WEEK 2

Day 1 1 hour ENGLISH	Day 2 1 hour MATH	Day 3 1 Hour READING	Day 4 1 Hour SCIENCE REASONING
Read material on Subject-Verb Agreement *Do Warm-Up Drill(s) and Practice Exercises* *Check answers* *Review material related to wrong answers (if time permits)*	*Read material on Exponents with Fractions and Percents* *Do warm-up drills* *Check answers* *Review material related to wrong answers (if time permits)*	*Read material on Prose Fiction passages* *Answer Sample Questions* *Do Warm-Up Drill* *Check answers and return to passage to review wrong answers (if time permits)*	*Read material on Conflicting Viewpoint Questions* *Answer sample questions and do warm-up drill* *Do Warm-Up Drill and check answers* *Review material and return to the passage to review incorrect answers (if time permits)*

- **Add or subtract time to fit your individual style.**
  Study plans should satisfy you and enable you to notice your progress. If you revise your study plan, be sure it encompasses everything you need to know for the exam.

- **After each study session, give yourself a treat of some kind.**
  You deserve a reward for having stuck to your plan for the day.

With two or more months to go . . .

A span of two or more months gives you plenty of time for a productive trek from the first to the last page of this book. Enroute from beginning to end, do the following:

- **Review the instructions on page 12 for test takers with six months to prepare.**
  These guidelines will serve you well, regardless of the time left before the exam.

- **Prepare a week-by-week study timetable.**
  Copy the timetable on page 13. But start with 90 minutes of study four times weekly instead of 60-minute study sessions. Six weeks before the exam add 15 minutes to each study session. During the last four weeks add still another 15 minutes.

- **As you get underway, read the introductory material in each of the subject chapters.**
  Knowing the content of each chapter will help you target the subjects to focus on. If science and math are your forte, devote more to the English and reading chapters.

- **Take the Diagnostic Exam.**
  Your scores will profile your strengths and weaknesses and help you pinpoint the topics to study most intensely during the weeks ahead. Take the test under the conditions explained earlier—a quiet place, three hours or three and a half if you take the optional Writing Test—and so forth.

- **Skim the sections on subjects you are least concerned about.**
  Don't waste time reviewing what you already know. Focus on what you don't know.

- **Take all the practice exams at the end of the book.**
  It's vital to be familiar with the structure of the ACT and the types of questions found in each test. Equally important is to become adept at pacing yourself through each of the ACT's four parts as well as the Writing Test, if you plan to take it.

With the test just around the corner—two weeks or less . . .

Considering that you're starting from scratch, psyche yourself for some heavy-duty cramming. Three or four hours a day would be best—or more if you can swing it. Here is how this book can help:

- **On the first day read the rest of this chapter, underlining as you go, particularly the sections that describe the structure of the ACT and explain the types of questions found on the exam.**
  Pay particular attention to "Getting Ready for Test Day," "Answering the Questions," and "Using Time Effectively." Familiarizing yourself with the exam may be the single most important step in getting ready.

- **Browse through the entire book.**
  Spend an hour browsing through the book. Stop at the beginning of each chapter for an overview of what to expect on each of the four tests—English, math, reading, and science—and the Writing Test, if you expect to take it. If science and math are your forte, spend more time on the English and reading chapters—or vice-versa.

- **Read all the test-taking tips throughout the book.**
  In just a few words, each tip highlights something to do—or not do—during the exam. If any tip puzzles you, read the accompanying text.

- **Do as many warm-up drills and practice exercises as you can.**
  Drills and exercises contain ACT-type questions. They also explain how to choose the correct answers. In short, they illustrate the thought processes you need in order to answer various types of questions.

- **Take the diagnostic exam plus at least two practice tests (the more, the better)—probably the most important thing you can do.**
  Take each test as though it were the real thing. Find a quiet place where you won't be interrupted for at least three hours. Before starting, cut an answer sheet from this book. Have on hand two #2 pencils with erasers, scrap paper, a calculator that works, and a clock or timer. Stick to the time limits for each test. If you take the Writing Test, give yourself a ten-minute break after the first three hours. Then go to work on the essay, using a pencil and standard 8½ × 11 lined composition paper.

- **After each exam, check your answers, read the answer explanations, and calculate your scores.**
  Read answer explanations for all questions, whether you got them right or wrong. Raw scores enable you to identify areas to study intensively, especially in English and math, which, unlike reading and science, contain specific content that you should know.

- **Use whatever time remains to study your weakest subject.**

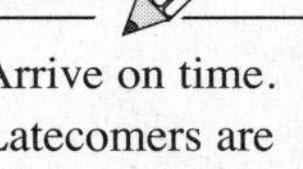

TIP

Arrive on time. Latecomers are not admitted.

On Test Day

Let common sense be your guide on test day. After a good night's sleep, get up early, eat a hearty breakfast, and arrive at the test site by 8:00 A.M. Arrive even earlier if you are not familiar with the location. At most testing sites students taking the ACT plus the ACT Writing Test will be assigned to a different room from those taking only the ACT. Be sure you go to the room reserved for the test for which you have registered.

If the weather is terrible, listen to the radio station that ordinarily carries school announcements. A postponed exam will be rescheduled. The new date and time will be mailed to you.

On the day of the test, bring with you:

1. Your ACT ticket of admission.
2. Three or more sharpened #2 pencils with erasers. If you are taking the Writing Test, toss a couple of extra pencils into your backpack.
3. Proper identification. In light of recent test security procedures, be sure to check the official ACT web site for what documentation you'll need to gain entry to the testing site. Otherwise, you may be turned away.

4. Calculators (optional). Although all math problems can be solved without a calculator, you may use one if you wish. Only certain calculators are authorized, however. See "Permitted and Prohibited Calculators" on the ACT web site (*www.actstudent.org*) or Chapter 2 for details. Don't bring a pocket organizer, tablet, writing pad, handheld or laptop computer, a calculator built into a cell phone, or any other non-approved electronic communication device. To be safe, put extra batteries in your pocket so you won't be stuck with a dead calculator halfway through the test.

5. Candy or gum, if you feel the need. (Eating snacks or anything more substantial is not permitted during the examination.)

   Be considerate of others: Avoid noisy wrappers and bubble-popping. Leave at home:
   - Books, notebooks, dictionaries, scrap paper.
   - iPods, smart phones, pagers, and all other digital communications devices.
   - Noisy jewelry, including watches that beep.

At the test site, stake out the room before you sit down. In a classroom, choose a seat away from the proctor's desk and away from any other place in the room where there may be distracting activity during the test, such as a water fountain. The same holds true for a gym or cafeteria; pick a seat away from potential distractions, as far as possible from the flow of traffic.

Wear something comfortable. On an unseasonable Saturday, test sites may be too hot or too cold, so dress for any eventuality. Following the first two tests, you'll be given a short break, but you won't be permitted to leave the building or the room without the proctor's permission. If you are taking the Writing Test, you'll have another break after the multiple-choice sections. Use the time-out to relax and to sharpen your pencils.

ROLE OF THE PROCTOR

Throughout the exam, listen attentively to the proctors' announcements. Proctors will distribute test materials, instruct you in test procedures, show you how to fill out the answer sheet, and answer administrative questions. They will also keep order in the exam room, and tell you when to start and stop work. The proctors must also prevent cheating. If proctors suspect that you are giving or receiving help, they'll dismiss you from the room and your test won't be scored. You'll also be dismissed for starting work before the test officially begins, for ignoring the proctor's command to stop work, for using an unauthorized calculator, for taking test material from the room, and for a host of other infractions that ACT authorities describe as "unruly," "confrontational," and "threatening." In other words, be cool and don't do anything that you'll regret later.

Do nothing that might be construed as cheating.

If you need assistance during the exam, raise your hand to summon a proctor. Don't talk to anyone else, and don't leave your seat without a proctor's permission.

Answering the Questions

Regardless of how quickly you like to work, read every word of every question. Don't read the first few words of the question. This habit is dangerous. Beware particularly of the presence of absolute words and phrases like *always, never, all of the following EXCEPT* ... and so on. Take such words seriously. A question containing an absolute demands a response that is absolute, too. However, questions that use such words as *mostly, usually,* and *generally* require a judgment call based on evidence you are given.

If a question stumps you, don't panic and don't let it slow you down. Mark it with your pencil and go on to questions that you can answer more easily. Later, come back to it. If you still can't come up with a decent answer, guess. You may get it right, and there is no penalty if you miss it. If you are revisiting several knotty questions, keep up your pace; don't use up all your time trying to unravel just one or two.

Dawdling over a stubborn question is never a good idea.

FOUR ANSWER CHOICES

For each question on the English, Reading, and Science Reasoning Tests, you are given four possible answers, and your task is to choose the best one. Sometimes a choice is partly true. For example, one answer to a reading question may be valid for only part of the reading passage. A better choice would be the answer that pertains to the whole passage. Therefore, it is very important to read all the choices before making your decision. Experts in testing say that the most obvious choice on a difficult question is usually wrong. Consequently, you should *look* for the answer that is most obvious, but you must not discount it as a possibility.

FIVE ANSWER CHOICES

Each problem on the Mathematics Test offers five possible answers. You have to choose the only correct one. Before making a choice try to predict the approximate answer. Then scan the choices to see which one comes closest to your prediction. The best choice may be the one you predict. Nevertheless, you should work out the solution to the problem in the space provided in the test booklet. If your solution fails to correspond with any of the choices, pick "None of these" as your answer. But double-check your calculations as well as the question itself, especially if your answer differs radically from any of the choices. If you plan to use a calculator, make sure it's working properly and is set in the correct mode.

You don't lose credit for a wrong answer, and you may make a lucky guess. Before you resort to guessing, though, try to eliminate any outrageous choices. By discarding one choice that you know is way off the mark, the chances of hitting the jackpot are one in three. By eliminating two wrong answers, they jump to fifty-fifty—pretty decent odds in any circumstances.

Answer every question. There is no penalty for guessing.

To complete an item, fill in the oval on your answer sheet that corresponds with the answer you've chosen. If you change your mind later, be sure to erase your original answer completely. While working on any of the tests, you may write in the exam booklet. Since there are no restrictions, you may underline, cross out, make any marks you wish.

Using Time Effectively

Each test on the ACT lasts a prescribed length of time. Once a test is over, you may not return to it. Nor are you permitted to work on a test that has not yet officially begun. After the first two tests, you'll have a 10- to 15-minute break.

To do your best on the ACT, it's useful to know approximately how much time you have to work on each problem or question. With practice, you will soon begin to sense whether you are working at a rate that will allow you to finish each test within its time limit.

TIP

It is faster to blacken the ovals on the answer sheet from the center outward than from the perimeter to the center. Try it.

TEST	CONTENT	LENGTH OF TIME PER QUESTION	COMMENTS
English 75 questions	5 passages, 15 questions each	30 seconds	Easy questions should take only a few seconds.
Mathematics 60 questions	Questions generally increase in difficulty from beginning to end.	Less than 60 seconds except for the hard ones	Spend as little time as possible on the easy questions to allow more time for the harder ones.
Reading 40 questions	4 passages, 10 questions each	3–4 minutes per passage, 4 minutes for 10 questions or about 25 seconds per question	Some passages may take more or less time to completely master.
Science Reasoning 40 questions	7 sets of questions with 5 to 7 questions per set; questions within a set often increase in difficulty	2 minutes per passage, 30 seconds for each question	Try to spend less than 5 minutes on the easier questions, allowing more time for the harder ones.
Essay	1 essay question	30 minutes	5–8 minutes planning time 15–20 minutes writing 5–8 minutes proofreading and editing

The periods of time allowed for each test are sufficient for almost every student to finish, although some students report having a problem finishing the reading and science sections. To answer all the questions, however, you must work deliberately. If you finish a test before the time is up, check your answers, especially those that you're unsure about. Make sure that you've blackened only one oval for each question. If time is about to be called and you haven't finished the test, don't panic. Just fill in answers at random on your answer sheet. A lucky guess or two will raise your score.

Just before test day, reread these pages. Knowing just what to expect and how to make the best use of the allotted time will work to your advantage during the exam.

AFTER THE TEST

About two and a half weeks after the test, scores are posted online. Writing Test scores are mailed about two weeks after that along with a printout of scores for all the multiple-choice questions. (Your scores will also be sent to your high school and to the colleges you designated on your ACT registration.) If you have questions or concerns about ACT test results, go to "Ask a Question" on the ACT web site.

To calculate test scores, the ACT uses the following procedure:

1. First, the ACT counts the number of questions you got right on each of the four multiple-choice tests. These are called *raw scores*. (No points are deducted for incorrect answers or unanswered questions—the reason that guessing is encouraged.)

2. The four raw scores are then converted to *scale scores* ranging from 1 (low) to 36 (high). Scale scores are averaged and rounded to the nearest whole number to give you a *composite score*—the score that you're most likely to utter when asked, "Hey, what did you get on the ACT?"

   Scale scores also provide evidence of your readiness for college work. The ACT has correlated certain minimum scale scores—called *benchmark* scores—with grades earned by college freshmen in selected courses.

   For example, a scale score of 22 on the ACT math test is the benchmark for a 50 percent chance of your earning a B or higher in a college algebra course. It's also the benchmark for a 75 percent chance of a C or higher. The same odds apply to the benchmark scores on other ACT tests:

Test	Benchmark Score	College Course
English	18	College Composition
Reading	21	Social Sciences/Humanities
Science	24	Biology

   In 2011 only 25 percent of ACT test-takers met or exceeded all four benchmark scores. On individual tests, 66 percent met or surpassed the English benchmark score. On the reading test, 52 percent met or exceeded the benchmark score. On the math test, 45 percent, and in science, 30 percent.

   Unfortunately, there are no statistics on the success rates of students who used this book to prepare for the ACT, but we expect the overall results to be a great deal higher.

TIP 

After taking the ACT twice, it is unusual for scores to rise high enough the third time to make a significant difference to a college.

3. In addition to a composite score and a scale score for each of the four tests, you'll receive *subscores* in English, math, and reading—12 subscores in all. No direct arithmetical relationship exists between subscores and individual test scores. In other words, the test scores in each subject are *not* the sum of the subscores. At best, the subscores will give you a general idea of your strengths and weaknesses in each academic area. A high subscore in algebra and a poor one in geometry, for instance, contains the message that you ought to immerse yourself for a while in the geometry section of this book.

4. If you took the ACT Writing Test, you'll get two additional scores: a Writing Test subscore reported on a scale of 2 (low) to 12 (high) and a combined English/Writing score reported on a scale of 1 to 36. The combined English/Writing score is calculated using weighted numbers. That is, the English test counts as two-thirds of the total, and the essay counts one-third. (Note: Your score on the multiple-choice English test will remain the same whether or not you took the Writing Test.)

   Along with these numerical results you'll also find a comment or two about your essay from the ACT readers. For a fee you can also arrange for a copy of the essay itself to be made available to your high school and to the colleges you listed on your ACT registration form.

COMPOSITE SCORES AND COLLEGE ENROLLMENT

Although ACT will shower you with scores of many kinds, the one score that seems to matter most is the composite score, the number that presumably indicates whether you'll qualify for admission to certain colleges or universities—or by implication, tells you that you have what it takes to do the work there. The ACT, however, advises you not to jump to any conclusions based on your composite score. In other words, don't overinterpret that score because no single test can measure your skills and the state of your knowledge with absolute precision.

Indeed, neither a very high nor very low ACT score will make or break an application for admission. While important, the score is just one of several criteria that admissions officials consider when making decisions about an applicant.

Let's say your composite score is 24. While a 24 may well keep you out of colleges that prefer 32s, there are always exceptions. The table on page 21, adapted from a study by the National Center for Educational Statistics, lists composite scores for the middle 50 percent of freshmen recently enrolled in a variety of institutions—from large state universities to small private colleges. For each college, you'll find two numbers. The higher one, in a column marked "75th Percentile," tells you that 75 percent of the freshman in the sample group earned an ACT composite score equal to or lower than the listed number. Similarly, the figure in the "25th Percentile" column indicates that 25 percent of the freshman in the sample group got composite scores equal to or less than the listed number. (To put it another way, 25 percent of the freshmen in the first group scored higher than the number listed, and 75 percent in the second group earned a score higher than the listed number.)

A complete list of colleges lies beyond the scope of this book, but if you expect to apply to an institution not listed on page 21, go to that college's web site and study its admissions standards. Look in particular at the average ACT score of its most recent freshman class. Based on that information, you may want to aim for more competitive or for less competitive colleges. Or you may decide to retake the ACT with the hope of improving your score.

Theoretically, you can take the ACT as often as you like, up to seven times—if you have the stomach for it. Years of experience show over half the students (about 57 percent) who've taken the ACT more than once raised their scores, but 22 percent did worse, and the scores of 21 percent stayed about the same.

How Colleges Use ACT Scores

Although ACT scores are used primarily for admissions, they are sometimes used to place freshmen in remedial, regular, or advanced courses. A college advisor may also use ACT scores to help you choose a major, schedule a realistic course load, pick extracurricular activities, define educational and career goals, and avoid a variety of potential academic problems. Based on the scores, you may also be eligible for certain scholarships or part-time campus jobs.

A Little Perspective

For better or worse, ACT scores affect you and your college plans. Like so many other matters that need your attention during junior and senior year, taking the ACT is one of the rites of passage between childhood and adulthood. To become familiar with the ins and outs of the ACT takes lots of effort and many hours of your time. Maybe you're already suffering from information overload—and we're only in the first chapter of this book. What's more, you should definitely check out the ACT web site. It contains many more details about every aspect of the ACT and will probably address every one of your concerns and questions, even those you didn't know you had.

It's normal to feel stressed, perhaps even overwhelmed, by the challenges of applying to college, keeping up your grades, and maintaining some sort of balance between work and play. Remember, though, that millions of students before you have met these challenges successfully. You can, too, particularly if you don't allow the experience to get you down. Grit your teeth if you must; be cheerful if you can.

College or University	**Composite ACT Scores** *(middle 50% of enrolled freshmen)* *75th Percentile*	*25th Percentile*
Amherst	34	29
Brown	34	29
Bryn Mawr	31	27
Carleton	33	29
Carnegie Mellon	33	29
Clemson	30	25
Colby	31	28
Colgate	32	29
Columbia	34	29
Connecticut	28	24
Cornell	33	29
Dartmouth	34	29
Davidson	32	28
Delaware	29	24
Denison	30	25
Dickinson	31	26
Duke	34	29
Emory	33	29
Florida	30	25
Georgetown	32	28
Georgia	29	25
Georgia Tech	31	27
Gettysburg	30	27
Grinnell	32	29
Hamilton	31	26
Harvard	34	31
Illinois Urbana/Champaign	31	26
Indiana	29	23
James Madison	26	22
Johns Hopkins	33	29
Kenyon	32	28
Lafayette	30	26
Macalester	32	28
Michigan	31	27
Middlebury	32	29
Minnesota	29	24
Minnesota-Morris	28	23

College or University	**Composite ACT Scores** *(middle 50% of enrolled freshmen)* *75th Percentile*	*25th Percentile*
Northwestern	34	30
Notre Dame	34	31
Oberlin	32	27
Ohio State	30	25
Penn State	28	24
Pitt	30	24
Pomona	34	29
Reed	33	29
Rice	34	30
Stanford	34	30
SUNY Binghamton	29	25
SUNY Geneseo	30	28
Swarthmore	33	27
Texas	30	24
Texas A&M	29	23
UCal Berkeley	32	26
UCal Davis	27	21
UCal Irvine	27	22
UCLA	31	24
UCal Merced	24	18
UCal Santa Barbara	28	23
UChicago	33	28
UNC Asheville	27	21
UNC Chapel Hill	31	28
UPenn	34	30
UVirginia	32	28
UWashington	29	23
UWisconsin	30	26
Vanderbilt	33	30
Vassar	32	29
Washington and Lee	31	28
Washington U	34	31
Wellesley	33	29
Wesleyan	33	29
Whitman	31	27
William and Mary	32	27
Williams	33	29
Yale	34	30

PART 2

DIAGNOSTIC EXAMINATION

Dress Rehearsal for the ACT

- Taking a Full-Length ACT
- Analyzing Your Answers
- What Your Answers Can Teach You
- How to Score Your Writing Test Essay
- What the Numbers Tell You
- Calculating Your ACT Scores

The purpose of this Diagnostic Examination is to help you identify your strengths and weaknesses. You should take the examination under simulated testing conditions and allow 2 hours and 55 minutes to answer the multiple-choice questions. Each of the tests should be taken within the time limit stated at the beginning of that test. Mark your answers directly on the Answer Sheet.

If you plan to take the ACT Writing Test, set aside an additional thirty minutes. Write your essay in pencil on the lined pages. Add extra sheets if necessary.

When you finish the entire examination, check your answers with the Answer Keys and fill in the Analysis Chart for each test. Rate your total score on each specific test by using the Performance Evaluation Chart on page 10. Then, carefully read the Answer Explanations. Pay particular attention to the explanations for questions you got wrong, but don't skip over those for questions you got right; you may pick up some shortcuts or alternative methods.

You can assess your strengths and weaknesses by examining the Question Analysis Charts. Your total scores and ratings indicate your overall performance on the individual tests. The subscores in the last column show how you did on specific passage types or content topics. Special attention should be given to weak areas when you review and do practice exercises in Part 3. If you write the essay, complete the self-evaluation guide, or better still, find an objective reader, preferably someone who knows about essay writing, to assess your work.

Now you are ready to take the Diagnostic Examination. Find a quiet room, take out your pencils, detach the Answer Sheet, check your watch, and begin.

Answer Sheet

DIAGNOSTIC TEST

Test 1

1 A B C D
2 F G H J
3 A B C D
4 F G H J
5 A B C D
6 F G H J
7 A B C D
8 F G H J
9 A B C D
10 F G H J
11 A B C D
12 F G H J
13 A B C D
14 F G H J
15 A B C D
16 F G H J
17 A B C D
18 F G H J
19 A B C D
20 F G H J
21 A B C D
22 F G H J
23 A B C D
24 F G H J
25 A B C D
26 F G H J
27 A B C D
28 F G H J
29 A B C D
30 F G H J
31 A B C D
32 F G H J
33 A B C D
34 F G H J
35 A B C D
36 F G H J
37 A B C D
38 F G H J
39 A B C D
40 F G H J
41 A B C D
42 F G H J
43 A B C D
44 F G H J
45 A B C D
46 F G H J
47 A B C D
48 F G H J
49 A B C D
50 F G H J
51 A B C D
52 F G H J
53 A B C D
54 F G H J
55 A B C D
56 F G H J
57 A B C D
58 F G H J
59 A B C D
60 F G H J
61 A B C D
62 F G H J
63 A B C D
64 F G H J
65 A B C D
66 F G H J
67 A B C D
68 F G H J
69 A B C D
70 F G H J
71 A B C D
72 F G H J
73 A B C D
74 F G H J
75 A B C D

Test 2

1 A B C D E
2 F G H J K
3 A B C D E
4 F G H J K
5 A B C D E
6 F G H J K
7 A B C D E
8 F G H J K
9 A B C D E
10 F G H J K
11 A B C D E
12 F G H J K
13 A B C D E
14 F G H J K
15 A B C D E
16 F G H J K
17 A B C D E
18 F G H J K
19 A B C D E
20 F G H J K
21 A B C D E
22 F G H J K
23 A B C D E
24 F G H J K
25 A B C D E
26 F G H J K
27 A B C D E
28 F G H J K
29 A B C D E
30 F G H J K
31 A B C D E
32 F G H J K
33 A B C D E
34 F G H J K
35 A B C D E
36 F G H J K
37 A B C D E
38 F G H J K
39 A B C D E
40 F G H J K
41 A B C D E
42 F G H J K
43 A B C D E
44 F G H J K
45 A B C D E
46 F G H J K
47 A B C D E
48 F G H J K
49 A B C D E
50 F G H J K
51 A B C D E
52 F G H J K
53 A B C D E
54 F G H J K
55 A B C D E
56 F G H J K
57 A B C D E
58 F G H J K
59 A B C D E
60 F G H J K

Answer Sheet

DIAGNOSTIC TEST

Test 3

1 Ⓐ Ⓑ Ⓒ Ⓓ	11 Ⓐ Ⓑ Ⓒ Ⓓ	21 Ⓐ Ⓑ Ⓒ Ⓓ	31 Ⓐ Ⓑ Ⓒ Ⓓ
2 Ⓕ Ⓖ Ⓗ Ⓙ	12 Ⓕ Ⓖ Ⓗ Ⓙ	22 Ⓕ Ⓖ Ⓗ Ⓙ	32 Ⓕ Ⓖ Ⓗ Ⓙ
3 Ⓐ Ⓑ Ⓒ Ⓓ	13 Ⓐ Ⓑ Ⓒ Ⓓ	23 Ⓐ Ⓑ Ⓒ Ⓓ	33 Ⓐ Ⓑ Ⓒ Ⓓ
4 Ⓕ Ⓖ Ⓗ Ⓙ	14 Ⓕ Ⓖ Ⓗ Ⓙ	24 Ⓕ Ⓖ Ⓗ Ⓙ	34 Ⓕ Ⓖ Ⓗ Ⓙ
5 Ⓐ Ⓑ Ⓒ Ⓓ	15 Ⓐ Ⓑ Ⓒ Ⓓ	25 Ⓐ Ⓑ Ⓒ Ⓓ	35 Ⓐ Ⓑ Ⓒ Ⓓ
6 Ⓕ Ⓖ Ⓗ Ⓙ	16 Ⓕ Ⓖ Ⓗ Ⓙ	26 Ⓕ Ⓖ Ⓗ Ⓙ	36 Ⓕ Ⓖ Ⓗ Ⓙ
7 Ⓐ Ⓑ Ⓒ Ⓓ	17 Ⓐ Ⓑ Ⓒ Ⓓ	27 Ⓐ Ⓑ Ⓒ Ⓓ	37 Ⓐ Ⓑ Ⓒ Ⓓ
8 Ⓕ Ⓖ Ⓗ Ⓙ	18 Ⓕ Ⓖ Ⓗ Ⓙ	28 Ⓕ Ⓖ Ⓗ Ⓙ	38 Ⓕ Ⓖ Ⓗ Ⓙ
9 Ⓐ Ⓑ Ⓒ Ⓓ	19 Ⓐ Ⓑ Ⓒ Ⓓ	29 Ⓐ Ⓑ Ⓒ Ⓓ	39 Ⓐ Ⓑ Ⓒ Ⓓ
10 Ⓕ Ⓖ Ⓗ Ⓙ	20 Ⓕ Ⓖ Ⓗ Ⓙ	30 Ⓕ Ⓖ Ⓗ Ⓙ	40 Ⓕ Ⓖ Ⓗ Ⓙ

Test 4

1 Ⓐ Ⓑ Ⓒ Ⓓ	11 Ⓐ Ⓑ Ⓒ Ⓓ	21 Ⓐ Ⓑ Ⓒ Ⓓ	31 Ⓐ Ⓑ Ⓒ Ⓓ
2 Ⓕ Ⓖ Ⓗ Ⓙ	12 Ⓕ Ⓖ Ⓗ Ⓙ	22 Ⓕ Ⓖ Ⓗ Ⓙ	32 Ⓕ Ⓖ Ⓗ Ⓙ
3 Ⓐ Ⓑ Ⓒ Ⓓ	13 Ⓐ Ⓑ Ⓒ Ⓓ	23 Ⓐ Ⓑ Ⓒ Ⓓ	33 Ⓐ Ⓑ Ⓒ Ⓓ
4 Ⓕ Ⓖ Ⓗ Ⓙ	14 Ⓕ Ⓖ Ⓗ Ⓙ	24 Ⓕ Ⓖ Ⓗ Ⓙ	34 Ⓕ Ⓖ Ⓗ Ⓙ
5 Ⓐ Ⓑ Ⓒ Ⓓ	15 Ⓐ Ⓑ Ⓒ Ⓓ	25 Ⓐ Ⓑ Ⓒ Ⓓ	35 Ⓐ Ⓑ Ⓒ Ⓓ
6 Ⓕ Ⓖ Ⓗ Ⓙ	16 Ⓕ Ⓖ Ⓗ Ⓙ	26 Ⓕ Ⓖ Ⓗ Ⓙ	36 Ⓕ Ⓖ Ⓗ Ⓙ
7 Ⓐ Ⓑ Ⓒ Ⓓ	17 Ⓐ Ⓑ Ⓒ Ⓓ	27 Ⓐ Ⓑ Ⓒ Ⓓ	37 Ⓐ Ⓑ Ⓒ Ⓓ
8 Ⓕ Ⓖ Ⓗ Ⓙ	18 Ⓕ Ⓖ Ⓗ Ⓙ	28 Ⓕ Ⓖ Ⓗ Ⓙ	38 Ⓕ Ⓖ Ⓗ Ⓙ
9 Ⓐ Ⓑ Ⓒ Ⓓ	19 Ⓐ Ⓑ Ⓒ Ⓓ	29 Ⓐ Ⓑ Ⓒ Ⓓ	39 Ⓐ Ⓑ Ⓒ Ⓓ
10 Ⓕ Ⓖ Ⓗ Ⓙ	20 Ⓕ Ⓖ Ⓗ Ⓙ	30 Ⓕ Ⓖ Ⓗ Ⓙ	40 Ⓕ Ⓖ Ⓗ Ⓙ

ENGLISH TEST

45 MINUTES—75 QUESTIONS

Directions: The following test consists of 75 underlined words and phrases in context, or general questions about the passages. Most of the underlined sections contain errors or inappropriate expressions. You are asked to compare each with the four alternatives in the answer column. If you consider the original version best, choose letter **A** or **F**: NO CHANGE. For each question, blacken on the answer sheet the letter of the alternative you think best. Read each passage through before answering the questions based on it.

Passage 1

(1)

Typical diseases associated with being overweight are hypertension,[1] or high blood pressure; atherosclerosis, or fatty deposits in blood vessels, which consequently for those reasons[2] restrict the flow of blood; and coronary heart disease. Other diseases occur far more often among the overweight than for those who have ordinary weight[3] including diabetes, respiratory ailments, gallbladder and kidney diseases, and some kinds of cancer.

(2)

Most all people[4] who are trying to lose weight are doing so mainly for health. In today's informed society, being overweight is no longer a symbol of good health and prosperity, as they used to think.[5] There are dangers

1. **A.** NO CHANGE
   B. are, hypertension
   C. are—hypertension
   D. are; hypertension

2. **F.** NO CHANGE
   G. which therefore in that manner
   H. which
   J. OMIT the underlined portion

3. **A.** NO CHANGE
   B. among normal-weighted people,
   C. others,
   D. among persons of normal weight,

4. **F.** NO CHANGE
   G. Among such people
   H. Most people
   J. Most of those people

5. **A.** NO CHANGE
   B. as it once has been.
   C. as was once thought to be.
   D. as it once was.

GO ON TO THE NEXT PAGE.

to one's well-being, as do, incidentally, being under-weight.[6] Doctors keep a close check on their patient's blood chemistry as never before now, in ordering[7] measuring blood samples for electrolytes, glucose, lipids, hemoglobin, and creatinine serum, and[8] without a doubt, they are very concerned with a general rise of weight.

(3)

Even more consequential is the looming chance of diabetes, especially as a man[9] reaches the ages above sixty five. Two/thirds[10] of all people who have maintained a weight of thirty or forty pounds above ideal weight for some years will be almost certain to notice the looming and frightening symptoms of *diabetic retinopathy* (changes in the blood vessels of the retina that are a major cause of blindness),[11] of *diabetic nephropathy*, which leads to kidney failure; or of *arteriosclerosis*, which may cause a stroke, heart failure, or gangrene. They will also notice a general lack of energy, and a lack of feeling in their aching feet. [12]

(4)

(1) Young people would do well to watch their weights for a lifetime. (2) Such people are likely to be constantly tired and unable to earn[13] much. (3) Eventually, diabetics are simply unable to be active in any endeavor. (4) The disease has many idiosyncrasies that they must cautiously pay attention to, like drinking to stave off thirst, they ought to maintain glucose[14] in the bloodstream, sustaining insulin, and many more. [15]

6. **F.** NO CHANGE
   G. as is, incidentally, being underweight.
   H. as does incidentally, being underweight.
   J. as does, incidentally, being underweight.

7. **A.** NO CHANGE
   B. DELETE in ordering
   C. quickly
   D. unabashedly

8. **F.** NO CHANGE
   G. serum, and,
   H. serum; and
   J. serum: and

9. **A.** NO CHANGE
   B. as a woman
   C. as men, women, and even the children
   D. as one

10. **F.** NO CHANGE
    G. Two thirds
    H. Two-thirds
    J. Two thirds—

11. **A.** NO CHANGE
    B. blindness);
    C. blindness):
    D. blindness)—

12. Choose the sequence of paragraph numbers up to this point (paragraphs 1–3) that makes the structure of the passage most logical.
    F. NO CHANGE
    G. 1, 3, 2
    H. 2, 3, 1
    J. 2, 1, 3

13. **A.** NO CHANGE
    B. to celebrate
    C. to do
    D. to cook

14. **F.** NO CHANGE
    G. maintaining a good supply of glucose
    H. maintaining much more glucose
    J. maintaining glucose

15. Choose the sequence of sentences that will make paragraph 4 most logical and final.
    A. NO CHANGE
    B. 3, 2, 4, 1
    C. 3, 4, 2, 1
    D. 1, 2, 4, 3

1 1 1 1 1 1 1 1 1 1 1

Passage 2

A convincing way to prove the need for nurses is the long lines in hospital waiting rooms. [16] An additional problem in most hospitals is the terrible food, which is usually prepared by contract service firms. [17] One only has to pick up a newspaper, or [18] turn on the radio to be informed about the very critical shortage of skilled nurses. The argument then begins about responsibility for the shortage. Without nurses, a hospital might as well pack away its sheets. [19] Yes, I wish it has not been shown that many nurses leave their profession, but they have always had the tendency of dropping out. [20]

[21] Hospitals have had to close wards and they have had to tell patients that they are unable to treat them [22]

16. **F.** NO CHANGE
    G. is to point to the long lines in hospital waiting rooms.
    H. are the long lines in hospital waiting rooms.
    J. always has been the long lines in hospital waiting rooms.

17. **A.** NO CHANGE
    B. Place this sentence at the end of the paragraph.
    C. Place this sentence at the beginning of the paragraph.
    D. OMIT this sentence.

18. **F.** NO CHANGE
    G. newspaper: or
    H. newspaper or
    J. or newspaper—or

19. **A.** NO CHANGE
    B. OMIT this sentence.
    C. Move this sentence to end of paragraph.
    D. Move this sentence to beginning paragraph.

20. **F.** NO CHANGE
    G. Yes, I wish it was not true that many nurses leave their profession, but they have always had the tendency of dropping out.
    H. Yes, I wish it were not true that many nurses leave their profession, but they have always had the tendency of dropping out.
    J. Yes, I wish it had not been true that many nurses leave their profession, but they have always has had the tendency of dropping out.

21. The writer could most effectively strengthen his arguments at this point by adding:
    A. a daily log from a critical care nursing station in a large, municipal hospital.
    B. a summary of the vacant nurse positions in all of the city's hospitals.
    C. testimony from two or three patients in a large hospital.
    D. a list of inactive nurses which explains why each nurse is not working.

22. **F.** NO CHANGE
    G. turn them out
    H. turn away patients
    J. tell patients "no go"

GO ON TO THE NEXT PAGE.

because of a lack of nursing staff. [23]

According to the Los Angeles Hospital Council, there is a 20 percent vacancy for budgeted, registered nurse positions. Therefore, there is a ready-made job market for graduates with Associate Degrees in nursing. The employment and career opportunities are greater <u>than other</u> [24] community college programs. Students all have jobs before graduation (contingent upon licensure) if they so desire. <u>This</u> [25] is further demonstrated by the waiting lists of applicants for programs, and <u>their being admitted</u> [26] to such rewarding programs has been a godsend to many.

The Associate Degree nursing programs are appealing to the disadvantaged individual who <u>could not afford</u> [27] the expenses and other requirements of university programs. Associate Degree programs attract ethnic minorities, <u>men, and older students</u> [28] who could not otherwise be served in the educational system. The Associate Degree nursing program provides disadvantaged people with a salable skill, thereby enabling them to enjoy a better way of life while meeting the nursing <u>shortage that</u> [29] helps all members of the community.

23. The first paragraph suggests that it is representing both sides of an "argument." How could the argument be made more fair or even-handed?
  A. Bolster the position that there is a critical shortage of nurses by giving statistics, pay scales, etc.
  B. Bolster the position that nurses are really in good supply by presenting numbers of nurses now available and of nursing students soon to be graduated.
  C. Bolster both positions with testimony of patients that have received adequate hospital care and patients that have received poor care.
  D. Bolster the position that nurses are really in good supply by compiling lists of registry applicants who have earned Master's Degrees in nursing.

24. **F.** NO CHANGE
  G. than still more
  H. than several more
  J. than those in other

25. **A.** NO CHANGE
  B. This need for more training
  C. This job glut
  D. This excess of jobs

26. **F.** NO CHANGE
  G. they being admitted
  H. their had been
  J. they having been

27. **A.** NO CHANGE
  B. has not been able to afford
  C. cannot afford
  D. up to now, could not afford

28. **F.** NO CHANGE
  G. men, older students
  H. men; older students
  J. men: older students

29. **A.** NO CHANGE
  B. shortage, a public service that
  C. shortage which
  D. shortage, a philosophy that

The health care profession has historically been represented by ethnic minorities, and a program at Los Angeles Mission College would help to correct this problem. [30]

30. This passage is probably written for readers who:
   F. are patients in hospitals.
   G. are other community college instructors.
   H. are members of a hospital governing board.
   J. are members of a state licensure panel or other group likely to rule on whether a nursing school should be opened at L.A. Mission College.

Passage 3

On the morning of June 8, 1988, Joyce McBride left her home to attend a garage sale. As she left, McBride locked her front door with a double dead-bolt lock that required a key <u>either to open it from inside or outside.</u> [31]

31. **A.** NO CHANGE
   B. to open it from inside or outside either.
   C. to either open it from inside or outside.
   D. to open it from either inside or outside.

While McBride was away, her next-door neighbor, Peggy Frobush, looked out her bathroom window and saw William Goode standing by McBride's front door. Peggy had known Goode for years; he was a good friend of her son, Chuck, and had been living in his car parked outside the <u>Frobushes' home.</u> [32] It <u>had appeared</u> [33] to her that Goode had just closed McBride's front door behind him. Thinking a burglary had just taken place, Peggy <u>screamed, "Police!"</u> [34] She noticed at that moment that

32. **F.** NO CHANGE
   G. Frobushe's home.
   H. Frobushes's home.
   J. Frobushes home.

33. **A.** NO CHANGE
   B. has appeared
   C. appeared
   D. appears

34. **F.** NO CHANGE
   G. screamed "Police"!
   H. screamed, "Police"!
   J. screamed "Police!"

GO ON TO THE NEXT PAGE.

1 1 1 1 1 1 1 1 1 1 1

McBride's back door was open. Peggy, by the way, is an extremely attractive woman. [36] The police told McBride about the burglary upon her return home. Several items were missing, including a guitar, power tools, and jewelry. Police investigators discovered the front-door dead-bolt shut and assigned as a cause the back door was the point of entry behind the house.

(1) These items were taken in the burglary. (2) Later that morning, Chuck approached a neighbor of McBride and offered to sell him a gold bracelet and necklace. (3) Chuck left the jewelry with the neighbor, who returned the articles to McBride. [39]

On July 15, 1988, Detective Bruno Pilsner interviewed Goode about the burglary. Goode told the detective he had been living in his broken-down car for several weeks, parking it outside the Frobushes' residence. In working on his car, Goode heard Chuck call to him from McBride's house. After walking to the front door, he saw his friend inside the residence. Chuck opened the front door and asked him to help take McBride's property, but Goode refused. He decided to leave when Peggy yelled for the police. [41]

35. **A.** NO CHANGE
    B. By the way, Peggy is an extremely attractive woman.
    C. Peggy is an extremely attractive woman, by the way.
    D. OMIT this sentence

36. **F.** NO CHANGE
    G. Begin a new paragraph with the following sentence.
    H. Delete the rest of this paragraph.
    J. Place the rest of this paragraph at the beginning of the passage.

37. **A.** NO CHANGE
    B. theorized that
    C. laid that fact on
    D. put the saddle on the right horse that

38. **F.** NO CHANGE
    G. on the nether side of the house.
    H. OMIT the underlined portion.
    J. toward the rear of the house.

39. Choose the sequence of sentences that will make this paragraph most logical.
    A. NO CHANGE
    B. 3, 2, 1
    C. 2, 3, 1
    D. 1, 3, 2

40. **F.** NO CHANGE
    G. While working
    H. For working
    J. As working

41. Suppose that at this point the writer decided to add more information about the police department in this town. Would this addition be an appropriate one, and, if so, which of the following would be most relevant to the passage as a whole?
    A. A brief biography of Detective Pilsner and his family
    B. A discussion of the structure of the local police department, including the duties of each branch
    C. No addition would be appropriate. This is a very lean summary of a case; additional detail is not required.
    D. A summary of exceptional cases Detective Pilsner has helped to solve

1 1 1 1 1 1 1 1 1 1 1

After further investigation, Goode was interviewed again. It was with no minor irritation that Detective Pilsner belabored[42] his earlier version because the front door could not have been opened without a key, he accused[43] Goode of planning the burglary with Chuck. Replying, "You are right," Goode told Pilsner the following story: Chuck, needing money to buy drugs, asked for Goode's help in burglarizing the McBride house. Goode agreed. Chuck planned to enter the house from the back and let Goode in through the front, thus[44] he could not open the door. Goode turned to leave when he heard Peggy scream, and fled the area on foot.

At trial, Goode denied participating in the crime. He testified that Chuck approached him that morning, told him he needed money for drugs, and asked for Goode's help in carrying tools from the McBride house. Goode's final version of the story was that he refused to participate. [45]

42. **F.** NO CHANGE
    G. Detective Pilsner was angry about
    H. Detective Pilsner pooh-poohed
    J. This time, Pilsner told Goode he did not believe

43. **A.** NO CHANGE
    B. a key he accused
    C. a key. He accused
    D. a key; he accused

44. **F.** NO CHANGE
    G. but
    H. however
    J. nevertheless

45. This passage was probably written for readers who:
    A. are detective and mystery fiction buffs.
    B. are law enforcement students learning about criminal behavior.
    C. need summary details about this case for a subsequent discussion or determination.
    D. are avid readers and would especially appreciate the technique and style of this author.

GO ON TO THE NEXT PAGE.

1 1 1 1 1 1 1 1 1 1 1

Passage 4

(1)

The person or persons suing someone are called the PLAINTIFFS; the person or persons being sued are called the DEFENDANTS. Neither plaintiffs <u>nor</u> 46 defendants may bring a lawyer to represent them in Small Claims Court.

(2)

<u>Having appeared on the Court Calendar,</u> 47 the plaintiffs simply explain why they feel the defendant owes them the money they have asked for, and present any evidence or witnesses they can to help them prove their case. After <u>having heard</u> 48 from both sides, the judge will decide who is right.

(3)

Any person who is eighteen or older may file suit in Small Claims Court. A minor may do so only if he or she has a parent or guardian <u>and who is to come</u> 49 along when the suit is filed. The judges of Small Claims Courts are members of the Justice and Municipal Courts. They set aside certain days and times to hold Small Claims <u>Court which</u> 50 may be different for each county. [51]

46. **F.** NO CHANGE
G. or
H. however or
J. and nor

47. **A.** NO CHANGE
B. When their suit comes before the judge,
C. When the Court Calendar determines the time of the hearing,
D. When the suit is brought before the Court Calendar,

48. **F.** NO CHANGE
G. they spoke
H. he heard
J. hearing

49. **A.** NO CHANGE
B. to have come
C. come
D. whom to come

50. **F.** NO CHANGE
G. Court, which
H. Court that
J. Court, whom

51. The writer could most effectively strengthen the passage at this point by adding which of the following?
A. A visual description of a typical Small Claims Court
B. A description of some of the more unusual small claims suits in recent years
C. A few examples to illustrate the general points being made
D. Testimony from both defendants and plaintiffs of what they think of the Small Claims Court

(4)

Small Claims Court is[52] a city or state court that handles minor lawsuits speedily and efficiently. Small Claims Courts can resolve issues regarding small debts, faulty products, or servicemen can provide poor service.[53] By the same token,[54] the maximum amount of money litigants can collect is $2500. If the suing party's[55] claim is larger, he[56] may either speak to an attorney about taking the case to a higher court, or may accept the $2500 and give up any claim to the rest.

(5)

In some cases, plaintiffs must file their suit at the court located in the district where the defendant lives or works at.[57] If, for example, the complaining party lives in Boston, but the store where a defective vacuum cleaner was bought is in Worcester, the plaintiff must file suit in Worcester A neighbor recently took me to Small Claims Court over my acacia trees.[58]

(6)

Unfortunately, there are usually no translators in Small Claims Court, so if either the plaintiff or the defendant does not speak English, it is advisable to bring along someone who can act as an interpreter. Also, due to the fact that[59] there are very few night courts, litigants will almost always have to attend court during working hours. [60]

52. **F.** NO CHANGE
G. are
H. claims to be
J. was

53. **A.** NO CHANGE
B. poor service is provided.
C. poor service.
D. poor service committed.

54. **F.** NO CHANGE
G. However,
H. Furthermore,
J. Granted that,

55. **A.** NO CHANGE
B. partys'
C. partys
D. parties

56. **F.** NO CHANGE
G. the defendant
H. the plaintiff
J. the judge

57. **A.** NO CHANGE
B. has worked
C. is working at
D. works

58. Choose the placement for this sentence that makes the information most logical.
F. NO CHANGE
G. Place at beginning of this paragraph
H. Place at beginning of next paragraph
J. DELETE the sentence

59. **A.** NO CHANGE
B. owing to the fact that
C. since
D. in the light of the fact that

60. Choose the sequence of paragraph numbers that makes the structure of the passage most logical.
F. NO CHANGE
G. 6, 1, 4, 2, 3, 5
H. 1, 4, 3, 5, 6, 2
J. 4, 1, 2, 3, 5, 6

GO ON TO THE NEXT PAGE.

Passage 5

(1)

Environmental issues appear frequently, especially in states where liberal groups are at odds with the establishment, in Nevada, for example, voters will be asked to withdraw from a five-state nuclear waste compact. Massachusetts will offer a measure that would ban the generation of electricity by nuclear plants that produce radioactive waste. Washington State voters will decide on the issue of whether to impose a tax on hazardous substances to help finance toxic waste cleanup. In general, throughout the nation, environmental initiatives are to be found everywhere, from bottle bills in Montana to surface-mine reclamation in South Dakota.

Many other issues will be brought up by initiatives in this year's general elections. Several states are voting on new minimum wage levels, and at least three are considering measures mandating AIDS testing. Others are deciding such mixed-up issues as personal property taxes, cigarette and beer taxes, mandatory health insurance, tuition tax credits, state park expansion, farm animal abuse, safety inspections, funding of abortions, homeless shelters, gambling, seat belt laws, official language laws, and school financing. [67]

(2)

Initiatives are citizen-sponsored ballot measures that circumvent the normal legislative process of placing referendums before the public. Considered by most advocates to be an important and useful safety valve for popular action when citizens are frustrated by state and

61. **A.** NO CHANGE
    B. establishment. In
    C. establishment in
    D. establishment; In

62. **F.** NO CHANGE
    G. on a tax
    H. whether a tax
    J. whether to impose a tax

63. **A.** NO CHANGE
    B. surface mine reclamation
    C. surface, mine reclamation
    D. surface and mine reclamation

64. **F.** NO CHANGE
    G. Begin new paragraph with this sentence.
    H. OMIT the underlined portion.
    J. Place this sentence at beginning of paragraph as it now exists.

65. **A.** NO CHANGE
    B. diverse
    C. wildly arrayed
    D. confusing

66. **F.** NO CHANGE
    G. laws and school
    H. laws, and school,
    J. laws and, school

67. Suppose at this point in the passage the writer wanted to add more information about the diversity of initiative subjects. Which of the following would be most relevant to the passage as a whole?
    A. Several detailed paragraphs about *one* really interesting initiative
    B. A history of the initiative process in England
    C. Two more paragraphs detailing more initiatives to be on ballots this year
    D. A summary of the election results

local legislatures, and which the 68 initiative process has been a significant factor in elections throughout this nation's history. In the 1970s, for example, the subject of most initiative propositions was state endorsement of a national nuclear freeze. During the late '70s and early '80s, the popular subject for initiatives was the taxpayers' revolt. In contrast, however 69 this year the initiative targets are very diverse, ranging from automobile insurance and tort liability and they also address mandatory 70 AIDS testing of prisoners. [71]

(3)

Some initiative watchers are alarmed by recent "judicial activism" that has seen judges nix 72 dozens of voter-sponsored referendums because petitions used to place measures on the ballot were not printed in Spanish or other languages that reflect the demographic makeup of the state, as well as in English. Other reasons that initiatives have been declared invalid is 73 that they address more than one subject, they 74 intrude upon the domain of the legislature, or they bear too colorful a title. [75]

68. **F.** NO CHANGE
    G. and the
    H. the
    J. which the

69. **A.** NO CHANGE
    B. In contrast,
    C. Moreover,
    D. In addition,

70. **F.** NO CHANGE
    G. to mandatory
    H. they address mandatory
    J. addressing

71. Readers are likely to regard the passage so far as best described by which of the following terms?
    A. Romantic
    B. Journalistic
    C. Fantastic
    D. Persuasive

72. **F.** NO CHANGE
    G. deep-six
    H. pull the plug on
    J. strike down

73. **A.** NO CHANGE
    B. have been
    C. are
    D. has been

74. **F.** NO CHANGE
    G. subject; They
    H. subject. They
    J. subject they

75. Choose the sequence of paragraph numbers that makes the structure of the passage most logical.
    A. NO CHANGE
    B. 3, 2, 1
    C. 2, 1, 3
    D. 1, 3, 2

If there is still time remaining, you may review your answers.

2 2 2 2 2 2 2 2 2 2 2

MATHEMATICS TEST

60 MINUTES—60 QUESTIONS

Directions: After solving each problem, darken the appropriate space on the answer sheet. Do not spend too much time on any one problem. Make a note of the ones that seem difficult, and return to them when you finish the others. Assume that the word *line* means "straight line," that geometric figures are not necessarily drawn to scale, and that all geometric figures lie in a plane.

DO YOUR FIGURING HERE

1. Which of the following is not a real number?

A. $\frac{0}{5}$

B. $-\sqrt{23}$

C. $\frac{12}{\sqrt{6}}$

D. $\frac{8}{2-2}$

E. π

2. What is the value of $7^2 - 2[3 + 2(5 - 1)]$?

F. 9
G. 940
H. 27
J. –8
K. –9

3. What is the solution set of $2x - 5 = 7 - 4x$?

A. {1}

B. {2}

C. $\left\{\frac{1}{2}\right\}$

D. {–2}

E. $\left\{\frac{-1}{3}\right\}$

4. What percent of 24 is 18?

F. 75%
G. 150%
H. 25%
J. $33\frac{1}{3}\%$
K. $133\frac{1}{3}\%$

2 2 2 2 2 2 2 2 2 2 2

DO YOUR FIGURING HERE

5. How many curtains can be made from 20 meters of cloth if each curtain requires $2\frac{1}{2}$ meters?

   A. 50
   B. 20
   C. 12
   D. 8
   E. 4

6. What is the simplified form of $2x - \{3x - 2[x - (1 - x)]\}$?

   F. $3x - 2$
   G. $-x - 2$
   H. $-4x - 1$
   J. $-x + 2$
   K. $3x - 2x^2$

7. Which of the following numbers is NOT prime?

   A. 43
   B. 51
   C. 73
   D. 97
   E. 101

8. Which of the following is a secant line?

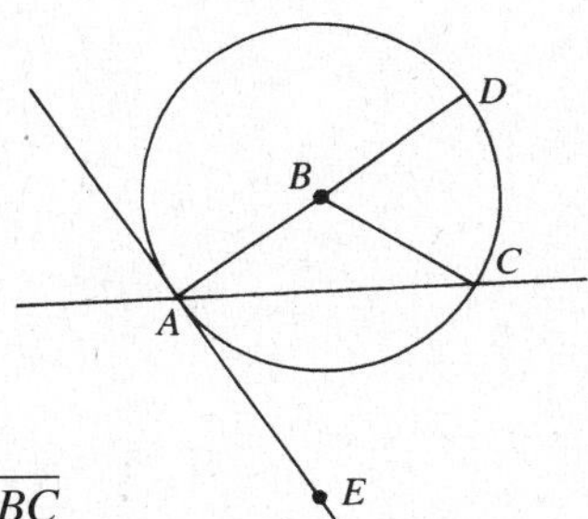

   F. Segment $\overline{BC}$
   G. Segment $\overline{AD}$
   H. Line $\overleftrightarrow{AC}$
   J. Line $\overleftrightarrow{AE}$
   K. Segment $\overline{AB}$

9. If $x = -2$ and $y = 3$, then $-x - xy^2 = ?$

   A. 16
   B. -34
   C. -38
   D. 20
   E. 144

GO ON TO THE NEXT PAGE.

2 2 2 2 2 2 2 2 2 2 2

DO YOUR FIGURING HERE

10. In the circle shown, $\overline{AB}$ is a tangent and $\overline{BD}$ is a secant. If the length of $\overline{AB}$ is 6 and the length of $\overline{BC}$ is 4, what is the length of $\overline{CD}$?

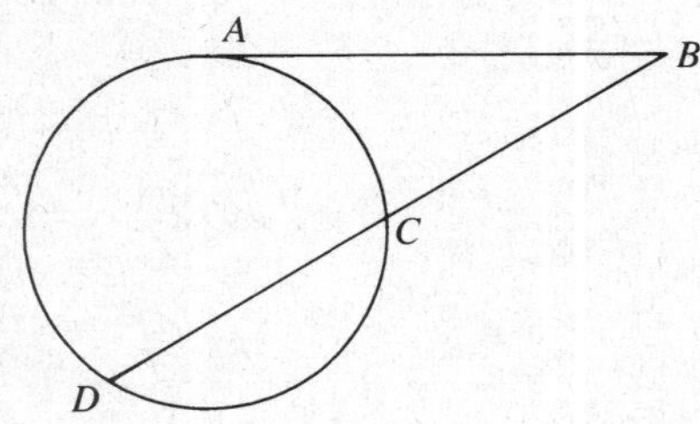

F. $2\sqrt{5}$

G. 8

H. $2\frac{2}{3}$

J. 5

K. 10

11. What is an equivalent expression, in simplest radical form, to $\sqrt[3]{4ab^2}\,\sqrt[3]{12a^4b^2}$?

A. $2ab\sqrt[3]{6a^2b}$

B. $\sqrt[3]{48a^5b^4}$

C. $\sqrt[6]{48a^5b^4}$

D. $16a^2b$

E. None of these

12. Which of the following is NOT a quadratic equation in one variable?

F. $3x^2 + 5 = 5x + 7$
G. $x(2x + 5) = 8$
H. $3^2 + 5x = 4^2 + 2x$
J. $x^2 = 16$
K. $(2x - 3)^2 = 5$

13. What is the simplified form of the expression $(3x - 1)^2$?

A. $9x^2 - 1$
B. $9x^2 - 6x + 1$
C. $9x^2 + 1$
D. $9x^2 + 6x + 1$
E. $9x + 1$

2 2 2 2 2 2 2 2 2 2 2 2

DO YOUR FIGURING HERE

14. If 2 less than five times a certain number is 1 more than twice the same number, which equation can be used to find the number?

F. $5(x - 2) = 2(x + 1)$
G. $5x + 1 = 2x - 2$
H. $2 - 5x = 1 + 2x$
J. $5x - 2 = 2x + 1$
K. $5(x - 2) = 2x + 1$

15. The diameter of a circle is one side of a triangle, and the third vertex is on the circle. What kind of triangle is formed?

A. Isosceles
B. Right
C. Acute
D. Scalene
E. Equilateral

16. Which of the following is equivalent to $|x - 1| \leq 3$?

F. $x \leq 4$
G. $x + 1 \leq 3$
H. $-2 \leq x \leq 4$
J. $x \leq -2$ or $x \geq 4$
K. $x \leq -2$ and $x \geq 4$

17. In the rectangular coordinate system, the point associated with the ordered pair $(-4, 0)$ is located in which quadrant?

A. I
B. II
C. III
D. IV
E. None of these

18. Which of the following ordered pairs satisfies the equation $3x - 2y = 5$?

F. $(-1, -1)$
G. $(1, 1)$
H. $(1, -1)$
J. $(-1, 1)$
K. $(5, -5)$

GO ON TO THE NEXT PAGE.

2 2 2 2 2 2 2 2 2 2 2

DO YOUR FIGURING HERE

19. In the diagram, lines m and n in a plane are cut by transversal l. Which statement would allow the conclusion that $m \parallel n$?

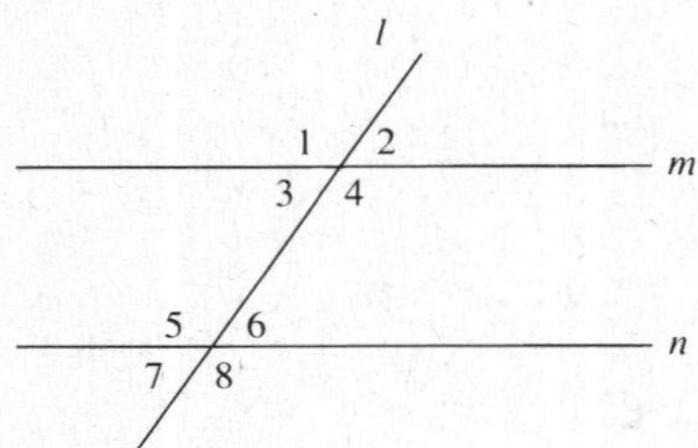

A. $m\angle 2 = m\angle 3$
B. $m\angle 2 = m\angle 6$
C. $m\angle 5 = m\angle 3$
D. $m\angle 2 + m\angle 4 = 180$
E. $m\angle 1 = m\angle 7$

20. If, in $\triangle ABC$, $\overline{BD}$ is drawn so that $AD = DC$, then what is BD?

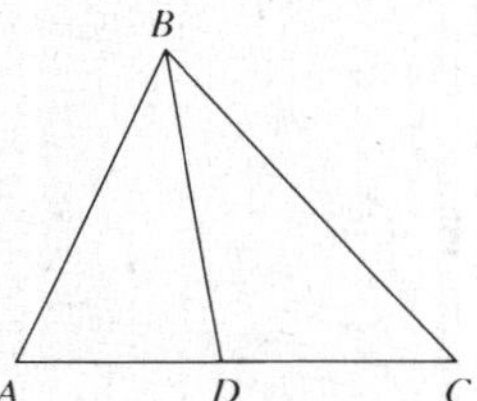

F. An angle bisector
G. An altitude
H. A median
J. A perpendicular bisector of $\overline{AC}$
K. A transversal

21. What is the sum of the fractions $\frac{5}{12}$ and $\frac{7}{18}$?

A. $\frac{3}{5}$

B. $\frac{29}{36}$

C. $\frac{1}{35}$

D. $\frac{1}{18}$

E. $\frac{2}{5}$

2 2 2 2 2 2 2 2 2 2 2

DO YOUR FIGURING HERE

22. When completely simplified,

$$\frac{2}{3} - \frac{2 - \frac{5}{6}}{2^3 - 1} \div \frac{1}{2} = ?$$

F. $\frac{1}{3}$

G. 1

H. $\frac{7}{12}$

J. $\frac{-32}{15}$

K. $\frac{5}{18}$

23. What is the value of $\log_3 27$?

A. 3

B. 9

C. $\frac{1}{3}$

D. $\frac{1}{9}$

E. 24

24. If $\sin \theta = \frac{1}{2}$, then $\cos \theta = ?$

F. $\frac{1}{2}$

G. $\frac{-1}{2}$

H. $\frac{\sqrt{3}}{2}$

J. $\frac{-\sqrt{3}}{2}$

K. $\frac{\pm\sqrt{3}}{2}$

25. In $\triangle ABC$, the length of $\overline{AC}$ is equal to the length of BC. If the measure of $\angle A$ is 40°, what is the measure of $\angle C$?

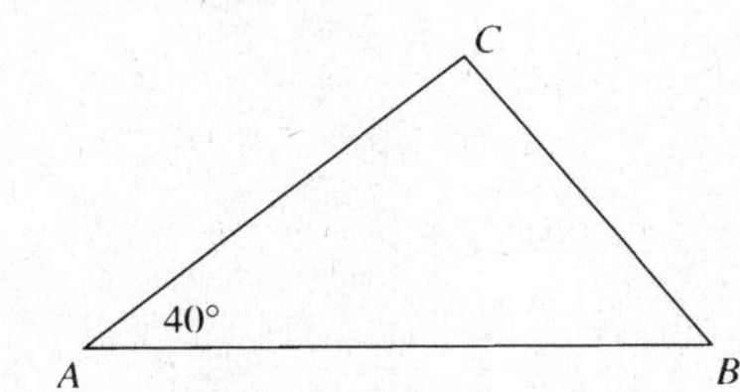

A. 50°
B. 60°
C. 80°
D. 100°
E. 140°

GO ON TO THE NEXT PAGE.

DO YOUR FIGURING HERE

26. Which is the largest of the following numbers?

F. 3.1415926
G. $\frac{22}{7}$
H. 3.14
J. 3.1416
K. All these numbers are equal.

27. If Joan's English assignment is to read 80 pages, and she has read $\frac{4}{5}$ of her assignment, how many pages does she have left to read?

A. 16
B. 20
C. 32
D. 48
E. 64

28. Which of the following is a pure imaginary number?

F. -4
G. $-\sqrt{4}$
H. $\sqrt{-4}$
J. $3 + 2i$
K. 8

29. Which equation corresponds to the accompanying graph?

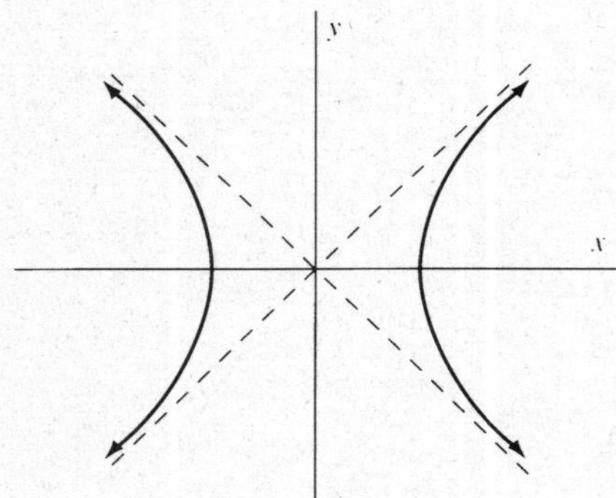

A. $x^2 - y^2 = 1$
B. $x^2 + y^2 = 1$
C. $x^2 + y = 1$
D. $x - y^2 = 1$
E. $x + y^2 = 1$

2 2 2 2 2 2 2 2 2 2 2

DO YOUR FIGURING HERE

30. What is the solution set of the following system of equations?

$$\begin{pmatrix} 2x + y = -1 \\ 3x - 2y = -19 \end{pmatrix}$$

F. {(2, –5)}
G. {(–3, 5)}
H. {(–7, –1)}
J. There is no solution.
K. There are infinitely many solutions.

31. What is the solution to this system of equations?

$$\begin{pmatrix} 5x - 2y = 3 \\ y = 4x - 3 \end{pmatrix}$$

A. {1}
B. {(1, 1)}
C. {(–1, –7)}
D. {(–1, –1)}
E. None of these

32. Which expression would be appropriate to complete the following equation in order for the equation to illustrate the identity property of addition: 5 + (7 + 0) = ?

F. (7 + 0) + 5
G. 5 + (0 + 7)
H. (5 + 7) + 0
J. 5 + 7
K. 12

33. If $a < b$, then $| a - b | + a + b = ?$

A. 0
B. $2a$
C. $2b$
D. $2a + 2b$
E. $a - b$

34. What is the set of prime factors of 6,440?

F. {2, 5, 161}
G. {2, 7, 23}
H. {2, 5, 7, 23}
J. {2, 5, 7}
K. {2, 3, 220}

DO YOUR FIGURING HERE

35. Which of the angles below are supplementary?

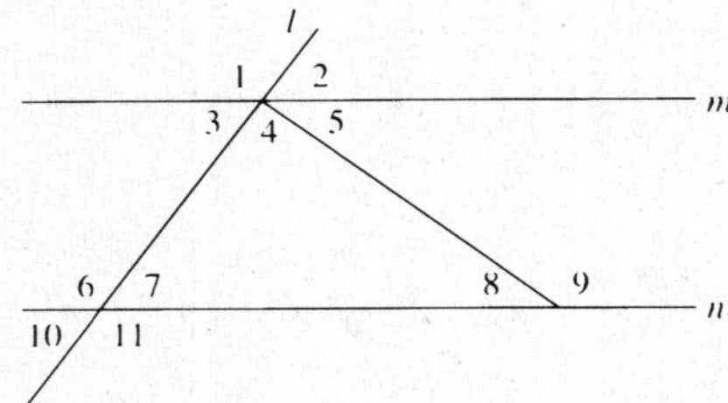

A. ∠ 6 and ∠ 11
B. ∠ 3, ∠ 4, and ∠ 5
C. ∠ 3 and ∠ 7
D. ∠ 8 and ∠ 9
E. ∠ 2 and ∠ 7

36. $13\frac{1}{4} - 7\frac{5}{8} = ?$

F. $5\frac{5}{8}$

G. $5\frac{7}{8}$

H. $6\frac{3}{8}$

J. $6\frac{1}{2}$

K. 5

37. What is the degree of the polynomial $3x^2y^3 + 5xy^2 - 7y$?

A. 0
B. 2
C. 5
D. 8
E. 9

38. What is the sum of the roots of $4x^2 + 3x - 8 = 0$?

F. $\frac{-4}{3}$

G. $\frac{1}{2}$

H. 2

J. $\frac{-3}{4}$

K. $\frac{3}{8}$

DO YOUR FIGURING HERE

39. What is the value of $16^{-3/4}$?

 A. This is undefined.
 B. 8
 C. $\frac{1}{8}$
 D. –8
 E. $\frac{-1}{8}$

40. Which of the following is not a conic section?

 F. Circle
 G. Parabola
 H. Hyperbola
 J. Exponential curve
 K. Ellipse

41. The trigonometric function sin 215° is equal to which of the following?

 A. sin 35°
 B. – cos 35°
 C. – cos 55°
 D. – sin 55°
 E. sin 55°

42. In how many orders can 6 different books be placed on a shelf?

 F. 1
 G. 6
 H. 12
 J. 36
 K. 720

43. What is the value of -2^{-2}?

 A. 4
 B. – 4
 C. $\frac{1}{4}$
 D. $\frac{-1}{4}$
 E. None of these

GO ON TO THE NEXT PAGE.

DO YOUR FIGURING HERE

44. A circle and a semicircle have the same area. If the circle has radius 1, what is the radius of the semicircle?

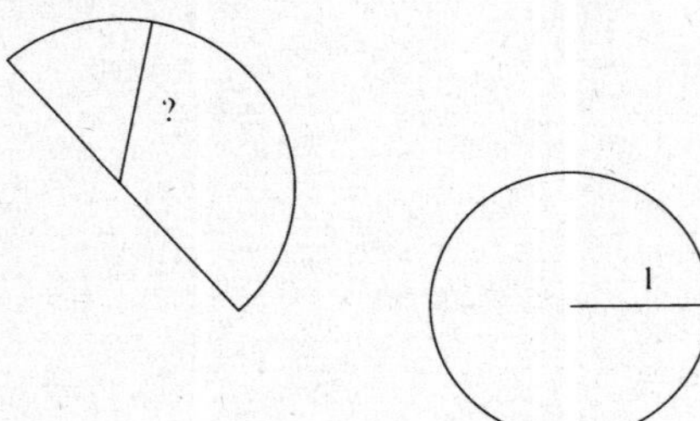

F. 2
G. 4
H. $\sqrt{2}$
J. $\pi\sqrt{2}$
K. 2π

45. What is the center of the circle whose equation is $x^2 + y^2 + 4x - 18y + 69 = 0$?

A. (–2, 9)
B. (2, – 9)
C. (4, –18)
D. (– 4, 18)
E. (0,0)

46. What is the distance between (5, 3) and (–2, 4)?

F. $\sqrt{38}$
G. $2\sqrt{10}$
H. $\sqrt{58}$
J. $5\sqrt{2}$
K. $\sqrt{10}$

47. What is the smallest positive angle that is co-terminal with 846°?

A. 234°
B. 126°
C. 36°
D. 54°
E. –234°

48. If a student received a score of 80% on a test in which 60 questions were answered correctly, how many questions were on the test?

F. 15
G. 30
H. 48
J. 75
K. 90

DO YOUR FIGURING HERE

49. $7(10^4) + 3(10^3) + 2(10^1) + 9(10^0)$ is the expanded form of what number?

    A. 7,329
    B. 70,329
    C. 73,029
    D. 73,209
    E. 7302.9

50. What is the probability of getting a sum of 8 on one roll of a fair pair of dice?

    F. 5

    G. 36

    H. $\frac{5}{36}$

    J. $\frac{1}{5}$

    K. $\frac{1}{8}$

51. If $\overline{AB}$ is a diameter, $\overline{AD} \parallel \overline{BC}$, and $m\angle BAD = 15°$, what is the measure of arc $\widehat{BC}$?

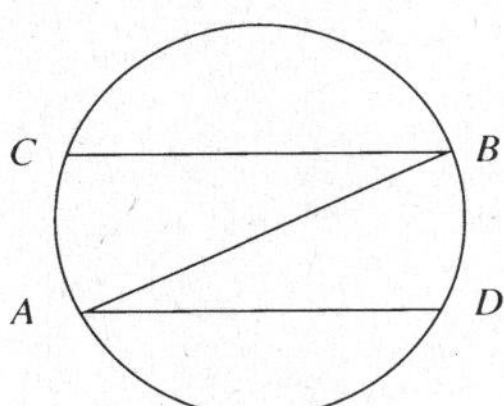

    A. 180°
    B. 165°
    C. 90°
    D. 75°
    E. None of these

52. What is the period of the function $y = 3 \sin 5\left(x + \frac{\pi}{12}\right)$?

    F. 3

    G. 5

    H. $-\frac{\pi}{12}$

    J. $\frac{2\pi}{5}$

    K. $\frac{\pi}{5}$

DO YOUR FIGURING HERE

53. What is the y-intercept of the graph of $y = x^2 - 2x - 8$?

    A. –8
    B. 8
    C. 4 and –2
    D. –4 and 2
    E. There are no y-intercepts.

54. What is the slope of the line whose equation is $2x - 5y = 7$?

    F. –2
    G. –5
    H. $\frac{5}{2}$
    J. $\frac{2}{5}$
    K. 2

55. In right triangle ABC ($\angle B$ is the right angle), altitude $\overline{BD}$ is drawn. If $AB = 4$ and $AD = 3$, what is the length of $\overline{AC}$?

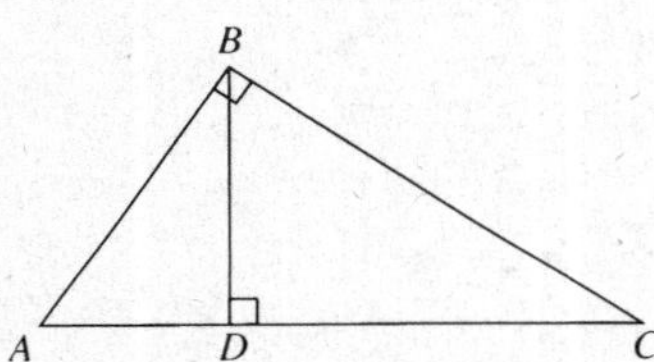

    A. 3
    B. 4
    C. $\frac{9}{4}$
    D. 12
    E. $\frac{16}{3}$

56. What is the sum of the interior angles of a hexagon?

    F. 360°
    G. 540°
    H. 720°
    J. 900°
    K. 1,080°

2 2 2 2 2 2 2 2 2 2 2

DO YOUR FIGURING HERE

57. If $\overline{AB}$ is a diameter, m $\angle CEB = 50°$, and m $\widehat{BC}$ = 20°, what is the measure of $\widehat{DB}$?

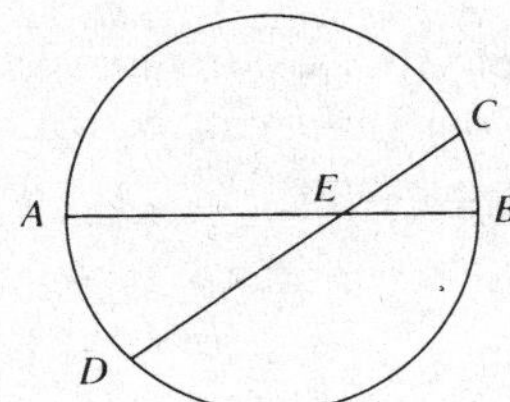

A. 160°
B. 130°
C. 100°
D. 80°
E. 70°

58. At a time when a 6-foot-tall man casts a shadow 10 feet long, a tree casts a shadow 85 feet long. What is the height, in feet, of the tree?

F. 51
G. 34
H. $141\frac{2}{3}$
J. 100
K. 89

59. In parallelogram *ABCD, AD* = 8, *AB* = 6, and $m\angle A = 60°$. What is its area?

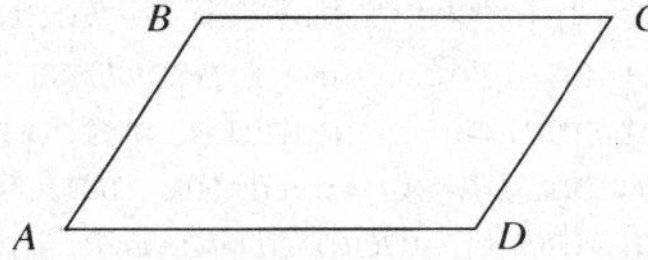

A. 24
B. 28
C. $24\sqrt{3}$
D. 48
E. $12\sqrt{3}$

60. If the measures of the angles of a triangle can be represented by $x + 15$, $3x - 75$, and $2x - 30$, what kind of triangle must it be?

F. Right
G. Equilateral
H. Obtuse
J. Scalene
K. No such triangle exists.

STOP

If there is still time remaining, you may review your answers.

3 3 3 3 3 3 3 3 3 3 3

READING TEST

35 MINUTES—40 QUESTIONS

Directions: This test consists of four passages, each followed by ten multiple-choice questions. Read each passage and then pick the best answer for each question. Fill in the spaces on your answer sheet that correspond to your choices. Refer to the passage as often as you wish while answering the questions.

Passage 1—Prose Fiction

This passage is an excerpt from a short story, "Buckthorne," by the 19th-century American author Washington Irving. The narrator of the passage recalls his boyhood years in a boarding school.

I was sent at an early age to a public school sorely against my mother's wishes; but my father insisted that it was the only way to make boys hardy. The school was kept by a conscientious prig of the ancient system who did his duty by the boys entrusted to his care; that is to say we were flogged soundly when we did not get our lessons. We were put into classes and thus flogged on in droves along the highways of knowledge, in much the same manner as cattle are driven to market, where those that are heavy in gait or short in leg have to suffer for the superior alertness of longer limbs of their companions.

For my part, I confess it with shame, I was an incorrigible laggard. I have always had the poetical feeling, that is to say I have always been an idle fellow and prone to play the vagabond. I used to get away from my books and school whenever I could and ramble about the fields. I was surrounded by seductions for such a temperament. The school house was an old fashioned, whitewashed mansion of wood and plaster, standing on the skirts of a beautiful village. Close by it was the venerable church with a tall Gothic spire. Before it spread a lovely green valley, with a little stream glistening along through willow groves; while a line of blue hills bounding the landscape gave rise to many a summer day dream as to the fairy land that lay beyond.

In spite of all the scourgings I suffered at that school to make me love my book I cannot but look back upon the place with fondness. Indeed I considered this frequent flagellation as the common lot of humanity and the regular mode in which scholars were made. My kind mother used to lament over the details of the sore trials I underwent in the cause of learning; but my father turned a deaf ear to her expostulations. He had been flogged through school himself and swore there was no other way of making a man of parts; though, let me speak it with true reverence, my father was but an indifferent illustration of his theory, for he was considered a grievous blockhead.

My poetical temperament evinced itself at a very early period. The village church was attended every Sunday by a neighbouring squire; the lord of the manor, whose park stretched quite to the village and whose spacious country seat seemed to take the church under its protection. Indeed you would have thought the church had been consecrated to him instead of to the Deity. The parish clerk bowed low before him and the vergers humbled themselves unto the dust in his presence. He always entered a little late and with some stir, striking his cane emphatically on the ground; swaying his hat in his hand, and looking loftily to the right and left as he walked slowly up the aisle, and parson, who always ate his Sunday dinner with him, never commenced service until he appeared. He sat with his family in a large pew gorgeously lined, humbling himself devoutly on velvet cushions and reading lessons of meekness and lowliness of spirit out of splendid gold and morocco prayer books. Whenever the parson spoke of the difficulty of a rich man's entering the kingdom of heaven, the eyes of the congregation would turn towards the "grand pew," and I thought the squire seemed pleased with the application.

The pomp of this pew and the aristocratical air of the family struck my imagination wonderfully and I fell desperately in love with a little daughter of the squire's, about twelve years of age. This freak of fancy made me more truant from my studies than ever. I used to stroll about the squire's park, and lurk near the house: to catch glimpses of this little damsel at the windows, or playing about the lawns; or walking out with her governess.

I had not enterprise, nor impudence enough to venture from my concealment; indeed I felt like an arrant poacher, until I read one or two of Ovid's Metamorphoses, when I pictured myself as some sylvan deity and she a coy wood nymph of whom I was in pursuit. There is something extremely delicious in these early awakenings of the tender passion. I can feel, even

3 3 3 3 3 3 3 3 3 3 3

at this moment, the thrilling of my boyish bosom, whenever by chance I caught a glimpse of her white frock fluttering among the shrubbery. I carried about in my bosom a volume of Waller, which I had purloined from my mother's library; and I applied to my little fair one all the compliments lavished upon Sacharissa.

At length I danced with her at a school ball. I was so awkward a booby that I dared scarcely speak to her; I was filled with awe and embarrassment in her presence; but I was so inspired that my poetical temperament for the first time broke out in verse and I fabricated some glowing lines, in which I berhymed the little lady under the favourite name of Sacharissa. I slipped the verses, trembling and blushing, into her hand the next Sunday as she came out of church. The little prude handed them to her mamma; the mamma handed them to the squire; the squire, who had no soul for poetry, sent them in dudgeon to the schoolmaster; and the schoolmaster, with a barbarity worthy of the dark ages, gave me a sound and peculiarly humiliating flogging for thus trespassing upon Parnassus.

Washington Irving, "Buckthorne," *Tales of a Traveller*

1. The narrator's father sent his son to a public school mainly:

   A. to toughen him up.
   B. to meet people from the upper class.
   C. because of its excellent curriculum.
   D. because the boy was a trouble maker.

2. The term "poetical feeling" (line 13), as used by the narrator, means that he:

   F. enjoyed writing poetry.
   G. views himself as a budding poet.
   H. was a romantic dreamer.
   J. loved reading poetry more than anything.

3. The speaker attributes his poor record in school to:

   A. too many distractions.
   B. a learning disability.
   C. friends who led him astray.
   D. being unhappy in a boarding school.

4. The narrator compares his schooling to a cattle drive (lines 7–11) in order to make the point that:

   F. students were grouped according to ability.
   G. the students were treated inhumanely.
   H. weak students were punished for their deficiencies.
   J. individuality was discouraged.

5. As a youth, the narrator believed that in order to learn in school you:

   A. should have small classes.
   B. had to be punished.
   C. should study hard.
   D. needed enthusiastic teachers.

6. The boy's attitude toward the country squire was shaped in part by:

   F. the influence of the schoolmaster.
   G. the squire's daughter.
   H. the teachings of the church.
   J. his observation of how others behaved.

7. The narrator introduces the squire into the passage (line 40) for the purpose of

   A. illustrating the evils of England's class structure.
   B. adding humor to the narrative.
   C. contrasting the personalities of the squire and the parson.
   D. pointing out similarities between his own father and the squire.

8. The name *Sacharissa* is:

   F. the first name of the girl with whom the narrator falls in love.
   G. a name invented by the narrator because he didn't know the girl's real name.
   H. the woman to whom the poet Waller wrote love poems.
   J. the name of a wood nymph in Ovid's *Metamorphosis*.

9. Which of the following best describes the narrator's feelings about the situations described in the passage?

   A. Amused by the trials of growing up.
   B. Bitter about the way he was treated by adults.
   C. Nostalgic about the days of his boyhood.
   D. Glad that those years are over and done with.

10. At the end of the passage the boy is flogged by the schoolmaster because he:

    F. embarrassed the girl.
    G. fell in love with someone above him.
    H. had illicit thoughts about the girl.
    J. wrote poetry.

GO ON TO THE NEXT PAGE.

Passage 2—Social Studies

This passage is adapted from a publication of the U.S. Department of Health and Human Services titled Stuttering: Hope Through Research. *The selection describes various symptoms of stuttering.*

Stuttering is a disorder in which the rhythmic flow, or fluency, of speech is disrupted by rapid-fire repetitions of sounds, prolonged vowels, and complete stops—verbal blocks. A stutterer's speech is often uncontrollable—sometimes faster, but usually slower than the average speaking rate. Sometimes, too, the voice changes in pitch, loudness, and inflection.

Observations of young children during the early stages of stuttering have led to a list of warning signs that can help identify a child who is developing a speech problem. Most children use "um's" and "ah's," and will repeat words or syllables as they learn to speak. It is not a serious concern if a child says, "I like to go and and and and play games," unless such repetitions occur often, more than once every 20 words or so.

Repeating whole words is not necessarily a sign of stuttering; however, repeating speech sounds or syllables such as in the song "K-K-K-Katy" is.

Sometimes a stutterer will exhibit tension while prolonging a sound. For example, the 8-year-old who says, "Annnnnnnd—and—thththen I I drank it" with lips trembling at the same time. Children who experience such a stuttering tremor usually become frightened, angry, and frustrated at their inability to speak. A further danger sign is a rise in pitch as the child draws out the syllable.

The appearance of a child or adult experiencing the most severe signs of stuttering is dramatic: As they struggle to get a word out, their whole face may contort, the jaw may jerk, the mouth open, tongue protrude, and eyes roll. Tension can spread through the whole body. A moment of overwhelming struggle occurs during the speech block. ...

While the symptoms of stuttering are easy to recognize, the underlying cause remains a mystery. Hippocrates thought that stuttering was due to dryness of the tongue, and he prescribed blistering substances to drain away the black bile responsible. A Roman physician recommended gargling and massages to strengthen a weak tongue. Seventeenth century scientist Francis Bacon suggested hot wine to thaw a "refrigerated" tongue. Too large a tongue was the fault, according to a 19th century Prussian physician, so he snipped pieces off stutterers' tongues. Alexander Melville Bell, father of the telephone inventor, insisted stuttering was simply a bad habit that could be overcome by reeducation.

Some theories today attribute stuttering to problems in the control of the muscles of speech. As recently as the fifties and sixties, however, stuttering was thought to arise from deep-rooted personality problems, and psychotherapy was recommended.

Stutterers represent the whole range of personality types, levels of emotional adjustment, and intelligence. Winston Churchill was a stutterer (or stammerer, as the English prefer to say). So were Sir Isaac Newton, King George VI of England, and writer Somerset Maugham.

There are more than 15 million stutterers in the world today and approximately 1 million in the United States alone.

Most stuttering begins after a child has mastered the basics of speech and is starting to talk automatically. One out of 30 children will then undergo a brief period of stuttering, lasting 6 months or so. Boys are four times as likely as girls to be stutterers.

Occasionally stuttering arises in an older child or even in an adult. It may follow an illness or an emotionally shattering event, such as a death in the family. Stuttering may also occur following brain injury, either due to head injury or after a stroke. No matter how the problem begins, stutterers generally experience their worst moments under conditions of stress or emotional tension: ordering in a crowded restaurant, talking over the telephone, speaking in public, asking the boss for a raise.

Stuttering does not develop in a predictable pattern. In children, speech difficulties can disappear for weeks or months only to return in full force. About 80 percent of children with a stuttering problem are able to speak normally by the time they are adults—whether they've had therapy or not. Adult stutterers have also been known to stop stuttering for no apparent reason.

Indeed, all stutterers can speak fluently some of the time. Most can also whisper smoothly, speak in unison, and sing with no hesitations. Country and western singer Mel Tillis is an example of a stutterer with a successful singing career.

Most stutterers also speak easily when they are prevented from hearing their own voices, when talking to pets and small children, or when addressing themselves in the mirror. All these instances of fluency demonstrate that nothing is basically wrong with the stutterer's speech machinery.

11. According to the passage, stuttering will be a life-long problem for:

    A. males who stuttered in childhood.
    B. males and females who began stuttering in childhood.
    C. only a small percentage of childhood stutterers.
    D. anyone who fails to get help.

12. The passage indicates that during moments of speech blockage, a stutterer may experience all of the following symptoms EXCEPT:

    F. facial distortion.
    G. severe frustration.
    H. body tension.
    J. trembling head and hands.

13. Based on information in the passage, which of the following situations is LEAST likely to occur?

    A. A man begins to stutter after a traumatic divorce.
    B. A schoolgirl temporarily stops stuttering during summer vacation.
    C. An actress stutters off stage but not during performances.
    D. A boy stutters mostly when telling bedtime stories to his baby sister.

14. One can infer from the passage that a parent whose young child repeats the same word over and over while learning to speak would be advised to:

    F. take the child to see a speech therapist.
    G. help the child relax while speaking.
    H. accept the fact that the child will be a stutterer.
    J. keep track of the frequency of repetitions.

15. According to the passage, young children usually begin to stutter:

    A. after learning to speak fluently.
    B. after a severe emotional shock.
    C. during prolonged periods of stress or tension.
    D. when they lack the vocabulary to express themselves.

16. Until the 19th century, authorities apparently regarded stuttering as:

    F. a sign of low intelligence.
    G. an emotional problem.
    H. a physical ailment.
    J. a lack of self-discipline.

17. One can infer from the passage that a stutterer may find relief by:

    A. avoiding situations that typically cause stuttering.
    B. practicing speech in front of a mirror.
    C. preparing what they have to say ahead of time.
    D. speaking more slowly.

18. One may assume that stuttering is NOT caused by a physical disorder of a person's speech apparatus because:

    F. all stutterers speak fluently from time to time.
    G. stuttering sometimes appears and disappears for no apparent reason.
    H. famous people, including athletes, have been stutterers.
    J. highly intelligent people have been known to stutter.

19. The author's main purpose in this passage is to point out that:

    A. treatment is available for stutterers identified early enough in life.
    B. the effects of stuttering are widely known, but uncertainty surrounds its causes.
    C. stutterers should not be held responsible for their speech disorder.
    D. the symptoms of stuttering are confusing and often misunderstood.

20. By pointing out that famous and successful people have been stutterers, the author means to imply all of the following EXCEPT that:

    F. stuttering is not a serious handicap in life.
    G. stuttering is unrelated to I.Q.
    H. the public is generally tolerant of stutterers.
    J. stuttering is not a personality disorder.

GO ON TO THE NEXT PAGE.

Passage 3—Humanities

This passage is adapted from "Wanted: A World Language," by Mario Pei. In this selection, Pei explains the difficulties of developing a single international language.

In the 17th century, French philosopher René Descartes came forth with a revolutionary idea. He proposed the creation of a language that could be used internationally by all sorts of people, peasants as well as scholars.

But Descartes made the mistake of concentrating on the logical aspects of such a language, the progression of ideas from the general to the specific. This logical structure exists in no living language, not even in the great classical tongues of antiquity, which are replete with illogical exceptions and arbitrary features.

While Descartes offered no sample of his ideal constructed language, several of his contemporaries immediately came to the fore with offerings. Some of their suggestions were quite ingenious, but all embodied the principle of logical progression at the expense of familiarity and ease. For example, Bishop John Wilkins' *Essay* of 1668 presents a language in which *Z* indicates animals in general, *Za* indicates fish, and successive consonants and vowels further restrict the concept to particular classes of fish.

But alongside these attempts at constructed languages which had no connection with any existing language, there was also a startlingly modern proposal, one made by the Bohemian scholar Comenius. He suggested the use of existing languages, not on a universal, but on a zonal basis (he actually proposed English and French for use in Western Europe, Russian as a common tongue for Eastern Europe). This type of solution, still widely advocated today, is in the nature of a temporary makeshift, because it does not supply us with one universal language, but merely makes the existing linguistic confusion a little easier to bear.

Since the days of Descartes, Wilkins, and Comenius, at least a thousand proposals of one description or another have been advanced. These include several distinct types:

1) The selection and use of an existing language, ancient or modern, such as Latin, French, or English.

2) The combination of two or more existing languages, either in zonal distribution, as advocated by Comenius and, much later, by Stalin; or existing side by side, like the Greek and Latin of antiquity. (The French *Monde Bilingue* organization, for instance, advocates that all English speakers learn French, all French speakers learn English, and all speakers of other tongues learn one or the other. This does not solve the problem of communicating when a Czech who has learned French meets a Japanese who has learned English.)

3) The choice of a modified national language, such as Basic English, which works with a reduced vocabulary made to serve all purposes by a process of substitution and paraphrase (*bush,* for instance, is replaced by *small tree; selfish* is replaced by *without thought of others*); or works with the modification applied not to the vocabulary, but to the system of spelling or the grammatical structure (*thru, filozofi,* would be samples of spelling; *goed, dood, oxes, mouses* instead of the irregular *went, did, oxen, mice* would be examples of grammar).

4) Blends of two or more existing languages, with words and constructions arbitrarily taken from one or another of the constituent languages.

5) Fully constructed languages showing no connection with any known languages (like the American Ro and Suma).

6) Constructed languages in which existing languages are freely utilized to supply, or at least to suggest, both vocabulary and grammatical structure, but with concern for component elements familiar to the greatest possible number of people with different language backgrounds (Volapük, Esperanto, Ido, Interlingua).

While many of these projects are impractical and present discouraging features, there are at least as many, of all the types outlined above, that could easily become operational. It is therefore not the lack of suitable schemes that has prevented, up to the time of writing, the adoption of a language for universal use. ...

The crux of the problem lies not in the principle, but in its application. *Which* language shall be adopted for international use? There are in existence some 3,000 natural languages, including the better-known classical ones, such as Latin and Greek; plus at least 1,000 fully constructed languages, or modified national tongues, that have been presented since the days of Descartes.

21. For a language to be designated "constructed," it must:

A. be different from any existing language.
B. have no connection whatever to any known language.
C. sound familiar to the greatest number of people, regardless of their native tongues.
D. combine elements from at least three existing languages.

3 3 3 3 3 3 3 3 3 3 3

22. Which of the following ideas is clearly indicated by the passage?

    F. Speakers of French are unwilling to replace their own tongue with a universal language.
    G. Josef Stalin advocated a language plan that no one had thought of before.
    H. Ancient Latin and Greek are the foundation of most modern languages.
    J. Natural languages are far more common than constructed languages.

23. The author's principal assumption is that:

    A. the world has too many languages.
    B. an international language will contribute to the formation of international government.
    C. a single international language will be beneficial to mankind.
    D. a universal language will simplify communications among Eastern and Western European nations.

24. The passage implies that the language proposed by Bishop John Wilkins is a:

    F. blend of two or more existing languages.
    G. type of zonal language.
    H. modified national language.
    J. constructed language.

25. The author of the passage believes that adoption of a universal language:

    A. is not as difficult as it may seem.
    B. will probably never happen.
    C. will occur when the right language is invented.
    D. will take place when linguists agree on which language to use.

26. The passage implies that Descartes' proposal for an international tongue failed because it:

    F. was illogical.
    G. contained too many exceptions to the rules of language.
    H. contradicted a basic principle of language usage.
    J. was too much like old Latin and Greek.

27. By calling Comenius's scheme for an international language "startlingly modern" (line 24), the author means that:

    A. Comenius devised a plan that could work in today's world.
    B. Comenius's proposal had never been thought of before.
    C. Comenius's ideas parallel the ideas of many 20th-century linguists.
    D. Comenius's language was simple and easy to learn.

28. Which of the following is the most valid generalization about the language types proposed for international use (lines 37 through 70)?

    F. They are simpler to use than most present-day languages.
    G. They are based on universal rules of grammar.
    H. They are rooted in existing languages.
    J. They appeal equally to all nationalities.

29. According to the passage, many proposals for an international language originated during the 17th century because:

    A. Descartes' proposal was incomplete.
    B. it was an enlightened time.
    C. it was a revolutionary era.
    D. international travel began to flourish.

30. The passage implies that, in order to be functional, a constructed language:

    F. must borrow from the widely spoken languages of the world.
    G. may not be based solely on logical principles.
    H. may use the grammar of English or of any other popular language.
    J. must be translatable into several thousand natural languages.

GO ON TO THE NEXT PAGE.

Passage 4—Natural Science

This passage, about undersea life in the very deepest parts of the ocean, comes from Rachel Carson's book, The Sea Around Us.

In their world of darkness, it would seem likely that some of the animals might have become blind, as has happened to some cave fauna. So, indeed, many of them have, compensating for the lack of eyes with marvelously developed feelers and long, slender fins and processes with which they grope their way, like so many blind men with canes, their whole knowledge of friends, enemies, or food coming to them through the sense of touch.

The last traces of plant life are left behind in the thin upper layer of water, for no plant can live below about 600 feet even in very clear water, and few find enough sunlight for their food-manufacturing activities below 200 feet. Since no animal can make its own food, the creatures of the deeper waters live a strange, almost parasitic existence of utter dependence on the upper layers. These hungry carnivores prey fiercely and relentlessly upon each other, yet the whole community is ultimately dependent upon the slow rain of descending food particles from above. The components of this never-ending rain are the dead and dying plants and animals from the surface, or from one of the intermediate layers. For each of the horizontal zones or communities of the sea that lie, in tier after tier, between the surface and the sea bottom, the food supply is different and in general poorer than for the layers above. There is a hint of the fierce and uncompromising competition for food in the saber-toothed jaws of some of the small, dragonlike fishes of the deeper waters, in the immense mouths and in the elastic and distensible bodies that make it possible for a fish to swallow another several times its size, enjoying swift repletion after a long fast.

Pressure, darkness, and—we should have added only a few years ago—silence, are the conditions of life in the deep sea. But we know now that the conception of the sea as a silent place is wholly false. Wide experience with hydrophones and other listening devices for the detection of submarines has proved that, around the shore lines of much of the world, there is the extraordinary uproar produced by fishes, shrimps, porpoises and probably other forms not yet identified. There has been little investigation as yet of sound in the deep, offshore areas, but when the crew of *Atlantis* lowered a hydrophone into deep water off Bermuda, they recorded strange mewing sounds, shrieks, and ghostly moans, the sources of which have not been traced. But fish of shallower zones have been captured and confined in aquaria, where their voices have been recorded for comparison with sounds heard at sea, and in many cases satisfactory identification can be made.

During the Second World War the hydrophone network set up by the United States Navy to protect the entrance to Chesapeake Bay was temporarily made useless when, in the spring of 1942, the speakers at the surface began to give forth, every evening, a sound described as being like "a pneumatic drill tearing up pavement." The extraneous noises that came over the hydrophones completely masked the sounds of the passage of ships. Eventually it was discovered that the sounds were the voices of fish known as croakers, which in the spring move into Chesapeake Bay from their offshore wintering grounds. As soon as the noise had been identified and analyzed, it was possible to screen it out with an electric filter, so that once more only the sounds of ships came through the speakers.

31. According to the passage, the layer of the ocean where food for animal life is most plentiful is:

A. the bottom.
B. an area below 600 feet deep.
C. the area between 200 and 600 feet in depth.
D. the uppermost layers of water.

32. Based on information in the passage, which of the following criteria is NOT likely to be used as a measure of underwater depth?

F. Noise level recorded by undersea microphones.
G. Pressure per square inch.
H. Amount of light.
J. Amount of plant life.

33. The passage indicates that many underwater animals cannot see because:

A. the lack of light has gradually eliminated their visual capability.
B. they use sound waves instead of light to navigate in the darkness.
C. they have learned to survive without seeing their enemies or their prey.
D. their acute sense of touch has made visual ability superfluous.

3 3 3 3 3 3 3 3 3 3 3

34. Based on information in the third paragraph, which of the following is most likely NOT a function of a hydrophone?

    F. To listen to the sound of undersea fauna.
    G. To search for unknown species of fish and other creatures.
    H. To monitor the passing of surface vessels.
    J. To detect submerged submarines.

35. It can be reasonably inferred from the passage that creatures living near the bottom of the sea are carnivorous because:

    A. they have developed sharp teeth and strong jaws with which to kill their prey.
    B. plants that grow far below the surface are not edible.
    C. animals cannot make their own food, so they eat each other.
    D. most surface vegetation is eaten before it sinks to the bottom of the sea.

36. The passage indicates that fish living far underwater sometimes do not eat for extended periods of time because:

    F. food is scarce at certain times of year.
    G. fish in the deepest parts of the ocean digest their food very slowly.
    H. weaker fish must compete for food with stronger fish.
    J. one large meal satisfies most fish for a long time.

37. Which of the following statements about the state of oceanographic research does the passage most clearly imply?

    A. Undersea research is still incomplete.
    B. Technology used in undersea studies is still in a very primitive stage of development.
    C. More undersea research is conducted near the shore than in mid-ocean.
    D. Military researchers have made several momentous discoveries about undersea life.

38. The phrase "enjoying swift repletion," as used in line 31, probably means that the fish:

    F. are in a state of being sated (*i.e.*, filled to capacity).
    G. seem to enjoy eating after a long fast.
    H. digest their prey very quickly.
    J. continue to hunt for food even after devouring their prey.

39. By using the phrase "saber-toothed" (line 27) to characterize some of the fishes that live in the deepest waters, the author is suggesting that the fishes:

    A. are still at an early stage of evolution.
    B. appear frightening to behold.
    C. are ferocious food-gatherers.
    D. are soon likely to become extinct.

40. The author's main purpose in the passage is to:

    F. show that the United States coast was threatened by the enemy in World War II.
    G. explain some of the complexities of deep-sea life.
    H. illustrate the main problems faced by undersea researchers.
    J. gain public support for oceanographic expeditions.

STOP

If there is still time remaining, you may review your answers.

4 4 4 4 4 4 4 4 4 4 4

SCIENCE REASONING TEST

35 MINUTES—40 QUESTIONS

Directions: This test consists of several distinct passages. Each passage is followed by a number of multiple-choice questions based on the passage. Study the passage, and then select the best answer to each question. You are allowed to reread the passage. Record your answer by blackening the appropriate space on the Answer Sheet.

Passage 1

In the diagram below, each point represents the average fat intake and rate of death from breast cancer for a particular country.

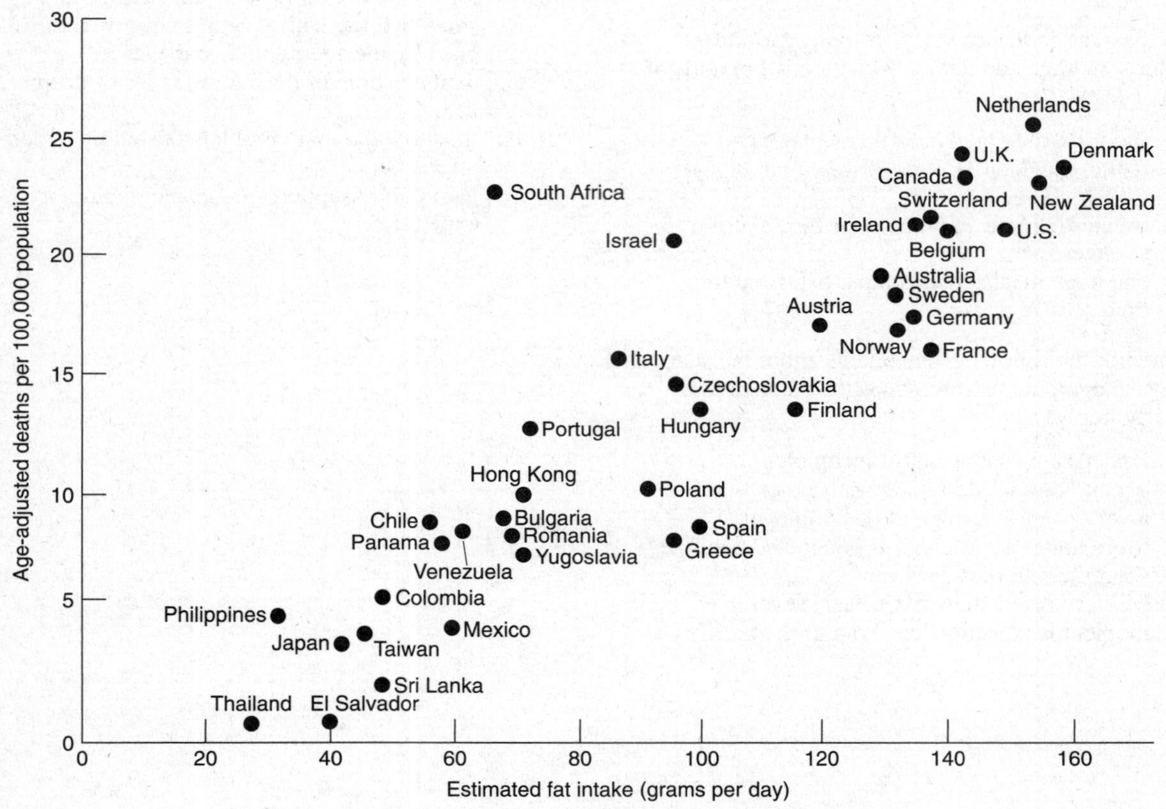

4 4 4 4 4 4 4 4 4 4

1. In countries where the death rate from breast cancer is about 13 or 14 per 100,000 of population, the average fat intake is:

   A. 60 g/day.
   B. from 70 to 120 g/day.
   C. from 60 to 90 g/day.
   D. 100 g/day.

2. Of the following pairs, which are two countries with about the same death rate, but drastically different fat intakes?

   F. Israel and Greece
   G. Austria and Germany
   H. France and Mexico
   J. Israel and the United States

3. What inference is suggested by the data?

   A. Consumption of fats is the cause of breast cancer.
   B. Women with breast cancer develop a craving for fatty foods.
   C. High levels of fat intake tend to promote the formation of breast cancers.
   D. Environmental pollution promotes a desire for fatty foods, and therefore, breast cancer.

4. For which country do the data suggest that some factor other than intake of fatty foods is causing many breast cancers?

   F. Thailand
   G. Philippines
   H. Netherlands
   J. South Africa

5. Why are the data points for Greece and Spain slightly below the general trend?

   A. The sunny Mediterranean climate offers some protection against breast cancer.
   B. For many reasons, there is considerable scatter in the points.
   C. Olive oil, rather than animal fats, is used in these countries.
   D. The scatter of the points implies that there is much unreliability in the data.

6. What additional evidence would tend to show that consumption of dietary fat is a chief contributor to the rate of breast cancer?

   F. Americans who move to Europe develop higher rates of breast cancer.
   G. With an increase in meat consumption, the rate of breast cancer in Japan is increasing.
   H. South Africans have a high level of fat in the diet.
   J. In the United States the rate of breast cancer is higher in whites than in blacks.

GO ON TO THE NEXT PAGE.

4 4 4 4 4 4 4 4 4 4 4

Passage 2

The chart below gives the 1998 death rate in the United States due to six chronic illnesses, and the change in this rate between 1980 and 1998. (Pulmonary refers to lungs.) It also states the risk factors known to be associated with each of these illnesses, as follows:

C: high cholesterol
H: hypertension (high blood pressure)
S: smoking
O: obesity
P: physical inactivity
D: poor diet

The graph shows how the incidence of 4 of these risk factors has changed since 1960.

THE SIX LEADING LIFESTYLE DISEASES

	DEATHS IN 1998 (THOUSANDS)	PERCENT CHANGE IN MORTALITY RATE, 1980–1998	LEADING RISK FACTORS
CORONARY HEART DISEASE	460	–47	C,H,S,O,P
STROKE	158	–38	C,H,S,O
LUNG CANCER	155	+6	S
CHRONIC OBSTRUCTIVE PULMONARY DISEASE	113	+34	S
DIABETES	65	+35	O
COLON CANCER	57	–24	D,P
ALL CAUSES	2,337	–19	

SOURCE: American Health Association. Changes in mortality rates are based on age-adjusted data.

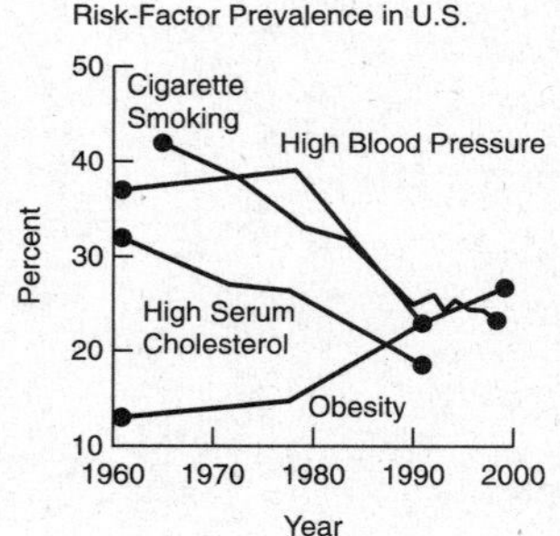

4 4 4 4 4 4 4 4 4 4

7. In 1998, how many Americans died of diseases that might have been prevented by regular exercise?

   A. 57,000
   B. 460,000
   C. 517,000
   D. 618,000

8. The decrease in deaths due to stroke caused by high blood pressure was probably not as good as it might have been because

   F. there has been little change in the rate of cigarette smoking.
   G. medication for high blood pressure has not improved.
   H. people are not exercising as much as they used to.
   J. the rate of obesity has been increasing.

9. The risk factors seem to be operating in the opposite direction from the change in mortality rate due to

   A. lung cancer
   B. heart disease
   C. diabetes
   D. colon cancer

10. What is a reasonable explanation for the increase in the incidence of lung cancer?

   F. Medication for hypertension has improved in recent years.
   G. The data do not cover the years before 1980.
   H. The graph does not include information about physical activity.
   J. Other factors, not considered here, enter into the liability to this disease.

11. A general statement about health that is implicit in this study is that

   A. chronic illness can be prevented by control of habits.
   B. lifestyle has a strong impact on survival.
   C. choices made while alive, not heredity, are the dominant factors in determining longevity.
   D. to prolong life, chronic illness should be treated medically.

12. What action that more people are taking in recent years could help to reverse a growing death rate?

   F. Taking steps to lower cholesterol level
   G. Adopting a healthier diet
   H. Dieting to lose weight
   J. Doing more exercise

GO ON TO THE NEXT PAGE.

Passage 3

A medical research worker is testing the effectiveness of an experimental vaccine in controlling cancer. His experimental animals are three different groups of mice. Strains A and B are purebred strains of laboratory white mice, whose susceptibilities to cancer are well known. The third group consists of mice trapped in the wild.

Experiment 1

All three groups were bred for several generations, and no treatment was given. Skin cancers developed at the following rates:

Strain A: 8%
Strain B: 62%
Wild mice: 3%

Experiment 2

All three groups were treated with applications of benzol, a known carcinogen. Skin cancers developed at these rates:

Strain A: 59%
Strain B: 98%
Wild mice: 14%

Experiment 3

All three groups were treated with benzol, followed by administration of the vaccine. Cancer rates were:

Strain A: 56%
Strain B: 61%
Wild mice: 14%

Experiment 4

All three groups were treated with benzol, followed by treatment with fexadrin, a chemical agent that is now in common use in the treatment of cancer. Cancer rates were:

Strain A: 32%
Strain B: 98%
Wild mice: 3%

13. Unless Experiment 1 were done, the scientist would not know:

 A. whether mice can develop skin cancer.
 B. how effective benzol is in producing cancers in these strains.
 C. whether wild mice can be compared with laboratory mice.
 D. if all laboratory-bred mice were alike.

14. One clear result of all these tests is the evidence that:

 F. the vaccine is completely ineffective.
 G. heredity influences the usefulness of the vaccine.
 H. there is no way to prevent skin cancer completely.
 J. neither of the two treatments will be effective in combating human cancers.

15. The experiments show that:

 A. the vaccine was generally more effective than fexadrin.
 B. fexadrin was generally more effective than the vaccine.
 C. where there is a strong hereditary tendency to develop cancer, the vaccine is more effective than fexadrin.
 D. In wild mice, neither the vaccine nor the chemical agent had any effect.

16. These experiments would be significant in developing treatment for human cancer only if:

 F. cancers produced in mice by benzol have properties similar to those of spontaneous human cancers.
 G. there is no hereditary tendency to develop cancer in human beings.
 H. humans have about the same rate of cancer as wild mice.
 J. human hereditary endowment is comparable to that of purebred laboratory mice.

17. Which of the following questions would it NOT be worthwhile to pursue further?

 A. Why do wild mice have such a low rate of cancer?
 B. Why does the vaccine have such a good effect in a strain with a strong hereditary susceptibility to cancer, but not in the other strains?
 C. Why does fexadrin have such a good effect in Strain A, but not in Strain B?
 D. How can benzol be altered chemically to increase the rate at which it produces cancer in lines of mice with hereditary susceptibility?

GO ON TO THE NEXT PAGE.

4 4 4 4 4 4 4 4 4 4 4

Passage 4

The diagram below shows the results of sampling the stomach contents of 5 species of fish. The data tell what percentage of each species were found to contain each of 6 kinds of food. A dot indicates that a particular species consumed none of the food in question.

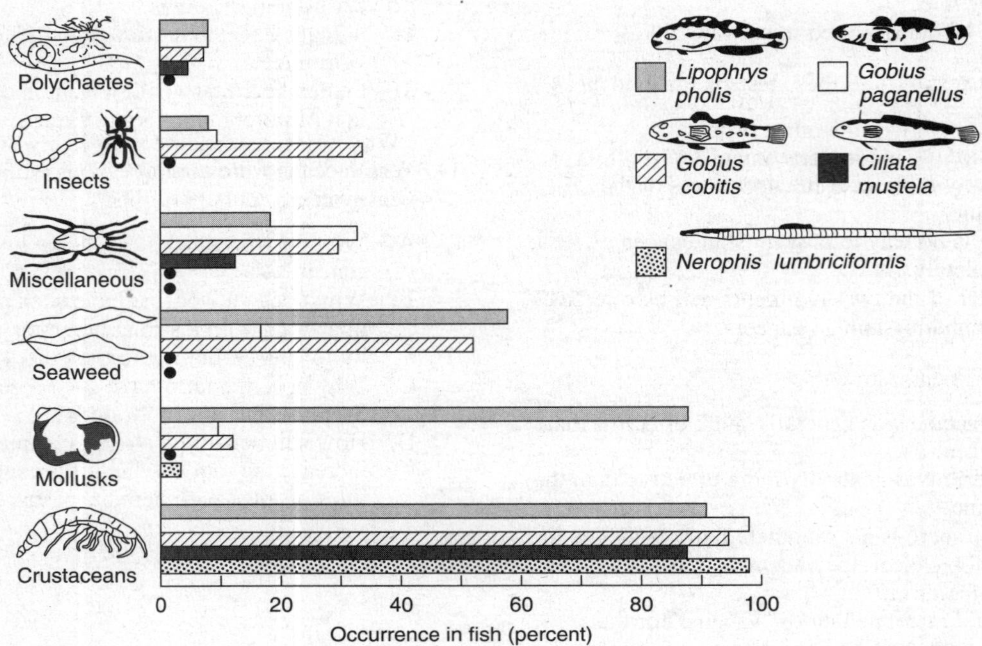

18. In which species did about one third of all individuals contain insects?

    F. *Lipophrys*
    G. *Nerophis*
    H. *G. paganellus*
    J. *G. cobitis*

19. Which statement correctly describes an aspect of the feeding habits of these fishes?

    A. Nonanimal food is used by more *Lipophrys* than by any of the other fishes.
    B. *Nerophis* cannot make any use of mollusks.
    C. *G. paganellus* uses a wider variety of food than any of the others.
    D. *G. cobitis* gets over 90% of its nourishment from crustaceans.

20. The data seem to suggest that:

    F. *G. cobitis* cannot digest plant food.
    G. all members of the genus *Gobius* have identical food choices.
    H. *Lipophrys* has jaws strong enough to crack shells.
    J. a long, thin fish prefers insect food.

21. In what way would a change in the food supply affect the population of the fishes?

    A. If polychaetes were eliminated from the supply, all five fish populations would suffer.
    B. Loss of crustaceans might completely eliminate the *Nerophis* population.
    C. Loss of mollusks might completely eliminate the *Lipophrys* population.
    D. Increase in the availability of insects would increase the population of *G. paganellus*.

22. Which fishes would be most likely to survive if crustaceans were completely wiped out in the ecosystem?

    F. *Nerophis* and *G. cobitis*
    G. *Lipophrys* and *G. cobitis*
    H. *G. paganellus* and *Ciliata*
    J. *Lipophrys* and *Ciliata*

GO ON TO THE NEXT PAGE.

Passage 5

A scientist is looking for a general rule that governs the viscous drag that a liquid exerts on a sphere moving through it. The viscous drag is a retarding force, tending to prevent any increase in the velocity of the sphere. If a sphere is dropped into a liquid, it will soon fall at a constant speed, at which the viscous drag is equal to the weight of the sphere.

Experiment 1

Steel spheres of various sizes were dropped into a tank containing a 2% solution of methyl cellulose. When they reached constant velocity, the speed of fall was measured.

Diameter of sphere (cm)	Velocity of fall (m/s)
0.5	0.21
1.0	0.82
1.5	1.80
2.0	3.25
2.5	5.03
3.0	7.25

Experiment 2

Spheres made of materials of different density, but all having a diameter of 1.0 cm, were dropped into a 2% solution of methyl cellulose, and the velocity of fall was measured.

Material	Density (g/cm^3)	Velocity of fall (m/s)
Tungsten	14.5	1.54
Lead	11.0	1.14
Brass	9.1	0.93
Steel	8.0	0.80
Gymalloy	5.2	0.48
Aluminum	2.7	0.19
Lignum vitae	1.3	0.03

Experiment 3

The same steel spheres as in Experiment 1 were now dropped through at 4% solution of methyl cellulose.

Diameter of sphere (cm)	Velocity of fall (m/s)
0.5	0.07
1.0	0.27
1.5	0.60
2.0	1.07
2.5	1.65
3.0	2.41

4 4 4 4 4 4 4 4 4 4

23. If Experiment 1 were repeated using a lead sphere instead of steel, in what way would the readings in the second column compare to those in the second column for steel?

 A. They would all be larger.
 B. They would all be smaller.
 C. They would all be the same.
 D. There is no way to predict the results.

24. The larger steel sphere falls faster than the small ones because it has a greater

 F. density
 G. weight
 H. volume
 J. surface area

25. If a 1.0-cm steel sphere falls at 0.50 m/s through honey, what would be the rate of fall of a 2.0-cm steel sphere?

 A. 0.25 m/s
 B. 0.50 m/s
 C. 1.00 m/s
 D. 2.00 m/s

26. What is a reasonable conclusion obtained by comparing the results of Experiments 1 and 3?

 F. Viscous drag is three times as great in a 2% solution of methyl cellulose as in a 4% solution.
 G. Steel spheres fall three times as fast in a 2% solution of methyl cellulose as in a 4% solution.
 H. Larger steel spheres fall faster than smaller ones in a 4% solution of methyl cellulose.
 J. Doubling the density of a solution of methyl cellulose raises its viscous drag by a factor of 3.

27. Which of the following spheres would probably NOT sink at all if placed in a 2% methyl cellulose solution?

 A. A 1.0-cm sphere of plastic with a density of 1.0 g/cm^3
 B. A 0.3-cm brass sphere with a density of 8.0 g/cm^3
 C. A 0.1-cm aluminum sphere with a density of 2.7 g/cm^3
 D. A 3.0-cm teakwood sphere with a density of 1.3 g/cm^3

GO ON TO THE NEXT PAGE.

Passage 6

The egg of a fruit fly hatches into a larva. After some days, the larva forms a shell around itself, turning into a pupa. In the pupa stage, it develops wings and legs and then emerges as an adult fly. The adult lives for some weeks.

Experiment 1

Eggs of a species of fruit fly, *Drosophila A,* were grown at different controlled temperatures, and the average number of days that the developing fly spent in each stage were recorded, as shown in the table below.

Temperature (° C)	Egg stage (days)	Larva stage (days)	Pupa stage (days)	Adult stage (days)
10	5	5	5	15
15	4	7	5	19
20	4	6	5	22
25	3	7	5	20
30	3	5	5	16

Experiment 2

An identical experiment was done with a different species, *Drosophila B:*

Temperature (° C)	Egg stage (days)	Larva stage (days)	Pupa stage (days)	Adult stage (days)
10	6	10	5	28
15	6	9	5	28
20	4	8	5	25
25	3	7	5	20
30	3	6	5	16

Experiment 3

Pupae of both species were moved from the 10° C room to the 25° C room as soon as the pupae formed. Adults of *Drosophila A* survived an average of 15 days, and of *Drosophila B* an average of 28 days.

28. In both species, which of the following effects is produced by higher temperatures?

    F. Faster development occurs through the egg stage.
    G. A larger fraction of the total life span is spent in the pupa stage.
    H. The larva stage is completed more quickly.
    J. Total life expectancy is greater.

29. Which of the following statements applies to both species?

    A. Larvae grow faster and larger at higher temperatures.
    B. The rate at which the egg grows into a larva is independent of temperature.
    C. The rate at which the larva changes into an adult is independent of temperature.
    D. Adults survive longer at lower temperatures.

30. Which of the following statements applies to *Drosophila B* but not to *Drosophila A?*

    F. At higher temperatures, development in the egg stage is speeded up.
    G. Life expectancy is greatest at the lower temperatures.
    H. The flies that pass through their developmental stages quickest have the longest life spans.
    J. The duration of the pupa stage is the same at all temperatures.

31. Which of the following statements about the probable natural habitat of the two species is suggested by the data?

    A. *Drosophila A* is a tropical species.
    B. *Drosophila B* is a tropical species.
    C. *Drosophila A* is a cold-weather species.
    D. *Drosophila B* is a cold-weather species.

32. Experiment 3 suggests that the life expectancy of a fruit fly depends largely on the temperature during what part of its life cycle?

    F. Pupa
    G. Egg or larva or both
    H. Egg only
    J. Adult

33. Which of the following hypotheses is suggested by all the data?

    A. Fruit flies develop faster at higher temperatures.
    B. Optimum temperatures differ among different species of fruit fly.
    C. Fruit flies that develop faster live longer.
    D. Higher temperatures reduce the life expectancy of fruit flies.

GO ON TO THE NEXT PAGE.

Passage 7

Mercury is a dangerous pollutant; it enters the water from the air and accumulates in the tissues of fish. It has been suggested that we severely limit the amount of fish we eat.

Scientist 1

Mercury is present in many kinds of rocks and in air polluted by the burning of fuels. It accumulates in the bodies of fish, particularly in carnivorous, freshwater sport fish. It is a nerve poison. Water polluted with mercury has poisoned whole populations of fish-eating people. A new study shows that mercury also damages the heart. Several hundred European men who had had heart attacks were assayed for mercury in the body by analyzing their toenail clippings. They were found to have more mercury in their bodies than a similar group who had not had heart attacks.

This suggests that we should limit our consumption of fish. Saltwater fish and seafood are safer since they have less mercury than freshwater fish. Children are especially vulnerable and should not be fed as much fish as adults.

Scientist 2

It is true that mercury is a nerve poison, but the amount in any fish we are likely to eat is too small to constitute a danger. Our water has been analyzed, and the amount of mercury in it is too little to threaten the health of adults. There is every reason to believe that fish are healthy foods. They contain a fatty acid known as DHA, which provides substantial protection against heart disease.

The study cited by Scientist 1 is not the last word. When it was repeated in the United States, no correlation between mercury and heart disease was found. A possible reason for this discrepancy might be that European waters contain some other pollutant, one not found in America. Scientists agree that we should not put too much faith in the results of an experiment unless it can be repeated in other venues.

The health benefits of fish are well established, and there is no reason for adults to limit their consumption. Perhaps as a precaution, pregnant women and young children, whose nervous systems are developing, should not eat too much freshwater fish.

4 4 4 4 4 4 4 4 4 4

34. What was the question being disputed in the two studies?
 - **F.** Does eating fish contribute to accumulation of mercury in the body?
 - **G.** Does mercury constitute a risk factor for heart disease?
 - **H.** Do freshwater fish contain mercury in their tissue?
 - **J.** Should we limit our consumption of fish?

35. Both of the experiments are based on the assumption that:
 - **A.** saltwater fish are safer than freshwater fish.
 - **B.** people are eating too much fish.
 - **C.** large concentrations of mercury are dangerous to the health.
 - **D.** eating fish is correlated with the amount of mercury in the toenails.

36. The two scientists would agree that:
 - **F.** freshwater fish contain dangerous levels of mercury.
 - **G.** at high levels, mercury is a health hazard.
 - **H.** steps should be taken to eliminate mercury from our rivers and streams.
 - **J.** mercury is a contributing factor for heart disease.

37. Scientist 2 suggests that a possible reason for the discrepancy between the two studies might be a difference between:
 - **A.** the kinds of pollution in the two venues.
 - **B.** the amount of mercury in European and American waters.
 - **C.** the fish-eating habits of Europeans and Americans.
 - **D.** the methods of evaluating the mercury content of bodily tissue.

38. Scientist 2's rebuttal of the position of Scientist 1 does NOT include:
 - **F.** pointing to the benefits of DHA in the tissues of fish.
 - **G.** claiming that the European study was flawed.
 - **H.** referring to studies of the acceptable levels of mercury in the diet.
 - **J.** noting the discrepancy between the results of the two studies.

39. Scientist 1 might suggest that an appropriate way to resolve the discrepancy would be to:
 - **A.** repeat the experiment in other venues.
 - **B.** submit the experimental results to a committee of experts.
 - **C.** do a similar experiment in a society that does not eat fish.
 - **D.** debate the issue in a scientific conference.

40. If Scientist 1's position is eventually verified, one outcome might be:
 - **F.** assaying the mercury content of toenails as part of a routine physical examination.
 - **G.** advising men who have had heart attacks to stop eating fish.
 - **H.** more trout fishermen releasing their catch instead of taking it home.
 - **J.** closing down of the tuna fishing industry.

STOP

If there is still time remaining, you may review your answers.

WRITING TEST (OPTIONAL)

30 MINUTES

Directions: Write an essay in response to the following prompt:

Prompt: Funding problems have forced your school administration to consider program cuts. Some members of the school community believe that the best way to save money is to reduce intramural and interscholastic athletics. They argue that only half the students in the school would be affected by such a cut.

Others say that the school should eliminate some arts and humanities offerings because these electives do not serve the basic educational mission of the school.

To save money, should the school reduce the athletic program or should it eliminate humanities and arts electives? In an essay, take a position on this question. You may write about either one of the two points of view. Alternatively, you may present a different point of view on the issue. Whatever your view, be sure to support your position with specific reasons and examples.

Use the lined paper provided. Add additional sheets if necessary.

ANSWER KEYS AND ANALYSIS CHARTS

ENGLISH TEST

1. A	16. G	31. D	46. F	61. B
2. H	17. D	32. F	47. B	62. J
3. D	18. H	33. C	48. J	63. A
4. H	19. B	34. F	49. C	64. G
5. D	20. H	35. D	50. G	65. B
6. J	21. B	36. G	51. C	66. F
7. B	22. H	37. B	52. F	67. C
8. G	23. B	38. H	53. C	68. H
9. D	24. J	39. C	54. G	69. B
10. H	25. B	40. G	55. A	70. G
11. B	26. F	41. C	56. H	71. B
12. J	27. C	42. J	57. D	72. J
13. C	28. F	43. C	58. J	73. C
14. J	29. B	44. G	59. C	74. F
15. B	30. J	45. C	60. J	75. C

Analysis Chart

Skills	Questions	Possible Score	Your Score
Usage/Mechanics			
Punctuation	1, 8, 10, 11, 28, 32, 34, 50, 55, 63, 66, 74	12	
Basic Grammar and Usage	5, 6, 18, 20, 24, 25, 26, 29, 46, 49, 56, 59, 70, 73	14	
Sentence Structure	16, 27, 33, 40, 43, 44, 47, 48, 52, 54, 57, 61, 68, 69	14	
Rhetorical Skills			
Strategy	23, 30, 35, 41, 45, 51, 58, 67	8	
Organization	3, 7, 12, 14, 15, 17, 19, 21, 31, 36, 39, 60, 64, 75	14	
Style	2, 4, 9, 13, 22, 37, 38, 42, 53, 62, 65, 71, 72	13	

Number correct: ______

MATHEMATICS TEST

1. D	13. B	25. D	37. C	49. C
2. H	14. J	26. G	38. J	50. H
3. B	15. B	27. A	39. C	51. E
4. F	16. H	28. H	40. J	52. J
5. D	17. E	29. A	41. C	53. A
6. F	18. H	30. G	42. K	54. J
7. B	19. B	31. B	43. D	55. E
8. H	20. H	32. J	44. H	56. H
9. D	21. B	33. C	45. A	57. C
10. J	22. F	34. H	46. J	58. F
11. A	23. A	35. D	47. B	59. C
12. H	24. K	36. F	48. J	60. G

Analysis Chart

Content Area	Skill Level: Basic Skills	Skill Level: Application	Skill Level: Analysis	Possible Score	Your Score
Pre-Algebra Algebra	1, 7, 17, 21, 26, 32, 34, 49	2, 3, 4, 6, 9, 13, 18, 22, 30, 36, 46, 48	5, 14, 27, 31	24	
Intermediate Algebra Coordinate Geometry	12, 23, 28, 37, 40, 50, 54	11, 16, 29, 38, 39, 43, 53	33, 42, 44, 45	18	
Geometry	8, 15, 19, 20, 35, 56	10, 25, 51, 55, 57, 58, 59, 60		14	
Trigonometry	47, 52	24, 41		4	

Number correct: ______

READING TEST

1. A	6. J	11. C	16. H	21. A	26. H	31. D	36. H
2. H	7. B	12. J	17. A	22. J	27. C	32. F	37. A
3. A	8. H	13. D	18. F	23. C	28. H	33. A	38. F
4. H	9. A	14. J	19. B	24. J	29. A	34. G	39. C
5. B	10. J	15. A	20. H	25. D	30. G	35. D	40. G

Analysis Chart

Passage Type	Referring	Reasoning	Possible Score	Your Score
Prose Fiction	1, 3, 5, 10	2, 4, 6, 7, 8, 9	10	
Social Studies	11, 12, 15	13, 14, 16, 17, 18, 19, 20	10	
Humanities	22, 25, 29	21, 23, 24, 26, 27, 28, 30	10	
Natural Science	31, 33, 34, 36	32, 35, 37, 38, 39, 40	10	

Number correct: ______

SCIENCE REASONING TEST

1. B	6. G	11. B	16. F	21. B	26. G	31. D	36. G
2. J	7. C	12. H	17. D	22. G	27. A	32. G	37. A
3. C	8. J	13. B	18. J	23. A	28. F	33. B	38. G
4. J	9. A	14. G	19. A	24. G	29. C	34. G	39. A
5. B	10. J	15. C	20. H	25. D	30. G	35. D	40. H

Analysis Chart

Kind of Questions	Skill Level: Understanding	Analysis	Generalization	Possible Score	Your Score
Data Representation	1, 2, 7, 18	3, 4, 5, 8, 9, 10, 19, 20	6, 11, 12, 21, 22	17	
Research Summaries	13, 14, 23, 28, 29	15, 24, 25, 30	16, 17, 26, 27, 31, 32, 33	16	
Conflicting Viewpoints	34, 35	36, 37, 38	39, 40	7	

Number correct: ______

In conducting your review and practice in Part 3, pay particular attention to those areas that need the most work, according to the Analysis Charts above.

COMPOSITE SCORE

To calculate your composite score (not including the Writing Test) follow these directions:

1. On the form below fill in the first column of blanks with the number of correct answers on each test.
2. Multiply each number by 36 and divide the product by the number of questions on each test. The results are your scale scores.
3. Add up your scale scores and divide by 4. The result should be rounded to the nearest whole number to determine your composite score.

	Number of correct answers				Scale score
English	______	× 36 =	______	÷ 75 =	______
Math	______	× 36 =	______	÷ 60 =	______
Reading	______	× 36 =	______	÷ 40 =	______
Science	______	× 36 =	______	÷ 40 =	______

Total ______ ÷ 4 = ______
Composite Score

No test can give you a totally precise measurement of your academic achievement. Rather, think of your composite score as the mid-point in a range of scores that can vary one or more points in either direction. A composite score of 24, for example, means that you scored somewhere between 22 and 26.

Answer Explanations: English Test

1. **A** No punctuation is necessary. A colon should not be used to introduce a list that is a complement or object of an element in the introductory statement. The other choices introduce errors, such as the semicolon, dash, and out-of-place comma, which only disrupt the sentence.
2. **H** The original version (F) as well as (G) are wordy. Omitting the underlined portion in the text cannot be a solution because the pronoun *which* is needed.
3. **D** Repetition of the preposition *among* creates a phrase that is parallel with the existing *among the overweight*. The description *normal weighted* is cumbersome. Choice (C), *others,* leaves the reader without enough information.
4. **H** All other options are either wordy or awkward.
5. **D** The only choice that employs the proper pronoun and tense is (D). The others either use a pronoun without a clear antecedent (A), omit a necessary pronoun (C), or use a tense incompatible with the tense of the sentence (B).
6. **J** The verb *does* must agree with its singular subject *being underweight*. In addition, the parenthetical adverb *incidentally* must be bracketed by two commas.
7. **B** Deletion is the only choice. All other options block the flow of ideas with meaningless adverbs.
8. **G** Choice (G) is the only option that properly sets off the following parenthetical phrase *without a doubt* with bracketing commas. In addition, (H) and (J) present punctuation that is unneeded and awkward.
9. **D** *As one* (D) is the only option that maintains neutral gender in the sentence, a requirement in this changing world.

10. **H** Option (H) supplies the standard expression for fractions today in written statements. All of the other choices are either incorrect, (G) or (J), or not used in writing, (J).

11. **B** This sentence presents three nouns with accompanying clauses of explanation. Of all the options, (B) is the only one with the required punctuation, namely with a semicolon after *blindness*.

12. **J** Choice (J) is the only option that begins with paragraph [2], clearly an introductory paragraph, followed by paragraph [1], which introduces the diseases the overweight most often contract, and finally, uses paragraph [3], which speaks of consequences. Because the paragraphs have subtle precursors, no other arrangement is possible.

13. **C** When people are tired and sick, they are unable *to do* as much (C). The other choices present verbs that are unsuitable in this context, *earn* (A), *celebrate* (B), and *cook* (D).

14. **J** Choice (J), *maintaining glucose,* is an economic expression at this final part of the essay. All three other choices are needlessly verbose.

15. **B** Sentence [1], *Young people would do well to watch their weights for a lifetime* is an ideal ending sentence for this essay. Sentence [3], *Eventually, diabetics are simply unable to be active in any endeavor*, is the ideal opening sentence. The sentences in (B) all have precursors in the construction; no other combination does.

16. **G** A *way* to prove the need for nurses is not the long lines, but rather *to point out* the long lines. As this sentence appears (F), the predicate is not compatible with the subject.

17. **D** While somewhat related, this sentence has no bearing on the main arguments of the passage.

18. **H** Choice (H) is the only correct option. The punctuation is meaningless in (F), (G), and (J): pairs, such as *pick up a newspaper or turn on the radio* require no punctuation. A set of three, would.

19. **B** This sentence is more remote in relevance than first appears. There is no reference to a hospital without nurses.

20. **H** The verbs are flatly wrong and confusing in all choices but (H). The text (F) confuses the present perfect passive *has not been shown* and the simple past perfect *have had.* (G) has *was* where the subjunctive *were* belongs; (J) mistakenly mixes the passive past perfect tense *had not been* and the present perfect tense *has had*.

21. **B** A summary of unfilled positions is the only information listed here that is appropriate in this paragraph. The other information is at least vaguely off the topic.

22. **H** The infinitive phrase (*to*) *turn away patients* is economical; the other choices are wordy (F), contain a pronoun without an antecedent (G), or are inappropriate in style (J).

23. **B** This paragraph really does not represent the opposing opinion very well and should support it with more detail.

24. **J** The opportunities are not greater than *programs,* but rather greater than opportunities *in* other programs.

25. **B** The pronoun *this* is almost never adequate alone; an explanatory noun is needed (*this need*). The other options supply nouns that are incompatible with the meaning of the sentence.

26. **F** The use of a possessive pronoun (*their*) is required before a gerund (*being admitted*). All other choices are improper English.

27. **C** The passage is written in the present tense.

28. **F** Separate three or more items in a series with commas and a conjunction.

29. **B** The pronoun *that* dangles without a clear antecedent like *service*. Meeting a shortage is not a philosophy (D).

30. **J** The target of this persuasive attempt to support the opening of another nursing school must be a body that can make such a decision.

31. **D** The conjunction *either* applies only to the words *inside* and *outside,* and so must be placed just before them.

32. **F** The plural of the proper name *Frobush* is *Frobushes;* the possessive is formed by adding the apostrophe after the pluralizing *s*.

33. **C** The tense of this passage is the simple past.

34. **F** A quotation must be separated from the preceding text by a comma; the exclamation point should be placed *inside* the quotation marks because the quoted utterance is the exclamation.

35. **D** This sentence has no bearing on the meaning of the passage and should be removed.

36. **G** A new paragraph begins at this point because a new subject (the police investigation) and line of action begin.

37. **B** Only the verb *theorized* results in an economical and meaningful sentence; the other options are either wordy or slang.

38. **H** The prepositional phrase *behind the house* is redundant; the words *back door* already convey that meaning.

39. **C** Choice (C) gives a clear, chronological report of the narrative. All other choices are awkward because they are not chronological.

40. **G** The phrase *While working* works best; the other options suggest the wrong meaning.

41. **C** From the outset, this narrative appears to be a very lean summary of a case; embellishment would be inappropriate.

42. **J** The correct answer maintains the strict, economical style of the passage; the other options are either incompatible in style or misleading in what they say.

43. **C** Without a period or semicolon, the sentence becomes a comma splice or run-on sentence. The period and new sentence options is most appropriate because of the significant statement made in the second clause—that is, Goode's being formally accused of a crime.

44. **G** The conjunction at the beginning of the second clause must logically signal contrast. The words *but* and *however* do just that, but *however,* being a conjunctive adverb, requires a semicolon. *But* is the only possible choice.

45. **C** Because of its sparse, businesslike style, this passage is clearly one that provides background for a subsequent discussion on a point of law or trial procedure.

46. **F** The correlative conjunction *neither* means "not one of two," and is followed by *nor; either* means "one of two" and is followed by *or.*

47. **B** The correct choice presents a concise adverb clause properly modifying the following verb *explain*. There is no need for reference to the court calendar.

48. **J** Only the gerund *hearing* maintains the sequence of tenses; all other choices confuse the time of the sentence.

49. **C** Only the infinitive *come,* with the *to* elliptically omitted, sounds natural in this position; the other options are awkward.

50. **G** The adjective clause *which may be different for each county* is nonrestrictive, modifying *days and times,* and therefore must be set off by a comma.

51. **C** Some specific details illustrating the plea of a plaintiff, for example, would support the general points made in this passage. The inappropriate alternative answers stray far from the thesis of the passage.

52. **F** Other options either disagree with the subject in number (G), employ a verb that makes little sense (H), or use the wrong tense (J).

53. **C** Choice (C) provides a crisp parallel statement. The other choices provide ideas that are not expressed in the same grammatical form, resulting in nonparallel sentences.

54. **G** A transitional word signaling contrast is needed here.

55. **A** A singular noun takes an apostrophe and *s* to indicate possession.

56. **H** Always use the principal noun enough to establish its presence in the sentence or paragraph.

57. **D** The correct answer (*works*) is parallel with the preceding verb (*lives*).

58. **J** Deletion (J) is the only possible choice; this sentence has no bearing on anything in the entire passage.

59. **C** The correct choice is concise and clear; the others are awkward, wordy, or ungrammatical.

60. **J** Paragraph 4 begins with a clear, simple sentence explaining the point of the selection.

61. **B** The two clauses that join at this point contain enough substance to require a full-fledged sentence for each. Options A and C are wrong because they create run-on sentences. In D the word after the semicolon is incorrectly capitalized.

62. **J** The correct choice is clear and economical; the others are either wordy or result in an incomplete statement.

63. **A** Hyphenate a compound adjective that precedes the noun it modifies.

64. **G** The topic abruptly and completely moves from environmental initiatives to other initiatives, mandating a new paragraph.

65. **B** The adjective *diverse* is in keeping with the style of the passage and the sense of what follows.

66. **F** The conjunction *and* that marks the end of this long series of nouns needs itself to be preceded by a comma.

67. **C** Only the correct answer addresses the issue posed in the question. The other options deal with irrelevant material.

68. **H** The participial phrase preceding the underlined matter of this question is subordinate; *initiative process* is the subject of the sentence, and cannot be introduced by a relative pronoun.

69. **B** *In contrast* and *however* are both transitions indicating contrast; only one is required. The other options signal addition.

70. **G** The idiom *ranging from ... to ...* is completed by choice G. The other choices disrupt the structure of the sentence.

71. **B** The facts presented are simple and sparse; that is, the passage is journalistic.

72. **J** The phrase *strike down* is the only one compatible with the rest of the passage; the other options represent colloquial usage or slang and are therefore unsuitable.

73. **C** The subject (*reasons*) is plural, and so the verb must be; options B and D change the tense inappropriately.

74. **F** The three clauses at the end of this sentence are members of a series and require separation by commas.

75. **C** Paragraph 2 clearly introduces the subject, and must be the first paragraph in the passage.

Answer Explanations: Mathematics Test

1. **D** Division by zero is undefined.

2. **H** Follow the order of operation rules.

$$\begin{aligned} 7^2 - 2[3 + 2(5 - 1)] &= 7^2 - 2[3 + 2(4)] \\ &= 7^2 - 2[3 + 8] \\ &= 7^2 - 2(11) \\ &= 7^2 - 22 \\ &= 49 - 22 = 27 \end{aligned}$$

3. **B**

$2x - 5 = 7 - 4x$	Add $4x$ to both sides.
$6x - 5 = 7$	Add 5 to both sides.
$6x = 12$	Divide both sides by 6.
$x = 2$	

4. **F** What percent of 24 is 18? P is unknown, $A = 18$, and $B = 24$. The percent proportion is

$$\frac{P}{100} = \frac{18}{24}\left(= \frac{3}{4}\right), P = 75$$

5. **D** The number of curtains, C, can be found by division.

$$\begin{aligned} C = 20 \div 2\tfrac{1}{2} &= 20 \div \frac{5}{2} \\ &= \frac{20}{1} \cdot \frac{2}{5} = 8 \end{aligned}$$

6. **F** $2x - \{3x - 2[x - (1 - x)]\}$

$$\begin{aligned} &= 2x - \{3x - 2[x - 1 + x]\} \\ &= 2x - \{3x - 2x + 2 - 2x\} \\ &= 2x - 3x + 2x - 2 + 2x \\ &= 3x - 2 \end{aligned}$$

7. **B** $51 = (3)(17)$

8. **H** A secant line intersects a circle in two points. Line $\overleftrightarrow{AC}$ is a secant.

9. **D** Substituting the given values into $-x - xy^2$ yields

$$\begin{aligned} -(-2) - (-2)(3^2) &= -(-2) - (-2)(9) \\ &= -(-2) - (-18) \\ &= 2 + 18 = 20 \end{aligned}$$

10. **J** The length of a tangent is the mean proportional between the length of a secant and the length of the external segment of the secant.

$$\frac{4}{6} = \frac{6}{CD + 4}$$

$$4(CD + 4) = 36$$
$$4CD + 16 = 36$$
$$4CD = 20$$
$$CD = 5$$

11. **A** These radicals can be multiplied since the indices are the same.

$\sqrt[3]{4ab^2}\,\sqrt[3]{12a^4b^2} = \sqrt[3]{48a^5b^4}$

Separate the radicand into cube and noncube factors.

$$= \sqrt[3]{(8a^3b^3)(6a^2b)}$$
$$= 2ab\sqrt[3]{6a^2b}$$

12. **H** A quadratic equation is one that is equivalent to $ax^2 + bx + c = 0$ for $a \neq 0$. Equation H is equivalent to

$$9 + 5x = 16 + 2x$$
$$3x - 7 = 0$$

This equation is linear.

13. **B** $(3x - 1)^2 = 9x^2 - 6x + 1$

14. **J** $5x - 2 = 2x + 1$

15. **B** Since an inscribed angle is measured by half of the intercepted arc, and the intercepted arc in a semicircle is 180°, the triangle must be a right triangle.

16. **H** Using the special rule about absolute value inequalities, we have

$$|x - 1| \leq 3$$
$$-3 \leq x - 1 \leq 3$$
$$-2 \leq x \leq 4$$

17. **E** Point (–4, 0) is located on the x-axis and is therefore not in any quadrant.

18. **H** Substitute each ordered pair into the equation.

(–1, –1)	3(–1) – 2(–1)	≠ 5
(1, 1)	3(1) – 2(1)	≠ 5
(1, –1)	3(1) – 2(–1)	= 5
(–1, 1)	3(–1) – 2(1)	≠ 5
(5, –5)	3(5) – 2(–5)	≠ 5

19. **B** If two lines in a plane are cut by a transversal so that a pair of corresponding angles are equal, the lines are parallel. Angles 2 and 6 are corresponding angles.

20. **H** A segment from a vertex of a triangle to the midpoint of the opposite side is a median. $\overline{BD}$ is a median.

21. **B** $\frac{5}{12} + \frac{7}{18} = \frac{15}{36} + \frac{14}{36}$ The LCD is 36.

$$= \frac{29}{36}$$

22. **F**

$$\frac{2}{3} - \frac{2 - \frac{5}{6}}{2^3 - 1} \div \frac{1}{2} = \frac{2}{3} - \frac{2 - \frac{5}{6}}{8 - 1} \div \frac{1}{2}$$

$$= \frac{2}{3} - \frac{2 - \frac{5}{6}}{7} \div \frac{1}{2} \quad \text{Multiply by 6.}$$

$$= \frac{2}{3} - \frac{12 - 5}{42} \div \frac{1}{2}$$

$$= \frac{2}{3} - \frac{7}{42} \div \frac{1}{2} = \frac{2}{3} - \frac{1}{6} \div \frac{1}{2} = \frac{2}{3} - \frac{1}{6} \cdot \frac{2}{1}$$

$$= \frac{2}{3} - \frac{1}{3} = \frac{1}{3}$$

23. **A** Let $x = \log_3 27$.

Then $3^x = 27 = 3^3$

$$x = 3$$

24. **K** From the identity $\cos^2\theta + \sin^2\theta = 1$, we have

$$\cos^2\theta + \left(\frac{1}{2}\right)^2 = 1$$
$$\cos^2\theta + \frac{1}{4} = 1$$
$$\cos^2\theta = \frac{3}{4}$$
$$\cos\theta = \pm\frac{\sqrt{3}}{2}$$

The ± sign is appropriate because, if all that is known is that the sine of the angle is $\frac{1}{2}$, the angle may be in either quadrant I or II, and in one of these quadrants the cosine is positive but in the other it is negative.

25. **D** Since $\triangle ABC$ is isosceles, $m\angle A = m\angle B = 40°$. The sum of the angles of any triangle = 180°.
$$m\angle C + 40° + 40° = 180°$$
$$m\angle C = 100°$$

26. **G** Compare the decimal forms of the four numbers.

3.1415926
$\frac{22}{7} = 3.\overline{142857}$
3.14
3.1416

Since $\frac{22}{7} = 3.\overline{142857}$ has the larger digit in the first position in which the digits differ, it is the largest number.

27. **A** Joan must read n pages, where
$$n = 80 - \frac{4}{5}(80)$$
$$= 80 - 64 = 16$$

28. **H** A pure imaginary number is a number of the type bi, where b is a real number and $i = \sqrt{-1}$. $\sqrt{-4} = 2i$.

29. **A** The graph is a hyperbola. The equations represent
A. Hyperbola B. Ellipse C., D., and E. Parabolas

30. **G** $2x + y = -1$
$3x - 2y = -19$ Multiply both sides of the top equation by 2.
$4x + 2y = -2$
$3x - 2y = -19$ Add the two equations.
$7x = -21$

$x = -3$ Substitute –3 into the top equation for x.
$2(-3) + y = -1$
$-6 + y = -1$
$y = 5$

31. **B** Use the substitution method.
$\begin{pmatrix} 5x - 2y = 3 \\ y = 4x - 3 \end{pmatrix}$ Substitute for y in the first equation.
$5x - 2(4x - 3) = 3$
$5x - 8x + 6 = 3$
$-3x + 6 = 3$
$-3x = -3$
$x = 1$ Substitute $x = 1$ in the second equation.
$y = 4(1) - 3 = 4 - 3 = 1$ The solution is $\{(1, 1)\}$.

32. **J** The identity property of addition states symbolically that
$$a + 0 = 0 + a = a$$
Therefore the appropriate right side of the given equation is 5 + 7.

33. **C** If $a < b$, then $a - b < 0$ and
$|a - b| = -(a - b) = b - a$
So $|a - b| + a + b = b - a + a + b$
$= 2b$

34. **H** $6{,}440 = (2)(2)(2)(5)(7)(23)$

35. **D** Supplementary angles are two angles whose sum is 180°. Angles 8 and 9 are supplementary.

36. **F**

$$\begin{array}{r} 13\frac{1}{4} \\ -7\frac{5}{8} \\ \hline \end{array} = \begin{array}{r} 13\frac{2}{8} \\ -7\frac{5}{8} \\ \hline 12\frac{10}{8} \\ -7\frac{5}{8} \\ \hline 5\frac{5}{8} \end{array}$$

We must borrow $1\left(=\frac{8}{8}\right)$ from the 13.

37. **C** The degree of a polynomial is the greatest of the degrees of all of its terms. The degree of each term is the sum of the exponents on the variables in that term. The degrees of the three terms of the given polynomial are 5, 3, 1, respectively.

38. **J** From the quadratic formula, the sum of the roots of any quadratic equation is $-\frac{b}{a}$. In the given quadratic equation, $a = 4$ and $b = 3$, so the sum of the roots is $-\frac{3}{4}$.

39. **C**

$$16^{-(3/4)} = \frac{1}{16^{(3/4)}}$$
$$= \frac{1}{(\sqrt[4]{16})^3}$$
$$= \frac{1}{2^3} \quad = \frac{1}{8}$$

40. **J** Exponential curves are not conic sections.

41. **C** Since 215° is in quadrant III, the value of the sine will be negative, and the reference angle is 215° – 180° = 35°. So sin 215° = –sin 35°. But this is not one of the options. Therefore, making use of the rule that states that cofunctions of complementary angles are equal, we have

$$-\sin 35° = -\cos (90° - 35°) = -\cos 55°$$

42. **K** The question is "How many permutations are there of 6 things taken 6 at a time?"

$${}_6P_6 = \frac{6!}{(6-6)!} = \frac{6!}{0!}$$
$$= \frac{6 \bullet 5 \bullet 4 \bullet 3 \bullet 2 \bullet 1}{1}$$
$$= 720$$

43. **D** The expression -2^{-2} is properly read as "the opposite of 2 to the negative second power." Hence

$$-(2^{-2}) = \frac{-1}{2^2}$$
$$= \frac{-1}{4}$$

44. **H** The area of the circle is $A = \pi r^2$ and the area of the semicircle is $A = \frac{1}{2}\pi r^2$. Since $r = 1$, $A = \pi$. Therefore

$$\frac{1}{2}\pi r^2 = \pi$$
$$\pi r^2 = 2\pi$$
$$r^2 = 2$$
$$r = \sqrt{2}$$

45. **A** The equation must be put into standard form,
$(x - h)^2 + (y - k)^2 = r^2$, by completing the square in each variable.
$x^2 + 4x \quad + y^2 - 18y \quad = -69$
$x^2 + 4x + 4 + y^2 - 18y + 81 \quad = -69 + 4 + 81$
$(x + 2)^2 + (y - 9)^2 \quad = 16$
The center is (–2, 9), and the radius is 4.

46. **J** This is an application of the distance formula
$d^2 = (x_1 - x_2)^2 + (y_1 - y_2)^2$

Here $d^2 = [5 - (-2)]^2 + (3 - 4)^2$
$= 7^2 + (-1)^2$
$= 49 + 1 = 50$
$d = \sqrt{50} = 5\sqrt{2}$

47. **B** Coterminal angles are found by adding or subtracting multiples of 360°.
$846° - 2(360°) = 846° - 720° = 126°$

48. **J** Rephrasing the problem in the format of a percent problem gives "60 is 80% of what number?"
$A = 60$, $P = 80\%$, B is unknown.

$$\frac{80}{100} = \frac{60}{B}$$

$$\frac{4}{5} = \frac{60}{B}$$

$$4B = 300$$

$$B = 75$$

49. **C** $7(10^4) + 3(10^3) + 2(10^1) + 9(10^0)$

$= 7(10{,}000) + 3(1{,}000) + 2(10) + 9(1)$
$= 70{,}000 + 3{,}000 + 20 + 9$
$= 73{,}029$

50. **H** The sample space contains 36 pairs of numbers. Among them are 2, 6; 3, 5; 4, 4; 5, 3; and 6, 2. Therefore, 5 out of 36 pairs satisfy the condition of having a sum of 8. P (sum of 8) = $\frac{5}{36}$.

51. **E** The measures of $\angle BAD$ and $\angle ABC$ are equal because $\overline{AD} \parallel \overline{BC}$. The measure of an inscribed angle is half of the intercepted arc, so the measure of arc AC is 30°. Since AB is a diameter, the measure of arc ACB is 180°. Therefore

$m\widehat{BC} = 180° - 30° = 150°$.

52. **J** The period of the sine function
$y = A \sin B(x - C)$ is $\frac{2\pi}{|B|}$
The period of the given function is $\frac{2\pi}{5}$

53. **A** The y-intercept of a graph is found at the ordered pairs where the x value is 0. Substituting $x = 0$, we find that $y = -8$.

54. **J** In the slope-intercept form of the equation of a line, $y = mx + b$, m is the slope. Solving the equation for y, we have

$$2x - 5y = 7$$

$$-5y = -2x + 7$$

$$y = \frac{2}{5}x - \frac{7}{5}$$

The slope of the graph is $\frac{2}{5}$

55. **E** In a right triangle, the leg $\overline{AB}$ is the mean proportional between its projection on the hypotenuse (the segment AD) and the entire hypotenuse.

$$\frac{3}{4} = \frac{4}{x}$$

$$3x = 16$$

$$x = \frac{16}{3}$$

56. **H** The sum of the interior angles of the n-gon is

$S = (n - 2)180°$
$S = (6 - 2)180°$
$= 4(180°) = 720°$

57. **C** The measure of an angle formed by the intersection of two chords in a circle is $\frac{1}{2}$ the sum of the measures of the intercepted arcs.

$$50 = \frac{1}{2}(20 + \text{m}\,\overset{\frown}{AD})$$

$$100 = 20 + \text{m}\,\overset{\frown}{AD}$$

$$\text{m}\,\overset{\frown}{AD} = 80$$

Since $\overline{AB}$ is a diameter,

$$\text{m}\,\overset{\frown}{AD} + \text{m}\,\overset{\frown}{DB} = 180$$

$$80 + \text{m}\,\overset{\frown}{DB} = 180$$

$$\text{m}\,\overset{\frown}{DB} = 100$$

58. **F** In similar triangles, the following ratios are equal:

$$\frac{6}{x} = \frac{10}{85}$$

$$10x = 510$$

$$x = 51$$

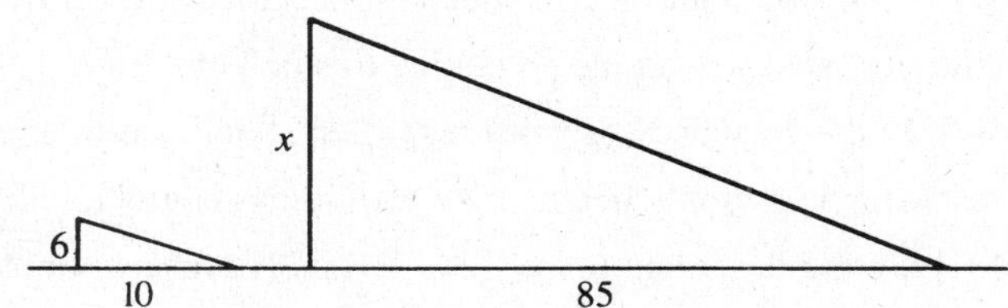

59. **C** Drawing a segment from $B \perp \overline{AD}$ forms a 30°-60°-90° triangle with hypotenuse 6. Therefore the length of the altitude of the parallelogram is $3\sqrt{3}$. The area of a parallelogram is $A = bh = 8(3\sqrt{3}) = 24\sqrt{3}$.

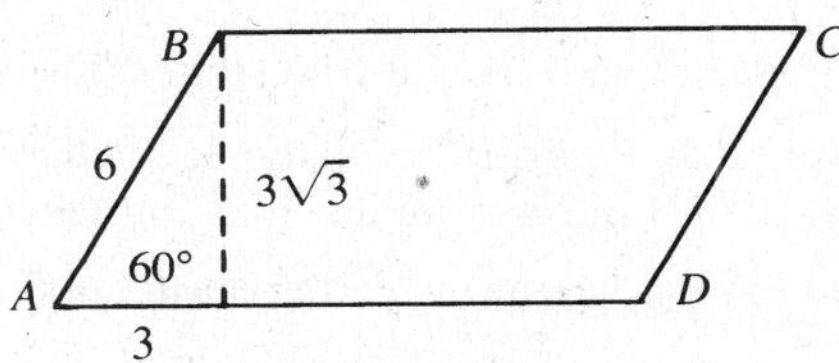

60. **G** The sum of the angles of a triangle equals 180°.

$$(x + 15) + (3x - 75) + (2x - 30) = 180$$
$$6x - 90 = 180$$
$$6x = 270$$
$$x = 45$$

Substituting 45 into each of the angle measures gives

$$45 + 15 = 60$$
$$3(45) - 75 = 135 - 75 = 60$$
$$2(45) - 30 = 90 - 30 = 60$$

All three angles of the triangle are equal, so the triangle is equilateral.

Answer Explanations: Reading Test

1. **A** The narrator says his father sent him to public school to make him "hardy" (line 3). Later he mentions that flogging was the way to make "a man of parts" (line 35), an expression that means a solid, well-rounded individual.

2. **H** The narrator defines the phrase in lines 14–15: "I have always been an idle fellow and prone to play the vagabond," that is, someone who likes to wander about aimlessly.

3. **A** The boy is distracted by "seductions" (line 17) such as the lovely green valley, the little stream, and the blue hills.
4. **H** Lines 9–11 say that inferior cattle—those that are slow or have short legs—suffer as a result.
5. **B** According to lines 28–30, as a youth, the narrator thought that flogging was a standard practice in education.
6. **J** Many details in the paragraph about the squire (lines 38–59) refer to people who humble themselves in the squire's presence.
7. **B** The passage was not written as a social or political commentary on England. And the passage is not meant to portray typical noblemen or members of the clergy. Rather, its main purpose is to recount in a personal and light-hearted manner the narrator's boyhood experiences.
8. **H** Lines 79–80 implies that Waller's poems were "lavished upon Sacharissa."
9. **A** The narrator's point of view throughout the passage is somewhat ironic, as though he is poking fun at the experiences and people of his youth.
10. **J** He is flogged for "trespassing on Parnassus" (lines 94–95), the mythical place where only Gods dwell. By writing poetry, he overstepped the acceptable boundaries of behavior for schoolboys.
11. **C** According to lines 75–77, 80 percent of childhood stutterers speak normally by the time they reach adulthood.
12. **J** Lines 20–32, which discuss signs of stuttering, include all the choices *except* trembling head and hands.
13. **D** Line 87 indicates that stutterers speak easily when talking to small children.
14. **J** Line 14 suggests that only a high frequency of word repetition should alert parents to a stuttering problem.
15. **A** Line 60 indicates that stuttering commonly begins after a child has begun to talk automatically.
16. **H** All the old antidotes for stuttering described in lines 36–45 involve forms of physical therapy.
17. **A** Lines 65–72 list stressful situations that provoke stuttering.
18. **F** If stuttering were a physical disorder, stutterers would probably never enjoy moments of speaking freely.
19. **B** Much of the passage raises questions about the causes of stuttering. Line 34 says that the "underlying cause remains a mystery."
20. **H** The passage never discusses attitudes toward people who stutter. Therefore, choice H is irrelevant.
21. **A** Items 5 and 6 at lines 62–70 imply that a constructed language is derived from several existing languages or is built from scratch. Either way, it must differ from any existing language.
22. **J** Lines 79–82 say that some 3,000 natural languages and at least 1,000 constructed languages exist.
23. **C** The premise implied throughout the passage is that mankind will be better off with a universal language. Choices A and B are too specific. Choice D refers to Comenius's proposal, which did *not* call for a universal language.
24. **J** Because the words of Wilkins' language, mentioned in lines 17–21, were newly coined, the language is considered a constructed language.
25. **D** Lines 79–84 make the point that there are plenty of languages to choose from, but an agreement about which language to use remains the major problem.
26. **H** Lines 8–11 explain that Descartes' logical scheme failed to reflect the way actual languages are constructed.
27. **C** Lines 29–30 say that the type of solution proposed by Comenius is "still widely advocated today."
28. **H** Of the six types of languages listed, four are based on existing languages.
29. **A** Lines 12–14 state that Descartes' contemporaries offered proposals because Descartes failed to offer an example of his scheme.
30. **G** Lines 15–17 make the point that languages built on logic alone won't work because they lack the familiarity and ease of natural languages.
31. **D** Lines 22–26 state that the food supply decreases as the water level deepens. Hence, the top layers contain the most food.
32. **F** Scientists once believed that silence reigned in the deepest ocean waters. That theory no longer holds true, according to the second paragraph.
33. **A** Lines 1–2 state that many of the animals have gradually become blind because they exist in a world of complete darkness.
34. **G** Several uses of hydrophones are described in lines 36–50. Searching for unknown species is not mentioned.

35. **D** Lines 17–22 explain that plants cannot grow in the undersea darkness and that dead and dying plants are eaten before they reach the bottom layers of ocean.

36. **H** In the battle for food described in lines 26–32, the weaker fish often lose. Therefore, they must wait for long periods of time to eat.

37. **A** Only this answer is supported by the passage. Oceanographers seem to be making new discoveries all the time.

38. **F** Repletion means the state of being full or being gorged with food or drink.

39. **C** The ferocity of the creatures is being emphasized. The other choices may merely call to mind the extinct saber-toothed tiger.

40. **G** While each of the choices may be somewhat valid, most of the passage is devoted to a description of life far below the surface of the sea.

Answer Explanations: Science Reasoning Test

1. **B** Find the position of 13 on the vertical scale, and move to the right horizontally from there. You will find yourself crossing Portugal, Hungary, and (a little higher) Finland. On the horizontal scale, Portugal is at 75 and Finland is at a little under 120.

2. **J** Israel and the United States are on the same horizontal line, both with about 20 deaths per 100,000. Their wide separation along this axis shows that they differ greatly in fat intake. Israel and Greece are on the same vertical line, so they have the same fat intake; the separation along this axis shows different death rates. Austria and Germany are not widely separated. France and Mexico are widely separated along both axes, showing that both the death rates and the fat intakes differ greatly.

3. **C** The general slope of the chart from lower left to upper right shows that there is a broad, general tendency for an increased rate of breast cancer in countries where the average fat intake is greatest. A is wrong because the data do not exclude many other possible causal relationships. B is wrong because the data for average fat intake are taken from the population as a whole, not just women with cancer. D is wrong because no evidence relating either diet or cancer to environmental pollution was presented.

4. **J** The point for South Africa is far above the general trend, indicating that this country has an extraordinarily high rate of breast cancer compared with its expected rate from the other data.

5. **B** The points of Greece and Spain are no further off the main trend than most of the others; many factors are involved in causing breast cancer. However, there is nothing in the data to implicate either sunshine or olive oil. D is wrong because many of the differences between countries are far too substantial to be blamed on uncertainty in the data.

6. **G** Although there may be many uncontrolled variables in changing Japan, the whole study seems to show a relationship between fat consumption and breast cancer, and this would be confirmed if the relationship held up in a single country. F is wrong because there is no significant difference between data for the United States and for Europe. H is wrong because this evidence would not represent additional data: South Africa is already on the chart. J is wrong because the chart gives no data distinguishing white from black Americans.

7. **C** These are the diseases marked P in the last column, 57,000 from colon cancer and 460,000 from coronary heart disease.

8. **J** Obesity is a risk factor for stroke, and the graph shows that it is on the rise. There has actually been a substantial drop in both cigarette smoking and hypertension. Lack of exercise is not a risk factor for stroke.

9. **A** Lung cancer showed a slight increase during the test period, even though smoking has decreased substantially. Diabetes goes up with the increase in obesity; heart disease and its risk factors are both decreasing; no information is given about the trend in one of the risk factors for colon cancer.

10. **J** No experiment can ever exclude the possibility that there are other factors operating that will affect the results. Earlier years, though interesting, do not invalidate the data for an 18-year period. Detailed information about hypertension medication or physical activity would not explain the contradiction.

11. **B** The entire study is an attempt to connect lifestyle to mortality from chronic disease. A is wrong because the study deals only with mortality, not with the incidence of chronic illness. Nothing in the study suggests that heredity is not a factor, in addition to the lifestyle choices. Medical treatment, while a good idea, is not addressed in the information given.

12. **H** Obesity, linked to diabetes, has increased in recent years.

13. **B** Since it is known at the outset that Strain B is much more likely to develop cancer than Strain A, answer choices A and D are wrong. The effectiveness of benzol in producing cancer in each of the three strains can only be discovered by comparing mice given benzol with mice that do not get it. Nothing prevents comparison with wild mice.

14. **G** The vaccine did have a strong effect only in strain B. Although the experiment gives no information about the usefulness of the treatments in humans, there is no reason to doubt that a method for complete prevention will someday be found. The differences among the three groups must be due to differences in heredity, since all received the same treatment.

15. **C** In Strain B, which has a hereditary cancer defect, the vaccine reduced the incidence of cancer from 98 percent to 61 percent, while fexadrin had no effect. Fexadrin was helpful in wild mice, but not at all in Strain B.

16. **F** The experiments were done on cancers produced in mice by exposure to benzol; if these are like human cancers, the results of the experiments might give a clue to an understanding of human cancer; if the two kinds of cancer are not alike, the information obtained from the experiments would not have any significance for human cancer. The other questions might be important but would be meaningless unless the condition in answer F was met.

17. **D** Answers to the questions in A, B, and C might provide valuable information about the causes of cancer and the physiological mechanisms that protect the body. But benzol already gives cancer to nearly all the mice in Strain B, and any increase is not likely to yield useful information.

18. **J** The bar for insect consumption is about 33%, much larger than for all the other species.

19. **A** The only nonanimal food shown is seaweed, and there the bar for *Lipophrys* is longer than any other. B is wrong because about 3% of the *Nerophis* sample contained mollusks. C is wrong because several of the fishes use food from all 5 groups. D is wrong because the graph shows only how many fishes contained the food, but *not* how much.

20. **H** Most *Lipophrys* stomachs contain mollusks, and the fish needs a strong jaw to crack the mollusk shells. F is wrong because *G. cobitis* eats seaweed. G is wrong because only two species of the genus *Gobius* were tested; there may be many others. The long, thin fish is *Nerophis*, whose stomachs contain mainly crustaceans, not insects.

21. **B** *Nerophis* seems to live almost entirely on crustaceans, since very few of these fishes have any other kind of food in their stomach. A is wrong because none of the fishes depends heavily on polychates. C is wrong because *Lipophrys* eats many other kinds of food as well as mollusks. D is wrong because *G. paganellus* eats many kinds of food.

22. **G** *Lipophrys* and *G. cobitis* eat a wide variety of food, while *Ciliata, Nerophis,* and *G. paganellus* depend very heavily on crustaceans.

23. **A** Experiment 2 shows that with equal diameters the denser lead sphere falls faster than the steel sphere. It is reasonable to suppose that this would hold true for any lead and steel spheres of equal diameter.

24. **G** In the statement, you are told that the rate of fall depends on the weight of the sphere. F is wrong because all steel spheres have the same density. There is no indication that surface area or volume is involved.

25. **D** The data of Experiment 1 show that the velocity of a 2.0-cm ball is four times as great as that of a 1.0-cm ball. There is no reason to believe that the rule would be any different in honey.

26. **G** Comparing the speeds of any pair of steel spheres in the two different media will reveal that the speed in the 2% solution is three times as great as in the 4% solution. Choice F is wrong because it has the effect reversed; if the speed is greater in the 2% solution, the drag must be smaller, not greater. H is wrong because this effect is seen in either of the two experiments, and no comparison is needed. J is wrong because there is no reason to believe that the density of a 4% solution is twice as great as the density of a 2% solution; in fact, it is not.

27. **A** Experiment 2 shows that, at any density larger than 1, the ball falls. However, as the density gets closer to 1, the speed of the ball slows up enormously and could be expected to drop to 0 when the density gets to 1.

28. **F** In both species, the length of time in the egg stage is smallest at higher temperatures. G is wrong because this is true for *Drosophila B,* but not for *Drosophila A,* where life span is maximum at 20°C. H is wrong because the duration of the larva stage for *Drosophila A* does not follow any clear rule. J is wrong because in both species, life is short at the highest temperature.

29. **C** The larva changes into an adult during the pupa stage, which always lasts just 5 days in both species. A is wrong because, in part, we have no information as to how large the larvae grow. B is wrong because the duration of the egg stage does in fact depend on temperature. D applies to *Drosophila B,* but not to *Drosophila A.*

30. **G** For *Drosophila B*, there is a clear decrease in duration of the adult stage as the temperature rises. F and J are wrong because these rules apply to both species. H is not true for either species.

31. **D** *Drosophila B* survives longest in the coldest weather, so it must be a cold-weather species.

32. **G** For both species, the duration of the adult stage is the same whether the pupae are kept at 10° or they are moved into a warmer room, so the temperature of the adult or pupa stage does not matter. The data show that the life span depends on the temperature in the pre-pupae stages, but do not distinguish between egg and larva stages.

33. **B** Optimum temperature for *Drosophila A* is about 20° C, and for *Drosophila B* 10° C. The other choices are wrong because the data are ambiguous for the larva stage of *Drosophila A*.

34. **G** The studies were attempts to find a relationship between mercury in the body tissues and heart disease. F and H are not at issue because Scientist 2 does not dispute these facts. J is wrong because this is not a hypothesis to be tested but a possible recommendation based on the study.

35. **D** Mercury in the toenails is used as a measure of the mercury taken in by eating fish.

36. **G** Both scientists acknowledge that high levels of mercury in the diet cause nerve damage. Scientist 2 has doubts that they affect the heart and thinks the levels in freshwaters are not dangerous.

37. **A** Scientist 2 thinks there might be many reasons for the discrepancy, but the only one he specifies is other kinds of pollutants.

38. **G** Scientist 2 does not impugn the quality of the European study; he tries to understand the discrepancy.

39. **A** The discrepancy is related to the venues of the studies, so this is the variable that should be tested in repeat experiments.

40. **H** Freshwater fish are the most dangerous, so the tuna industry is not involved. Choices F and G are far out of proportion to the problem.

Answer Explanations: Writing Test

Essays written in response to the prompt will vary. Below are responses that represent three levels of performance: Outstanding, Good, and Poor. Each essay is followed by a brief critique by an ACT essay evaluator and a grade scaled from 6 (high) to 1 (low). Once you have read the essays and critiques, rate your own essay using the Essay Self-Assessment.

Note: Each essay appears as written by a student.

Sample Essay 1 by Betsy

Funding problems are forcing program cuts. In my opinion, reduce intramural and interscholastic athletics. Also eliminate some arts and humanities offerings. However, there is one thing that must not be cut under any circumstances, Mr. Hannan's Television Production class.

I have been interested in television and radio for most of my life. My first exposure to television production was at 5 years old when a national television crew came to my kindergarten classroom and I was chosen to speak on camera. As I got older, my studies have always included voice, dance, acting, and public speaking on camera. When I was 9, I took a course called "Me On TV", which was an introduction to work in front of the camera. More recently, I have auditioned for and obtained paid professional work as an actress and vocalist. You can hear my voiceover on the local cable channel announcing future programs. I am the youngest staff member at the station, where I am learning from professionals from CBS and CNN who live in the community and volunteer their time at the station.

My interest in the television-radio academic area expanded in high school. During my junior and senior year I have been Mr. Hannan's assistant in production, working with 9th graders just being introduced to television studies. I have also enrolled in courses in television and video production where have gotten expe-

rience in writing, producing, acting in, and editing my own videos. Two of my videos have been chosen for the video library at the George Eastman House International Museum of Photography and Film in Rochester, New York, and can be seen on YouTube.

This past summer I continued my interest at the New York State summer program for Media Arts at Ithaca College, where I was able to sharpen my video producation skills, making a video project that won second prize. This year in school, every morning, my classmates and I produce, direct, and anchor a daily television news program cablecast live throughout the school and the community.

As you can see, television has been important to me. Therefore, I again urge the administration not to cut Television Production from the school program. After I graduate this June, many younger people will pick up where I left off. Don't take away from them the kind of opportunities I have had.

Critique: The weakest part of the essay is probably its opening, where the writer repeats almost verbatim the text of the prompt. She quickly redeems herself, however, by forcefully articulating the main idea of the essay, that the television production course must be preserved. The remainder of the piece shows specifically why she feels passionately about the issue.

The writer has refused to be drawn into the issue of which budget should be cut. Instead, she concentrates on preserving a single television-production course, part of the "arts and humanities" program at her school. This approach enables her to support her essay's main idea with concrete details derived from her own experience, proving beyond question her passion for television production. In the final paragraph she reiterates the point of the essay and makes the claim that she supports the television course not for selfish reasons but because it's the right thing to do for students yet to come.

Although the essay is not perfect, considering that the writer had only thirty minutes, it is an exemplary piece of work. Score: **6**

Sample Essay 2 by Keith

Math at this High school is mandatory. It is in most High schools. Whether it be basic math, geometry, algebra, trig, or calculus that is mandatory, varies from school to school, but math is required for graduation and to attend college. No doubt math is basicly is a useful thing to those people who somehow find enjoyment in it or who plan to be math teachers or even architects. It is basicly a waist of time for those like me who have little or no interest in math, so I reccommend that to save money the math program be cut from the budget before intramural and interscholastic athletics or arts and humanities.

The Math teachers at the High school, when asked the question, "Why must I take this math course if I plan no future for myself in that area?" I was given answers such as "Well can it really hurt you?", another said "Because I said so and it is just good for you." (So is flaxseed oil.) Even the statement that, "Keith, why do you ask so many questions?" arose.

The real reason, lies with the result of the math courses. The side effects of the courses are to learn a little math. The main purpose, is to develop the reasoning abilities of our young minds. This, even I can agree, can have some merit. It can be used to some advantage in latter life. But I also think that a course entitled "Objective Reasoning" or "Reasoning for the High School Student" could handle the task of teaching us to reason clearly. A course like this could contain such things as solving everyday problems, dealing with complex moral and ethical issues, complex word problems and yes, even some math.

Math could be tought in such a manner that its' main benefits would be interesting. I think that a course, like the one I suggested, should replace math for those people who have no desire to know mathematics.

Critique: The main idea of the essay is clearly stated at the end of the first paragraph. By using quotations in the next paragraph the writer dramatically supports his viewpoint, although the impact of his argument is diluted by awkward sentence structure. The third and fourth paragraphs offer constructive ideas, but in proposing to substitute courses in reasoning in place of math courses, the writer loses sight of the chief reason for writing the essay—to address the issue of program cuts. On the whole the writer conveys ideas reasonably well, but mechanical flaws, needless repetition, and a pedestrian style create the impression that he has not yet fully gained control of the craft of essay writing. Score: **4**

Sample Essay 3 by Gilbert

Through my life, I have lived in an enviroment where hard work and ability to utilize talent has proved a rewarding experience. Weather in school or football team, those who demonstrate these qualties are always the most successful in intro-scholastic and intro-mural atheletics. For I believe that sports is where I will be able to apply my working effort best. Also, I know that sports will always present interesting and challenging situations to me and other students.

Although I have come to realize that I have many talents that will present me with many opportunities, I believe that my strongest talents are best suited for a career in sports. These talents include my ability to work well with numbers and solving problems But more importantly they include my ability to analyze and my ability to work well with people. Perfecting my ability to work with people is something that sports will help me achieve. Communicating with and understanding people are talents that are necessary in sports career, but I believe that these, combined with my other talents create a strong potential for me to succeed.

Critique: Instead of putting the essay's main idea in a prominent, attention-grabbing place, the writer has tucked it into the middle of the first paragraph. Yet, the essay's statement of purpose is relatively clear. Less clear, however, is how its main point relates to the assertion made in the first two sentences—that success comes to those who work hard and use their talents.

The second paragraph consists largely of generalities that apply not just to a career in sports but also to almost any career or endeavor. As a consequence, it fails to argue compellingly that athletic programs should not be cut. In fact, only by implication is the essay related to the topic that prompted it. Rather than offer specific reasons for keeping the school's sports program intact, the writer does little more than claim to possess personal qualities appropriate to a sports-related career.

Overall, the essay is sincere but aimless. Score: **2**

Essay Self-Assessment

Before evaluating your own essay, read pages 433–434 on evaluating ACT essays. Then complete the following checklist. Focus on both the strengths and weaknesses of your essay.

	Yes!	Mostly	Hardly	No
Does the essay address the ACT prompt?	____	____	____	____
Is the topic sufficiently narrowed?	____	____	____	____
Is the essay's main idea clear?	____	____	____	____
Have you written an introduction?	____	____	____	____
Does the essay sound natural?	____	____	____	____
Have you used plain words?	____	____	____	____
Have you used precise language?	____	____	____	____
Does your essay have a clear focus?	____	____	____	____
Do all parts fit together coherently?	____	____	____	____
Is each sentence accurately worded?	____	____	____	____
Have you trimmed needless words?	____	____	____	____
Do you show more than tell?	____	____	____	____
Have you used active verbs?	____	____	____	____
Is the language fresh?	____	____	____	____
Do you include verbal surprises?	____	____	____	____
Are the sentences varied?	____	____	____	____
Is sentence length balanced?	____	____	____	____
Does the essay have a conclusion?	____	____	____	____
Is the essay mostly error-free?	____	____	____	____

Identify the three greatest strengths of your essay:

1)____

2) ____

3) ____

Name three specific things that you could do to improve your essay:

1)____

2) ____

3) ____

Circle the score your essay deserves: 6 5 4 3 2 1

Table for Calculating the Combined English/Writing Test Score

Instructions:

1. Find your Writing Test subscore (2–12) along the top of the table.
2. Find your English Test score on the left or right side.
3. Your combined score will appear in the table where the two scores intersect. For instance, a 10 on the Writing Test and a 25 on the English Test will yield a Combined English/Writing Test score of 26.

English Test Score	Writing Test Subscore											English Test Score
	2	3	4	5	6	7	8	9	10	11	12	
1	1	2	3	4	5	6	7	8	9	10	11	**1**
2	2	3	4	5	6	6	7	8	9	10	11	**2**
3	2	3	4	5	6	7	8	9	10	11	12	**3**
4	3	4	5	6	7	8	9	10	11	12	13	**4**
5	4	5	6	7	8	9	10	11	12	12	13	**5**
6	5	6	7	7	8	9	10	11	12	13	14	**6**
7	5	6	7	8	9	10	11	12	13	14	15	**7**
8	6	7	8	9	10	11	12	13	14	15	16	**8**
9	7	8	9	10	11	12	13	13	14	15	16	**9**
10	8	9	9	10	11	12	13	14	15	16	17	**10**
11	8	9	10	11	12	13	14	15	16	17	18	**11**
12	9	10	11	12	13	14	15	16	17	18	19	**12**
13	10	11	12	13	14	14	15	16	17	18	19	**13**
14	10	11	12	13	14	15	16	17	18	19	20	**14**
15	11	12	13	14	15	16	17	18	19	20	21	**15**
16	12	13	14	15	16	17	18	19	20	20	21	**16**
17	13	14	15	16	16	17	18	19	20	21	22	**17**
18	13	14	15	16	17	18	19	20	21	22	23	**18**
19	14	15	16	17	18	19	20	21	22	23	24	**19**
20	15	16	17	18	19	20	21	21	22	23	24	**20**
21	16	17	17	18	19	20	21	22	23	24	25	**21**
22	16	17	18	19	20	21	22	23	24	25	26	**22**
23	17	18	19	20	21	22	23	24	25	26	27	**23**
24	18	19	20	21	22	23	23	24	25	26	27	**24**
25	18	19	20	21	22	23	24	25	26	27	28	**25**
26	19	20	21	22	23	24	25	26	27	28	29	**26**
27	20	21	22	23	24	25	26	27	28	28	29	**27**
28	21	22	23	24	24	26	26	27	28	29	30	**28**

Table for Calculating the Combined English/Writing Test Score (cont.)

English Test Score	Writing Test Subscore 2	3	4	5	6	7	8	9	10	11	12	English Test Score
29	21	22	23	24	25	26	27	28	29	30	31	**29**
30	22	23	24	25	26	27	28	29	30	31	32	**30**
31	23	24	25	26	27	28	29	30	30	31	32	**31**
32	24	25	25	26	27	28	29	30	31	32	33	**32**
33	25	25	26	27	28	29	30	31	32	33	34	**33**
34	26	26	27	28	29	30	31	32	33	34	35	**34**
35	26	27	28	28	30	31	31	32	33	34	35	**35**
36	26	27	28	29	30	31	32	33	34	35	36	**36**

Calculating Your Combined English/Writing Test Score

English Test Score _____

Essay Score ___ multiply by 2 = _____

Combined Score (See table): _____

PART 3

TAKING THE ACT

CHAPTER 1

English Review and Practice

- Punctuation
- Basic Grammar and Usage
- Sentence Mechanics
- Writing Strategy
- Organization
- Style
- Word Choice

The English Test consists of 75 multiple-choice questions based on five prose passages with portions of their text underlined and numbered. Next to each numbered part are four responses corresponding to the test item. Sometimes the question will attempt to measure your understanding of usage and mechanics. You will have to decide whether to leave the underlined text as it is or substitute one of the choices. Other questions will attempt to measure your understanding of rhetorical skills, such as the order of items within a passage, the organization of a passage, or the appropriateness or consistency of the language. Questions measuring rhetorical skills may ask you to select how a general statement might be better supported or whether a different arrangement of the passage's parts might be more meaningful. You have 45 minutes to complete the 75 items.

Here is a quick view of the test itself. Read this passage and answer the questions. Do not refer to the correct answers (given below each set of choices) until you have tried to answer the questions yourself.

Sample Passage

All creatures in the animal kingdom have the instincts of curiosity and fear. Man alone was endowed with <u>imagination, which</u> [1] was bound to complicate matters for him. Whereas a fox, let us say, was able to shrug off the mysteries of the heavens and such whims of nature as lightning and earthquakes, man <u>has demanded</u> [2] an explanation.

And so began the myths, the ancient creeds, witchcraft, astrology, <u>they told fantastic tales</u> [3] of wanderings into the unknown reaches of space and time, the distortions of the mental and physical capabilities of man himself. Evidently, these "explanations" were not enough: Man developed a thirst for something *beyond* the ever-growing knowledge brought to him by empirical scientific research. The French call this *le culte de merveilleux*. We call it science fiction. [4]

1. **A.** NO CHANGE
   B. imagination; which
   C. imagination, a fact that
   D. imagination, on which

2. **F.** NO CHANGE
   G. had been demanding
   H. demanded
   J. demands

3. **A.** NO CHANGE
   B. fantastic tales
   C. They were told fantastic tales
   D. fireside stories

4. If the writer wanted to include more information about the early history of science fiction, which of the following would be most effective for the passage as a whole?
   F. A listing of current science fiction writers
   G. A discussion of recent science fiction movies
   H. A discussion of the "fantastic tales" that were the origin of science fiction
   J. A discussion of witchcraft

Correct Answers:

1. **C** 3. **B**
2. **H** 4. **H**

The *Usage/Mechanics* questions test your understanding of punctuation, grammar, and sentence structure. These questions stress the use of *clear, effective, concise* language. Inappropriate or incorrect choices can often be detected by the way in which they confuse the structure of the sentence or obscure its meaning. A description of the three categories follows, together with the percentage of the test devoted to each.

1. *Punctuation* ✓	13%	These questions concern the use of punctuation marks (apostrophes, colons, commas, dashes, exclamation points, hyphens, parentheses, question marks, quotation marks, and semicolons) and, in particular, their function in clarifying the *meaning of the prose selection.*
2. *Basic Grammar and Usage* ✓	16%	Items in this category test your knowledge and understanding of verbs, adverbs, and adjectives; subject-verb agreement, and agreement of pronoun and antecedent; and the proper use of connectives.
3. *Sentence Structure* ✓	24%	These items deal with the makeup of the sentence, including the relationship of clauses, the correct use and placement of modifiers, parallelism, and consistency in point-of-view and tense.

The *Rhetorical Skills* questions refer to a specific portion of the text or to the passage as a whole, including the logical sequence of sentences or paragraphs, and the order, appropriateness, or sufficiency of supporting details. You may be asked to choose a term that describes the passage, such as "critical," "emotional," "dispassionate," or "accusatory." Or you may be asked to select a phrase that describes the type of reader for whom the selection is intended. The *Rhetorical Skills* questions are almost equally distributed among three categories: strategy, organization, and style.

1. *Strategy* ✓	16%	Questions on strategy involve examination of some of the options the author has decided upon. Chief among these is the author's choice of supporting material. Is it effective, appropriate, and sufficient in amount and quality? Another author option is the choice of writing vehicle—for example, the descriptive essay, the persuasive essay, the biography, or the comparison-contrast model. You will be asked to make some judgments concerning the writer's handling of these options.
2. *Organization* ✓	15%	Questions on organization will most often involve rearrangement of sentences in a paragraph or paragraphs within a passage. You may also be asked to spot extraneous material that has little or nothing to do with the main idea, and to indicate places where additional material might strengthen the paragraph.
3. *Style* ✓	16%	In these questions, you may be asked to choose an adjective that best describes the style of the prose passage, to select the best phrase of several that have the same words but in a different order, or to choose alternative words. You will be asked to select text that matches the style and tone of the passage, and to choose words or phrases that most concisely express an idea.

LONG-RANGE STRATEGY

As a student planning to take the ACT test, you are already engaged in what is probably the most important of the long-term strategies, that is, learning as much as you can about the test and about the questions you are expected to answer. The English Test questions are quite straightforward, not tricky or devious. They seek to measure your ability to recognize clear and meaningful prose, and to identify word combinations that are either incorrect or less effective than others.

If you feel unsure of your prose "ear" (the language sense you have developed over the years), your best strategy is to review this chapter several times. As you examine each section, think of the materials presented to you as a general review of problem areas, rather than as specific data to memorize or master. The English language has too many options to commit to memory. In each lesson, try to see the general rule and its purpose.

TIP

Go over any item that you find unfamiliar or difficult several times.

Work on your trouble spots by taking the practice exercises more than once and by reviewing the answers and explanations as often as necessary, since the explanations themselves will help serve as mini-reviews.

More suggestions:

- If you have enough time before you take the actual test, improve your prose "ear" by reading good, informative prose under relaxed conditions, perhaps even on a daily, limited basis.

- Be sure you understand the format of the English Test, the time limitations, the number and types of questions, and the form of the answer sheet.
- Discuss the test frankly with your English teacher. Ask about your strengths and weaknesses in the skills to be tested. Does your teacher see anything in your habits or work that suggests problems you may have with the test? If so, how can you deal with those problems?
- Search out all avenues of help. Perhaps your school counselor has practice tests or other materials on test taking. Also, if there are ACT study groups in your school or community, join one, by all means. The additional practice will give you confidence, and you will find that sharing problems with other prospective test-takers is another good way to build confidence. Consult the on-line help at the www.act.org web site.
- Talk with your friends and family about the test and any fears you might have. Keep in mind that the ACT is only one of several means by which you will be evaluated and your admission to a college or university determined. Do not magnify its importance to the degree that you cannot prepare or perform effectively.

Anxiety affects your perception and use of language. Before you take the ACT test, you should come to terms in your own mind that you will do your best and that nobody, including yourself, has a right to ask more of you than that.

Now, look over the Test-taking Tactics that follow, and practice the habits and skills that will help you do your best.

SHORT-RANGE STRATEGY

1. **Concentrate.** On the morning of the test, reduce as many of your distractions, obligations, and plans as possible. Have no social events planned—either before or after the test—so that your full attention is on your answers. Leave adequate time to arrive at the test center. It is better to be a little early.
2. **Work carefully.** Before you arrive, be familiar with the test directions. When the test begins, listen carefully to any directions read to you by a proctor or played on a tape. In marking the answer sheet, be sure to put each answer in the right space. If you skip a question because it is taking too much time, be careful to skip the corresponding space on the answer sheet. Focus only on the test; block out any distractions.

TACTICS

1. **Pace yourself.** You have 45 minutes to answer 75 questions, or roughly nine minutes for each passage and its questions. It is wise to assume that some passages and some questions will be more difficult for you, so that you may wish to complete others that are easier and to return to the more difficult ones before the test ends. Occasionally, stop to check the time, to be sure you are working at a good pace and will have time both to complete the test and to review your work.
2. **Read with a purpose.** The five passages cover a wide range of topics and are written in different styles. In responding to questions, you should be aware of these differences in writing style. Before you begin to answer the questions, quickly skim the passage. Then, answer each question in light of its context. If you are unsure of a question or your answer, read the sentences immediately before and after the sentence with the underlined part.
3. **Carefully examine the underlined parts.** Think about the principles of usage involved in each question and focus on the one that applies. Many of the questions concern more than one aspect of usage, especially in the answer options. Be sure that the answer you choose does not introduce another error while correcting the first!

4. **Decide on the best answer.** As you approach each question, it is probably best to think how the underlined portion would be expressed in standard written English. If it already seems correct, you should mark NO CHANGE. If your own conversion seems better, check the answers to see if it matches one of them. If it does not, choose the answer you think best. If the choice is too difficult, try substituting each option for the underlined part, being sure to examine it in the context of the question sentence, the preceding sentence, and the following sentence.

PUNCTUATION

The Comma

Among its many functions, the comma is used to set off independent clauses, items in a series, coordinate adjectives, parenthetical expressions, and nonrestrictive phrases or clauses.

Use a comma to separate independent clauses joined by a coordinating conjunction (*and, but, for, or, nor, yet,* or *so*).

EXAMPLES: He wanted to be a salesman, but no jobs were available.
The people refused to send their children to school, and the school building stood empty the entire year.

Be sure you understand that this rule applies to the joining of *independent clauses,* that is, complete sentences. The use of the coordinating conjunction to join compound subjects (*Bush* and *Gore* debated three times), pairs of phrases (The food at that restaurant is prepared *without care* and *without taste*), compound verbs (Phil *ran* the office and *acted* as athletic director), or the like does not require the comma.

Use commas to separate items in a series.

EXAMPLES: Friendly, small, and innovative are adjectives that accurately characterize this college.
He went to the basement, set the trap, and returned to the kitchen to wait.

TIP

Ignoring the need for commas is probably one of the most universal errors in student writing. The chances are good that you will be tested on that rule. *She rose, showered, and had breakfast. (Correct)*

Use a comma to separate coordinate adjectives modifying the same noun.

EXAMPLES: He washed his low-slung, shiny, souped-up pickup.
Himalayan cats have long, silky, heavy fur.

To test whether adjectives are coordinate, reverse their order or insert *and* between them. If the phrase still makes sense, they are coordinate adjectives and require a comma. The first example makes sense using either method: *souped-up, shiny, low-slung pickup,* or *low-slung and shiny and souped-up pickup.*

Non-coordinate adjectives have a special relationship with the nouns they modify. To some degree, they create a word group that itself is modified. They should not be preceded by commas.

EXAMPLE: They all admired the tall, powerful *football player.*

In this sentence, *football* is a non-coordinate adjective, different from the coordinate adjectives *tall* and *powerful*. You cannot put *and* between *powerful* and *football* nor can you move the word *football*. Other examples of non-coordinate adjectives are *doll* house, *art* museum, *computer* science, and *wheat* bread.

Use commas to set off nonrestrictive (amplifying or explanatory) phrases and clauses from the rest of the sentence.

PARTICIPIAL PHRASE: Having spent his last penny, Luster tried to borrow a quarter from his boss.
PREPOSITIONAL PHRASE: At the beginning of each game, a noted singer gives his rendition of "The Star-Spangled Banner."
ADVERBIAL CLAUSE: When the composer was finished with the prelude, she began work on the first movement.

Use a comma to set off contrasting and nonessential phrases and clauses.

EXAMPLES: Mary Jennings, who was my best friend, dropped the class.
The first offer on the Blake house, which had been on the market for almost a month, was very disappointing.

Be sure to distinguish between these *nonrestrictive* interrupters and the *restrictive modifiers,* which are *not* set off by commas. Nonrestrictive modifiers add information but do not limit or change the meaning of the sentence. Note how the meaning changes when the clause is restrictive.

RESTRICTIVE: The young woman who was my best student dropped the class.

The young woman is now identified as the best student. Here is another example of a nonrestrictive clause:

EXAMPLE: Cardiac patients who have artificial valve implants are required to take anticoagulants for the rest of their lives.

Use a comma to set off nonrestrictive phrases and clauses that follow the main clause.

EXAMPLES: Jessica wanted to see the ice show, not the circus.
Few fans thought the reigning heavyweight champion could win, although he was superior to the challenger in every category.

Use the commas to set off an appositive. An appositive is a noun or noun phrase that renames or explains the noun it follows.

EXAMPLE: The novel, a mystery about a secret island off the Washington coast, was an instant bestseller.

Use commas to set off words in direct address. Words in direct address identify the one being spoken to.

EXAMPLE: Excuse me, Beth, but aren't you late for your tennis lesson?

A comma can take the place of an omitted word or phrase.

EXAMPLE: The Capitol Bank is located in a shopping mall; the Investors Bank, in the heart of town.

A comma is sometimes needed for clarity.

EXAMPLES: Ever since, we have taken the plane rather than the train.
In May, Marcia went to Washington, D.C.

AVOID using a comma:

When it occurs after a subject or a verb. (Commas interrupt and disturb the direct link of subject to verb or verb to object/complement.)

FAULTY: The retiring teacher, was applauded more than he expected.
REVISED: The retiring teacher was applauded more than he expected.

When it separates a pair of words, phrases, or subordinate clauses joined by ***and, or,*** or ***nor***. (Do not use a comma unless the parts of the sentence are main clauses.)

FAULTY: The Pacific Pelican population has been seriously affected by DDT, and by greedy fishermen.
REVISED: The Pacific Pelican population has been seriously affected by DDT and by greedy fishermen.

When the comma occurs after ***and, but, although, because,*** or another conjunction. The coordinating conjunctions (and, but, for, or, yet) and the subordination conjunctions (although, because, when, since, and so on) are not followed by commas.

FAULTY: Secluded little islands in the Pacific are restful and, alluring.
REVISED: Secluded little islands in the Pacific are restful and alluring.

FAULTY: Although, most families eat around their television sets, mine does not.
REVISED: Although most families eat around their television sets, mine does not.

When the comma sets off a series. (Delete any commas introducing a series.)

FAULTY: Secretaries today need skills in, typing on a computer, using a calculator, and organizing the work flow.
REVISED: Secretaries today need skills in typing on a computer, using a calculator, and organizing the work flow.

TIP

Learn to recognize where commas are never used; for example, between subjects and verbs or after conjunctions.

When the comma sets off restrictive, essential elements. (Commas do not set off essential elements which limit the meaning of the word they refer to).

FAULTY: Even people, who are fit, should be wary of falling on a hike.
REVISED: Even people who are fit should be wary of falling on a hike.

FAULTY: Lois Lowry's work, *The Giver,* won a Newbery Award.
REVISED: Lois Lowry's work *The Giver* won a Newbery Award.

The Semicolon

The semicolon is a straightforward mark of punctuation with several capabilities. However, to understand all uses of this versatile mark, read this explanation several times until you grasp it well.

The semicolon is generally used to separate coordinate elements in a sentence, that is, items of the same grammatical nature. Most often, it is used between related ideas that require punctuation weaker than a period, but stronger than a comma. In addition, the semicolon divides three or more items in a series when the items themselves contain commas.

Use a semicolon between related independent clauses not joined by a coordinating conjunction.

EXAMPLES: A mature male gorilla may be six feet tall and weigh 400 pounds or more; his enormous arms can span eight feet.
New York has twelve major stadiums; Los Angeles has fifteen.

Use a semicolon between independent clauses joined by a transitional word (conjunctive adverb).

Frequently, two independent clauses are joined, not by a coordinating conjunction, but by a transitional word (conjunctive adverb) introducing the second clause. A semicolon must be used between the clauses, because these transitional words (*accordingly, also, consequently, finally, furthermore, however, indeed, meanwhile, nevertheless, similarly, still, therefore, thus,* and the like) are *not* connecting words.

EXAMPLE: A female coyote will not bear pups if her diet consists of fewer than fifty rodents a week; thus, Mother Nature achieves a population balance.

Use a semicolon to separate coordinate clauses if the clauses themselves have commas.

EXAMPLE: The warranty on the car covered extensive repairs to the electrical system, front end, transmission, fuel injection system, and valves; but the amount of time and inconvenience involved in returning each time to the dealer cannot be ignored.

Use a semicolon to separate items in a series when the items themselves contain internal punctuation.

Normally, three or more items in a series are set off by commas; however, when they are made more complex by commas and other punctuation, they are separated by semicolons.

EXAMPLE: The trio was composed of a cellist named Grosz, who had been a European virtuoso for many years; a pianist who had won a major music festival in 1954, 1955, and 1958; and a violinist who had studied in Budapest, Vienna, and Munich.

AVOID using a semicolon:

When the semicolon separates a subordinate clause or a phrase from a main clause. (The semicolon is not used to separate clauses and phrases from a main clause.)

FAULTY: Many forms of wildlife are becoming extinct; because of the encroachment of humans on the animals' territory and habitat.

REVISED: Many forms of wildlife are becoming extinct because of the encroachment of humans on the animals' territory and habitat.

When the semicolon introduces a series or explanation. (Colons and dashes, not semicolons, are used to introduce series and explanations.)

FAULTY: Sue and Matt quickly stowed the supplies they needed into the canoe; the sleeping bags, four large jugs of water, spare boots and socks, and enough food to last them three days.

REVISED: Sue and Matt quickly stowed the supplies they needed into the canoe—the sleeping bags, four large jugs of water, spare boots and socks, and enough food to last them three days.

The Colon, Hyphen, and Apostrophe

The Colon

The colon is a signal that something is to follow: a rephrased statement, a list or series, or a formal quotation. Use a colon in a sentence if you can logically insert *namely* after it.

Use a colon at the end of a complete statement to show anticipation—that is, to show that amplifying details follow, such as a list, a series of items, a formal quotation, or an explanation.

EXAMPLES: Of all the gauges in an airplane cockpit, three are crucial: the altimeter, the gas gauge, and the crash-warning indicator.
After five minutes of silence, the actor uttered those famous words: "To be or not to be; that is the question."
A popover has four common ingredients: flour, milk, salt, and butter.

TIP

Be sure of the use of the colon. Colons appear frequently on the test.

Problems that occur in the use of the colon usually result from the following lapses:

1. A complete statement (independent clause) does not precede the colon.

INCORRECT: Tasks that I must complete today: mow the lawn, read two chapters of history, and tidy my room.
CORRECT: I must complete several tasks today: mow the lawn, read two chapters of history, and tidy my room.

2. A colon incorrectly separates essential parts of a sentence.

INCORRECT: In updating my computer, I added: a hard disk, a laser printer, and a fine-resolution monitor. (The colon separates the verb from its direct objects.)
CORRECT: In updating my computer, I added some new components: a hard disk, a laser printer, and a fine-resolution monitor.
ALSO CORRECT: In updating my computer, I added a hard disk, a laser printer, and a fine-resolution monitor.

3. There is more than one colon in a sentence.

INCORRECT: The success of the action depended upon three variables: that the weather would hold out, that the supplies would arrive on time, and that the enemy would be short on three things: planes, ammunition, and food.
CORRECT: The success of the action depended upon three variables: that the weather would hold out, that the supplies would arrive on time, and that the enemy would be short on planes, ammunition, and food.

Hyphen

The hyphen has two main uses: to divide syllables at the end of a line and to link words in certain combinations. It is also used in compound numbers from twenty-one to ninety-nine.

Hyphenate a compound adjective (an adjective made up of two or more words) when it precedes the noun it modifies. The hyphen is ordinarily not used when the words follow the noun.

EXAMPLES: She wore a well-used raincoat.
BUT
Her raincoat was well used.

NOTE: A compound adjective with an adverbial *-ly* modifier is never hyphenated: the *poorly designed* interchange.

Apostrophe

In addition to indicating possession, the apostrophe is used to take the place of omitted numbers (class of '02) and omitted letters or words in contractions (wasn't [was not], o'clock [of the clock]), and to indicate plurals that might otherwise be confusing (A's [not As]).

Make sure apostrophes have meaning. Do not make the error of adding an apostrophe where it has no meaning and is ungrammatical.

Use an apostrophe to show the possessive case of nouns and indefinite pronouns.

1. The possessive case of singular nouns (either common or proper) is indicated by adding an apostrophe and an s.

   EXAMPLES: George's speech, the senator's campaign, anyone's opinion, the boss's office, Charles's book.

2. The possessive case of plural nouns ending in *s* is formed by adding only the apostrophe.

   EXAMPLES: the girls' softball team, the waitresses' union, the Harrisons' antique cars.

   NOTE: Irregular plurals, such as *men* or *children,* form the possessive by adding an apostrophe and an *s:* men's, children's.

A common error is to confuse possessive pronouns and contractions, particularly *its* and *it's* (meaning it is) *their* and *they're (they are),* and *whose* and *who's (who is)*. Possessive pronouns have no apostrophe.

AVOID using an apostrophe:

When it is a plural noun. (Do not fall into the habit of adding an apostrophe when possession is not indicated.)

FAULTY: The Perkins' and the Rists' were going fishing together.
REVISED: The Perkins and the Rists were going fishing together.

When you are using a personal pronoun. (*His, hers, its, ours, yours, theirs,* and *whose* are possessives, serving to provide possessive forms of the pronouns *he, she, it, we, you, they,* and *who*.)

FAULTY: The hairbrush used by Nichol was clearly her's.
REVISED: The hairbrush used by Nichol was clearly hers.

The Dash, Question Mark, and Exclamation Point

Dash

The main function of the dash, like parentheses, is to enclose information within a sentence. Dashes are generally more forceful and therefore should be used sparingly, since they highlight the ideas and items they enclose.

TIP 

Use dashes sparingly. The main function of the dash, like parentheses, is to enclose information within a sentence. Dashes are generally more forceful and, therefore, should be used prudently.

Use dashes to indicate hesitation, or a sudden break in thought or sentence structure, or to set off appositives and other explanatory or parenthetical elements.

The dash adds emphasis to any part of a sentence that can be separated from the rest of the sentence.

EXAMPLE: The skydiver—in spite of his broken leg—set a new record for endurance.

Some specific uses of the dash are:

1. To interrupt continuity of prose

   EXAMPLE: "I really can't tolerate—Well, never mind."

2. To emphasize appositives

   EXAMPLE: The items she had asked for in the new car—tape deck, mileage computer, stick shift—were all included.

3. To set off phrases or clauses containing commas

When a modifier itself contains commas, dashes can make its boundaries clear.

EXAMPLE: General Motors—which has manufactured tanks, cannons, and mobile cranes—has always been far more than an automobile assembler.

4. To set off parenthetical elements

EXAMPLE: The child was sitting—actually sprawling—at his desk.

AVOID using a dash:

When commas, semicolons, and periods are more suitable. (Also, when you have used dashes already in the writing; more dashes can lend a jumpy or breathy atmosphere.)

FAULTY: My friend Phil Petersen—who lives across the street from me—does not believe in letting his children—five-year-old Josh and eight-year-old Melanie—watch television. He believes that watching the devil's box—the television set—introduces his children to all the evils in the world.

REVISED: My friend Phil Petersen, who lives across the street from me, does not believe in letting his five-year-old Josh and eight-year-old Melanie watch television. He believes that watching the devil's box—the television set—introduces his children to all the evils in the world.

Question Mark

A question mark indicates the end of a direct question. A question mark in parentheses signals doubt or uncertainty about a fact such as a date or a number.

Use a question mark after a direct question.

EXAMPLES: When are we going to eat?
Ask yourself, what are the odds of winning?
(It is also correct to capitalize the word *what*.)

A question mark in parentheses may be used to express doubt.

EXAMPLE: The Dean's notes, published in 1774 (?), are considered the novel's origin.

NOTE: The use of the question mark as a mark of irony or sarcasm is not usually considered proper: The superintendent's important (?) announcements took all morning.

The question mark is unlikely to cause you trouble on the English test. Problems mainly occur (a) because of failure to distinguish between *direct* and *indirect* questions (an *indirect* question is always followed by a period: My friend asked why I didn't have my car.) or (b) because of mistaken combination of question marks with other punctuation marks. A question mark should never be combined with a comma, period, exclamation point, or other question mark.

Exclamation Point

An exclamation point is an indicator of strong *emotional* feelings, such as anger, joy, shock, surprise, or fear. It may also be used to express irony or emphasis. Like the dash, it should be used sparingly.

Use an exclamation point after a command, an interjection, an exclamation, or some other expression of strong emotion.

COMMAND: Stop!
INTERJECTION: Wow! Fire! Help!
EMOTIONAL EXPRESSION: Don't tell me you won again! How wonderful!

An exclamation point should not be used with commas, periods, other exclamation points, or question marks.

Use exclamation points sparingly and tastefully.

FAULTY: A year after declaring California fiscally sound, the governor was forced to declare an 81 billion dollar deficit!
REVISED: A year after declaring California fiscally sound, the governor was forced to declare an 81 billion dollar deficit.

Quotation Marks and Parentheses

Quotation Marks

One of the main uses of quotation marks is to signal the exact words of a writer or speaker. Quotation marks are also used to enclose the titles of short literary or musical works (articles, short stories or poems, songs), as well as words used in a special way.

Watch punctuation of quotations. When a quotation is structurally part of a sentence, remember to begin with a lowercase letter even though the original quotation is a separate sentence beginning with a capital letter.

EXAMPLE: FDR told a worried nation that "there is nothing to fear but fear itself."

However, when the quotation is not structurally integrated with the rest of the sentence, the intitial letter is capitalized.

EXAMPLE: FDR's sage words of wisdom, "There is nothing to fear but fear itself," soothed a worried nation.

Enclose direct quotations in quotation marks.

EXAMPLE: "We will wage war wherever it takes us," Winston Churchill pledged.

Quotation marks should enclose only the exact words of the person quoted.

EXAMPLE: Winston Churchill pledged that "we will wage war wherever it takes us." (NOT ... pledged "that we will ...")

NOTE: When a quoted sentence is interrupted by a phrase such as *he said* or *she replied,* two pairs of quotation marks must be used, one for each part of the quotation. The first word of the second part of the quoted material should not be capitalized unless it is a proper noun or the pronoun *I*.

EXAMPLE: "There are two sorts of contests between men," John Locke argued, "one managed by law, the other by force."

Use single quotation marks to enclose a quotation inside another quotation.

EXAMPLE: "My favorite saying, 'A day without a slice of apple pie is a day lost,' " said Dr. Annaheim, "is causing me to be in trouble with health addicts."

Commas and periods *always* belong *inside* quotation marks; semicolons and colons, outside. Question marks and exclamation points are placed inside the quotation marks when they are part of the quotation; otherwise, they are placed outside.

EXAMPLE: What did he mean when he said, "I know the answer already"?
"The case is closed!" the attorney exclaimed.

AVOID using quotation marks:

When the quotation marks are used to set off a simple title. (Quotation marks are not used around titles unless they contain or are themselves direct quotations.)

FAULTY: "My Great Adventure Last Vacation"
REVISED: My Great Adventure Last Vacation

FAULTY: "Optimism in William Faulkner's The Bear."
REVISED: Optimism in William Faulkner's "The Bear."

When they use ordinary nicknames or esoteric terms that are not being explained.

FAULTY: Birds of the Alaskan "tundra" are Canada Geese and Golden Plovers.
REVISED: Birds of the Alaskan tundra are Canada Geese and Golden Plovers.

TIP 

Make sure your diction is grammatical. To rid youself of grammatical lapses remember these two rules:
1. Commas and periods ALWAYS belong inside quotation marks (page 112).
2. Use a possessive pronoun before a gerund (page 125).

When the quotation marks are used to justify or apologize for slang or trite phrases that are not appropriate for your writing. (If slang is effective, employ it without quotation marks.)

FAULTY: The President's State of the Union speech was "flat as a pancake" and "heavy as lead."
REVISED: The President's State of the Union speech was flat as a pancake and heavy as lead.

Parentheses

Parentheses, like dashes, are used to set off words of explanation and other secondary supporting details—figures, data, examples—that are not really part of the main sentence or paragraph. Parentheses are less emphatic than dashes and should be reserved for ideas that have no essential connection with the rest of the sentence.

Use parentheses to enclose an explanatory or parenthetical element that is not closely connected with the rest of the sentence.

EXAMPLE: The speech that he gave on Sunday (under extremely difficult circumstances, it should be noted) was his best.

If the parenthetical item is an independent sentence that stands alone, capitalize the first word and place a period inside the end parenthesis. If it is a complete sentence within another complete sentence, do not begin it with a capital letter or end it with a period. A question mark or exclamation point that is part of the parenthetical element should be placed inside the parenthesis.

EXAMPLES: On Easter, I always think of the hot cross buns I used to buy for two cents apiece. (At the time, the year was 1939, and I was three years old.) Congressman Jones (he was the man who once proposed having no entrance standards for community college students) gave a speech decrying the lack of basic skills on campuses today. The absurd placement of the child-care center (fifteen feet from a classroom building!) was amateur architecture at its worst.

AVOID using unneeded parentheses:

Always use parentheses sparingly. Too many in a text will distract and confuse the reader.

FAULTY: The basic food pyramid has changed considerably. The old version (which was posted in every classroom and doctor's office in the land) had sugar and nuts at the top (the narrowest part) and grain and starches at the bottom (the widest part).

REVISED: The basic food pyramid has changed considerably. The old version, which was posted in every classroom and doctor's office in the land, had sugar and nuts at the top, which was the narrowest part, and grain and starches at the bottom, the widest part.

Warm-Up Drill

Decide whether the punctuation or capitalization at each numbered point is correct or incorrect. Then place a check in the proper column.

CORRECT	INCORRECT	
_______	_______	1. He had said that "he was nobody to fool with." (1)
_______	_______	2. Fred wrote a poem for Barbara, which he entitled "Barbaric Barbara." (2)
_______	_______	3. Joseph Pummell (he was the senator who authored the antifraud bill.) (3) offered to speak at our first meeting.
_______	_______	4. "I knew for sure," she said, "when he didn't ask me to the prom". (4)
_______	_______	5. The measure designed to lower inflationary pressures on the economy resulted in a cost-of-living increase of 12 per-cent (some measure, some reduction!). (5)
_______	_______	6. "There is no doubt," he asserted, " (6) That the enormous national debt will be a major problem in the next century."

ANSWERS AND EXPLANATIONS

1. INCORRECT. Only the actual words spoken can be in quotation marks. *He was* would not be part of the speaker's words.
2. CORRECT. Quotation marks are used for titles of shorter literary works.
3. INCORRECT. A complete sentence enclosed in parentheses within another sentence does not take a period.
4. INCORRECT. A period always belongs inside the quotation mark.
5. CORRECT. An exclamation point that is part of the parenthetical phrase is placed within the parentheses.
6. INCORRECT. The second part of a quoted sentence interrupted by a phrase like *he asserted* does not begin with a capital unless the first word is a proper noun or *I*.

Practice Exercises

What lies behind the creative genius of our greatest authors [1] has been the subject of speculation over the past two centuries. There is little doubt that many of the worlds [2] creative geniuses experienced miserable lives [3] most often, they suffered a personal and extreme brand of deprivation that profoundly affected the quality of their daily lives. Almost always, [4] the depth of their misery is related to the greatness of their genius. One who reads both Emily Bronte's *Wuthering Heights* [5] and the best known [6] critical discussions about her work cannot escape the conclusion, [7] that Emily was the product of a punitive and abusive environment, [8] it is difficult to avoid the further conclusion that the strength and authenticity of her novel [9] the vulnerabilities and palpable yearnings of its main characters—are related however, faintly [10] to her personal affliction.

1. **A.** NO CHANGE
   B. authors'
   C. authors,
   D. author's

2. **F.** NO CHANGE
   G. world's
   H. worlds'
   J. world's,

3. **A.** NO CHANGE
   B. lives:
   C. lives;
   D. lives,

4. **F.** NO CHANGE
   G. always;
   H. always—
   J. always:

5. **A.** NO CHANGE
   B. "Wuthering Heights"
   C. Wuthering Heights
   D. Wuthering-Heights

6. **F.** NO CHANGE
   G. best, known
   H. best-known
   J. "best known"

7. **A.** NO CHANGE
   B. conclusion;
   C. conclusion—
   D. conclusion

8. **F.** NO CHANGE
   G. environment;
   H. environment—
   J. environment?

9. **A.** NO CHANGE
   B. novel;
   C. novel—
   D. novel:

10. **F.** NO CHANGE
    G. related; however faintly,
    H. related, however faintly,
    J. related (however faintly)

ANSWERS AND EXPLANATIONS

1. **(A)** The noun *authors* is a simple object in this sentence and requires no punctuation.
2. **(G)** The plural *geniuses* are a possession of the world and require that it signal that possession with an apostrophe.
3. **(B)** The words occurring after *lives* form an independent clause and so must be set off with a stronger mark of punctuation. The colon is the best choice in this context because the following statement gives specific focus to the general statement made in the sentence's introductory clause.
4. **(F)** Set off introductory phrases with a comma.
5. **(A)** Underline (set in italics) novels and other larger works of literature.
6. **(H)** Hyphenate compound adjectives preceding the noun they modify.
7. **(D)** The adjective clause following the noun *conclusion* is a restrictive modifier and so does not take separating punctuation.
8. **(G)** The clause that follows necessitates a strong mark of punctuation. Since it is closely related in meaning to the previous independent clause, the most appropriate choice is the semicolon.
9. **(C)** The dash at the end of this phrase requires a matching dash at the beginning. Dashes are appropriately used to give special emphasis to parenthetical phrases such as this one.
10. **(H)** The phrase *however faintly* is parenthetical and must be set off by commas.

BASIC GRAMMAR AND USAGE

Subject-Verb Agreement

Nouns, verbs, and pronouns often have special forms or endings that indicate *number*—that is, whether the word is singular or plural. A verb must agree in number with the noun or pronoun that is its subject.

A verb agrees in number with its subject.

A singular subject requires a singular verb; a plural subject, a plural verb.

SINGULAR	PLURAL
The *house has* three bathrooms.	Many *houses have* more than one bathroom.
UCLA is my choice.	*UCLA, Berkeley, and Stanford are* my favorites.
Mandy, together with the other girls, *wants* a pizza for lunch.	*Mandy and the other girls want* a pizza for lunch.

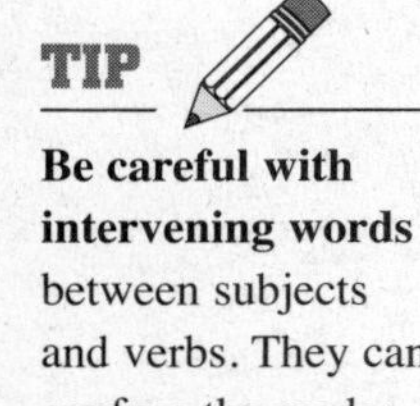

Be careful with intervening words between subjects and verbs. They can confuse the reader.

Do not let **intervening words obscure the relationship between subject and verb.** Find the subject and make the verb agree with it.

EXAMPLES: A column of wounded prisoners, townspeople, and exhausted soldiers *was spotted* struggling over the horizon. (*Was spotted* agrees with its subject, *column,* not with the intervening plural nouns.)

She, her brother, and her friends from upstate *have* always *bought* tickets to the rock concert. (The verb agrees with the plural subject.)

Singular subjects followed by such words and phrases as *along with, as well as, in addition to, together with,* or *with* require singular verbs.

EXAMPLE: The *carrier,* together with three destroyers and two frigates, *was dispatched* to the Mediterranean Sea.

Indefinite pronouns like *anybody, each, either, everyone, neither,* and *one* are always singular, and take a singular verb, regardless of intervening words. Other indefinite pronouns, like *all, any, none* or *some* may be either singular or plural. *Both, few, many,* and *several* are always plural.

EXAMPLES: *Neither* of my children *has* an interest in music.
All is not lost BUT *all* of us *are going*.
Few of the golfers *were* professionals.

Compound subjects joined by *and* usually take a plural verb. (An exception is a compound subject that names one person, thing, or idea: *Ham and eggs is* a favorite breakfast.)

EXAMPLES: The *Toyota* and the *Ford are* low on gas.
The *Pendletons,* the *Riveras,* and the *Kleins are coming* to dinner.

In sentences that begin with *there is* or *there are,* the subject follows the verb, and the verb must agree with it.

EXAMPLES: There *are* (verb) many *reasons* (subject) for the war in the Middle East.

Singular subjects joined by *or* or *nor* take a singular verb. If one subject is singular and the other plural, the verb should agree with the nearer subject.

EXAMPLES: Either the *vegetable* or the *pan is creating* this awful taste. (Singular subjects)
Either the *pan* or the *vegetables are creating* this awful taste. (The verb agrees with the nearer subject.)

"Collective noun" is another term for designating a noun that is singular in form but which denotes a collection of individuals (e.g., army, orchestra, crowd). It is treated as singular when the collection is thought of as a whole, but as a plural when the individual members are thought of as acting separately.

SINGULAR: The *number* of homeless families *increases* every year.
The *committee has* the serious responsibility of selecting a new dean.

Notice that the same nouns are considered plural when the reference is to individual members of the group.

PLURAL: A *number* of homeless people *were* ill enough to require hospitalization.
The *committee have* not *agreed* on a date for the picnic.

NOTE: A good rule to follow with *number, total,* and similar nouns is that, preceded by *the, number* is singular; preceded by *a,* it is plural. Another test: *A number of* should be treated as plural if it signifies several or many.

Words like *aeronautics, cybernetics, mathematics, physics,* or *news* and *dollars,* are plural in form but usually singular in usage.

EXAMPLES: *Mathematics is* a subject essential to the sciences.
Eighty-five *dollars* for that coat *is* a bargain.

Warm-Up Drill

Decide whether the verb in the following sentences should be singular or plural. Then indicate your answer by placing a check in the appropriate space.

1. Some of us is ( ) are ( ) studying for the test.
2. The Board of Trustees is ( ) are ( ) making a decision about tuition increases this Wednesday.
3. The committee is ( ) are ( ) arriving in Chicago at different times.
4. There is ( ) are ( ) several options available to the opera buff in Chicago.
5. A large shipment of automotive parts has ( ) have ( ) been delayed.
6. Peanuts is ( ) are ( ) high in cholesterol.
7. Neither the mechanics nor the shop manager was ( ) were ( ) able to solve the problem.
8. Hospital expense, as well as doctor's, is ( ) are ( ) skyrocketing.
9. The cat and the dog is ( ) are ( ) getting a flea bath today.
10. Few of us realize ( ) realizes ( ) how much work went into the senior prom.

ANSWERS AND EXPLANATIONS

1. ARE studying. The indefinite pronoun *some* here signifies more than one and consequently requires a plural verb.
2. IS making. The Board of Trustees is a single body acting officially as a legal entity.
3. ARE arriving. The reference is clearly to individual members of the committee; therefore, the verb is plural.
4. ARE. The subject of the sentence is *options,* and the plural verb *are* agrees in number.
5. HAS been delayed. The subject of the sentence, *shipment* requires a singular verb.
6. ARE. The plural subject *peanuts* requires a plural verb.
7. WAS. If a singular subject and a plural subject are joined by *nor,* the verb agrees with the nearer subject ("manager *was*").
8. IS skyrocketing. The singular subject *expense* requires a singular verb.
9. ARE getting. Use a plural verb with two singular subjects joined by *and*.
10. REALIZE. The subject of this sentence is the indefinite pronoun *few,* which requires the plural verb *realize*.

Principal Parts of Verbs

All verbs have four principal parts: the *present* (NOW), the *past* (YESTERDAY), the *present participle* (the -ING form of the verb), and the *past participle* (the form of the verb with HAVE). To find the principal parts of a verb, just remember the clues NOW, YESTERDAY, -ING, and HAVE.

PRESENT: (you) *work* (NOW)
PAST: (you) *worked* (YESTERDAY)
PRESENT PARTICIPLE: (you are) *workING*
PAST PARTICIPLE: (you HAVE) *worked*

PRESENT: (he) *buys* (NOW)
PAST: (he) *bought* (YESTERDAY)
PRESENT PARTICIPLE: (he is) *buyING*
PAST PARTICIPLE: (he HAS) *bought*

Participles are used:

1. as part of the main verb of the sentence

   EXAMPLES: Sylvia *was buying* a dress.
   Ed *had swum* a mile last Sunday.

2. as an adjective

   EXAMPLE: *Protesting* loudly at the podium, Mr. McCracken insisted that an environmental study be held. (The present participle *protesting* modifies the noun *Mr. McCracken.*)

3. As a noun

   A gerund is the present participle, or *-ing* form of the verb, used as a noun.

   EXAMPLE: SMOKING is indisputably a danger to one's health. (The gerund *smoking* is the subject of this sentence.)

When the main verb is separated from its helping verbs (like *has, have, be, does*) by intervening parts of a sentence, sometimes, through omission, an error in verb formation results. The verb formation *did not swum,* for example, is obviously wrong when seen out of context, but notice how difficult it is to spot in a sentence.

INCORRECT: Florence Chadwick *had swum* the English Channel twice before in treacherously cold weather, but last winter she *did not.*
CORRECT: Florence Chadwick *had swum* the English Channel twice before in treacherously cold weather, but last winter she *did not swim.*
INCORRECT: The rebel groups never *have* and never *will surrender* to any government forces.
CORRECT: The rebel groups never *have surrendered* and never *will surrender* to any government forces.

Another error involving principal parts of verbs results from a confusion of the simple past and the past participle. As in the preceding examples, such errors are more likely to occur in sentences where subject and verb are separated by modifiers.

EXAMPLES:	**PRESENT**	**PAST**	**PAST PARTICIPLE**
We *saw* (not *seen*) the dog just last week.	see	saw	seen
The Dodgers finally *did* (not *done*) it.	do	did	done
My family had *gone* (not *went*) there for several summers.	go	went	gone
The music *began* (not *begun*) as the ship slid into the sea.	begin	began	begun
Jose Conseco had *broken* (not *broke*) his favorite bat.	break	broke	broken
The guests had *eaten* (not *ate*) before the wedding party arrived.	eat	ate	eaten
The Liberty Bell had *rung* (not *rang*) every Fourth of July for a century.	ring	rang	rung

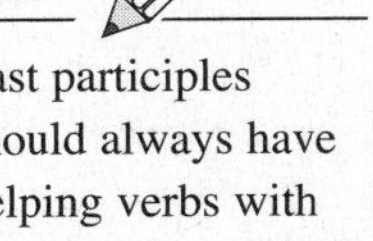

Past participles should always have helping verbs with them, such as "has," "have," or "had."

Verbs like *sit, set, rise, raise, lie,* and *lay* cause trouble because of similarity of form.

EXAMPLES:	PRESENT	PAST	PAST PARTICIPLE
My cats usually *lie* (not *lay*) in the sun.	lie (to recline)	lay	lain
The President *lay* (not *laid*) down for his afternoon rest.	lay (to place)	laid	laid
The wounded soldier had *lain* (not *laid*) on the battlefield for three days.			
If you *lay* (not *lie*) your jacket on the counter, it may become soiled.			
Phillip *laid* (not *lay*) the new sod on the prepared soil.			

EXAMPLES:	PRESENT	PAST	PAST PARTICIPLE
The contractors have recently *laid* (not *lain*) the fresh cement for our new driveway.			
At the sound of "Hail to the Chief," everyone usually *rises* (not *raises*).	rise (to get up or move up)	rose	risen
The flag *rose* (not *raised*) to the strains of "The Marine Hymn."	raise (to cause to rise)	raised	raised
We feel that the faculty and staff have *risen* (not *raised*) to the challenge.			
The college trustees intend to *raise* (not *rise*) student fees.			
The students *raised* (not *rose*) the dress-code issue again.			
The neighbors had *raised* (not *risen*) the third side of the barn by noon.			

Some errors arise from the confusion of the present tense with another principal part. Look at the following examples:

EXAMPLES: The students protested that the test was *supposed* (not *suppose*) to be on Chapter 3.
They *used* (not *use*) to have dinner together every Friday.
Shirley *came* (not *come*) to see how you are.

The following list of principal parts features verbs that sometimes cause trouble in speaking and writing.

PRESENT	PAST	PAST PARTICIPLE
become	became	become
begin	began	begun
bid (offer)	bid	bid
bid (command)	bade	bidden
bite	bit	bit, bitten
blow	blew	blown
break	broke	broken
bring	brought	brought
burst	burst	burst
catch	caught	caught
choose	chose	chosen
come	came	come

PRESENT	PAST	PAST PARTICIPLE
dive	dived, dove	dived
do	did	done
drag	dragged	dragged
draw	drew	drawn
drink	drank	drunk
drive	drove	driven
eat	ate	eaten
fall	fell	fallen
fly	flew	flown
forget	forgot	forgot, forgotten
freeze	froze	frozen
get	got	got, gotten
give	gave	given
go	went	gone
grow	grew	grown
hang (suspend)	hung	hung
hang (execute)	hanged	hanged
know	knew	known
lay	laid	laid
lead	led	led
lend	lent	lent
lie (recline)	lay	lain
lie (speak falsely)	lied	lied
lose	lost	lost
pay	paid	paid
prove	proved	proved, proven
raise	raised	raised
ride	rode	ridden
ring	rang, rung	rung
rise	rose	risen
run	ran	run
see	saw	seen
shake	shook	shaken
shrink	shrank	shrunk
sing	sang, sung	sung
sink	sank, sunk	sunk
speak	spoke	spoken
spring	sprang	sprung
steal	stole	stolen
swim	swam	swum
swing	swung	swung
take	took	taken
tear	tore	torn
throw	threw	thrown
wear	wore	worn
weave	wove	woven
wring	wrung	wrung
write	wrote	written

Warm-Up Drill

Find the verb errors in the following sentences. Not every sentence has an error. Place a check in the appropriate column.

CORRECT	INCORRECT	
_______	_______	1. Within five minutes, the fireman had climbed the ladder, plowed his way through mountains of debris, and did the impossible by putting out the fire.
_______	_______	2. The play was completely staged by July and began in early August.
_______	_______	3. She was very weary and simply wanted to lay down until dinner.
_______	_______	4. The price of football tickets had rose dramatically since 1974.
_______	_______	5. The New Zealand crew had lost a man overboard and tore the spinnaker.
_______	_______	6. He had driven his bike to the trail head, run to the lake, and swum to the base camp.
_______	_______	7. When we were down at the lake on weekends, we use to sit on the sand and watch the girls.
_______	_______	8. After my mother removed the sheets from the washer, my sister hanged them on the line.

ANSWERS AND EXPLANATIONS

1. INCORRECT. *Had climbed,* [had] *plowed,* and [had] *done*.
2. INCORRECT. *Was staged* and [was] *begun*.
3. INCORRECT. The infinitive form of the verb *lie* (meaning *to recline*) is *to lie*.
4. INCORRECT. *Rose* is the past tense of the verb *rise;* the past participle required here is *risen*.
5. INCORRECT. *Had lost* and [had] *torn*.
6. CORRECT.
7. INCORRECT. The past tense *used* is needed here.
8. INCORRECT. The past tense of *hang* (to suspend) is *hung*.

Verb Forms and Verbals

A high percentage of verb-related errors occurs because the reader confuses *verb forms*— that is, the different forms that an action word can assume—with entirely different structures known as *verbals*—words formed from verbs but not used as verbs in a sentence. Known as *participles, gerunds,* and *infinitives,* verbals form important phrases within the sentence.

Infinitives

An infinitive is ordinarily preceded by *to* and is used as a noun, an adjective, or an adverb.

NOUN: *To err* is human. (Subject)

ADJECTIVE: The survivors had little *to celebrate*. (*To celebrate* modifies the noun *little*.)
ADVERB: *To please* his children, Jerry bought a new pool. (*To please* modifies the verb *bought*.)

Sometimes, infinitives omit the word *to*.

EXAMPLES: Who dares [to] *challenge* a champion?
Please [to] *go*.
Make him [to] turn on the radio.
We saw him [to] leave.

Because both gerunds and participles have an *-ing* ending, they can be harder to distinguish between. However, a sentence that equates the two presents an error in parallel structure. If you understand the function of each in the sentence, you will be sure to spot this error if it occurs on the ACT English test.

Gerunds

A gerund always ends in *-ing* and functions as a noun.

SUBJECT: *Writing* is very rewarding.
SUBJECTIVE COMPLEMENT: My favorite occupation is *binding* books.
DIRECT OBJECT: He now regrets *resigning*.
OBJECT OF PREPOSITION: After *sealing* the letter, he went for a walk.

Participle

A participle acts as an adjective in the sentence.

EXAMPLES: *Growling* threateningly, the gorilla intimidated the crowd. (*Growling* modifies *gorilla*.)
The floor *invaded* by termites was made of oak. (*Invaded* modifies *floor*.)

There are two forms of participles, present and past. Present participles end in *-ing;* past participles assume many different forms (e.g., *bought, granted, shown, heard, hung, hidden, shot, torn*).

Other verb forms that may give trouble are the progressive and the passive. Progressive verb forms are regular action words that emphasize continuing action: "I *am running*" rather than "I *run*." Passive verbs transform the sentence in such a way that the subject is receiving action instead of performing it: "I *was given*" instead of "I *gave*."

Note the similarities of form in the following groups:

VERBS: *Simple*—I *hit* the clay target fifty times.
Progressive—I *am hitting* the ball better than ever.
Passive—I *was hit* by a snowball.
VERBALS: *Infinitive*—*To hit* a child is considered criminal.
Gerund—*Hitting* golf balls at a driving range is essential preparation for a match.
Participle—The man *hitting the ball* is also the coach.

Pronouns

Pronouns are most often employed as substitutes for nouns, but some can also be used as adjectives or conjunctions. To master pronouns and be able to spot errors in their use, you need to understand pronoun *case* (nominative, possessive, objective), pronoun *number* (singular or plural), and pronoun *class* (personal, demonstrative, interrogative, relative, indefinite).

TIP

A persistent error is to confuse possessive pronouns and contractions, particularly *its* and *it's* (meaning it is), *their* and *they're* (*they are*), and *whose* and *who's* (*who is*). Possessive pronouns have no apostrophes.

Personal Pronouns

A personal pronoun indicates by its form the person or thing it takes the place of: the person speaking (first person), the person spoken to (second person), or the person or thing spoken about (third person).

First-Person Pronouns		
	SINGULAR	PLURAL
Nominative case	I	we
Possessive case	my, mine	our, ours
Objective case	me	us
Second-Person Pronouns		
Nominative case	you	you
Possessive case	your, yours	your, yours
Objective case	you	you
Third-Person Pronouns		
Nominative case	he, she, it	they
Possessive case	his, hers, its	their, theirs
Objective case	him, her, it	them

Some common errors in pronoun case occur frequently in everyday speech and may well appear on the ACT. Study the following applications to see if you have been using the correct forms.

Use the nominative case of a pronoun in a compound subject.

EXAMPLE: Betty and *I* watched the Olympics on television.

Use the nominative case of a pronoun following any form of the verb *to be*. This use may not sound right to you, but it is standard written English, the language of the ACT.

EXAMPLE: It is *she*. The winner was *I*.

Use the objective case when the pronoun is the object of a preposition.

EXAMPLES: This is just between you and *me*.
Doug looks like *me*. (Like, as well as *but,* can be used as a preposition.)
Nadine made coffee for Allan, Ken, and *me*.

When there are intervening words, eliminate them to find the correct pronoun to use. "Nadine made coffee for *I*" sounds ridiculous, yet some people might say, "Nadine made coffee for *Allan, Ken, and I*." Similarly, in the sentence *"We (Us) homeowners want better roads,"* eliminate the word *homeowners* to find the correct word: *"We want better roads."*

Use the objective case when the pronoun is the object of a verb.

EXAMPLE: The noise frightened Karen and *me*.

Use the nominative case for pronouns that are subjects of elliptical clauses (clauses that are incomplete or unexpressed).

As and *than* are subordinating conjunctions that introduce elliptical clauses. Complete the clause to determine the pronoun case.

EXAMPLES: My children are as excited as *I* [am].
She raked more than *he* [raked].

Use a possessive pronoun before a gerund.

Just as you would say *My car,* you would also say *My smoking* bothers her.

Possessive pronoun/gerund combination drill

If you have the habit of using objective-case pronouns with gerunds and gerund phrases, a very common error, here is an easy way to develop an ear for using the correct pronoun case.

Gerunds are always nouns. Therefore, any pronoun placed before them must always be a possessive pronoun. The following sentences are all correct. Just read the list several times, preferably aloud. Read them once a week until you use the possessive naturally with gerunds.

1. She resented *my going out* and having business lunches.
2. *Your wanting* to get up and leave was obvious to everyone.
3. *Her having* to cook dinner as well as take care of the children was the last straw.
4. The girls were irritated at *our referring to* the old fraternity all evening.
5. *Your wanting* to rebuild the city is very moving to me.
6. George resented *their imposing* a filing fee for new candidates.
7. The commission ruled against *my giving away* free balloons at the fair.
8. *Your car pooling* can help rid the city of gridlock.
9. Edna began to feel embarrassed at *his jumping* into every conversation and immediately monopolizing it.
10. *Our letting* Brock eat table scraps produced a spoiled animal.
11. *Your sponsoring* our son will not be forgotten.
12. *Their having* turned their backs on Kuwait and Saudi Arabia could possibly signify the end of the PLO.
13. *My getting* married should have no impact on you.
14. He felt strongly that he did not have to explain *his enlisting* in the navy to anyone.
15. The world in general deeply resented *Saddam Hussein's setting* those oil fires and *causing* the world's largest oil leak.
16. *The industrial world's treating* oil as the only economical source of energy has brought us to a critical state of dependence.
17. *Janet's brushing* her hair every night has certainly made a difference in her appearance.
18. The house mistress felt that *Yvonne's* obvious *flaunting* of her attractiveness would lead to some animosity among the girls.
19. *Her knowing* that he did not have much money and yet *ordering* prime rib and lobster tails was an example of raw greed.
20. *Bertha's consuming* four entire chickens in front of the Jungle Chicken stand was not the kind of endorsement the management wanted.
21. Mary thinks *Phil's chewing* gum is the reason they did not get the part.
22. *Jill's losing* her wallet started off a very bad day.
23. The whole city was shocked by *his refusing* to take the oath.
24. *Their running* and *jumping* on our grass is going to ruin our front lawn.
25. *My taking* lunch to work every day has saved hundreds of dollars so far.

Global Pronouns

Global pronouns are *this, which*, or *it* when they refer to general ideas or statements used in previous paragraphs. Any pronoun should refer to a specific noun rather than to a general or suggested antecedent. The following sentence contains an example of an unclear global pronoun.

EXAMPLE: The profits the college made from the rodeo were large, *which* the faculty knew almost immediately.

Demonstrative Pronouns

Demonstrative pronouns (*this, that, these, those*) take the place of things being pointed out.

EXAMPLES: *These* are Mary's.
I don't like *this*.

They are called demonstrative adjectives when used before nouns:
EXAMPLE: *These seats* are comfortable.

INCORRECT: *Them* are the new watches I ordered.
CORRECT: *Those* are the new watches I ordered. (Demonstrative pronoun)

Do not substitute a personal pronoun for a demonstrative pronoun or a demonstrative adjective.

INCORRECT: Look at *them* diamonds!
CORRECT: Look at *those* diamonds! (Demonstrative adjective)

Interrogative Pronouns

Interrogative pronouns (*who, whom, whose, which,* and *what*) are used in questions. *Who, which,* and *what* are used as subjects and are in the nominative case. *Whose* is in the possessive case. *Whom* is in the objective case, and, like all objects, it is the receiver of action in the sentence.

The most common error involving interrogative pronouns is the tendency to use *who* instead of *whom*.

When the pronoun is receiving the action, the objective form *whom* must be used.

INCORRECT: *Who* did you contact?
CORRECT: *Whom* did you contact? (You did contact whom?)

When the pronoun is performing the action, the nominative *who* must be used.

INCORRECT: *Whom* did you say is running the dance?
CORRECT: *Who* did you say is running the dance? (*Who* is the subject of *is running*.)

Relative Pronouns

Relative pronouns (*who, whom, whose, which, what,* and *that*) refer to people and things. When a relative pronoun is the subject of a subordinate clause, the clause becomes an adjective modifying a noun in the sentence.

EXAMPLE: The rumor *that plagued him all his life* was a lie. (*That* [subject] *plagued him all his life* modifies *rumor.*)

That can also act as a conjunction to introduce a subordinate clause.

EXAMPLE: Bob knew *that* Boston would win.

Remember that the case of a relative pronoun is established by its function inside its clause.

EXAMPLE: Aimee is the girl who needs your advice. (*Who* is the subject of the verb *needs* within the clause.)

EXAMPLE: Coach Shanks is the person whom we must thank. (*Whom* is the object of *must thank*.)

Indefinite Pronouns

Indefinite pronouns (*all, another, any, both, each, either, everyone, many, neither, one, several, some,* and similar words) represent an indefinite number of persons or things. Many of these words also function as adjectives ("*several* men").

Indefinite pronouns present few problems. One thing to remember:

Use a singular pronoun with an indefinite antecedent like *one, everyone,* and *anybody.*

INCORRECT: Everyone needs to prepare *themselves* for retirement.
CORRECT: Everyone needs to prepare *himself* (or *herself*) for retirement.

And a final caution:

The antecedent of a pronoun should be clear, specific, and close to the pronoun. Reword the sentence if necessary.

CONFUSING: The coach told Eric that *he* could practice after school.
CLEAR: The coach said that Eric could practice after school.

Watch for references to inaccessible or distant antecedents.

EXAMPLE: The law books are housed in a gleaming new library with electronic retrieval chutes, personal elevators to the ten stack levels, and student aides who will fetch and carry for all the visiting scholars. *They* are color coded according to function. (The pronoun *they* is too far removed from its antecedent *books*.)

SENTENCE STRUCTURE

In addition to a NO CHANGE response, the questions on the ACT English Test that deal with sentence structure will offer three alternatives, each one a restructuring of the underlined part. Errors in sentence structure include such items as sentence fragments, run-on sentences, misplaced modifiers, and lack of parallelism. These topics are reviewed in this section.

Sentence Fragments

A sentence fragment is a part of a sentence that has been punctuated as if it were a complete sentence. It does not express a complete thought but depends upon a nearby independent clause for its full meaning. It should be made a part of that complete sentence.

INCORRECT: I was not able to pick up my child at her school. *Having been caught in heavy traffic*. (Participial phrase)
REVISED: Having been caught in heavy traffic, I was not able to pick up my child at her school.

OR

I was not able to pick up my child at her school. I had been caught in heavy traffic.

INCORRECT: The cat sat on the water heater. *Unable to get warm*. (Adjective phrase)
REVISED: Unable to get warm, the cat sat on the water heater.

INCORRECT: The salesman tightened the wire around the burlap feed bag with a spinner. *Which twists wire loops until they are secure*. (Adjective clause)
REVISED: The salesman tightened the wire around the burlap feed bag with a spinner, which twists wire loops until they are secure.

INCORRECT: We will probably try to find another insurance company. *When our policy expires.* (Adverb clause)
REVISED: When our policy expires, we will probably try to find another insurance company.

Run-on Sentences

Probably the most common error in writing occurs when two sentences are run together as one. There are two types of run-on sentences: the *fused* sentence, which has no punctuation mark between its two independent clauses, and the *comma splice,* which substitutes a comma where either a period or a semicolon is needed.

FUSED: Jean had no luck at the store they were out of raincoats.
COMMA SPLICE: She surprised us all with her visit, she was on her way to New York.

To correct a run-on sentence, use a period, a semicolon, or a coordinating conjunction (*and, but, or, nor, for*) to separate independent clauses.

Note the following examples of run-on sentences and the suggested revisions.

FUSED: Eric is a bodybuilder he eats only large amounts of meat.
REVISED: Eric is a bodybuilder; he eats only large amounts of meat.

COMMA SPLICE: He had never seen Alex so prepared, he even had backup copies of his study sheets!
REVISED: He had never seen Alex so prepared. He even had backup copies of his study sheets!

COMMA SPLICE: His father was an artist, his mother was an accountant.
REVISED: His father was an artist, and his mother was an accountant.

Connectives

Connectives that join elements of equal rank are called coordinating conjunctions (*and, but, or, nor, so, for, yet*). Connectives that introduce a less important element are called subordinating conjunctions (*after, although, since, when*).

Coordinating conjunctions link words, phrases, and clauses that are of equal importance.

EXAMPLES: The pilot *and* the crew boarded the plane.
The road ran through the valley *and* along the river.

Compound sentences are formed when coordinating conjunctions link two independent clauses.

EXAMPLE: You can sign the loan papers on Friday, *or* you can sign them on Monday.

Subordinating conjunctions are used in sentences to connect clauses that are not equal in rank—that is, in sentences in which one idea is made subordinate to another. There are many subordinating conjunctions. Some of the important ones are *after, as, because, before, if, in order that, once, since, unless, until, whenever,* and *wherever.*

EXAMPLES: We covered up the newly planted citrus trees *when* the temperature began to drop.
Until I saw her in person, I thought Cher was a tall woman.

Another form of connective is the *conjunctive adverb*. It is actually an adverb that functions as a coordinating conjunction. The principal conjunctive adverbs are *accordingly, also, besides, certainly, consequently, finally, furthermore, however, incidentally, instead, likewise, nevertheless, otherwise, similarly,* and *undoubtedly*. When they join clauses, conjunctive adverbs are usually preceded by a semicolon and followed by a comma.

EXAMPLE: I understand you wish to see a Broadway musical; *undoubtedly,* you'll have to get tickets far in advance for one of the hit shows.

Coordination can be overdone. If every significant idea in every sentence is given equal weight, there is no *main* idea.

FAULTY COORDINATION: The real power in the company lies with Mr. Stark, and he currently owns 55 percent of the stock; in addition to that, his mother is semiretired as president of the firm.

REVISED: The real power in the company lies with Mr. Stark, who currently owns 55 percent of the stock and whose mother is semiretired as president of the firm.

Notice that subordinating two of the independent clauses tightens the sentence and adds focus.

Subordination of too many parts of a sentence, however, can be just as confusing. Look at the following example:

EXCESSIVE SUBORDINATION: Standing on the corner were many aliens who had entered the country illegally, and most of whom had applied for amnesty, and even more important to them though, who had families back in Mexico or El Salvador who needed food and shelter.

REVISED: Standing on the corner were many illegal aliens, most of whom had applied for amnesty. Even more important to them, though, was the fact that they had families needing food and shelter back in Mexico or El Salvador.

Notice how proper coordination and subordination helps clarify a confusing stream of excessively entwined modifiers.

You must also keep in mind the *logic* of subordination. What you choose to subordinate in a sentence has to make sense to the reader. For example, the sentence "Sue happened to glance at the sky, amazed to see an enormous flying saucer hovering over the barn" gives greater importance to the fact that Sue glanced at the sky. A more logical version of that sentence is, "Happening to glance at the sky, Sue was amazed to see an enormous flying saucer hovering over the barn."

BACKWARD SUBORDINATION: She studied medicine with great intensity for fifteen years, becoming a doctor.

LOGICAL REVISION: She became a doctor, having studied medicine with great intensity for fifteen years.

BACKWARD SUBORDINATION: The pitcher momentarily let the runner on first base take a wide lead, when he stole second.

LOGICAL REVISION: The runner stole second when the pitcher momentarily let him take a wide lead.

BACKWARD SUBORDINATION: He ran over with a fire extinguisher, saving the driver's life.

LOGICAL REVISION: Running over with a fire extinguisher, he saved the driver's life.

Modifiers

Adjectives and Adverbs

The purpose of adjectives and adverbs is to describe, limit, color—in other words, to *modify* other words. Adjectives modify nouns or pronouns, and generally precede the words they modify. Adverbs describe verbs, adjectives or other adverbs. Some words can be used as either adjectives (He has an *early appointment*) or adverbs (He *arrived early*).

ADJECTIVES: *fuzzy* peach
impressive view
sour milk

ADVERBS: He grumbled *loudly.*
She smiled *broadly.*
It poured *unmercifully.*

Although most adverbs end in *-ly,* some do not (*fast, hard, long, straight*). A few adjectives also have an *-ly* ending (*lovely* day, *lively* discussion).

Adjectives

Problems that students face with adjectives frequently relate to the use of degrees of comparison. There are three degrees: the *positive*—the original form of the word (*straight*); the *comparative*—used to compare two persons or things (*straighter*); and the *superlative*—used to compare more than two persons or things (*straightest*). If not understood, the spelling and form changes involved can sometimes confuse the unwary student.

1. Most adjectives form the comparative and superlative degrees by adding *-er* and *-est*:

POSITIVE: nice
COMPARATIVE: nicer
SUPERLATIVE: nicest

2. Other adjectives form the comparative and superlative by using *more* and *most:*

POSITIVE: challenging
COMPARATIVE: more challenging
SUPERLATIVE: most challenging

3. Some adjectives change completely as they form the comparative and superlative degrees:

POSITIVE: little
COMPARATIVE: less
SUPERLATIVE: least

Be alert for double comparisons, which incorrectly use *more* or *most* with adjectives that already express a degree: *more softer* or *most strongest*.

Also, watch for the illogical use of the comparative or the superlative with adjectives that cannot be compared, such as *square, round, perfect, unique*. It is meaningless to write *rounder* or *most perfect*.

When comparing only two nouns, use the comparative degree: Mars is the *larger* of the two planets. When comparing more than two, use the superlative: Gibson is the *most dangerous* hitter on their team.

Adverbs

Adverbs (either as words, phrases, or clauses) describe the words they modify by indicating *when, how, where, why, in what order,* or *how often*.

WHEN: He studied *until 10:00 every night.*
HOW: She testified *with quiet dignity.*
WHERE: Bring the paper *here.*
WHY: They rejected the offer *because it was too little.*
IN WHAT ORDER: *One after another,* the townspeople told the judge their story.

NOTE: *Anywheres, nowheres,* and *somewheres* are incorrect adverb forms. Use *anywhere, nowhere, somewhere.*

The adjectives *good* and *bad* should not be used as adverbs.

NOT
She doesn't sing so *good*.
He wants that job *bad*.
BUT
She doesn't sing so *well*.
He wants that job *badly*.

Standard English requires the use of a formal adverb form rather than a colloquial version.

NOT
This was a *real* good clambake.
He *sure* doesn't look happy.
BUT
This was a *really* good clambake.
He *surely* doesn't look happy.

Probably the most persistent and frustrating errors in the English language involve either *incorrect modification* or else *inexact modification* that is difficult to pin down.

In most cases, if you can keep your eye on the *word or phrase being modified,* it is easier to avoid the following pitfalls.

Misplaced Modifiers

To avoid confusion or ambiguity, place the modifying words, phrases, or clauses near the words they modify.

Misplaced Adverb Modifiers

Adverbs like *scarcely, nearly, merely, just, even,* and *almost* must be placed near the words they modify.

CONFUSED: Last week during the cold spell, I *nearly* lost all of my flowers.
CLEAR: Last week during the cold spell, I lost *nearly* all of my flowers. (The adverb *nearly* modifies the pronoun *all.*)

CONFUSED: Acme *just* cleaned my rugs last month.
CLEAR: Acme cleaned my rugs *just* last month. (The adverb *just* modifies the adverbial phrase *last month.*)

Misplaced Phrase Modifiers

CONFUSED: *To plant tomatoes,* it was a good growing year.
CLEAR: It was a good growing year *to plant tomatoes*.

CONFUSED: *Like a sleek projectile,* the passengers saw the new train approach the station.
CLEAR: The passengers saw the new train approach the station *like a sleek projectile*.

Misplaced Clause Modifiers

CONFUSED: He packed all of his books and documents into his van, *which he was donating to the library.*
CLEAR: He packed all of his books and documents, *which he was donating to the library,* into his van.

CONFUSED: The new series of seminars will focus on how to prevent inflation, *which will benefit us all.*
CLEAR: The new series of seminars, *which will benefit us all,* will focus on how to prevent inflation.

TIP

Watch for dangling constructions. A dangling participle, gerund, or infinitive sounds vaguely humorous. Example: *Calling Pizza Hut, a large cheese pizza was ordered.*

Dangling Constructions

A dangling modifier literally hangs in the air; there is no logical word in the sentence for it to modify. Frequently it is placed close to the wrong noun or verb, causing the sentence to sound ridiculous: *Driving through the park, several chipmunks could be seen.*

Dangling Participles

A participle is a form of the verb that is used as an adjective. Unless there is a logical word for it to modify, the participial phrase will dangle, modifying either the wrong noun or none at all.

INCORRECT: Having run out of gas, John was late for dinner.
REVISED: Because the car ran out of gas, John was late for dinner.

INCORRECT: Driving along the parkway, several deer were spotted.
REVISED: Driving along the parkway, we spotted several deer.

Dangling Gerunds

A gerund is the *-ing* form of a verb serving as a noun (*Smoking is bad for your health*). When a gerund is used as the object of a preposition ("by *hiding*," "after *escaping*," "upon *realizing*"), the phrase can dangle if the actor that it modifies is missing.

INCORRECT: After putting a bloodworm on my hook, the flounders began to bite.
REVISED: After putting a bloodworm on my hook, I found that the flounders began to bite.

INCORRECT: In designing our house addition, a bathroom was forgotten.
REVISED: In designing our house addition, we forgot to add a bathroom.

Dangling Infinitives

Unlike the participle and the gerund, the infinitive performs more than one job in a sentence. While the participle acts like an adjective, and the gerund like a noun, the infinitive phrase can take the part of a noun, adjective, or adverb. Note the following examples of dangling infinitive phrases:

INCORRECT: To skate like a champion, practice is essential.
REVISED: To skate like a champion, one must practice.

INCORRECT: To make a good impression, a shirt and tie should be worn to the interview.
REVISED: To make a good impression, Jeff should wear a shirt and tie to the interview.

Illogical Comparisons

Occasionally, a writer will mistakenly compare items that are not comparable.

INCORRECT: Her *salary* was lower than a clerk. (The *salary* is incorrectly compared with a *clerk*.)
CORRECT: Her *salary* was lower than a *clerk's*.

INCORRECT: The cultural *events* in Orlando are as diversified as *any other large city*. *Events* are being compared with a large city.
CORRECT: The cultural events in Orlando are as diversified as *those in any other large city*.

Another form of illogical comparison results when a writer fails to exclude from the rest of the group the item being compared.

INCORRECT: She is taller than *any girl* in her class.
CORRECT: She is taller than *any other girl* in her class.

Warm-Up Drill

In the following sentences, find the errors that involve modifiers. Not every sentence has an error. Place a check in the appropriate column to indicate whether the sentence is correct or incorrect.

CORRECT	INCORRECT	
_______	_______	1. The corn was roasted by the boys skewered on the ends of long, pointed sticks.
_______	_______	2. It was still pouring, so Uncle Maurice went out to the sty to feed the hogs with an umbrella.
_______	_______	3. Coming nearer to it, the building certainly seemed dilapidated.
_______	_______	4. Henry's sales record will be as good as any of the top salespeople.
_______	_______	5. Coiled in a corner of the garage and ready to spring, Mrs. Lampert was surprised by a rattlesnake.
_______	_______	6. Having been asked to speak at the senior dinner, Fred spent many evenings preparing his speech.
_______	_______	7. To be well baked, you have to leave the pork roast in the oven for three hours.
_______	_______	8. We saw the impressive Concorde on the porch this morning.

ANSWERS AND EXPLANATIONS

1. INCORRECT. The participial phrase *skewered on the ends of long, pointed sticks* should be placed closer to corn, the noun it is intended to modify: *Skewered ... sticks, the corn ...*

2. INCORRECT. The prepositional phrase *with an umbrella* is misplaced. It seems to modify the *hogs* or *to feed* but should modify the verb *went*.

3. INCORRECT. This sentence is missing the noun that the participial phrase *Coming nearer to it* is meant to modify. A corrected version might be *Coming nearer to the building, we noticed that it certainly seemed dilapidated*.

4. INCORRECT. This sentence contains an illogical comparison. The correct sentence should include the pronoun *that: Henry's sales record will be as good as that of any of the top salespeople*.

5. INCORRECT. The participial phrase beginning this sentence seems to modify *Mrs. Lampert*. It should modify *rattlesnake*. The correction, of course, is to place the participial phrase close to the word *rattlesnake*.

6. CORRECT. The participial phrase is placed close to *Fred,* the noun it logically modifies.

7. INCORRECT. The infinitive phrase *To be well baked* here incorrectly modifies *you* instead of *roast,* the noun it is intended for.

8. INCORRECT. The Concorde was not on the porch, as this sentence seems to imply. Revised: *As we sat on the porch this morning, we saw the impressive Concorde*.

Practice Exercises

The life of famed watchmaker Abraham-Louis Breguet was, from beginning to end (1747-1823). A [1] steady progression toward fame and fortune. Breguet soon revealed a lively interest that developed into a veritable passion for things mechanical in his stepfather's shop. [2] He studied with the famed jeweler Abbot Marie for twelve years, his vocation [3] was henceforth decided. Living in the Swiss cantons [4] on the French border, watch-making had already been developed on a large scale by refugee French families, because [5] it was limited almost exclusively to inexpensive products. Young Breguet, on the contrary, demonstrating very early a decided disgust for shoddy workmanship, as well as a genius for precision work, had an attitude he never lost. [6]

In 1802, Breguet, receiving the gold medal at an exhibition of industrial products, sat at the table of the first consul. [7] Throughout his reign, Napoleon's interest in the works of the watch master, principally those of

1. **A.** NO CHANGE
   B. (1747-1823), a
   C. (1747-1823) a
   D. (1747-1823); a

2. **F.** NO CHANGE
   G. (Place at the beginning of the sentence).
   H. (Place after the verb *revealed*).
   J. (Delete altogether; the phrase is not related).

3. **A.** NO CHANGE
   B. years his vocation
   C. years, then his vocation
   D. years, and his vocation

4. **F.** NO CHANGE
   G. (Place this phrase after *border*).
   H. (Place this phrase after *families*).
   J. (Delete altogether; the phrase is not related).

5. **A.** NO CHANGE
   B. but
   C. even though
   D. however

6. **F.** NO CHANGE
   G. Young Breguet, on the contrary, demonstrating very early a decided disgust for shoddy workmanship, as well as a genius for precision work, an attitude he never lost.
   H. Young Breguet, on the contrary, demonstrated very early a decided disgust for shoddy workmanship, as well as a genius for precision work, an attitude he never lost.
   J. Young Breguet, on the contrary, demonstrated very early a decided disgust for shoddy workmanship, as well as a genius for precision work, and had an attitude he never lost.

7. **A.** NO CHANGE
   B. In 1802, Breguet, receiving the gold medal at an exhibition of industrial products, sitting at the table of the first consul.
   C. In 1802, Breguet, received the gold medal at an exhibition of industrial products and sat at the table of the first consul.
   D. In 1802, Breguet sat at the table of the first consul, receiving the gold medal at an exhibition of industrial products.

high precision, never slackened. <u>The face studded with brilliant diamonds and rubies, Napoleon acquired Breguet's most ambitious creation the day after it was completed.</u> 8

8. **F.** NO CHANGE
G. The face studded with brilliant diamonds and rubies, Breguet's most ambitious creation, the day after it was completed, was acquired by Napoleon.
H. The face studded with brilliant diamonds and rubies the day after it was completed, Napoleon acquired Breguet's most ambitious creation.
J. Napoleon acquired Breguet's most ambitious creation, the face studded with brilliant diamonds and rubies, the day after it was completed.

<u>The fall of the empire did not affect either his fortunes adversely or his renown, which had spread throughout Europe.</u> 9 The exhibition of 1819 in which Breguet presented a collection of his most important works was a triumphant compendium of his life, <u>by then more than seventy years old.</u> 10

9. **A.** NO CHANGE
B. The fall of the empire did not adversely affect either his fortunes or his renown, which had spread throughout Europe.
C. Adversely, the fall of the empire did not affect either his fortunes or his renown, which had spread throughout Europe.
D. The fall of the empire did not affect either his fortunes or his renown adversely, which had spread throughout Europe.

10. **F.** NO CHANGE
G. (Place this phrase at the beginning of the sentence).
H. (Place this phrase, bracketed with commas, after the word *Breguet*).
J. (Delete this phrase; it is not relevant).

ANSWERS AND EXPLANATIONS

1. **(B)** This sentence contains the parenthetical interruption "from beginning to end (1747-1823)," which must be set off by commas. Any stronger mark of punctuation after the parentheses results in two fragmented sentences.

2. **(G)** The only logical position in this sentence for the prepositional phrase *in his stepfather's shop* is at the beginning of the sentence where it will correctly modify the noun *Breguet*.

3. **(D)** A compound sentence is the most appropriate vehicle for these two ideas of equal importance. A comma is used before the coordinating conjunction that joins coordinate clauses.

4. **(H)** The only logical position in this sentence for the participial phrase *Living in the Swiss cantons* is next to the noun it logically modifies, *families*.

5. **(B)** Only a connective signaling contrast like *but* makes sense in this context, especially in the light of the next sentence.

6. **(H)** This choice allows the main clause to emphasize the major characteristic of the subject, and correctly subordinates the parenthetical phrase, "an attitude he never lost."

7. **(C)** The act of receiving the gold medal is logically as important as sitting with the first consul, and should not be subordinated in a participial phrase.

8. **(J)** The phrase *The face studded with brilliant diamonds and rubies* modifies the noun *creation* and so must be placed next to it.

9. **(B)** The adverb *adversely* logically modifies only the verb *affect* and should be placed near it.

10. **(H)** The phrase *By then more than seventy years old* appropriately modifies the noun *Breguet* and should be placed next to it, set off by commas since it is a parenthetical addition.

Consistency and Tense

Verbs in Subordinate Clauses

Because *tense* indicates the time of the action and *voice* indicates whether the subject is the agent of the action (*active:* Tom *saw*) or the recipient of the action (*passive:* Tom *was seen*), both of these verb forms are central to the consistency of a sentence or passage.

TIP 

Be alert for sentences that omit a needed verb, preposition, or conjunction. Faulty: *The Coast Guard always has and always will assist boaters in distress.* Correct: *The Coast Guard always has assisted and always will assist boaters in distress.*

Tense

A verb in a subordinate clause should relate logically in tense to the verb in the principal clause. Avoid any unnecessary shift.

INCORRECT: As the wedding *began* [past], the bride's mother *starts* [present] to cry.
CORRECT: As the wedding *began* [past], the bride's mother *started* [past] to cry.

INCORRECT: He *had intended* [past perfect] to finish his third novel by the end of the year, but he *has been very sick* [present perfect] until Thanksgiving.
CORRECT: He *had intended* [past perfect] to finish his third novel by the end of the year, but he *was very sick* [past] until Thanksgiving.

INCORRECT: By the time the fire *had been extinguished* [past perfect], the priceless paintings *had been destroyed* [past perfect].
CORRECT: By the time the fire *was extinguished* [past], the priceless paintings *had been destroyed* [past perfect]. (The past perfect expresses action that took place before the simple past.)

Voice

A verb in a subordinate clause should relate logically in voice to the verb in the main clause. It is generally better to avoid voice shifts within a sentence.

INCORRECT: Sighs of appreciation *could be heard* [passive] as the waiters *brought* [active] huge trays of roast beef and Yorkshire pudding.
REVISED: The guests *sighed* [active] with appreciation as the waiters *brought* [active] huge trays of roast beef and Yorkshire pudding.

INCORRECT: If the fishing boat *had been reached* [passive] in time, the Coast Guard *might have saved* [active] it with floats. (Note that the subject shifts as well as the voice.)
CORRECT: If it *had reached* [active] the fishing boat in time, the Coast Guard *might have saved* [active] it with floats.

The Present Infinitive

Always use the present infinitive (to run, to see), after a perfect tense (a tense that uses some form of the helping verb ***have*** or ***had***).

EXAMPLES: He *has decided to order* the Jaguar Model S-1. (Present Perfect + Present Infinitive)
They *had hoped to hold* a spring picnic. (Past Perfect + Present Infinitive)

Keep in mind that the ACT test offers three substitute choices for each underlined part. Frequently, even though you may not remember the grammatical terms involved, your prose sense will lead you to the right answer.

Look at the following set of responses. Which is correct?

A. Fran would of wanted to see the show.
B. Fran would have wanted to had seen the show.
C. Fran would have wanted to have seen the show.
D. Fran would have wanted to see the show.

Choice **D** is correct. If you selected this answer, did you apply the grammatical principle involved (use the present infinitive after a perfect tense), or were you guided by your prose "ear"? Chances are that it may have been your own language sense that suggested this answer. The point is that you already possess language sense that should help you on the test. With more preparation, you should do even better.

The Subjunctive Mood

Verbs may be expressed in one of three moods: the *indicative,* used to declare a fact or ask a question; the *imperative,* used to express a command; and the *subjunctive,* generally used to indicate doubt or to express a wish or request or a condition contrary to fact. The first two moods are fairly clear-cut.

INDICATIVE: This cake is tasty. Who baked it?
IMPERATIVE: Please leave now. Go home.

NOTE: The imperative mood has only one subject (*you*) and one tense (the present).

The subjunctive mood presents more of a problem. It suggests *possibilities, maybes, could have beens,* or *wishes that it had been,* and its uses are sometimes more difficult to understand. The subjunctive mood appears more frequently in formal English than in standard written English.

Notice the following uses, including some traditional ones:

EXAMPLES: I insist that the new road *be started* this spring.
The company requires that the check *be certified*.
Had she been certain of her facts, she would have challenged the teacher.
If need *be,* we can use our pension money.
Should the swarm *reappear,* I will call a beekeeper.
If he *were* honest, he would return all the money.
I move that the budget *be accepted*.
Far *be* it from me to suggest that he is lying.
Would that I *were* sixteen again!
I wish I *were* on a plane to Tahiti.

NOTE: Today, the subjunctive is most often used to express doubt, wishes, or conditions contrary to fact. However, the indicative can also be used for some of these same feelings.

SUBJUNCTIVE MOOD: If it *be* true, I will be delighted.
INDICATIVE MOOD: If it *is* true, I will be delighted.

Special Use of the Present Tense

Use the present tense to express universally true statements or timeless facts.

EXAMPLES: Ice *forms* at 32° (F).
The rainy season seldom *arrives* in California.
She told the campers that mosquitos *are* part of nature.

The Historical Present

In writing about a poem or describing events in fiction or plays, use the present tense. This convention is called the *historical present*.

EXAMPLE: In *A Tale of Two Cities,* Dr. Manette *is restored* to his daughter after twenty years in jail.

Warm-Up Drill

In the following sentences, find any errors in mood or tense. Not every sentence has an error. Place a check in the appropriate column to indicate whether the sentence is correct or incorrect.

CORRECT	INCORRECT	
_______	_______	1. If I knew about winning the lottery, I would not have sold my boat.
_______	_______	2. In his poem "In Memoriam," Tennyson spoke of his sorrow at the death of his friend Arthur Henry Hallam.
_______	_______	3. They have decided to have gone on a trip.
_______	_______	4. By the time the tide had covered the sand castles, we had already put the children to bed.
_______	_______	5. Groans and catcalls could be heard as the opposing team took the field.
_______	_______	6. When the earthquake struck, we all run out of our houses.
_______	_______	7. If I was you, I would take the job.
_______	_______	8. If we reach an accord by Monday, we will offer it to the membership by Monday night.

ANSWERS AND EXPLANATIONS

1. INCORRECT. The past tense *knew* does not go back in time far enough to permit the use of the present perfect tense later in the sentence. The correction is to change *knew* to *had known* (the past perfect).
2. INCORRECT. Use the historical present for statements about literary works (*Tennyson … speaks*).
3. INCORRECT. Use the present infinitive after a perfect tense.
4. INCORRECT. Watch the sequence of tenses: The children had been put to bed *before* the tide covered the sand castles. *Covered* is the correct tense.
5. INCORRECT. Both the subject and the voice shift in this sentence. Revised: *The opposing team heard groans and catcalls as they took the field.*
6. INCORRECT. Maintain a consistent verb tense: *When the earthquake struck* [past], *we all ran* [past] *out of our houses.*
7. INCORRECT. Use the subjunctive mood for a condition contrary to fact: *If I were you …*
8. CORRECT. There are no awkward shifts of subjects or voice in this sentence. The sequence of tenses is also correct.

Predication

Predication refers to the process of joining the *naming* part of the sentence (the *subject*) to the *doing* or *describing* part of the sentence (the *predicate*).

SUBJECT	PREDICATE
People	are buying more fish.
Cecelia	is a counselor.

It is not likely that a writer or reader will have trouble linking the subjects and predicates of sentences as short as these. It is in the use of longer, more detailed sentences that predication errors come about. Illogical predication equates unlike constructions and ideas. Look at the following incorrect examples.

INCORRECT: By working at such technical plants as Lockheed and Bendix gives the engineering students insight into what will be expected of them. (*By working* does not give them insight; *working* does.)

According to one authority, the ages of thirty to forty are subject to the most pressures concerning self-identity. (The *ages* are not subject to the pressures, but rather the *people* of those ages.)

The sheer simplicity of frozen food may soon replace home-cooked meals. (*Simplicity* will not replace the meals; *frozen food* will, *because* of its simplicity of preparation.)

Paying bills on time causes many worries for young families. (*Paying* bills does not cause worries, but *not paying* them does.)

Is When, Is Where, Is Because

The use of *is when, is where, is because* is always incorrect. The reason is simple: *when, where,* and *because* introduce adverbial clauses; and a noun subject followed by a form of the verb *to be* must be equated with a noun structure, not with an adverb clause.

INCORRECT: Lepidopterology *is where you study butterflies and moths*.

CORRECT: Lepidopterology *is the study of butterflies and moths*. (Here, the adverb clause *where you study* ... has been changed to a subject complement: *lepidopterology = study*.)

INCORRECT: The reason they won *is because they had better coaching*.

CORRECT: The reason they won *is that they had better coaching*. (The noun clause *that they had better coaching* equates with the noun *reason*.)

OR

They *won because* they had better coaching. (The adverb clause modifies the verb *won*.)

Warm-Up Drill

In the following sentences, find any errors in predication. Not every sentence has an error. Place a check in the appropriate column to indicate whether the sentence is correct or incorrect.

CORRECT	INCORRECT	
_______	_______	1. By building a more efficient engine will save fuel.
_______	_______	2. Maintaining a healthy weight causes problems for many millions of Americans.

_______ _______ 3. Vertigo is when people become dizzy and are unable to maintain their balance.

_______ _______ 4. Heart failure results from the inability of the heart to pump enough blood to maintain normal bodily functions.

_______ _______ 5. Niagara Falls is an inspiring experience.

_______ _______ 6. The reason that our team did not win was because our key players had injuries.

ANSWERS AND EXPLANATIONS

1. INCORRECT. *Building* a more efficient engine may save fuel, but not *by building*.
2. INCORRECT. The problem does not lie in *maintaining* a healthy weight. It lies in *not maintaining* a healthy weight.
3. INCORRECT. *Is when* is always incorrect. Revised: *Vertigo is a condition in which …*
4. CORRECT. This sentence has no errors in predications.
5. INCORRECT. A place (*Niagara Falls*) cannot be an experience.
6. INCORRECT. Equate a noun (*reason*) with a noun structure (the clause *that our key players had injuries*).

Parallelism

Parallel ideas in a sentence should be expressed in the same grammatical form. If they are not, the sentence will be unbalanced.

TIP

When dealing with parallel constructions, be sure to read the whole sentences twice, checking each component for true parallelism.

A series of coordinated elements should be parallel in form.

INCORRECT: He enjoys *plays, exhibitions,* and *to walk* every morning. (An infinitive is paired with two nouns.)
CORRECT: He enjoys *going* to plays, *visiting* exhibitions, and *walking* every morning.
OR
He enjoys *plays, exhibitions,* and morning *walks*.

INCORRECT: The union wanted *pay increases for every employee* and *that there would be shorter working hours*. (A noun is paired with a noun clause.)
CORRECT: The union wanted *pay increases* and shorter *working hours* for every employee.

The constructions that follow correlative conjunctions (*both-and, either-or, neither-nor, not only-but also, whether-or*) should be parallel in form.

INCORRECT: He was *neither qualified* to lead this country *nor was he willing*.
CORRECT: He was *neither qualified nor willing* to lead this country.

Do not use *and* before *which* or *who* unless the sentence has a previously expressed *which* or *who* clause with which to be parallel.

INCORRECT: She is a well-known surgeon from New York, and who has written many books on brain surgery.
CORRECT: She is a well-known surgeon from New York, who has lectured at many medical schools and who has written many books on brain surgery.

NOTE: A sentence may lack parallelism even though its parts are *grammatically* parallel. If the ideas are not logically equal, then the flow of ideas is not parallel.

INCORRECT: The dean introduced new faculty members, explained some curriculum strategies, began an exploratory discussion of the accreditation process, *spilled coffee on his tie,* reviewed the budget for the fiscal year, and *went to lunch with Don Love.* (Although the italicized phrases are grammatically parallel, they are not parallel with the other ideas expressed.)

Warm-Up Drill

In the following sentences, find any errors in parallelism. Not every sentence has an error. Place a check in the appropriate column to indicate whether the sentence is correct or incorrect.

CORRECT	INCORRECT	
_______	_______	1. William Faulkner wrote *As I Lay Dying, The Sound and the Fury, Sartoris,* and he was also the author of *The Reivers.*
_______	_______	2. Cluster secretaries answer calls about special programs, file important papers, sort mail, and they do typing and stuffing envelopes.
_______	_______	3. He bought a new scooter with an electric starter, and which has dual pipes and a digital clock.
_______	_______	4. My sister's tamale pie is made with ground meat, chili seasoning, olives, and it has onions and beans as well.
_______	_______	5. Playing racquetball is more taxing than to jog or play basketball.
_______	_______	6. The union stood firm on its demands for a realistic wage, a better health plan, and a more generous pension package.
_______	_______	7. The pool is eighteen feet in length and twelve feet wide.
_______	_______	8. Most citizens felt gas rationing to be a necessity and fair.

ANSWERS AND EXPLANATIONS

1. INCORRECT. *Made parallel:* William Faulkner wrote *As I Lay Dying, The Sound and the Fury, Sartoris,* and *The Reivers.* (*He was also the author of* is unnecessary.)

2. INCORRECT. *Made parallel:* Cluster secretaries answer calls about special programs, file important papers, sort mail, type, and stuff envelopes.

3. INCORRECT. *Made parallel:* He bought a new scooter with an electric starter, dual pipes, and a digital clock. (A sentence that contains *and which* is not parallel unless it has a previously expressed *which* clause.)

4. INCORRECT. *Made parallel:* My sister's tamale pie is made with ground meat, chili seasoning, olives, onions, and beans.

5. INCORRECT. *Made parallel:* Playing racquetball is more taxing than jogging or playing basketball. (In the original, the infinitives *to jog* and [*to*] *play* are not parallel with the gerund phrase *playing racquetball*.

6. CORRECT. The structures in this sentence—*wage, plan,* and *package*—are parallel.

7. INCORRECT. *Made parallel:* The pool is eighteen feet long and twelve feet wide. (Or match the phrase *in length* with the phrase *in width*.)

8. INCORRECT. *Made parallel:* Most citizens felt gas rationing to be necessary and fair. (In the original sentence, an adjective, *fair,* is paired with a noun, *necessity*.)

Transitional Words and Phrases

Words of transition are clues that help the reader to follow the writer's flow of ideas. Confusion can result, however, when an illogical or incorrect connective is used. The following list includes more commonly used transitional words and phrases, and the concepts they suggest.

TIP 

Be careful with words of transition. Words of transition are clues that help the reader to follow the writer's flow of ideas. Confusion can result, however, when an illogical or incorrect connective is used.

Concept	
Addition	also, furthermore, moreover, similarly, too
Cause and Effect	accordingly, as a result, consequently, hence, so, therefore, thus
Concession	granted that, it is true that, no doubt, to be sure
Conclusion	in short, that is, to conclude, to sum up
Contrast	although, but, however, nevertheless, on the contrary, on the other hand
Example	for example, for instance

Watch for errors in logical use of transitional words. For example:

INCORRECT: At many gas stations, drivers have to pump their own gasoline; *therefore,* at Ken's Union Station, full service is still the rule.

CORRECT: At many gas stations, drivers have to pump their own gasoline; *however,* at Ken's Union Station, full service is still the rule.

Warm-Up Drill

In the following sentences, find any transition errors. Not every sentence has an error. Place a check in the appropriate column to indicate whether the sentence is correct or incorrect.

CORRECT	INCORRECT	
_______	_______	1. Her apple pie won a blue ribbon at the county fair; nevertheless, we all wanted the recipe.
_______	_______	2. Bud and Jake climbed to the top of the falls, and Jake had a fear of heights.
_______	_______	3. I have been meaning to learn more about electronics, so I just bought a book on the subject.
_______	_______	4. I have just finished preparing my tax return after four weeks of figuring and frustration; furthermore, I refuse to fill out any other forms for at least a month!
_______	_______	5. Maria has spent almost twelve years of her academic life studying medicine; however, she feels well qualified to treat sick people.

ANSWERS AND EXPLANATIONS

1. INCORRECT. The connective *nevertheless* is obviously illogical here, with its implication of contrast. A better transitional word might be *consequently*.
2. INCORRECT. A contrast like *although* is needed in this sentence.
3. CORRECT. This is a typical cause-and-effect sentence, correctly using the word *so*.
4. INCORRECT. The speaker refuses to fill out another form *because of* his work on the tax return. Needed here is a causal transition like *as a result*.
5. INCORRECT. The connective *however* does not make sense here because it implies contrast. A causal word like *accordingly* is required.

Practice Exercises

Crime and Punishment by Fyodor Dostoevsky is a topical novel dealing with philosophical doctrines, political,[1] and social issues widely discussed in Russia just after the 1861 reforms. By most critical essays,[2] treating Dostoevsky's work has employed[3] psychological or biological points of view. Because *Crime and Punishment* is a passionate, masterly portrayal of internal psychological conflict, a general assumption has evolved in the general critical world that the author wrote, at least in part, from personal experience. Nevertheless,[4] Dostoevsky's biography has been endlessly probed, explored, and it was thoroughly analyzed.[5]

In 1849, Dostoevsky was convicted of consorting with known radical factions; however, he was sentenced[6] to a four-year prison term. Many critical commentaries

1. **A.** NO CHANGE
   B. politically
   C. politics
   D. that are political

2. **F.** NO CHANGE
   G. Because of most critical essays
   H. Most critical essays,
   J. Most critical essays

3. **A.** NO CHANGE
   B. have employed
   C. should employ
   D. employ

4. **F.** NO CHANGE
   G. Hence,
   H. On the contrary,
   J. Furthermore

5. **A.** NO CHANGE
   B. and being analyzed.
   C. and analyzed.
   D. subject to analysis.

6. **F.** NO CHANGE
   G. factions, yet, he was sentenced
   H. factions and was sentenced
   J. factions; moreover, he was sentenced

on *Crime and Punishment* consider this experience formative and essential, certainly a major source of the creative impulses that eventually resulted in the execution of the novel. The epilogue of the novel <u>had been set</u> [7] in Siberia, where he was imprisoned.

7. **A.** NO CHANGE
   B. is set
   C. was set
   D. has been set

When <u>talking</u> [8] to his fellow prisoners, he must have focused on crime and guilt and thought about the

8. **F.** NO CHANGE
   G. having talked
   H. he had talked
   J. having been talking

psychology of the criminal mind <u>granted that</u> [9] he lived among hardened convicts. One must ask, though, why he waited until 1865 to write *Crime and Punishment*.

9. **A.** NO CHANGE
   B. as
   C. knowing that
   D. considering that

One possible answer <u>is because</u> [10] he wrote the novel in part to speak against foreign ideas adopted by the Russian radicals of the 1860s.

10. **F.** NO CHANGE
    G. is when
    H. is where
    J. is that

ANSWERS AND EXPLANATIONS

1. **(C)** A noun is necessary in this position to be parallel with the other noun objects in this series, *doctrines* and *issues*.

2. **(J)** As it stands, this sentence contains an error in predication, beginning with one construction, *By most critical essays,* and continuing with a different one, *treating Dostoevsky's work has employed ... points of view*. It is incorrect to separate a subject from its verb, as in choice H.

3. **(D)** The verb must agree with its plural subject *essays* and maintain the established present tense.

4. **(G)** The logic of the sentence requires a cause/effect transitional marker like *Hence,* not the contrast or addition markers suggested by the alternative choices.

5. **(C)** The parallel series of past participles in this sentence requires this option: *has been probed, explored, and analyzed*.

6. **(H)** The logic of this sentence requires a transitional word suggesting either *cause* or *addition*. Since the acts of *conviction* and *sentencing* seem to be of equal weight, the conjunction *and* is a sound choice.

7. **(B)** Use the historical present tense when relating events that occur in fiction.

8. **(F)** The present participle is used for an action going on at the same time as the main verb.

9. **(B)** The use of the subordinating conjunction *as* is a sound choice in this position because it creates an adverb clause that modifies the verbs *focused* and *thought*. The other choices create modifiers of the subject to little effect.

10. **(J)** Only the use of the words *is that* in this spot forms a noun structure that equates with the noun *answer*. The other choices form adverb clauses that cannot equate with the noun.

ORGANIZATION

The Main Idea

If a passage of prose can be viewed as a liquid and boiled in a pan until just one drop is left, that one drop can be considered the *essence* or *main idea* of that passage. It is essential to realize that every piece of writing that can stand on its own has one *main idea* from which the entire work, no matter how large or small, is derived.

TIP 

The main idea must always be a complete sentence, not a word or a topic. Only a sentence is able to express the *idea* of the passage.

It should not be too difficult to discover the central idea in each of the short selections that generally make up the ACT English Test. If you get in the habit of formulating the main idea as you read each passage, you will find that the rhetorical questions, especially those concerning organization, can be answered more easily.

For example, a passage might be about exercise (the *topic*). But what does it state about exercise? If the selection points out that exercise makes a person more alert, more fit, more productive, and more likely to live longer, the central idea is probably something similar to "Exercise is essential to a healthy, productive life." On the other hand, if statements are made concerning bruised heel bones, pulled hamstrings, shinsplints, and muscle pain, then the main idea might be something similar to "Exercise can do more harm than good."

Whatever sentence you decide expresses the main idea of the passage, you must test it to make sure it really does represent the thrust of the entire selection. For example, you can ask, "In what way can exercise do more harm than good?" Or, "In what way is exercise essential to a healthy, productive life?" If every sentence and paragraph in the passage pertains to the main idea you have chosen, then you know your choice is sound. However, if you find that the passage contains sentences and paragraphs that support other ideas, then you need to start over and formulate another main idea.

Questions that test your ability to determine the central idea can be expressed in a number of ways:

The main point the author makes is ...
The author seems chiefly concerned with ...
The main idea of this passage is ...
Which of the following titles could best be used for this selection?
Which of these statements best expresses the idea of the passage?

Supporting Material

The supporting material that makes up the larger portion of most selections (often called the *body of the writing*) contains the essential material of the work—specific details, anecdotes, allusions, references, or reasons—by which a writer substantiates the main thought.

Keep in mind that supporting material may vary considerably from one context to another. The specific details in a report on a scientific discovery, for example, may be very different from the kind of detail needed in a biographical selection.

Try to be continually mindful of the logical order of paragraphs within a selection, and of the logical order of sentences within each paragraph. Transitional words and phrases usually highlight paragraph or essay coherence, and should be of great help when you are asked whether or not a sentence or paragraph is out of place.

At times, the English Test will include a question about the readers or audience for whom the selection is intended. The relative quality and sophistication of the supporting details will supply the basis for the answer to such questions. For example, a selection intended for children would probably include simple explanations and supporting details that would be unnecessary or inappropriate for adult readers.

Transition

Transitional words and phrases make clear the relationship between phrases, clauses, and sentences, and lend coherence to the sequence of paragraphs.

A transitional paragraph is used to link the main parts of an essay. Such a paragraph may be just a single sentence that eases the progression from one idea to the next:

EXAMPLE: Sometimes a solution is based upon a study of the past. Let us review what has taken place in new architecture so far this century.

Most of the time, however, transitions are individual words or phrases that provide transition while signaling a concept like addition, contrast, example, or time. The following list will show you the functions of some transitions.

CONCEPTS	TRANSITIONS
Addition and continuation	also, and, another, besides, finally, likewise, furthermore, in addition, indeed, moreover, similarly, then, too
Cause and effect	accordingly, as, as a result, because, consequently, for this reason, since, then, therefore, thus
Concession	certainly, granted that, it is true that, no doubt, of course, still, to be sure
Conclusion or repetition	in other words, in particular, in short, in summary, once again, that is, to repeat
Contrast or limitation	although, but, however, if, in contrast, instead, nevertheless, on the contrary, on the other hand, otherwise, provided that, still, yet
Example	for example, for instance, in particular, likewise, specifically, that is, to illustrate
Place	above, behind, below, elsewhere, here, in back of, north of, on this side, there, to the right of, underneath
Time	afterward, before, earlier, eventually, immediately, later, meanwhile, next, now, since, soon, until

Openings and Closings

Being able to spot beginning and ending paragraphs is important when you are asked on the ACT to rearrange paragraphs that are obviously scrambled. The beginning paragraph will often include signals that will help you determine the proper order of subsequent paragraphs.

The *opening paragraph* is crucial. In a few words, the author must make clear the central purpose of the work and also persuade the reader to continue reading. Sometimes, authors will use the opening paragraph to establish their authority for the task or to create a question in the reader's mind that he or she needs or hopes to have answered—by continuing to read.

TIP

Be sure to end with an effective closing paragraph.

> The land that became the United States was in colonial times an extension of the Old World into the New. Through the centuries, the descendants of the original colonists blended their European heritage into the new Nation that evolved. But for the courage and resourcefulness of the Europeans who first explored and settled the unknown wilderness, that evolution would not have been possible.

The simplest *closing paragraphs* summarize the gist of the entire passage in a sentence or two. Others invite or challenge the reader to engage in further research on the topic. A good concluding paragraph will complete the passage logically and clearly, leaving the reader with the certainty that the main idea has been adequately developed.

The amalgamation of such rich and diverse national, cultural, and racial elements into a free and democratic society has created the United States of America—a blending of cultures, languages, and traditions that mirrors the hopes and aspirations of all mankind.

WORD CHOICE

Diction

Some of the questions on the English Test will require you to decide the appropriateness of a word in its context. In a technical passage about the development of the transistor, for example, the use of a flowery or ornate word or phrase would stand out as inappropriate. Similarly, words that are illiterate or colloquial, or used in spoken English, for the most part, are not appropriate in a formal literary passage. In general, most language can be categorized as either formal, informal (colloquial), or popular.

A word is *appropriate* if it fits the reader, occasion, and purpose for which the writing is intended.

Formal Diction

Formal diction is seldom used in everyday conversation and writing. It is found in writing that serves a serious purpose (for example, a research paper) and concerns weighty or substantial topics, such as death, crime, philosophy, scholarship, science, and literature.

Formal language employs a more scholarly vocabulary than popular English (*eccentric* for *strange, extenuation* for *excuse, immaculate* for *clean, tantamount* for *equivalent,* and so on). Another characteristic is grammatical exactness.

Informal Diction

Informal diction is *colloquial* language, that is, the language of everyday conversation. It includes contractions (always improper in formal writing), slang, colloquialisms, dialect and turns of phrase peculiar to local areas (*provincialisms*), and shortened word forms (*TV* for *television*, *phone* for *telephone, CD* for *compact disc,* for example).

Popular Diction

Popular diction lies somewhere between formal and informal (colloquial) diction. It is not as free as colloquial, nor does it include slang or provincialisms, but it relaxes many of the rules and restrictions of formal written English. Generally, popular diction is the language of mass-media publications. Its aim is to appeal to and communicate clearly with the average reader.

The following expressions have no place in formal prose.

Cool it.	yeah
guys	turn-on
high (intoxicated)	guts
spaced-out (on drugs)	I've had it!
for sure	stuck-up
creep (obnoxious person)	an awful lot
macho	screwball

This list contains some common misspellings, provincialisms, illiterate expressions, and incorrect forms to be avoided.

NOT	BUT
aggravate	annoy; exasperate
a half an hour	a half hour or half an hour
alot	a lot
alright	all right
and etc.	etc. or et cetera
anywheres	anywhere
being that, being as how	as, because, since
can't seem to	seem unable to
considerable sick	quite sick
dark-complected	dark-complexioned
different than	different from
hadn't ought	ought not
heighth	height
irregardless	regardless, irrespective
no-account; no-good	worthless
off of	off, from
out loud	aloud
outside of	except; beside
should of, would of	should have, would have
the reason is because	the reason is that
tote	carry
try and give	try to give
use to	used to
visit with	visit
won him	beat him

Some colloquialisms and short forms are appropriate in everyday conversation and informal writing, but should not be used in formal written English.

NOT	BUT
ad	advertisement
at about; at around	about; around
can't help but	cannot help but
center around	center on
get going	go
guess so, reckon so	think, suppose
has got to go	has to go
he is liable to be there	he is likely to be there
hold on	wait
kids	children
kind of a, sort of a	kind of, sort of
mighty hard	very hard
okay	all right
out loud	aloud
packs quite a punch	delivers a strong blow
phone	telephone
show up	appear to be superior
TV	television
wait a bit	wait

Wordiness

To avoid wordiness, eliminate language that either duplicates what has already been expressed or adds nothing to the sense of the statement.

TIP

Beware of wordiness. Wordy sentences either duplicate what has already been expressed or add nothing to the sense of the statement.

WORDY: At the present time, you can call up the library on the telephone if you want to receive that particular information.
REVISED: Now you can call the library for that information.

WORDY: A factor in the cause of the decline in stock prices was unwarranted growth.
REVISED: One cause of the decline in stock prices was unwarranted growth.
OR
A factor in the decline in stock prices ...

WORDY: As a pet, the llama is easygoing in its habits and has a friendly personality.
REVISED: As a pet, the llama is easygoing and friendly.

Expressions like *there are* and *it is* can add unnecessary words to your sentences.

EXAMPLES: [There are] several people at school [who] have promised to help with the gardening at the new campus.
[It is] the way you swing the club [that] amazes me.

A *redundant* expression is characterized by unnecessary repetition. To say *adequate enough* is to be redundant, because *adequate* and *enough* have nearly the same meaning.

EXAMPLES: The two clubs joined [together] to feed the poor at Christmas.
They circled [around] the field.
For a list of ski areas in the state, refer [back] to page 25.

Avoid redundancies and roundabout phrases (*circumlocutions*) like the following:

WORDY	CONCISE
advance planning	planning
contributing factor	factor
due to the fact that	because
during the course of	during
exact same symptoms	same symptoms; exact symptoms
for the purpose of	for
in the event that	if
in the near future	soon
large in size	large
past experience	experience
past history	history
revert back	revert
sufficient enough	sufficient; enough

TIP 

Watch for redundancies. A redundant expression is characterized by unnecessary repetition. To say *adequate enough* is to be redundant because *adequate* and *enough* have nearly the same meaning.

SAMPLE ENGLISH TEST

The ACT English Test consists of five prose passages and 75 questions, with a 45-minute time limit. The test is designed to measure your ability to discern and remedy errors and awkwardness in punctuation, grammar and usage, and sentence structure. You will also find questions about the prose—for whom the passage is intended, for example, or how the paragraph or sentence might be improved with reorganization or additional material.

The following two practice passages are intended to familiarize you with questions that approximate those on the ACT. Each passage is accompanied by 30 multiple-choice questions. These passages are approximately double the length of the ones on the actual test. If you wish to time yourself, allow 18 minutes to read each passage and answer the questions.

Directions: The following test consists of 60 items. Some concern underlined words and phrases in context; others ask general questions about the passages. Most of the underlined sections contain errors or inappropriate expressions. You are asked to compare each with the four alternatives in the answer column. If you consider the original version best, choose letter **A** or **F:** NO CHANGE. For each question, select the alternative you think best. Read each passage through before answering the questions based on it.

NOTE: Answers and explanations can be found at the end of each passage.

Passage 1

A peaceful oasis in the midst of the bustling San Fernando Valley, San Fernando Mission has been declared a historic cultural monument by the City of Los Angeles, according to a bronze plaque at the entrance to the mission. In addition to being an active <u>religion</u> [1] center, <u>many tourists come to the mission each year</u> [2] to stroll through the well-tended grounds and <u>they admire</u> [3] the unique architecture of the restored mission buildings.

The entrance to the mission quadrangle opens <u>onto</u> [4] the east garden, a large, <u>grass covered</u> [5] courtyard in the middle of which is a flower-shaped fountain modeled

1. **A.** NO CHANGE
   B. religions
   C. religious
   D. more religious

2. **F.** NO CHANGE
   G. many tourists are invited to the Mission each year
   H. it is a place where many tourists come each year
   J. people come

3. **A.** NO CHANGE
   B. they were admiring
   C. admiring
   D. admire

4. **F.** NO CHANGE
   G. out into
   H. wide into
   J. for

5. **A.** NO CHANGE
   B. grass-covered
   C. grass covering
   D. grass, covered

after one that stands in Cordova, Spain. Wind rustles through the branches of the trees, and water tinkles in the fountain, also[6] the sounds of traffic outside the walls only accentuate the tranquility of the setting. Strolling about the grounds, the smell of spring flowers scenting the air and the sunlight warm upon your back, one can easily[7] imagine being back two hundred years during the time of the founding of the mission. The present-day mission compound, however, with its air of serenity and unhurried repose, is nothing like the mission in its heyday, when it was the scene of bustling activity and the labor was diligent[8] by hundreds of Indians under the direction of a few Spanish Franciscan padres.

San Fernando Mission, founded in 1779 by Padre Fermin Lasuen and named for a saintly king of thirteenth-century Spain, it was[9] the seventeenth of California's twenty-one missions stretching[10] in a chain from San Francisco to San Diego. The purpose of the mission chain was to create centers of Christian civilization who would want[11] to convert the California Indians and prepare them for Spanish citizenship.

Mission San Francisco was established centrally[12] between the missions of San Buenaventura and San Gabriel, at a distance of one day's journey from each. The site chosen[13] for the mission—land[14] that had been used by Don Francisco Reyes, first mayor of the Pueblo de Los Angeles, to graze cattle—was rich in water, in

6. **F.** NO CHANGE
   G. while
   H. moreover,
   J. furthermore,

7. **A.** NO CHANGE
   B. you can easily
   C. it seems easy to
   D. one easily

8. **F.** NO CHANGE
   G. diligent labor
   H. the labor was industrious
   J. labor that was diligent

9. **A.** NO CHANGE
   B. it had been
   C. it will be
   D. was

10. **F.** NO CHANGE
    G. and it stretched
    H. that was stretching
    J. widely stretched out

11. **A.** NO CHANGE
    B. which was hoping
    C. seeking
    D. needing

12. **F.** NO CHANGE
    G. in a great spot
    H. well within and
    J. OMIT the underlined phrase.

13. **A.** NO CHANGE
    B. cite chosen
    C. sight chose
    D. site choosed

14. **F.** NO CHANGE
    G. Mission: land
    H. Mission; land
    J. Mission. Land

fertile, arable soil, and <u>it had an Indian population,</u> [15] all necessary elements for a successful mission.

15. **A.** NO CHANGE
    B. there also were Indians,
    C. it had Indians,
    D. in an Indian population,

The chapel—an exact replica of the original, which was built between 1804 and 1806 and destroyed by the 1971 earthquake—is long and narrow, with adobe walls decorated by frescoes of native designs. The overall effect of the frescoes, the colorful Spanish altar hangings, and the Stations of the Cross <u>are,</u> [16] as one writer put it, "a glorious, if barbaric spectacle!"

16. **F.** NO CHANGE
    G. was
    H. is
    J. will have been

Although there <u>is a number of</u> [17] windows on the south wall of the chapel, there is only one window on the north wall. It is not known whether this architectural detail was meant to keep out cold winds from the nearby mountains or <u>as a defense against a potential attack by hostile Indians.</u> [18]

17. **A.** NO CHANGE
    B. were a number of
    C. are a number of
    D. should be a number of

18. **F.** NO CHANGE
    G. hostile Indians.
    H. defending against an Indian attack.
    J. an attack against hostile Indians.

Behind the chapel is a cemetery, where many of the natives and other early settlers attached to the mission were buried. Only a few wooden crosses and <u>there is one large gravestone</u> [19] mark the final resting places of approximately 2,000 persons buried there. Beyond the burial grounds is a <u>fountain: fed</u> [20] by a small stream and surrounded <u>in</u> [21] foliage and a flower garden.

19. **A.** NO CHANGE
    B. one large gravestone
    C. there might have been a gravestone
    D. there most likely is a gravestone

20. **F.** NO CHANGE
    G. fountain. Fed
    H. fountain; fed
    J. fountain fed

21. **A.** NO CHANGE
    B. overhead in the
    C. about with
    D. by

<u>Across the compound, stands</u> [22] the "convento"—the largest original mission building in California—with its famous corridor of twenty-one Roman arches that today

22. **F.** NO CHANGE
    G. Across the compound, stood
    H. Across the compound stands
    J. Across the compound, is standing

front San Fernando Mission Road. Two stories high, with
23

23. **A.** NO CHANGE
    B. fronts
    C. fronting
    D. fronted

four-foot-thick adobe walls that keeps the inside cool on
24

24. **F.** NO CHANGE
    G. walls, that keep
    H. walls that keep
    J. walls, that keeps

even the hottest summer day. It served as living quarters
25
for the missionaries and visitors in the early 1800's.

25. **A.** NO CHANGE
    B. day, it
    C. day—it
    D. day: it

Tourists taking pictures inside the mission should bring
26
high-speed color film.
26

26. **F.** NO CHANGE
    G. Retain the position of this sentence in the passage but place it in its own paragraph.
    H. Move this sentence to the beginning of the paragraph.
    J. OMIT the underlined sentence.

Just inside the entrance hall an atmosphere is able to
27
be felt of great age, perhaps due in part to the stillness
27
that seems to echo within the brick-floored rooms. Then

27. **A.** NO CHANGE
    B. may be feeling an atmosphere
    C. one feels an atmosphere
    D. an atmosphere can be felt

again, this feeling might be due to the odor, emanating
28
from the nearby wine cellar, a musty smell that grows
stronger as one moves slowly down the whitewashed

28. **F.** NO CHANGE
    G. odor; emanating
    H. odor. Emanating
    J. odor emanating

stairs—past a deep tub cut from rock where grapes were
29
once pressed underfoot. [30]

29. **A.** NO CHANGE
    B. stairs, passed
    C. stairs; passed
    D. stairs, past

30. Is the mention of the odor appropriate and effective at the end of this passage?
    F. No, because it introduces a new element at the end of the passage.
    G. Yes, because the musty odors of old buildings and old wine presses appropriately reflect the age of this historic mission.
    H. Yes, because the description of the odor is somewhat suspenseful, and mentioning it gives a mysterious quality to the passage.
    J. No, because an odor is generally perceived as offensive.

Answer Key

1. C	6. G	11. C	16. H	21. D	26. J
2. H	7. B	12. J	17. C	22. H	27. C
3. D	8. G	13. A	18. G	23. B	28. J
4. F	9. D	14. F	19. B	24. H	29. D
5. B	10. F	15. D	20. J	25. B	30. G

Answer Explanations

1. **(C)** The underlined word is intended to modify the noun *center* and so must be an adjective.
2. **(H)** The introductory phrase *In addition to being an active [religious] center* clearly refers to the mission, not the tourists. Therefore, the main clause must begin with the word *mission* or with the referent pronoun *it*.
3. **(D)** The infinitive *to admire* is parallel in construction with *to stroll,* with which it is paired: *to stroll ... and [to] admire*.
4. **(F)** No other choice is idiomatically correct.
5. **(B)** Hyphenate a compound adjective that precedes the noun it modifies.
6. **(G)** Conjunctive adverbs (such as *also, moreover,* and *furthermore*) used to join clauses must be preceded by a semicolon. *While,* a subordinating conjunction used to introduce an adverb clause, is properly preceded by a comma.
7. **(B)** Avoid a shift in point of view, from the second person *your* to the third person *one*. Choice C incorrectly makes *it* the word modified by the introductory participial phrase.
8. **(G)** The prepositional phrase *of bustling activity* requires a parallel object, *diligent labor.* Choice J is wordy.
9. **(D)** The sentence has two subjects: *San Fernando/it. It* is unnecessary.
10. **(F)** The participial phrase *stretching in a chain* ... correctly modifies the noun *missions*. Choice G incorrectly uses *it* to refer to the plural word *missions*. H also incorrectly uses a singular form, *was,* which does not agree with *missions,* the antecedent of *that*. J is wordy.
11. **(C)** The other options either carry meanings inappropriate to the sense of the passage or contain faulty grammar.
12. **(J)** *Centrally* repeats the idea of *at a distance of one day's journey from each. In a great spot* is too colloquial for this passage. Choice H is wordy.
13. **(A)** The correct word to use here is *site,* meaning location. The verb forms *chose* and *choosed* in choices C and D are incorrect.
14. **(F)** A pair of dashes precedes and follows an interrupting parenthetical element.
15. **(D)** Only this option is parallel with the other prepositional phrases: *in water, in ... soil,* and *in ... population*.
16. **(H)** The singular subject *effect* requires the singular verb *is*. The predominant tense of the passage is the present.

17. **(C)** The phrase *a number of* is plural in meaning and takes the plural verb *are*. Choice B is wrong, since the predominant tense of the passage is the present. D changes the meaning of the clause.

18. **(G)** The infinitive phrase *to keep out* needs a parallel second object: *to keep out cold winds ... or hostile Indians*.

19. **(B)** A simple noun is needed to form the other half of the compound subject: *crosses and ... gravestone*.

20. **(J)** The participial phrase *fed by a small stream* is a restrictive modifier and should not be separated from the noun it modifies, *fountain,* by a punctuation mark. Choice G introduces a sentence fragment.

21. **(D)** The correct idiom is *surrounded by*.

22. **(H)** In an inverted sentence, do not use a comma to separate a short adverb construction from the verb it modifies.

23. **(B)** The subject of the verb *front* is the relative pronoun *that,* which refers to the singular noun *corridor,* not the plural *arches*. Thus, the correct verb form is *fronts*. Choice C is a participle, not a verb form. D shifts to the past tense.

24. **(H)** The subject of the verb *keep* is the relative pronoun *that,* which refers to the plural noun *walls*. Do not use a comma to separate a restrictive clause from the word it modifies (G and J).

25. **(B)** A comma is used to separate the introductory phrase *two stories high ... day* from the main clause of the sentence. Choice A creates a sentence fragment.

26. **(J)** This sentence has no bearing on the topic of the passage.

27. **(C)** As a rule, it is better to avoid the passive voice. The active voice is more direct and forceful.

28. **(J)** The participial phrase *emanating from the nearby wine cellar* is a restrictive modifier and cannot be set off by commas. Choice H introduces a sentence fragment.

29. **(D)** A comma is called for at this point for clarity. A dash is too great a mark of separation. Choices B and C incorrectly substitute the verb form *passed* for the preposition *past*.

30. **(G)** This descriptive paragraph adds a meaningful sense impression to the passage.

Passage 2

Each of the paragraphs in this passage is numbered, but may not be in the most logical position. The last question asks you to select the correct number.

(1)

Sometime around the middle of January, after reading about standard organic gardening techniques, prospective home gardeners should make a list of the vegetables most enjoyed by their families. Sitting down with a few seed catalogs, preferably those from local companies such as Santa Rosa Gardening Co. or Burbank Farms,—whose [1] catalogs contain detailing [2] planting instructions for Southern California, including the proper planting dates for each of the distinct climatic regions—they should review the directions for growing vegetables, narrowing the choices to crops easy to grow. And although January is an ideal time here to plant such winter vegetables such as [3] beets, broccoli, peas, lettuce, and swiss chard, novice gardeners might do well to plan a spring garden as a first effort. For one thing, summer vegetables like tomatoes, zucchini, and beans are easy to grow, they require [4] little in the way of additional care once they have been planted and are growing well. And for another, spring—traditionally a time of renewal—seems the right time of year to begin a gardening project.

1. **A.** NO CHANGE
   B. Farms—whose
   C. Farms; whose
   D. Farms. Whose

2. **F.** NO CHANGE
   G. details of
   H. detailed
   J. in detailed

3. **A.** NO CHANGE
   B. like
   C. such as;
   D. as

4. **F.** NO CHANGE
   G. grow. Since these vegetables require
   H. grow. Requiring
   J. grow, requiring

(2)

These differences make it impossible that gardeners [5] in Southern California to follow in an explicit way [6] the advice given in nationally circulated magazines and

5. **A.** NO CHANGE
   B. to be a gardener
   C. to go on being a gardener
   D. for gardeners

6. **F.** NO CHANGE
   G. explicitly
   H. in a more explicit way
   J. explicitly and definitely

books on organic gardening. Instead, these methods <u>must be adopted</u> [7] to the particular climate in this area. Some suggestions follow that may be helpful to fellow gardeners in the San Fernando Valley region.

7. **A.** NO CHANGE
   B. should be adopted
   C. must be adapted
   D. must adopt

(3)

Just as organic gardening differs from gardening with the help of a chemical <u>company. Gardening</u> [8] in Southern California differs dramatically from gardening in almost every other part of the country. For one thing, crops <u>will be planted</u> [9] here almost any time during the year, whereas spring gardens are the rule in most other parts of the country. Diversity of weather systems within the relatively small area that <u>encompassing</u> [10] Southern California is another distinction. For instance, coastal communities experience cool, damp weather for much of the year, while the San Fernando and San Gabriel valleys are blistering hot in summer and cold in <u>winter—some</u> [11] inland valleys even encounter frost and freezing temperatures! Thus, although these areas <u>separate</u> [12] by fewer than fifty miles, the climates are disparate, necessitating the use of distinct gardening techniques for each locale.

8. **F.** NO CHANGE
   G. company; gardening
   H. company, gardening
   J. company: gardening

9. **A.** NO CHANGE
   B. can be planted
   C. have been planted
   D. ought to be planted

10. **F.** NO CHANGE
    G. encompassed
    H. has encompassed
    J. encompasses

11. **A.** NO CHANGE
    B. winter;—some
    C. winter—Some
    D. winter, some

12. **F.** NO CHANGE
    G. are separated
    H. must be separated
    J. were separated

(4)

After deciding what vegetables to grow, <u>a rough draft is made</u> [13] of the garden, which should be located in an area of <u>flat well-drained</u> [14] ground that <u>has gotten</u> [15] at least six full hours of sun daily. Taller-growing crops should be put on the north side of the garden so that

13. **A.** NO CHANGE
    B. a rough draft should be made
    C. the gardener should make a rough draft
    D. it is necessary to make a rough draft

14. **F.** NO CHANGE
    G. flat, well-drained
    H. flat, well drained
    J. flat and well drained

15. **A.** NO CHANGE
    B. will have gotten
    C. got
    D. gets

they do not shade any low-growing vegetables; except [16] those that cannot survive the intense summer sun. The latter include lettuce and many other greens. The rows, or beds, should be wide enough to accommodate the particular kind of a [17] crop to be grown. The wider the rows, of course, the more crops the garden will have produced. [18] This [19] is known as "intensive gardening" and is ideal for small backyard gardens. One suggestion is to make the beds three feet wide, with enough space between them to allow easy access for cultivating, weeding, and to harvest [20] mature plants. However, two-foot beds are also okay. [21]

(5)

After the plan has been drawn up and the seeds will be ordered, [22] the next step is to prepare the soil properly, one [23] of the most important procedures in insuring a successful harvest. Testing the soil for deficiencies is a must; soil-testing [24] kits are available from most home improvement stores and gardening centers. The organic gardening books and magazines mentioned earlier go into heavy detail [25] regarding soil composition, testing, and preparation. Following their

16. **F.** NO CHANGE
    G. vegetables except
    H. vegetables: except
    J. vegetables. Except

17. **A.** NO CHANGE
    B. kind of a
    C. kinds of a
    D. OMIT the underlined words.

18. **F.** NO CHANGE
    G. would of produced.
    H. will produce.
    J. is producing.

19. **A.** NO CHANGE
    B. This close spacing
    C. Which
    D. This here

20. **F.** NO CHANGE
    G. harvesting
    H. to be harvesting
    J. so we can harvest the

21. **A.** NO CHANGE
    B. alright.
    C. all right.
    D. allright.

22. **F.** NO CHANGE
    G. should be ordered,
    H. were ordered,
    J. have been ordered,

23. **A.** NO CHANGE
    B. properly. One
    C. properly; one
    D. properly, it is one

24. **F.** NO CHANGE
    G. must, as soil-testing
    H. must, soil-testing
    J. must because soil-testing

25. **A.** NO CHANGE
    B. much detail
    C. exquisite detail
    D. alot of detail

recommendations will contribute <u>for the success</u> [26] of the gardening project.

(6)

<u>Once the condition of the soil is ascertained by the person doing the gardening, deficient elements (such as phosphorus, potassium, magnesium, or sulphur) can be added.</u> [27] In addition to these <u>minerals; however,</u> [28] enough fertilizer to get the seedlings off to a good start should be incorporated into the soil. [29] [30]

26. **F.** NO CHANGE
    G. in the success
    H. to the success
    J. for the successfulness

27. **A.** NO CHANGE
    B. Once the condition of the soil is ascertained by the gardener, elements that are lacking in sufficient quantity (such as phosphorus, potassium, magnesium, or sulphur) can be added by the gardener.
    C. Once the gardener ascertains the condition of the soil, he or she can add deficient elements (such as phosphorus, potassium, magnesium, or sulphur).
    D. Once, the gardener ascertains the condition of the soil, deficient elements (such as: phosphorus, potassium, magnesium, or sulphur) can be added.

28. **F.** NO CHANGE
    G. minerals however,
    H. minerals, however—
    J. minerals, however,

29. This passage is most likely directed to readers who:
    A. are experts in gardening and need little advice.
    B. are residents of Southern California and have never had a garden.
    C. are residents of Freeport, Maine, and are just curious about gardening in a warmer state.
    D. have gardened so much that they hope never to see another bud.

30. Select the correct order of the numbered paragraphs so that the passage will read in logical sequence.
    F. NO CHANGE
    G. 3, 2, 1, 4, 5, 6
    H. 1, 2, 4, 5, 3, 6
    J. 4, 2, 3, 1, 5, 6

Answer Key

1. B	6. G	11. A	16. G	21. C	26. H
2. H	7. C	12. G	17. D	22. J	27. C
3. D	8. H	13. C	18. H	23. A	28. J
4. J	9. B	14. G	19. B	24. F	29. B
5. D	10. J	15. D	20. G	25. B	30. G

Answer Explanations

1. **(B)** A pair of dashes is used to separate a parenthetical element from the rest of the sentence; a comma is not used with the dash. Choice D introduces a sentence fragment.

2. **(H)** The correct choice is the past participle *detailed,* which acts as an adjective to modify the noun phrase *planting instructions*. The present participle *detailing* carries meaning that does not apply to this sentence. Choice J adds a word that does not make sense in the structure of the sentence.

3. **(D)** The sentence already contains the word *such (such winter vegetables as)*. Choice B offers an ungrammatical construction, *such ... like*.

4. **(J)** This is the only correct option. The other choices produce sentence fragments or a comma splice.

5. **(D)** Idiomatic English requires the construction *impossible for gardeners ... to follow.*

6. **(G)** The other choices are wordy or redundant.

7. **(C)** The correct word here is *adapted,* meaning modified to suit. *Adopted* means taken as is.

8. **(H)** Use a comma to separate an introductory adverb clause from the main clause.

9. **(B)** The verb phrase *can be planted* also means *are planted* in the context of this sentence. The other options do not carry this essential additional meaning.

10. **(J)** Use the present tense to express generally true statements.

11. **(A)** A dash is used for emphasis to separate a parenthetical comment from the rest of the sentence. It is not used together with a semicolon. Choice C incorrectly capitalizes the word *some*. D introduces a comma splice.

12. **(G)** The passive voice is required when the subject is acted upon. The present tense is consistent with the rest of the passage.

13. **(C)** Without a logical noun to modify (*gardener,* for example), the introductory phrase would dangle.

14. **(G)** Place a comma between coordinate adjectives. The compound adjective *well-drained* takes a hyphen when it precedes the noun it modifies.

15. **(D)** The predominant tense in this passage is the present.

16. **(G)** Do not use a punctuation mark to separate a restrictive phrase from the word it modifies. The phrase beginning *except those* ... limits *low-growing vegetables*. Choice J would create a sentence fragment.

17. **(D)** The other choices are unnecessarily wordy and also introduce an error. (*Kind of a* is not idiomatic English.)

18. **(H)** The simple future tense, showing expectation, is appropriate here, because the passage is set in the present tense. *Would of* is incorrect grammatically.

19. **(B)** The pronoun *This* needs a specific antecedent for clear reference. Since there is none, the meaning of *this* has to be clarified. Choice C introduces a sentence fragment. D is redundant, as *here* repeats the meaning of *this*.

20. **(G)** The gerund *harvesting* is required, to be parallel with the other gerunds, *cultivating* and *weeding*.

21. **(C)** Choice A is colloquial. B and D are misspellings.

22. **(J)** The verb must agree in tense with *has been drawn*.

23. **(A)** Set off a nonrestrictive appositive phrase with a comma. Choice B introduces a sentence fragment; D, a comma splice.

24. **(F)** A semicolon is used to separate clauses that are closely related. The transitional words in Choices G and J change the meaning. H creates a comma-splice sentence.

25. **(B)** The other options are either inappropriate or incorrect.

26. **(H)** The correct idiom is *contribute to*.

27. **(C)** The passive voice (*is ascertained* and *can be added*) is less forceful and usually results in more wordy sentences than the active voice. Choice D incorrectly places a comma after the conjunction *Once* and a colon after *such as*.

28. **(J)** The word *however* is used here as an adverb, not as a conjunctive adverb introducing a clause, and so should be set off by commas as a simple parenthetical word.

29. **(B)** The references to the southwestern climate, to aids for novice gardeners, and to gardening techniques indicate that this article is addressed primarily to first-time gardeners in Southern California.

30. **(G)** Paragraph (3) is clearly the introduction to this passage; it makes general statements about the topic that are supported by data in subsequent paragraphs. The phrase *These differences* that begins paragraph (2) directly relates to the ending of paragraph (3). The step-by-step process begins with paragraph (1) and continues in order with paragraphs (4), (5), and (6).

The English Review and Practice section is designed to help you prepare for the ACT Test. Everything is presented with the test in mind. It is not a summary of all points in English; it is a summary of all points in English that you need to know for the best experience with the English part of the ACT. The more you familiarize yourself with this material, the better the score you will achieve.

Go over this review and practice material several times. Those parts of it that you feel unsure of you should revisit even more. Familiarize yourself with the ACT English answer sheets. Take the practice test under the same conditions you will be in when you finally take the official test. Do not receive any phone calls, talk to anyone, or listen to music. An empty classroom would be ideal if it is available to you. When you are finished, evaluate your results on the practice test. Ask yourself whether or not you had enough time, whether you left too many questions unanswered, whether you made any careless mistakes, and whether you should go over any sections again.

CHAPTER 2

Mathematics Review and Practice

- Arithmetic/Pre-Algebra
- Algebra and Coordinate Geometry
- Solving Word Problems
- Systems of Linear Equations
- Conic Sections
- Nonlinear Systems
- Geometry
- Trigonometry

The ACT test in mathematics is a 60-minute test designed to evaluate your mathematical achievement in courses commonly taught in high school. This test includes questions from the areas of pre-algebra, algebra, plane geometry, intermediate algebra, coordinate geometry, and trigonometry.

The 60 questions on the test are classified by topic and skill level according to the following chart:

Topic	Basic Skills	Application	Analysis	Total
Pre-Algebra Algebra	8	12	4	24
Intermediate Algebra Coordinate Geometry	7	7	4	18
Plane Geometry	6	8	0	14
Trigonometry	2	2	0	4

The questions in the Basic Skills category cover recognition and simple application of elementary concepts such as subsets of real numbers, terms and relationships concerning operations, and axioms of the real number system. The Application questions require you to apply one or two concepts to the solution of a problem. The questions in the Analysis category usually require the application of several concepts to obtain the solution. Frequently this type of question is posed as a typical "word problem."

The emphasis in this test is on your ability to reason with numbers and mathematical concepts. No very complicated formulas or procedures will be involved in the solution of the problems.

For each question five potential answers are given, only one of which is correct. The answers may be designated as **A**, **B**, **C**, **D**, **E** or **F**, **G**, **H**, **J**, **K**. For some questions the last choice (either **E** or **K**) may be "None of the above." (In this book the alternative form "None of these" is used.)

Strategy

To be in the best position to do well on the ACT mathematics test, a review of the mathematics material covered on the test should be planned. Included in this chapter is a review that should be read with a pencil in hand. There are many examples of problems with detailed commentary on their solutions, as well as many practice exercises. The practice exercises also have complete solutions and explanations. The best plan is to work each practice problem on your own, and then check your solution with the one given in this book. If your answer is the same, you can be reasonably sure you did the problem correctly, even though your procedure may be different. There is no claim that there is only one way to do any given problem. Also, the chapter is intended to be review, not a textbook on mathematics. No attempt is made to prove most statements; they are merely presented as facts. If you want justification for a given statement or if you want more practice on a particular topic, consult a textbook that covers the material in a non-review manner.

A reasonable time period to review the material in the mathematics section of this book may be 2 or 3 months. This would leave time to search for additional help if you find that you need it.

The best long-range strategy for preparation for this or any other test is to do well in the courses that you take in school. Although the ACT test is not necessarily like the tests that you had in these courses, much of the same material is covered; and if you have retained the fundamental concepts, you should be able to do well on the ACT test. As in many skills, however, the level of mathematics ability decreases with time if you do not practice continuously. Therefore, even if you have done very well in course work, it would be wise to spend time on this review chapter.

Tactics

After you have reviewed the mathematics chapter and done the practice exercises, you should be ready to take the mathematics tests in this book. The following techniques will be helpful in taking model or actual ACT mathematics tests:

1. *Pace yourself.* The ACT mathematics test is a 60-question, 60-minute test to determine your mathematical achievement. Keep in mind as you take the test that the average amount of time allotted to each question is 1 minute. This means that you must work quickly and use the time that remains to try the more difficult questions again.
2. *Know the directions.* The ACT directions state that figures are not necessarily drawn to scale. You may also assume that geometric figures lie in a plane and that the word *line* means a straight line. Keep these directions in mind during the test. Mark your answer carefully on the appropriate answer sheet.
3. *Work efficiently.* You should work through each question, taking each step in order, rather than try to answer the question by working backward from the proposed answers; usually too much time is required to eliminate incorrect responses. Once you have an answer, try to locate it among the response choices. If it is there, mark the answer sheet quickly but accurately and go on to the next question.

STUMPED?

If your answer is not among the choices, there are three possibilities:

1. You misread or misunderstood the question. Reread the question carefully. Be sure that you answer the question that was asked.
2. You made a mistake in the solution of the problem. Quickly review your steps, looking for errors. Perhaps your answer is equivalent to one of the choices by a simple manipulation.
3. You solved the problem correctly, and the correct answer is "None of the above."

If the search for a correct answer takes too much time, mark the question so that you can return to it after you have answered all of the others. Then

1. *Evaluate your method.* If you find that a question involves a very complicated computation or a very involved procedure for its solution, you should re-evaluate your method. The problems on the ACT do not require lengthy computations or proofs. In many cases computations can be done more easily if products are left in factored form until the very last step in order to make use of cancellation. (This is particularly true in the evaluation of combinations and permutations.)
2. *Draw on your knowledge.* Although the questions do not require the application of complicated formulas, you should know certain basic formulas such as those for the areas of squares, rectangles, triangles, and so on, perimeters, simple interest, uniform motion ($d = rt$), and the Pythagorean theorem. You should also know the definitions of terms and operations, such as prime numbers, composite numbers, union of sets, intersection of sets, axioms of the real number system, the axioms of equality and inequality (used to solve equations and inequalities), the trigonometric functions, and some of the simpler identities.
3. *Guess when necessary.* When you return to questions that you abandoned temporarily because they took too much time, consider eliminating any response that is not reasonable, given the proper interpretation of the problem. If then the solution still eludes you, guess. There is no penalty for guessing.
4. *Check if possible.* If time remains when you have finished the test to your satisfaction, go back to see that you have answered each question, and check your answers.

Use of Calculators

Some calculators may be used on the ACT. No questions on the ACT require the use of any calculator, but if you are accustomed to using a calculator in your classes or while doing your homework, you may bring your calculator to the test and use it to assist you on any question or to verify your answer. Be sure that you are very familiar with any calculator that you plan to use. Do not purchase one the day before the test and expect it to do you any good.

Any calculator may be used with the exception of the following:

- no pocket organizers or electronic notepads with pen-input devices
- no laptop or similar computers
- no device with a standard typewriter keyboard
- no calculator with symbolic algebra ability
- no calculator with the ability to communicate with another calculator unless the communication port is disabled
- no calculator that requires a power cord
- no calculator that has a sound function unless the sound function is disabled

The following calculators are some specific models that are not allowed.

Texas Instruments	TI-89
Texas Instruments	TI-92
Casio	CFX-9970G
Casio	ALGEBRA FX-2.0
Hewlett-Packard	HP-49G

Because the introduction of new models occurs regularly, a comprehensive list of disallowed models is not given. Use the above guidelines to determine whether a specific calculator will be allowed. The supervisors of the test will give the final word on the acceptability of the calculator you bring to the test.

Four-function, scientific, and graphing calculators are acceptable if they meet the guidelines above. Be sure that any calculator you plan to use is in good repair with adequate batteries (bring extras if you wish). You may not store any test data in your calculator. You may not share a calculator with another test-taker, and it may be used only on the mathematics portion of the test.

ARITHMETIC/PRE-ALGEBRA

Real Numbers

The set of real numbers has several very important subsets:

$N = \{1, 2, 3, \ldots\}$ Natural (or counting) numbers.

$W = \{0, 1, 2, 3, \ldots\}$ Whole numbers.

$J = \{\ldots, -3, -2, -1, 0, 1, 2, 3, \ldots\}$ Integers.

$Q = \{x|x \text{ can be written in the form } \frac{p}{q}, p \text{ and } q \in J, q \neq 0\}$ Rational numbers.

$I = \{x|x \in R \text{ and } x \notin Q)$ Irrational numbers.

$R = Q \cup I$ Real numbers.

The set of rational numbers is the set of all numbers that can be written as fractions. The irrational numbers are the real numbers that cannot be written as fractions. The real numbers are all those, rational and irrational, that are found on a number line.

The following Venn diagram shows the relationships among the subsets of real numbers:

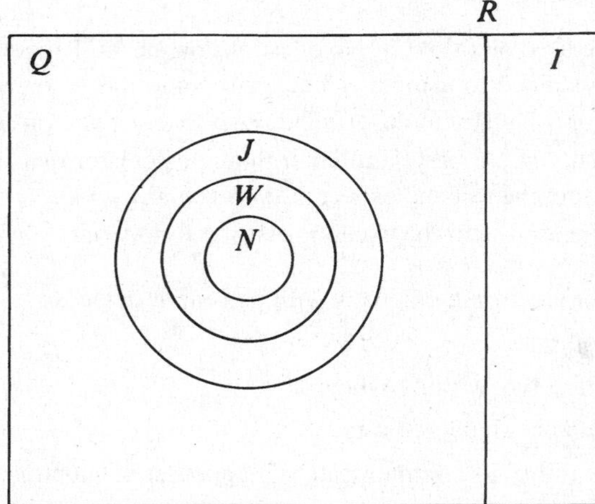

It is important to be able to categorize numbers according to the subsets above. All integers are rational numbers because any integer can easily be written as a fraction by placing the integer in the numerator and the number 1 in the denominator. $-3 = \frac{-3}{1}$

Real numbers that are written in decimal form fall into two basic types:

1. There are those that terminate. (One may think of this type as having an infinitely long string of zeros after the last nonzero digit.) All such decimals represent rational numbers. For example, 23.346 is twenty-three and three hundred forty-six thousandths. Therefore an appropriate fraction would be $23\frac{346}{1000}$ or $\frac{23346}{1000}$.

2. Some decimals do not terminate, and these fall into two types:

a. Some nonterminating decimals repeat. All repeating decimals represent rational numbers. For example:

- $\frac{1}{3} = 0.3333\ldots = 0.\overline{3}$
- $\frac{5}{6} = 0.83333\ldots = 0.8\overline{3}$
- $\frac{3}{11} = 0.27272727\ldots = 0.\overline{27}$

b. Other nonterminating decimals do not repeat. A number of this type cannot be written as a fraction and is therefore irrational. For example:

- $\sqrt{2} = 1.414213\ldots$
- $\sqrt[3]{7} = 1.912931\ldots$
- $\pi = 3.1415926\ldots$

Warm-Up Drill

1. Change $\frac{7}{8}$ to decimal form.
2. Change $\frac{8}{7}$ to decimal form.
3. Find a fraction equivalent to 3.8.
4. Find a fraction equivalent to $3.\overline{8}$.
5. Find a fraction equivalent to 0.21.
6. Find a fraction equivalent to $0.\overline{21}$.
7. Categorize each of the following numbers. Choose the appropriate letter(s) from the following list: *N, W, J, Q, I, R*.

   a. 0
   b. 2
   c. $\frac{5}{9}$
   d. -5
   e. $\sqrt{5}$
   f. $\sqrt{64}$
   g. $\sqrt{-9}$
   h. 3.1416
   i. $3.\overline{1416}$

SOLUTIONS

1. $\frac{7}{8} = 0.875$ This is merely a division problem; divide the denominator into the numerator. The zero to the left of the decimal point is optional.

2. $\frac{8}{7} = 1.\overline{142857}$

3. $3.8 = 3\frac{8}{10} = \frac{38}{10} = \frac{19}{5}$

4. $3.\overline{8} = 3\frac{8}{9} = \frac{35}{9}$

5. $0.21 = \frac{21}{100}$

6. $0.\overline{21} = \frac{21}{99} = \frac{7}{33}$ If the repeating block consists of one digit, place the repeating digit over 9; if the repeating block has two digits, place the repeating digits over 99; if the repeating block has three digits, place the repeating digits over 999, etc. If the repeating part does not begin immediately after the decimal point, first multiply by an appropriate power of 10 to place the decimal point immediately at the left of the repeating block. Follow the directions above, and then divide by the same power of 10.

For example:
$$2.3\overline{7} = \left(\frac{1}{10}\right)23.\overline{7}$$
$$= \frac{1}{10}(23.\overline{7})$$
$$= \frac{1}{10}\left(23\frac{7}{9}\right)$$
$$= \left(\frac{1}{10}\right)\frac{214}{9}$$
$$= \frac{214}{90} = \frac{107}{45}$$

7. a. W, J, Q, R
   b. N, W, J, Q, R
   c. Q, R
   d. J, Q, R
   e. I, R
   f. W, N, J, Q, R ($\sqrt{64} = 8$)
   g. $\sqrt{-9}$ is not a real number.
   h. Q, R (3.1416 is a rational approximation for π.)
   i. Q, R

Scientific Notation

Very large and very small numbers can be written conveniently using *scientific notation*. A number in scientific notation is written as a product of a number between 1 and 10 and an appropriate power of 10:

$$a(10^n) \text{ for } 1 \le a < 10 \text{ and } n \text{ an integer}$$

Example: The distance between the earth and the sun is about 94,000,000 miles. Express this number in scientific notation.

The number a between 1 and 10 is found by placing a decimal point after the first nonzero digit reading from left to right. So $a = 9.4$. The exponent is the number of places needed to move the decimal point from where it is placed back to where it was originally, in this case seven places to the right. Scientific notation is $9.4(10^7)$.

Example: One angstrom is 0.00000001 centimeter. Express this number in scientific notation.

The number between 1 and 10 is $a = 1$. The decimal point must be moved eight places to the left, so $n = -8$. Scientific notation is $1(10^{-8})$.

Example: Express $23.8(10^{-4})$ in scientific notation.

First express the number in standard form by moving the decimal point four places to the left: $23.8(10^{-4}) = 0.00238$.

For scientific notation, the number between 1 and 10 is $a = 2.38$, and the decimal point must be moved three places to the left. Scientific notation is $2.38(10^{-3})$.

Warm-Up Drill

Write in standard form.

1. Avogadro's number: $6.0225(10^{23})$
2. $2.04(10^{-6})$

Write in scientific notation.

3. 370,500
4. 5.83
5. $421(10^4)$

SOLUTIONS

1. 602,250,000,000,000,000,000,000
2. 0.00000204
3. $3.705(10^5)$
4. $5.83(10^0)$
5. $421(10^4) = 4210000 = 4.21(10^6)$

Three Meanings of the Symbol "–"

Many students have problems with this symbol: –. The reason these problems occur is that the symbol actually has three distinct meanings. A clear understanding of these three meanings can go a long way toward correcting errors made with signs.

1. When this symbol appears between two numbers, it always means "subtract." Thus 7 – 4 can be read either as "7 subtract 4" or "7 minus 4."
2. When the symbol appears to the left of a numeral, it is properly read as "negative." Thus, –8 is read as "negative 8." The word *negative* means that the number is located to the left of zero on the number line.

3. In any other position, however, the symbol "–" should be read as "opposite." In particular:

$-x$ means the opposite of x.
$-(-9)$ means the opposite of negative 9.
$-(a + b)$ means the opposite of the sum of a and b.
$-[-(-8)]$ means the opposite of the opposite of negative 8.
-5^2 means the opposite of 5 squared.

Operations with Signed Numbers

Absolute Value

The absolute value of any number is its distance from the origin on a number line. The symbol for this operation is $|x|$. An alternative (and more algebraic) definition of absolute value is

$$|x| = \begin{cases} x \text{ if } x \geq 0 \\ -x \text{ if } x < 0 \end{cases} \qquad \textit{opposite} \text{ of } x, \text{ not } \textit{negative}$$

Addition

TIP

Many students incorrectly say, "Subtract and take the sign of the larger number."

If the two numbers are either both positive or both negative, add the absolute values of the numbers and prefix the answer with the sign that is common to the original numbers.

$$(-2) + (-5) = -7 \qquad 5 + 3 = 8 \qquad -4 + (-6) = -10$$

If the two numbers have opposite signs, subtract the absolute values of the numbers (the smaller from the larger) and prefix the answer with the sign of the original number that has the larger absolute value.

$$-7 + 9 = 2 \qquad 4 + (-3) = 1 \qquad 5 + (-9) = -4$$

Subtraction

The definition of subtraction is

$$a - b = a + (-b)$$

This definition says, "a minus b equals a plus the opposite of b." In other words, to subtract, add the opposite of the number following the subtraction sign.

TIP

Change two things for each subtraction: the operation sign and the sign of the number following the subtraction sign.

- $2 - 5$
  $= 2 + (-5)$
  $= -3$
  Change the operation to addition and replace the number following the subtraction sign by its opposite. Follow the rules for addition.
- $5 - (-3)$
  $= 5 + 3$
  $= 8$
  Change to addition, replace second number by its opposite. Add.
- $-7 - 8$
  $= -7 + (-8)$
  $= -15$
  Change to addition, replace second number by its opposite. Add.
- $-2 - (-4)$
  $= -2 + 4$
  $= 2$

Multiplication

To multiply two numbers, multiply their absolute values and prefix the answer with a sign determined by the following rule:

If the two numbers have the same sign, the product is positive, +. The sign of a positive number is always optional. If the two numbers have opposite signs, the product is negative, –.

$$(-3)(4) = -12 \qquad (-5)(-4) = 20 \qquad 3(-7) = -21$$

TIP

If multiplying more than two numbers, multiply two at a time.

Division

The rule for division is similar to the rule for multiplication. Divide the absolute values of the numbers, and prefix the answer with a sign determined by the following rule:

If the two numbers have the same sign, choose +. If the two numbers have opposite signs, choose –.

Of course, division by zero is undefined.

$-15 \div 3 = -5$

$\frac{-28}{-7} = 4$

$\frac{0}{-8} = 0$

$\frac{-8}{0}$ is undefined.

$\frac{0}{0}$ is undefined.

Exponents

For whole numbers, n, and real numbers, x,:

$$x^n = x \cdot x \cdot x \cdot \ldots \cdot x \qquad (n \text{ factors of the base } x)$$

$$x^1 = x$$

$$x^0 = 1, x \neq 0$$

It is important to remember that any exponent always refers only to the symbol immediately to its left. Thus:

$5^3 = 5 \cdot 5 \cdot 5 = 25 \cdot 5 = 125$

$-2^4 = -(2 \cdot 2 \cdot 2 \cdot 2) = -16$ (-2^4 is read as "the opposite of 2 to the fourth power.")

$2(-3x)^2 = 2[(-3x)(-3x)] = 2(9x^2) = 18x^2$ (In this expression the symbol immediately to the left of the exponent is the parenthesis and parentheses come in pairs.)

Roots

The definition is

$$a \text{ is the } n\text{th root of } b \text{ if and only if } a^n = b$$

An immediate consequence of the definition is that there are no real, even roots of negative numbers because any real number raised to an even power is always positive. Also, any positive real number has two real square roots, one positive and the other negative.

The radical sign is used in the context of roots. However, in the case of *n*th roots when *n* is even, the symbol represents the *principal* *n*th root. The principal *n*th root is always the positive root. Thus:

$$\sqrt{9} = 3 \qquad \text{(and not } -3\text{)}$$

Odd roots, on the other hand, do not have this problem—the odd root of a positive number is positive, and the odd root of a negative number is negative.

Order of Operation Rules

So that everyone gets the same answer for an expression like

$$1 + 3 \cdot 4 \qquad \text{or} \qquad -2^2,$$

the order in which operations are to be performed must be defined.

ORDER OF OPERATION RULES

1. Perform all operations inside grouping symbols first. Grouping symbols include parentheses: ( ), brackets: [ ], braces: { }, and a bar: $\frac{2+3}{7}$ or $\sqrt{9+16}$.
2. Do all roots and exponents in order from left to right.
3. Do all multiplications and divisions in order from left to right. (This rule does NOT say, "Do all multiplications and then do all divisions.")
4. Do all additions and subtractions (and opposites) in order from left to right.

Warm-Up Drill

Perform the indicated operations.

1. $3 - 5 \cdot 7$
2. $-2(3 - 4)^3 - 2$
3. $5\{2[3(4 + 1) - 3] - 2\} - 7$
4. $\frac{3(-4)}{2} + (-2)^2(3) - (-3)(-3)^2 + \frac{-5}{-1}$
5. $\sqrt{(-3)^2 + 4^2}$
6. -5^2
7. $(-5)^2$
8. $\sqrt{49}$
9. $-\sqrt{64}$
10. $\sqrt{-100}$

SOLUTIONS

1. $\mathbf{3 - 5 \cdot 7} = 3 - 35 = 3 + (-35) = -32$

2. $\mathbf{-2(3-4)^3 - 2} = -2[3 + (-4)]^3 - 2$
$= -2(-1)^3 - 2$
$= -2(-1) - 2 = 2 - 2$
$= 2 + (-2) = 0$

3. $\mathbf{5\{2[3(4+1) - 3] - 2\} - 7}$
$= 5\{2[3(5) - 3] - 2\} - 7$
$= 5\{2[15 - 3] - 2\} - 7$
$= 5\{2[15 + (-3)] - 2\} - 7$
$= 5\{2[12] - 2\} - 7$
$= 5\{24 - 2\} - 7$
$= 5\{24 + (-2)\} - 7$
$= 5\{22\} - 7 = 110 - 7$
$= 110 + (-7) = 103$

(These steps show excruciating detail. Many steps may be omitted by experienced students.)

4. $\dfrac{3(-4)}{2} + (-2)^2(3) - (-3)(-3)^2 + \dfrac{-5}{-1}$

$= \dfrac{3(-4)}{2} + 4(3) - (-3)(9) + \dfrac{-5}{-1}$

$= \dfrac{-12}{2} + 12 - (-27) + 5$
$= -6 + 12 - (-27) + 5$
$= -6 + 12 + 27 + 5$
$= 6 + 27 + 5$
$= 33 + 5 = 38$

(All multiplications and divisions are done before any additions or subtractions).

5. $\mathbf{\sqrt{(-3)^2 + 4^2} = \sqrt{9 + 16}}$ (The bar is a grouping symbol.)

$= \sqrt{25} = 5$

6. -5^2 means "the opposite of five squared"

$-5^2 = -(5 \cdot 5) = -25$

7. $(-5)^2$ means "negative five, squared"

$(-5)^2 = (-5) \cdot (-5) = 25$

8. 7

9. -8 (the opposite of $\sqrt{64}$)

10. Undefined in real numbers.

Prime and Composite Numbers

A whole number is *prime* if and only if it has exactly two factors.
A whole number greater than 1 is *composite* if and only if it is not prime.
Both of these definitions involve whole numbers, so examine each whole number.

Number	Factors	Conclusion
0	0, 1, 2, . . .	Neither prime nor composite
1	1	Neither prime nor composite
2	1, 2	Prime
3	1, 3	Prime
4	1, 2, 4	Composite
5	1, 5	Prime
6	1, 2, 3	Composite
7	1, 7	Prime
8	1, 2, 4, 8	Composite

A prime number must be a whole number that has exactly two factors. There are an infinite number of primes, but it is very difficult to determine whether a very large number is prime.

It is a good idea to memorize the primes up to 20. They are 2, 3, 5, 7, 11, 13, 17, and 19.

Every whole number has 1 as a factor, and every whole number is a factor of itself; therefore each whole number greater than 1 has at least two factors. The task then is to determine whether there is another factor in addition to the number 1 and the number itself. If there is another factor, then the number is not prime; it is composite. Consider these examples:

- 51 has 1 and 51 as factors. Examining other whole numbers to determine divisibility, we find that 0 is not a factor, 2 is not, 3 is a factor; therefore 51 is composite.
- 61 has 1 and 61 as factors. Examining other whole numbers:

  0 is a factor of 0 only. (Don't bother with 0.)

  2 is not a factor; 2 divides even numbers only.

  3 is not.

  4 is not. If 4 were a factor, then 2 would also be a factor and 2 has already been tested. Don't bother with 4.

  5 is not.

  6 is not. If it were, then both 2 and 3 would also be factors. *Test the prime numbers only.*

  7 is not.

  11 is not.

  Must all the prime numbers up to 61 be tested? No, you must test only those up to the approximate square root of the number. The square root of the number is passed when the quotient is smaller than the divisor. If no other factor has been found, the number is prime. If another factor is found, the number is composite.

  Since $\frac{61}{11} = 5 +$, and 5 is smaller than 11; the conclusion is that 61 is prime.

Here's another example. To determine whether or not 97 is prime, only the primes up to 11 need to be tested as factors.

2 is not a factor.

3 is not.

5 is not.

7 is not.

11 is not, and the quotient is less than 11.

Therefore 97 is prime.

To categorize any number as prime or composite up to 200, only the primes up to 13 need to be tested.

Warm-Up Drill

Determine whether each of the following numbers is prime or composite:

1. 143 2. 151 3. –5 4. 79 5. 1 6. 89 7. 91

SOLUTIONS

1. Composite (The factors are 1, 11, 13, 143.)
2. Prime
3. Neither (According to the definitions, both prime and composite numbers are whole numbers.).
4. Prime
5. Neither
6. Prime
7. Composite

Prime Factorization

It is important to be able to express a whole number as a product of prime factors. For example, $12 = 2 \cdot 2 \cdot 3 = 2^2 \cdot 3$. There are two useful methods to accomplish this task.

Method 1: Factor tree. Find the prime factorization of 72. First name any two factors of 72 (not necessarily prime), say 8 and 9. Each of these numbers can be factored. Continue this until all factors are prime. It is convenient to arrange these numbers in a tree.

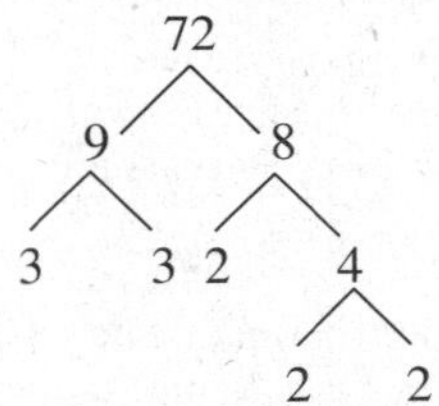

$$72 = 2 \cdot 2 \cdot 2 \cdot 3 \cdot 3$$

Method 2: Repeated division by primes. Determine the prime factorization of 120. First name any prime number that divides 120, and perform the division; then repeat the process with the quotient until the last quotient is also prime. The factorization consists of all the prime divisors and the last quotient.

TIP

Determining prime factors is easy to do with a calculator.

$$\begin{array}{r} 5 \\ 3\overline{)15} \\ 2\overline{)30} \\ 2\overline{)60} \\ 2\overline{)120} \end{array}$$

$$120 = 2 \cdot 2 \cdot 2 \cdot 3 \cdot 5$$

Therefore, the prime factorization is $120 = 2 \cdot 2 \cdot 2 \cdot 3 \cdot 5 = 2^3 \cdot 3 \cdot 5$.

Warm-Up Drill

Determine the prime factorization of each of the following numbers:

1. 50 2. 300 3. 73 4. 1617 5. 243

SOLUTIONS

1. $50 = 2 \cdot 5^2$
2. $300 = 2^2 \cdot 3 \cdot 5^2$
3. 73 is prime, so there is no prime factorization. In particular, the answer is not $1 \cdot 73$.
4. $1617 = 3 \cdot 7^2 \cdot 11$
5. $243 = 3^5$

Lowest Common Multiples and Greatest Common Factors

The list of factors of any whole number is always finite, and the list of multiples is infinite. For example, the factors of 12 are 1, 2, 3, 4, 6, and 12, whereas the multiples of 12 are 12, 24, 36, 48, . . .

Given any two natural numbers, it is frequently necessary to find the lowest (or least) common multiple (LCM).

Example 1: To find the LCM of 54 and 60, first find the prime factorizations:

$$54 = 2 \cdot 3^3 \qquad 60 = 2^2 \cdot 3 \cdot 5$$

Use each factor the greater number of times that it appears in either factorization. In other words, use the factor 2 twice, the factor 3 three times, and the factor 5 once. Therefore the LCM of 54 and 60 is $2^2 \cdot 3^3 \cdot 5 = 540$.

Find the LCM of 80 and 90.

$$80 = 2 \cdot 2 \cdot 2 \cdot 2 \cdot 5$$
$$90 = 2 \cdot 3 \cdot 3 \cdot 5$$

Use the factor 2 four times, 3 twice, and 5 once. The LCM is $2 \cdot 2 \cdot 2 \cdot 2 \cdot 3 \cdot 3 \cdot 5 = 720$.

Sometimes it is necessary to find the largest number that is in the list of factors of two numbers, that is, the greatest common factor (GCF) (also called greatest common divisor, GCD). This operation could also become difficult without the following process using factorization.

Example 2: To find the GCF of 96 and 108, first find the prime factorizations:

$$96 = 2^5 \cdot 3 \qquad 108 = 2^2 \cdot 3^3$$

Any factor that occurs in both lists is a common factor, so to find the GCF use each common factor the smaller number of times that it appears in either factorization. Thus the GCF of 96 and 108 is $2^2 \cdot 3 = 12$.

Find the GCF of 80 and 90. Use the same factorization from above.

$$80 = 2 \cdot 2 \cdot 2 \cdot 2 \cdot 5$$
$$90 = 2 \cdot 3 \cdot 3 \cdot 5$$

The only factors that appear in both lists are one factor of 2 and one factor of 5. The GCF is $2 \cdot 5 = 10$.

Warm-Up Drill

Find the lowest common multiple of each of the following groups of numbers:

1. 28 and 70
2. 72 and 150
3. 24, 48, and 60
   Find the greatest common factor of each of the following groups of numbers:
4. 70 and 120
5. 180 and 300
6. 24, 54, and 72
7. 108 and 245

SOLUTIONS

1. $28 = 2^2 \cdot 7$ and $70 = 2 \cdot 5 \cdot 7$
   Choose 2 twice, 5 once, and 7 once.
   The LMC is $2^2 \cdot 5 \cdot 7 = 140$.
2. $72 = 2^3 \cdot 3^2$ and $150 = 2 \cdot 3 \cdot 5^2$
   Choose 2 three times, 3 twice, and 5 twice.
   The LCM is $2^3 \cdot 3^2 \cdot 5^2 = 1800$.
3. $24 = 2^3 \cdot 3$, $48 = 2^4 \cdot 3$, and $60 = 2^2 \cdot 3 \cdot 5$
   The LCM is $2^4 \cdot 3 \cdot 5 = 240$.
4. $70 = 2 \cdot 5 \cdot 7$ and $120 = 2^3 \cdot 3 \cdot 5$
   Choose 2 once and 5 once.
   The GCF is $2 \cdot 5 = 10$.
5. $180 = 2^2 \cdot 3^2 \cdot 5$ and $300 = 2^2 \cdot 3 \cdot 5^2$
   Choose 2 twice, 3 once, and 5 once.
   The GCF is $2^2 \cdot 3 \cdot 5 = 60$.
6. 6
7. 1

Practice Exercises

The following sample questions represent ways in which the reviewed skills might be tested on the ACT.

1. Which of the following is not a rational number?

   A. 3.14
   B. $7.\overline{4}$
   C. 0
   D. $-\sqrt{4}$
   E. $\sqrt{5}$

2. $-2 - [-3^2 + (-1)^2] = ?$

   F. −12
   G. 6
   H. 16
   J. −18
   K. 8

3. Which of the following numbers is prime?

   A. 51
   B. 52
   C. 53
   D. 54
   E. 55

4. What is the greatest common factor (GCF) of 48 and 90?

   F. 6
   G. 8
   H. 9
   J. 480
   K. 720

5. What is the lowest common multiple (LCM) of 24 and 42?

   A. 6
   B. 24
   C. 42
   D. 168
   E. 1008

6. What is the product of GCF (20, 30) and LCM (20, 30)?

   F. 1
   G. 20
   H. 30
   J. 60
   K. 600

ANSWERS AND EXPLANATIONS

1. **(E)** Each of the other numbers can be written as a fraction.

$$3.14 = \frac{314}{100}$$

$$7.\overline{4} = 7\frac{4}{9} = \frac{67}{9}$$

$$0 = \frac{0}{1}$$

$$-\sqrt{4} = -2 = \frac{-2}{1}$$

There is no fraction equivalent to $\sqrt{5}$.

2. **(G)** $-2 - [-3^2 + (-1)^2]$
$= -2 - [-9 + 1]$
$= -2 - [-8]$
$= -2 + 8$
$= 6$

3. **(C)** Only 53 has exactly two factors, namely 1 and 53.
$51 = 1 \cdot 51 = 3 \cdot 17$
$52 = 1 \cdot 52 = 2 \cdot 26 = 4 \cdot 13$
$54 = 1 \cdot 54 = 2 \cdot 27 = 3 \cdot 18 = 6 \cdot 9$
$55 = 1 \cdot 55 = 5 \cdot 11$

4. **(F)** $48 = \underline{2} \cdot 2 \cdot 2 \cdot \underline{3}$
$90 = \underline{2} \cdot \underline{3} \cdot 3 \cdot 5$
Choose the prime factors in both lists.
$2 \cdot 3 = 6$ is the GCF.

5. **(D)** $24 = 2 \cdot 2 \cdot 2 \cdot 3$
$42 = 2 \cdot 3 \cdot 7$
Use each prime factor the greater number of times it appears in either list. $2 \cdot 2 \cdot 2 \cdot 3 \cdot 7 = 168$ is the LCM.

6. **(K)** GCF (20, 30) = 10
LCM (20, 30) = 60 and $10 \cdot 60 = 600$
The product of the LCM and GCF of any two numbers is equal to the product of the original numbers.

Fractions

A rational number can always be expressed as a fraction in which the numerator (the top number) is an integer and the denominator is a natural number. (Notice that zero is not a natural number.) If the absolute value of the numerator is greater than or equal to the denominator, the fraction is called *improper;* otherwise it is a *proper* fraction. Two fractions are *equivalent* if they represent the same number. An easy way to tell whether two fractions are equivalent is to cross-multiply. If the products are equal, then the fractions are equivalent and the rational numbers are equal:

$$\frac{a}{b} = \frac{c}{d} \quad \text{if and only if} \quad ad = bc, \quad b, d \neq 0$$

The Fundamental Principle of Fractions states that any fraction is equivalent to a fraction obtained by multiplying the numerator and denominator by the same nonzero number:

$$\frac{a}{b} = \frac{ak}{bk}, \quad b, k \neq 0$$

This property is used to reduce fractions to lowest terms:

$$\frac{12}{18} = \frac{2 \cdot 6}{3 \cdot 6} = \frac{2}{3}$$

$$\frac{90}{108} = \frac{45}{54}(k = 2) \qquad \text{(This reduction can be done in stages.)}$$

$$= \frac{5}{6}(k = 9)$$

This same property is used to rewrite a fraction so that it has a specific denominator:

$$\frac{5}{9} = \frac{?}{63} = \frac{35}{63}(k = 7)$$

$$\frac{5}{8} = \frac{?}{120} = \frac{75}{120}(k = 15)$$

Warm-Up Drill

Reduce each fraction to lowest terms.

1. $\frac{20}{50}$

2. $\frac{18}{30}$

3. $\frac{60}{84}$

4. $\frac{108}{162}$

Rewrite each fraction so that it has the specified denominator.

5. $\frac{4}{5}=\frac{?}{70}$ 6. $\frac{5}{8}=\frac{?}{96}$ 7. $\frac{7}{12}=\frac{?}{180}$

SOLUTIONS

1. $\frac{2}{5}(k=10)$
2. $\frac{3}{5}(k=6)$
3. $\frac{5}{7}(k=12)$
4. $\frac{2}{3}(k=54)$
5. $\frac{56}{70}(k=14)$
6. $\frac{60}{96}(k=12)$
7. $\frac{105}{180}(k=15)$

Proper and Improper Fractions and Mixed Numbers

An improper fraction can be changed to a mixed number or a whole number. A mixed number is a special form that represents the sum of a whole number and a proper fraction:

$$\frac{7}{5}=1+\frac{2}{5}=1\frac{2}{5}$$

To determine the mixed number that is equivalent to an improper fraction, divide the denominator into the numerator. The quotient becomes the whole number part of the mixed number, and the remainder becomes the numerator of the fraction part of the mixed number.

Warm-Up Drill

Change each improper fraction to a corresponding mixed number.

1. $\frac{23}{5}$ 2. $\frac{87}{13}$ 3. $\frac{105}{7}$ 4. $\frac{72}{16}$

Change each mixed number to a corresponding improper fraction.

5. $7\frac{3}{4}$ 6. $12\frac{3}{7}$ 7. $5\frac{11}{12}$

SOLUTIONS

1. $4\frac{3}{5}$
2. $6\frac{9}{13}$
3. 15 (not a mixed number)
4. $4\frac{1}{2}$ (Be sure to reduce the fraction to lowest terms.)
5. $7\frac{3}{4}=\frac{31}{4}$ (The numerator is 7(4) + 3 = 31.)
6. $\frac{87}{7}$
7. $\frac{71}{12}$

Operations with Fractions

Addition and Subtraction

The rules for addition and subtraction of fractions are as follows:

$$\frac{a}{b}+\frac{c}{b}=\frac{a+c}{b} \quad \text{and} \quad \frac{a}{b}-\frac{c}{b}=\frac{a-c}{b}, \qquad b\neq 0$$

TIP 

One of the more complicated operations in arithmetic is adding and subtracting fractions and mixed numbers.

To add or subtract fractions with the same denominator, add or subtract the numerators and keep the same denominator. These rules are very easy to apply; however, difficulty with these operations comes in four areas:

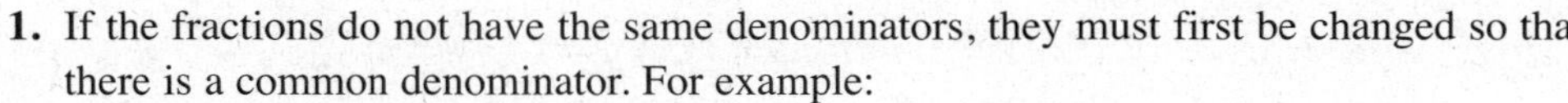

1. If the fractions do not have the same denominators, they must first be changed so that there is a common denominator. For example:

   - $\frac{3}{4}+\frac{1}{8}=\frac{6}{8}+\frac{1}{8}=\frac{7}{8}$ The lowest common denominator (LCD) is the lowest common multiple of the denominators.
   - $\frac{5}{12}+\frac{7}{16}=\frac{20}{48}+\frac{21}{48}=\frac{41}{48}$ The LCM of 12 and 16 is 48.

2. If the numbers to be added or subtracted are given as mixed numbers, there are two methods of performing the operations. For example:

   - $3\frac{2}{3}+5\frac{1}{2}=3\frac{4}{6}+5\frac{3}{6}$ Add the fraction parts and whole number parts separately.

     $=8\frac{7}{6}$ Since the fraction part is an improper fraction, the answer must be expressed in simplest form.

     $=8+1\frac{1}{6}=9\frac{1}{6}$

   OR

   - $3\frac{2}{3}+5\frac{1}{2}=\frac{11}{3}+\frac{11}{2}$ Write each mixed number as an improper fraction and then add according to the rule.

     $=\frac{22}{6}+\frac{33}{6}$

     $=\frac{55}{6}=9\frac{1}{6}$ Change the answer back to a mixed number:

TIP

On the ACT, rational answers are expressed in simplest form.

3. The answers must normally be expressed in simplest form.

   $\frac{1}{5}+\frac{1}{2}=\frac{1}{6}+\frac{3}{6}=\frac{4}{6}=\frac{2}{3}$ The answer has been reduced.

4. In subtraction of mixed numbers, borrowing or regrouping must be done carefully.

   $5\frac{2}{3}-1\frac{3}{4}=5\frac{8}{12}-1\frac{9}{12}$ Borrow 1 from the 5 and add it to the fraction part of the mixed number

   $=4\frac{20}{12}-1\frac{9}{12}$ $\left(1+\frac{8}{12}=\frac{20}{12}\right)$.

   $=3\frac{11}{12}$

Some calculators will perform operations with fractions.

Warm-Up Drill

Add or subtract as indicated, and express the answer in simplest form.

1. $\frac{4}{9}+\frac{2}{9}$
2. $\frac{5}{7}+\frac{2}{21}$
3. $\frac{3}{7}-\frac{1}{9}$
4. $\frac{7}{20}+\frac{3}{16}$
5. $4\frac{1}{2}-2\frac{1}{3}$
6. $8-5\frac{5}{8}$
7. $3\frac{2}{5}-1\frac{3}{4}$
8. $6\frac{7}{8}+2\frac{2}{3}$
9. $\left(-2\frac{3}{5}\right)+1\frac{1}{2}$
10. $\left(-17\frac{8}{9}\right)-5\frac{11}{12}$

SOLUTIONS

1. $\mathbf{\frac{4}{9}+\frac{2}{9}}=\frac{6}{9}=\frac{2}{3}$

2. $\mathbf{\frac{5}{7}+\frac{2}{21}}=\frac{15}{21}+\frac{2}{21}=\frac{17}{21}$

3. $\mathbf{\frac{3}{7}-\frac{1}{9}}=\frac{27}{63}-\frac{7}{63}=\frac{20}{63}$

4. $\mathbf{\frac{7}{20}+\frac{3}{16}}=\frac{28}{80}+\frac{15}{80}$ LCM of 20 and 16 is 80.

   $=\frac{43}{80}$

5. $\mathbf{4\frac{1}{2}-2\frac{1}{3}}=4\frac{3}{6}-2\frac{2}{6}=2\frac{1}{6}$

6. $\mathbf{8-5\frac{5}{8}}=7\frac{8}{8}-5\frac{5}{8}$ Borrow 1 from 8.

   $=2\frac{3}{8}$

7. $\mathbf{3\frac{2}{5}-1\frac{3}{4}}=3\frac{8}{20}-1\frac{15}{20}$ Borrow 1 from 3 and add to the fraction part.

   $=2\frac{28}{20}-1\frac{15}{20}$

   $=1\frac{13}{20}$

8. $\mathbf{6\frac{7}{8}+2\frac{2}{3}}=6\frac{21}{24}+2\frac{16}{24}$

$=8\frac{37}{24}=8+1\frac{13}{24}$

$=9\frac{13}{24}$

9. $\mathbf{\left(-2\frac{3}{5}\right)+1\frac{1}{2}}$

$=\left(-2\frac{6}{10}\right)+1\frac{5}{10}$

$=-1\frac{1}{10}$

TIP

All rules of signs that apply to positive and negative integers apply also to fractions.

10. $\mathbf{\left(-17\frac{8}{9}\right)-5\frac{11}{12}}=\left(-17\frac{8}{9}\right)+\left(-5\frac{11}{12}\right)$

$=\left(-17\frac{64}{72}\right)+\left(-5\frac{66}{72}\right)$

$=-22\frac{130}{72}$

$=-\left(22+1\frac{58}{72}\right)=-23\frac{29}{36}$

Multiplication

The rule for multiplication of fractions is as follows:

$$\frac{a}{b}\cdot\frac{c}{d}=\frac{ac}{bd}, \qquad b,\ d\neq 0$$

To multiply any two fractions, multiply the numerators and denominators separately.

Division

The rule for division is as follows:

$$\frac{a}{b}\div\frac{c}{d}=\frac{a}{b}\cdot\frac{d}{c}, \qquad b,\ c,\ d\neq 0$$

This rule states that, to divide fractions, one must replace the divisor with its reciprocal and change the operation to multiplication. Here are some examples:

- $\frac{2}{3}\cdot\frac{5}{7}=\frac{10}{21}$
- $\frac{3}{4}\cdot\frac{8}{9}=\frac{24}{36}=\frac{2}{3}$ All answers must be reduced.
- $\frac{5}{12}\cdot\frac{8}{9}=\frac{5}{\cancel{12}_{3}}\cdot\frac{\cancel{8}^{2}}{9}=\frac{5}{3}\cdot\frac{2}{9}=\frac{10}{27}$

TIP

The common factors in the numerators and denominators are normally divided out before actually multiplying. This is called *canceling*.

- $2\frac{1}{2}\cdot 3\frac{5}{6}=\frac{5}{2}\cdot\frac{23}{6}$
  $=\frac{115}{12}=9\frac{7}{12}$

  Mixed numbers must be changed to improper fractions before multiplying.

- $\left(-3\frac{4}{5}\right)\cdot\left(-6\frac{1}{3}\right)=\left(\frac{-19}{5}\right)\cdot\left(\frac{-19}{3}\right)$
  $=\frac{361}{15}=24\frac{1}{15}$

  The same rules of signs apply.

- $\frac{2}{5}\div\frac{3}{8}=\frac{2}{5}\cdot\frac{8}{3}$
  $=\frac{16}{15}=1\frac{1}{15}$

  The reciprocal of $\frac{3}{8}$ is $\frac{8}{3}$.

- $7\frac{1}{4}\div\left(-2\frac{3}{5}\right)=\frac{29}{4}\div\left(\frac{-13}{5}\right)$

  Change to improper fractions.

  $=\frac{29}{4}\cdot\left(\frac{-5}{13}\right)$

  Replace divisor by reciprocal, and change operation to multiplication.

  $=\frac{-145}{52}=-2\frac{41}{52}$

Exponents with Fractions

It is important to recall that an exponent always applies only to the immediately preceding symbol. Thus, to raise any fraction to a power, parentheses are necessary. For example:

$$\left(\frac{2}{3}\right)^2=\frac{4}{9} \qquad \frac{2^2}{3}\neq\frac{4}{9}$$

Complex Fractions

If the numerator or the denominator, or both, themselves contain fractions, the expression is called a *complex fraction*. There are two methods to simplify complex fractions:

1. Treat the complex fraction as a division-of-fractions problem. For example:

$$\frac{\frac{2}{3}+\frac{3}{4}}{2-\frac{5}{6}}=\frac{\frac{8}{12}+\frac{9}{12}}{\frac{12}{6}-\frac{5}{6}}=\frac{\frac{17}{12}}{\frac{7}{6}}$$

$$=\frac{17}{12}\cdot\frac{6}{7}=\frac{17}{\underset{2}{\cancel{12}}}\cdot\frac{\overset{1}{\cancel{6}}}{7}$$

(Cancel the 6.)

$$=\frac{17}{14}=1\frac{3}{14}$$

2. Multiply the numerator and denominator by the lowest common denominator of the fractions within both numerator and denominator. For example:

$$\frac{\frac{5}{6}+\frac{1}{2}}{\frac{7}{8}-\frac{3}{4}}=\frac{24\left(\frac{5}{6}+\frac{1}{2}\right)}{24\left(\frac{7}{8}-\frac{3}{4}\right)}$$

$$=\frac{20+12}{21-18}=\frac{32}{3}=10\frac{2}{3}$$

This is usually the more efficient method.

Warm-Up Drill

Find the reciprocal of each of the following rational numbers:

1. $7\frac{3}{5}$ 2. $\frac{-2}{5}$ 3. $\frac{1}{8}$ 4. 6 5. 0

Perform the indicated operations, and express the answers in simplest form.

6. $-2\frac{4}{9}\cdot 4\frac{1}{2}$

7. $3\frac{1}{3}\div 1\frac{3}{7}$

8. $\frac{3}{7}\div\frac{3}{14}$

9. $\dfrac{\frac{1}{4}+\frac{1}{2}}{\frac{1}{3}+\frac{1}{4}}$

10. $\dfrac{3-\frac{3}{4}}{-4+\frac{1}{2}}$

SOLUTIONS

1. $7\frac{3}{5}=\frac{38}{5}$ so the reciprocal is $\frac{5}{38}$.

2. $\frac{-5}{2}=-2\frac{1}{2}$

3. $\frac{8}{1}=8$

4. $\frac{1}{6}$

5. Zero is the only real number that has no reciprocal. This is part of the reason that 0 may not be chosen as the divisor.

6. $-2\frac{4}{9}\cdot 4\frac{1}{2}=\frac{-22}{9}\cdot\frac{9}{2}$ Cancel both 2 and 9.

$$=\frac{\overset{-11}{\cancel{-22}}}{\underset{1}{\cancel{9}}}\cdot\frac{\overset{1}{\cancel{9}}}{\underset{1}{\cancel{2}}}=-11$$

7. $3\frac{1}{3}\div 1\frac{3}{7}=\frac{10}{3}\div\frac{10}{7}$ Change to improper fractions.

$=\frac{10}{3}\cdot\frac{7}{10}$ Replace divisor.

$=\frac{\overset{1}{\cancel{10}}}{3}\cdot\frac{7}{\underset{1}{\cancel{10}}}$ Cancel.

$$=\frac{7}{3}=2\frac{1}{3}$$

8. $\frac{3}{7}\div\frac{3}{14}=\frac{3}{7}\cdot\frac{14}{3}$

$=\frac{\overset{1}{\cancel{3}}}{\underset{1}{\cancel{7}}}\cdot\frac{\overset{2}{\cancel{14}}}{\underset{1}{\cancel{3}}}=2$ Cancel.

9. $$\frac{\frac{1}{4}+\frac{1}{2}}{\frac{1}{3}+\frac{1}{4}}$$

$=\frac{12\left(\frac{1}{4}+\frac{1}{2}\right)}{12\left(\frac{1}{3}+\frac{1}{4}\right)}$ (LCD is 12.)

$$=\frac{3+6}{4+3}=\frac{9}{7}=1\frac{2}{7}$$

10. $$\frac{3-\frac{3}{4}}{-4+\frac{1}{2}}$$

$=\frac{4\left(3-\frac{3}{4}\right)}{4\left(-4+\frac{1}{2}\right)}$ (LCD is 4.)

$$=\frac{12-3}{-16+2}$$

$$=\frac{9}{-14}=\frac{-9}{14}$$

Practice Exercises

The following sample questions represent ways in which the reviewed skills might be tested on the ACT.

1. $3\frac{1}{2}+7\frac{3}{4}=?$

   A. $10\frac{5}{4}$

   B. $11\frac{1}{4}$

   C. $10\frac{2}{3}$

   D. 11

   E. None of these.

2. $5-3\frac{3}{5}=?$

   F. $2\frac{3}{5}$

   G. $2\frac{2}{5}$

   H. $1\frac{2}{5}$

   J. $1\frac{3}{5}$

   K. None of these.

3. $1\frac{2}{3}\cdot 2\frac{1}{4}=?$

   A. $2\frac{1}{6}$

   B. $\frac{20}{27}$

   C. $1\frac{1}{6}$

   D. $3\frac{3}{4}$

   E. None of these.

4. $7\frac{1}{2}\div 5=?$

   F. $35\frac{1}{2}$

   G. $37\frac{1}{2}$

   H. $1\frac{1}{2}$

   J. $\frac{2}{3}$

   K. None of these.

5. $\dfrac{3-\frac{1}{2}}{\frac{2}{3}+\frac{3}{4}}=?$

   A. $1\frac{13}{17}$

   B. $\frac{17}{30}$

   C. $\frac{-3}{17}$

   D. $3\frac{1}{2}$

   E. None of these.

ANSWERS AND EXPLANATIONS

1. **(B)**

$3\frac{1}{2}+7\frac{3}{4}$

$=3\frac{2}{4}+7\frac{3}{4}$ — Rewrite with common denominators.

$=10\frac{5}{4}=10+1+\frac{1}{4}=11\frac{1}{4}$ — Add whole numbers and fractions.

Simplify.

2. **(H)** $5-3\frac{3}{5}$ Borrow (regroup) 1 $\left(\frac{5}{5}\right)$ from the 5.

$=4\frac{5}{5}-3\frac{3}{5}$ Subtract whole numbers and fractions separately.

$=1\frac{2}{5}$

3. **(D)** $1\frac{2}{3}\cdot 2\frac{1}{4}$ Rewrite as improper fractions.

$=\frac{5}{3}\cdot\frac{9}{4}$

$=\frac{5}{\cancel{3}_1}\cdot\frac{\cancel{9}^3}{4}$ Cancel common factors.

$=\frac{15}{4}=3\frac{3}{4}$

4. **(H)** $7\frac{1}{2}\div 5$ Rewrite as improper fractions.

$=\frac{15}{2}\div\frac{5}{1}$ Invert and multiply.

$=\frac{15}{2}\cdot\frac{1}{5}$ Cancel.

$=\frac{\cancel{15}^3}{2}\cdot\frac{1}{\cancel{5}_1}=\frac{3}{2}=1\frac{1}{2}$ Multiply and simplify.

5. **(A)** $\dfrac{3-\frac{1}{2}}{\frac{2}{3}+\frac{3}{4}}$ The LCM of the denominators is 12.

$=\dfrac{12\left(3-\frac{1}{2}\right)}{12\left(\frac{2}{3}+\frac{3}{4}\right)}$ Multiply top and bottom by the LCM.

$=\frac{36-6}{8+9}=\frac{30}{17}=1\frac{13}{17}$

Percents

The word *percent* literally means hundredths, so 25% means $\frac{25}{100}$, which reduces to $\frac{1}{4}$. Since "hundredths" could also be interpreted as divided by 100, and dividing by 100 can most efficiently be accomplished by moving the decimal point two places to the left, 25% is also 0.25.

RULES WORTH MEMORIZING

1. To change a percent to a fraction, omit the percent sign, divide by 100, and reduce the fraction.
2. To change a percent to a decimal, omit the percent sign and move the decimal point two places to the left.

To change either a fraction or a decimal to a percent, the rules above are reversed:

1. To change a fraction to a percent, (do the division to get a decimal) multiply by 100 and attach a percent sign.
2. To change a decimal to a percent, move the decimal point two places to the right and attach a percent sign.

Examples:
Change each percent to both a fraction and a decimal.

1. 78% Fraction: $\frac{78}{100}=\frac{39}{50}$ Decimal: 0.78

2. 8% Fraction $\frac{8}{100}=\frac{2}{25}$ Decimal: 0.08

3. 2.5% Fraction: $\frac{2.5}{100}=\frac{25}{1000}$ (Multiply numerator and denominator by 10.)

$=\frac{1}{40}$

Decimal: 0.025

4. $3\frac{1}{3}\%$ Fraction: $\left(3\frac{1}{3}\right)\div 100=\frac{10}{3}\div 100=\frac{10}{3}\cdot\frac{1}{100}=\frac{1}{3}\cdot\frac{1}{10}=\frac{1}{30}$

Decimal: $3\frac{1}{3}\%=3.333\ldots\%=0.0\overline{3}$

5. $86\frac{2}{3}\%$ Fraction: $\left(86\frac{2}{3}\right)\div 100=\frac{260}{3}\div 100=\frac{260}{3}\cdot\frac{1}{100}=\frac{13}{3}\cdot\frac{1}{5}=\frac{13}{15}$

Decimal: $86\frac{2}{3}\%=86.666\ldots\%=0.8\overline{6}$

Change each number to a percent.

6. $\frac{4}{5}$ $\frac{4}{5}(100)\%=\frac{400}{5}\%=80\%$

7. 7 7(100)% = 700%

8. $\frac{3}{8}$ $\frac{3}{8}(100)\%=\frac{3}{8}\left(\frac{100}{1}\right)\%$

$=\frac{3}{2}\left(\frac{25}{1}\right)\%=\frac{75}{2}\%=37\frac{1}{2}\%$ or 37.5%

9. 0.34 0.34 = 0.34(100)% = 34%

10. 0.005 0.005 = 0.005(100)% = 0.5%

Warm-Up Drill

Change each percent to both a fraction and a decimal.

1. 53% 2. 129% 3. $12\frac{1}{2}\%$ 4. 0.1% 5. 200%

Change each number to a percent.

6. 0.8 7. $\frac{5}{8}$ 8. $\frac{3}{5}$ 9. 0.003 10. $\frac{3}{11}$

SOLUTIONS

1. Fraction: $\frac{53}{100}$

   Decimal: 0.53

2. Fraction: $\frac{129}{100} = 1\frac{29}{100}$

   Decimal: 1.29

3. Fraction: $12\frac{1}{2} \div 100 = \frac{25}{2} \cdot \frac{1}{100}$
   $= \frac{1}{2} \cdot \frac{1}{4} = \frac{1}{8}$

   Decimal: $0.12\frac{1}{2} = 0.125$

4. Fraction: $\frac{0.1}{100} = \frac{1}{1000}$

   Decimal: 0.001

5. Fraction: $\frac{200}{100} = 2$

   Decimal: 2

6. $0.8 = 0.8(100)\% = 80\%$

7. $\frac{5}{8} = \frac{5}{8}(100\%) = \frac{500}{8}\% = 62\frac{1}{2}\%$ *or* 62.5%

8. $\frac{3}{5} = \frac{3}{5}(100)\% = \frac{300}{5}\% = 60\%$

9. $0.003 = 0.003(100)\% = 0.3\%$

10. $\frac{3}{11} = \frac{3}{11}(100)\% = \frac{300}{11}\% = 27.\overline{27}\% = 27\frac{3}{11}\%$

Applications of Percent

Most percent applications are variations of this sentence:

A is P percent of B.

In this sentence, A is the amount (or percentage), P is the percent (or rate), and B is the base. The key to solving a percent problem is to translate the problem into the form of the sentence above. Consider the following example:

The enrollment in an algebra class dropped from 30 students to 27. What percent of the class dropped out?

In this problem we are asked to find the percent, P.

The base is always the quantity before any change, 30.

The number of students that dropped out is the amount (or percentage), 3. So the sentence is

3 is P percent of 30.

Once the problem has been written in the proper form, there are two methods of solving the problem:

1. An equation may be written:

$$A = (P\%)B$$

Of course a percent sign is not written in the equation, so the percent must first be changed to either a fraction or a decimal.

If the unknown in the equation is A, multiply $(P\%)$ times B.

If the unknown is either $(P\%)$ or B, divide A by the other quantity.

2. A proportion may be written.

$$\frac{P}{100} = \frac{A}{B}$$

To solve any proportion, $\frac{x}{y} = \frac{z}{w}$, first cross-multiply, and then divide by the coefficient of the unknown.

In the problem above, $\frac{P}{100} = \frac{3}{30}$, $\begin{aligned} 30P &= 300 \\ P &= 10 \end{aligned}$ 10% of the students dropped.

Examples:

1. What is 22% of 1086?

A is unknown, $P = 22\%$, and $B = 1086$. Substituting into the percent equation gives

$$A = (0.22)(1086) = \underline{238.92}$$

2. Find 12% of 350.

A is unknown, $P = 12\%$, and $B = 350$. Substituting into the percent proportion gives

$$\frac{12}{100} = \frac{A}{350}$$

$$100A = 4200 \quad \text{Cross-multiply.}$$

$$A = \underline{42} \quad \text{Divide by 100.}$$

3. 4 is what percent of 80?

$A = 4$, P is unknown, and $B = 80$.

$$4 = P(80)$$

$$P = 4 \div 80 = 0.05 = \underline{5\%}$$

4. What percent of 75 is 90?
$A = 90$, P is unknown, and $B = 75$.

$$\frac{P}{100} = \frac{90}{75}$$
$$75P = 9000$$
$$P = 120$$

The answer is <u>120%</u>.

5. 35.1 is 78% of what number?
$A = 35.1$, $P = 78\%$, and B is unknown.

$$35.1 = (0.78)B \qquad \text{Divide by } 0.78.$$
$$B = \underline{45}$$

6. A student got a grade of 85% on a test in which she answered 3 questions incorrectly. How many questions were on the test?

The 3 wrong answers represent 15% (100%–85%) of the questions on the test. Therefore we have this question: 3 is 15% of what number?

$A = 3$, $P = 15\%$, and B is unknown.

$$3 = (0.15)B \qquad \text{Divide by } 0.15.$$
$$B = 20$$

There were <u>20</u> questions on the test.

7. A house worth $120,000 is in an area where real estate is increasing in value at the rate of 8% per year. How much will the house be worth in 1 year?

The amount that the house will increase in value in 1 year is 8% of the original value of the house. Hence the amount of increase is 8% of $120,000.

A is unknown, $P = 8\%$, and $B = 120{,}000$.

$$A = (0.08)(120{,}000) = 9600$$

The value of the house in 1 year will be $120,000 + 9600 = <u>$129,600</u>.

This problem could also be done by the following method:
The value in 1 year will be 108% of the present value. Hence the new value is 108% of $120,000.

$$A = 1.08(120{,}000) = 129{,}600$$

When approached in this manner, the problem is called a *percent-increase* type. If an amount decreases over time, the problem can be approached similarly, but it is then called a *percent-decrease* type. For example:

On a diet James's weight decreased 10%. If he now weighs 126 pounds, what was his original weight?

James's new weight is 90% (100% – 10%) of his original weight. Therefore 126 is 90% of the original weight.

$A = 126$, $P = 90\%$, and B is unknown.

$$\frac{90}{100} = \frac{126}{B}$$
$$90B = 12600$$
$$B = 140$$

James originally weighed <u>140 pounds</u>.

Warm-Up Drill

Solve the following proportions:

1. $\frac{x}{4} = \frac{8}{15}$

2. $\frac{5}{9} = \frac{t}{12}$

3. $\frac{7.2}{12} = \frac{5.4}{z}$

Write both the percent equation and the percent proportion for each sentence. Then answer the question.

4. What number is 30% of 58?
5. 24 is what percent of 33?
6. 1.8 is 80% of what number?

Solve the following percent problems:

7. How much interest is earned in 1 year on an investment of $25,000 at 12% annual interest?
8. Last month Dale's paycheck was $840.00. If she is to receive a raise of 5% on this month's check, what should be the amount of this month's check?
9. In the fall semester Alice enrolled in 20 units. If she wants to decrease her load 15% in the spring semester, how many units should she take?
10. Jon paid $24.00 for a sweater that was advertised on sale at 10% off. What was the original price of the sweater?

SOLUTIONS

1. $\mathbf{\frac{x}{4} = \frac{8}{15}}$

   $15x = 32$

   $x = 2\frac{2}{15}$

2. $\mathbf{\frac{5}{9} = \frac{t}{12}}$

   $9t = 60$

   $t = 6\frac{2}{3}$

3. $\mathbf{\frac{7.2}{12} = \frac{5.4}{z}}$

   $7.2z = 64.8$

   $z = 9$

4. Equation: $A = 0.3(58)$

   Proportion: $\frac{30}{100} = \frac{A}{58}$: $A = 17.4$

5. Equation: $24 = P(33)$

   Proportion: $\frac{P}{100} = \frac{24}{33}$: 24 is $72\frac{8}{11}$% of 33.

6. Equation: $1.8 = 0.8B$

   Proportion: $\frac{80}{100} = \frac{1.8}{B}$: $B = 2.25$

7. Interest is 12% of \$25,000.
   A is unknown, $P = 12\%$, and $B = 25{,}000$
   $A = 0.12(25{,}000) = 3000$
   The interest is \$3000.

8. This is a percent-increase type of problem.
   Dale's new salary is 105% (100% + 5%) of her old salary.
   The new salary is 105% of \$840.
   A is unknown, $P = 105\%$, $B = 840$.
   $A = 1.05(840) = 882$
   Dale's new salary is \$882.

9. This is a percent-decrease type of problem.
   The spring semester load is 85% of the fall semester load.
   The spring load is 85% of 20.
   A is unknown, $P = 85\%$, and $B = 20$.
   $A = 0.85(20) = 17$
   The spring load is 17 units.

10. The sale price is 90% of the original price.
    $A = 24$, $P = 90\%$, B is unknown.
    $24 = 0.9B$

    $B = 26.66\frac{2}{3}$

    The original price was \$26.67.

Statistics

Scientists frequently need to interpret data that arise from an experiment. The data are usually obtained in random fashion and are presented in a large array of numbers. One of the purposes of statistics is to "make sense" of such an array. There are three basic characteristics of data that are most helpful:

1. Where is the middle? The middle is a measure of central tendency, also called the average.
2. How are the data spread out? The spread is represented by a measure of dispersion.
3. What do the data look like graphically?
   In the following discussion, examples will be based on this sample of data:

   $$4, 7, 2, 8, 7, 4, 8, 10, 1, 4$$

   For many applications of statistics, it is helpful to have the data ranked from the smallest to largest:

   $$1, 2, 4, 4, 4, 7, 7, 8, 8, 10$$

Averages

The statistic that most people refer to as the average is the *mean*. The mean is found by dividing the sum of the data by the number of items in the data set. For example, the mean of the sample data given above is

$$\frac{1+2+4+4+4+7+7+8+8+10}{10}=\frac{55}{10}=5.5$$

Most scientific calculators have an automatic mean function, usually designated by the symbol $\bar{x}$.

The item of data that occurs most frequently is called the *mode*. In our sample data, the number 4 occurs three times, more than any other item, so 4 is the mode. If no one item of data occurs more than any other, the set of data has no mode. If two items of data occur with equal frequency, greater than any other, the data set is said to be bimodal.

The number that lies exactly in the middle of the ranked data is called the *median*. If the data set contains an odd number of items, the median is the middle number at the $\frac{n+1}{2}$ position, where n is the number of items of data. If the data set has an even number of items, the median is the mean of the two data items in the middle. Since our sample data has ten items and the two items in the middle are 4 and 7, the median is $\frac{4+7}{2}=5.5$

Range

The difference between the largest item of data and the smallest is called the *range*. In our sample data 10 is the largest item and 1 is the smallest, so the range is 10 – 1 = 9.

Graphic Displays of Data

Information about a collection of data can be gained easily from a graphical display. Graphs of data can take many forms. Bar charts, histograms, pie charts, and broken-line graphs are a few of the types of graphs commonly used in statistics.

The data in our sample may be displayed in this frequency distribution and in the accompanying bar chart.

Data Item	Frequency
1	1
2	1
4	3
7	2
8	2
10	1

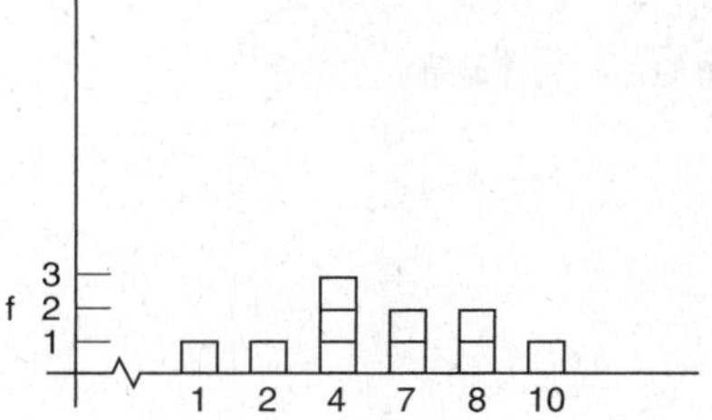

Warm-Up Drill

Given this set of data: 6, 5, 4, 6, 1, 6, 6, 1, 5

1. Find the mean.
2. Find the median.
3. Find the mode.
4. Find the range.

Given the following frequency distribution:

Data Item	Frequency
5	2
6	5
7	8
8	3
9	1
10	1

5. Find the mode.
6. How many items of data are in this data set?
7. Find the mean.
8. Find the median.
9. Find the range.

SOLUTIONS

First, rank the data: 1, 1, 4, 5, 5, 6, 6, 6, 6.

1. Add the data and divide by 9: $\frac{40}{9} = 4\frac{4}{9}$.
2. Since there is an odd number of items of data, the middle number is the median. The fifth number from either end is 5.
3. The most frequently occurring item of data is 6.
4. The range is $6 - 1 = 5$.
5. The most frequently occurring item of data is 7; it occurs eight times.
6. The number of items of data is the sum of the frequencies: 20.
7. Since 5 occurs twice, 6 occurs five times, etc., it is easy to find the sum of the products of the classes and their frequencies and then divide by 20:

Class	Frequency	Product
5	2	10
6	5	30
7	8	56
8	3	24
9	1	9
10	1	10
	Sum of products =	139

The mean is $\frac{139}{20} = 6.95$.

8. The median is the mean of the tenth and eleventh items of data, counting from either direction. Since both of these numbers are in the 7 class, the median is 7.

9. The range is 10 – 5 = 5.

Probability

Probability is a number assigned to the likelihood of the occurrence of an event. The probability of an event that is sure to happen is 1, and the probability of an event that is sure not to happen is 0. All other probabilities are numbers between 0 and 1. The probability of event A is denoted by $P(A)$.

An experiment is any procedure that has a random output, i.e., the results of the experiment occur randomly. The *sample space* of an experiment is the set of all possible outcomes. For example:

> The sample space for the experiment of tossing two coins and noting heads (H) or tails (T) of each coin is:
>
> {HH, HT, TH, TT}
>
> The sample space for the experiment of rolling one die and noting the number of spots on top is:
>
> {1, 2, 3, 4, 5, 6}

TIP 

If the probability of an event is close to 1, the event is likely to occur; if it is close to 0, the event is likely not to occur.

The probability of any event is the fraction $\frac{a}{b}$ where a is the count of the number of items in the sample space that show the given event and b is the number of items in the sample space.

If A is the event of both coins showing heads (HH), then the probability of event A, $P(A) = \frac{1}{4}$ (the number of outcomes in the sample space that show 2 heads divided by the number of items in the sample space).

If B is the event of a number less than 3 showing when a die is rolled, then $P(B) = \frac{2}{6} = \frac{1}{3}$.

Warm-Up Drill

Find the sample space for each experiment.

Experiment 1. Tossing three coins.
Experiment 2. Rolling two dice.
Experiment 3. Drawing one card from a standard deck of 52 cards.
Experiment 4. Flipping one coin and then rolling one die.

Determine the probability of each event.

5. Experiment 1:
   a. A, the event that all three coins show T.
   b. B, the event that at least two coins show T.
   c. C, the event that all three coins land on edge.

6. In Experiment 2:
   a. D, the event that both dice show even number of spots.
   b. E, the event that the sum of spots showing is 5.
   c. F, the event that the sum of spots showing is 1.

7. Experiment 3:
   a. G, the event that the ace of hearts is drawn.
   b. H, the event that an ace is drawn.
   c. I, the event that a heart is drawn.
   d. J, the event of drawing a red card.
8. In Experiment 4:
   a. K, the event of head on the coin and even number on the die.
   b. L, the event of tail on the coin and a number less than 6 on the die.
9. Nine people were asked, "How many brothers or sisters do you have?" The results of this survey are recorded in the accompanying table.

Number of brothers or sisters	Number who responded
0	2
1	3
2	1
3	2
5	1

A person from the original group of nine was chosen at random. Find the probability that the chosen person was one who responded:

   a. 0
   b. 5
   c. 6
   d. fewer than 2

SOLUTIONS

1. {HHH, HHT, HTH, THH, HTT, THT, TTH, TTT}
2. The sample space is the set of all ordered pairs of numbers 1 through 6. Consider a table:

Second die

		1	2	3	4	5	6
	1	11	12	13	14	15	16
	2	21	22	23	24	25	26
First	3	31	32	33	34	35	36
die	4	41	42	43	44	45	46
	5	51	52	53	54	55	56
	6	61	62	63	64	65	66

There are 36 items in this sample space.

3. This sample space consists of the set of all 52 cards.
4. {H1, H2, H3, H4, H5, H6, T1, T2, T3, T4, T5, T6}

5. a $P(A) = \frac{1}{8}$

   b. $P(B) = \frac{4}{8} = \frac{1}{2}$

   c. $P(C) = 0$ (Well, maybe.)

6. a. $P(D) = \frac{9}{36} = \frac{1}{4}$

   b. $P(E) = \frac{4}{36} = \frac{1}{9}$

   c. $P(F) = 0$

7. a. $P(G) = \frac{1}{52}$

   b. $P(H) = \frac{4}{52} = \frac{1}{13}$

   c. $P(I) = \frac{13}{52} = \frac{1}{4}$

   d. $P(J) = \frac{26}{52} = \frac{1}{2}$

8. a. $P(K) = \frac{3}{12} = \frac{1}{4}$

   b. $P(L) = \frac{5}{12}$

9. a. P(0 brothers or sisters) $= \frac{2}{9}$

   b. P(5 brothers or sisters) $= \frac{1}{9}$

   c. P(6 brothers or sisters) $= 0$

   d. P(fewer than 2 brothers or sisters) $=$ P(0 or 1 brothers or sisters) $= \frac{5}{9}$

Practice Exercises

The following sample questions represent ways in which the reviewed skills might be tested on the ACT.

1. Which of the following is not equivalent to the others?

   A. $\frac{3}{8}$
   B. 0.375
   C. $37\frac{1}{2}\%$
   D. 375%
   E. $\frac{15}{40}$

2. $(0.2)^3 = ?$

   F. 0.8
   G. 0.6
   H. 0.0008
   J. 0.008
   K. $\frac{3}{5}$

3. What is 15% of 40?

   A. 600
   B. 60
   C. 6
   D. $266\frac{2}{3}$
   E. 25

4. Corey received 10 toys for his birthday and 12 toys for Christmas. By what percent did the number of toys increase?

   F. 10%
   G. 12%
   H. 20%
   J. 2%
   K. $16\frac{2}{3}\%$

5. A card is drawn from a standard, well-shuffled deck of 52 cards. What is the probability that it is a face card (J, Q, or K)?

   A. $\frac{12}{52} = \frac{3}{13}$
   B. $\frac{1}{3}$
   C. $\frac{3}{10}$
   D. $\frac{4}{52} = \frac{1}{13}$
   E. None of these.

ANSWERS AND EXPLANATIONS

1. **(D)** All of the others are equivalent to $\frac{3}{8}$. Only 375% is different. It is equivalent to

   $\frac{375}{100} = \frac{15}{4}$.

2. **(J)** $(0.2)^3$

   $= (0.2)(0.2)(0.2)$ Keep track of the decimal places.

   $= (0.04)(0.2)$

   $= 0.008$

3. **(C)** "What is 15% of 40?" translates to a proportion as follows:

   $\frac{15}{100} = \frac{A}{40}$ Cross multiply.

   $100A = 600$ Divide by 100.

   $A = 6$

4. **(H)** Corey received 2 more toys at Christmas than he received at his birthday. Therefore the question is "2 is what percent of 10?"

$\frac{P}{100}=\frac{2}{10}$	Cross multiply.
$10P = 200$	Divide by 10.
$P = 20$	Be sure to attach a % sign.

Corey received 20% more toys at Christmas.

5. **(A)** There are 12 face cards in a standard deck. Twelve outcomes in the event divided by 52 items in the sample space give a probability of $\frac{12}{52}=\frac{3}{13}$.

ALGEBRA AND COORDINATE GEOMETRY

If $a = b$, then b may be substituted for a in any expression with no change in meaning.
Examples:

Evaluate each expression if $a = 3$, $b = -2$, and $c = -5$. (The rules for order of operations given previously are important. See page 172.)

1. $a + b - c$ $\quad 3 + (-2) - (-5) = 3 + (-2) + 5$
$= 1 + 5 = 6$

2. ab^2c $\quad 3(-2)^2(-5) = 3(4)(-5)$
$= 12(-5) = -60$

3. $ab + ac - bc$ $\quad 3(-2) + 3(-5) - (-2)(-5) = -6 + (-15) - 10$
$= -6 + (-15) + (-10)$
$= -21 + (-10) = -31$

Any of these three examples may be done using a calculator.

Warm-Up Drill

If $x = -2$, $y = 4$, and $z = -3$, evaluate the following expressions:

1. $x - yz$
2. $7(x + y + z)$
3. $\frac{x-y}{z}$
4. $xy + yz$
5. xyz^2

If $a=\frac{1}{2}$, $b=\frac{-2}{3}$, and $c = -1$, evaluate the following expressions.

6. $a + b$
7. ab^2c
8. $2a - 3b + c$
9. $\frac{1}{a}+\frac{1}{b}$
10. $a(b + c)$

SOLUTIONS

1. $x - yz = -2 - 4(-3)$
$= -2 - (-12)$
$= -2 + 12 = 10$

2. $7(x + y + z) = 7[(-2) + 4 + (-3)]$
$= 7[2 + (-3)]$
$= 7(-1) = -7$

3. $\frac{x-y}{z} = \frac{(-2)-4}{-3}$
$= \frac{(-2)+(-4)}{-3}$
$= \frac{-6}{-3} = 2$

4. $xy + yz = -2(4) + 4(-3)$
$= -8 + (-12) = -20$

5. $xyz^2 = -2(4)(-3)^2$
$= -2(4)(9)$
$= -8(9) = -72$

6. $a+b = \frac{1}{2} + \left(\frac{-2}{3}\right) = \frac{3}{6} + \left(\frac{-4}{6}\right) = \frac{-1}{6}$

7. $ab^2c = \frac{1}{2}\left(\frac{-2}{3}\right)^2(-1) = \frac{1}{2}\left(\frac{4}{9}\right)(-1) = \frac{-2}{9}$

8. $2a - 3b + c = 2\left(\frac{1}{2}\right) - 3\left(\frac{-2}{3}\right) + (-1) = 1 - (-2) + (-1) = 1 + 2 + (-1) = 2$

9. $\frac{1}{a} + \frac{1}{b} = \frac{1}{\frac{1}{2}} + \frac{1}{\frac{-2}{3}} = 2 + \frac{-3}{2} = \frac{4}{2} + \frac{-3}{2} = \frac{1}{2}$

10. $a(b+c) = \frac{1}{2}\left(\frac{-2}{3} + (-1)\right) = \frac{1}{2}\left(\frac{-2}{3} + \frac{-3}{3}\right) = \frac{1}{2}\left(\frac{-5}{3}\right) = \frac{-5}{6}$

Equations

An equation is almost any meaningful mathematical sentence that contains an equal sign. Some equations are true, some are false, and some are open or conditional.

$5 = 5$	True
$\frac{2}{3} = \frac{2}{3}$	True
$x + 1 = x + 1$	True for every replacement of x
$7 = 9$	False
$x + 3 = x + 1$	False for every replacement of x
$x + 2 = 5$	Open; true if $x = 3$ only

The set of numbers that makes an open equation true when substituted for the variable is called the *solution set*. The numbers themselves are called the *solution*. (The solution set of the equation $2x + 1 = 7$ is {3}.)

Equations that have the same solution set are called *equivalent* equations. There are two basic rules to use in order to solve equations. The application of either rule guarantees that an equivalent equation will result.

Addition Property of Equality

1. If $a = b$, then $a + c = b + c$ for any number c.

Multiplication Property of Equality

2. If $a = b$, then $ac = bc$ for any number $c \neq 0$.

The process of solving an equation is to produce a sequence of equivalent equations, the last one of which looks like

$$x = \text{constant}$$

from which the solution set can easily be found.

Since subtraction can be done by adding the opposite of the second number, there is no need for a subtraction axiom of equality. And division can be done by multiplying by the reciprocal of the divisor, so there is no need for a division axiom of equality.

Examples:

Solve each of the following:

1. $3x - 15 = 9$ — Rule 1. Add 15 to both sides of equation.

$$3x - 15 \underline{+15} = 9 \underline{+15}$$

$$3x = 24$$

$$3x\left(\frac{1}{3}\right) = 24\left(\frac{1}{3}\right)$$ Rule 2. Multiply both sides of $\frac{1}{3}$ or divide by 3.

$$x = 8$$

The solution set is {8}.

2. $4z + 2 = -2(z + 2)$ — First use distributive property to simplify.

$$4z + 2 = -2z - 4$$

$$4z + 2 \underline{+2z} = -2z - 4 \underline{+2z}$$ Add $2z$ to both sides.

$$6z + 2 = -4$$

$$6z + 2 \underline{-2} = -4 \underline{-2}$$ Add -2 to both sides.

$$6z = -6$$

$$6z\left(\frac{1}{6}\right) = -6\left(\frac{1}{6}\right)$$ Multiply both sides by $\frac{1}{6}$, or divide by 6.

$$z = -1$$

The solution set is {–1}.

3. $\frac{2x-1}{3}-\frac{x+3}{6}=\frac{1}{2}$

Multiply both sides by the lowest common denominator, 6.

$$6\left(\frac{2x-1}{3}-\frac{x+3}{6}\right)=\left(\frac{1}{2}\right)6$$

$2(2x - 1) - (x + 3) = 3$ Simplify

$4x - 2 - x - 3 = 3$

$3x - 5 = 3$

$3x = 8$ Divide by 3.

$x = \frac{8}{3}$ The solution set is $\left\{\frac{8}{3}\right\}$.

TIP

An equation with more than one letter is called a *literal* equation and its solution is another equation, not a set.

4. Solve for x: $3x - 2y = 7$

$$3x-2y+2y=7+2y$$
$$3x=7+2y$$
$$3x\left(\frac{1}{3}\right)=(7+2y)\left(\frac{1}{3}\right)$$
$$x=\frac{7+2y}{3} \text{ or } x=\frac{7}{3}+\frac{2}{3}y$$

Warm-Up Drill

Solve the following equations:

1. $2x - 5 = 3$
2. $5x - 6 = 2x + 9$
3. $4(x + 3) = 2(3x - 5) + 4$
4. $2x + 2(3x + 2) - 9 = (3x - 9) + 3$
5. $3(m - 4) - (4m - 11) = -5$
6. $1.2(x + 5) = 3(2x - 8) + 23.28$
7. $\frac{2x+1}{3}+\frac{1}{4}=\frac{2x-1}{6}$
8. $\frac{3y-1}{5}-\frac{2y+1}{4}=1$
9. Solve for x: $3x + 7y = 5$
10. Solve for b: $A = \frac{1}{2}(b + B)h$

SOLUTIONS

1. $\mathbf{2x - 5 = 3}$ Add 5 to both sides.

$2x = 8$ Multiply by $\frac{1}{2}$. (This is the same as dividing by 2.)

$x = 4$ Solution set is $\{4\}$.

2. $\mathbf{5x - 6 = 2x + 9}$ Add $-2x$ to both sides.
$3x - 6 = 9$ Add 6 to both sides.
$3x = 15$ Divide by 3.
$x = 5$ Solution set is $\{5\}$.

3. $\mathbf{4(x + 3) = 2(3x - 5) + 4}$ Use distributive property.
$4x + 12 = 6x - 10 + 4$ Combine similar terms.
$4x + 12 = 6x - 6$ Subtract $4x$ from both sides.
$12 = 2x - 6$ Add 6 to both sides.
$18 = 2x$ Divide by 2.
$9 = x$ Solution set is $\{9\}$.

4. $\mathbf{2x + 2(3x + 2) - 9 = (3x - 9) + 3}$ Use distributive property.
$2x + 6x + 4 - 9 = 3x - 9 + 3$ Combine similar terms.
$8x - 5 = 3x - 6$ Subtract $3x$ from both sides.
$5x - 5 = -6$ Add 5 to both sides.
$5x = -1$ Divide by 5.
$x = -1$ Solution set is $\left\{\frac{-1}{5}\right\}$.

5. $\mathbf{3(m - 4) - (4m - 11) = -5}$
$3m - 12 - 4m + 11 = -5$
$-m - 1 = -5$
$-m = -4$
$m = 4$ Solution set is $\{4\}$.

6. $\mathbf{1.2(x+5) = 3(2x-8) + 23.28}$ Multiply by 100.
$120(x+5) = 300(2x-8) + 2328$
$120x + 600 = 600x - 2400 + 2328$
$120x + 600 = 600x - 72$
$600 = 480x - 72$
$672 = 480x$
$x = \frac{672}{480} = 1.4$ Solution set is $\{1.4\}$.

7. $\mathbf{\frac{2x+1}{3} + \frac{1}{4} = \frac{2x-1}{6}}$ Multiply by 12.
$4(2x+1) + 3 = 2(2x-1)$
$8x + 4 + 3 = 4x - 2$
$8x + 7 = 4x - 2$
$4x + 7 = -2$
$4x = -9$
$x = -\frac{9}{4}$ Solution set is $\left\{\frac{-9}{2}\right\}$.

8. $$\mathbf{\frac{3y-1}{5}-\frac{2y+1}{4}=1} \qquad \text{Multiply by 20.}$$
$$4(3y-1)-5(2y+1)=20$$
$$12y-4-10y-5=20$$
$$2y-9=20$$
$$2y=29$$
$$y=\frac{29}{2} \qquad \text{Solution set is } \left\{\frac{29}{2}\right\}.$$

9. $$\mathbf{3x+7y=5}$$
$$3x=-7y+5$$
$$x=\frac{-7y+5}{3} \text{ or } x=\frac{-7}{3}y+\frac{5}{3}$$

10. $$\mathbf{A=\frac{1}{2}(b+A)h} \qquad \text{Multiply by 2.}$$
$$2A=(b+B)h$$
$$2A=bh+Bh$$
$$2A-Bh=bh$$
$$\frac{2A-Bh}{h}=b \qquad b=\frac{2A}{h}-B \text{ is also correct.}$$

Inequalities

Inequalities may contain any one of the following symbols:

$<$	less than
$>$	greater than
$\leq$	less than or equal to
$\geq$	greater than or equal to

Expressions such as

$$a<x<b \quad \text{and} \quad b \geq x > a$$

are most easily translated as "between." That is,

$a<x<b$	means x is between a and b.
$b \geq x > a$	means x is between b and a, including b.

The rules for solving linear inequalities with one variable are similar to those used to solve equations.

Addition Property of Inequality

1. If $a < b$, then $a + c < b + c$. Any number may be added to both sides of an inequality without changing the sense of the inequality.

Multiplication Property of Inequality

2. If $a < b$, then:

a. $ac < bc$ if $c > 0$.

b. $ac > bc$ if $c < 0$.

If both sides of an inequality are multiplied by a positive number, the sense of the inequality is not changed.

If both sides of an inequality are multiplied by a negative number, however, the sense of the inequality must be reversed.

TIP

Use caution when multiplying both sides of an inequality by a negative number. Many students forget to reverse the inequality sign.

Examples:

Solve each inequality and graph the solution set on a number line.

1. $x - 3(x - 1) < 7$

$x - 3x + 3 < 7$

$-2x + 3 < 7$

$-2x < 4$

$x > -2$ (Reverse the inequality symbol.)

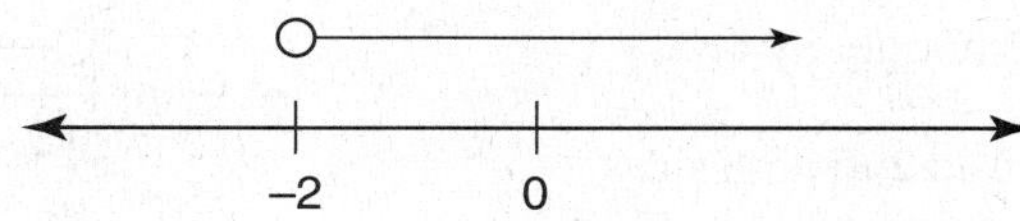

Often it is convenient to show the solution set, $\{x|x > -2\}$, on a number line. An open circle at –2 indicates that –2 is not included in the solution set. A closed circle would indicate that a particular number is included.

2. $-3 \leq 2x - 1 < 9$

$-2 \leq 2x < 10$ Add 1 to all three parts.

$-1 \leq x < 5$ Divide all three parts by 2.

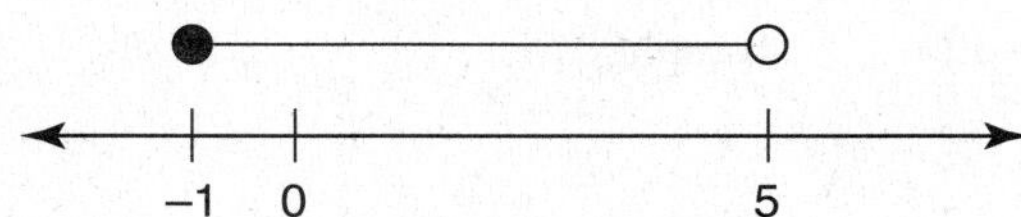

Some students will graph the solution on the number line.

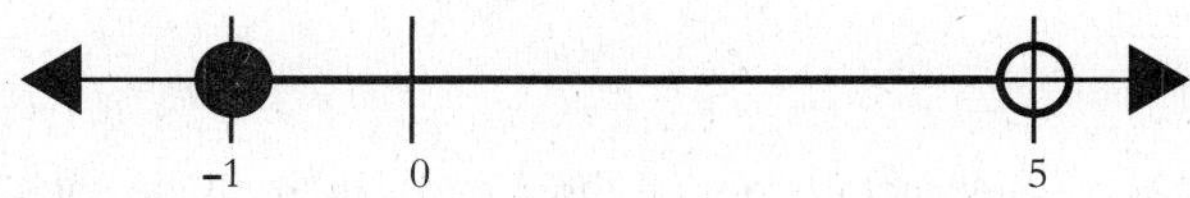

Warm-Up Drill

Solve the following inequalities:

1. $3x + 1 > 16$
2. $\frac{3x-2}{4} > 2$
3. $\frac{3x-2}{-5} \geq 4$
4. $2(3x - 5) + 7 > x + 12$
5. $-6 \leq 2x + 4 \leq 12$

SOLUTIONS

1. $\mathbf{3x + 1 > 16}$ Add –1 to both sides.

$3x > 15$ Multiply by $\frac{1}{3}$ (or divide by 3).

$x > 5$

2. $\mathbf{\frac{3x-2}{4} > 2}$ Multiply by 4.

$3x - 2 > 8$ Add 2 to both sides.

$3x > 10$ Divide by 3.

$x > \frac{10}{3}$

3. 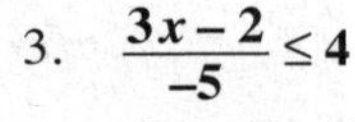

$\mathbf{\frac{3x-2}{-5} \leq 4}$ Multiply by –5. Reverse sense of inequality.

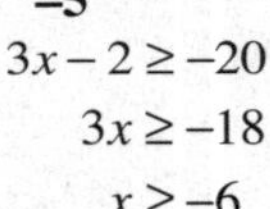

$3x - 2 \geq -20$

$3x \geq -18$

$x \geq -6$

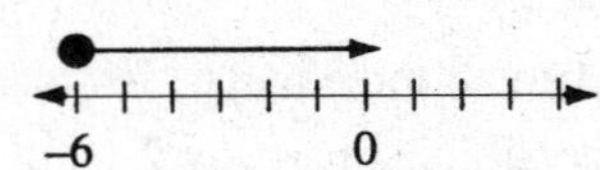

4. $\mathbf{2(3x - 5) + 7 > x + 12}$ Simplify first.

$6x - 10 + 7 > x + 12$

$6x - 3 > x + 12$ Subtract x from both sides.

$5x - 3 > 12$

$5x > 15$

$x > 3$

5. $\mathbf{-6 \leq 2x + 4 \leq 12}$ Subtract 4 from all three parts, then divide each part by 2.

$-10 \leq 2x \leq 8$

$-5 \leq x \leq 4$

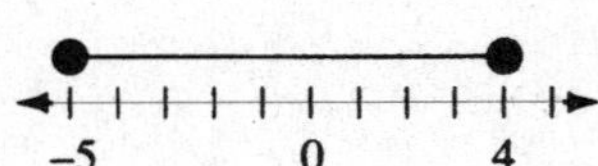

Operations on Polynomials

Addition and Subtraction

To add or subtract polynomials, first use the distributive property as needed to get rid of parentheses and then combine similar terms. Usually the terms of a polynomial are arranged in the order of descending degree in a specified variable. For example:

$$\begin{aligned}(3x^2 + 5x - 4) + (2x^2 - 7x - 3) &= 3x^2 + 5x - 4 + 2x^2 - 7x - 3\\ &= 5x^2 - 2x - 7\end{aligned}$$

$$\begin{aligned}(2x^2 - 6xy + 3y^2) - (x^2 - xy + 2y^2) &= 2x^2 - 6xy + 3y^2 - x^2 + xy - 2y^2\\ &= x^2 - 5xy + y^2\end{aligned}$$

Multiplication

Multiplication of a monomial by a polynomial of several terms is merely an extension of the distributive property.

$$-2a(3a^2 - 5a + 8) = -6a^3 + 10a^2 - 16a$$

Multiplication of two polynomials of more than one term each is also an extension of the distributive property. It is easier, however, to follow the rule "Multiply each term of one polynomial by each term of the other polynomial and then simplify."

$$\begin{aligned}(a + b - c)(2a - b + c) &= a(2a - b + c) + b(2a - b + c) - c(2a - b + c)\\ &= 2a^2 - ab + ac + 2ab - b^2 + bc - 2ac + bc - c^2\\ &= 2a^2 + ab - ac - b^2 + 2bc - c^2\end{aligned}$$

Multiplication of two binomials is such a common operation that a special procedure has been devised to make it easy to do mentally.

Consider the product of two binomials:

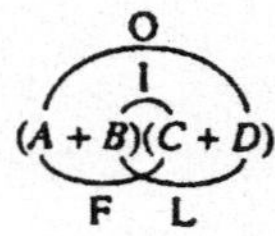

Call A and C the First terms of the binomials.
Call A and D the Outer terms.
Call B and C the Inner terms.
Call B and D the Last terms.
The product can be found by following the acronym FOIL.
For example, to multiply $(2x + 3)(x + 4)$;

Multiply the **First** terms: $(2x)(x) = 2x^2$.
Multiply the **Outer** terms: $(2x)(4) = 8x$.
Multiply the **Inner** terms: $(3)(x) = 3x$.
Multiply the **Last** terms: $(3)(4) = 12$.

Since the Outer product and the Inner product are similar terms, combine them and write the answer:

$$2x^2 + 11x + 12$$

You **must** understand FOIL for the ACT.

Three products occur frequently and deserve special attention:

Sum and difference binomials: $(A + B)(A - B) = A^2 - B^2$
Square of a binomial: $(A \pm B)^2 = A^2 \pm 2AB + B^2$
Cube of a binomial: $(A \pm B)^3 = A^3 \pm 3A^2B + 3AB^2 \pm B^3$

Examples:

1. $(3x - 5)(3x + 5) = 9x^2 - 25$
2. $(5x - 2y)^2 = 25x^2 - 20xy + 4y^2$
3. $(x + 4)^3 = x^3 + 12x^2 + 48x + 64$

Warm-Up Drill

Perform the indicated operations. Express each answer in the order of descending degree in some variable.

1. $(5x + 3xy - 8y) - (y - 6yx + 2x)$
2. $(2x - 3) - [(4x + 7) - (5x - 2)]$
3. $-3ab(4a^2 - 5ab + 2b^2)$
4. $(2x - 3)(4x^2 + 6x + 9)$
5. $(x + 3)(x - 5)$
6. $(3x + 1)(2x + 5)$
7. $2x(x - 8)(2x - 5)$
8. $(3x + 8)(3x - 8)$
9. $(3x + 5)^2$
10. $(x - 2)^3$

SOLUTIONS

1. $\mathbf{(5x + 3xy - 8y) - (y - 6yx + 2x)}$
$= 5x + 3xy - 8y - y + 6yx - 2x$
$= 3x + 9xy - 9y$

2. $\mathbf{(2x - 3) - [(4x + 7) - (5x - 2)]}$ Do inner grouping symbols first.
$= (2x - 3) - [4x + 7 - 5x + 2]$
$= 2x - 3 - 4x - 7 + 5x - 2$
$= 3x - 12$

3. $\mathbf{-3ab(4a^2 - 5ab + 2b^2)}$
$= -12a^3b + 15a^2b^2 - 6ab^3$

4. Multiply each term of the second polynomial first by $2x$ and then by -3:
$\mathbf{(2x - 3)(4x^2 + 6x + 9)}$
$= 8x^3 + 12x^2 + 18x - 12x^2 - 18x - 27$
$= 8x^3 - 27$

5. $\mathbf{(x + 3)(x - 5)}$ — Use FOIL.
   $= x^2 - 5x + 3x - 15$ — Try not to write this line.
   $= x^2 - 2x - 15$

6. $\mathbf{(3x + 1)(2x + 5)}$ — Use FOIL. Do the Outer and Inner mentally.
   $= 6x^2 + 17x + 5$

7. $\mathbf{2x(x - 8)(2x - 5)}$ — Multiply the binomials first.
   $= 2x(2x^2 - 21x + 40)$
   $= 4x^3 - 42x^2 + 80x$

8. $\mathbf{(3x + 8)(3x - 8)}$ — This is an example of sum and difference binomials, one of the special types.
   $= 9x^2 - 64$

9. $\mathbf{(3x + 5)^2}$ — This is a binomial square. The middle term is 2 times the product of the terms of the binomial.
   $= 9x^2 + 30x + 25$

10. $\mathbf{(x - 2)^3}$ — This is a binomial cube. The second term, for example, is found by squaring the first term, multiplying by the second term, and then multiplying by 3.
    $= x^3 - 6x^2 + 12x - 8$

Division

We can interpret the rule for addition and subtraction of fractions as a method of dividing a polynomial by a monomial.

$$\frac{a+b}{c} = \frac{a}{c} + \frac{b}{c} \quad \text{or} \quad \frac{a-b}{c} = \frac{a}{c} - \frac{b}{c}, \qquad c \neq 0$$

This rule means that each term of the polynomial in the numerator is to be divided by the monomial in the denominator.

Here are two examples:

- $\dfrac{4x-8}{2} = \dfrac{4x}{2} - \dfrac{8}{2} = 2x - 4$
- $\dfrac{3x^3 - 6x^2 + 9x}{-3x} = -x^2 + 2x - 3$

Sometimes the rule for division of exponential expressions is needed:

$$\frac{x^m}{x^n} = x^{m-n}$$

This rule and others are reviewed in the section entitled Laws of Exponents, pages 236–237.

The procedure for dividing a polynomial by a binomial (or other polynomial) is similar to that for whole number division. Consider the division problem

$$x-3\overline{)2x^2+5x-1}$$

Divide the first term of the divisor into the first term of the dividend, x into $2x^2$. Place the quotient above the first term of the dividend.

$$\begin{array}{r l} & 2x \\ x-3 & \overline{)2x^2+5x-1} \end{array}$$

Multiply $2x$ time $x-3$, place the product under $2x^2+5x$, and subtract. Remember to follow the rule for subtraction; change the sign of the subtrahend (the bottom expression) and add.

$$\begin{array}{r l} & 2x \\ x-3 & \overline{)2x^2+5x-1} \\ & \;\;2x \;-\; 6x \\ & \overline{\qquad\quad 11x} \end{array}$$

Bring the next term down from the dividend, and repeat the process. Divide x into $11x$. Then multiply and subtract.

$$\begin{array}{r l} & 2x \\ x-3 & \overline{)2x^2+5x-1} \\ & \;\;2x \;-\; 6x \\ & \overline{\qquad\quad 11x-\;\;1} \\ & \qquad\quad 11x-33 \\ & \qquad\qquad \overline{\quad\;\; 32} \end{array}$$

The answer may be written as either

$$2x+11 \text{ remainder } 32 \qquad \text{or} \qquad 2x+11+\frac{32}{x-3}$$

$$\begin{array}{r l} & 2x^2-2x-2 \\ 2x-1 & \overline{)4x^3-6x^2-2x+1} \\ & \;\;4x^3-2x^2 \\ & \overline{\qquad -4x^2-\;2x} \\ & \qquad -4x^2+\;2x \\ & \qquad \overline{\qquad\quad -4x+1} \\ & \qquad\qquad\quad -4x+2 \\ & \qquad\qquad\quad \overline{\qquad\; -1} \end{array}$$

The answer is $2x^2-2x-2+\dfrac{-1}{2x-1}$.

When the divisor in algebraic division is of degree greater than 1, the signal to stop the division process comes when the degree of the remainder is smaller than the degree of the divisor.

A polynomial can be easily divided by a first-degree binomial of the type $x - a$ by a procedure called *synthetic division*. To demonstrate, we will consider the first division problem done above. The coefficients of the dividend are aligned in descending degree. (The variables are not written.) The constant term of the divisor is written with the opposite sign to the left of the coefficients of the dividend. In this problem, 3 is placed to the left of the row of numbers, 2 5 –1:

TIP 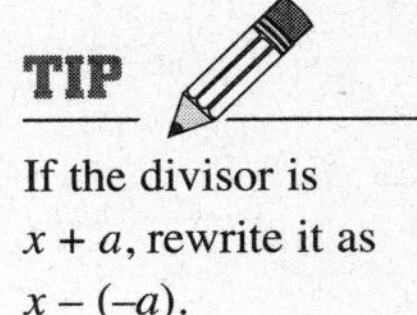

If the divisor is $x + a$, rewrite it as $x - (-a)$.

$$\begin{array}{r|rrr} 3 & 2 & 5 & -1 \\ \hline \end{array}$$

The procedure is as follows:

1. Bring the first coefficient of the dividend down to the bottom row under the line.
2. Multiply the number on the left of the top row, that is, the divisor, by the number on the bottom row.
3. Place this product above the line and under the next number to the right.
4. Add the numbers in that column, place the sum under the line, and repeat steps 2, 3, and 4.

In the bottom row, the last number is the remainder, and the others are the coefficients of the quotient in order of descending degree.

$$\begin{array}{r|rrl} 3 & 2 & 5 & -1 \\ & & 6 & 33 \\ \hline & 2 & 11 & 32 \rightarrow 2x + 11 \text{ remainder } 32 \end{array}$$

Here is another example: $(2x^3 - 5x + 7) \div (x + 2)$.

$$\begin{array}{r|rrrl} -2 & 2 & 0 & -5 & 7 \\ & & -4 & 8 & -6 \\ \hline & 2 & -4 & 3 & 1 \rightarrow 2x^2 - 4x + 3 \text{ remainder } 1 \end{array}$$

Warm-Up Drill

1. $(-48x^2y^3z) \div (-16xy^2z)$
2. $(25x^3 - 10x^2 + 5x) \div (5x)$

Use synthetic division to find the quotient and the remainder in each of the following problems:

3. $(x^2 - 3x - 18) \div (x - 6)$
4. $(x^3 - x^2 + 3x + 1) \div (x - 3)$
5. $(2x^3 - 3x^2 + 5) \div (x + 2)$

SOLUTIONS

1. $3xy$
2. $5x^2 - 2x + 1$
3. $\mathbf{(x^2 - 3x - 18) \div (x - 6)}$

$$\begin{array}{r|rrr} 6 & 1 & -3 & -18 \\ & & 6 & 18 \\ \hline & 1 & 3 & 0 \end{array}$$

The answer is $x + 3$.

4. $(x^3 - x^2 + 3x + 1) \div (x - 3)$

$$\begin{array}{r|rrrr} 3 & 1 & -1 & 3 & 1 \\ & & 3 & 6 & 27 \\ \hline & 1 & 2 & 9 & 28 \end{array}$$

The answer is $x^2 + 2x + 9$ remainder 28.

5. $(2x^3 - 3x^2 + 5) \div (x + 2)$

$$\begin{array}{r|rrrr} -2 & 2 & -3 & 0 & 5 \\ & & -4 & 14 & -28 \\ \hline & 2 & -7 & 14 & -23 \end{array}$$

The answer is $2x^2 - 7x + 14$ remainder -23.

Factoring

The process of factoring involves changing an expression from addition or subtraction to multiplication—creating factors. The property underlying all factoring rules is the distributive property:

$$ab + ac = a(b + c)$$

If an expression has a *common factor* other than 1 in all of its terms, use distributive property to factor it out. Here are some examples:

- $4ab^2 + 2a^2b = 2ab(2b + a)$
- $39x^5y^3 - 26x^7y^2 + 52x^8y^5 = 13x^5y^2(3y - 2x^2 + 4x^3y^3)$ The common factor chosen should be the greatest common factor of the terms. Choose the exponent on each variable to be the smallest exponent on that variable in the expression.

TIP

Notice that the left has the *sum* of terms, while the right has the *product* of factors.

- $-25x^3y^2 - 20x^4y^3 + 15x^5y^4 - 50x^6y^2 = -5x^3y^2(5 + 4xy - 3x^2y^2 + 10x^3)$ If the first term is negative, choose a negative common factor.
- $(x + 5)(x - 6) + (x + 5)(x - 1) = (x + 5)[(x - 6) + (x - 1)] = (x + 5)(2x - 7)$ The common factor is the binomial $(x + 5)$.
- $pq + 3rq + pm + 3rm = (pq + 3rq) + (pm + 3rm) = q(p + 3r) + m(p + 3r) = (p + 3r)(q + m)$ The trick is to group so that each group has a common factor.
- $8x^2 + 6xy - 12xy - 9y^2 = (8x^2 + 6xy) - (12xy + 9y^2) = 2x(4x + 3y) - 3y(4x + 3y) = (4x + 3y)(2x - 3y)$ Be very careful of signs.

Warm-Up Drill

Factor completely,

1. $8x^3y^3 - 12x^2y^2$
2. $28a^2b - 14ab^2 + 7ab$
3. $-6a^5b^5 - 8a^4b^4 - 4a^3b^2$
4. $7m^3n^3 + 6$
5. $9x(3x + 2y) - 5y(3x + 2y)$
6. $5x^2y^2 + 10x^2 - 7y^2 - 14$
7. $6x^2y^2 - 6xy - 24xy^2 + 24y$
8. $4x^3 + 8x - 3x - 6$
9. $4x^3 + 16x^2 + 6x^2 + 24x$

SOLUTIONS

1. $4x^2y^2(2xy - 3)$
2. $7ab(4a - 2b + 1)$ The 1 is easy to miss but very important.
3. $-2a^3b^2(3a^2b^3 + 4ab^2 + 2)$
4. The terms of this binomial have no common factor other than 1. It is not factorable. A non-factorable polynomial is said to be prime.
5. $(3x + 2y)(9x - 5y)$
6. $\mathbf{5x^2y^2 + 10x^2 - 7y^2 - 14}$
   $(5x^2y^2 + 10x^2) - (7y^2 + 14)$ Group, being careful of signs.
   $= 5x^2(y^2 + 2) - 7(y^2 + 2)$
   $= (y^2 + 2)(5x^2 - 7)$
7. $\mathbf{6x^2y^2 - 6xy - 24xy^2 + 24y}$
   $6y(x^2y - x - 4xy + 4)$ $6y$ is a common factor.
   $6y[x(xy - 1) - 4(xy - 1)]$ Group in pairs and find common factors in each.
   $6y(xy - 1)(x - 4)$
8. $4x^3 + 8x - 3x - 6$
   $= (4x^2 + 8x) - (3x - 6)$ Group.
   $= 4x(x + 2) - 3(x + 2)$
   $= (x + 2)(4x - 3)$
9. $4x^3 + 16x^2 + 6x^2 + 24x$
   $= 2x(2x^2 + 8x + 3x + 12)$ $2x$ is a common factor.
   $= 2x[(2x^2 + 8x) + (3x + 12)]$ Group.
   $= 2x[2x(x + 4) + 3(x + 4)]$
   $= 2x(x + 4)(2x + 3)$

Difference of Squares and Sum and Difference of Cubes

The following products are the bases for factoring special types of binomials:

$(a + b)(a - b) = a^2 - b^2$ Difference of squares.

$(a + b)(a^2 - ab + b^2) = a^3 + b^3$ Sum of cubes.

$(a - b)(a^2 + ab + b^2) = a^3 - b^3$ Difference of cubes.

Here is an example of each type:

- $25 - 49x^2 = (5 + 7x)(5 - 7x)$ Difference of squares.
- $x^3 + 8 = (x + 2)(x^2 - 2x + 4)$ Sum of cubes. Watch signs carefully.
- $125x^3 - 64y^3 = (5x - 4y)(25x^2 + 20xy + 16y^2)$ Difference of cubes.

Factoring Trinomials of the Type $x^2 + Bx + C$

When two binomials of the type $(x + a)(x + b)$ are multiplied, a trinomial of the type $x^2 + Bx + C$ results, in which C is the product of a and b and B is the sum of a and b. To factor such a trinomial, look for two factors of C whose sum is B.

Examples:

Factor each of the following:

1. $x^2 + 7x + 12$ Search the factors of 12 to find a pair whose sum is 7. The factors of 12 in pairs are 1, 12; 2, 6; and 3, 4. The sum is 7. The answer is $(x + 3)(x + 4)$.
2. $x^2 - 8x + 15$ The factors of 15 are 1 and 15 or 3 and 5. The answer is $(x - 3)(x - 5)$.
3. $x^2 - 3x - 40$ Since the sign of the third term is negative, the signs in the two binomials are different, and the middle term is the sum of two numbers with different signs. Search for a pair of factors so that the difference is 3, and adjust signs. The answer is $(x - 8)(x + 5)$.
4. $x^2 + 5x - 66$ Look for two factors of 66 whose difference is 5: 6, 11. The answer is $(x - 6)(x + 11)$.

Factoring Trinomials of the Type $Ax^2 + Bx + C$

The leading coefficient of this type of polynomial is always something other than 1. The procedure is to multiply the coefficients of the first and third terms and look for a pair of factors of that number whose sum or difference is the second coefficient. Rewrite the second term using those numbers, then group and factor.

Examples:

1. $2x^2 + 5x - 12$ — Multiply 2 times 12. Look for two factors of 24 whose difference (because the 12 is negative) is 5.

   $24 = (3)(8)$

   $2x^2 + 8x - 3x - 12$ — Rewrite $5x$ using the numbers above.

   $(2x^2 + 8x) - (3x + 12)$ — Group.

   $2x(x + 4) - 3(x + 4)$ — Factor out the common factor in each group.

   $(x + 4)(2x - 3)$ — Factor out the common factor $(x + 4)$.

2. $24x^2 - 14x - 3$ — $24 \cdot 3 = 72$

   $24x^2 - 18x + 4x - 3$ — $72 = 18 \cdot 4$

   $(24x^2 - 18x) + (4x - 3)$

   $6x(4x - 3) + 1(4x - 3)$

   $(4x - 3)(6x + 1)$

3. $24x^2 - 34x + 5$ — $24 \cdot 5 = 120$

   $24x^2 - 4x - 30x + 5$ — $120 = 30 \cdot 4$

   $(24x^2 - 4x) - (30x - 5)$

   $4x(6x - 1) - 5(6x - 1)$

   $(6x - 1)(4x - 5)$

This type of trinomial can also be factored by a method best described as "trial and error." Given a trinomial of the appropriate type, begin with either the first or third term (whichever one has fewer factors). Look for obvious factors of that number to place in the binomial factors.

4. $6x^2 + 19x + 10$

$(2x$	$)(3x$	$)$
	2	5
	5	2 ←
	1	10
	10	1

There are two possibilities for the first terms of the binomials. Guessing that the correct choice is $2x$ and $3x$, list the factors of 10 and check them, adding the outer and inner products in the hope of getting $19x$. The answer is $(2x + 5)(3x + 2)$.

5. $8x^2 - 2x - 3$	There are two possibilities for the first terms of the binomials and only one for the second terms, so begin there, and list the factors of $8x$. Since the sign of the third term is negative, subtract the outer and inner products in the hope of getting $2x$. Then adjust the signs to make the middle term negative. The answer is $(2x + 1)(4x - 3)$.
(1)(3)	
$2x$ $4x \leftarrow$	
$4x$ $2x$	
x $8x$	
$8x$ x	

Perfect Square Trinomials

If the first and last terms of a trinomial are squares, it is worth considering the special form of a perfect square trinomial:

$$a^2 + 2ab + b^2 = (a + b)^2$$

For example, $x^2 + 10x + 25$ is a perfect square trinomial. The correct factorization is $(x + 5)^2$. [The factorization $(x + 5)(x + 5)$ is also correct.]

GENERAL STRATEGY FOR FACTORING A POLYNOMIAL

1. If a polynomial has a common factor, *always* factor that first.
2. If there is no common factor (or if the common factor has already been factored out):
   a. factor a binomial according to the rule for the difference of squares or the sum or difference of cubes;
   b. factor a trinomial according to the appropriate rule;
   c. consider factoring by grouping if there are more than three terms.
3. Look for tricks.

TIP

The ACT would not likely require you to use a trick.

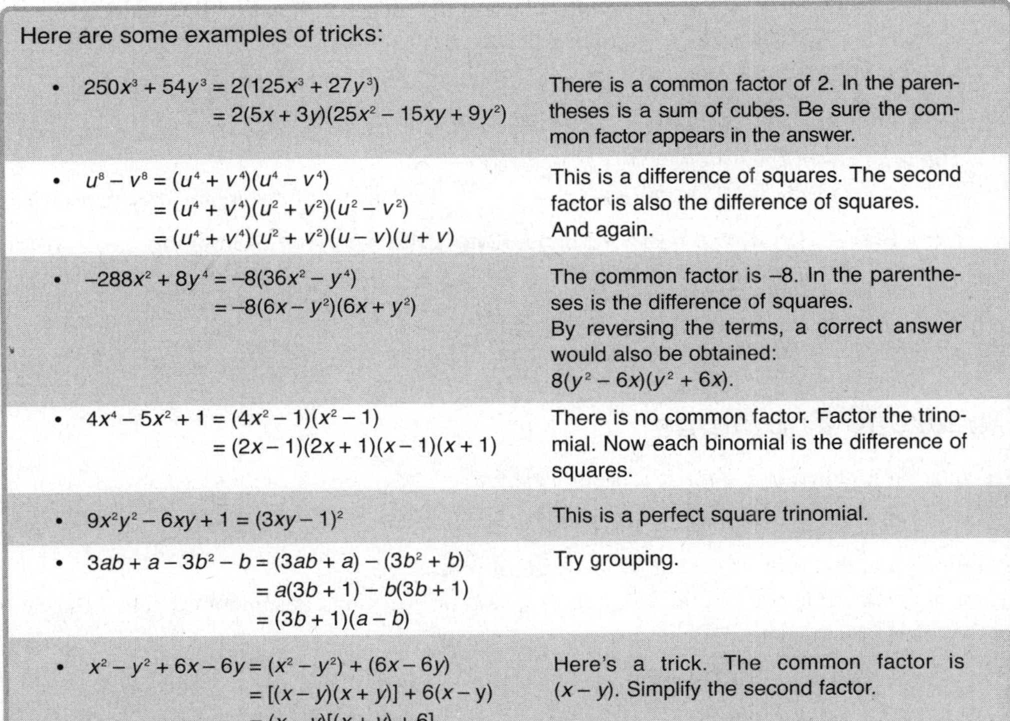

Here are some examples of tricks:

• $250x^3 + 54y^3 = 2(125x^3 + 27y^3)$ $= 2(5x + 3y)(25x^2 - 15xy + 9y^2)$	There is a common factor of 2. In the parentheses is a sum of cubes. Be sure the common factor appears in the answer.
• $u^8 - v^8 = (u^4 + v^4)(u^4 - v^4)$ $= (u^4 + v^4)(u^2 + v^2)(u^2 - v^2)$ $= (u^4 + v^4)(u^2 + v^2)(u - v)(u + v)$	This is a difference of squares. The second factor is also the difference of squares. And again.
• $-288x^2 + 8y^4 = -8(36x^2 - y^4)$ $= -8(6x - y^2)(6x + y^2)$	The common factor is −8. In the parentheses is the difference of squares. By reversing the terms, a correct answer would also be obtained: $8(y^2 - 6x)(y^2 + 6x)$.
• $4x^4 - 5x^2 + 1 = (4x^2 - 1)(x^2 - 1)$ $= (2x - 1)(2x + 1)(x - 1)(x + 1)$	There is no common factor. Factor the trinomial. Now each binomial is the difference of squares.
• $9x^2y^2 - 6xy + 1 = (3xy - 1)^2$	This is a perfect square trinomial.
• $3ab + a - 3b^2 - b = (3ab + a) - (3b^2 + b)$ $= a(3b + 1) - b(3b + 1)$ $= (3b + 1)(a - b)$	Try grouping.
• $x^2 - y^2 + 6x - 6y = (x^2 - y^2) + (6x - 6y)$ $= [(x - y)(x + y)] + 6(x - y)$ $= (x - y)[(x + y) + 6]$ $= (x - y)(x + y + 6)$	Here's a trick. The common factor is $(x - y)$. Simplify the second factor.

Warm-Up Drill

Factor completely.

1. $5x^2y^2 - 10xy$
2. $x^2 - 4x - 21$
3. $2x^2 - x - 10$
4. $-5x^2 - 15xy + 50y^2$
5. $8a^3 - b^3$
6. $6y^2 + y - 40$
7. $9x^2 + 30xy + 25y^2$
8. $16u^4 - v^4$
9. $6x^2 - 14xy - 21xy + 49y^2$
10. $x^{2n} - 6x^n + 5$

SOLUTIONS

1. $\mathbf{5x^2y^2 - 10xy} = 5xy(xy - 2)$
2. $\mathbf{x^2 - 4x - 21} = (x - 7)(x + 3)$
3. $2x^2 - x - 10$ Multiply 2 times 10. Look for factors of 20 whose difference is 1. Rewrite $-x$ using those two numbers. Group and find common factors in each group.
   $2x^2 - 5x + 4x - 10$
   $x(2x - 5) + 2(2x - 5)$
   $(2x - 5)(x + 2)$
4. $\mathbf{-5x^2 - 15xy + 50y^2} = -5(x^2 + 3xy - 10y^2)$ -5 is the common factor.
   $= -5(x + 5y)(x - 2y)$
5. $\mathbf{8a^3} - \mathbf{b^3} = (2a - b)(4a^2 + 2ab + b^2)$ Difference of cubes.
6. $6y^2 + y - 40$ Multiply first and last coefficients. $6 \cdot 40 = 240 = 16 \cdot 15$, factors whose difference is 1. Rewrite the middle term, group and factor.
   $= 6y^2 + 16y - 15y - 40$
   $= 2y(3y + 8) - 5(3y + 8)$
   $= (3y + 8)(2y - 5)$
7. $\mathbf{9x^2 + 30xy + 25y^2} = (3x + 5y)^2$ A perfect square trinomial.
8. $\mathbf{16u^4} - v^4 = (4u^2 + v^2)(4u^2 - v^2)$
   $= (4u^2 + v^2)(2u + v)(2u - v)$ Two layers of difference of squares.
9. $\mathbf{6x^2 - 14xy - 21xy + 49y^2} = (6x^2 - 14xy) - (21xy - 49y^2)$ Grouping.
   $= 2x(3x - 7y) - 7y(3x - 7y)$
   $= (3x - 7y)(2x - 7y)$
10. $\mathbf{x^{2n} - 6x^n + 5} = (x^n - 5)(x^n - 1)$

Quadratic Equations

An equation is called *quadratic* if it is equivalent to

$$ax^2 + bx + c = 0, \quad a \neq 0$$

An equation in this form is said to be in *standard* form.

An important rule used in the solution of quadratic equations is sometimes called the Zero Product Principle:

$$\text{If } AB = 0, \quad \text{then } A = 0 \quad \text{or} \quad B = 0.$$

Examples:

Solve each of the following:

1. $x^2 + 8x + 15 = 0$ Factor.

$(x + 5)(x + 3) = 0$ Zero product principle

$x + 5 = 0$ or $x + 3 = 0$

$x = -5$ or $x = -3$

The solution set is $\{-5, -3\}$.

2. $3x^2 + 5 = 2x$

$3x^2 - 2x + 5 = 0$ Standard form.

$(3x - 5)(x + 1) = 0$ Factor.

$3x - 5 = 0$ or $x + 1 = 0$ Zero product principle

$x = \frac{5}{3}$ or $x = -1$ Solve each linear equation.

The solution set is $\left\{\frac{5}{3}, -1\right\}$.

If the coefficient of the linear term in the standard form of the quadratic equation is zero ($b = 0$), it is easier to solve the equation by isolating x^2 and taking the square root of both sides, remembering that there are two solutions to such an equation—one positive and the other negative.

Examples:

Solve each of the following:

1. $x^2 - 49 = 0$

$x^2 = 49$ Isolate x^2.

$x = \pm 7$ Take the square root of each side.

The solution set is $\{7, -7\}$.

2. $2x^2 - 10 = 0$

$2x^2 = 10$

$x^2 = 5$

$x = \pm \sqrt{5}$.

The solution set is $\{\sqrt{5}, -\sqrt{5}\}$.

The Quadratic Formula

All quadratic equations can be solved by using the quadratic formula:

$$x = \frac{-b \pm \sqrt{b^2 - 4ac}}{2a}$$

The radicand of the quadratic formula, $b^2 - 4ac$, is called the *discriminant*. The discriminant allows one to describe the nature of the solution of the equation without actually solving it. The following rules apply if the coefficients are rational:

If the discriminant is:	then the solution is:
0	one rational number
positive square	two unequal rationals
positive nonsquare	two unequal irrationals
negative	two unequal complex numbers (conjugates; see page 273)

An immediate consequence of the quadratic formula is the following theorem:

If r_1 and r_2 are the roots of the quadratic equation

$$ax^2 + bx + c = 0$$

then

$$r_1 + r_2 = \frac{-b}{a} \quad \text{and} \quad r_1 \cdot r_2 = \frac{c}{a}$$

These relationships are useful for checking the solution to a quadratic equation.

Example: Solve and check the solutions to this quadratic equation.

$$10x^2 - 11x - 6 = 0$$

This equation can be solved by factoring:

$$10x^2 - 11x - 6 = (2x - 3)(5x + 2) = 0$$

$$2x - 3 = 0 \qquad 5x + 2 = 0$$

$$x = \frac{3}{2} \qquad x = \frac{-2}{5}$$

Add these numbers. The sum should be $\frac{-b}{a} = \frac{11}{10}$.

$$\frac{3}{2} + \frac{-2}{5} = \frac{15}{10} + \frac{-4}{10} = \frac{11}{10}$$

Multiply these numbers. The product should be $\frac{c}{a} = \frac{-6}{10} = \frac{-3}{5}$.

$$\left(\frac{3}{2}\right)\left(\frac{-2}{5}\right) = \frac{-3}{5}$$

The sum and product constitute a check for the quadratic equation. The solution is $\left\{\frac{3}{2}, \frac{-2}{5}\right\}$.

Warm-Up Drill

Solve the following quadratic equations:

1. $x^2 - 3x - 4 = 0$
2. $x^2 + 9 = 6x$
3. $2x^2 + 10x = 0$
4. $3x^2 - 75 = 0$
5. $x^2 - 2x - 5 = 0$

Use the discriminant to describe the roots of these equations:

6. $3x^2 - 2x + 4 = 0$
7. $2x^2 + 11x - 40 = 0$
8. $x^2 = x + 1$

Without solving, find the sum and product of the roots of these equations:

9. $2x^2 + 9x - 35 = 0$
10. $7x^2 + \frac{1}{2}x = 0$
11. $x^2 + 7x + 6 = 0$

SOLUTIONS

1. $\mathbf{x^2 - 3x - 4 = 0}$

$(x - 4)(x + 1) = 0$ — Factor the left side.

$x - 4 = 0$ or $x + 1 = 0$

$x = 4 \qquad x = -1$ — Set each factor equal to zero. Solve each equation.

The solution set is $\{4, -1\}$.

2. $\mathbf{x^2 + 9 = 6x}$

$x^2 - 6x + 9 = 0$	The equation is in standard form.
$(x - 3)^2 = 0$	Factor.
$x - 3 = 0$	Set factor equal to zero.
$x = 3$	Solve.

The solution set is {3}.

3. $\mathbf{2x^2 + 10x = 0}$

$2x(x + 5) = 0$	Factor.
$2x = 0$ or $x + 5 = 0$	Set each factor equal to zero.
$x = 0 \quad x = -5$	Solve.

The solution set is {0, –5}.

4. $\mathbf{3x^2 - 75 = 0}$

$3(x^2 - 25) = 0$	
$3(x - 5)(x + 5) = 0$	Factor.
$x - 5 = 0$ or $x + 5 = 0$	Set each variable factor equal to zero.
$x = 5 \quad x = -5$	Solve.

The solution set is {5, –5}.

5. The left side is not factorable, so use the quadratic formula.

$$\mathbf{x^2 - 2x - 5 = 0}$$

$$a = 1, b = -2, c = -5$$

$$x = \frac{-b \pm \sqrt{b^2 - 4ac}}{2a}$$

$$= \frac{2 \pm \sqrt{(-2)^2 - 4(1)(-5)}}{2(1)}$$

$$= \frac{2 \pm \sqrt{4 - (-20)}}{2} = \frac{2 \pm \sqrt{24}}{2}$$

$$= \frac{2 \pm 2\sqrt{6}}{2} = 1 \pm \sqrt{6}$$

6. The discriminant is

$$(-2)^2 - 4(3)(4) = 4 - 48 = -44 < 0$$

Therefore there are two unequal complex solutions.

7. The discriminant is

$$(11)^2 - 4(2)(-40) = 121 - (-320) = 441$$

which is a positive square ($441 = 21^2$).
Therefore there are two unequal rational solutions.

8. The equation must first be in standard form:
$x^2 - x - 1 = 0$. The discriminant is

$$(-1)^2 - 4(1)(-1) = 1 - (-4) = 5$$

which is a positive nonsquare.
Therefore the solution set consists of two unequal irrational numbers.

9. Sum: $\frac{-b}{a}=\frac{-9}{2}$ Product: $\frac{c}{a}=\frac{-35}{2}$

10. Sum: $\frac{-b}{a}=\frac{2}{7}=\frac{-1}{14}$ Product: $\frac{c}{a}=\frac{0}{7}=0$

11. Sum: $\frac{-b}{a}=\frac{-7}{1}=-7$ Product: $\frac{c}{a}=\frac{6}{1}=6$

Fractions

TIP

Be sure you understand the difference between "terms" and "factors."

Algebraic fractions can be reduced by using the Fundamental Principle of Fractions:

$$\frac{a}{b}=\frac{ak}{bk},\ b,\ k\neq 0$$

Multiplication and Division

Multiplication and division of fractions are merely extensions of the same procedure. It is important to factor all expressions first and to cancel only common *factors* from any numerator and any denominator. Most errors are made by attempting to cancel *terms,* not factors.
Examples:

TIP

$a-b$ and $b-a$ are opposites and when canceled give -1.

1. Reduce: $\frac{15x+7x^2-2x^3}{x^2-8x+15}$

$\frac{x\cancel{(5-x)}^{-1}(3+2x)}{(x-3)\cancel{(x-5)}}$ Factor.

$\frac{-x(3+2x)}{(x-3)}$

The factors $(x-5)$ and $(5-x)$ are not equal, but they are opposites. Therefore, when canceled, these factors yield -1.

2. Multiply: $\frac{a^3+a^2b}{5a}\cdot\frac{25}{3a+3b}$

$\frac{a^2(a+b)}{5a}\cdot\frac{25}{3(a+b)}$ Cancel a, $(a+b)$, and 5.

$\frac{\cancel{a^2}^{a}\cancel{(a+b)}}{\cancel{5}\cancel{a}}\cdot\frac{\cancel{25}^{5}}{3\cancel{(a+b)}}$

$\frac{5a}{3}$

3. Divide: $\frac{x-y}{4x+4y}\div\frac{x^2-2xy+y^2}{x^2-y^2}$

$\frac{x-y}{4(x+y)}\div\frac{(x-y)}{(x-y)(x+y)}$ Factor.

$\frac{\cancel{x-y}}{4\cancel{(x+y)}}\cdot\frac{\cancel{(x-y)}\cancel{(x+y)}}{\cancel{(x-y)}^{2}}$ Invert second fraction and cancel.

$\frac{1}{4}$

Addition and Subtraction

The same rules for addition and subtraction that are used in arithmetic apply to the addition and subtraction of algebraic fractions.

$$\frac{a}{b} \pm \frac{c}{b} = \frac{a \pm c}{b}, \; b \neq 0$$

Examples:

1. Add: $\frac{3}{5x} + \frac{5-6x}{10x^2}$

First find the lowest common denominator.

$5 \cdot x$ Use each factor the greater number of

$2 \cdot 5 \cdot x \cdot x$ times it appears. The LCD is $10x^2$

Rewrite each fraction so that the denominators of the fractions are the same. Then add the numerators and reduce, if possible.

$$\frac{6x}{10x^2} + \frac{5-6x}{10x^2} = \frac{6x+(5-6x)}{10x^2}$$
$$= \frac{5}{10x^2} = \frac{1}{2x^2}$$

TIP  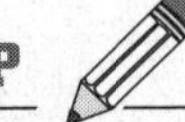

Addition and subtraction of algebraic fractions are two of the most complicated operations in algebra. Breaking the operations into manageable steps, however, can reduce any confusion.

2. Subtract: $\frac{3}{x^2-5x+6} - \frac{2}{x^2-x-2}$

Factor each denominator: $(x-2)(x-3)$
$(x-2)(x+1)$

Therefore the LCD is $(x-2)(x-3)(x+1)$. The numerator and denominator of the first fraction must be multiplied by the factor $(x+1)$, and those in the second fraction by $(x-3)$,

$$\frac{3(x+1)}{(x-2)(x-3)(x+1)} - \frac{2(x-3)}{(x-2)(x-3)(x+1)} = \frac{3(x+1)-2(x-3)}{(x-2)(x-3)(x+1)}$$
$$= \frac{3x+3-2x+6}{(x-2)(x-3)(x+1)}$$
$$= \frac{x+9}{(x-2)(x-3)(x+1)}$$

Fractional Equations

An equation that has a variable in a denominator is a *fractional* equation. In addition to the usual procedure for solving equations, care must be exercised to see that the proposed solution set does not contain numbers that would make any denominator zero. The proposed solution set must be checked, and the extraneous solutions omitted.

Example:

Solve: $2 + \frac{4}{x-2} = \frac{8}{x^2-2x}$ Multiply both sides by the LCD: $x(x-2)$

$$x(x-2)\left(2+\frac{4}{x-2}\right) = \left(\frac{8}{x^2-2x}\right)x(x-2) \qquad x \neq 0,2$$
$$2x(x-2)+4x = 8$$
$$2x^2-4x+4x = 8$$
$$2x^2-8 = 0$$
$$2(x-2)(x+2) = 0$$
$$x-2=0 \qquad x+2=0$$
$$x=2 \qquad x=-2$$

But $x \neq 0,2$, so the only solution is $\{-2\}$.

Solve: $\frac{7}{z-5}-\frac{6}{z+3}=\frac{48}{z^2-2z-15}$

$7(z + 3) - 6(z - 5) = 48$ Multiply by $(z - 5)(z + 3)$, $z \neq 5, -3$.

$7z + 21 - 6z + 30 = 48$

$z + 51 = 48$

$z = -3$ But -3 makes the second denominator zero, so the solution set is empty.

Warm-Up Drill

Perform the indicated operations and simplify.

1. $\frac{x^2-16}{x}\cdot\frac{3}{4-x}$

2. $\frac{z^2-z-6}{z-6}\cdot\frac{z^2-6z}{z^2+2z-15}$

3. $\frac{a^3-b^3}{a^2-b^2}\div\frac{a^2+ab+b^2}{a^2+ab}$

4. $\frac{2}{x+1}+\frac{6}{x-1}$

5. $\frac{2x}{2x^2-x-1}-\frac{3x}{3x^2-5x+2}$

6. $\frac{\frac{3}{x}-5}{6+\frac{1}{x}}$

7. $\frac{\frac{3}{x}-\frac{2}{y}}{\frac{9y^2-4x^2}{xy}}$

Solve each equation.

8. $\frac{5y}{y+1}-\frac{y}{3y+3}=\frac{-56}{6y+6}$

9. $\frac{2}{x-3}-\frac{3}{x+3}=\frac{12}{x^2-9}$

SOLUTIONS

1. $\frac{(x-4)(x+4)}{x}\cdot\frac{3}{4-x}$

$=\frac{-1(x+4)}{x}\cdot\frac{3}{1}$ $(x - 4)$ and $(4 - x)$ are opposites.

$=\frac{-3(x+4)}{x}$

2. $\frac{(z-3)(z+2)}{z-6}\cdot\frac{z(z-6)}{(z+5)(z-3)}$

$=\frac{z+2}{1}\cdot\frac{z}{z+5}$

$=\frac{z(z+2)}{z+5}$

3. $\frac{(a-b)(a^2+ab+b^2)}{(a-b)(a+b)} \cdot \frac{a(a+b)}{a^2+ab+b^2}$

$= \frac{1}{1} \cdot \frac{a}{1} = a$

4. The LCD is $(x + 1)(x - 1)$.

$\frac{2(x-1)}{(x+1)(x-1)} + \frac{6(x+1)}{(x+1)(x-1)}$

$= \frac{2x-2+6x+6}{(x+1)(x-1)}$

$= \frac{8x+4}{(x+1)(x-1)}$

5. Factor each denominator:

$(2x + 1)(x - 1)$

$(3x - 2)(x - 1)$

The LCD is $(2x + 1)(3x - 2)(x - 1)$.

$\frac{2x(3x-2)}{(2x+1)(3x-2)(x-1)} - \frac{3x(2x+1)}{(2x+1)(3x-2)(x-1)}$

$= \frac{2x(3x-2)-3x(2x+1)}{(2x+1)(3x-2)(x-1)}$

$= \frac{6x^2-4x-6x^2-3x}{(2x+1)(3x-2)(x-1)}$

$= \frac{-7x}{(2x+1)(3x-2)(x-1)}$

6. Multiply the numerator and denominator by the LCD, which is x.

$\frac{3-5x}{6x+1}$ (Complex fractions; see pages 184–185.)

7. Multiply the numerator and denominator by the LCD, which is xy.

$\frac{3y-2x}{9y^2-4x^2} = \frac{3y-2x}{(3y-2x)(3y+2x)}$

$= \frac{1}{3y+2x}$

8. Multiply both sides of the equation by the LCD, which is $6(y + 1)$.

$30y - 2y = -56$

$28y = -56$

$y = -2$

The solution set is $\{-2\}$. The only restricted value is -1.

9. Multiply by the LCD, which is $(x - 3)(x + 3)$. The restricted values are 3 and -3.

$2(x + 3) - 3(x - 3) = 12$

$2x + 6 - 3x + 9 = 12$

$-x + 15 = 12$

$-x = -3$

$x = 3$

Because 3 is a restricted value, the solution set is empty.

Practice Exercises

The following sample questions represent ways in which the reviewed skills might be tested on the ACT.

1. Find the solution set: $1-\frac{2x-1}{6}=\frac{3x}{8}$

   A. $\{28\}$
   B. $\left\{\frac{28}{17}\right\}$
   C. $\left\{\frac{7}{5}\right\}$
   D. $\left\{\frac{20}{17}\right\}$
   E. $\{\}$

2. Solve: $4(x-3) > 9(x+2)$

   F. $\{x|x < -1\}$
   G. $\{x|x > -1\}$
   H. $\{x|x > -6\}$
   J. $\{x|x < -6\}$
   K. $\left\{x\middle|x > \frac{-6}{5}\right\}$

3. Divide: $(2x^3 - x + 4) \div (x - 2)$

   A. $2x^2 + 4x + 7$ remainder 18
   B. $2x + 3$ remainder 10
   C. $2x - 5$ remainder 14
   D. $2x^2 - 4x + 7$ remainder -10
   E. $2x^2 + 3x + 6$ remainder 16

4. Factor completely over integers: $4x^2 - 4x - 15$

   F. $(2x - 5)(2x - 3)$
   G. $(4x + 5)(x - 3)$
   H. $(2x + 3)(2x - 5)$
   J. $(2x - 15)(2x + 1)$
   K. $(2x - 3)(2x + 5)$

5. Solve: $(x - 1)(x + 9) = 11$

   A. $\{-10, 2\}$
   B. $\{10, -2\}$
   C. $\{12, 2\}$
   D. $\{1, -9\}$
   E. $\{-1, 9\}$

ANSWERS AND EXPLANATIONS

1. **(B)**

$$1-\frac{2x-1}{6}=\frac{3x}{8}$$
$$24\left(1-\frac{2x-1}{6}\right)=\left(\frac{3x}{8}\right)24$$
$$24-4(2x-1)=9x$$
$$24-8x+4=9x$$
$$24-8x+4=9x$$
$$28-8x=9x$$
$$28=17x$$
$$x=\frac{28}{17}$$

The solution set is $\left\{\frac{28}{17}\right\}$.

2. **(J)** $4(x - 3) > 9(x + 2)$

$4x - 12 > 9x + 18$
$-5x - 12 > 18$
$-5x > 30$ Reverse sense of inequality when
$x < -6$ dividing by a negative number.

The solution set is $\{x|x < -6\}$.

3. **(A)** Use synthetic division:

$$\begin{array}{r|rrrr} 2 & 2 & 0 & -1 & 4 \\ & & 4 & 8 & 14 \\ \hline & 2 & 4 & 7 & 18 \end{array}$$

The quotient is $2x^2 + 4x + 7$ remainder 18.

4. **(H)** $4x^2 - 4x - 15$
$= 4x^2 + 6x - 10x - 15$
$= 2x(2x + 3) - 5(2x + 3)$
$= (2x + 3)(2x - 5)$

Multiply the first and last coefficients.
$4 \cdot 15 = 60 = 6 \cdot 10$
Factors of 60 whose difference is 4.

5. **(A)** $(x - 1)(x + 9) = 11$
$x^2 + 8x - 9 = 11$
$x^2 + 8x - 20 = 0$
$(x + 10)(x - 2) = 0$
$x + 10 = 0 \qquad x - 2 = 0$
$x = -10 \qquad x = 2$
The solution set is $\{-10, 2\}$.

Word Problems

Word Problem 1:

Two-thirds of the graduating class of Limerick Avenue Elementary School are girls, and 25% of the girls are also in the band. If there are eight graduating girls in the band, how many are in the graduating class?

Solution:

If $25\% = \frac{1}{4}$ of the girls are in the band, and that number is eight, then there must be $4 \cdot 8 = 32$ girls in the graduating class. The number of girls in the graduating class represents $\frac{2}{3}$ of all the graduating students. Let x equal the number of students in the graduating class. Then:

$\frac{2}{3}x = 32$ Multiply both sides by $\frac{2}{3}$.

$\frac{3}{2} \cdot \frac{2}{3}x = 32 \cdot \frac{3}{2}$

$x = 48$ There are 48 students in the graduating class.

Word Problem 2:

A plumber has a pipe that is ten feet long from which he needs to cut pieces that are each 1 foot 4 inches long. How many pieces can he cut from the ten-foot-long pipe, and how long is the remaining unused piece?

Solution:

First, change all measurements to inches and divide: 1 foot 4 inches = 16 inches; 10 feet = 120 inches.

$$120 \div 16 = 7\frac{1}{2}$$

The plumber can cut 7 pieces, each 1 foot 4 inches, from the long pipe, and there will be a piece that represents $\frac{1}{2}$ of one of the 1 foot 4 inches pieces left. One-half of 1 foot 4 inches is 8 inches—the length of the remaining unused piece.

Word Problem 3:

The average cost of three books for Jason's classes is \$74.16. What should the average cost of the next two books that he buys be so that his average for all five books is \$90?

Solution:

If the average cost of three books is \$74.16, it's as if each book cost exactly that amount. If x represents the average cost of the next two books, then:

$$\frac{3(74.16)+2x}{5}=90 \quad \text{Multiply both sides by 5.}$$

$$222.48+2x=450 \quad \text{Subtract 222.48 from both sides.}$$

$$2x=227.52$$

$$x=113.76 \quad \text{The average cost of the next two books is \$113.76.}$$

Word Problem 4:

Linda commutes a one-way total of 40 miles to work each day—part by car and part by train. If the ratio of the distance traveled by car to the distance traveled by train is 1 to 9, how far does she ride on the train?

Solution:

Suppose she divides her total trip of 40 miles into 10, (1 + 9), equal parts of 4 miles each. Then she drives her car for one of them and rides the train for nine of them. Therefore, she rides the train 36 miles.

This problem could also be solved by using an equation:

$$x + 9x = 40$$

Word Problem 5:

On the last day of her yard sale, Carol placed a sign on her books that read, "Fifty cents each or 5 for \$2.00." What percent would a customer save on each book by buying five?

Solution:

The cost of each book when buying five is 2.00 ÷ 5 = 0.40. Therefore the customer saves 10 cents on each book. But the question is "What percent…," so the interpretation is: 10 is what percent of 50? (the original cost)

So the proportion is:

$$\frac{10}{50}=\frac{P}{100} \quad \text{Cross multiply.}$$

$$50P=1000 \quad \text{Divide by 50.}$$

$$P=20 \quad \text{The customer saves 20\% on each book.}$$

In this section, certain typical word problems of the kind found in most algebra courses will be solved in detail with hints given to aid in their solution.

1. *Read the problem carefully,* often several times until the meaning of the problem is clear.
2. *Make a sketch or diagram* if it would help make the problem clear.
3. *Choose a variable* to represent an unknown quantity in the problem. Many times it is helpful to put the variable where the question is.
4. *Represent all other unknown quantities* in terms of the chosen variable.
5. *Write an equation.* Many times a well-known formula can be used. Other times a literal translation of the problem leads to the equation. This is the most difficult step in the procedure.
6. *Solve the equation.*
7. *Answer the question.*

Example 1: Uniform motion problem

One train starts from Des Moines and travels toward Dallas at 40 miles per hour at the same time that a second train starts from Dallas and travels toward Des Moines on a parallel track. If the distance between Dallas and Des Moines is 1080 miles on these tracks and the trains pass each other in 12 hours, what is the speed of the second train?

Solution:

A diagram may help organize the information in the problem.

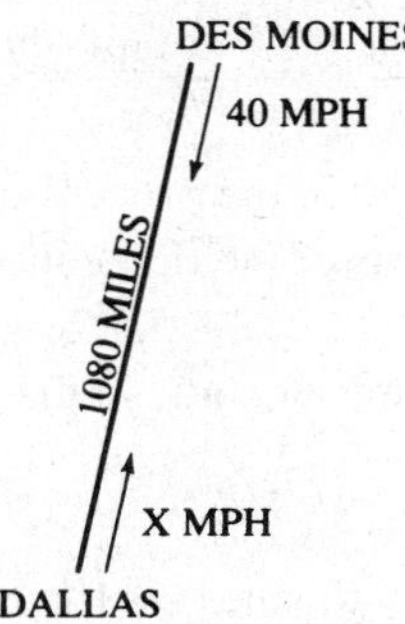

In all problems involving uniform motion, the following formula applies:

$$d = rt$$

A chart constructed with the aid of this formula will help to find an equation that can be used to answer the problem. Let us choose to let the variable represent the speed of the second train. When all else fails, put the variable in the chart where the question is.

	d =	r •	t
To Dallas		40	12
From Dallas		x	12

When two boxes in any row are filled in, let the formula fill in the third box. In this case the formula indicates that the distances traveled by each train are $40(12) = 480$ and $12x$.

	d =	r •	t
To Dallas	480	40	12
From Dallas	$12x$	x	12

As is common with this type of problem, one piece of information did not get into the chart—the total distance between the cities, 1080 miles. Use this information to write the equation:

Total distance = 1080 miles

The sum of the entries in the d column total 1080

$$480 + 12x = 1080$$

Solve this equation.

$$12x = 600$$
$$x = 50$$

Therefore the speed of the second train is 50 miles per hour.

Example 2: Mixture problem

A nurse needs 20 ml of a 30% alcohol solution. The only solutions available are 25% and 50%. How many milliliters of each should be mixed in order to obtain the required solution?

Solution:

A diagram of the physical situation will be helpful. Draw three containers, two whose contents will be mixed together to obtain the third. Under each container describe the contents, and inside the containers label the quantity that it holds.

$$\underset{25\%}{\lfloor x \text{ ml} \rfloor} + \underset{50\%}{\lfloor (20-x) \text{ ml} \rfloor} = \underset{30\%}{\lfloor 20 \text{ ml} \rfloor}$$

The amount of alcohol does not change in the process of mixing. This is the basis of the equation. Twenty-five percent of the contents of the first container is alcohol; 50% of the second container is alcohol. Together they contain $0.25x + 0.5(20 - x)$ ml of alcohol. Thirty percent of the final mixture [0.3(20)] is supposed to be alcohol, so the equation is:

$$0.25x + 0.5(20 - x) = 0.3(20)$$

To solve this equation, first multiply both sides by 100 to get rid of the decimal numbers.

TIP

Multiply outside parentheses and *not inside.*

$$\begin{aligned} 25x + 50(20 - x) &= 30(20) \\ 25x + 1000 - 50x &= 600 \\ -25x + 1000 &= 600 \\ -25x &= -400 \\ x &= 16 \end{aligned}$$

The nurse must mix 16 ml of the 25% solution with 4 ml of the 50% solution in order to obtain 20 ml of a solution that is 30% alcohol.

Example 3: Consecutive integer problem

The sum of three consecutive odd integers is 87. Find the integers.

If the problem is about consecutive integers, let the integers be represented by

$$\begin{aligned} &x \\ &x + 1 \\ \text{and} \quad &x + 2 \end{aligned}$$

If the problem is about consecutive even or consecutive odd integers, let them be represented by

$$\begin{aligned} &x \\ &x + 2 \\ \text{and} \quad &x + 4 \end{aligned}$$

Solution:

The sum of three consecutive odd integers is represented by

$$x + (x + 2) + (x + 4)$$

The problem states that this sum is equal to 87. Therefore the equation is

$$x + (x + 2) + (x + 4) = 87$$

To solve this equation first simplify the left side.

$$\begin{aligned} 3x + 6 &= 87 \\ 3x &= 81 \\ x &= 27 \end{aligned}$$

The three consecutive odd integers are

$$\begin{aligned} x &= 27 \\ x + 2 &= 29 \\ \text{and } x + 4 &= 31 \end{aligned}$$

Example 4: Geometric problem

The length of a rectangle is 4 meters more than 5 times its width. Find the dimensions of the rectangle if its perimeter is 68 meters.

Solution:

Always draw a diagram for geometric type problems.

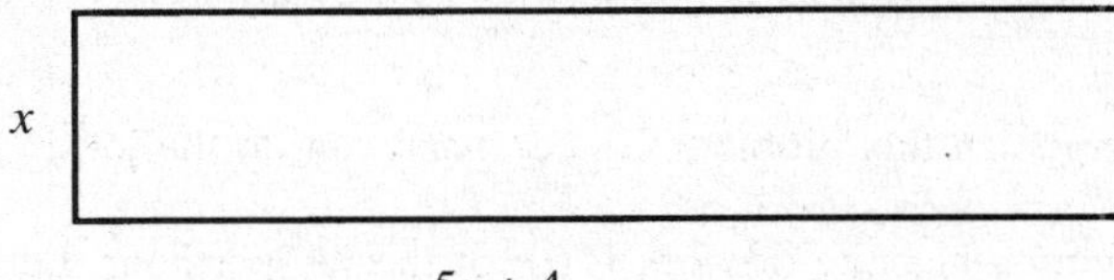

If x represents the width of the rectangle then the length is $5x + 4$. One must know certain formulas that apply to geometric figures. In this case the perimeter of a rectangle is: $P = 2l + 2w$. Therefore the equation is:

$$68 = 2(5x + 4) + 2x$$

To solve this equation, first simplify the right side.

$$\begin{aligned} 68 &= 10x + 8 + 2x \\ 68 &= 12x + 8 \\ 60 &= 12x \\ 5 &= x \end{aligned}$$

Then $5x + 4 = 29$.
The width of the rectangle is 5 meters and its length is 29 meters.

Example 5: Age problem

Lisa is now six years older than Cheryl. In two years, Lisa will be twice as old as Cheryl. How old is each girl now?

Solution:

A chart will aid in organizing this problem. Make a chart with one row for each person and the first column headed "Now." Since the problem makes a statement about two years from now, let the other column heading be "2 years hence."

	Now	2 years hence
Lisa	$x + 6$	
Cheryl	x	

Let the column heading fill in the second column—add 2 to each value of the first column.

	Now	2 years hence
Lisa	$x + 6$	$x + 8$
Cheryl	x	$x + 2$

Now Lisa's age in two years $(x + 8)$ is twice Cheryl's age in two years $(x + 2)$. Therefore the equation is:

$$x + 8 = 2(x + 2)$$

To solve this equation, first simplify the right side.

$$\begin{aligned} x + 8 &= 2x + 4 \\ 8 &= x + 4 \\ 4 &= x \end{aligned}$$

Cheryl is now 4 years old and Lisa is 10 years old.

Example 6: Work problem

Diana can type a batch of 100 form letters in six hours. When Frankie helps, they can do the job together in four hours. How long will it have taken Frankie to do the job if he worked alone?

Solution:

The formula that applies to this type of problem states that the amount of work accomplished is equal to the rate of work times the amount of time spent working.

$$w = rt$$

A chart will help to organize this problem. Since Diana can do the job in 6 hours, she can do $\frac{1}{6}$ of the job in one hour—her rate of work is $\frac{1}{6}$ of the job per hour. Let the amount of time that it would take Frankie to do the job be x, then his rate is $\frac{1}{x}$ part of the job per hour. Both work for 4 hours. (The 100 is extra information not needed in the solution of the problem.)

	w =	r •	t
Diana		$\frac{1}{6}$	4
Frankie		$\frac{1}{x}$	4

Let the formula fill in the third column of the chart.

	w =	r •	t
Diana	$\frac{2}{3}$	$\frac{1}{6}$	4
Frankie	$\frac{4}{x}$	$\frac{1}{x}$	4

Diana does $\frac{2}{3}$ of the work, and Frankie does $\frac{4}{x}$ part of the work. A completed job in this type of problem is always represented by the number 1 (*one* completed job.)
The equation therefore is:

$$\frac{2}{3}+\frac{4}{x}=1$$

To solve this equation, first multiply by the common denominator, $3x$.

$$2x + 12 = 3x$$
$$12 = x$$

It would take Frankie 12 hours to do the job alone.

Example 7: Time problem

Elizabeth agreed to do a certain job for $48.00. She was able to finish the job in two hours less time than she had anticipated it would take. As a result she earned $2 per hour more than she would have if the job had taken the anticipated amount of time. How long did she anticipate that the job would take to complete?

Solution:

Let x represent the amount of time she had anticipated it would take her to complete the job. Then $x - 2$ represents the amount of time it actually took her to do the job. Let's organize the information:

	Total price	Number of hours	Price per hour
Anticipated	\$48	x	$\frac{48}{x}$
Actually	\$48	$x-2$	$\frac{48}{x-2}$

The problem states that she actually earned \$2 per hour more than she had anticipated. The equation is therefore

$$\frac{48}{x-2} = \frac{48}{x} + 2 \qquad \text{Multiply both sides by } x(x - 2).$$

$$48x = 48(x - 2) + 2x(x - 2)$$
$$48x = 48x - 96 + 2x^2 - 4x$$

This equation is quadratic, so write it in standard form and factor.

$$0 = 2x^2 - 4x - 96$$
$$0 = 2(x^2 - 2x - 48)$$
$$0 = 2(x - 8)(x + 6)$$
$$x - 8 = 0 \qquad x + 6 = 0$$
$$x = 8 \qquad x = -6$$

The solution set is $\{8, -6\}$.

The solution -6 is obviously extraneous. The answer is:

Elizabeth anticipated that it would take her 8 hours to do the job.

Warm-Up Drill

1. An airplane has just enough fuel for a five-hour flight. How far can it fly on a round trip on which, during the first leg of the trip, it flies with the wind at 225 miles per hour and, during the return trip, it flies against the wind at 180 miles per hour?
2. A race car needs a fuel mixture that is 20% alcohol. How many liters of a 10% alcohol fuel mixture must be combined with 100 liters of a 40% alcohol mixture in order to obtain the required percentage of alcohol?
3. Find four consecutive even integers whose sum is 100.
4. Find the dimensions of a rectangle whose perimeter is 38 m and whose area is 84 square meters.
5. Diane was 24 years old when her daughter Heidi was born. In how many years will Diane be four years less than five times Heidi's age?
6. One pipe can fill a tank in four hours; another pipe can fill the same tank in three hours. If both pipes flow at the same time, how long will it take to fill the tank?
7. Clarice purchased some very breakable items for sale in her shop. She paid \$100 for these items, but she discovered that three of the items had broken and could not be sold. When she sold the remaining items for \$5 more per item than she paid for them she discovered that her total profit turned out to be only \$5. How many items did she purchase?

SOLUTIONS

1. Create a chart. Let x be the one way distance traveled.

	d =	r ·	t
With wind	x	225	
Against wind	x	180	

Let the formula fill in the third box in each row of the chart, that is, $t = \frac{d}{r}$.

	d =	r ·	t
With wind	x	225	$\frac{x}{225}$
Against wind	x	180	$\frac{x}{180}$

The sum of the times of the two legs of the trip must be five hours:

$$\frac{x}{225} + \frac{x}{180} = 5$$

Multiply both sides by the common denominator, 900.

$$4x + 5x = 4500$$
$$9x = 4500$$
$$x = 500$$

The one-way distance is 500 miles; therefore the total round-trip distance is 1000 miles.

2. Set up a diagram of containers.

$$\underset{10\%}{\lfloor x \rfloor} + \underset{40\%}{\lfloor 100 \rfloor} = \underset{20\%}{\lfloor x + 100 \rfloor}$$

The amount of alcohol did not change in the mixing process. Therefore the equation is:

$$.1x + .4(100) = .2(x + 100)$$

To solve this equation, first multiply by 10 to get rid of the decimals.

$$x + 4(100) = 2(x + 100)$$
$$x + 400 = 2x + 200$$
$$400 = x + 200$$
$$200 = x$$

One must use 200 liters of the 10% alcohol fuel mixture.

3. The equation is:

$$x + (x + 2) + (x + 4) + (x + 6) = 100$$
$$4x + 12 = 100$$
$$4x = 88$$
$$x = 22$$

The four consecutive even integers are 22, 24, 26, and 28.

4. Draw a diagram.

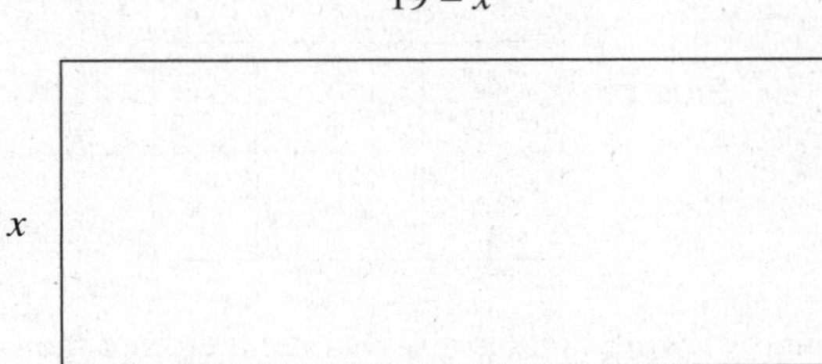

Since the perimeter is 38, then the sum of one length and one width must be half of 38. Therefore if the width is represented by x then the length is $19 - x$.
The equation is therefore:

$$x(19 - x) = 84$$
$$19x - x^2 = 84$$
$$0 = x^2 - 19x + 84$$
$$0 = (x - 12)(x - 7)$$
$$x - 12 = 0 \text{ or } x - 7 = 0$$
$$x = 12 \qquad x = 7$$

If 12 were the width then the length would be 7 (the length is $19 - x$). The width is always the smaller dimension of a rectangle, so 12 is an extraneous solution of the equation.

The width of the rectangle is 7 m and the length is 12 m.

5. Create a chart.

	Age at birth	x years hence
Diane	24	$24 + x$
Heidi	0	x

According to the words of the problem. Diane's age in the future must be 4 less than 5 times Heidi's age then. Therefore the equation is:

$$24 + x = 5x - 4$$
$$24 = 4x - 4$$
$$28 = 4x$$
$$7 = x$$

Therefore this condition will happen in 7 years from Heidi's birth; that is, when Heidi is 7 years old.

6. Create a chart.

	w =	r ·	t
Pipe 1		$\frac{1}{4}$	x
Pipe 2		$\frac{1}{3}$	x

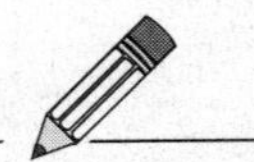

The ACT will not likely require you to do an entire word problem.

Let the formula fill in the third box in each row.

	w =	r •	t
Pipe 1	$\frac{x}{4}$	$\frac{1}{4}$	x
Pipe 2	$\frac{x}{3}$	$\frac{1}{3}$	x

The sum of the amounts of work done is always one; therefore the equation is:

$$\frac{x}{4}+\frac{x}{3}=1$$

Multiply by the common denominator.

$$3x + 4x = 12$$
$$7x = 12$$
$$x = \frac{12}{7} = 1\frac{5}{7}$$

The tank will be filled in $1\frac{5}{7}$ hours.

7. Organize the information.

	Price	No. of items	Price per item
Items purchased	$100	x	$\frac{100}{x}$
Items sold	$105	$x - 3$	$\frac{105}{x-3}$

The selling price is $5 more per item than the purchasing price. The equation is therefore:

$$\frac{105}{x-3} = \frac{100}{x} + 5 \qquad \text{Multiply both sides by } x(x-3).$$
$$105x = 100(x - 3) + 5x(x - 3)$$
$$105x = 100x - 300 + 5x^2 - 15x$$
$$0 = 5x^2 - 20x - 300$$
$$0 = 5(x^2 - 4x - 60)$$
$$0 = 5(x - 10)(x + 6)$$
$$x - 10 = 0 \qquad x + 6 = 0$$
$$x = 10 \qquad x = -6$$

The solution set is {10, –6}.

The solution –6 is obviously extraneous. The answer is:

Clarice purchased 10 items originally.

Laws of Exponents

The following laws of exponents apply to all real-number exponents:

1. $x^m \cdot x^n = x^{m+n}$

2. $(x^m)^n = x^{mn}$

3. $(xy)^m = x^m \cdot y^m$

4. $\frac{x^m}{x^n} = x^{m-n}, x \neq 0$

5. $\left(\frac{x}{y}\right)^m = \left(\frac{x^m}{y^m}\right), y \neq 0$

6. $x^0 = 1, x \neq 0$

7. $x^{-m} = \frac{1}{x^m}, x \neq 0$

a. $\left(\frac{x}{y}\right)^{-m} = \left(\frac{y}{x}\right)^m, x, y \neq 0$

b. $\frac{a}{x^{-m}} = ax^m, x \neq 0$

Here are some examples:

- $x^{5/3} \cdot x^{-2/3} = x^{3/3} = x^1 = x$
- $(x^{3/2})^4 = x^6$
- $(x^3y)^3 = x^9y^3$
- $\frac{x^5}{x^6} = x^{-1} = \frac{1}{x^1} = \frac{1}{x}$
- $\frac{a^3b}{a^{-2}b^2} = a^{3-(-2)}\, b^{1-2} = a^5b^{-1} = \frac{a^5}{b}$
- $\left(\frac{x^2}{y^4}\right)^{-3} = \left(\frac{y^4}{x^2}\right)^3 = \frac{y^{12}}{x^6}$
- $\frac{3^{-2}}{3^{-3}} = 3^{-2-(-3)} = 3^1 = 3$

Warm-Up Drill

Simplify and write without negative exponents.

1. $\frac{x^{10}}{x^4}$
2. $\left(\frac{4x^3}{y^2}\right)^3$
3. $\left(\frac{a^2b^3}{2a^{-2}b}\right)^{-2}$
4. $\frac{2}{a^{-7}}$
5. $\left(\frac{3}{2}\right)^0$
6. $3x^0$
7. $4x^{-2}$
8. $\frac{3x^5y^{-3}}{6y^2}$
9. $(x^6y^{-2})^{-2}$
10. $\left(\frac{2a^{-5}b^9}{c^8}\right)^{-3}$

SOLUTIONS

1. $\frac{x^{10}}{x^4} = x^{10-4} = x^6$

2. $\left(\frac{4x^3}{y^2}\right)^3 = \frac{4^3x^9}{y^6} = \frac{64x^9}{y^6}$

3. $\left(\frac{a^2b^3}{2a^{-2}b}\right)^{-2} = \left(\frac{2a^{-2}b}{a^2b^3}\right)^2 = \frac{2^2a^{-4}b^2}{a^4b^6}$

$= 4a^{-4-4}b^{2-6} = 4a^{-8}b^{-4} = \frac{4}{a^8b^4}$

4. $\frac{2}{a^{-7}} = 2a^7$

5. $\left(\frac{3}{2}\right)^0 = 1$

6. $3x^0 = 3(1) = 3$ An exponent applies only to the immediately preceding symbol.

7. $\frac{4}{x^2}$ Not $\frac{1}{4x^2}$. The exponent applies only to x.

8. $\frac{3x^5y^{-3}}{6y^2} = \frac{1}{2}x^5y^{-3-2} = \frac{1}{2}x^5y^{-5} = \frac{1}{2}x^5\left(\frac{1}{y^5}\right) = \frac{x^5}{2y^5}$

9. $(x^6y^{-2})^{-2} = \left(\frac{x^6}{y^2}\right)^{-2} = \left(\frac{y^2}{x^6}\right)^2 = \frac{y^4}{x^{12}}$

10. $\left(\frac{2a^{-5}b^9}{c^8}\right)^{-3} = \left(\frac{2b^9}{a^5c^8}\right)^{-3} = \left(\frac{a^5c^8}{2b^9}\right)^3 = \frac{a^{15}c^{24}}{8b^{27}}$

Roots and Fractional Exponents

The definition of an nth root is as follows:

a is an nth root of b if and only if $a^n = b$.

The symbol for the nth root of b is $\sqrt[n]{b}$. The number in the notch of the radical, n, is the index, and b is the radicand. According to the definition, this is the number that, when raised to the nth power, yields b. If n is even and b is negative, the nth root of b is not a real number. The laws of exponents apply to all real-number exponents, and $(b^{1/n})^n = b^1 = b$. Since both $\sqrt[n]{b}$ and $b^{1/n}$ give the same result when raised to the nth power, they are defined to be equal: $\sqrt[n]{b} = b^{1/n}$.

The definition of a fractional exponent is as follows:

$a^{p/q} = \sqrt[q]{a^p} = \left(\sqrt[q]{a}\right)^p$ for all real numbers a and integers p and q for which p and q have no common factor and a is not negative if q is even. All of the previous laws of exponents apply to fractional exponents also.

Example 1: $8^{2/3} = \left(\sqrt[3]{8}\right)^2 = 2^2 = 4$

Example 2: $(-125)^{-1/3} = \frac{1}{(-125)^{1/3}} = \frac{1}{\sqrt[3]{-125}} = \frac{1}{-5} = \frac{-1}{5}$

Example 3: $\frac{\sqrt{3}}{\sqrt[3]{3}} = \frac{3^{1/2}}{3^{1/3}} = 3^{1/2-1/3} = 3^{1/6} = \sqrt[6]{3}$

Simplest Radical Form

A radical expression is said to be in simplest radical form (SRF) if the following conditions are met:

1. The radicand has no perfect nth-power factors.
2. There are no fractions in the radicand.
3. There are no radicals in a denominator.

Here are some examples of these rules:

- $\sqrt{12}$ is not in simplest radical form because the radicand has $4 = 2^2$ as a factor. To put $\sqrt{12}$ in SRF, factor the radicand so that one factor is the largest square factor of the radicand. Then use the rule of radicals.

$$\sqrt[n]{xy} = (\sqrt[n]{x})(\sqrt[n]{y}) \text{ for all defined radicals.}$$

The square factor can be extracted from the radical.

$$\sqrt{12} = \sqrt{4 \cdot 3} = \sqrt{4} \cdot \sqrt{3} = 2\sqrt{3}$$

- $\sqrt[3]{32x^3y^8} = \sqrt[3]{(8x^3y^6)(4y^2)}$ Separate the radicand into cube and noncube factors.

$$= \sqrt[3]{8x^3y^6} \cdot \sqrt[3]{4y^2}$$

$$= 2xy^2\sqrt[3]{4y^2}$$

- $\sqrt{\dfrac{5}{8}}$ is not in SRF because of rule 2 above. To simplify, multiply the numerator and denominator by some number in order to make the denominator a perfect square. Then use the rule of radicals

$$\sqrt[n]{\frac{x}{y}} = \frac{\sqrt[n]{x}}{\sqrt[n]{y}} \text{ for all defined radicals.}$$

$$\sqrt{\frac{5}{8}} = \sqrt{\frac{5 \cdot 2}{8 \cdot 2}} = \sqrt{\frac{10}{16}} = \frac{\sqrt{10}}{\sqrt{16}} = \frac{\sqrt{10}}{4}$$

- $\dfrac{7}{\sqrt[3]{12}}$ is not in SRF because of rule 3 above. To simplify, multiply the numerator and denominator by an appropriate radical to make the bottom radicand a perfect nth power.

$$\frac{7}{\sqrt[3]{12}} = \frac{7\sqrt[3]{18}}{\sqrt[3]{12}\sqrt[3]{18}} = \frac{7\sqrt[3]{18}}{\sqrt[3]{216}} = \frac{7\sqrt[3]{18}}{6}$$

Since $12 = 2 \cdot 2 \cdot 3$, one more 2 and two 3's are needed to make a perfect cube. Multiply by $2 \cdot 3 \cdot 3 = 18$ in the radical.

- $\dfrac{2}{3 - \sqrt{2}}$ is not in SRF because of rule 3 above. To simplify, multiply by an appropriate radical expression, sometimes called the *conjugate* of the denominator. In this case, multiply the numerator and denominator by $3 + \sqrt{2}$.

$$\frac{2(3 + \sqrt{2})}{(3 - \sqrt{2})(3 + \sqrt{2})} = \frac{2(3 + \sqrt{2})}{9 - 2} = \frac{2(3 + \sqrt{2})}{7} = \frac{6 + 2\sqrt{2}}{7}$$

Warm-Up Drill

Simplify. Assume all variables are non-negative.

1. $2^{1/3} \cdot 2^{1/4}$
2. $\dfrac{1}{8^{-4/3}}$
3. $\sqrt{500}$
4. $\sqrt{20x^6}$
5. $\sqrt[4]{x^5y^7}$
6. $\sqrt{\dfrac{5}{12}}$
7. $\dfrac{6}{\sqrt{3}}$
8. $\dfrac{4}{\sqrt{6}-4}$
9. $\sqrt[8]{4x^6y^{10}}$
10. $\sqrt[3]{1080x^4y^6z^8}$
11. $\dfrac{10}{\sqrt[3]{18}}$

SOLUTIONS

1. $\mathbf{2^{1/3} \cdot 2^{1/4}} = 2^{1/3+1/4} = 2^{7/12}$

2. $\mathbf{\dfrac{1}{8^{-4/3}}} = 8^{4/3} = (\sqrt[3]{8})^4 = 2^4 = 16$

3. $\mathbf{\sqrt{500}} = \sqrt{(100 \cdot 5)} = \sqrt{100} \cdot \sqrt{5} = 10\sqrt{5}$

4. $\mathbf{\sqrt{20x^6}} = \sqrt{(4x^6)(5)} = \sqrt{4x^6}\sqrt{5} = 2x^3\sqrt{5}$

5. $\mathbf{\sqrt[4]{x^5y^7}} = \sqrt[4]{(x^4y^4)(xy^3)}$

   $= \sqrt[4]{x^4y^4} \cdot \sqrt[4]{xy^3} = xy\sqrt[4]{xy^3}$

6. $\mathbf{\sqrt{\dfrac{5}{12}}} = \sqrt{\dfrac{15}{36}}$ Multiply by $\dfrac{3}{3}$ to make the denominator a square.

   $= \dfrac{\sqrt{15}}{\sqrt{36}} = \dfrac{\sqrt{15}}{6}$

7. $\mathbf{\dfrac{6}{\sqrt{3}}} = \dfrac{6\sqrt{3}}{\sqrt{9}}$ Multiply by $\dfrac{\sqrt{3}}{\sqrt{3}}$ to make the denominator a square.

   $= \dfrac{6\sqrt{3}}{3} = 2\sqrt{3}$

8. $\mathbf{\dfrac{4}{\sqrt{6}-4}}$

   $= \dfrac{4(\sqrt{6}+4)}{(\sqrt{6}-4)(\sqrt{6}+4)}$ Multiply the numerator and denominator by the conjugate of the denominator.

   $= \dfrac{4(\sqrt{6}+4)}{6-16}$

   $= \dfrac{4(\sqrt{6}+4)}{-10} = \dfrac{-2(\sqrt{6}+4)}{5} = \dfrac{-2\sqrt{6}-8}{5}$ Reduce the fraction.

9. $\mathbf{\sqrt[8]{4x^6y^{10}}} = \sqrt[4]{\sqrt{4x^6y^{10}}} = \sqrt[4]{2x^3y^5} = \sqrt[4]{y^4 \cdot 2x^3y} = \sqrt[4]{y^4} \cdot \sqrt[4]{2x^3y} = y\sqrt[4]{2x^3y}$

10. Look for the largest cube factor of the radicand.

$$1080x^4y^6z^8 = 2^3 \cdot 3^3 \cdot 5 \cdot x^3 \cdot x \cdot y^6 \cdot z^6 \cdot z^2$$

$$\begin{aligned} \text{So } \sqrt[3]{1080x^4y^6z^8} &= \sqrt[3]{2^3 \cdot 3^3 \cdot x^3 \cdot y^6 \cdot z^6 \cdot (5xz^2)} \\ &= \sqrt[3]{2^3 \cdot 3^3 \cdot x^3 \cdot y^6 \cdot z^6} \cdot \sqrt[3]{5xz^2} \\ &= 2 \cdot 3 \cdot x \cdot y^2 \cdot z^2 \cdot \sqrt[3]{5xz^2} \\ &= 6xy^2z^2\sqrt[3]{5xz^2} \end{aligned}$$

11. $\dfrac{10}{\sqrt[3]{18}} = \dfrac{10\sqrt[3]{12}}{\sqrt[3]{18}\sqrt[3]{12}} = \dfrac{10\sqrt[3]{12}}{\sqrt[3]{216}} = \dfrac{10\sqrt[3]{12}}{6} = \dfrac{5\sqrt[3]{12}}{3}$

Operations with Radicals

All of the following discussion assumes that the radicals represent real numbers, that is, there are no even roots of negative numbers.

Any radicals with the same index may be multiplied or divided according to the following rules:

$$\sqrt[n]{x}\,\sqrt[n]{y} = \sqrt[n]{xy} \text{ and } \frac{\sqrt[n]{x}}{\sqrt[n]{y}} = \sqrt[n]{\frac{x}{y}}$$

Radicals may be added and subtracted only if both the indices and the radicands are the same.

$$a\sqrt[n]{x} \pm b\sqrt[n]{x} = (a \pm b)\sqrt[n]{x}$$

Warm-Up Drill

Perform the indicated operations and simplify. Assume all variables are non-negative.

1. $5\sqrt{8} - 3\sqrt{72} + 3\sqrt{50}$
2. $6\sqrt[3]{128m} - 3\sqrt[3]{16m}$
3. $\sqrt{2}(\sqrt{32} - \sqrt{9})$
4. $(\sqrt{7} + \sqrt{3})(\sqrt{7} - \sqrt{3})$
5. $(4\sqrt{5})^2$
6. $(\sqrt{6} - \sqrt{2})^2$
7. $\dfrac{\sqrt{3} + 1}{\sqrt{5} + \sqrt{3}}$
8. $(9 + 3\sqrt{6})(8 + 2\sqrt{6})$

SOLUTIONS

1. $\mathbf{5\sqrt{8} - 3\sqrt{72} + 3\sqrt{50}}$

   Simplify each radical first.

   $5\sqrt{8} = 5 \cdot 2\sqrt{2} = 10\sqrt{2}$

   $3\sqrt{72} = 3 \cdot 6\sqrt{2} = 18\sqrt{2}$

   $3\sqrt{50} = 3 \cdot 5\sqrt{2} = 15\sqrt{2}$

   $10\sqrt{2} - 18\sqrt{2} + 15\sqrt{2} = 7\sqrt{2}$

2. $\mathbf{6\sqrt[3]{128m} - 3\sqrt[3]{16m}}$

$6\sqrt[3]{128m} = 6\sqrt[3]{(64)(2m)}$

$= 6 \cdot 4\sqrt[3]{2m} = 24\sqrt[3]{2m}$

$3\sqrt[3]{16m} = 3\sqrt[3]{(8)(2m)}$

$= 3 \cdot 2\sqrt[3]{2m} = 6\sqrt[3]{2m}$

$24\sqrt[3]{2m} - 6\sqrt[3]{2m} = 18\sqrt[3]{2m}$

3. $\mathbf{\sqrt{2}(\sqrt{32} - \sqrt{9})}$ Apply the distributive property.

$= \sqrt{64} - \sqrt{18}$

$= 8 - \sqrt{9 \cdot 2} = 8 - 3\sqrt{2}$

4. $\mathbf{(\sqrt{7} + \sqrt{3})(\sqrt{7} - \sqrt{3})}$

$= \sqrt{49} - \sqrt{9}$ This is the same FOIL for binomials.

$= 7 - 3 = 4$

5. $\mathbf{(4\sqrt{5})^2} = 16\sqrt{25}$ Square each factor.

$= 16 \cdot 5 = 80$

6. $\mathbf{(\sqrt{6} - \sqrt{2})^2}$

$= \sqrt{36} - 2\sqrt{12} + \sqrt{4}$ Use the same pattern as squaring a binomial. Then

$= 6 - 4\sqrt{3} + 2 = 8 - 4\sqrt{3}$ simplify.

7. $\mathbf{\dfrac{\sqrt{3} + 1}{\sqrt{5} + \sqrt{3}}}$

$= \dfrac{(\sqrt{3} + 1)(\sqrt{5} - \sqrt{3})}{(\sqrt{5} + \sqrt{3})(\sqrt{5} - \sqrt{3})}$ Multiply the numerator and denominator by the conjugate of the denominator.

$= \dfrac{\sqrt{15} - \sqrt{9} + \sqrt{5} - \sqrt{3}}{\sqrt{25} - \sqrt{9}}$

$= \dfrac{\sqrt{15} + \sqrt{5} - \sqrt{3} - 3}{2}$

8. $(9 + 3\sqrt{6})(8 + 2\sqrt{6})$ $= 72 + 18\sqrt{6} + 24\sqrt{6} + 6\sqrt{36}$ Like FOIL.

$= 72 + 42\sqrt{6} + 6 \cdot 6$

$= 72 + 42\sqrt{6} + 36$

$= 108 + 42\sqrt{6}$

Radical Equations

TIP

You cannot find the square root of negative numbers.

The procedure for solving radical equations is to raise both sides of the equation to the nth power at an appropriate point. This does not always assure that equivalent equations will result; therefore the potential solutions must be checked in the original equation. Solutions are not lost in the process, but frequently extraneous solutions are introduced and must be eliminated.

Examples:

Solve each of the following:

1. $\sqrt{3x+1} - 4 = 0$ Isolate the radical term first, if possible.

$\sqrt{3x+1} = 4$ Square both sides. This eliminates the radical on the left.

$3x + 1 = 16$

$3x = 15$

$x = 5$

Check: $\sqrt{3 \cdot 5 + 1} - 4 = \sqrt{16} - 4 = 0$

The solution set is {5}.

2. $x = \sqrt{x^2 - 4x - 8}$ Square both sides.

$x^2 = x^2 - 4x - 8$

$0 = -4x - 8$

$4x = -8$

$x = -2$

Check $-2 \neq \sqrt{(-2)^2 - 4(-2) - 8} = \sqrt{+4 - (-8) - 8} = \sqrt{4} = 2$

Since $-2 \neq 2$, -2 is not a solution.

The solution set is empty.

3. $\sqrt{x^2 - 3x + 3} = x - 1$ Be sure to square the binomial on the right.

$x^2 - 3x + 3 = x^2 - 2x + 1$

$-3x + 3 = -2x + 1$

$3 = x + 1$

$2 = x$

Check: $\sqrt{2^2 - 3 \cdot 2 + 3} = 2 - 1$

$\sqrt{4 - 6 + 3} = 1$

$\sqrt{1} = 1$

The solution set is {2}.

4. $\sqrt{x+6} - \sqrt{x-2} = 2$ Separate the radicals.

$\sqrt{x+6} = \sqrt{x-2} + 2$ Carefully square both sides.

$x + 6 = x - 2 + 4\sqrt{x-2} + 4$

$6 = 2 + 4\sqrt{x-2}$

$4 = 4\sqrt{x-2}$

$1 = \sqrt{x-2}$ Square again.

$1 = x - 2$

$3 = x$

Check $\sqrt{3+6} - \sqrt{3-2} = \sqrt{9} - \sqrt{1} = 3 - 1 = 2$

The solution set is {3}.

Warm-Up Drill

Solve.

1. $\sqrt{5x-1}+3=0$
2. $\sqrt{y^2-4y+9}=y-1$
3. $\sqrt{5x+6}+\sqrt{3x+4}=2$

SOLUTIONS

1. $\mathbf{\sqrt{5x-1}+3=0}$

$\sqrt{5x-1}=-3$ Square both sides.

$5x-1=9$

$5x=10$

$x=2$

Check: $\sqrt{5\cdot 2-1}+3=\sqrt{9}+3$

$=3+3=6\neq 0$

The solution set is empty.

2. $\mathbf{\sqrt{y^2-4y+9}=y-1}$ Square both sides.

$y^2-4y+9=y^2-2y+1$

$8=2y$

$4=y$

Check: $\sqrt{4^2-4\cdot 4+9}=4-1$

$\sqrt{16-16+9}=3$

$\sqrt{9}=3$

The solution set is $\{4\}$.

3. $\mathbf{\sqrt{5x+6}+\sqrt{3x+4}=2}$ Separate the radicals.

$\sqrt{5x+6}=2-\sqrt{3x+4}$ Square both sides.

$5x+6=4-4\sqrt{3x+4}+3x+4$

$2x-2=-4\sqrt{3x+4}$

$x-1=-2\sqrt{3x+4}$ Square again.

$x^2-2x+1=4(3x+4)=12x+16$

$x^2-14x-15=0$

$(x-15)(x+1)=0$

$x-15=0$ or $x+1=0$

$x=15$ or $x=-1$

Check 15: $\sqrt{5\cdot 15+6}+\sqrt{3\cdot 15+4}$

$=\sqrt{81}+\sqrt{49}$

$=9+7$

$=16\neq 2$

15 is not a solution.

Check 1: $\sqrt{5(-1)+6}+\sqrt{3(-1)+4}$

$=\sqrt{1}+\sqrt{1}$

$=1+1=2$

The solution set is $\{-1\}$.

Practice Exercises

The following sample questions represent ways in which the reviewed skills might be tested on the ACT.

1. Which equation could be used to solve the following problem?

   The sum of the squares of two consecutive whole numbers is 85. Find the whole numbers.

   A. $[x + (x + 1)]^2 = 85$
   B. $x^2 + x^2 + 1 = 85$
   C. $x^2 + (x + 2)^2 = 85$
   D. $x^2 + (x + 1)^2 = 85$
   E. None of these.

2. Simplify: $-2x^{-2}$

   F. $\frac{1}{4x^2}$
   G. $\frac{-1}{4x^2}$
   H. $\frac{-1}{2x^2}$
   J. $\frac{-2}{x^2}$
   K. $4x^2$

3. Express in simplest radical form: $\frac{-12}{\sqrt{20}}$

   A. $\frac{-6}{\sqrt{5}}$
   B. $\frac{-6\sqrt{5}}{5}$
   C. $\frac{-3\sqrt{20}}{5}$
   D. $\frac{-3}{\sqrt{5}}$
   E. $\frac{-3\sqrt{5}}{5}$

4. Simplify: $2\sqrt{18} - \sqrt{50}$

   F. 1
   G. 60
   H. $\sqrt{2}$
   J. $-7\sqrt{2}$
   K. None of these.

5. Solve: $\sqrt{x - 1} = x - 3$

   A. $\{5, 2\}$
   B. $\{2\}$
   C. $\{-5, -2\}$
   D. $\{\ \}$
   E. $\{5\}$

ANSWERS AND EXPLANATIONS

1. **(D)** Two consecutive whole numbers may be represented by x and $x + 1$. Therefore the sum of their squares is $x^2 + (x + 1)^2$.

2. **(J)** Any exponent applies only to the immediate preceding symbol.

3. **(B)** $\frac{-12}{\sqrt{20}}$ To make the radicand in the denominator

   $\frac{-12}{\sqrt{20}} \cdot \frac{\sqrt{5}}{\sqrt{5}}$ a perfect square, multiply top and bottom

   $\frac{-12\sqrt{5}}{\sqrt{100}}$ by $\sqrt{5}$.

   $\frac{\overset{-6}{\cancel{-12}}\sqrt{5}}{\underset{5}{\cancel{10}}}$ Reduce.

4. **(H)** $2\sqrt{18} - \sqrt{50}$
$= 2\sqrt{9 \cdot 2} - \sqrt{25 \cdot 2}$
$= 2 \cdot 3\sqrt{2} - 5\sqrt{2}$
$= 6\sqrt{2} - 5\sqrt{2} = \sqrt{2}$

5. **(E)** $\sqrt{x - 1} = x - 3$ Square both sides.
$x - 1 = x^2 - 6x + 9$
$0 = x^2 - 7x + 10$
$(x - 5)(x - 2) = 0$
$x - 5 = 0 \qquad x - 2 = 0$
$x = 5, x = 2$
2 is extraneous. The solution set is $\{5\}$.

Distance Formula

The distance between any two points on a number line can be found by taking the absolute value of the difference of the coordinates.

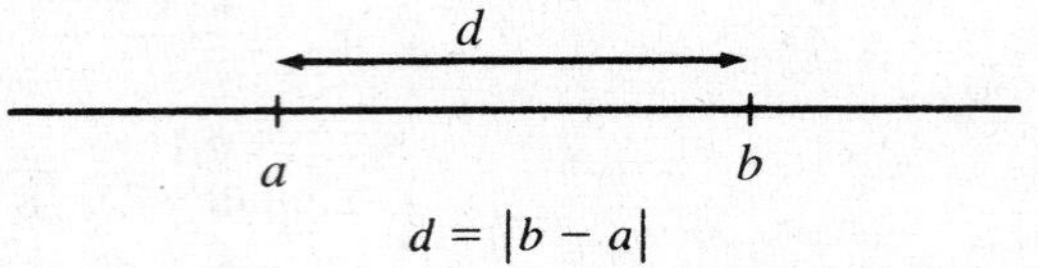

$$d = |b - a|$$

The distance between any two points (x_1, y_1) and (x_2, y_2) in the plane can be found by the distance formula, which is a result of the Pythagorean Theorem.

$$d = \sqrt{(x_2 - x_1)^2 + (y_2 - y_1)^2}$$

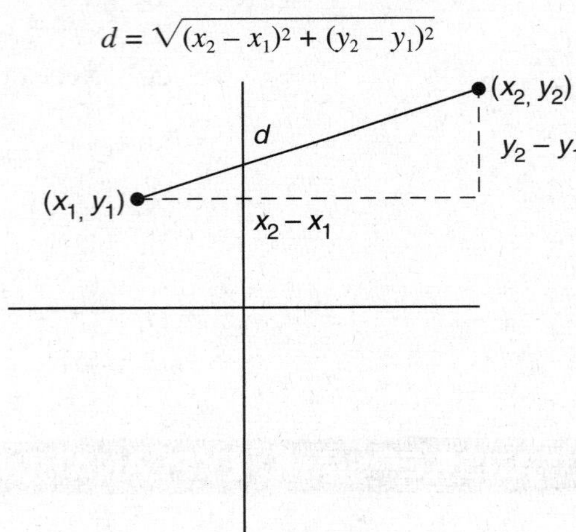

Midpoint Formula

The midpoint of the segment between two points $A\ (x_1, y_1)$ and $B\ (x_2, y_2)$ is found by averaging the x-coordinates and the y-coordinates

$$\text{midpoint of } \overline{AB}: \left(\frac{x_1 + x_2}{2}, \frac{y_1 + y_2}{2}\right)$$

Warm-Up Drill

1. Find the distance between the following points on a number line:
   a. 6 and 15
   b. –3 and –11
   c. –5 and 12
2. Find the distance between the following points in the plane:
   a. (2, 5) and (5, 9)
   b. (–4, 8) and (6, 1)
   c. (0, –5) and (–3, –2)
   d. $(\sqrt{2}, -1)$ and $(3\sqrt{2}, -5)$
3. Find the midpoint of the segment between each pair of points in problem 2 above.
4. Determine if the triangle with vertices at *A* (–1, 1), *B* (1, 3), and *C* (6, –2) is a right triangle or not.

SOLUTIONS

1. a. $|15 - 6| = 9$

   b. $|-11 - (-3)| = |-8| = 8$

   c. $|12 - (-5)| = |17| = 17$

2. a. $d = \sqrt{(5-2)^2 + (9-5)^2} = \sqrt{3^2 + 4^2} = \sqrt{9 + 16} = \sqrt{25} = 5$

   b. $\sqrt{[6-(-4)]^2 + (1-8)^2} = \sqrt{10^2 + (-7)^2} = \sqrt{100 + 49} = \sqrt{149}$

   c. $\sqrt{(-3-0)^2 + [-2-(-5)]^2} = \sqrt{(-3)^2 + 3^2} = \sqrt{9+9} = \sqrt{18} = 3\sqrt{2}$

   d. $\sqrt{(3\sqrt{2} - \sqrt{2})^2 + [-5-(-1)]^2} = \sqrt{(2\sqrt{2})^2 + (-4)^2} = \sqrt{8+16} = \sqrt{24} = 2\sqrt{6}$

3. a. $\left(\frac{2+5}{2}, \frac{5+9}{2}\right) = \left(\frac{7}{2}, 7\right)$

   b. $\left(1, \frac{9}{2}\right)$

   c. $\left(\frac{-3}{2}, \frac{-7}{2}\right)$

   d. $(2\sqrt{2}, -3)$

4. Find the length of each side:

   $AB = \sqrt{[1-(-1)]^2 + (3-1)^2} = \sqrt{2^2 + 2^2} = \sqrt{8} = 2\sqrt{2}$

   $BC = \sqrt{(6-1)^2 + (-2-3)^2} = \sqrt{5^2 + (-5)^2} = \sqrt{50} = 5\sqrt{2}$

   $AC = \sqrt{[6-(-1)]^2 + [-2-1]^2} = \sqrt{7^2 + (-3)^2} = \sqrt{58}$

   Then check to see whether or not these lengths satisfy the Pythagorean Theorem.

$$(2\sqrt{2})^2 + (5\sqrt{2})^2 \stackrel{?}{=} (\sqrt{58})^2$$
$$8 + 50 = 58$$

   Therefore, yes, $\triangle ABC$ is a right triangle.

Linear Equations

The graph of every linear equation is a line in the rectangular coordinate system. A linear equation is one that is equivalent to $Ax + By = C$ in which not both A and B are zero. A linear equation written in the form $Ax + By = C$ is in *standard form*.

TIP

A graphing calculator may help with linear equations.

The two ordered pairs obtained by choosing each variable in turn to be 0 are the coordinates of the intercepts of the graph of a linear equation. In other words, by choosing $x = 0$, one obtains the ordered pair $(0, b)$, the y-intercept. The ordered pair $(a, 0)$ is the x-intercept.

For any two ordered pairs (x_1, y_1) and (x_2, y_2) on the graph of a linear equation, the following is called the *slope formula:*

$$m = \frac{y_2 - y_1}{x_2 - x_1} \text{ if } x_1 \neq x_2$$

If $x_1 = x_2$, then the line is vertical, and it has no slope. If $y_1 = y_2$, then the line is horizontal, and it has slope 0. Zero slope is very different from no slope.

Slopes of parallel lines are equal. The product of the slopes of perpendicular lines is –1. Of course neither of these statements is true if either line is vertical because vertical lines have no slope. But on the other hand, all vertical lines are parallel to each other and every vertical line is perpendicular to every horizontal line.

A linear equation written in the form

$$y = mx + b$$

is said to be in *slope-intercept* form because the coefficient of x is the slope of the line m and b is the y-intercept. This form is most useful for determining the slope of a line, given its equation.

When an equation is written in this form, the right side of the equation may be entered into a graphing calculator. By choosing an appropriate viewing window, you can graph the equation on the calculator screen. Then by using the *trace* function on the calculator, you can find specific ordered pairs on the graph.

Equations whose graphs are vertical lines cannot be graphed on a graphing calculator. The equations of all vertical lines are of the type $x =$ *constant,* so there is no way to solve for the variable y.

We derive the *point-slope* form of the equation of the line from the slope formula:

$$y - y_1 = m(x - x_1)$$

in which m is the slope and (x_1, y_1) is a given fixed point on the line. This form is most useful for determining the equation of a line with certain given characteristics.

Warm-Up Drill

Graph.

1. $x + 2y = 3$
2. $5x - 2y = 7$
3. $x + 2 = 0$

Find the slope of the line:

4. through (2, 3) and (–1, 5)
5. with equation $2x - 3y = 5$
6. perpendicular to the line with equation $4x - 3y = 8$.

Find the standard form of the equation of the line:

7. through (–3, 4) with slope $m = \frac{5}{8}$
8. through (–8, 1) and (3, 5)
9. through (5,–2) and parallel to the line with equation $3x + 2y = 8$.
10. through (–1,–3) and perpendicular to the line with equation $x - 3y = -1$.

SOLUTIONS

1. It is a good idea to find three ordered pairs for each linear equation; the third one serves as a built-in check. Three ordered pairs: (1, 1) (3, 0), (–3, 3).

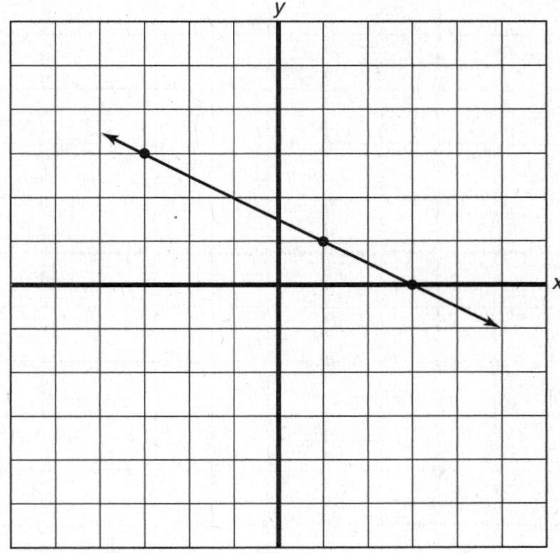

2. Three ordered pairs: (1, –1), (3, 4), (–1, –6). (It is actually more likely that ordered pairs like $\left(2, \frac{3}{2}\right)$ would show up. No matter; fractions are OK.)

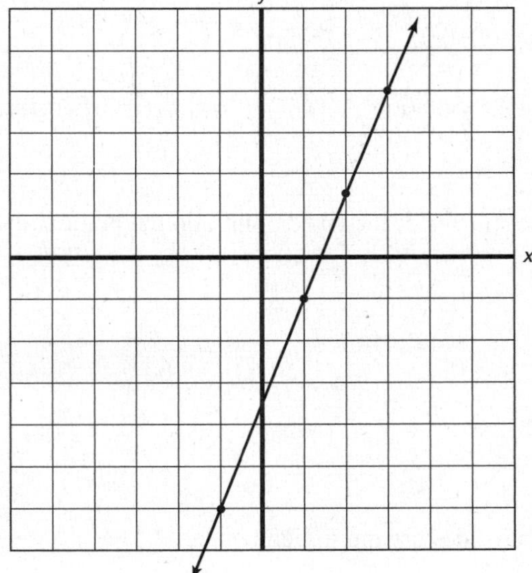

3. Because the y-variable is not in the equation, its value may be chosen to be any convenient number as long as $x = -2$. Three ordered pairs: $(-2, 0)$, $(-2, 3)$, $(-2, -4)$.

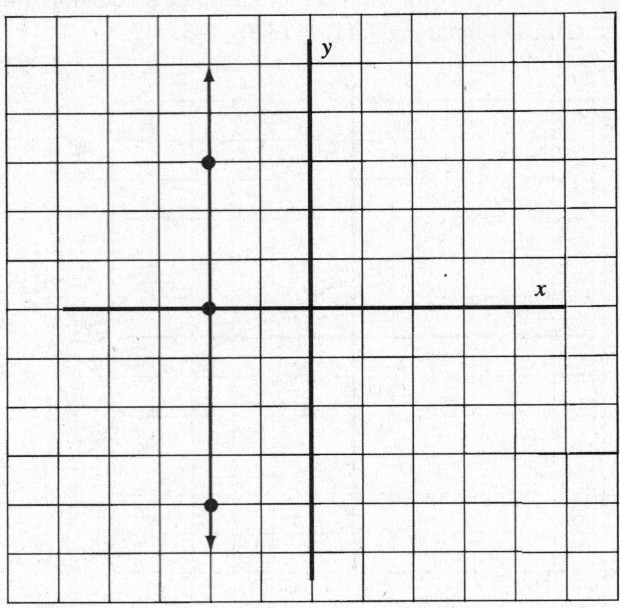

4. $\frac{y_2 - y_1}{x_2 - x_1} = \frac{5 - 3}{-1 - 2} = \frac{2}{-3} = \frac{-2}{3}$

5. Solve the equation for y: $y = \frac{2}{3}x - \frac{5}{3}$.
   The slope is the coefficient of x: $\frac{2}{3}$.

6. The slope of the line whose equation is $4x - 3y = 8$ is $\frac{4}{3}$. Then the slope of the line perpendicular to that line is $\frac{-3}{4}$.

7. Plug the slope and the coordinates of the fixed point into the point-slope form:
   $y - 4 = \frac{5}{8}[x - (-3)]$
   $y - 4 = \frac{5}{8}(x + 3)$ Multiply by 8.
   $8y - 32 = 5(x + 3)$
   $8y - 32 = 5x + 15$
   $-5x + 8y = 47$
   or
   $5x - 8y = -47$ if both sides are multiplied by -1.

8. First find the slope: $m = \frac{5 - 1}{3 - (-8)} = \frac{4}{11}$.
   Choose either ordered pair, and plug into the point-slope form:
   $y - 5 = \frac{4}{11}(x - 3)$
   $11y - 55 = 4(x - 3)$
   $11y - 55 = 4x - 12$
   $-4x + 11y = 43$
   or
   $4x - 11y = -43$

9. Find the slope of the given line:
   $3x + 2y = 8$
   $2y = -3x + 8$
   $y = \frac{-3}{2}x + 4$ The slope is $\frac{-3}{2}$.
   Now use the point-slope form:
   $y - (-2) = \frac{-3}{2}(x - 5)$
   $y + 2 = \frac{-3}{2}(x - 5)$
   $2y + 4 = -3x + 15$
   $3x + 2y = 11$
   [An easier method is to plug the coordinates of the point into the left side of the equation.
   $3x + 2y = 3(5) + 2(-2) = 15 + (-4) = 11$]
10. Find the slope of the given line:
   $x - 3y = -1$
   $-3y = -x - 1$
   $y = \frac{1}{3}x + \frac{1}{3}$ The slope is $\frac{1}{3}$.
   Therefore the slope of the line that is perpendicular to it is -3. Use the point-slope form.
   $y - (-3) = -3(x - (-1))$
   $y + 3 = -3(x + 1)$
   $y + 3 = -3x - 3$
   $3x + y = -6$

SYSTEMS OF LINEAR EQUATIONS

A group of two or more equations considered together is called a system of equations (or simultaneous equations). The solution of a system of equations is the set of all points of intersection of their graphs. There are several methods for solving a system of equations, the least efficient being the graphing method. Two algebraic methods, the addition method and the substitution method, are both more efficient than graphing and always work.

The Addition Method

In the addition method, multiply both sides of one or both of the equations by constants so that a variable is eliminated by adding the left sides and right sides of the equations.

TIP

The addition method is also known as the *elimination method* or the *elimination by addition method.*

Example: Solve the system: $\begin{pmatrix} 2x + 3y = 11 \\ 3x - 4y = 8 \end{pmatrix}$

Multiply both sides of the first equation by 4, and the second equation by 3.

$$\begin{pmatrix} 8x + 12y = 44 \\ 9x - 12y = 24 \end{pmatrix}$$

Add the left sides and the right sides of the equations.

$$17x = 68$$

This equation is easy to solve; divide both sides by 17.

$$x = 4$$

If the equations were graphed, they would intersect at a point with x-value 4: {(4, ?)}. To find the y-value, substitute $x = 4$ into either of the original equations, say, the first one:

$$2(4) + 3y = 11$$
$$8 + 3y = 11$$
$$3y = 3$$
$$y = 1$$

The solution to the system is {(4, 1)}.

Example: Solve the system: $\begin{pmatrix} 4x - 3y = -2 \\ 6x + 5y = -1 \end{pmatrix}$

Multiply both sides of the first equation by 5, and the second by 3.

$$\begin{pmatrix} 20x - 15y = -10 \\ 18x + 15y = -3 \end{pmatrix}$$

Add the left sides and the right sides of the equations

$38x = -13$ Divide both sides by 38.

$$x = \frac{-13}{38}$$

Instead of substituting this number, it is easier to eliminate the other variable to solve for y. Multiply both sides of the first equation by 3, and the second by –2.

$$\begin{pmatrix} 12x - 9y = -6 \\ -12x - 10y = 2 \end{pmatrix}$$

Add the left sides and the right sides of the equations.

$-19y = -4$ Divide both sides by –19.

$$y = \frac{4}{19}$$

The solution to the system is $\left\{\left(\frac{-13}{38}, \frac{4}{19}\right)\right\}$.

This answer is impossible to read from a graph.

Warm-Up Drill

Solve the following systems of equations.

1. $\begin{pmatrix} x - 3y = 4 \\ 2x - 3y = 5 \end{pmatrix}$

2. $\begin{pmatrix} 2x + 5y = 4 \\ 3x - 2y = 6 \end{pmatrix}$

3. $\begin{pmatrix} x + 3y = -2 \\ 2x - 7y = 3 \end{pmatrix}$

SOLUTIONS

1. $\begin{pmatrix} x-3y=4 \\ 2x-3y=5 \end{pmatrix}$ Multiply both sides of the first equation by –1.

$\begin{pmatrix} -x+3y=-4 \\ 2x-3y=5 \end{pmatrix}$ Add the left sides and the right sides.

$x = 1$ Substitute into the first equation.

$1 - 3y = 4$

$-3y = 3$

$y = -1$ The solution is $\{(1, -1)\}$.

2. $\begin{pmatrix} 2x+5y=4 \\ 3x-2y=6 \end{pmatrix}$ Multiply both sides of the first equation by 2, and the second by 5. Then add the left sides and right sides.

$\begin{pmatrix} 4x+10y=8 \\ 15x-10y=30 \end{pmatrix}$

$19x = 38$

$x = 2$ Substitute into the second equation.

$3(2) - 2y = 6$

$6 - 2y = 6$

$-2y = 0$

$y = 0$ The solution is $\{(2, 0)\}$.

3. $\begin{pmatrix} x+3y=-2 \\ 2x-7y=3 \end{pmatrix}$ Multiply both sides of the first equation by –2.

$\begin{pmatrix} -2x-6y=4 \\ 2x-7y=3 \end{pmatrix}$ Add.

$-13y = 7$

$y = \frac{-7}{13}$

It may be easier to eliminate the other variable than to substitute. Multiply both sides of the first equation by 7 and the second by 3.

$\begin{pmatrix} 7x+21y=-14 \\ 6x-21y=9 \end{pmatrix}$ Add.

$13x = -5$

$x = \frac{-5}{13}$ The solution is $\left\{\left(\frac{-7}{13}, \frac{-5}{13}\right)\right\}$.

The Substitution Method

Although all linear systems can be solved by the addition method, it may be more efficient to use the substitution method, particularly if one of the equations is in the form

$$y = mx + b \quad \text{or} \quad x = ny + c$$

Example: Solve: $\begin{pmatrix} y = 2x - 1 \\ x - 3y = 13 \end{pmatrix}$

$\begin{pmatrix} y = \boxed{2x - 1} \\ \downarrow \\ x - 3y = 13 \end{pmatrix}$ Substitute for y in the second equation.

$x - 3(2x - 1) = 13$ Simplify.

$x - 6x + 3 = 13$

$-5x + 3 = 13$ Subtract 3 and divide by -5.

$-5x = 10$

$x = -2$ Now substitute into the circled expression above.

$y = 2(-2) - 1 = -4 - 1 = -5$ The solution is $\{(-2, -5)\}$.

Example: Solve: $\begin{pmatrix} 3x - 4y = -10 \\ x = 6 - y \end{pmatrix}$

$\begin{pmatrix} 3x - 4y = -10 \\ \nwarrow \\ x = \boxed{6 - y} \end{pmatrix}$ Substitute for x in the first equation.

$3(6 - y) - 4y = -10$ Solve for y.

$18 - 3y - 4y = -10$

$18 - 7y = -10$

$-7y = -28$

$y = 4$ Substitute into the circled expression above.

$x = 6 - 4 = 2$ The solution is $\{(2, 4)\}$.

Warm-Up Drill

Solve each system of equations.

1. $\begin{pmatrix} y = \frac{5}{2}x - 2 \\ 3x - y = 4 \end{pmatrix}$ 2. $\begin{pmatrix} 5x + 3y = 7 \\ x - y = 3 \end{pmatrix}$ 3. $\begin{pmatrix} 2x + 3y = -1 \\ 5x - 4y = 3 \end{pmatrix}$

SOLUTIONS

1. Use the substitution method.

$\begin{pmatrix} y = \frac{5}{2}x - 2 \\ 3x - y = 4 \end{pmatrix}$ Substitute for y in the second equation.

$3x - \left(\frac{5}{2}x - 2\right) = 4$ Get rid of parentheses.

$3x - \frac{5}{2}x + 2 = 4$ Multiply both sides by 2.

$6x - 5x + 4 = 8$

$x + 4 = 8$

$x = 4$ Substitute into the second equation.

$3(4) - y = 4$

$12 - y = 4$

$-y = -8$

$y = 8$ The solution is $\{(4, 8)\}$.

2. $\begin{pmatrix} 5x + 3y = 7 \\ x - y = 3 \end{pmatrix}$ Either method could reasonably be used. We'll use substitution.

Solve the second equation for x: $x = y + 3$ (circled)
Substitute for x in the first equation:

$5(y + 3) + 3y = 7$

$5y + 15 + 3y = 7$

$8y + 15 = 7$

$8y = -8$

$y = -1$ Substitute into the circled expression above.

$x = -1 + 3 = 2$ The solution is $\{(2, -1)\}$.

3. $\begin{pmatrix} 2x + 3y = -1 \\ 5x - 4y = 3 \end{pmatrix}$ This system is solved more easily by the addition method.

Multiply both sides of the first equation by 4 and the second by 3.

$\begin{pmatrix} 8x + 12y = -4 \\ 15x - 12y = 9 \end{pmatrix}$ Add the left sides and the right sides.

$23x = 5$

$x = \frac{5}{23}$ Solve for y by multiplying the first equation by 5 and the second by –2.

$\begin{pmatrix} 10x + 15y = -5 \\ -10x + 8y = -6 \end{pmatrix}$ Add.

$23y = -11$

$y = \frac{-11}{23}$ The solution is. $\left\{\left(\frac{5}{23}, \frac{-11}{23}\right)\right\}$.

Special Cases

If, in the process of solving a system of equations, both variables disappear and a false equation results, then the solution set is empty. This is an indication that the graphs of the equations are parallel lines.

Example: Solve: $\begin{pmatrix} 2x - y = -1 \\ 4x - 2y = 5 \end{pmatrix}$

$\begin{pmatrix} 2x - y = -1 \\ 4x - 2y = 5 \end{pmatrix}$ Multiply both sides of the first equation by –2.

$\begin{pmatrix} -4x + 2y = 2 \\ 4x - 2y = 5 \end{pmatrix}$ Add the left sides and right sides of the equations.

$0 = 7$ Both variables are gone, and the resulting equation is false. The solution is { }.

If both variables disappear and a true equation results, then the solution consists of all the points on the line because the graphs of the equations are the same line. The lines coincide and intersect everywhere along their length. The answer can be expressed in several ways:

1. All points on the line
2. An infinite number of points
3. $\{(x, y) | ax + by = c\}$

Example: Solve: $\begin{pmatrix} 3x-2y=6 \\ y=\frac{3}{2}x-3 \end{pmatrix}$

$\begin{pmatrix} 3x-2y=6 \\ y=\frac{3}{2}x-3 \end{pmatrix}$ Substitute for y in the first equation.

$3x-2\left(\frac{3}{2}x-3\right)=6$

$3x - 3x + 6 = 6$

$6 = 6$ Both variables are gone; a true equation results.

The solution is *all points on the line*.

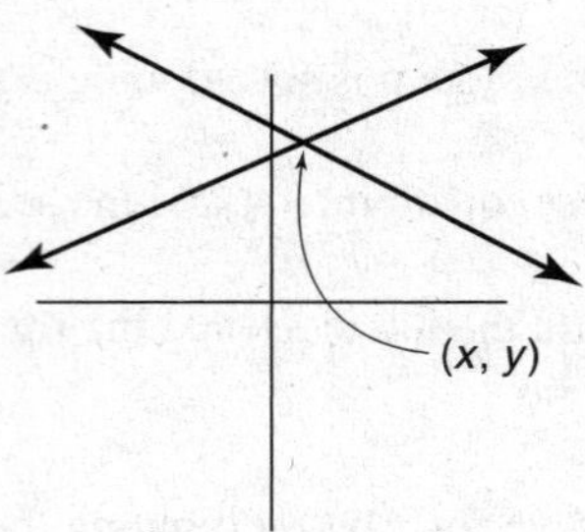

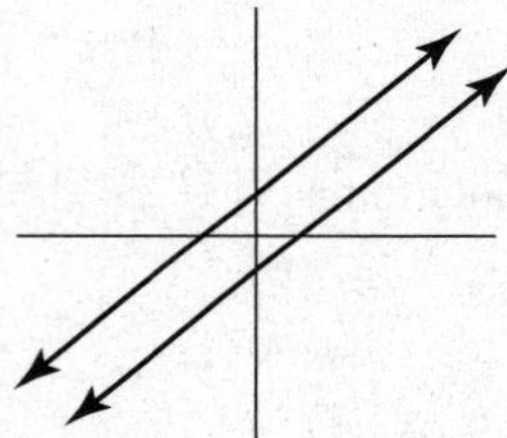

No solution

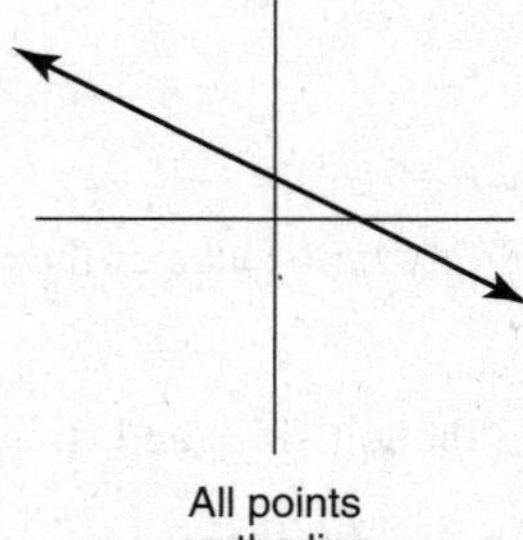

All points on the line

Warm-Up Drill

Solve each system of equations.

1. $\begin{pmatrix} x+y=-8 \\ x-y=2 \end{pmatrix}$ 2. $\begin{pmatrix} x=\frac{1}{3}y+2 \\ 3x-y=6 \end{pmatrix}$ 3. $\begin{pmatrix} 2x+y=-4 \\ 6x+3y=-1 \end{pmatrix}$

SOLUTIONS

1. $\begin{pmatrix} x+y=-8 \\ x-y=2 \end{pmatrix}$ Add the left sides and the right sides of the equations.

$2x = -6$

$x = -3$ Substitute into either equation, say, the first.

$-3 + y = -8$

$y = -5$ The solution is $\{(-3, -5)\}$.

2. $\begin{pmatrix} x=\frac{1}{3}y+2 \\ 3x-y=6 \end{pmatrix}$ Use the substitution method.

$3\left(\frac{1}{3}y+2\right)-y=6$ Simplify.

$y + 6 - y = 6$

$6 = 6$ Both variables are gone, resulting in a true equation.

The solution is *all points on the line*.

3. $\begin{pmatrix} 2x+y=-4 \\ 6x+3y=-1 \end{pmatrix}$ Multiply both sides of the first equation by –3.

$\begin{pmatrix} -6x-3y=12 \\ 6x+3y=-1 \end{pmatrix}$ Add.

$0 = 11$ Both variables are gone, resulting in a false equation.

The solution is the empty set, { }.

CONIC SECTIONS

Circle

The equation of the circle in the plane comes from the distance formula:

$$(x - h)^2 + (y - k)^2 = r^2$$

For an equation in this form the center of the circle is (h, k), and its radius is r.

Ellipse

The equation of an ellipse is:

$\frac{x^2}{a^2} + \frac{y^2}{b^2} = 1$ or $\frac{x^2}{b^2} + \frac{y^2}{a^2} = 1$ Center at the origin. The larger denominator is always a^2.

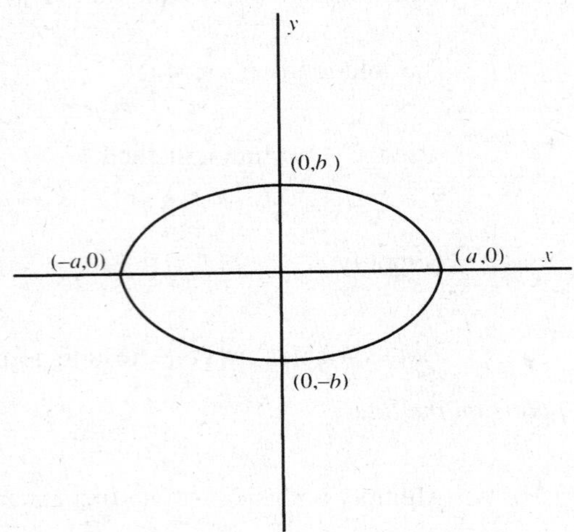

The major axis is a segment of length $2a$, and the minor axis is $2b$. The foci are located along the major axis at a distance $c = \sqrt{a^2 - b^2}$ from the center.

If the center is not at the origin, the equation of an ellipse with major axis oriented horizontally is

$$\frac{(x - h)^2}{a^2} + \frac{(y - k)^2}{b^2} = 1$$

The center is at (h, k).

If the larger denominator is under the variable y, then the major axis is vertical, and the foci are located c units from the center in a vertical direction.

Parabola

The equation of a parabola is either

$$y - k = a(x - h)^2 \qquad \text{or} \qquad x - h = a(y - k)^2$$

In both cases the vertex is at the point (h, k). In the first case the parabola is oriented vertically, so that there is a maximum or a minimum point, depending on whether a is negative or positive, respectively. In the second case the parabola is oriented horizontally, and there is a point farthest to the left or farthest to the right depending on whether a is positive or negative.

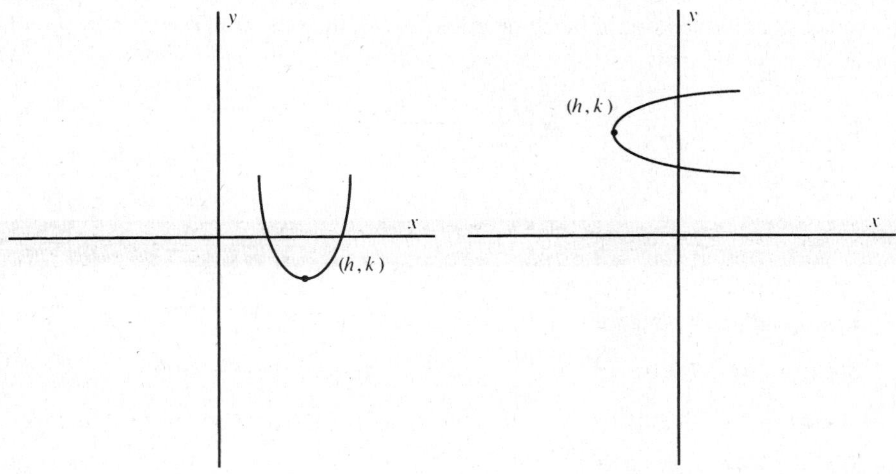

Hyperbola

The equation of a hyperbola is:

$$\frac{x^2}{a^2} - \frac{y^2}{b^2} = 1 \qquad \text{or} \qquad \frac{y^2}{a^2} - \frac{x^2}{b^2} = 1$$

Center at the origin. The positive term identifies a^2. It is not the larger value as with an ellipse.

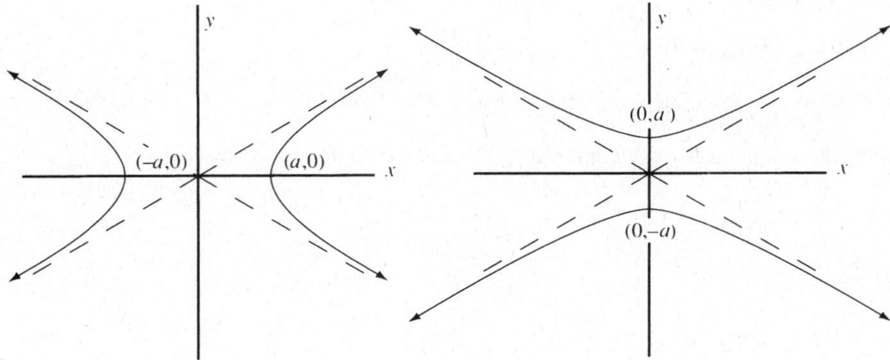

The segment of length $2a$ between the intercepts is called the *transverse axis*. The segment perpendicular to the transverse axis at its midpoint (the center of the hyperbola) of length $2b$ is called the *conjugate axis*.

If the positive term contains the y-variable, then the transverse axis is vertical and the conjugate axis is horizontal.

The foci of the hyperbola are located along the line containing the transverse axis at a distance $c = \sqrt{a^2 + b^2}$ from the center.

The asymptotes of a hyperbola with a horizontal transverse axis are two lines that intersect at the center of the hyperbola and have equations

$$\frac{x}{a} + \frac{y}{b} = 0 \quad \text{and} \quad \frac{x}{a} - \frac{y}{b} = 0$$

The easiest way to find these equations is to factor the left side of the equation in standard form and set each factor equal to zero. (The left side will always be a difference of squares.)

If the center is not at the origin [at some point (h, k)], then the equation of a hyperbola with a horizontal transverse axis is

$$\frac{(x-h)^2}{a^2} - \frac{(y-k)^2}{b^2} = 1$$

Warm-Up Drill

Discuss the graph of each equation.

1. $x^2 + y^2 - 10x - 4y - 7 = 0$
2. $x - 2 = (y - 1)^2$
3. $\frac{(x-3)^2}{25} + \frac{(y+4)^2}{16} = 1$
4. $4x^2 - 25y^2 = -100$
5. $y = x^2 - 6x + 2$

SOLUTIONS

1. $\mathbf{x^2 + y^2 - 10x - 4y - 7 = 0}$ Complete the square in each variable:

$$x^2 - 10x \qquad + y^2 - 4y \qquad = 7$$

Take half of the coefficient of each linear term, square it, and add the result to both sides of the equation.

$x^2 - 10x \underline{+ 25} + y^2 - 4y \underline{+ 4} = 7 \underline{+ 25 + 4}$

$(x - 5)^2 + (y - 2)^2 = 36$ Standard form.

The graph is a circle with center at (5, 2) and radius 6.

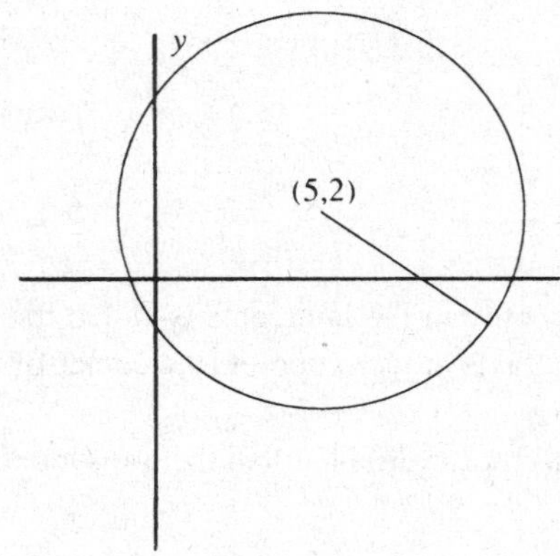

2. Written as $x - 2 = (y - 1)^2$, this equation is the standard form of the equation for a parabola oriented horizontally with a vertex at (2, 1), which happens to be the point farthest to the left. Locating a couple of other points gives the graph.

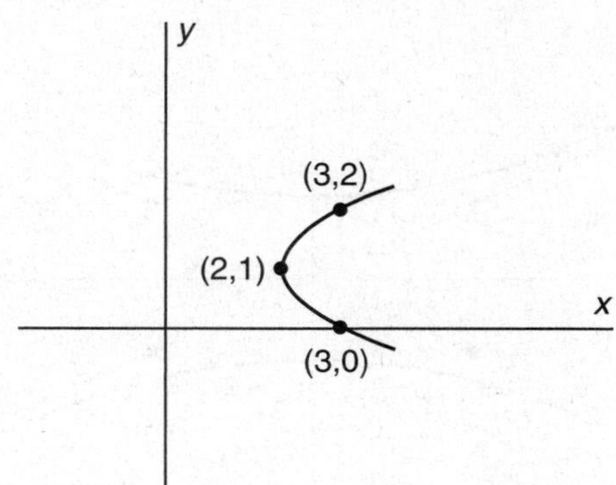

3. $\frac{(x-3)^2}{25} + \frac{(y+4)^2}{16} = 1$ This is the standard form of an equation of an ellipse with major axis horizontal, of length $2a = 10$, minor axis of length $2b = 8$, and center at point (3, –4).

The foci are located $c = \sqrt{5^2 - 4^2} = \sqrt{9} = 3$ units horizontally from the center, (3 + 3, –4) and (3 – 3, –4).

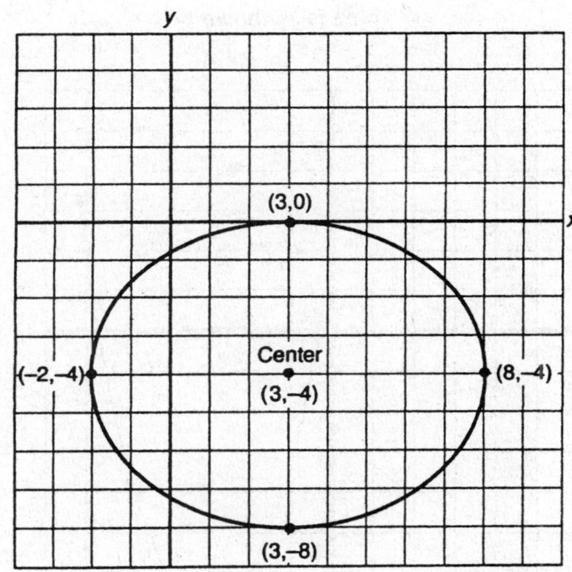

4. $4x^2 - 25y^2 = -100$ To obtain the standard form, divide both sides by –100:

$$\frac{y^2}{4} - \frac{x^2}{25} = 1$$

The graph of this equation is a hyperbola with center at the origin and with transverse axis vertical, of length $2a = 4$, and conjugate axis horizontal, of length $2b = 10$. The asymptote equations are

$$\frac{y}{2} + \frac{x}{5} = 0 \quad \text{and} \quad \frac{y}{2} - \frac{x}{5} = 0$$

The foci are located $c = \sqrt{2^5 + 5^2} = \sqrt{29}$ units from the center along the line containing the transverse axis, that is, at $(0, \sqrt{29})$ and $(0, -\sqrt{29})$.

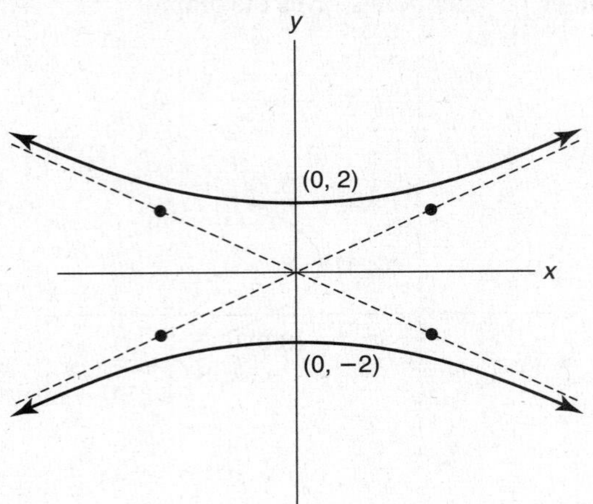

5. $\mathbf{y = x^2 - 6x + 2}$ — Complete the square in x.

$y = x^2 - 6x \underline{+ 9} + 2 \underline{- 9}$

$y = (x - 3)^2 - 7$

$y + 7 = (x - 3)^2$ — This is standard form for a parabola oriented vertically with vertex (minimum point) at $(3, -7)$. When a couple of other points are chosen the graph is as shown below.

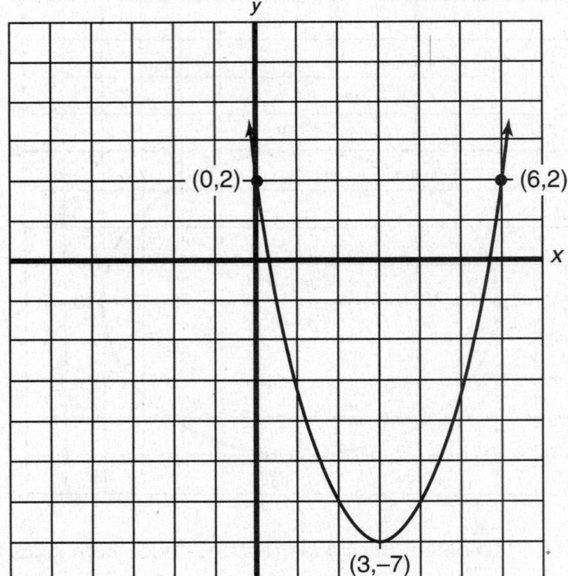

Practice Exercises

The following sample questions represent ways in which the reviewed skills might be tested on the ACT.

1. Find the distance between (–2, 1) and (5, –4).

   A. $2\sqrt{6}$
   B. $\sqrt{74}$
   C. $3\sqrt{2}$
   D. $\sqrt{82}$
   E. $2\sqrt{5}$

2. Find the slope of the line through (5, –2) and (–1, –5).

   F. $\frac{-7}{4}$
   G. 2
   H. $\frac{-1}{2}$
   J. $\frac{1}{2}$
   K. –2

3. Find the standard form of the equation of the line through (4, –8) with slope $\frac{-3}{5}$.

   A. $3x + 5y = -28$
   B. $3x + 5y = 28$
   C. $5x - 3y = -4$
   D. $3x + 5y = -4$
   E. None of these.

4. Which equation's graph is a parabola?

   F. $4x^2 + 2y^2 = 25$
   G. $3x^2 - 5y^2 = 15$
   H. $5x + 2y = 7$
   J. $y = -3x^2 + 2x + 1$
   K. $x^2 + y^2 = 5$

5. What is the center of the circle with equation $x^2 + y^2 -2x + 4y - 5 = 0$?

   A. (2, –4)
   B. (–2, 4)
   C. (1, –2)
   D. (–1, 2)
   E. $\sqrt{10}$

ANSWERS AND EXPLANATIONS

1. **(B)** Apply the distance formula

   $$d = \sqrt{(x_2 - x_1)^2 + (y_2 - y_1)^2}.$$

   $$d = \sqrt{(5 - (-2))^2 + (-4 - 1)^2}$$

   $$\sqrt{7^2 + (-5)^2} = \sqrt{49 + 25} = \sqrt{74}$$

2. **(J)** Apply the slope formula $m = \frac{y_2 - y_1}{x_2 - x_1}$.

   $$m = \frac{-5 - (-2)}{-1 - 5} = \frac{-3}{-6} = \frac{1}{2}$$

3. **(A)** Apply the point-slope form of the equation of the line.

   $$y - (-8) = \frac{-3}{5}(x - 4)$$

   $$5(y + 8) = 5\left[\frac{-3}{5}(x - 4)\right]$$

   $$5y + 40 = -3(x - 4)$$

   $$5y + 40 = -3x + 12$$

   $$3x + 5y = -28$$

4. **(J)** The graphs of the others given are:
(F) ellipse
(G) hyperbola
(H) line
(K) circle

5. **(C)** Complete the square in both x and y:
$x^2 + y^2 - 2x + 4y - 5 = 0$
$(x^2 - 2x \quad) + (y^2 + 4y \quad) = 5$
$(x^2 - 2x + 1) + (y^2 + 4y + 4) =$
$5 + 1 + 4$
$(x - 1)^2 + (y + 2)^2 = 10$

Add the square of half of the coefficients of x and y to both sides. The center is $(1, -2)$.

Functions

A function is a set of ordered pairs of real numbers in which no two ordered pairs have the same first component.

An example of a function according to this definition is

$$f = \{(1, 1), (2, 4), (3, 9), (4, 16), (5, 25)\}$$

The equation $f(x) = y$, read as "f of x equals y," is special notation for functions to indicate that the ordered pair, $(x, y,)$ is in the function. In the example, $f(4) = 16$ conveys the same information as $(4, 16) \in f$.

The *domain* of a function is the set of all first components of the ordered pairs in the function. The *range* is the set of all second components of the ordered pairs. In the example:

$$\text{Domain} = \{1, 2, 3, 4, 5\}$$
$$\text{Range} = \{1, 4, 9, 16, 25\}$$

Many times a function is given by the rule that generates the ordered pairs, rather than by the ordered pairs themselves. For example, $g(x) = x^2$. The domain in this case should always be chosen to be the largest set of real numbers for which the defining rule makes sense—no division by 0 or square roots of negative numbers. The range is usually a more difficult question; it can be determined by examining the rule itself or by observing the graph of the function.

TIP

Range is almost always a more difficult concept to understand than domain.

Consider the defining rules for functions f and g:

$$f(x) = x^2 \qquad \text{and} \qquad g(x) = \frac{1}{x-1}$$

Domain of f: R (all real numbers)
Range of f: $\{y|y \geq 0\}$
Domain of g: $\{x|x \in R \text{ and } x \neq 1\}$
Range of g: $\{y|y \in R \text{ and } y \neq 0\}$ (A graph is the best tool to determine this.)

Other functions can also be created by the usual operations of addition, subtraction, multiplication, and division. For example:

$$(f + g)(x) = f(x) + g(x) = x^2 + \frac{1}{x-1}$$

or

$$\left(\frac{f}{g}\right)(x) = \frac{f(x)}{g(x)} = \frac{x^2}{\frac{1}{x-1}} = x^2(x - 1) \text{ if } x \neq 1$$

The domain of all functions defined in this manner is the intersection of the domains of the original functions except for the quotient. The domain of the quotient also omits numbers for which the second function value is 0.

Another useful combination of functions is called the *composite function:*

$$(f \circ g)(x) = f(g(x)) = f\left(\frac{1}{x-1}\right) = \left(\frac{1}{x-1}\right)^2$$

or

$$(g \circ f)(x) = g(f(x)) = g(x^2) = \frac{1}{x^2 - 1}$$

The domain of $f \circ g$, for example, consists of all numbers in the domain of g such that their function values $g(x)$ are contained in the domain of f.

Domain of $f \circ g$: same as domain of g
Domain of $g \circ f$: $\{x | x \in R \text{ and } x \neq \pm 1\}$

Warm-Up Drill

Find the domain and range of each function (1–3).

1. $f(x) = x^2 + 1$
2. $g(x) = \dfrac{1}{x}$
3. $h(x) = \sqrt{x-1}$
4. Determine the composition function $f \circ g$ and its domain for the functions given in exercises 1 and 2.
5. Determine the difference function $g - h$ and its domain for the functions given in exercises 2 and 3.

SOLUTIONS

1. Domain: R
   Range: $\{y \mid y \in R \text{ and } y \geq 1\}$
2. Domain: $\{x \mid x \in R \text{ and } x \neq 0\}$
   Range: $\{y \mid y \in R \text{ and } y \neq 0\}$
3. Domain: $\{x \mid x \in R \text{ and } x \geq 1\}$
   Range: $\{y \mid y \in R \text{ and } y \geq 0\}$
4. $(f \circ g)(x) = f(g(x)) = f\left(\dfrac{1}{x}\right) = \left(\dfrac{1}{x}\right)^2 + 1$
   Domain: $\{x \mid x \in R \text{ and } x \neq 0\}$
5. $(g - h)(x) = g(x) - h(x) = \dfrac{1}{x} - \sqrt{x-1}$
   Domain: $\{x \mid x \in R \text{ and } x \geq 1\} = D_g \cap D_h$

Exponential and Logarithmic Functions

An *exponential function* is any function of the type

$$f(x) = a^x \qquad \text{for any positive number } a, a \neq 1.$$

The following is a definition of a *logarithmic function:*

$$y = \log_a x \qquad \text{if and only if} \qquad x = a^y.$$

Logarithmic functions are inverses of exponential functions. The inverse of a function, if it exists, is found by reversing all of the ordered pairs in the function. The same effect can be achieved by reversing the roles of x and y in the equation. Consequently, the graphs of inverse functions are always symmetric to the line $y = x$.

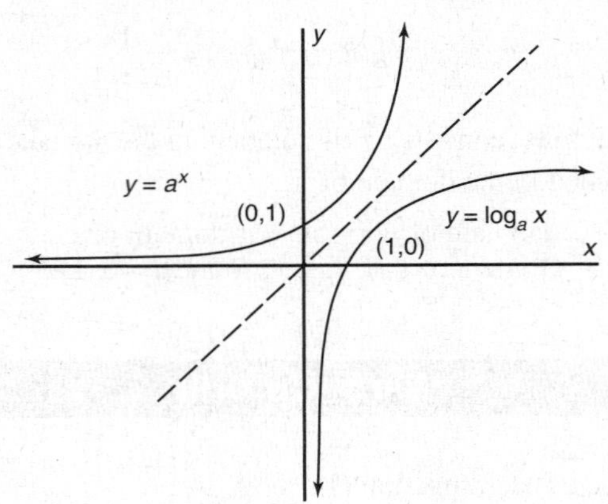

Six fundamental properties of logarithms are easily derived from the definition given above:

1. $\log_a(xy) = \log_a x + \log_a y$ The logarithm of a product is the sum of the logarithms.
2. $\log_a\left(\frac{x}{y}\right) = \log_a x - \log_a y$ The logarithm of a quotient is the difference of the logarithms.
3. $\log_a x^n = n \log_a x$ The logarithm of a power is that power multiplied by the logarithm.
4. $\log_a a^x = x$ and $a^{\log_a x} = x$
5. $\log_a 1 = 0$
6. $\log_a a = 1$

When no base is indicated, the base is understood to be 10. Base 10 logarithms are called common logs.

Examples:

1. Write as a logarithmic equation: $2^5 = 32$.

$$\log_2 32 = 5$$

2. Write as an exponential equation: $\log_2 \frac{1}{8} = -3$.

$$2^{-3} = \frac{1}{8}$$

Evaluate the following logarithms:

3. $\log_8 64$ Let the value of the logarithm be x, and change to the corresponding exponential form.

$$x = \log_8 64$$
$$8^x = 64$$

The answer is easily seen to be 2. So $\log_8 64 = 2$

4. $\log_5 \frac{1}{25} = x$

$$5^x = \frac{1}{25} = 5^{-2} \qquad \text{So } x = -2.$$

5. $\log_6 \sqrt{6^3} = x$

$$6^x = \sqrt{6^3} = (6^3)^{1/2} = 6^{3/2} \qquad \text{So } x = \frac{3}{2}.$$

Solve each equation.

6. $\log_x 9 = \frac{1}{2}$ Change to exponential form.

$x^{1/2} = 9$ Square both sides.

$x = 81$

The solution set is {81}.

7. $\log_{1/2} x = -3$

$$x = \left(\frac{1}{2}\right)^{-3}$$

$$x = 2^3 = 8$$

The solution set is {8}.

8. $4^x = 7$ Take the logarithm of each side.

$\log_a 4^x = \log_a 7$ Any convenient base will do.

$x \log_a 4 = \log_a 7$

$x = \frac{\log_a 7}{\log_a 4}$ It would require a calculator or tables to continue to find a decimal answer.

9. $\log x + \log (3x - 5) = \log 2$ Apply the first rule of logarithms to the left side.

$\log[x(3x - 5)] = \log 2$ If $a = b$, then $10^a = 10^b$.

$$x(3x - 5) = 2$$

$$3x^2 - 5x - 2 = 0$$

$$(3x + 1)(x - 2) = 0$$

$$x = \frac{-1}{3} \text{ or } x = 2$$

Each potential solution must be checked.

Check $\frac{-1}{3}$: $\log\left(\frac{-1}{3}\right)$ does not exist. There are no logarithms of negative numbers.

Eliminate $\frac{-1}{3}$.

Check 2: $\log 2 + \log(3 \cdot 2 - 5) = \log 2 + \log 1$ $\quad \log_a 1 = 0$ in any base

$= \log 2 + 0 = \log 2$

The solution set is {2}.

10. Write as a single logarithm:

$$2 \log x + \frac{1}{2} \log y - \frac{3}{2} \log z - 3 \log a$$

Applying property 3 of logarithms gives:

$$\log x^2 + \log y^{1/2} - \log z^{3/2} - \log a^3$$

Applying rules 1 and 2, together with properties of radicals, we have

$$\log \frac{x^2\sqrt{y}}{a^3\sqrt{z^3}}$$

Warm-Up Drill

1. Write as a logarithmic equation:
$8^{-(1/3)} = \frac{1}{2}$
2. Write as an exponential equation:
$\log_{1/4} 16 = -2$
Evaluate.
3. $\log_3 \frac{1}{9}$
4. $\log_3 \sqrt{3^5}$
5. $\log_3 27^{1/2}$

Solve the following:

6. $\log_x 125 = -3$
7. $\log_x 4 = 1$
8. $\log_5 x = 0$
9. $\log_2 (x + 5) - \log_2 (x - 1) = \log_2 3$
10. Write as a single logarithm:
$\log_b 2 + 2 \log_b 3 - \log_b 5$

SOLUTIONS

1. $\log_8 \frac{1}{2} = -\frac{1}{3}$
2. $\left(\frac{1}{4}\right)^{-2} = 16$
3. $\boldsymbol{\log_3 \frac{1}{9} = x}$
$3^x = \frac{1}{9} = 9^{-1} = (3^2)^{-1} = 3^{-2}$ So $x = -2$.
4. $\boldsymbol{\log_3 \sqrt{3^5} = x}$
$3^x = \sqrt{3^5} = (3^5)^{1/2} = 3^{5/2}$ So $x = \frac{5}{2}$.
5. $\boldsymbol{\log_3 27^{1/2} = x}$
$3^x = 27^{1/2} = (3^3)^{1/2} = 3^{3/2}$ So $x = \frac{3}{2}$.
6. $\boldsymbol{\log_x 125 = -3}$ Write the equation in exponential form.
$x^{-3} = 125$ Raise both sides to the $\frac{-1}{3}$ power.
$x = 125^{-(1/3)}$
$= \sqrt[3]{\frac{1}{125}} = \frac{1}{5}$
7. $\boldsymbol{\log_x 4 = 1}$ $x^1 = 4$ A rule is $\log_b b = 1$. The logarithm of the base is always 1.
$x = 4$
8. $\boldsymbol{\log_5 x = 0}$ $5^0 = x$ A rule is $\log_b 1 = 0$. The logarithm of 1 in any base is 0.
$x = 1$
9. $\boldsymbol{\log_2(x + 5) - \log_2(x - 1) = \log_2 3}$
$\log_2 \frac{x+5}{x-1} = \log_2 3$ Apply rule 2.
$\frac{x+5}{x-1} = 3$ If $a = b$, then $2^a = 2^b$.

$$x + 5 = 3(x - 1) \qquad \text{Multiply by } x - 1.$$
$$x + 5 = 3x - 3$$
$$5 = 2x - 3$$
$$8 = 2x$$
$$4 = x$$

Check 4: $\log_2 9 - \log_2 3 = \log_2 \frac{9}{3}$
$= \log_2 3$

The solution set is {4}.

10. $\log_b \frac{2 \cdot 3^2}{5} = \log_b \frac{18}{5}$

Sequences and Series

A *sequence* (also called a *progression*) is a function whose domain is the set of natural numbers, $N = \{1, 2, 3, \ldots\}$. Consider the sequence 1, 4, 9, ..., whose terms are the squares of the natural numbers. It is common to use subscripts and write $a_1 = 1, a_2 = 4, a_3 = 9, \ldots$ instead of $a(1) = 1$, $a(2) = 4, a(3) = 9, \ldots$, as in other functions. The general or nth term for this function is $a_n = n^2$.

If any term of a sequence is obtained by adding a constant to the preceding term, the sequence is called *arithmetic*. The terms of an arithmetic sequence therefore are:

$a_1 = a$
$a_2 = a + d$ The constant d is the *common difference*.
$a_3 = a + 2d$
$a_4 = a + 3d$
...
$a_n = a + (n - 1)d$ This is the formula for the nth term of an arithmetic sequence.

The sequence of the sums of the first n terms of an arithmetic sequence is called the *series* associated with the given sequence. The following are formulas for the sum of the first n terms of an arithmetic sequence.

$$S_n = \frac{n}{2}[2a + (n - 1)d] \quad \text{or} \quad S_n = \frac{n}{2}(a_1 + a_n)$$

$$S_n = \sum_{i=1}^{n} a_i$$

A sequence is *geometric* if any term is obtained by multiplying the preceding term by a nonzero constant. The terms of geometric sequence then are as follows:

$a_1 = a$
$a_2 = ar$ The constant r is called the *common ratio*.
$a_3 = ar^2$
$a_4 = ar^3$
...
$a_n = ar^{n-1}$ This is the formula for the nth term of a geometric sequence.

The sum of the first n terms of a geometric sequence is:

$$S_n = \frac{a - ar^n}{1 - r} = \sum_{i=1}^{n} a_i$$

If $|r| < 1$, then the sum of the infinite sequence can be found:

$$S_\infty = \frac{a}{1 - r}$$

Warm-Up Drill

Write the first five terms of each of the following sequences, whose nth term is given:

1. $a_n = 2n - 1$
2. $a_n = n^2 + n$
3. $a_n = 3^n$
4. Which of the above sequences is arithmetic?
5. Which of the above sequences is geometric?
6. Find the 25th term of the sequence whose nth term is $a_n = 3n + 2$.
7. Find the eighth term of the sequence whose first three terms are 4, 2, 1.
8. Find the sum of this series:

   $$\sum_{i=1}^{50} (2i - 1) = 1 + 3 + 5 + \cdots + 99$$

9. Find the sum of the first 20 terms of the sequence whose nth term is $a_n = (-2)^n$.
10. Find the sum: $0.9 + 0.09 + 0.009 + \cdots$.

SOLUTIONS

1. 1, 3, 5, 7, 9
2. 2, 6, 12, 20, 30
3. 3, 9, 27, 81, 243
4. $a_n = 2n - 1$ is arithmetic. The common difference is 2.
5. $a_n = 3^n$ is geometric. The common ratio is 3.
6. $\boldsymbol{a_n = 3n + 2}$ is arithmetic with first term 5 and common difference 3. The 25th term is $a_{25} = 5 + 24(3) = 5 + 72 = 78$
7. **4, 2, 1, . . .** is geometric with first term 4 and common ratio $\frac{1}{2}$. The eighth term is $a_8 = 4\left(\frac{1}{2}\right)^7 = 4\left(\frac{1}{128}\right) = \frac{1}{32}$
8. $\boldsymbol{\sum_{i=1}^{50} (2n - 1) = 1 + 3 + 5 + \cdots + 99}$ is arithmetic with first term 1 and common difference 2. Using the formula, we obtain

   $$S_{50} = \frac{50}{2}[2(1) + 49(2)] = 25(2 + 98)$$
   $$= 25(100) = 2500$$

9. $\boldsymbol{a_n = (-2)^n}$ is geometric with first term -2 and common ratio -2. The series of the first 20 terms is

   $$S_{20} = \frac{(-2) - (-2)(-2)^{20}}{1 - (-2)}$$
   $$= \frac{(-2) - (-2)(1{,}048{,}576)}{3}$$
   $$= \frac{(-2) - (-2{,}097{,}152)}{3}$$
   $$= \frac{(-2) + 2{,}097{,}152}{3}$$
   $$= \frac{2{,}097{,}150}{3}$$
   $$= 699{,}050$$

10. **0.9 + 0.09 + 0.009 +** ⋯ is geometric with first term 0.9 and common ratio 0.1. Since the common ratio is between –1 and 1, the formula for an infinite geometric series applies:

$$S_\infty = \frac{0.9}{1-0.1} = \frac{0.9}{0.9} = 1$$

The Binomial Theorem

The expression $n!$ (read as "n factorial") is defined as follows:

$$n! = n(n-1)(n-2)(n-3)\cdots 2\cdot 1$$
$$1! = 1$$
$$0! = 1$$

Factorials allow easy counting of certain arrangements (or permutations) and combinations. The number of permutations of n things taken r at a time is

$${}_nP_r = \frac{n!}{(n-r)!} \qquad \text{(The notation } P_{n,r} \text{ is also used.)}$$

For example, if one has 20 different books and a shelf that will hold 8 of them, how many different arrangements of those books on the shelf are possible?

$${}_{20}P_8 = \frac{20!}{(20-8)!} = 20\cdot 19\cdot 18\cdots\cdot 13 = 5{,}079{,}110{,}400$$

The number of combinations of n things taken r at a time is

$${}_nC_r = \frac{n!}{r!(n-r)!} \qquad \text{(The notation } C_{n,r} \text{ and } \binom{n}{r} \text{ are also used.)}$$

The difference is that permutations are concerned with order, whereas combinations are not. For example, the number of different combinations of the 20 books on the shelf that will hold 8 books is

$${}_{20}C_8 = \frac{20!}{8!12!} = 125{,}970$$

TIP 

Most scientific calculators have combination and permutation functions. Familiarize yourself with them.

The combination numbers turn out to be useful in the formula to raise a binomial to a power. This formula is known as the Binomial Theorem.

$$(a+b)^n = {}_nC_0a^n + {}_nC_1a^{n-1}b^1 + {}_nC_2a^{n-2}b^2 + \cdots + {}_nC_ra^{n-r}b^r + \cdots + {}_nC_nb^n$$

The coefficients of the terms in the Binomial Theorem are found in the nth row of Pascal's triangle, an array of numbers in which each entry other than the 1 at the end of each row is found by adding the two numbers immediately above it.

PASCAL'S TRIANGLE

```
            1              Row 0
          1   1            Row 1
        1   2   1          Row 2
      1   3   3   1
    1   4   6   4   1
  1   5  10  10   5   1
1   6  15  20  15   6   1
```

Using Pascal's triangle, we can easily write the expansion of $(x+y)^6$ as follows:

$$(x+y)^6 = 1x^6 + 6x^5y + 15x^4y^2 + 20x^3y^3 + 15x^2y^4 + 6xy^5 + 1y^6$$

Warm-Up Drill

Evaluate.

1. 7!
2. ${}_8P_3$
3. ${}_{10}C_4$
4. In how many ways can the 3 officers of a club—president, vice president, and secretary—be chosen from a membership of 12 people?
5. How many 4-member committees can be selected from a club that has 16 members?
6. Expand $(2x - 3)^4$.
7. What is the fifth term of the binomial expansion of $(x - 2)^6$?

SOLUTIONS

1. $\mathbf{7!} = 7 \cdot 6 \cdot 5 \cdot 4 \cdot 3 \cdot 2 \cdot 1 = 5040$

2. $${}_8\mathbf{P}_3 = \frac{8!}{(8-3)!} = \frac{8 \cdot 7 \cdot 6 \cdot 5 \cdot 4 \cdot 3 \cdot 2 \cdot 1}{5 \cdot 4 \cdot 3 \cdot 2 \cdot 1} = 8 \cdot 7 \cdot 6 = 336$$

3. $${}_{10}\mathbf{C}_4 = \frac{10!}{4!(10-4)!}$$
   $$= \frac{10!}{4!6!} \qquad \text{Cancel 6!}$$
   $$= \frac{10 \cdot \overset{3}{\cancel{9}} \cdot \cancel{8} \cdot 7}{\cancel{4} \cdot \cancel{3} \cdot \cancel{2} \cdot 1} \qquad \text{Cancel common factors.}$$
   $$= 10 \cdot 3 \cdot 1 \cdot 7 = 210$$

4. This question concerns order, so the correct answer is
   $${}_{12}P_3 = \frac{12!}{(12-3)!} = 12 \cdot 11 \cdot 10 = 1320$$

5. Order on a committee is not important, so this is a combination question.
   $${}_{16}C_4 = \frac{16!}{4!(16-4)!} = \frac{16 \cdot 15 \cdot 14 \cdot 13}{4 \cdot 3 \cdot 2 \cdot 1} \qquad \text{Cancel.}$$
   $$= 4 \cdot 5 \cdot 7 \cdot 13 = 1820$$

6. Use the fourth row of Pascal's triangle.
   $$(2x-3)^4 = 1(2x)^4 + 4(2x)^3(-3) + 6(2x)^2(-3)^2 + 4(2x)(-3)^3 + 1(-3)^4$$
   $$= 16x^4 - 96x^3 + 216x^2 - 216x + 81$$

7. The coefficients of the expansion of $\mathbf{(x - 2)^6}$ are the numbers in the sixth row of Pascal's triangle. They are also the combination numbers. The fifth one is ${}_6C_4$, so the fifth term is
   $${}_6C_4(x)^2(-2)^4 = 15x^2(16) = 240x^2$$

   [Notice that the exponent on the second factor, (–2), is the same as the number on the right of the combination symbol.]

Complex Numbers

A complex number is any number in the form $a + bi$, in which a and b are real numbers and $i = \sqrt{-1}$. The real number a is called the *real* part of the imaginary number, and the real number b is called the *imaginary* part. Complex numbers are equal if and only if the real parts are equal and the imaginary parts are equal.

$$a + bi = c + di \text{ if and only if } a = c \text{ and } b = d$$

The following are the definitions of the operations on complex numbers:

- *Absolute value:* $|a + bi| = \sqrt{a^2 + b^2}$. (Note that i is not used in the radicand.) The absolute value of a complex number is called its modulus.
- *Conjugate:* The conjugate of $a + bi$ is $a - bi$. (Change the sign of the imaginary part.)
- *Addition:* $(a + bi) + (c + di) = (a + c) + (b + d)i$ (Add the real parts and add the imaginary parts separately.)
- *Subtraction:* $(a + bi) - (c + di) = (a - c) + (b - d)i$ (Subtract the real parts and subtract the imaginary parts.)
- *Multiplication:* $(a + bi)(c + di) = (ac - bd) + (ad + bc)i$ (Rather than use the definition, it is common to treat the complex numbers like binomials and multiply by the FOIL method.)
- *Division:* $\frac{a + bi}{c + di} = \frac{(a + bi)(c - di)}{(c + di)(c - di)}$ (Multiply the numerator and denominator by the conjugate of the denominator.)

Here are some examples:

- $(2 + 3i) + (-5 + 7i) = -3 + 10i$
- $(7 - 8i) - (-6 - 3i) = 13 - 5i$
- $i^2 = -1$
- $i^3 = -i$
- $i^4 = 1$
- $i^{27} = (i^4)^6(i^3) = 1^6(-i) = -i$
- $(2 + 5i)(-3 + i) = -6 + 2i - 15i + 5i^2$
  $= -6 - 13i + 5(-1)$
  $= -6 - 13i - 5 = -11 - 13i$
- $(5 + 6i)(5 - 6i) = 25 - 36i^2$ (The outer and inner products cancel out.)
  $= 25 - 36(-1)$
  $= 25 + 36 = 61$
- $\frac{4 + 3i}{3 - i} = \frac{(4 + 3i)(3 + i)}{(3 - i)(3 + i)}$
  $= \frac{9 + 13i}{10} = \frac{9}{10} + \frac{13}{10}i$
- $\frac{1}{i} = \frac{1(-i)}{i(-i)} = \frac{-i}{-i^2} = \frac{-i}{-(-1)} = \frac{-i}{1} = -i$

TIP 

The easy method is to divide the exponent by 4. Match the remainder with the exponents in the first four powers of i:

$i^1 = i,\ i^2 = -1,\ i^3 = -i,\ i^4 = i^0 = 1$

TIP 

So i is definitely not a real number. If any *real* number is squared, the result is always positive.

Warm-Up Drill

Perform the indicated operations. Express answers in the standard form, $a + bi$.

1. $\sqrt{-125}$
2. $\sqrt{-9} \cdot \sqrt{-36}$
3. $(-3 + 2i) + (4 + 5i)$
4. $(-3 - 4i) - (-1 - i)$
5. $2i(4 - 3i)$
6. $(7 + 3i)(-5 + i)$
7. $(-5 + 2i)^2$
8. $\dfrac{4i}{1 - i}$
9. i^{98}
10. $|2 + 5i|$

SOLUTIONS

1. $\boldsymbol{\sqrt{-125}} = \sqrt{(-1)(25)(5)} = \sqrt{-1} \cdot \sqrt{25} \cdot \sqrt{5} = i \cdot 5 \cdot \sqrt{5} = 5i\sqrt{5}$

2. $\boldsymbol{\sqrt{-9} \cdot \sqrt{-36}} = (3i)(6i) = 18i^2 = 18(-1) = -18$

   (The rule from algebra, $\sqrt{ab} = \sqrt{a}\sqrt{b}$, does not apply to this problem because the factors are not real numbers.)

3. $\boldsymbol{(-3 + 2i) + (4 + 5i)} = 1 + 7i$

4. $\boldsymbol{(-3 - 4i) - (-1 - i)} = -2 - 3i$

5. $\boldsymbol{2i(4 - 3i)} = 8i - 6i^2 = 8i - 6(-1)$
   $= 8i + 6 = 6 + 8i$

6. $\boldsymbol{(7 + 3i)(-5 + i)} = -35 + 7i - 15i + 3i^2$
   $= -35 - 8i + 3(-1)$
   $= -35 - 8i - 3 = -38 - 8i$

7. $\boldsymbol{(-5 + 2i)^2} = 25 - 2(5)(2i) + 4i^2$ Use the rule for squaring a binomial.
   $= 25 - 20i + 4(-1)$
   $= 21 - 20i$

8. $\boldsymbol{\dfrac{4i}{1 - i}} = \dfrac{4i(1 + i)}{(1 - i)(1 + i)} = \dfrac{4i - 4}{1 - i^2}$
   $= \dfrac{-4 + 4i}{2} = -2 + 2i$

9. $\boldsymbol{i^{98}} = i^2 = -1$ Divide 98 by 4. The remainder is 2.

10. $\boldsymbol{|2 + 5i|} = \sqrt{2^2 + 5^2} = \sqrt{29}$

Practice Exercises

The following sample questions represent ways in which the reviewed skills might be tested on the ACT.

1. Solve: $\begin{pmatrix} x + 5y = -2 \\ 3x - 4y = -25 \end{pmatrix}$

   A. $\{(1, -7)\}$
   B. $\{(7, -1)\}$
   C. $\{(-1, 7)\}$
   D. $\{(-7, 1)\}$
   E. $\{\ \}$

2. What is the value of $\log_4 8$?

   F. $\frac{2}{3}$
   G. $\frac{3}{2}$
   H. 2
   J. $\frac{1}{2}$
   K. $(\sqrt{4})^3$

3. If $\log_b 2 = x$ and $\log_b 3 = y$, express $\log_b 12$ in terms of x and y.

   A. $x^2 + y$
   B. $2xy$
   C. $2x + y$
   D. $x + 2y$
   E. x^2y

4. What is the fifteenth term of the arithmetic sequence that begins:

   $$0, 3, 6, 9, \ldots?$$

   F. 42
   G. 45
   H. 15
   J. 39
   K. 48

5. What is the product of $2 + i$ and $3 - 2i$?

   A. 8
   B. $4 - i$
   C. $4 - 7i$
   D. $6 - 2i$
   E. $8 - i$

ANSWERS AND EXPLANATIONS

1. **(D)** Multiply both sides of the first equation by –3 and add:

$$\begin{pmatrix} -3x - 15y = 6 \\ 3x - 4y = -25 \end{pmatrix}$$
$$-19y = -19$$

$y = 1$ Substitute $y = 1$ into either
$x + 5(1) = -2$ original equation, say the first.
$x = -7$ The solution set is $\{(-7, 1)\}$.

2. **(G)** Call the value x: $\log_4 8 = x$ Rewrite in exponential form.
$4^x = 8$
$(2^2)^x = 2^3$ Express both sides with a common base.
$2^{2x} = 2^3$ Set the exponents equal.
$2x = 3$
$x = \frac{3}{2}$

3. **(C)** $\log_b 12 = \log_b 2^2 \cdot 3 = 2 \log_b 2 + \log_b 3 = 2x + y$

4. **(F)** The nth term of any arithmetic sequence is given by the formula $a_n = a_1 + (n - 1)d$ in which a_1 is the first term and d is the common difference between successive terms.

$$a_{15} = 0 + (15 - 1)3 = 0 + 14 \cdot 3 = 42$$

5. **(E)** Multiply them as you would multiply binomials, but remember that $i^2 = -1$.

$$(2 + i)(3 - 2i) = 6 - 4i + 3i - 2i^2 =$$
$$6 - i - 2(-1) = 6 - i + 2 = 8 - i.$$

GEOMETRY

Angles

An *angle* is the union of two rays with a common endpoint.

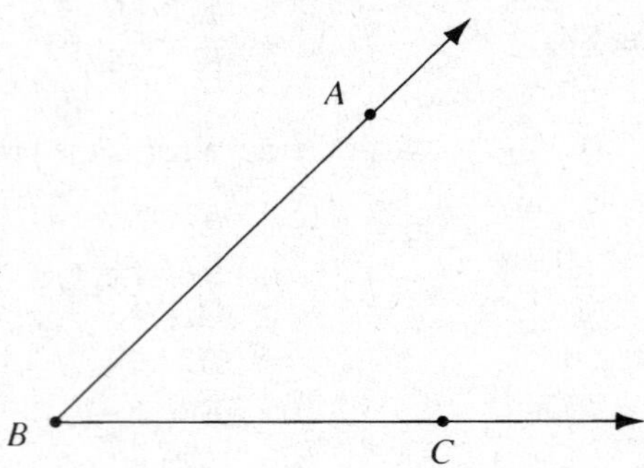

The angle shown above consists of $\overrightarrow{BA}$ and $\overrightarrow{BC}$. The common endpoint B is called the *vertex*.

Two angles that have the same measure are called *congruent*.

Angles can be classified according to their measure.

- The measure of an *acute angle* is between 0° and 90°.
- A *right angle* measures 90°.
- The measure of an *obtuse angle* is between 90° and 180°.
- A *straight angle* measures 180°.
- The measure of a *reflex angle* is greater than 180° but less than 360°.

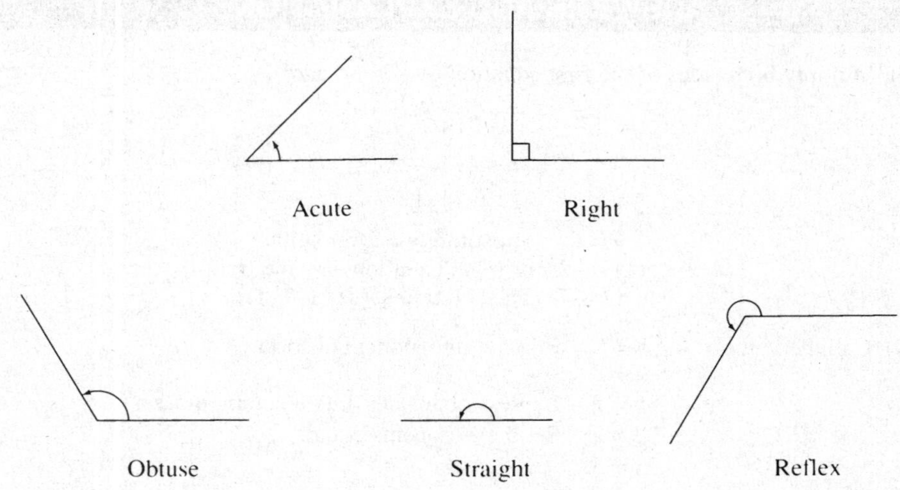

Two angles are called *adjacent* if they have a common side and the interiors of the angles do not intersect.

A segment, a ray, or a line that contains the vertex of an angle such that it forms two congruent adjacent angles with the sides of the angle is called the *angle bisector.*

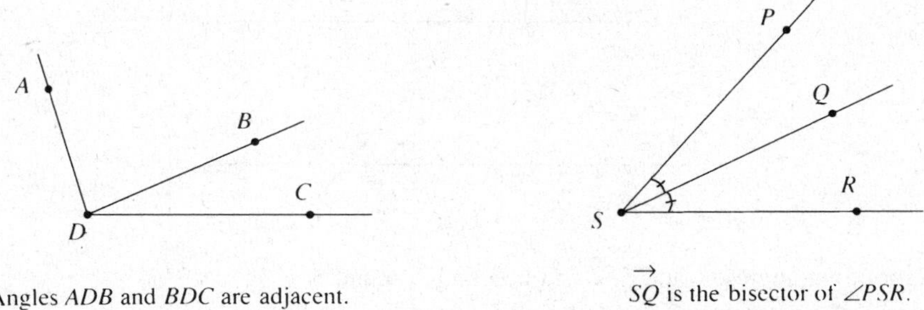

Angles *ADB* and *BDC* are adjacent.

$\overrightarrow{SQ}$ is the bisector of $\angle PSR$.

There are always two pairs of *vertical angles* formed by the intersection of two lines. In the figure shown below, angles *AEB* and *DEC* are vertical angles, and angles *AED* and *BEC* are also vertical angles.

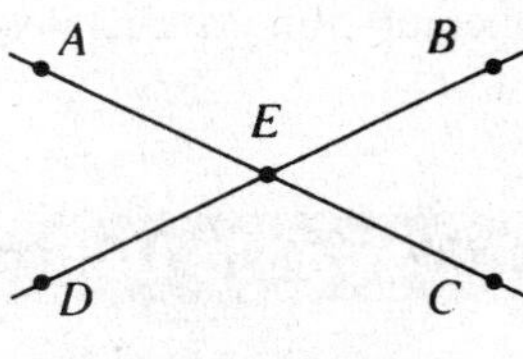

Angles *AED* and *BEC* are vertical angles.

Two angles are *complementary* if their sum is 90°. Two angles are *supplementary* if their sum is 180°. Notice that both definitions specify two angles. These definitions do not apply to three or more angles.

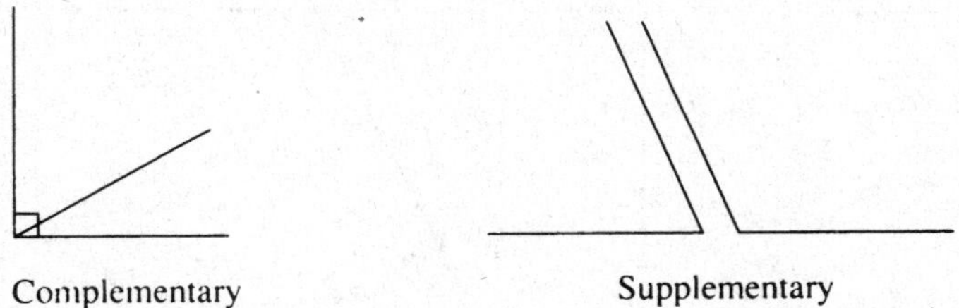

Complementary

Supplementary

Perpendicular lines are two lines that intersect to form a right angle. Of course, if there is one right angle, then there must be four of them.

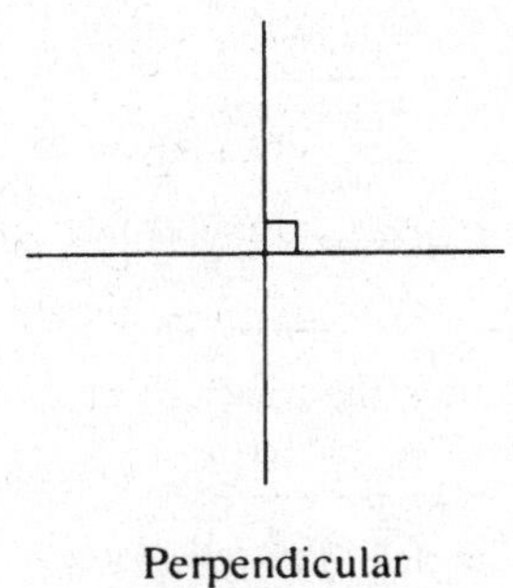

Perpendicular Lines

If two parallel lines are intersected by a third line (called the *transversal*), then the following angles are congruent:

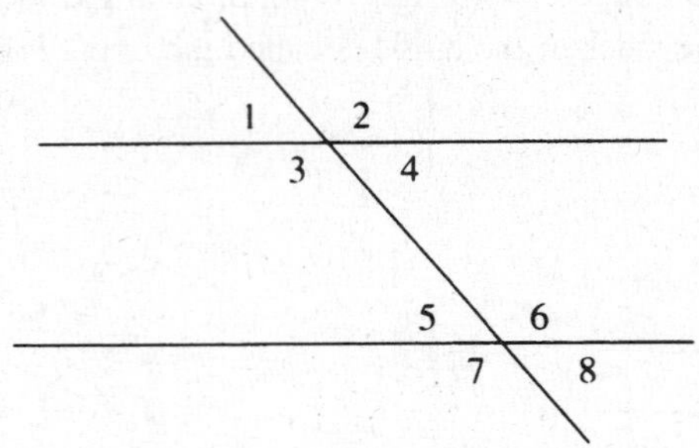

Corresponding angles: 1 and 5, 2 and 6, 3 and 7, 4 and 8
Alternate interior angles: 3 and 6, 4 and 5
Alternate exterior angles: 1 and 8, 2 and 7
Vertical angles: 1 and 4, 2 and 3, 5 and 8, 6 and 7

Interior angles on the same side of the transversal are supplementary. Angles 4 and 6 are supplementary, and 3 and 5 are supplementary. Exterior angles on the same side of the transversal are also supplementary: 2 and 8, 1 and 7.

Warm-Up Drill

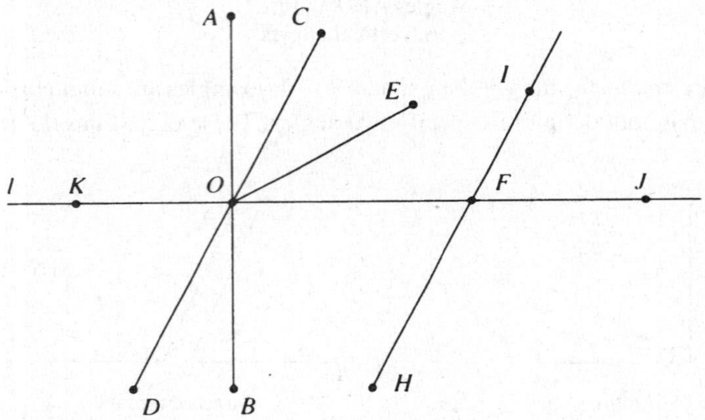

In the diagram, segment $\overline{AB}$ is perpendicular to ($\perp$) line l. Segment $\overline{CD}$ is parallel to ($\parallel$) segment $\overline{FH}$. Point O is the midpoint of segment $\overline{AB}$. Angle COE and $\angle EOF$ are congruent.

1. The measure of $\angle AOF$ is ________________.
2. Angle AOC and $\angle$ ________________ are vertical angles.
3. Angle COF and $\angle$ ________________ are alternate interior angles.
4. Angle HFJ and $\angle DOF$ are ________________ angles.
5. If the measure of $\angle COF$ is 80°, then the measure of $\angle OFI$ is ________________.
6. Angle DOB and $\angle BOF$ are ________________ angles.
7. Name a pair of complementary angles in the diagram.
8. Name a pair of supplementary angles in the diagram.
9. ________________ is a bisector of segment $\overline{AB}$.
10. ________________ is a bisector of $\angle COF$.

SOLUTIONS

1. Since segment $\overline{AB} \perp l$, the measure of $\angle AOF$ is 90°.
2. Angle *DOB*.
3. Angle *OFH*.
4. Corresponding.
5. Interior angles on the same side of the transversal are supplementary, so the measure of $\angle OFI$ is 180° – 80° = 100°.
6. Adjacent.
7. There are several pairs of complementary angles: *AOC* and *COF, AOE* and *EOF, KOD* and *DOB, COF* and *DOB,* for example.
8. There are several pairs of supplementary angles: *KOA* and *AOF, KOC* and *COF, KOE* and *EOF, AOD* and *DOB, OFI* and *IFJ,* for example.
9. Either segment $\overline{KF}$, segment $\overline{OC}$, segment $\overline{OD}$, segment $\overline{OE}$, line *l*, or ray $\overline{OF}$, for example.
10. Segment $\overline{OE}$.

Polygons

If two polygons have their angles congruent in sequence and their corresponding sides have the same ratio, then the polygons are similar.

If two polygons have the same size and shape (that is, they would coincide if one was placed on top of the other), they are congruent. Congruent polygons are also similar, and the ratio of corresponding sides is 1.

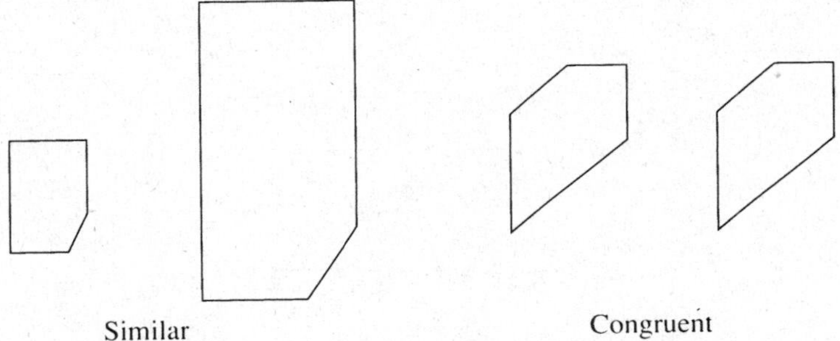

If all of the angles of a polygon are congruent and the sides are also congruent, the polygon is regular.

A diagonal of a polygon is a segment with endpoints at two nonadjacent vertices. The only polygons with no diagonals are triangles.

Triangles

A *triangle* is a polygon with three sides. Triangles may be classified according to the lengths of their sides.

- An *equilateral triangle* has three congruent sides.
- An *isosceles triangle* has at least two congruent sides.
- A *scalene triangle* has no two congruent sides.

A triangle may also be classified according to the measure of its angles.

- An *equiangular triangle* has three congruent angles.
- An *acute triangle* has all acute angles.
- A *right triangle* has one right angle.
- An *obtuse triangle* has one obtuse angle.

An *altitude* of a triangle is a segment from a vertex perpendicular to the opposite side (the base). Each triangle has three altitudes, and the lines that contain all three intersect at a point. The area of any triangle is $\frac{1}{2}$ of the product of the length of an altitude and the length of the base to that altitude:

$$A = \frac{1}{2}bh$$

An *angle bisector* of a triangle is a segment that bisects one of the angles of the triangle. The three angle bisectors of a triangle intersect at a point. This point is the center of a circle that is inscribed in the triangle.

A *median* of a triangle is a segment with one endpoint at a vertex and the other endpoint at the midpoint of the opposite side. The three medians of a triangle intersect at a point.

The three perpendicular bisectors of the sides of a triangle meet at a point. This point is the center of a circle circumscribed about the triangle.

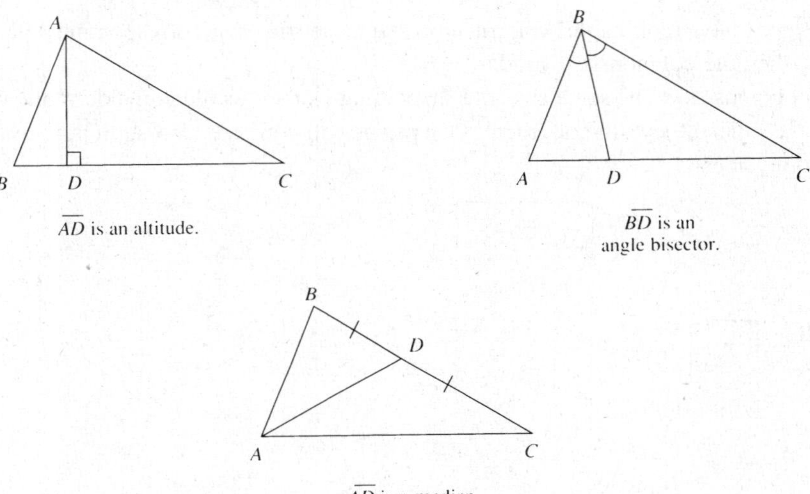

$\overline{AD}$ is an altitude.

$\overline{BD}$ is an angle bisector.

$\overline{AD}$ is a median.

The following are important properties of triangles:

1. Base angles of an isosceles triangle are congruent. (If two sides are the same length, then the angles opposite those sides are congruent.)

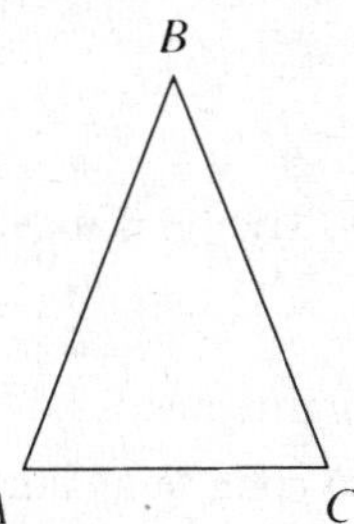

If $AB = BC$, then $m\angle A = m\angle C$.

2. The sum of the measures of the angles of any triangle is 180°. Therefore the sum of the measures of the angles of an n-sided polygon is $(n - 2)(180°)$.

3. The angles of an equilateral triangle are congruent. They each have measure 60°.
4. If two sides of a triangle are unequal, then the angles opposite those sides are unequal in the same order.
5. The sum of the lengths of any two sides of a triangle must be greater than the length of the third side.
6. The sum of the exterior angles of a triangle (taking one at each vertex) is 360°. An exterior angle is formed by extending one side of a triangle through the vertex.
7. If the sides of a right triangle have lengths a, b, and c (c is the length of the hypotenuse), then these numbers satisfy the Pythagorean Theorem:

$$a^2 + b^2 = c^2$$

8. If an altitude is drawn from the right angle of a right triangle, it separates the hypotenuse into two segments.

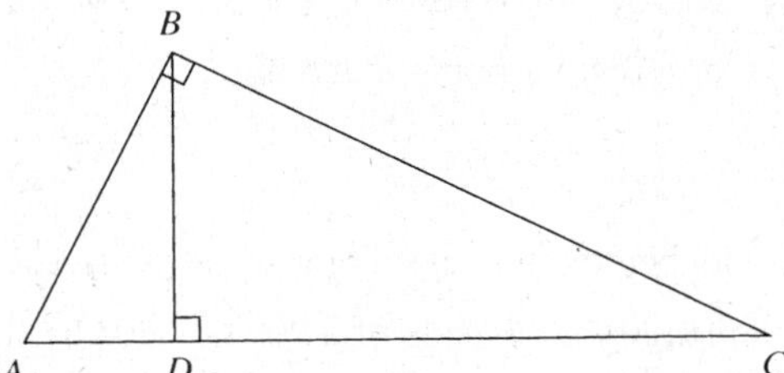

The following are true because of similarity of the three triangles: $\triangle ABC$, $\triangle ADB$, and $\triangle BDC$.

a. The altitude is the mean proportional between the two segments of the hypotenuse.

$$\frac{AD}{BD} = \frac{BD}{DC}$$

b. Either leg is the mean proportional between the hypotenuse and the nearer segment of the hypotenuse.

$$\frac{AD}{AB} = \frac{AB}{AC}, \qquad \frac{DC}{BC} = \frac{BC}{AC}$$

9. In an isosceles right triangle, the legs are congruent and the length of the hypotenuse is $\sqrt{2}$ times the length of a leg.

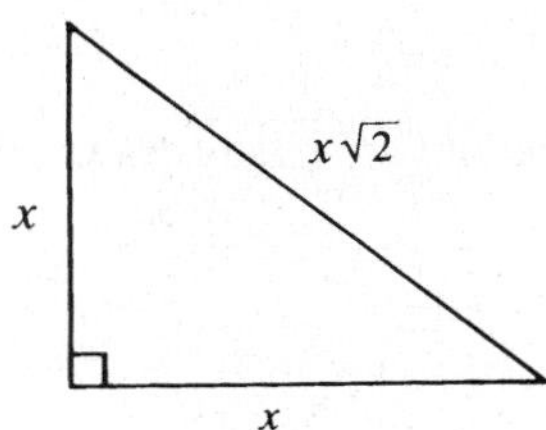

10. In a 30°-60°-90° right triangle, the length of the hypotenuse is twice the length of the shorter leg, and the length of the longer leg is $\sqrt{3}$ times the length of the shorter leg.

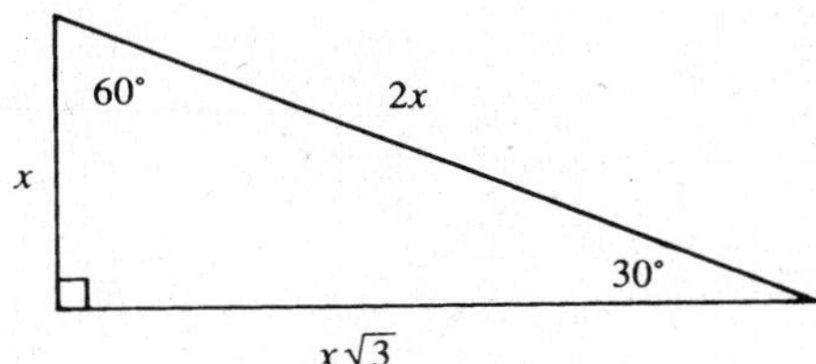

Warm-Up Drill

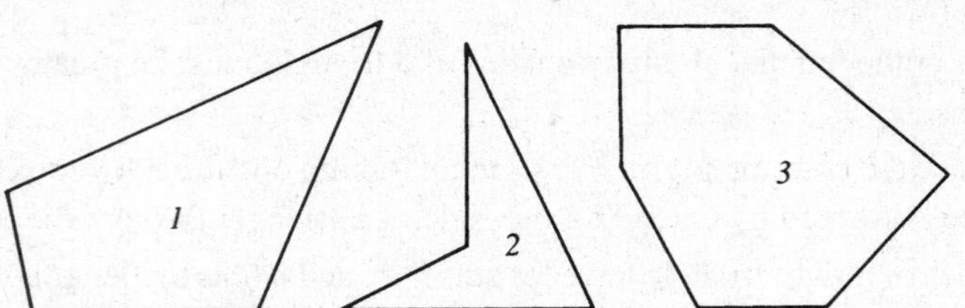

1. Which, if any, of the polygons in the diagram is (are) convex?
2. Which, if any, of the polygons is (are) concave?
3. What is the sum of the interior angles of the first polygon?
4. What is the sum of the exterior angles (taking one at each vertex) in the first polygon?
5. What is another name for a regular polygon having:
   a. four sides?
   b. three sides?
6. How many diagonals can be drawn in a polygon of seven sides?
7. In each case below, the length of one side of a 30°-60°-90° triangle is given. Find the lengths of the other two sides.

	Shorter Leg	Longer Leg	Hypotenuse
a.	8		
b.		3	
c.			12

8. In each case below, the length of one side of a 45°-45°-90° triangle is given. Find the length of the other sides.

	Legs	Hypotenuse
a.	9	
b.	$8\sqrt{3}$	
c.		16
d.		$5\sqrt{5}$

9. For right triangle ABC, in which altitude $\overline{CD}$ is drawn, find the indicated part for the given information in each question.
   a. $AD = 4$, $BD = 12$
      i. Find AC.
      ii. Find CD.
      iii. Find BC.
   b. $BC = 12$, $AB = 13$
      i. Find AC.
      ii. Find BD.
      iii. Find CD.

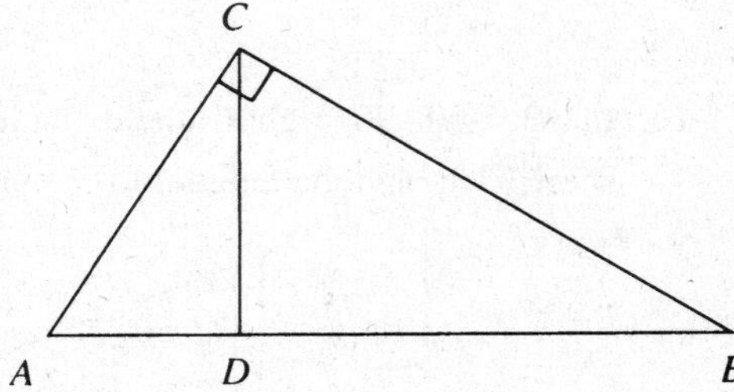

SOLUTIONS

1. Polygons 1 and 3 are convex.
2. Polygon 2 is concave.
3. The sum of the interior angles of any polygon is $(n - 2)180°$.
   $(4 - 2)180° = 2(180°) = 360°$
4. The sum of the exterior angles (taking one at each vertex) for any polygon is always 360°.
5. a. Square
   b. Equilateral triangle
6. In a polygon of 7 sides, four diagonals can be drawn from one vertex, then four more from an adjacent vertex, three from another, two from another, and finally 1 from the last vertex. So $4 + 4 + 3 + 2 + 1 = 14$ diagonals can be drawn in a polygon of seven sides.
7. a. Hypotenuse: $2(8) = 16$

   Longer leg: $8\sqrt{3}$

   b. Shorter leg: $\frac{3}{\sqrt{3}} = \sqrt{3}$ Divide the length of the longer leg by $\sqrt{3}$.

   Hypotenuse: $2\sqrt{3}$

   c. Shorter leg: 6 Divide by 2.

   Longer leg: $6\sqrt{3}$
8. a. Hypotenuse: $9\sqrt{2}$

   b. Hypotenuse: $(8\sqrt{3})\sqrt{2} = 8\sqrt{6}$

   c. Legs: $\frac{16}{\sqrt{2}} = 8\sqrt{2}$

   d. Legs: $\frac{5\sqrt{5}}{\sqrt{2}} = \frac{5\sqrt{10}}{2}$
9. a. i. AC is the mean proportional between the hypotenuse and the nearer segment of the hypotenuse.

   $\frac{4}{AC} = \frac{AC}{16}$

   $AC^2 = 64$

   $AC = 8$

   ii. CD is the mean proportional between the two segments of the hypotenuse.

   $\frac{4}{CD} = \frac{CD}{12}$

   $CD^2 = 48$

   $CD = \sqrt{48} = 4\sqrt{3}$

   iii. $\frac{12}{BC} = \frac{BC}{16}$

   $BC^2 = 192$

   $BC = \sqrt{192} = 8\sqrt{3}$

b. i. The Pythagorean Theorem applies.

$$AC^2 + 12^2 = 13^2$$
$$AC^2 + 144 = 169$$
$$AC^2 = 25$$
$$AC = 5$$

ii. 12 is the mean proportional between BD and 13.

$$\frac{BD}{12} = \frac{12}{13}$$
$$13BD = 144$$
$$BD = \frac{144}{13} = 11\frac{1}{13}$$

iii. Since $BD = \frac{144}{13}$, $AD = \frac{25}{13}$, and CD is the mean proportional between the two segments of the hypotenuse.

$$\frac{\frac{25}{13}}{CD} = \frac{CD}{\frac{144}{13}}$$

$$CD^2 = \frac{25}{13} \cdot \frac{144}{13}$$

$$CD = \frac{5 \cdot 12}{13} = \frac{60}{13} = 4\frac{8}{13}$$

Similar Triangles

Similar triangles have angles of the same measure and sides with the same ratio in pairs.

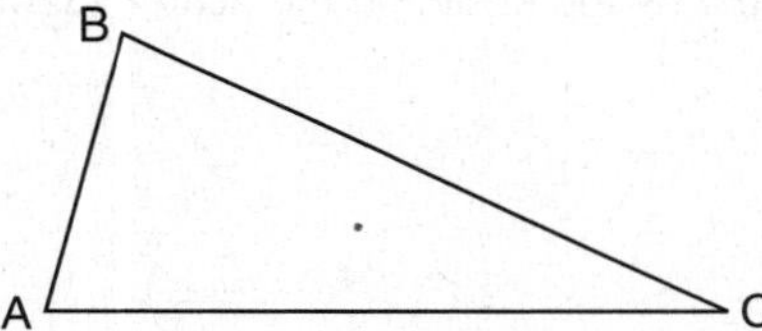

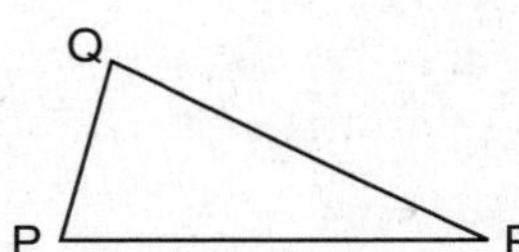

If $\triangle ABC$ is similar to $\triangle PQR$, then $m\angle A = m\angle P$, $m\angle B = m\angle Q$, and $m\angle C = m\angle R$, and $\frac{AB}{PQ} = \frac{BC}{QR} = \frac{AC}{PR}$. If any two pairs of angles of two triangles have the same measure, then the triangles are similar, but if two pairs of sides have the same ratio, the triangles are not necessarily similar.

Example: In the accompanying diagram, $\overline{AB}$ is parallel to $\overline{DE}$. Determine $DE = x$.

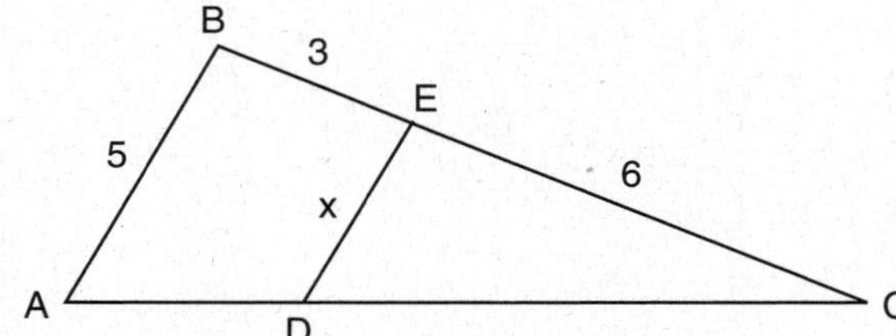

Angle C is in both triangles ABC and DEC, and because $\overline{AB}$ is parallel to $\overline{DE}$, then $m\angle BAC = m\angle EDC$. So the triangles are similar, and the corresponding sides have the same ratio.

$$\frac{x}{5} = \frac{6}{9} \qquad \text{Cross multiply.}$$
$$9x = 30$$
$$x = \frac{30}{9} = 3\frac{1}{3}$$

Warm-Up Drill

At a time when a 6-foot post casts a 2-foot shadow, a tree casts a 12-foot shadow. How tall is the tree?

SOLUTION

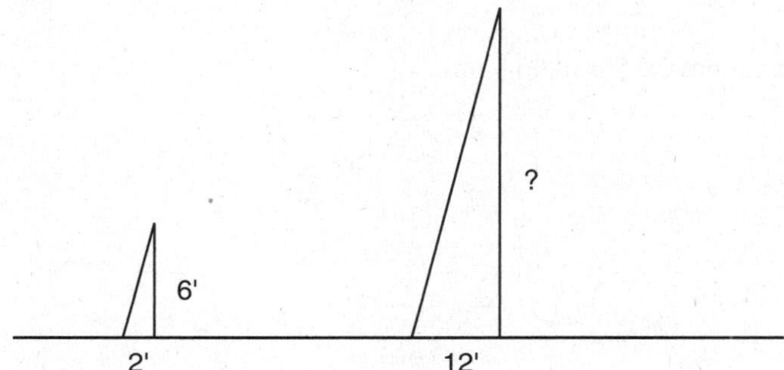

Two similar triangles are formed.

$$\frac{6}{2} = \frac{x}{12}$$
$$2x = 72$$
$$x = 36 \qquad \text{The tree is 36 feet tall.}$$

Quadrilaterals

A *quadrilateral* is a polygon with four sides. The following are definitions of certain quadrilaterals with special characteristics:

- A *trapezoid* has one pair of opposite sides parallel.

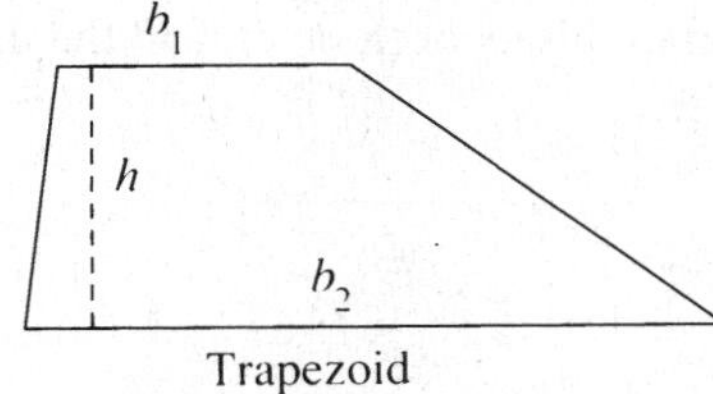

Trapezoid

- A *parallelogram* has both pairs of opposite sides parallel.

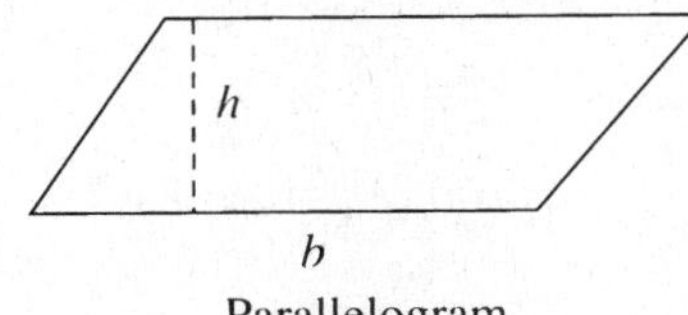

Parallelogram

- A *rectangle* is a parallelogram with a right angle (and, hence, four right angles).

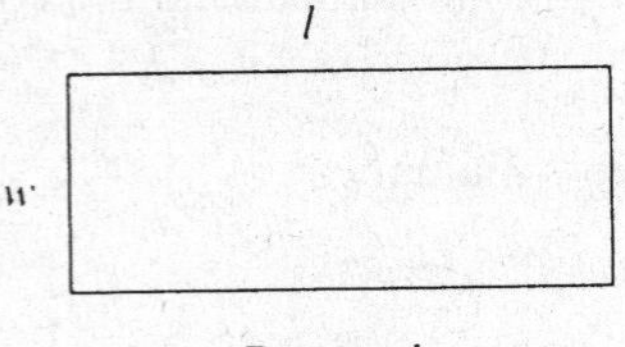

Rectangle

- A *square* is an equilateral rectangle or a regular quadrilateral.

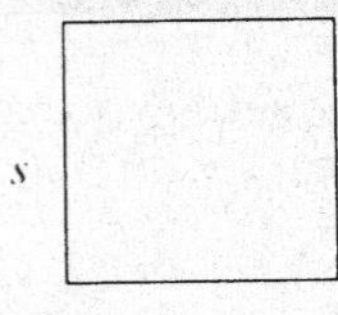

Square

- A *rhombus* is an equilateral parallelogram.

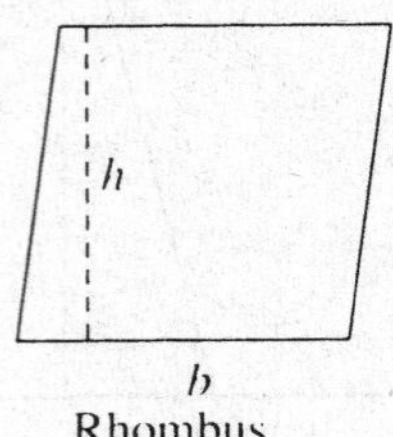

Rhombus

Areas of Quadrilaterals

The following are area formulas for the quadrilaterals defined above:

Trapezoid: $A = \frac{1}{2}h\,(b_1 + b_2)$

Parallelogram: $A = hb$

Rectangle: $A = lw$

Square: $A = s^2$

Rhombus: $A = hb = \frac{1}{2}$ (product of diagonals)

The diagonals of a parallelogram bisect each other, and the diagonals of a rhombus are perpendicular bisectors of each other.

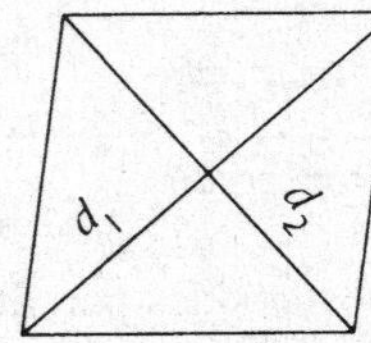

Warm-Up Drill

State whether each of the following is true or false:

1. All squares are rectangles.
2. All rhombuses are squares.
3. All rectangles are quadrilaterals.
4. All trapezoids are polygons.
5. All parallelograms are rhombuses.
6. 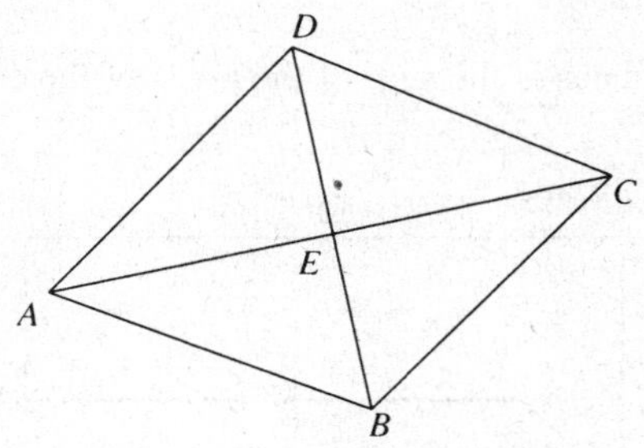

   Given: Rhombus *ABCD*, length of $\overline{DB} = 8$, length of $\overline{AC} = 12$.

   Find: a. *DE*.
   b. *AE*.
   c. Area of rhombus *ABCD*.
   d. *DC*.

7. 

   Given: Trapezoid *ABCD*, $\overline{AB} \parallel \overline{DC}$, $\overline{AD} \perp \overline{DC}$, $AB = 5$, $DC = 8$, $AD = 3$.

   Find: a. Area of trapezoid *ABCD*.
   b. Perimeter of trapezoid *ABCD*.

SOLUTIONS

1. True
2. False
3. True
4. True
5. False
6. a. $DE = \frac{1}{2}DB = 4$
   b. $AE = 6$
   c. Area of rhombus $= \frac{1}{2}$ (product of diagonals)
   $= \frac{1}{2}(8)(12) = 48$
   d. $DC = \sqrt{4^2 + 6^2} = \sqrt{16 + 36} = \sqrt{52} = 2\sqrt{13}$

7. a. Area of trapezoid $= \frac{1}{2}h(b_1 + b_2)$

$= \frac{1}{2}(3)(5 + 8)$

$= \frac{39}{2} = 19\frac{1}{2}$

b. Since the triangular portion of the trapezoid is a 45°–45°–90° triangle, the length of the slanted side is $3\sqrt{2}$, and the perimeter is

$5 + 3 + 8 + 3\sqrt{2} = 16 + 3\sqrt{2}$

Areas of Irregular Shapes

The area of many irregular shapes is the sum of the areas of the component parts that compose the irregular shape.

Example: Find the area of this shape.

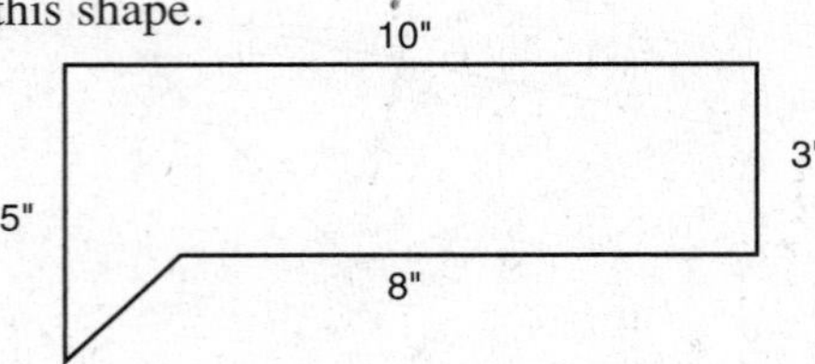

Divide the region into smaller parts in order to apply the area formulas. One way this could be done is to draw a segment to create a rectangle and a triangle.

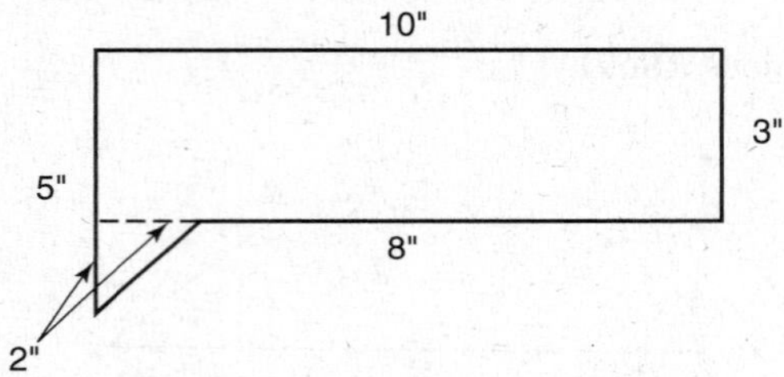

The area of the rectangle is (3)(10) = 30 square inches. The triangle has legs each 2". Its area is $\frac{1}{2}(2)(2) = 2$ square inches. The area of the entire region is 30 + 2 = 32 square inches.

Example: Find the area of this region.

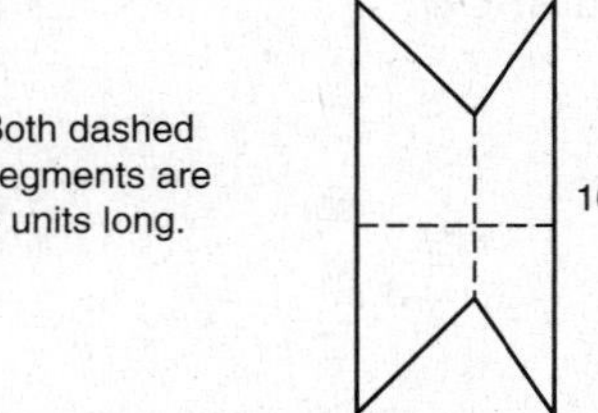

Consider separating this region along the vertical dashed line. There are two trapezoids both with bases 10 and 6. The sum of the heights of the trapezoids is 6. The area of the trapezoid on the left is

$$A_1 = \frac{1}{2}(6 - x)(10 + 6)$$

The area of the trapezoid on the right is

$$A_2 = \frac{1}{2}x(10 + 6)$$

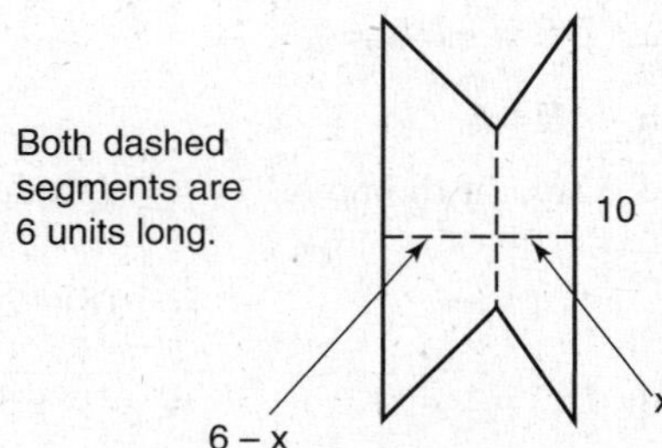

So $A_1 + A_2 = \left[\frac{1}{2}(6-x)(16)\right] + \left[\frac{1}{2}x(16)\right] = 8(6-x) + 8x = 48 - 8x + 8x = 48$

The area is 48 square units.
(This area could also have been determined by subtracting the areas of the two triangles from the big 6 by 10 rectangle. Do you see that it doesn't matter that the heights of the triangles are unknown?)

Warm-Up Drill

Find the area of this region.

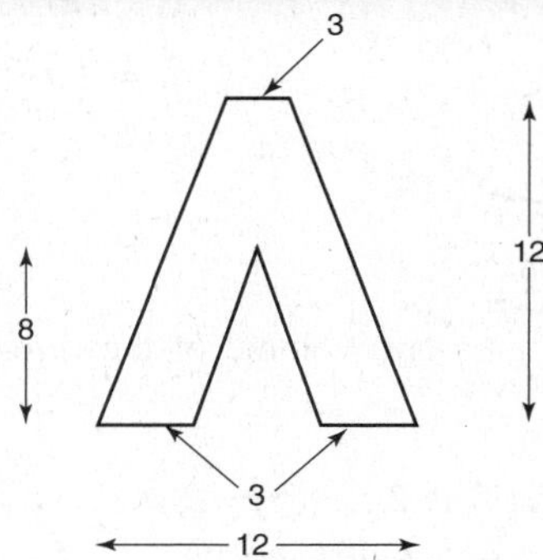

SOLUTION

The area of this region is the area of a trapezoid minus the area of a triangle. The area of the trapezoid A_1 is

$A_1 = \frac{1}{2}(12)(12+3) = 90$

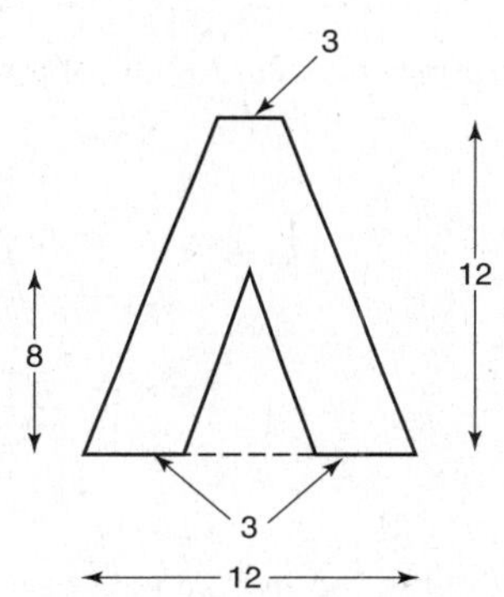

The area of the triangle A_2 is

$A_2 = \frac{1}{2}(6)(8) = 24$

Therefore the area of the given region is $A_1 - A_2 = 90 - 24 = 66$ square units.

Total Surface Area and Volume of 3-Dimensional Objects

There are reasonable formulas to find the total surface area and volume of rectangular solids, right circular cylinders and cones, and spheres.

Rectangular solids

$S = 2lw + 2lh + 2wh$
$V = lwh$

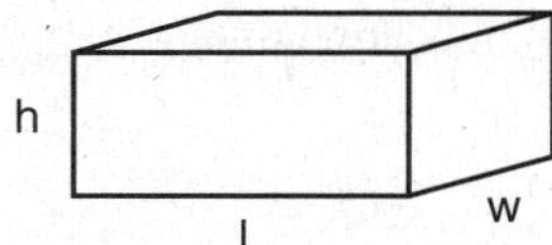

Right circular cylinders

$S = 2\pi r^2 + 2\pi rh$
$V = \pi r^2 h$

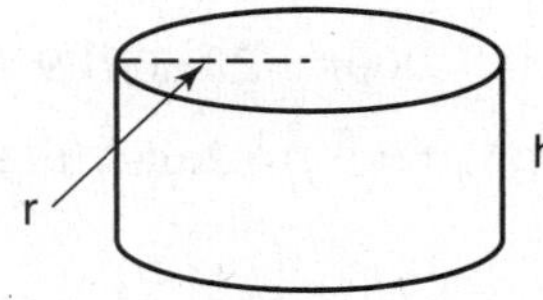

Right circular cones

$S = \pi r\sqrt{r^2 + h^2}$

$V = \frac{1}{3}\pi r^2 h$

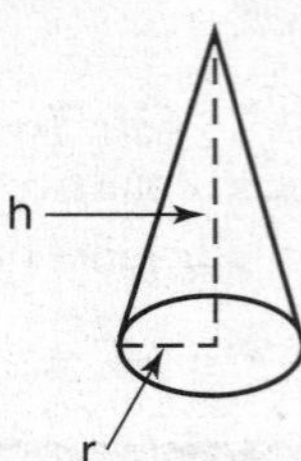

Spheres

$S = 4\pi r^2$

$V = \frac{4}{3}\pi r^3$

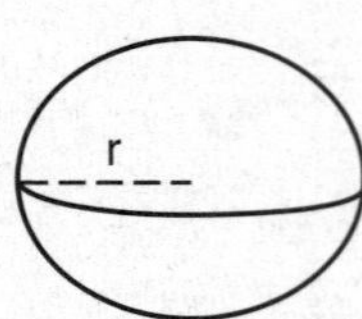

Example: Find the total surface area and volume of the right circular cylinder with radius 3 inches and height 5 inches.

$$S = 2\pi r^2 + 2\pi rh = 2\pi(3^2) + 2\pi(3)(5) = 18\pi + 30\pi = 48\pi \text{ square inches}$$
$$V = \pi r^2 h = \pi(3^2)(5) = 45\pi \text{ cubic inches}$$

Example: Determine the slant height of a right circular cone with radius 3 and height 4.

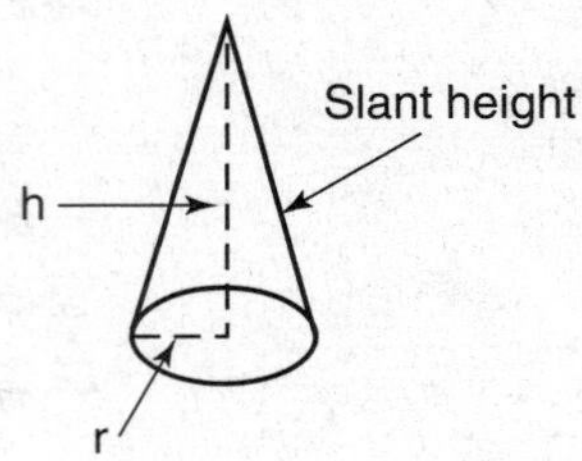

The slant height is the hypotenuse of a right triangle with legs the height and the radius. Use the Pythagorean theorem:

$$\text{Slant height} = \sqrt{r^2 + h^2} = \sqrt{3^2 + 4^2} = \sqrt{9 + 16} = \sqrt{25} = 5 \text{ units}$$

Warm-Up Drill

1. Find the total surface area and volume of a rectangular solid with dimensions 3 inches by 1 foot by 8 inches.
2. Find the surface area and volume of a sphere with radius 4000 miles.

SOLUTIONS

1. All measurements must be in the same units, so convert 1 foot to 12 inches.

   $S = 2lw + 2lh + 2wh = 2(3)(12) + 2(3)(8) + 2(12)(8) = 72 + 48 + 192 = 312$ square in.

   $V = lwh = (3)(12)(8) = 288$ cubic in.

2. $S = 4\pi r^2 = 4\pi(4000^2) = 64{,}000{,}000\pi \approx 201{,}061{,}930$ square miles

   $V = \frac{4}{3}\pi r^3 = \frac{4}{3}\pi(4000^3) = \frac{4}{3}\pi(6.4(10^{10})) \approx 2.68(10^{11})$ cubic miles

Circles

A *circle* is the set of points in a plane that are a given fixed distance from a given point. The given distance is called the *radius* and the fixed point is the *center.* A segment whose endpoints are on the circle is called a *chord*. A chord that also contains the center is a *diameter* (the longest chord). A line that contains a chord of a circle is a *secant line*. A line that contains only one point of a circle is a *tangent line*.

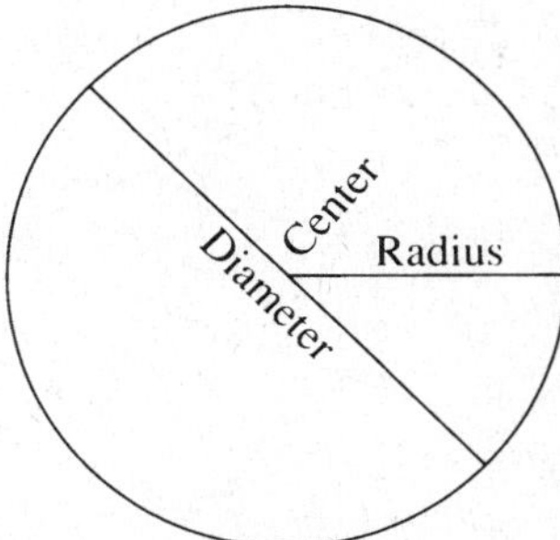

The length around a circle is called its *circumference*. The formula for the circumference is

$C = \pi d$ (π times diameter) or $C = 2\pi r$ (2π times radius)

The area formula for a circle is

$$A = \pi r^2$$

A *central angle* is an angle with its vertex at the center of a circle. The measure of a central angle is the same as the measure of its intercepted arc. Thus there are 360° of arc in a circle.

An *inscribed angle* is an angle formed by two chords of a circle; its vertex is on the circle. The measure of an inscribed angle is one-half the measure of its intercepted arc.

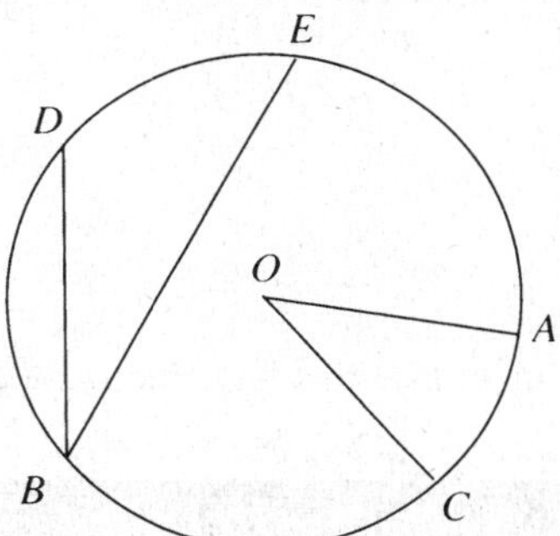

Angle *AOC* is a central angle.
Angle *DBE* is inscribed.

If two chords intersect inside a circle, the measures of the angles formed are one half of the sum of the measures of the intercepted arcs.

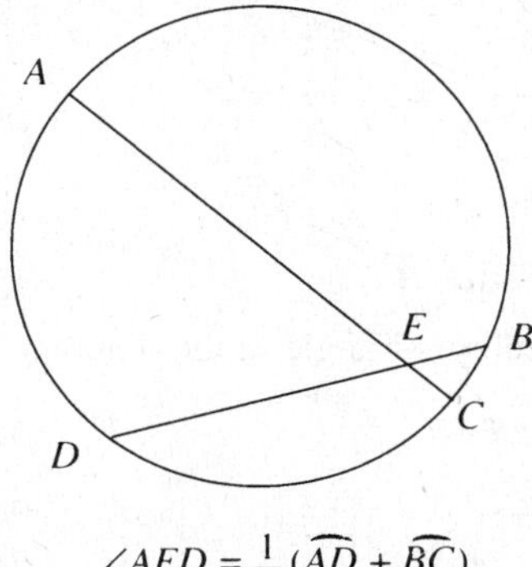

$$\angle AED = \frac{1}{2}(\overset{\frown}{AD} + \overset{\frown}{BC})$$

If secant lines intersect outside a circle, the measure of the angle formed is one half of the difference of the measures of the intercepted arcs.

If a secant and a tangent line intersect outside a circle, the measure of the angle formed is one half of the difference of the measures of the intercepted arcs.

If two tangent lines intersect outside a circle, the measure of the angle formed is one half of the difference of the measures of the intercepted arcs.

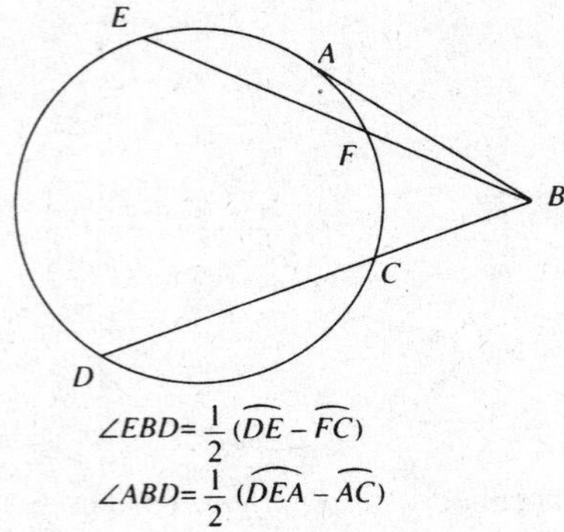

$$\angle EBD = \frac{1}{2}(\overparen{DE} - \overparen{FC})$$

$$\angle ABD = \frac{1}{2}(\overparen{DEA} - \overparen{AC})$$

The measure of the angle formed by a tangent line and a chord from the point of tangency is one half of the measure of the intercepted arc.

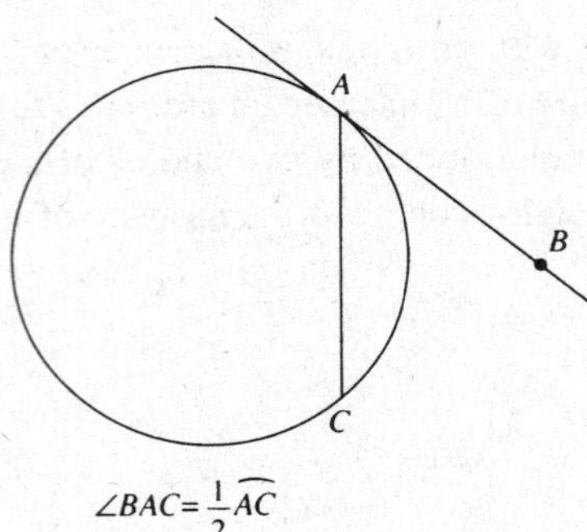

$$\angle BAC = \frac{1}{2}\overparen{AC}$$

Concentric circles are circles in a plane that have the same center.

Warm-Up Drill

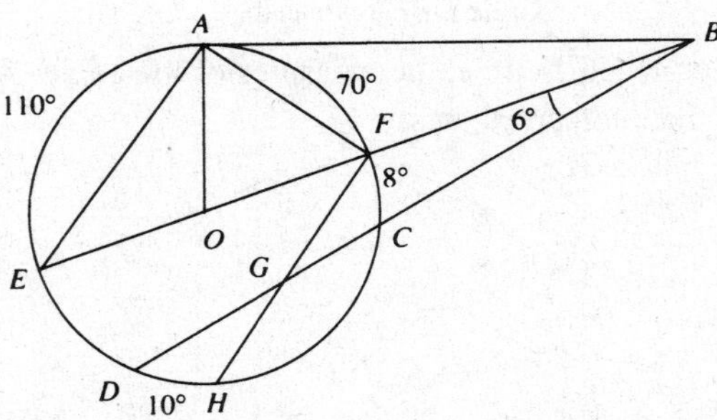

Find the measure of the indicated arc or angle in the diagram. (*0* is the center)

1. $\overparen{DE}$
2. $\overparen{DC}$
3. $\angle AOF$
4. $\angle EAF$
5. $\angle EFA$
6. $\angle OAF$
7. $\angle ABE$
8. $\angle BAF$
9. $\angle FGC$

SOLUTIONS

1. $6 \circeq \frac{1}{2}(\overparen{DE} - 8)$

$$12 \circeq \overparen{DE} - 8$$

$$\overparen{DE} \circeq 20$$

2. Since $\overline{EF}$ is a diameter, arc EDF must be 180°.

$$\overparen{DE} + \overparen{DC} + \overparen{CF} \circeq 180$$

$$20 + \overparen{DC} + 8 \circeq 180$$

$$\overparen{DC} \circeq 152$$

3. A central angle has the same measure as its intercepted arc.

$$\angle AOF \circeq 70$$

4. The measure of an inscribed angle is $\frac{1}{2}$ of the measure of the intercepted arc.

$$\angle EAF \circeq \frac{1}{2}(180) = 90$$

5. $\angle EFA \circeq \frac{1}{2}(110) = 55$

6. The sum of the three angles of a triangle is 180°. So

$$\angle AOF + \angle EFA + \angle OAF \circeq 70 + 55 + \angle AOF$$

$$\circeq 125 + \angle OAF \circeq 180$$

$$\angle OAF \circeq 55$$

7. The measure of an angle formed by a tangent and a secant line is $\frac{1}{2}$ of the difference of the measures of the intercepted arcs.

$$\angle ABE \circeq \frac{1}{2}(110 - 70) = \frac{1}{2}(40) = 20$$

8. The measure of an angle formed by a tangent and a chord intersecting at the point of tangency is $\frac{1}{2}$ of the measure of the intercepted arc.

$$\angle BAF \circeq \frac{1}{2}(70) = 35$$

9. The measure of an angle formed by the intersection of two chords in a circle is $\frac{1}{2}$ of the sum of the measures of the intercepted arcs.

$$\angle FGC \circeq \frac{1}{2}(8 + 10) = \frac{1}{2}(18) = 9$$

Relationships Among Chords, Secants, and Tangents

If two chords intersect in a circle, the product of the lengths of the segments of one chord is equal to the product of the lengths of the segments of the other.

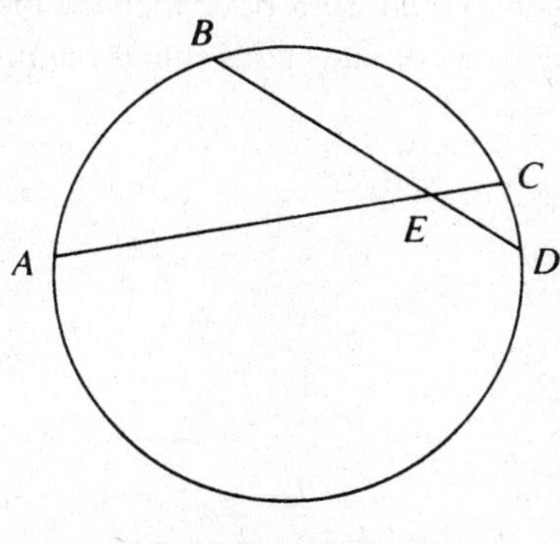

$(BE)\,(ED) = (AE)\,(EC)$

If a tangent and a secant intersect outside a circle, the length of the tangent is the mean proportional between the length of the secant and the length of its external segment.

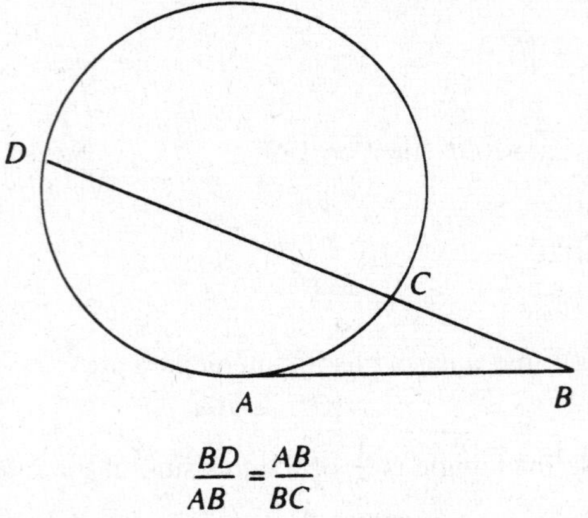

$$\frac{BD}{AB} = \frac{AB}{BC}$$

If two secants intersect outside a circle, the product of the length of one secant and the length of its external segment equals the product of the length of the other secant and the length of its external segment.

Warm-Up Drill

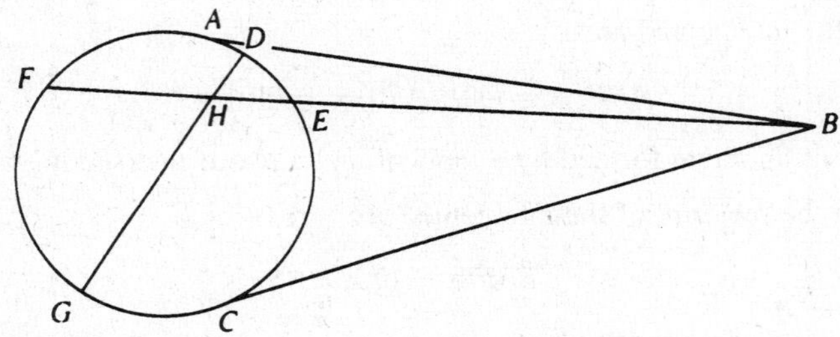

1. If $FE = 8$, $GH = 8$, and $HD = 2$, find FH.
2. If $BF = 12$ and $FE = 5$, find:
   a. AB
   b. BC

SOLUTIONS

1. Let the length of one segment of chord $\overline{FE}$ be x; then the other segment is $8 - x$. The product of the lengths of the segments of one chord equals the product of the lengths of the segments of the other.

   $x(8 - x) = 8(2)$
   $8x - x^2 = 16$
   $0 = x^2 - 8x + 16$
   $0 = (x - 4)^2$
   $x - 4 = 0$
   $x = 4$ So $FH = 4$.

2. a. The length of a tangent is the mean proportional between a secant and its external segment. The external segment is $BE = 12 - 5 = 7$.

$$\frac{12}{AB} = \frac{AB}{7}$$

$$AB^2 = 84$$

$$AB = \sqrt{84} = 2\sqrt{21}$$

b. Tangents to a circle from a common external point have the same length.

$$AB = BC = 2\sqrt{21}$$

TRIGONOMETRY

Angles

An angle is in standard position if its initial side is the positive x-axis and the vertex is at the origin. If the terminal side of the angle then lies in quadrant I, the angle is called a quadrant I angle: if it lies in quadrant II, it is called a quadrant II angle; etc. A positive angle is measured counterclockwise, and a negative angle is measured clockwise from the positive x-axis.

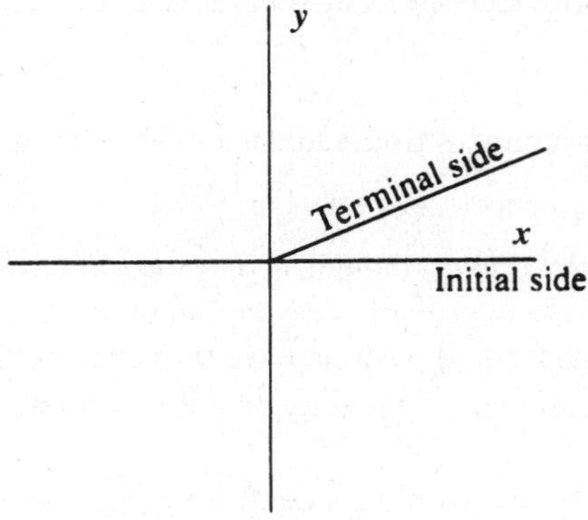

Standard Position

There are several measurement systems for angles. Two of them will be reviewed here.

1. Degree-minute-second: 1 degree $= 1° = \frac{1}{360}$ of a revolution

   1 minute $= 1' = \frac{1}{60}^{\circ}$

   1 second $= 1'' = \frac{1}{60}'$

2. Radians: 1 radian is the central angle subtended by an arc equal in length to the radius of the circle.

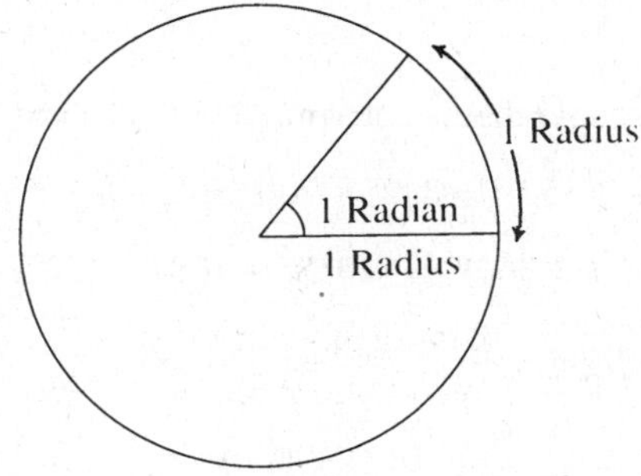

The formula for the circumference of a circle, $C = 2\pi r$, shows that there are 2π radii in the circumference of a circle. Therefore there are 2π radians in one complete revolution.

2π radians = 360° (The equal sign is used here to mean that the two numbers measure the same angle.)

Therefore:

TIP

Most angles of interest are multiples of these five, so memorize them.

$$\pi \text{ radians} = 180°$$

$$\frac{\pi}{2} \text{ radians} = 90°$$

$$\frac{\pi}{3} \text{ radians} = 60°$$

$$\frac{\pi}{4} \text{ radians} = 45°$$

$$\frac{\pi}{6} \text{ radians} = 30°$$

Generally, to convert an angle measurement from degrees to radians, multiply the number of degrees by $\frac{\pi}{180}$. The measurement of an angle in radians is commonly expressed in terms of π. ($1° = \frac{\pi}{180}$ radians.)

To convert an angle measurement from radians to degrees, multiply the number of radians by $\frac{180}{\pi}$. The π normally cancels. (1 radian = $\frac{180°}{\pi}$.)

Any statement made below, even though it may be phrased with the angles measured in degrees, will be true also if the angles are measured in radians.

If two different angles in standard position have the same terminal side, the angles are called *coterminal*. Coterminal angles can be found by adding or subtracting multiples of 360° or 2π to or from the original angle.

The acute angle formed by the terminal side of the angle and the nearer portion of the x-axis is called the *reference* angle.

Examples:

Convert from degree measure to radian measure.

1. $150° = 150\left(\frac{\pi}{180}\right) \text{ radians} = \frac{5\pi}{6} \text{ radians}$

2. $-240° = -240\left(\frac{\pi}{180}\right) \text{ radians} = \frac{-4\pi}{3} \text{ radians}$

Convert from radian measure to degree measure.

3. $\frac{11\pi}{6} \text{ radians} = \frac{11\pi}{6}\left(\frac{180}{\pi}\right)^{\circ} = 330°$

4. $\frac{-3\pi}{4} \text{ radians} = \frac{-3\pi}{4}\left(\frac{180}{\pi}\right)^{\circ} = -135°$

Find the smallest positive angle that is coterminal with each of the following:

5. 832° $\quad 832° - 2(360)° = 832° - 720° = 112°$

6. −1058° $\quad -1058° + 3(360)° = -1058° + 1080° = 22°$

7. $\frac{23\pi}{4}$ $\quad \frac{23\pi}{4} - 2(2\pi) = \frac{23\pi}{4} - \frac{16\pi}{4} = \frac{7\pi}{4}$

8. $\frac{-11\pi}{3}$ $\quad \frac{-11\pi}{3} + 2(2\pi) = \frac{-11\pi}{3} + \frac{12\pi}{3} = \frac{\pi}{3}$

Determine the reference angle for each angle given.

9. 140° For an angle, θ, in quadrant II, the reference angle is $180° - \theta$. $180° - 140° = 40°$

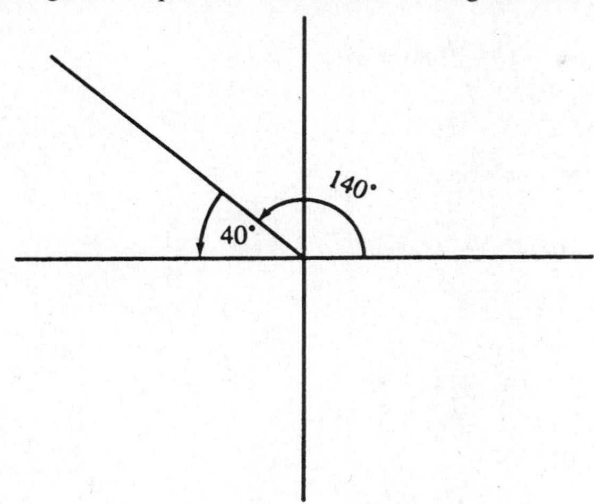

10. 215° For an angle, θ, in quadrant III, the reference angle is $\theta - 180°$. $215° - 180° = 35°$

11. 307° For an angle, θ, in quadrant IV, the reference angle is $360° - \theta$. $360° - 307° = 53°$

12. $\frac{-7\pi}{3}$ If necessary, first find the smallest positive angle that is coterminal with the original angle. Then use the rules above with radians instead of degrees.

$$\frac{-7\pi}{3} + 2(2\pi) = \frac{-7\pi}{3} + \frac{12\pi}{3} = \frac{5\pi}{3} \text{ (quad. IV)}$$

Reference angle is $2\pi - \frac{5\pi}{3} = \frac{6\pi}{3} - \frac{5\pi}{3} = \frac{\pi}{3}$.

Warm-Up Drill

Convert from degree measure to radian measure.

1. 210°
2. –540°

Convert from radian measure to degree measure.

3. $\frac{5\pi}{4}$
4. $\frac{7\pi}{9}$

Find: a. The smallest positive angle that is coterminal with the given angle
b. The reference angle

5. 478°
6. –815°
7. $\frac{11\pi}{3}$
8. $\frac{-17\pi}{6}$

SOLUTIONS

1. $210\left(\frac{\pi}{180}\right) = \frac{7\pi}{6}$
2. $-540\left(\frac{\pi}{180}\right) = -3\pi$
3. $\frac{5\pi}{4}\left(\frac{180}{\pi}\right) = 225$
4. $\frac{7\pi}{9}\left(\frac{180}{\pi}\right) = 140$

5. a. $478 - 360 = 118$
   $118°$ is in quad. II.
   b. $180 - 118 = 62$

6. a. $-815 + 3(360) = -815 + 1080 = 265$
   $265°$ is in quad. III.
   b. $265 - 180 = 85$

7. a. $\frac{11\pi}{3} - 2\pi = \frac{11\pi}{3} - \frac{6\pi}{3} = \frac{5\pi}{3}$
   $\frac{5\pi}{3}$ is in quad. IV.
   b. $2\pi - \frac{5\pi}{3} = \frac{6\pi}{3} - \frac{5\pi}{3} = \frac{\pi}{3}$

8. a. $\frac{-17\pi}{6} + 2(2\pi) = \frac{-17\pi}{6} + \frac{24\pi}{6} = \frac{7\pi}{6}$
   $\frac{7\pi}{6}$ is in quad. III.
   b. $\frac{7\pi}{6} - \pi = \frac{\pi}{6}$

Definitions of Trigonometric Functions

Choose a point, (x, y), on the terminal side of an angle, θ, in standard position. The distance from the origin is $r = \sqrt{x^2 + y^2}$

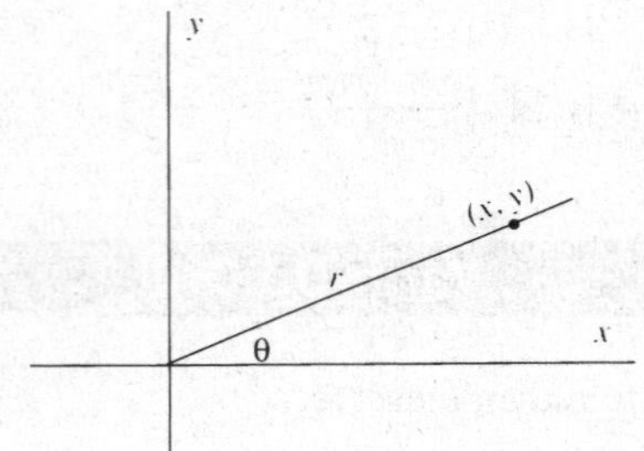

$\sin\theta = \frac{y}{r}$		Sine
$\cos\theta = \frac{x}{r}$		Cosine
$\tan\theta = \frac{y}{x}$,	$x \neq 0, \theta \neq 90° \pm 180n°$	Tangent
$\csc\theta = \frac{r}{y}$,	$y \neq 0, \theta \neq \pm 180n°$	Cosecant
$\sec\theta = \frac{r}{x}$,	$x \neq 0, \theta \neq 90° \pm 180n°$	Secant
$\cot\theta = \frac{x}{y}$,	$y \neq 0, \theta \neq \pm 180n°$	Cotangent

In each case above, $n = 0, 1, 2, \ldots$.

For an angle, θ, in quadrant I, both of the coordinates of a point on the terminal side of θ are positive; and since r is always positive, all of the six trigonometric functions have positive values.

In quadrant II the value of x is negative and both y and r are positive, so the values of the functions sine and cosecant are positive while the other four are negative.

In quadrant III the values of both x and y are negative, so the values of the tangent and cotangent are positive while the other four are negative.

In quadrant IV the values of x and r are positive and y is negative, so the values of the functions cosine and secant are positive while the other four are negative.

This information should be memorized for the four quadrants:

I: All positive.
II: Sine and cosecant positive, others negative.
III: Tangent and cotangent positive, others negative.
IV: Cosine and secant positive, others negative.

ASTC is a helpful mnemonic aid.

The domains of the six trigonometric functions are sets of angles in standard position.
Domain of sine: All angles
Domain of cosine: All angles
Domain of tangent: All angles except those coterminal with 90° or 270°
Domain of cosecant: All angles except those coterminal with 0° or 180°
Domain of secant: Same as for tangent
Domain of cotangent: Same as for cosecant

The ranges of the trigonometric functions are subsets of real numbers.
Range of sine: $\{y \mid -1 \le y \le 1\}$
Range of cosine: $\{y \mid -1 \le y \le 1\}$
Range of tangent: R(All real numbers)
Range of secant: $\{y \mid y \le -1 \quad \text{or} \quad y \ge 1\}$
Range of cosecant: Same as for secant
Range of cotangent: R

The following useful rule can easily be derived:

A function of any angle is equal to ± the same function of the reference angle. The sign of the function value is determined by ASTC.

Warm-Up Drill

Name the six trigonometric function values for the angle θ in standard position with the given point on the terminal side.

1. $(-3, 4)$
2. $(-2, -6)$

Name the quadrant in which the angle θ must lie for the following to be true:

3. $\sin\theta > 0$ and $\tan\theta < 0$
4. $\cos\theta < 0$ and $\csc > 0$
5. $\cot\theta > 0$ and $\sec\theta < 0$
6. $\sec\theta > 0$ and $\sin\theta < 0$

Find the remaining five function values, given the following information:

7. $\tan\theta = \frac{1}{2}$ and $\sin\theta$ is negative
8. $\sec\theta = \frac{-\sqrt{2}}{5}$ and $\tan\theta < 0$
9. $\sin\theta = \frac{-\sqrt{3}}{5}$ and $\cos\theta > 0$
10. Express each function as a function of its reference angle.
    a. $\sin 233°$
    b. $\tan(-57°)$
    c. $\cos\frac{5\pi}{6}$
    d. $\sec 680°$

SOLUTIONS

1. First $r = \sqrt{(-3)^2 + 4^2} = \sqrt{25} = 5$
   $\sin\theta = \frac{4}{5}$ $\csc\theta = \frac{5}{4}$
   $\cos\theta = \frac{-3}{5}$ $\sec\theta = \frac{-5}{3}$
   $\tan\theta = \frac{-4}{3}$ $\cot\theta = \frac{-3}{4}$
2. $r = \sqrt{(-2)^2 + (-6)^2} = \sqrt{40} = 2\sqrt{10}$
   $\sin\theta = \frac{-6}{2\sqrt{10}} = \frac{-3\sqrt{10}}{10}$
   $\cos\theta = \frac{-2}{2\sqrt{10}} = \frac{-\sqrt{10}}{10}$
   $\tan\theta = \frac{-6}{-2} = 3$
   $\csc\theta = \frac{2\sqrt{10}}{-6} = \frac{-\sqrt{10}}{3}$
   $\sec\theta = \frac{-2\sqrt{10}}{2} = -\sqrt{10}$
   $\cot\theta = \frac{-2}{-6} = \frac{1}{3}$
3. ASTC indicates that the sine is positive in quads. I and II, while the tangent is negative in quads. II and IV. Both are true only in quad. II.
4. $\cos\theta < 0$ in II and III
   $\csc\theta >$ in I and II
   Both are true only in quad. II.
5. $\cot\theta > 0$ in I and III
   $\sec\theta < 0$ in II and III
   Both are true only in quad. III.
6. $\sec\theta > 0$ in I and IV
   $\sin\theta < 0$ in III and IV
   Both are true only in quad. IV.
7. Since $\tan\theta = \frac{1}{2}$ (>0) and $\sin\theta < 0$, angle θ must be in quad. III. And since
   $$\tan\theta = \frac{y}{x} = \frac{1}{2} = \frac{-1}{-2}$$
   choose a point (–2, –1) on the terminal side of θ.

   $r = \sqrt{2^2 + 1^2} = \sqrt{5}$
   $\sin\theta = \frac{-1}{\sqrt{5}} = \frac{-\sqrt{5}}{5}$
   $\cos\theta = \frac{-2}{\sqrt{5}} = \frac{-2\sqrt{5}}{5}$
   $\tan\theta$ is given.
   $\csc\theta = \frac{\sqrt{5}}{-1} = -\sqrt{5}$
   $\sec\theta = \frac{-\sqrt{5}}{2}$
   $\cot\theta = \frac{2}{1} = 2$

8. The secant is given as $\frac{-\sqrt{2}}{5}$, which is not in the range of the secant function. There is no angle that satisfies the conditions given; therefore there are no function values.

9. Here $\sin \theta = \frac{-\sqrt{3}}{5}$ (< 0) and $\cos \theta > 0$, which occurs only in quad. IV. Since

$$\sin \theta = \frac{y}{r} = \frac{-\sqrt{3}}{5}$$

choose a point $(x, -\sqrt{3})$ with $r = 5$. Substitute into the distance formula to find x:

$$5 = \sqrt{x^2 + (-\sqrt{3})^2} = \sqrt{x^2 + 3}$$
$$25 = x^2 + 3$$
$$22 = x^2$$
$$\pm\sqrt{22} = x$$

Choose the positive sign because the point is in quad. IV: $x = \sqrt{22}$.

$\sin \theta$ is given. $\qquad \csc \theta = \frac{5}{-\sqrt{3}} = \frac{-5\sqrt{3}}{3}$

$\cos \theta = \frac{\sqrt{22}}{5} \qquad \sec \theta = \frac{5}{\sqrt{22}} = \frac{5\sqrt{22}}{22}$

$\tan \theta = \frac{-\sqrt{3}}{\sqrt{22}} = \frac{-\sqrt{66}}{22} \qquad \cot \theta = \frac{\sqrt{22}}{-\sqrt{3}} = \frac{-\sqrt{66}}{3}$

10. a. 233° is in quad. III and the reference angle is 233 – 180 = 53. So

$$\sin 233° = -\sin 53°$$

b. –57° is in quad. IV and the reference angle is 57°. So

$$\tan(-57°) = -\tan 57°$$

c. $\frac{5\pi}{6}$ is in quad. II and the reference angle is $\pi - \frac{5\pi}{6} = \frac{\pi}{6}$. So

$$\cos \frac{5\pi}{6} = -\cos \frac{\pi}{6}$$

d. 680° is coterminal with 320°, which is in quad. IV and its reference angle is 360 – 320 = 40. So

$$\sec 680° = \sec 40°$$

Trigonometric Function Values of Special Angles

The values of the trigonometric functions in the following table occur frequently enough that they should be memorized.

Angle	sin	cos	tan
0°	0	1	0
30°	$\frac{1}{2}$	$\frac{\sqrt{3}}{2}$	$\frac{\sqrt{3}}{3}$
45°	$\frac{\sqrt{2}}{2}$	$\frac{\sqrt{2}}{2}$	1
60°	$\frac{\sqrt{3}}{2}$	$\frac{1}{2}$	$\sqrt{3}$
90°	1	0	undef.

The function values of angles in other quadrants for which the reference angle is 30°, 45°, or 60° may be found by using the rule that a function of any angle is equal to ± the same function of the reference angle, the sign being determined by ASTC.

Here are some examples:

- $\tan 240° = \tan 60° = \sqrt{3}$
- $\sin 330° = -\sin 30° = \frac{-1}{2}$
- $\cos(-210°) = -\cos 30° = \frac{-\sqrt{3}}{2}$

Warm-Up Drill

Determine each function value.

1. $\sin 225°$
2. $\tan 480°$
3. $\sec(-300°)$
4. $\cos \frac{11\pi}{6}$
5. $\sin 270°$
6. $\csc \frac{13\pi}{6}$
7. $\cos\left(\frac{-13\pi}{4}\right)$
8. $\tan(-660°)$

SOLUTIONS

1. $\mathbf{\sin 225°} = -\sin 45° = \frac{-\sqrt{2}}{2}$ 225° is in quad. III where $\sin\theta < 0$.

2. $\mathbf{\tan 480°} = \tan 120°$ 120° is the smallest positive coterminal angle. 120° is in quad. II.
$= -\tan 60°$ 60° is the reference angle.
$= -\sqrt{3}$

3. $\mathbf{\sec(-300°)} = \sec 60°$ 60° is the smallest positive coterminal angle and the reference angle.
$$= \frac{1}{\cos 60°} = \frac{1}{\frac{1}{2}} = 2$$

4. $\mathbf{\cos \frac{11\pi}{6}} = \cos\frac{\pi}{6}$
$= \frac{\sqrt{3}}{2}$ Since $\frac{\pi}{6} = 30°$.

5. Since **270°** is not in a quadrant, the rule does not apply. Instead, choose a point on the terminal side of 270°.

   The point (0, –1) is on the terminal side and $r = 1$. So

$$\sin 270° = \frac{y}{r} = \frac{-1}{1} = -1$$

6. $\csc \frac{13\pi}{6} = +\csc\left(\frac{\pi}{6}\right)$ $\qquad \frac{13\pi}{6}$ is in quad. I where $\csc\theta > 0$.

$$= \frac{1}{\sin\left(\frac{\pi}{6}\right)}$$

$$= \frac{1}{\frac{1}{2}} = 2$$

7. $\cos\left(\frac{-13\pi}{4}\right) = -\cos\frac{\pi}{4}$ $\qquad \frac{-13\pi}{4} + \frac{2(8\pi)}{4} = \frac{3\pi}{4}$ in quad. II where $\cos\theta < 0$.

$$= \frac{-\sqrt{2}}{2}$$ The reference angle is $\frac{\pi}{4}$.

8. $\tan(-660°) = \tan 60°$ $\qquad -660 + 2(360) = 60$. 60° is in quad. I where

$= \sqrt{3}$ $\qquad \tan\theta > 0$.

Solving Right Triangles

Right triangles may be solved by trigonometric means by interpreting the definitions as ratios of the lengths of the sides.

$$\sin A = \frac{\text{length of side opposite } A}{\text{length of hypotenuse}} = \frac{\text{opp}}{\text{hyp}}$$

$$\cos A = \frac{\text{length of side adjacent to } A}{\text{length of hypotenuse}} = \frac{\text{adj}}{\text{hyp}}$$

$$\tan A = \frac{\text{opp}}{\text{adj}}$$

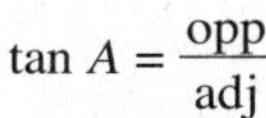

$$\csc A = \frac{\text{hyp}}{\text{opp}}$$

$$\sec A = \frac{\text{hyp}}{\text{adj}}$$

$$\cot A = \frac{\text{adj}}{\text{opp}}$$

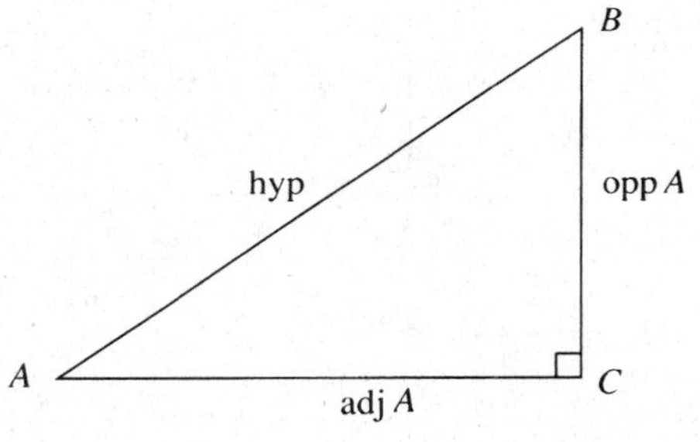

TIP

Since the acute angles of a right triangle are always complementary, the following rule applies:

Cofunctions of complementary angles are equal.

Here are some examples:

- $\sin 83° = \cos(90 - 83)° = \cos 7°$
- $\tan 27° = \cot(90 - 27)° = \cot 63°$
- $\csc\frac{\pi}{5} = \sec\left(\frac{\pi}{2} - \frac{\pi}{5}\right) = \sec\frac{3\pi}{10}$

Given right triangle *ABC* with right angle *C*, $\angle B = 33°$, and side $b = 12.5$. (The sides of a triangle are labeled with the lowercase letter of the angle opposite.) Solve for the remaining parts of the triangle.

- $\angle A = (90 - 33)° = 57°$
- $\tan 33° = \frac{\text{opp}}{\text{adj}} = \frac{12.5}{a}$

$$a = \frac{12.5}{\tan 33°} = 19.2 \text{ (by calculator)}$$

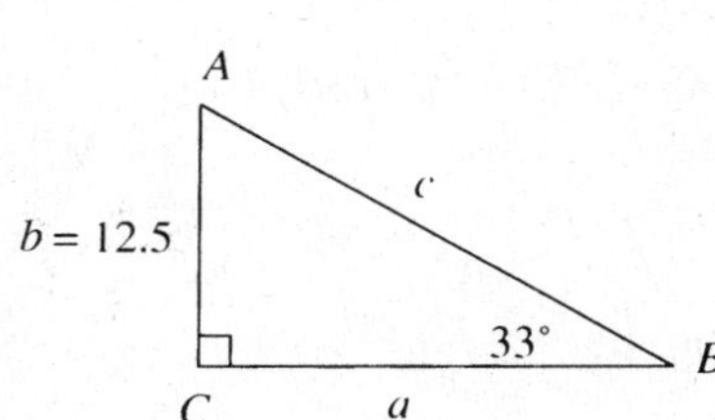

- $\sin 33° = \frac{\text{opp}}{\text{hyp}} = \frac{12.5}{c}$

$$c = \frac{12.5}{\sin 33°} = 23.0 \text{ (by calculator)}$$

A scientific calculator is indispensable in trigonometry.

Warm-Up Drill

1. Solve right triangle ABC using the following information: Given right angle C, $\angle A = 15°$ and side $c = 8.74$.
2. Solve $\triangle ABC$.

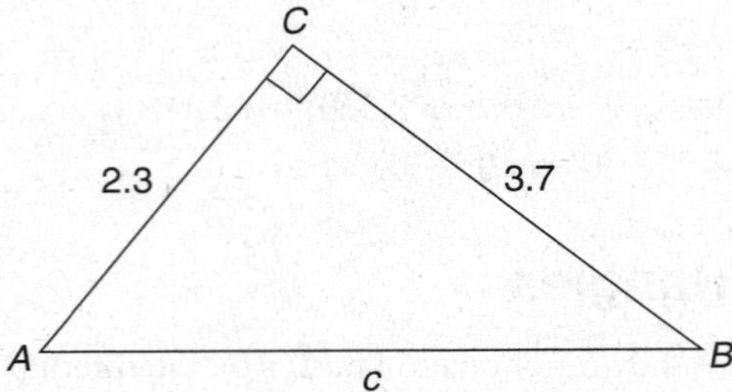

SOLUTIONS

1.

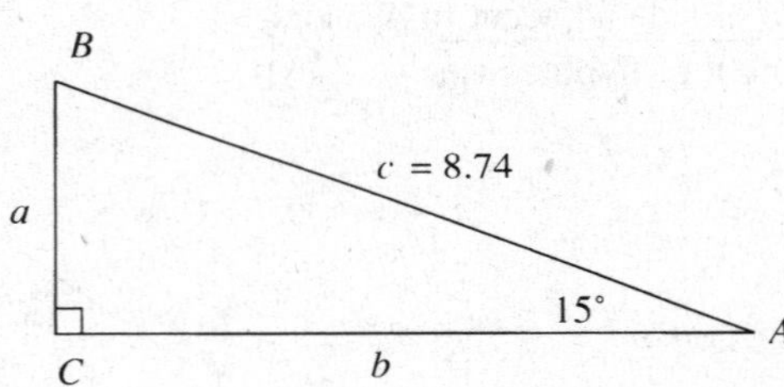

$$\angle B = (90 - 15)° = 75°$$

$$\sin 15° = \frac{a}{8.74}$$

$$a = 8.74 \sin 15° = 2.26$$

$$\cos 15° = \frac{b}{8.74}$$

$$b = 8.74 \cos 15° = 8.44$$

2. $\tan A = \frac{3.7}{2.3}$

$$\angle A = 58.1°$$

$$\angle B = (90 - 58.1)° = 31.9°$$

$$\sin A = \frac{3.7}{c}$$

$$c = \frac{3.7}{\sin A} = \frac{3.7}{\sin 58.1°} = 4.4$$

Graphs

Each of the trigonometric functions is periodic. A *periodic function f* is any function for which the following is true for some number *p:*

$$f(x + p) = f(x) \text{ for all } x \text{ in the domain}$$

If *p* is the smallest number for which this equation is true, then *p* is called the *period*.

Since $\sin(\theta + 2\pi) = \sin\theta$:
$\cos(\theta + 2\pi) = \cos\theta$,
$\csc(\theta + 2\pi) = \csc\theta$,
$\sec(\theta + 2\pi) = \sec\theta$.

These all show that the functions are periodic with period 2π.

Since $\tan(\theta + \pi) = \tan\theta$:
$\cot(\theta + \pi) = \cot\theta$.

The period of tangent and cotangent is π.

Identities

An *identity* is an equation that is true for all elements in the domains for which the functions involved are defined. There are many identities in trigonometry. Memorize these:

- *Reciprocal identities*

$$\sin x = \frac{1}{\csc x} \qquad \csc x = \frac{1}{\sin x}$$

$$\cos x = \frac{1}{\sec x} \qquad \sec x = \frac{1}{\cos x}$$

$$\tan x = \frac{1}{\cot x} \qquad \cot x = \frac{1}{\tan x}$$

- *Quotient identities*

$$\tan x = \frac{\sin x}{\cos x} \qquad \cot x = \frac{\cos y}{\sin x}$$

- *Pythagorean identities*

$\sin^2 x + \cos^2 x = 1$ Note that $\sin^2 x = (\sin x)^2$.

$\tan^2 x + 1 = \sec^2 x$

$1 + \cot^2 x = \csc^2 x$

- *Sum and difference identities*

($\pm$ and $\mp$ are different; if one is –, the other is +.)

$\cos(A \pm B) = \cos A \cos B \mp \sin A \sin B$

$\sin(A \pm B) = \sin A \cos B \pm \sin B \cos A$

$$\tan(A \pm B) = \frac{\tan A \pm \tan B}{1 \mp \tan A \tan B}$$

- *Double-angle identities*

$\sin 2A = 2 \sin A \cos A$

$\cos 2A = \cos^2 A - \sin^2 A = 2\cos^2 A - 1 = 1 - 2\sin^2 A$

$$\tan 2A = \frac{2 \tan A}{1 - \tan^2 A}$$

- *Half-angle identities*

$$\sin\frac{A}{2} = \pm\sqrt{\frac{1-\cos A}{2}}$$

$$\cos\frac{A}{2} = \pm\sqrt{\frac{1+\cos A}{2}}$$

$$\tan\frac{A}{2} = \pm\sqrt{\frac{1-\cos A}{1+\cos A}} = \frac{\sin A}{1+\cos A} = \frac{1-\cos A}{\sin A}$$

Warm-Up Drill

Use the identities above to find each function value.

1. cos 15°
2. tan 75°
3. sin 195°
4. $\cos\frac{\pi}{8}$
5. sin 2*A*, given that $\sin A = \frac{3}{4}$ and *a* is in quadrant I.
6. tan 2*A*, given that $\sin A = \frac{-2}{5}$ and *A* is in quadrant III.

SOLUTIONS

1. Find two angles whose difference is 15° (45° and 30° will do).

$$\textbf{cos 15°} = \cos(45-30)°$$
$$= \cos 45 \cos 30 + \sin 45 \sin 30$$
$$= \left(\frac{\sqrt{2}}{2}\right)\left(\frac{\sqrt{3}}{2}\right) + \left(\frac{\sqrt{2}}{2}\right)\left(\frac{1}{2}\right)$$
$$= \frac{\sqrt{6}}{4} + \frac{\sqrt{2}}{4}$$
$$= \frac{\sqrt{6}+\sqrt{2}}{4}$$

2. Several choices are possible. Choose the half-angle tangent formula.

$$\textbf{tan 75°} = \tan\frac{1}{2}(150°) = \frac{\sin 150°}{1+\cos 150°}$$
$$= \frac{\frac{1}{2}}{1+\frac{-\sqrt{3}}{2}}$$
$$= \frac{1}{2-\sqrt{3}} = 2+\sqrt{3}$$

3. **sin 195°** $= \sin(150 + 45)°$

$= \sin 150 \cos 45 + \sin 45 \cos 150$

$= \left(\frac{1}{2}\right)\left(\frac{\sqrt{2}}{2}\right) + \left(\frac{\sqrt{2}}{2}\right)\left(\frac{-\sqrt{3}}{2}\right)$

$= \frac{\sqrt{2}}{4} + \frac{-\sqrt{6}}{4} = \frac{\sqrt{2}-\sqrt{6}}{4}$

4. $\mathbf{\cos \frac{\pi}{8}}$ $= \cos \frac{\left(\frac{\pi}{4}\right)}{2} = \sqrt{\frac{1+\cos\left(\frac{\pi}{4}\right)}{2}}$

$= \pm\sqrt{\frac{1+\frac{\sqrt{2}}{2}}{2}}$

$= \pm\sqrt{\frac{2+\sqrt{2}}{4}}$ Choose the positive sign because $\frac{\pi}{8}$ is in quad. I.

$= \frac{\sqrt{2+\sqrt{2}}}{2}$

5. Since $\sin A = \frac{3}{4}$ and A is in quad. I,

$\sin^2 A + \cos^2 A = 1$

$\left(\frac{3}{4}\right)^2 + \cos^2 A = 1$

$\frac{9}{16} + \cos^2 A = 1$

$\cos^2 A = \frac{7}{16}$

$\cos A = \frac{\sqrt{7}}{4}$ Choose the positive sign.

So

$\sin 2A = 2 \sin A \cos A = 2\left(\frac{3}{4}\right)\left(\frac{\sqrt{7}}{4}\right) = \frac{3\sqrt{7}}{8}$.

6. Since $\sin A = \frac{-2}{5}$ and A is in quad. III,

$\cos A = -\sqrt{1-\sin^2 A}$

$= -\sqrt{1-\left(\frac{-2}{5}\right)^2}$

$= -\sqrt{1-\frac{4}{25}} = -\sqrt{\frac{21}{25}} = \frac{-\sqrt{21}}{5}$

So

$$\tan A = \frac{\sin A}{\cos A} = \frac{\frac{-2}{5}}{\frac{-\sqrt{21}}{5}} = \frac{2}{\sqrt{21}} = \frac{2\sqrt{21}}{21}$$

Then

$$\tan 2A = \frac{2\tan A}{1 - \tan^2 A}$$

$$= \frac{2\left(\frac{2\sqrt{21}}{21}\right)}{1 - \left(\frac{2\sqrt{21}}{21}\right)^2}$$

$$= \frac{\frac{4\sqrt{21}}{21}}{1 - \frac{4}{21}} = \frac{4\sqrt{21}}{17}$$

Solution of Nonright Triangles

The Law of Sines says that in any triangle the ratio of the sine of an angle to the length of the opposite side is constant.

$$\frac{\sin A}{a} = \frac{\sin B}{b} = \frac{\sin C}{c}$$

This law is useful in the solution of a triangle in which the given information is in the order ASA (Angle, Side, Angle), AAS, or SSA (the ambiguous case).

The Law of Cosines is useful in the solution of triangles for which the data are given in the order SAS or SSS.

$$a^2 = b^2 + c^2 - 2bc \cos A$$
$$b^2 = a^2 + c^2 - 2ac \cos B$$
$$c^2 = a^2 + b^2 - 2ab \cos C$$

Warm-Up Drill

1. Solve $\triangle ABC$, given: $A = 25°$, $B = 70°$, $c = 3.7$ cm.
2. Find the largest angle of a triangle with sides 51 cm, 35 cm, and 72 cm.

SOLUTIONS

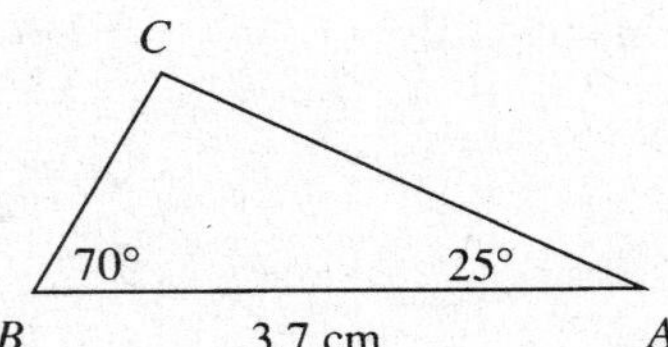

1. The data given are of the type ASA (the side is between the two angles). The Law of Sines applies:

   First find C: $C = 180 - (25 + 70) = 85$

$$\frac{\sin 25°}{a} = \frac{\sin 70°}{b} = \frac{\sin 85°}{3.7}$$

Solve two proportions:

$$a = \frac{3.7 \sin 25°}{\sin 85°} = 1.57 \text{ (by calculator)}$$

$$b = \frac{3.7 \sin 70°}{\sin 85°} = 3.49 \text{ (by calculator)}$$

2. The largest angle of a triangle is opposite the longest side. The Law of Cosines may be written in the alternative form for finding an angle.

$$\cos A = \frac{b^2 + c^2 - a^2}{2bc}$$

$$= \frac{51^2 + 35^2 - 72^2}{2(51)(35)}$$

$$= -0.3804$$

So

$$A \doteqdot 112 \quad [\cos^{-1}(-0.3804) \doteqdot 112]$$

Practice Exercises

The following sample questions represent ways in which the reviewed skills might be tested on the ACT.

1. If, in the right triangle ABC, m$\angle A = 60°$ and $AB = 12$, what is BC?

A. 12
B. 6
C. $6\sqrt{3}$
D. $6\sqrt{2}$
E. $4\sqrt{3}$

2. If m $\overset{\frown}{AB} = 105°$ and $\overline{AC}$ is a diameter, find the measure of $\angle ADB$.

F. 15°
G. 30°
H. 45°
J. $7\frac{1}{2}°$
K. $52\frac{1}{2}°$

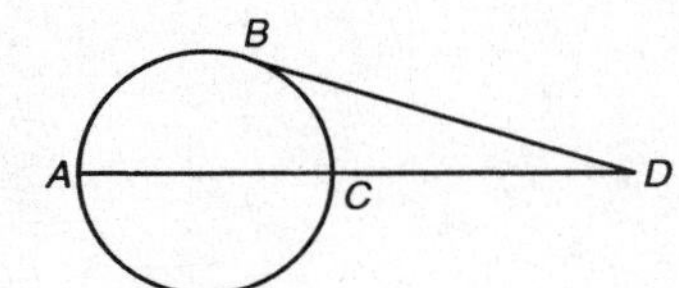

3. Chords $\overline{AB}$ and $\overline{CD}$ intersect in a circle such that $CE = 4$ and $DE = 2$. If $BE = 1$, what is AE?

A. 6
B. 8
C. 4
D. 9
E. 10

4. What is the smallest positive angle that is coterminal with –815°?

F. 85°
G. –95°
H. 625°
J. 265°
K. None of these.

5. If $\sin A = x$ and x is in quadrant I, what is the value of $\sin 2A$?

A. $2x$
B. $\frac{x}{2}$
C. $x^2 + 1$
D. $\sqrt{1 - 2x^2}$
E. $2x\sqrt{1 - x^2}$

ANSWERS AND EXPLANATIONS

1. **(C)** In a 30-60-90° triangle the shorter leg is half of the hypotenuse and the longer leg (*BC*) is $\sqrt{3}$ times the shorter leg.

2. **(F)** The angle formed by a tangent line and a secant line intersecting outside a circle has measure equal to half of the difference of the intercepted arcs. Since arc *AB* is given to be 105°, then arc *BC* must be

   $75°(= 180° - 105°). \frac{1}{2}(105 - 75) = \frac{1}{2}(30) = 15.$

3. **(B)** The product of the segments of two intersecting chords in a circle must be equal.
   $(CE)(DE) = (AE)(BE)$
   $(4)(2) = (AE)(1)$
   $8 = AE$

4. **(J)** Coterminal angles are found by adding or subtracting multiples of 360°. $-815 + 3(360) = -815 + 1080 = 265$.

5. **(E)** Apply the double angle identity $\sin 2A = 2\sin A\cos A$ and the Pythagorean identity $\cos A = \pm\sqrt{1 - \sin^2 A}$, choosing the positive sign because *A* is in quadrant I. $\sin 2A = 2x\sqrt{1 - x^2}$.

SAMPLE MATHEMATICS TEST

The following test is representative of the ACT mathematics tests except that it is half as long. All content areas and skill levels are presented in approximate proportions to the actual test. Allow yourself 30 minutes to do the 30 questions. Try to simulate actual test conditions.

Directions: Do not spend too much time on any one problem. Make a note of the ones that seem difficult, and return to them when you finish the others. Assume that the word line means "straight line," that geometric figures are not necessarily drawn to scale, and that all geometric figures lie in a plane.

1. What is the value of $5 \cdot 3^2 - 3(4 + 2 \cdot 3)$?

   A. 195
   B. 171
   C. 150
   D. 15
   E. –9

2. Which of the following is NOT an irrational number?

   F. π
   G. $\sqrt{2}$
   H. 3.1416
   J. 3.101001000100001 . . .
   K. $\sqrt[3]{9}$

3. If a student received a score of 85% on a test on which he got six questions wrong, how many questions were on the test?

   A. 5
   B. 40
   C. 90
   D. 510
   E. None of these

4. On the diagram, which of the following is a chord?

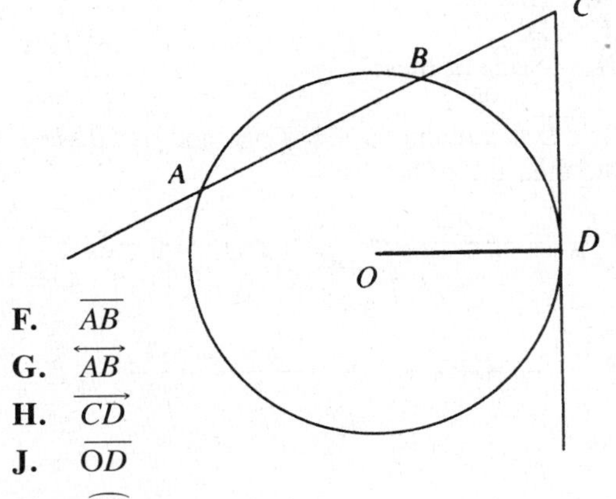

   F. $\overline{AB}$
   G. $\overleftrightarrow{AB}$
   H. $\overrightarrow{CD}$
   J. $\overline{OD}$
   K. $\overparen{BD}$

5. What is the solution of $5 - 2[3x - (x - 2)] = 1 - x$?

   A. $\{0\}$
   B. $\{1\}$
   C. $\left\{\frac{8}{3}\right\}$
   D. $\left\{\frac{-5}{7}\right\}$
   E. $\left\{\frac{-21}{19}\right\}$

6. If $a = -9$, which of the following expressions represents an integer?

   F. $-\sqrt{a}$
   G. $\sqrt{\frac{1}{-a}}$
   H. $\sqrt{-a}$
   J. $\sqrt{a+5}$
   K. None of these

7. $2\frac{7}{8} + 5\frac{5}{12} = ?$

   A. 8
   B. $8\frac{7}{24}$
   C. $2\frac{13}{24}$
   D. $3\frac{1}{2}$
   E. $7\frac{3}{5}$

8. Which of the following is a polynomial of degree 3?

   F. $3x + 1$
   G. $4x^2 + x + 1$
   H. $(2x^2 + 1)^3$
   J. $\frac{1}{x^2}$
   K. $5x^3 - 2x^2 + x - 3$

9. What is the simplified form of $x - \{5 - 3[2x - 3(x + 2)]\}$?

A. $-8x - 3$
B. $16x - 23$
C. $-2x - 23$
D. $-2x + 13$
E. $-9x - 12$

10. Which expression would be appropriate to complete the following equation in order for it to illustrate the associative property of multiplication: $(ab)(c + d) = ?$

F. $(ba)(c + d)$
G. $abc + abd$
H. $(c + d)(ab)$
J. $a[b(c + d)]$
K. $(ab)(d + c)$

11. What is the expanded form of $(5x - 2)^2$?

A. $25x^2 + 4$
B. $25x^2 - 20x + 4$
C. $25x^2 + 10x + 4$
D. $5x^2 - 4$
E. $25x + 4$

12. Which of the following numbers is prime?

F. -5
G. 0
H. 1
J. 51
K. None of these

13. Jack is 4 years older than Jill. If 3 years ago Jack was 2 years less than twice Jill's age then, what equation can be used to determine how old each person is now?

A. $2(x - 3) - 2 = x + 1$
B. $2(x + 1) - 2 = x - 3$
C. $2(x - 3) = (x + 1) - 2$
D. $2(x + 1) = (x - 3) - 2$
E. $x + 1 = 2(x - 3)$

14. What is the slope of the line whose equation is $x + 2y = 5 - (x + y)$?

F. $\frac{5}{3}$
G. -2
H. $\frac{-2}{3}$
J. $\frac{-3}{2}$
K. -1

15. What is the solution set of $x(x - 3) = 18$?

A. $\{0, 3\}$
B. $\{18, 21\}$
C. $\{-6, 3\}$
D. $\{6, -3\}$
E. $\{9\}$

16. What is the center of the ellipse whose equation is $\frac{(x-2)^2}{9} + \frac{(y+4)^2}{25} = 1$?

F. The origin
G. $(3, 5)$
H. $(2, -4)$
J. $(-2, 4)$
K. $(9, 25)$

17. What is an equivalent expression, in simplest radical form, to $\sqrt[3]{\frac{16a^4}{b^2c}}$?

A. $\frac{4a^2\sqrt{c}}{bc}$
B. $2a\sqrt[3]{\frac{2a}{b^2c}}$
C. $\frac{\sqrt[3]{16a^4bc^2}}{bc}$
D. $\frac{2a\sqrt[3]{2abc^2}}{bc}$
E. $\frac{4a^2\sqrt[3]{c}}{bc}$

18. In which quadrant does the terminal side of angle θ lie if $\sin\theta > 0$ and $\tan\theta < 0$?

F. I
G. II
H. III
J. IV
K. None of these

19. If $\overline{CD}$ is a diameter, $\overline{CD} \parallel \overline{AB}$, and $m\angle BCD = 50°$, the measure of arc $AB = ?$

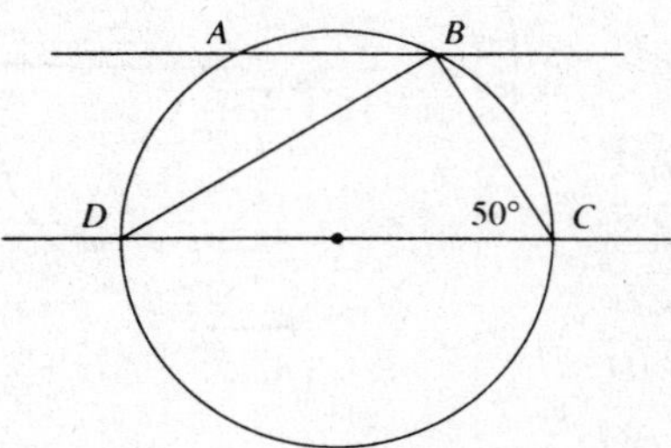

A. 100°
B. 50°
C. 25°
D. 20°
E. 10°

20. How many 4-person committees can be formed from a club of 12 people?

F. 11,880
G. 495
H. 48
J. 3
K. 1

21. What is the graph of the solution set of $|x - 1| \leq 5$?

A.
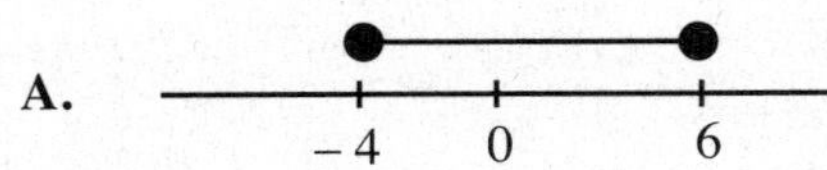

B.
–4 0 6

C.
–4 0 6

D.
–4 0 6

E.
–4 0 6

22. If $\triangle ABC \sim \triangle DEF$, and the sides have the measures indicated, what is the length of $\overline{BC}$?

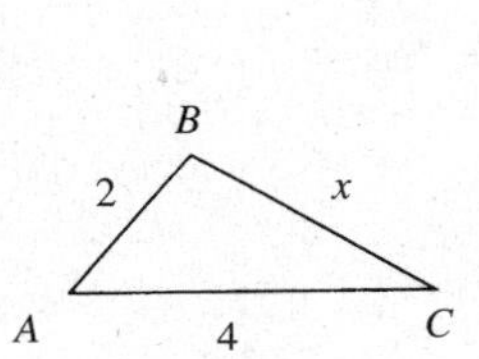

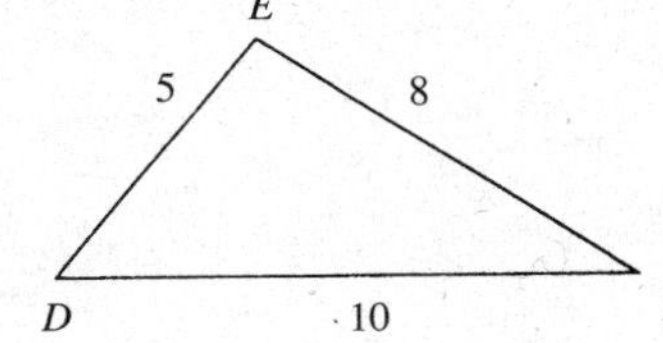

F. $1\frac{1}{4}$

G. 3

H. $3\frac{1}{5}$

J. 5
K. 20

23. Points $A(1,0)$, $B(8,0)$, and $C(3,4)$ are the vertices of a triangle. What is the area of this triangle?

A. 5
B. $10\frac{1}{2}$
C. 14
D. 16
E. 28

24. If
$A = \{1, 3, 5, \ldots\}$
and
$B = \{x \mid x = 2n - 1, n \in \{1, 2, 3, 4, 5\}\}$
which of the following statements is true of sets A and B?

F. $A \subseteq B$
G. B is an infinite set.
H. $A \cap B = \phi$
J. $A \cup B = A$
K. $A \cap B = A$

25. Given that tangent $\overline{AB}$ is 4 cm and radius $\overline{CD}$ is 3 cm, the length of segment $\overline{BC}$ = ?

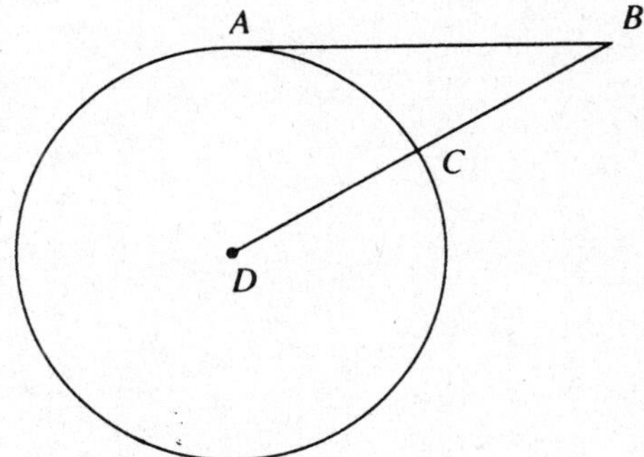

A. 1
B. 2
C. 3
D. 4
E. 5

26. What is the probability of exactly one head showing when two coins are tossed?

F. $\frac{1}{4}$

G. $\frac{3}{4}$

H. 1

J. $\frac{1}{2}$

K. 0

27. Working alone, Bill can paint a room in 12 hours. When Tom helps him, the job takes only 8 hours. How many hours would it take Tom to do the job alone?

A. 4
B. 10
C. 20
D. 24
E. 48

28. In $\triangle ABC$, $m\angle B = 30°$, $m\angle A = 60°$, and $AC = 4$ cm. What is the length of $\overline{AB}$?

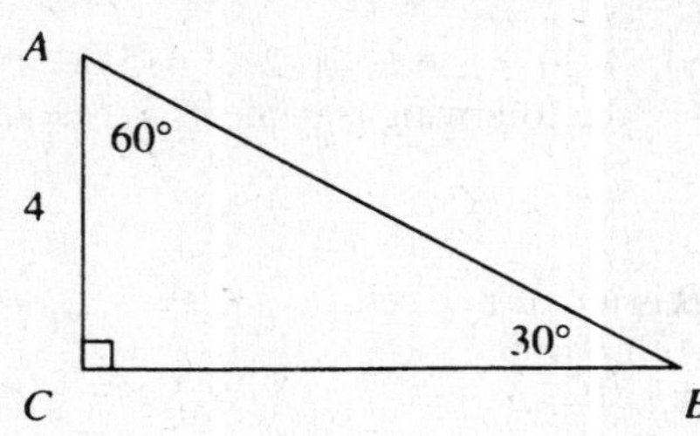

F. $4\sqrt{3}$
G. 8
H. $4\sqrt{2}$
J. $\frac{4\sqrt{3}}{3}$
K. $\frac{8\sqrt{3}}{3}$

29. Which of the following statements is false?

A. Every rectangle is a quadrilateral.
B. Every square is a rhombus.
C. Every trapezoid is a parallelogram.
D. Every rhombus is a parallelogram.
E. None of these statements is false.

30. If $\tan 25° = 0.4663$, then $\tan 875° = ?$

F. 0.4663
G. –0.4663
H. $\frac{1}{0.4663}$
J. $-\frac{1}{0.4663}$
K. 35(0.4663)

Answer Key

1. D	6. H	11. B	16. H	21. A	26. J
2. H	7. B	12. K	17. D	22. H	27. D
3. B	8. K	13. A	18. G	23. C	28. G
4. F	9. C	14. H	19. D	24. J	29. C
5. A	10. J	15. D	20. G	25. B	30. G

Answer Explanations

1. **(D)** Follow the order of operation rules.

$$
\begin{aligned}
5 \cdot 3^2 - 3(4 + 2 \cdot 3) &= 5 \cdot 3^2 - 3(4 + 6)\\
&= 5 \cdot 3^2 - 3(10)\\
&= 5 \cdot 9 - 3(10)\\
&= 45 - 30 = 15
\end{aligned}
$$

2. **(H)** $3.1416 = \frac{31{,}416}{10{,}000}$

3. **(B)** If 85% were correct, then 100% – 85% = 15% were wrong, and 6 is 15% of the total number of questions on the test. $A = 6$, $P = 15\%$, and B is unknown. The percent proportion is

$$\frac{15}{100} = \frac{6}{B}$$
$$15B = 600$$
$$B = 40$$

4. **(F)** By definition.

5. **(A)** $5 - 2[3x - (x - 2)] = 1 - x$

$$
\begin{aligned}
5 - 2[3x - x + 2] &= 1 - x && \text{Simplify the left side.}\\
5 - 6x + 2x - 4 &= 1 - x\\
-4x + 1 &= 1 - x\\
-3x + 1 &= 1 && \text{Add } x \text{ to both sides.}\\
-3x &= 0 && \text{Add } -1 \text{ to both sides.}\\
x &= 0 && \text{Divide both sides by } -3.
\end{aligned}
$$

6. **(H)** $\sqrt{-a} = \sqrt{-(-9)} = \sqrt{9} = 3$, which is an integer.

7. **(B)** $2\frac{7}{8} + 5\frac{5}{12} = 2\frac{21}{24} + 5\frac{10}{24}$

$$= 7\frac{31}{24}$$
$$= 7 + 1 + \frac{7}{24} = 8\frac{7}{24}$$

8. **(K)** The largest exponent on the variable in K is 3.

9. **(C)** $x - \{5 - 3[2x - 3(x + 2)]\}$

$$
\begin{aligned}
&= x - \{5 - 3[2x - 3x - 6]\}\\
&= x - \{5 - 6x + 9x + 18\}\\
&= x - 5 + 6x - 9x - 18\\
&= -2x - 23
\end{aligned}
$$

10. **(J)** Regrouping the multiplication gives

$$(ab)(c + d) = a[b(c + d)]$$

11. **(B)** Following the pattern for squaring a binomial, we have

$$(a + b)^2 = a^2 + 2ab + b^2$$
$$(5x - 2)^2 = 25x^2 - 20x + 4$$

12. **(K)** Prime numbers are whole numbers that have exactly two different factors. Of the answer choices:
–5 is not a whole number.
0 has many factors.
1 has only one factor.
51 = (1)(52) = (3)(17)

13. **(A)**

	Now	3 Years Ago
Jack	$x + 4$	$x + 1$
Jill	x	$x - 3$

Since Jack's age 3 years ago was 2 less than twice Jill's age then, $x + 1 = 2(x - 3) - 2$.

14. **(H)** To find the slope of a line from its equation, put the equation in slope-intercept form, $y = mx + b$.

$$\begin{aligned} x + 2y &= 5 - (x + y) \\ &= 5 - x - y \\ 3y &= -2x + 5 \\ y &= \frac{-2}{3}x + \frac{5}{3} \end{aligned}$$

15. **(D)** $x(x - 3) = 18$

$$\begin{aligned} x^2 - 3x &= 18 \\ x^2 - 3x - 18 &= 0 \\ (x - 6)(x + 3) &= 0 \end{aligned}$$

Set each factor equal to 0.

$$x - 6 = 0 \quad x + 3 = 0$$
$$x = 6 \quad x = -3$$

16. **(H)** The center of an ellipse whose equation is

$$\frac{(x - h)^2}{a^2} + \frac{(y - k)^2}{b^2} = 1$$

is (h, k). The given equation's graph has its center at $(2, -4)$.

17. **(D)** First multiply the numerator and denominator of the radicand by bc^2 to make the denominator a perfect cube.

$$\sqrt[3]{\frac{16a^4 \cdot bc^2}{b^2c \cdot bc^2}} = \frac{\sqrt[3]{16a^4bc^2}}{\sqrt[3]{b^3c^3}}$$

$$= \frac{\sqrt[3]{16a^4bc^2}}{bc}$$ Now separate the radicand into cube and noncube factors.

$$= \frac{\sqrt[3]{8a^3 \cdot 2abc^2}}{bc}$$

$$= \frac{2a\sqrt[3]{2abc^2}}{bc}$$

18. **(G)** The value of the sine function is positive in quadrants I and II, and the tangent function is negative in quadrants II and IV. Both of these conditions are satisfied only in quadrant II.

19. **(D)** Since $\overline{CD}$ is a diameter, $\angle DBC = 90°$. Therefore $\angle BDC = 40°$ and arc $\widehat{BC} = 2(40°) = 80°$. Parallel lines cut off equal arcs in a circle, so arc $\widehat{AD} = 80°$ also.

Therefore

$$\text{arc } \widehat{AB} = 180° - [2(80°)] = 180° - 160° = 20°$$

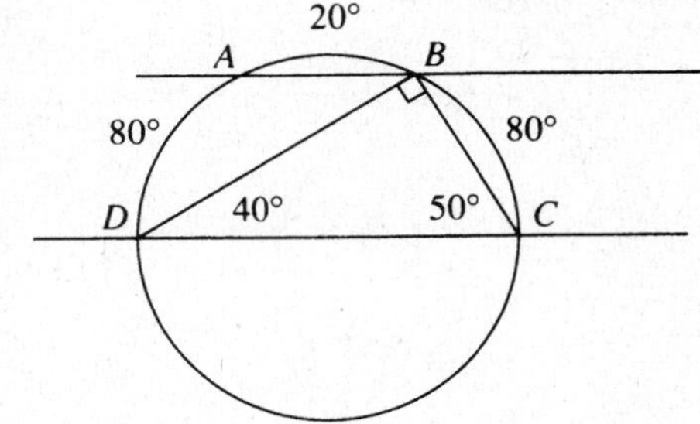

20. **(G)** Order in a committee is not important, so this is a combination, not a permutation, problem.

$$\begin{aligned} {}_{12}C_4 &= \frac{12!}{4!(12-4)!} = \frac{12!}{4! \cdot 8!} \\ &= \frac{12 \cdot 11 \cdot 10 \cdot 9}{4 \cdot 3 \cdot 2 \cdot 1} \\ &= \frac{1 \cdot 11 \cdot 5 \cdot 9}{1} = 495 \end{aligned}$$

21. **(A)** Using the special rule for absolute value inequalities, we have $|x - 1| \leq 5$ equivalent to

$$-5 \leq x - 1 \leq 5 \quad \text{or} \quad -4 \leq x \leq 6$$

22. **(H)** In similar triangles, corresponding sides have the same ratio.

$$\frac{2}{5} = \frac{x}{8}$$

$$5x = 16$$

$$x = 3\frac{1}{5}$$

23. **(C)** The length of the base of the triangle is 7, and the length of the altitude is 4. Therefore the area is

$$A = \frac{1}{2}bh = \frac{1}{2}(7)(4) = 14$$

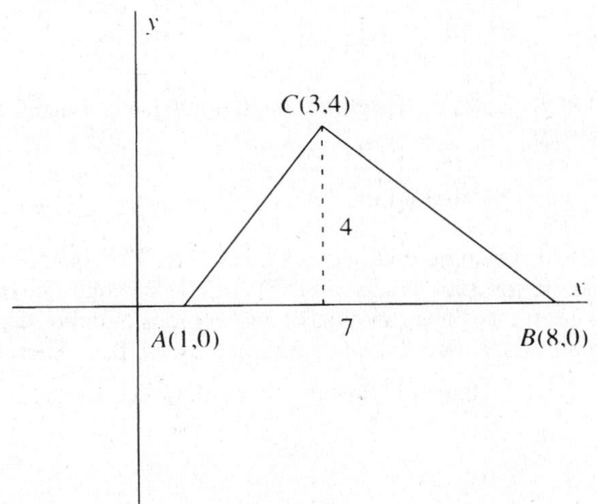

24. **(J)** $A = \{1, 3, 5, \ldots\}$ and $B = \{1, 3, 5, 7, 9\}$. The only statement that is true is $A \cup B = A$.

25. **(B)** The length of a tangent is the mean proportional between the length of a secant and the length of the external segment of the secant.

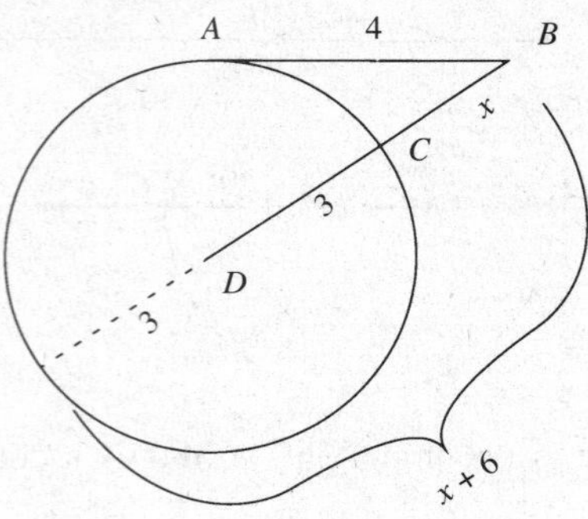

$$\frac{x}{4} = \frac{4}{x+6}$$
$$x(x + 6) = 16$$
$$x^2 + 6x - 16 = 0$$
$$(x + 8)(x - 2) = 0$$
$$x + 8 = 0 \qquad x - 2 = 0$$
$$x = -8 \qquad x = 2$$

26. **(J)** The sample space is {HH, HT, TH, TT}. Among the four elements in the sample space are two that have exactly one head. P (exactly one head) = $\frac{2}{4} = \frac{1}{2}$.

27. **(D)** Create a chart in which the data always apply to what the workers do *together.* Since Bill can do the job *alone* in 12 hours, his rate of work is $\frac{1}{12}$ of the job per hour. Suppose it takes Tom x hours to do the job alone; then his rate is $\frac{1}{x}$ part of the job per hour.

	W =	r ·	t
Bill	$\frac{2}{3}$	$\frac{1}{12}$	8
Tom	$\frac{8}{x}$	$\frac{1}{x}$	8

The total of the (W) column is 1 (one job completed).

$\frac{2}{3} + \frac{8}{x} = 1$ Multiply both sides by $3x$.

$2x + 24 = 3x$

$x = 24$

28. **(G)** In a (30-60-90)° triangle, the length of the hypotenuse is twice the length of the shorter leg, so $AB = 8$.

29. **(C)** A trapezoid is not a parallelogram.

30. **(G)** The smallest positive angle that is coterminal with 875° is 155°, which is in quadrant II. The reference angle for 155° is (180 – 155)° = 25°. In quadrant II the value of the tangent is negative. The rule is "The function of any angle is equal to the same function of the reference angle except for a sign that is determined by ASTC." Therefore

$$\tan 875° = -\tan 25° = -0.4663.$$

The Reading Test

CHAPTER 3

- A Preview of the Test
- Getting a Fix on the Passages
- Reading Passages for Practice
- Answering Two Types of Questions
- A 35-Minute Warm-Up for the Real Thing
- What the Results Tell You

Knowing the variety and the amount of reading that await you in college, the writers of the ACT have included a 35-minute Reading Test in the examination. Answering the questions gives you an opportunity to show your ability to read and understand the kind of materials required in college coursework. The test contains reading passages, each about 750 words, from four content areas.

Content Area	Subject	# of Questions	% of Test
1. Prose Fiction	novel or short story	10	25
2. Social Studies	anthropology, archaeology, business, economics, education, geography, history, political science, psychology and sociology	10	25
3. Humanities	architecture, art, dance, ethics, film, language, literary criticism, music, philosophy, radio, television, and theater	10	25
4. Natural Science	anatomy, astronomy, biology, botany, chemistry, ecology, geology, medicine, meteorology, microbiology, natural history, physiology, physics, technology, and zoology	10	25

Scoring: Two subscores reported:

1) Prose Fiction and Humanities — 20 questions
2) Social Studies and Natural Science — 20 questions

The passages are meant to be comprehensible to college-bound high school students. They aren't supposed to stump, trick, or frustrate you. On the other hand, they aren't totally transparent. To grasp them you'll have to read carefully and thoughtfully, being ever alert to all the facts and ideas they contain. Everything you need to know to answer the questions is right in the passage, although you may have a slight advantage if you happen to know something about the topic.

Each passage is followed by 10 multiple-choice questions—40 questions in all. Fourteen of the questions test what the passages say explicitly. These are what the ACT calls *referring* questions, because they "refer" precisely to what is stated in the passages.

Many more of the questions—almost twice as many—ask what the passage implies or suggests. The ACT calls these *reasoning* questions, because they call for answers that you must reason out by interpreting ideas, making generalizations, and drawing inferences and conclusions.

In general, the ten questions about each passage are arranged according to level of difficulty, the easiest question being first and the hardest, last. The questions ask what the author of the passage thinks and says—not what readers believe the author ought to think or say.

In addition to the total score, two subscores are reported. One is for Prose Fiction and Humanities, the other for the Social Studies and Natural Science reading passages.

TEST-TAKING TACTICS

You've probably observed that people cope with tests in a variety of ways. Considering the number of different test-taking styles, it would take a very long list to describe every tactic that has helped other students taking the ACT Reading Test. What works for them may not work for you and vice versa. Nevertheless, some tactics help everyone, regardless of ability or test-taking style. Many of the following tactics can improve your score. Give them an honest chance to work for you.

1. **Pace yourself.** You have less than nine minutes per passage. If you spend five minutes reading a passage, you still have four minutes left to answer ten questions, or almost 25 seconds per question. These numbers may vary, depending on the level of difficulty of the passage or the questions.

2. **Understand the test directions.** Know what the directions say before you walk into the exam room. The directions will be similar to the following:

   > This test consists of four passages, each followed by ten multiple-choice questions. Read each passage and then pick the best answer for each question. Fill in the spaces on your answer sheet that correspond to your choices. Refer to the passage as often as you wish while answering the questions.

3. **Decide on a reading technique.** On the ACT, different approaches to a reading passage carry different gains and losses.

Option	Technique	Gains/Losses
A	*Read the passage carefully from start to finish.* Don't try to remember every detail. As you read, ask yourself, "What is this passage really about?" You can usually get the general idea in two or three lines. When finished reading, state the author's main point. Even an incorrect statement gives you an idea to focus on as you work on the questions.	Takes longer at the start, but allows you to make up the time later.
B	*Skim the passage for its general idea.* Read faster than you normally would to figure out the type of passage it is: fiction, humanities, social science, or natural science. At the same time, try to sense what the author is saying. Read the passage just intently enough to get an impression of its content. Don't expect to keep details in mind. Refer to the passage as you answer the questions.	Saves time and keeps your mind free of needless details.
C	*Skim the passage to get its general meaning; then go back and read it more thoroughly.* Two readings, one fast and one slow, enable you to grasp the passage better than if you read it only once. During your second reading, confirm that your first impression was accurate. Proceed to the questions.	Requires the most time but offers you the firmest grip on the passage.
D	Read the questions first; then read the passage.	Alerts you to the content of the passage. (For details, see Tactic 7.)

4. **Concentrate on paragraph openings and closings.** Since ACT passages are generally written in standard English prose, most of them are constructed according to a common pattern—that is, they consist of two or more paragraphs. Except for paragraphs in fictional passages, most have a topic sentence supported by specific detail. More often than not, the topic sentence is located near the beginning of the paragraph. Sometimes, too, the final sentence of the paragraph suggests, perhaps with a mere phrase or two, the main point of the paragraph.

   When reading quickly for the gist of a passage, focus on paragraph openings and closings. Skip the material in between until you need the details to answer certain questions.

Knowing how passages are constructed can speed up your reading and also guide your search for answers to the questions.

5. **Use paragraphs as clues to help you understand the passage.** Writers generally take pains to organize their material. They decide what goes first, second, third. Usually, the arrangement follows a logical order, although sometimes material is arranged to build suspense or to surprise the reader. Most often, though, paragraphs are used to build the main idea of a passage. Each paragraph in some way reinforces the author's point.

   Sometimes, authors state their main point early in the passage. They use the remaining paragraphs to support what they said at the beginning. At other times, authors reverse the process, writing several paragraphs that lead inevitably to the main idea. Occasionally, a main idea shows up somewhere in the middle of a passage, and, at other times, it doesn't appear at all. Rather, it's implied by the contents of the whole passage. It's so apparent that to state it outright is unnecessary.

   There's no need on the ACT to figure out the main point of each paragraph. The point of one paragraph in a difficult passage, though, may provide a clue to the meaning of the whole passage. Understanding the second paragraph, for example, may clarify the point of the first one, and the two together may reveal the intent of the entire passage.

6. Decide whether to use an underlining technique.

Option A. *Underline key ideas and phrases.* Since you have a pencil in your hand during the ACT, use it to highlight the important points of a reading passage. When you come to an idea that sounds important, quickly draw a line under it or put a checkmark next to it in the margin. Underlining may be better, because you'll be rereading the words as your pencil glides along. On the other hand, underlining is time-consuming. Whatever you do, though, use your pencil sparingly or you may end up with most of the passage underlined or checked.

Option B. *Don't underline anything.* The rationale here is that, without having read the passage at least once, you can't know what's important. Furthermore, underlining takes time and you may be wasting valuable seconds drawing lines under material that won't help you answer the questions. The time you spend underlining might better be spent rereading the passage or studying the questions. Anyway, a 750-word passage won't contain so much material that you can't remember most of it when you start to look for answers to the questions.

Option C. *Underline answers only.* After you have read the questions and returned to the passage, use your pencil to identify tentative answers to the questions. Underline only a word or two, no more than is necessary to attract your attention when you look back to the passage for answers. Consider using checks or other marks; they take less time than underlining but serve the same purpose.

7. Decide when to read the questions.

Option A. *Read the questions before you read the passage.* Because it's almost impossible to remember ten, or even five or six, questions about material you haven't read, just review the questions in order to become acquainted with the kinds of information you are expected to draw out of the passage. Identify the questions as "MI" (main idea), "SD" (specific detail), "Interp" (interpretation of phrase or idea), and so on. (You can devise your own system.) When a question refers to a specific line number, go directly to the passage and mark that line with a check or asterisk. Better still, write the number of the question in the margin (e.g., #3, #8, etc.). Later, when you read the passage, you'll know instantly that you must read that line attentively because it may give you, or at least strongly suggest, the right answer.

When you know the questions beforehand, you can read a passage more purposefully. Instead of reading for a general impression, you can look for the main idea of the passage, seek out specific details, and locate the meaning of a phrase or idea. Exercising this option requires you to become familiar with the varieties of questions typically asked on the ACT, an effort that could save you precious time during the test itself.

Option B. *Read the questions after you read the passage.* With the passage fresh in your mind, you can probably answer two or three questions immediately. On other questions, you can eliminate one or two obviously wrong choices. Just "x" them and forget them. With a few questions and choices eliminated, direct your second reading of the passage to the remaining questions. You'll read still more purposefully if you note the question types beforehand, as suggested by Option A.

Option C. *Read the questions one by one, not as a group.* After reading the passage, start with the first question and answer it by referring to the passage. Then go on to the next question. This approach is slow but thorough. It's comfortable, too, since you needn't keep large amounts of information in mind all at once, just a question at a time. Don't be a slave to the order of the questions. If you can't answer a question, skip it for the time being and go on to the next one. Go back later if you have time. Whatever you do, don't even think of answering a question before reading the passage from start to finish. Misguided students first read a question, then start to read the passage in search of an answer. Before they know it, time runs out, and they're far from finishing.

8. **Suspend your prior knowledge.** Occasionally, a reading passage may deal with a subject you know about. Because all the questions are derived from the passage in front of you, all your answers should be, too. Cast aside your prior knowledge and read both passage and questions with an open mind.

9. **Identify each question by type (referring or reasoning).** With experience you can learn to spot question types quickly. Without getting bogged down in making small distinctions, label each question by its type. Usually the wording of a question will tell you whether you can find the answer by *referring* directly to the passage or by using your *reasoning* powers. Questions that ask what a passage *indicates,* as in "What does the second paragraph indicate about . . .?", are almost always referring questions. Other referring questions can often be recognized by their straightforward wording and by certain tag phrases such as

Identify question types by their wording.

"according to the passage, . . ."
"the passage clearly indicates . . ."
"the passage says . . ."

The words used in reasoning questions vary according to the intent of the questions. Those that begin with something like "On the basis of information in the passage, which . . .?" are usually reasoning questions, which can also be identified by such tag phrases as

"infer from the passage that . . ."
"the passage implies that . . ."
"the passage suggests that . . ."
"probably means that . . ."
"one can conclude that . . ."
"the main idea . . ."
"the main thought . . ."
"the primary purpose . . ."

With a little practice you can easily learn to identify referring and reasoning questions. Once you know how to distinguish between them, you can vary your approach to find the right answers. For example, when a question asks you to identify what the author of the passage *says,* you'll know instantly that you are dealing with a referring question and that you should search the passage for explicit material. In contrast, a question that asks about the main thought of a passage calls for a different approach, perhaps rereading the passage's opening and closing paragraphs and inferring the author's purpose.

Identifying your strengths and weaknesses will enable you to practice the skills needed to boost your score. If, for instance, you repeatedly stumble on questions that ask you to reason out the main idea of a passage, you may be reading the passages too slowly, paying too much attention to details to recognize the main flow of ideas. The problem can be remedied by consciously pressing yourself to read faster.

On the actual test, answer first the types of questions you rarely get wrong on ACT practice exercises, perhaps the main idea questions or those that ask about specific details. Then devote the bulk of your time to the types that have given you more trouble. The order in which you answer the questions is completely up to you. You alone know which question types you customarily handle with ease and which types give you trouble.

10. **Answer general questions before detail questions.** General questions usually ask you to identify the author's point of view or the main idea of the passage. A reader with a good understanding of the whole passage can often answer general questions without rereading a word. That's not always so with detail questions. When you're asked for a specific fact or for an interpretation of a word or phrase, you may have to return to a particular place in the passage to find the answer. That takes time, and, since speed is impor-

Answer easy questions first.

tant on the ACT, it makes sense to get the easier questions out of the way before tackling the more time-consuming ones.

Some people claim that broad questions are harder than questions about details because you need to understand the whole passage to answer them. Don't believe it. They're neither harder nor easier. As with so much in life, it all depends. . . . In any case, the first five questions about a reading passage are usually detail questions. The general questions come later.

11. **Do the easy passages first.** If you've always experienced success with natural science passages, and you have trouble with fiction, go first to the natural science passage, even if it's last on the test. In other words, try to lead with your strength, whatever it may be. If you're equally good in everything, then stick with the order of the test.

12. **Stay alert for "switchbacks."** These are the words and phrases frequently used to alert you to shifts in thought. The most common switchback word is *but*. You may know *but* as a harmless conjunction, but it may turn into a trap for an unwary reader. (Notice how the second *but* in the preceding sentence is meant to shift your concept of the word—i.e., think of *but* not merely as a harmless conjunction, *but* think of it also as a trap!) If you ignore *but,* you miss half the point. Here's another example:

Candidates for public office don't need to be wealthy, *but* money helps.

Other switchback words and phrases that function like *but* include *although* ("*Although* candidates for public office don't need to be wealthy, money helps"), *however, nevertheless, on the other hand, even though, while, in spite of, despite, regardless of.*

In your normal reading, you may hardly notice switchback words. On the ACT, however, pay attention to them. Many questions are asked about sentences that contain switchbacks. The reason: a test must contain questions that trap careless readers. Therefore, don't rush past the switchbacks in your hurry to read the passages and find answers. In fact, you can improve your vigilance by scanning a few of the practice passages in this book with the sole purpose of finding switchbacks. Circle them. In no time you'll start to pick them up almost automatically.

SUMMARY OF TEST-TAKING TACTICS

1. Pace yourself.
2. Understand the test directions.
3. Decide on a reading technique.
   Option A: Read the passage carefully from start to finish.
   Option B: Skim the passage for its general idea.
   Option C: Skim the passage to get its general meaning; then go back and read it more thoroughly.
4. Concentrate on paragraph openings and closings.
5. Use paragraphs as clues to help you understand the passage.
6. Decide whether to use an underlining technique.
   Option A: Underline key ideas and phrases.
   Option B: Don't underline anything.
   Option C: Underline answers only.

7. Decide when to read the questions.
   Option A: Read the questions before you read the passage.
   Option B: Read the questions after you read the passage.
   Option C: Read the questions one by one, not as a group.
8. Suspend your prior knowledge.
9. Identify each question by type.
10. Answer general questions before detail questions.
11. Do the easy passages first.
12. Stay alert for "switchbacks."

   ... and a thirteenth for good measure: *Practice, practice, practice!* Then decide: Which of these twelve tactics help you to do your best?

PROSE FICTION

Passages

Before you read a word of the prose fiction passage, you'll probably recognize its distinctive look: quotation marks, several short lines of text, frequently indented sentences. Even without dialogue, though, you'll know that it's fiction before you've read more than a few lines. It will be a piece of a story, perhaps describing a place, portraying a person, or showing characters in action.

Fiction comes in many forms and styles, from simple folk stories and fairy tales to confusing, nearly impenetrable novels and short stories. On the ACT the passage is straightforward, and you are asked to demonstrate that you can use clues found in the text to determine where and when the action takes place, to understand what is going on and to recognize the human emotions or conflicts that motivate the characters.

Here, for example, is a prose passage consisting only of dialogue.* As you read it, identify the characters, the time and place, and the situation:

"I'd like you to do that assignment before you leave today."

"I can't. I have to go home. My mother wants me to shovel the walk."

"But I insist. You have to do it."

"I'm not going to."

"Listen, Charles, you were absent all last week with an earache and runny nose. Now you have to make up the work. I've put the assignment on the board."

"No!"

"Yes."

"Make me. I dare you."

"Oh, Charles, dear, I can't make you. You know that, but I just want you to do well in my class. Don't you understand?"

"I don't care. Math is so stupid."

"Math isn't stupid."

"It is!"

---

*The passages used for illustration and practice exercises in this chapter may be shorter or longer than the 750 words typical of ACT passages. Accordingly, you should not be concerned with time when doing the practice exercises.

"Look, Charles, I can't stay here all day and argue. I have to eat. After lunch I'm going to call your mother and ask her if you can stay."

"Don't."

"Why not?"

"Just don't."

"But why?"

"Just don't call her. I'll stay, O.K."

"You mean you don't want to get into trouble?"

"She'll get mad and won't let me play."

"Play what?"

"With my friends."

"Why?"

"Just forget it, O.K.? I'll stay and do math."

"Good, Charles. I knew you'd see it my way. I'll see you at three o'clock."

Although the author doesn't tell you who is talking in the dialogue, it's pretty obvious after a line or two. Nor are you told the place, the time, the season, and the circumstances of the conversation, but you can deduce all those details by paying attention to the speakers' words. Likewise, you should be able to tell Charles's approximate age and whether the teacher is a man or a woman. You may also conclude that Charles is a stubborn little kid, but one who knows when he's beaten. Perhaps you've inferred, too, that the teacher has a mean streak, not because she forces Charles to stay after school, but because she insists on having the last word. She provokes Charles, trying to prove that she's the boss.

TIP

Questions or prose fiction often focus on the speaker or narrator, and on setting, character traits, tone, and use of language.

By carefully reading the following segment of a well-known short story, you'll see the wealth of information that can be crammed into just a few lines of narration.

As the men trooped heavily back into the front room, the two little windows presented views of a turmoiling sea of snow. The huge arms of the wind were making attempts—mighty, circular, futile—to embrace the flakes as they sped. A gate-post like a still man with a blanched face stood aghast amid this profligate fury. In a hearty voice Scully announced the presence of a blizzard. The guests of the blue hotel, lighting their pipes, assented with grunts of lazy masculine contentment. No island of the sea could be exempt in the degree of this little room with its humming stove. Johnnie, son of Scully, in a tone which defined his opinion of his ability as a card-player, challenged the old farmer of both grey and sandy whiskers to a game of High-Five. The farmer agreed with a contemptuous and bitter scoff. They sat close to the stove, and squared their knees under a wide board. The cowboy and the Easterner watched the game with interest. The Swede remained near the window, aloof, but with a countenance that showed signs of an inexplicable excitement.

Stephen Crane, *The Blue Hotel*

Analysis

From this passage you should be able to make several observations about the hotel and about the breed of men gathered there. Do you recognize that Johnnie is a braggart and that the farmer would like to prove that Johnnie is more hot air than substance? Do you realize that the other men, except for the Swede, are curious about the outcome of the card game? Do you also notice that these are tough, hard men, accustomed to being outdoors, but now caught inside a small, smoky room that contrasts sharply to the raging blizzard outside? Do you sense a tension in the room, suggested most forcefully by the contest between the two card players sitting with squared knees under a wide board and also somewhat by the Swede's face that showed signs of an "inexplicable excitement"?

Perhaps you didn't see all that during your first reading of the passage. That's not surprising. The author, a nineteenth-century writer, used language and sentence structure more akin to his own time than to ours. Also, you may have been puzzled by some of the vocabulary—*turmoiling, blanched, aghast, profligate, countenance*—words you don't run into every day. Yet, those words are not out of reach. Their meanings can be figured out from context. The word *turmoiling,* for example, is practically defined for you in the next sentence: "mighty, circular," the furious motion of snowflakes in a storm.

During your second reading of the passage you'll probably notice ideas you hadn't noticed the first time. Even if you find nothing new, however, remember that the ACT doesn't expect you to do a profound analysis of the text. Just use the questions as a guide. Some questions will refer to details you may have overlooked. They may also illuminate nuances and highlight shades of meaning in the passage that you failed to see on your own.

Read the passage once to see what it's about, twice to observe details and find shades of meaning.

A typical prose fiction passage consists of both dialogue and narration. Questions often pertain to the *narrator, setting, character, tone,* and *use of language* in a passage. You may also be asked to *identify main ideas, draw inferences about the relationship of characters, speculate on events that may have preceded or will follow the passage,* and much more. In short, you may expect questions on anything that the author has done to convey meaning or create an effect.

Prose fiction passages come from contemporary novels and stories, and also, as in the following instance, from works written generations ago.

Presently, Claude came up the bank with two shining, dripping pails. "Now may I sit down with you for a few minutes?"

Moving to make room for him beside her, Enid noticed that his thin face was heavily beaded with perspiration. His pocket handkerchief was wet and sandy, so she gave him her own, with a proprietary air. "Why, Claude, you look quite tired! Have you been over-doing? Where were you before you came here?"

"I was out in the country with your father, looking at his alfalfa."

"And he walked you all over the field in the hot sun, I suppose?"

Claude laughed. "He did."

"Well, I'll scold him tonight. You stay here and rest. I am going to drive Gladys home."

Gladys protested, but at last consented that they should both drive her home in Claude's car. They lingered awhile, however, listening to the soft, amiable bubbling of the spring; a wise unobtrusive voice, murmuring night and day, continually telling the truth to people who could not understand it.

When they went back to the house Enid stopped long enough to cut a bunch of heliotrope for Mrs. Farmer,—though with the sinking of the sun its rich perfume had already vanished. They left Gladys and her flowers and cresses at the gate of the white cottage, now half hidden by gaudy trumpet vines.

Claude turned his car and went back along the dim, twilight road with Enid. "I usually like to see Gladys, but when I found her with you this afternoon, I was terribly disappointed for a minute. I'd just been talking with your father, and I wanted to come straight to you. Do you think you could marry me, Enid?"

"I don't think it would be for the best, Claude." She spoke sadly.

He took her passive hand. "Why not?"

"My mind is full of other plans. Marriage is for most girls, but not for all."

Enid had taken off her hat. In the low evening light Claude studied her pale face under her brown hair. There was something graceful and charming about the way she held her head, something that suggested both submissiveness and great firmness. "I've had those dreams, too, Enid; but now my thoughts don't get any further than you. If you could care ever so little for me to start on, I'd be willing to risk the rest."

She sighed. "You know I care for you. I've never made any secret of it. But we're happy as we are, aren't we?"

"No, I'm not. I've got to have some life of my own, or I'll go to pieces. If you won't have me, I'll try South America,—and I won't come back until I am an old man and you are an old woman."

Enid looked at him, and they both smiled.

The mill house was black except for a light in one upstairs window. Claude sprang out of the car and lifted Enid gently to the ground. She let him kiss her soft cool mouth, and her long lashes. In the pale, dusty dusk, lit only by a few white stars, and with the chill of the creek already in the air, she seemed to Claude like a shivering little ghost come up from the rushes where the old mill-dam used to be. A terrible melancholy clutched at the boy's heart. He hadn't thought it would be like this. He drove home feeling weak and broken. Was there nothing in the world outside to answer to his own feelings, and was every turn to be a fresh disappointment? Why was life so mysteriously hard? This country itself was sad, he thought, looking about him,—and you could no more change that than you could change the story in an unhappy human face. He wished to God he were sick again; the world was too rough a place to get about in.

Adapted from Willa Cather, *One of Ours*, 1922

Analysis

Most of this passage focuses on a conversation during which Claude, a young man, proposes marriage to Enid. The events occur alongside a stream and inside a car driving along a road and then parked outside the home of Enid's friend, Gladys. Facts in the passage reveal that Claude has already asked Enid's father for permission to marry the girl but that Enid, in spite of her declaration, "You know I care for you," spurns Claude's proposal. Whether she truthfully cares for him or feigns affection just to spare his feelings remains unclear. What do you make of the kiss that Claude plants on Enid's "soft cool mouth, and her long lashes?" Is it a good-bye kiss, or does she allow it just to keep him interested?

TIP

Answering some prose fiction questions requires reading between the lines.

Enid's rejection shatters Claude. Like a spoiled and spiteful little boy, he threatens to run off to South America. We can't be sure whether or not he is joking because afterward nothing but an ambiguous smile passes between him and Enid. Is Enid turned off by Claude's feeble attempt to gain sympathy? Or does she truly pity him? Were this passage on the ACT, you might be given a question or two about that issue.

Having been turned down, Claude drives home feeling weak and broken. What inference can be drawn about Claude from his response to Enid? What does his pathetic wish to be "sick again" tell you about him?

ACT questions are apt to ask you to analyze the complex relationship between such characters as Enid and Claude. Other questions may focus on an individual's values and attitudes. You might also be asked to identify the narrator's point of view. Within a few lines in this passage we learn the private thoughts of both Claude and Enid. Even the narrator himself comments on the bubbling spring: "a wise unobtrusive voice, murmuring night and day, continually telling the truth to people who could not understand it." Does this observation relate to the events in the passage or is it merely a poetic diversion from the main narrative? An ACT question could be asked about that. Still other questions on the exam test your sense of language. That is, you could be asked to identify the meaning or connotation of certain words and phrases used in the passage.

Sample Questions

The ACT prose fiction passage is always followed by four questions that refer directly to information presented in the passage (*referring* questions) and by six questions that require you to interpret, or read between the lines of, the narrative. These so-called *reasoning* questions test both your ability to uncover levels of meaning and the depth of your understanding.

Rarely are the answers to reasoning questions stated outright. Instead, they are implied. Sometimes an implication almost jumps off the page and shouts "Here I am," but far more often it remains buried in the text until you dig it out. Therefore, take nothing for granted. Frankly, no foolproof method exists for figuring out answers to all reasoning questions. The best thing to do is to stay alert and keep constantly in mind the overall purpose of the passage and how each detail contributes to achieving that purpose.

TIP

As you search the passage for evidence to support your answer choice, consider every word as a potentially useful clue.

It may seem that referring questions are easier to answer than reasoning questions. In general, that may be true, but not always. For instance, you can probably answer without difficulty the sample reasoning questions that follow the short-story excerpt below. The sample referring questions, though, offer more of a challenge.

The following passage comes from a well-known Civil War tale. The story's protagonist, Peyton Farquhar, is a Southerner about to be hanged as a spy. The action takes place as he stands on a railroad bridge with a noose around his neck.

> He closed his eyes in order to fix his last thoughts upon his wife and children. The water, touched to gold by the early sun, the brooding mists under the banks at some distance down the stream, the fort, the soldiers, the piece of drift—all had distracted him. And now he became conscious of a new disturbance. Striking through the thought of his dear ones was a sound which he could neither ignore nor understand, a sharp, distinct, metallic percussion like the stroke of a blacksmith's hammer upon the anvil; it had the same ringing quality. He wondered what it was, and whether immeasurably distant or near by—it seemed both. Its recurrence was regular, but as slow as the tolling of a death knell. He awaited each stroke with impatience and—he knew not why—apprehension. The intervals of silence grew progressively longer; the delays became maddening. With their greater infrequency the sounds increased in strength and sharpness. They hurt his ear like the thrust of a knife; he feared he would shriek. What he heard was the ticking of his watch.
>
> Ambrose Bierce, *An Occurrence at Owl Creek Bridge*

Sample Referring Questions:

1. The passage indicates that, just before being put to death, Farquhar tries to think about

   A. the beauty of his surroundings.
   B. anything other than his impending doom.
   C. his family.
   D. why this is happening to him.

   To answer this and other referring questions, skim the passage in search of words that correspond to each choice. Sometimes a choice will repeat the words in the passage, but be wary of such duplication. The repetition may be a trap. More than likely, the choices will paraphrase or summarize ideas in the passage. Where you find a thought or idea that seems closely related to the choice, read it carefully to determine whether it's the answer you need.

   Choice **A** summarizes in a phrase all the beauty that Farquhar sees. If you read the second sentence to its end, however, you see that the beauty of nature has distracted him from what he really wants to think about. **B** refers to an idea not mentioned in the passage. **C** paraphrases the contents of the first sentence. "Family" is clearly a synonym for "wife and children." Choice **C** is the correct answer. **D** refers to an idea not mentioned in the passage.

   Question 1 is a relatively easy referring question. Here is a more challenging one:

2. According to the passage, which emotion did Farquhar NOT experience during the moment before he was hanged?

   F. Frustration
   G. Impatience
   H. Fear
   J. Sorrow

To find the best answer, you must search the entire passage for an example of each emotion that Farquhar feels. The one you *don't* find is the answer. Obviously, it's more of a challenge to find three wrong answers than to find a single correct one. As you did for question 1, skim the passage for words and ideas that correspond to each choice.

Choice **F** names the emotion that Farquhar experiences as he tries in vain to shut out the pounding in his ears. **G** names Farquhar's emotion as he waits impatiently for each stroke. **H** names an emotion that Farquhar feels while resisting the urge to shriek out loud. **J** refers to an emotion *not* mentioned in the passage. Therefore, **J** is the correct answer.

Sample Reasoning Questions:

3. Based on information in the passage, Farquhar probably "feared he would shriek," because he doesn't want:

   A. his wife and children to hear his screams.
   B. the soldiers to know that he is scared of dying.
   C. to disturb the peacefulness of early morning.
   D. to lose control of himself.

   To answer this question, you must infer why Farquhar might want to keep himself from shrieking. Consider the likelihood of each choice:

   Choice **A** could not be correct, because Farquhar's family is not at the scene. **B** implies that Farquhar is scared, but nothing in the passage suggests that he is afraid to die. **C** is unrelated to Farquhar's state of mind. **D** is correct. Farquhar, a spy, is portrayed as a highly rational person, one who masters his fears and emotions. It would be out of character, even moments before death, for him to lose his calm.

4. The ticking of the watch in Farquhar's ears signifies:

   F. that each second just before death grows increasingly important.
   G. that the pressure has made Farquhar crazy.
   H. the footsteps of the approaching executioner.
   J. the excited pounding of Farquhar's heart.

   To answer this reasoning question, you must interpret the beating sound inside Farquhar's head, using clues from the passage. Examine the possibilities of each choice:

   Choice **F** describes Farquhar's condition. Since he has just moments to live, each remaining second of life acquires importance. **F** is the correct answer. **G** raises a valid point. A man on the verge of execution might well lose his mind, but Farquhar shows no symptoms of insanity. **H** contradicts information in the last sentence of the passage, that the beating sound is the tick of Farquhar's watch. **J** may accurately describe Farquhar's physical state. His heart probably is racing, but we are told that the sound comes from the ticking of his watch.

It often helps to be acquainted with referring and reasoning questions in order to decide quickly whether to skim the passage for the answer or whether to think about more general meanings and implications. True comprehension, however, lies not in identifying question types. More important is to read the whole passage carefully.

Now try another passage for practice. It comes from "The Ice Palace" (1920), a short story by F. Scott Fitzgerald that examines the cultural as well as the social differences between the North and the South.

As you read the excerpt, use the tactics for reading ACT passages suggested earlier in this chapter. Also, try one of the suggested approaches to answering the questions. Compare your approach to that suggested after each question.

In November Harry Bellamy, tall, broad, and brisk, came down from his Northern city to spend four days. His intention was to settle a matter that had been hanging fire since he and Sally Carrol had met in Asheville, North Carolina, in midsummer. The settlement took only a quiet afternoon and an evening in front of a glowing open fire, for Harry Bellamy had everything she wanted; and, besides, she loved him—loved him with that side of her she kept especially for loving. Sally Carrol had several rather clearly defined sides.

On his last afternoon they walked, and she found their steps tending half-unconsciously toward one of her favorite haunts, the cemetery. When it came in sight, gray-white and golden-green under the cheerful late sun, she paused, irresolute, by the iron gate.

"Are you mournful by nature, Harry" she asked with a faint smile.

"Mournful? Not I."

"Then let's go in here. It depresses some folks, but I like it."

They passed through the gateway and followed a path that led through a wavy valley of graves—dusty-gray and mouldy for the fifties; quaintly carved with flowers and jars for the seventies; ornate and hideous for the nineties, with fat marble cherubs lying in sodden sleep on stone pillows, and great impossible growths of nameless granite flowers. Occasionally they saw a kneeling figure with tributary flowers, but over most of the graves lay silence and withered leaves with only the fragrance that their own shadowy memories could waken in living minds.

They reached the top of the hill where they were fronted by a tall, round headstone, freckled with dark spots of damp and half grown over with vines.

"Margery Lee," she read; "1844–1873. Wasn't she nice? She died when she was twenty-nine. Dear Margery Lee," she added softly. "Can't you see her, Harry?"

"Yes, Sally Carroll."

He felt a little hand insert itself into his.

"She was dark, I think; and she always wore her hair with a ribbon in it, and gorgeous hoop-skirts of alice blue and old rose."

"Yes."

"Oh, she was sweet, Harry! And she was the sort of girl born to stand on a wide, pillared porch and welcome folks in. I think perhaps a lot of men went away to war meanin' to come back to her; but maybe none of 'em ever did."

He stooped down close to the stone, hunting for any record of marriage.

"There's nothing here to show."

"Of course not. How could there be anything there better than just 'Margery Lee,' and that eloquent date?"

She drew close to him and an unexpected lump came into his throat as her yellow hair brushed his cheek.

"You see how she was, don't you, Harry?"

"I see," he added gently. "I see through your precious eyes. You're beautiful now, so I know she must have been."

Silent and close they stood, and he could feel her shoulders trembling a little. An ambling breeze swept up the hill and stirred the brim of her floppidy hat.

"Let's go down there!"

She was pointing to a flat stretch on the other side of the hill where along the green turf were a thousand grayish-white crosses stretching in endless, ordered rows like the stacked arms of a battalion.

"Those are the Confederate dead," said Sally Carrol simply.

They walked along and read the inscriptions, always only a name and a date, sometimes quite indecipherable.

"The last row is the saddest—see, 'way over there. Every cross has just a date on it, and the word 'Unknown.'"

She looked at him and her eyes brimmed with tears.

"I can't tell you how real it is to me, darling—if you don't know."

"How you feel about it is beautiful to me."

"No, no, it's not me, it's them—that old time that I've tried to have live in me. These were just men, unimportant evidently or they wouldn't have been 'unknown'; but they died for the most beautiful thing in the world—the dead South. You see," she continued, her voice still husky, her eyes glistening with tears, "people have these dreams they fasten onto things, and I've always grown up with that dream. It was so easy because it was all dead and there weren't any disillusions comin' to me. I've tried to live up to those past standards of *noblesse oblige*—there's just the last remnants of it, you know, like the roses of an old garden dying all round us—streaks of strange courtliness and chivalry in some of these boys and in stories I used to hear from a Confederate soldier who lived next door, and a few old folks. Oh, Harry, there was something, there was something! I couldn't ever make you understand, but it was there."

"I understand," he assured her again quietly.

Sally Carrol smiled and dried her eyes on the tip of a handkerchief protruding from his breast pocket.

"You don't feel depressed, do you, lover? Even when I cry I'm happy here, and I get a sort of strength from it."

Hand in hand they turned and walked slowly away. Finding soft grass she drew him down to a seat beside her with their backs against the remnants of a low broken wall.

"Wish those three old women would clear out," he complained. "I want to kiss you, Sally Carrol."

"Me, too."

They waited impatiently for the three bent figures to move off, and then she kissed him until the sky seemed to fade out and all her smiles and tears to vanish in an ecstasy of eternal seconds.

1. It is reasonable to infer from the passage that the *matter* referred to in line 2 pertains to:

A. something that Sally had said to Harry last summer.
B. the question of Sally and Harry's future together.
C. reasons that Sally had been in Asheville.
D. rumors that Harry had heard about Sally's romances.

The phrase "reasonable to infer" tells you that the answer must be dug from beneath the surface or between the lines of the passage. The author alludes to an unspecified *matter* that has brought Harry down from a Northern city. Your task is to search for clues that will identify that *matter*. Start by re-reading not only line 2 but also lines 1 and 3 in order to understand the larger context in which the word is used. You'll quickly see that the "matter" had been "hanging fire" since last summer. In other words, some sort of issue between Sally and Harry has remained unsettled for several months. What the issue is becomes more evident in lines 3–7. Apparently, it's related to the growth of mutually amorous feelings that have sprung up between the young man and woman.

Choice **A** is intriguing, but the passage fails to mention any particular words that Sally had said to Harry last summer. Choice **B** is supported by lines 5 and 6, which indicate that Sally loved Harry. Indeed, Harry, we are told, has everything that Sally wants in a man, an attitude suggesting that she had at last found her true love. **B** is the best answer. Choice **C** is unimportant to Harry. Either he already knows why Sally had been in Asheville or he doesn't care. **D** may be a trap for readers who see Sally as a flirt because she has a side that is "kept especially for loving" (line 6). But nothing in the portrait of Sally says that she jumps casually into and out of romances.

2. The narrator indicates that Sally loves Harry because:

   F. he is different from the boys she knew in her hometown.
   G. he is good-looking, masculine, and energetic.
   H. he has come on his own to visit her for four days.
   J. he possesses all the qualities she wanted in a boy.

The question's introductory phrase, "The narrator indicates," signifies that the answer will be a thought or idea specifically stated in the passage. Skim the passage in search of a word, thought, or idea that corresponds to *love,* the key word in the question. You'll find love mentioned in lines 5–6: "she loved him—loved him with that side of her she kept especially for loving," an attribute that explains Sally's ardor for Harry.

Choice **J** paraphrases the very reason that attracts Sally to Harry: he "had everything she wanted." **J**, therefore, is the best answer. **F** is a reasonable choice, but the passage includes nothing about her attitude toward hometown boys. **G** lists qualities that may have turned Sally's head, but there is something more to Harry that captures Sally's affection. **H** is true but is unrelated to Sally's fondness for Harry.

3. As it is used in the passage (line 10) the word *irresolute* most nearly means:

   A. thoughtful.
   B. determined.
   C. hesitant.
   D. irrelevant.

Almost every ACT includes one or more vocabulary questions that ask you to identify the meaning of a word in a specific context. Sometimes the meaning corresponds with the word's most common dictionary definition. At other times, you'll have to find a secondary meaning. On occasion, the context gives the word an unusual twist. But you can depend on the context to provide sufficient evidence for you to answer the question.

As used in the passage, *irresolute* describes Sally's state of mind as she pauses at the cemetery gate. At that moment she is unsure whether to invite Harry to go with her to the valley of graves. "It depresses some folks," she says. Even if you'd never heard of the word *irresolute*, Sally's hesitancy would help you determine its meaning.

Choice **A** is a possibility because Sally pauses, perhaps to think things out. Choice **B**, virtually an antonym of irresolute, make little sense in the context, and **D** is no better. That leaves **C**, an answer preferable to **A** because of the question Sally asks, "Are you mournful by nature?" She has hesitated at the gate to make certain that Harry will be all right visiting a cemetery. **C** is the best answer.

4. The details and events in the passage suggest that the relationship between Harry Bellamy and Sally Carrol can most accurately be described as:

   F. trusting, as evinced by a shared love of risky adventures.
   G. selfish, as shown by occasional insensitivity to the needs of the other.
   H. charitable, as illustrated by their generosity toward others.
   J. tender, based on their willingness to share intimate feelings.

This is a broad question that tests your ability to interpret aspects of the entire passage. To answer it you must study all choices and quickly review the main "details and events" described in the passage. Notice that each choice has two parts—an introductory adjective, followed by an example meant to illustrate the quality stated by the adjective. When you choose your answer, be sure that both parts accurately depict the way Harry and Sally behave with each other.

Choice **F** is a possibility because Harry and Sally share a mutual trust. The illustrative example, however, disqualifies **F** as a good answer because there is nothing risky or adventurous about Harry and Sally's stroll through the cemetery. Eliminate **G** as a reasonable choice because neither Harry nor Sally shows signs of selfishness or insensitivity to others' needs. **H** is an equally dubious choice. It's true that Sally grows weepy over the Confederate dead, but her feelings don't necessarily reflect a generous nature. That leaves **J** as the best choice. Indeed, Harry and Sally express affection for each other, especially in the second half of the passage. He tells her, for example, "I see through your precious eyes. You're beautiful now" (line 41). She calls him "darling" (line 55) and "lover" (line 71). Even more to the point are Sally's poignant revelations about her nostalgia for the Old South (lines 57–67).

5. Which of the following is NOT included in the narrator's descriptions of the cemetery?

   A. An orderly arrangement of graves
   B. An ornate stone entrance to the burial ground
   C. Carvings on headstones
   D. Visitors paying their respects to the dead

TIP

Stay alert for questions containing "NOT" and "EXCEPT." They ask you to find something that is *not* in the passage.

Unlike most ACT questions, this one asks you to identify something that does NOT exist in the passage. To find the correct answer, you must refer to all the sections in the passage that describe the cemetery, beginning in line 9 and continuing on and off to the end of the passage. (As you read, use your pencil to highlight specific details.)

Eliminate **A** because the narrator says in lines 47–48 that crosses stretch "in endless, ordered rows like the stacked arms of a battalion." **C** is not a good answer because almost an entire paragraph (lines 15–21) is devoted to the carvings on gravestones. The reference to kneeling figures with "tributary flowers" (line 19) rules out **D** as an answer. Only **B** is not mentioned in the passage. In fact, lines 10–11 indicate that that gate to the cemetery is made of iron. **B**, therefore, is the best answer.

6. As she is portrayed in the passage, Sally can best be described as

   F. generous and considerate.
   G. morbid and depressed.
   H. sentimental and compassionate.
   J. high-strung and nervous.

The phrasing of the question suggests that you won't find the answer stated verbatim in the passage. Rather, you'll need to consider the portrayal of Sally and draw conclusions about her personality from everything she thinks, says, and does. In fact, because the author focuses mainly on Sally, the question tests your understanding of virtually the entire passage. As you search for the best answer, therefore, do a quick review. You won't have time during the ACT to reread the whole passage to answer a single question, but spot-checking the text will refresh your memory of Sally's traits. Each choice consists of two adjectives. Be sure that both adjectives apply.

Choice **F** has promise because Sally is neither *un*generous nor *in*considerate. But the absence of unfavorable traits doesn't necessarily prove the existence of favorable opposites. Choice **G** may also have appeal because Sally's obsession with dead soldiers suggests a kind of morbidity. Whether she is depressed, however, is questionable. Note that she says in line 14, "It [visiting the cemetery] depresses some folks, but I like it." **H** most accurately captures Sally's character. She revels in nostalgia for the Old South and feels acutely for the dead soldiers, especially for the unknowns. **H** is the best answer. **J** is the least valid answer; Sally does nothing to suggest that she is neurotic.

7. Given evidence throughout the passage, Margery Lee is most likely:

   A. an idealized figure imagined by Sally.
   B. a spinster who died in childbirth.
   C. an obscure ancestor of Sally's.
   D. a well-known celebrity from the past.

This question concerns Sally's puzzling reaction to Margery Lee's headstone (lines 24–37). Why does Sally describe Margery Lee? Are Sally's words true, or do they represent a figurative rendering of the truth? Only when you can reasonably explain Sally's motives can you choose the best answer. According to the question, you are being asked to determine from evidence in the passage why Sally talks at length about a woman who died decades ago, a woman she never met or knew. The episode in the cemetery provides a telling clue: Sally apparently has an intense love for the Old South. In fact, she admits to Harry that she has tried to have that old time "live in" her.

Choice **A** fits Sally's propensity to empathize with the "dead South." Indeed, she imagines Margery Lee as the epitome of a Southern belle in both manners and looks. She may, in fact, be describing how she herself would have looked and acted back then. **A** is the best choice. **B** is a far cry from anything that Sally has in mind, for a sexual scandal has no place in Sally's thoughts. **C** could make sense, although there is nothing in the passage to suggest that Margery Lee is kin to Sally. Nor does the passage allude to **D**.

8. Sally weeps for all of the following reasons EXCEPT:

   F. the realization that she'll never be like Margery Lee.
   G. her estrangement from the modern world.
   H. the anonymity of the dead soldiers.
   J. the passing of the old South.

The capitalized EXCEPT is a signal to skim the passage in search of a direct or indirect reference to each of the four choices. The one that you don't find is the answer. To identify what causes Sally's tears, skim the text both before and after Harry feels Sally's trembling shoulders (line 43). What has stirred her? Before line 43, only Sally's encounter with the grave of Margery Lee could have moved her to tears. Afterward, visions of the faded beauty of the old South and soldiers' willingness to die for beauty have the power to bring tears to her eyes.

Choice **F** alludes to Sally's identification with the long-dead Margery Lee. Because Sally's eyes brim with tears after she and Harry come upon the graves of the unknown soldiers (lines 52–53), eliminate **H**. Also rule out **J** because Sally's eyes glisten "with tears" (line 60) after explaining to Harry that the soldiers made a sacrifice for "the most beautiful thing in the world—the dead South" (line 59). Someone stuck in the past may indeed feel alienated from the modern world, but if Sally does feel estranged, nothing in the passage suggests that it causes her to weep. Therefore, **G** is the best answer.

9. While explaining her attachment to the "dead South" (lines 57–67), Sally is most worried that:

   A. she cannot accurately express her emotions.
   B. she may burst into tears at any moment.
   C. Harry will fail to understand.
   D. Harry will think she is a silly fool.

To answer this question your task is not to interpret what Sally says, but how she feels about confiding her most intimate thoughts to Harry. An analysis of the dialogue that both precedes and follows Sally's explanation leads to the correct answer.

Choice **A** could not be right; Sally conveys her feelings convincingly; there is no doubt that she is enamored of a time and place that no longer exist. As for **B**, Sally tends to weep easily. In fact, her eyes brim with tears (line 54) even before she begins to confide in Harry. Discard **D** as an answer because Harry's affectionate statement, "How you feel about it is beautiful to me," has already assured her that he accepts her without reservation just as she is. The process of elimination leaves **C** as the best answer. Indeed, in line 55 Sally is concerned that Harry may not have grasped the reality of her feelings. Moments later (lines 66–67), she declares, "Oh, Harry, there was something . . . I couldn't ever make you understand, but it was there."

10. It is reasonable to infer from the passage that Harry said, "I wish those three old women would clear out" (line 75) because he:

   F. is uncomfortable about showing affection in public.
   G. has concerns about Sally's reputation.
   H. does not want to embarrass the old women.
   J. has more on his mind than just a kiss.

This question asks you to interpret a character's thoughts. To find the best answer, look for evidence in the last lines of the passage. Does the reference to three old women surprise you? Who are these women? Where did they come from? The fact is that they are the kneeling figures placing flowers on graves earlier in the passage (line 19). Their presence obviously annoys Harry. Why they irk him can be inferred from lines 75–76.

Choice **F** reveals the source of Harry's wish to be alone. **F** is the best answer. **G** alludes to something that may be true, but nothing in the passage suggests that the three old women either knew Sally or had the slightest awareness that she and Harry were in the cemetery. **H** has no merit whatsoever. If anyone were to be embarrassed by the ardent kiss that ends the passage, it would be the lovers, not the old women. **J** may indeed reflect Harry's innermost desires, but the passage stops short of saying so.

Warm-Up Drill

While answering the ten questions about the following prose fiction passage, use the strategies you learned as you studied the sample questions in this chapter. Answers and explanations follow the questions.

This is an excerpt from *Work: A Story of Experience* by the 19th century American author Louisa May Alcott. In the passage, Christie, the novel's protagonist, has just begun a new job as a housekeeper with the well-to-do Stuart family.

. . . Christie got on excellently, for she did her best, and found both pleasure and profit in her new employment. It gave her real satisfaction to keep the handsome rooms in order, to polish plate, and spread bountiful meals. There was an atmosphere of ease and comfort about her which contrasted agreeably with the shabbiness of Mrs. Flint's boarding-house, and the bare simplicity of the old home. Like most young people, Christie loved luxury, and was sensible enough to see and value the comforts of her situation, and to wonder why more girls placed as she was did not choose a life like this rather than the confinements of a sewing-room, or the fatigue and publicity of a shop.

She did not learn to love her mistress, because Mrs. Stuart evidently considered herself as one belonging to a superior race of beings, and had no desire to establish any of the friendly relations that may become so helpful and pleasant to both mistress and maid. She made a royal progress through her dominions every morning, issued orders, found fault liberally, bestowed praise sparingly, and took no more personal interest in her servants than if they were clocks, to be wound up once a day, and sent away the moment they got out of repair.

Mr. Stuart was absent from morning till night, and all Christie ever knew about him was that he was a kind-hearted, hot-tempered, and very conceited man; fond of his wife, proud of the society they managed to draw about them, and bent on making his way in the world at any cost.

If masters and mistresses knew how skilfully they are studied, criticized, and imitated by their servants, they would take more heed to their ways, and set better examples, perhaps. Mrs. Stuart never dreamed that her quiet, respectful Jane* kept a sharp eye on all her movements, smiled covertly at her affectations, envied her accomplishments, and practiced certain little elegancies that struck her fancy.

Mr. Stuart would have become apoplectic with indignation if he had known that this too intelligent table-girl often contrasted her master with his guests, and dared to think him wanting in good breeding when he boasted of his money, flattered a great man, or laid plans to lure some lion into his house. When he lost his temper, she always wanted to laugh; he bounced and bumbled about so like an angry blue-bottle fly; and when he got himself up elaborately for a party, this disrespectful hussy confided to Hepsey, the cook, her opinion that "master was a fat dandy, with nothing to be vain of but his clothes,"—a sacreligious remark which would have caused her to be summarily ejected from the house if it reached the august ears of master or mistress.

"My father was a gentleman; and I shall never forget it, though I do go out to service. I've got no rich friends to help me up, but, sooner or later, I mean to find a place among cultivated people; and while I'm working and waiting, I can be fitting myself to fill that place like a gentlewoman, as I am."

---

* Mrs. Stuart chooses to call her new housekeeper "Jane" instead of Christie.

With this ambition in her mind, Christie took notes of all that went on in the polite world of which she got frequent glimpses while "living out." Mrs. Stuart received one evening of each week, and on those occasions Christie, with an extra frill on her white apron, served the company, and enjoyed herself more than they did, if the truth had been known.

While helping the ladies with their wraps, she observed their manners, how they carried themselves, and how they bedecked themselves in finery, not to mention the flood of gossip they talked while shaking out their flounces and settling their topknots.

Later in the evening, when she passed cups and glasses, this demure-looking damsel heard much fine discourse, saw many famous beings, and improved her mind with surreptitious studies of the rich and great when on parade.

After a time, however, Christie got rather tired of it, for there was an elegant sameness about these evenings that became intensely wearisome to the unititiated, but she fancied that as each had his part to play he managed to do it with spirit. Night after night the wag told his stories, the poet read his poems, the singers warbled, the pretty women simpered and dressed, the heavy scientific was duly discussed by the elect precious, and Mrs. Stuart, in amazing costumes, sailed to and fro in her most swan-like manner; while my lord stirred up the lions he had captured, till they roared their best, great and small.

1. It can most reasonably be inferred from the first paragraph (lines 1–9) that prior to being employed by the Stuarts, Christie:
   A. had never held a job.
   B. had been a shopkeeper.
   C. had run away from home.
   D. had experience as a domestic worker.

2. Which of the following best describes Christie's attitude toward her new job?
   F. She can hardly wait to quit and find a higher-paying position.
   G. She considers herself fortunate.
   H. The job stimulates and excites her.
   J. She is bored by the work but proud to be earning a living.

3. Based on information in the first and second paragraphs (lines 1–16), Christie and Mrs. Stuart are alike in which of the following ways?
   A. They are conceited and egotistical.
   B. They enjoy being among handsome and costly surroundings.
   C. They prefer the company of men rather than women.
   D. They delight in good food and fine wine.

4. Until the end of the third paragraph (line 20), the passage is written from Christie's point of view. The next two paragraphs are written from the point of view of:
   F. Mr. Stuart.
   G. Mrs. Stuart.
   H. Christie as an older person.
   J. The author of the passage.

5. The reference to "quiet, respectful Jane" (line 23) is meant to reinforce the point that:
   A. Mrs. Stuart neither knows nor cares about the people who work for her.
   B. Christie is bashful in Mrs. Stuart's presence.
   C. Mrs. Stuart suffers from delusions of grandeur.
   D. Christie is awed by and slightly afraid of Mrs. Stuart.

6. The statement that Christie "dared to think of him [Mr. Stuart] wanting in good breeding" (lines 27–28), helps to establish that:
   F. Christie can be no less snobbish than Mrs. Stuart.
   G. Christie has impeccable manners.
   H. Christie knows right from wrong.
   J. the guests are not impressed with Mr. Stuart's wealth.

7. Christie's private thoughts, spelled out in lines 35–38, reveal that Christie:
   A. has secured her position with the Stuarts under false pretenses.
   B. expects to use her current position as a stepping stone.
   C. has become reconciled to her status in life.
   D. thinks that the duties of a housekeeper are beneath her.

8. Christie enjoys Mrs. Stuart's weekly parties (lines 44–46) mainly because she:
   F. takes pleasure in dressing up in an elegant maid's costume.
   G. uses them as an opportunity to observe and learn the customs of polite society.
   H. aspires to be just like the ladies she serves.
   J. looks forward to ridiculing the ladies' manners and behavior when the party ends.

9. Christie's observation that "each had his part to play" (line 52) is meant to show:
   A. why she had more fun than the guests at Mrs. Stuart's parties.
   B. that the guests grew tired of the Stuarts' weekly parties.
   C. that the Stuarts' friends only pretended to enjoy each other's company.
   D. that the party guests behaved in predictable ways.

10. The author uses the words "lion" (line 29) and "lions" (line 56) as a metaphor for:
    F. rich and powerful men.
    G. loud and boisterous men.
    H. business associates of Mr. Stuart.
    J. people from whom Mr. Stuart wants to borrow money.

ANSWERS AND EXPLANATIONS

1. **(D)** The first paragraph contrasts the agreeable surroundings in the Stuart home with the shabbiness of Mrs. Flint's boarding house (lines 4–5), where Christie once worked in a similar capacity. Choice A is contradicted by the reference to Mrs. Flint's boarding house. B is wrong because in lines 8–9 Christie actually states her objection to working in a shop. C cannot be supported by the content of the paragraph.

2. **(G)** According to the first paragraph, Christie found pleasure, profit, and satisfaction in her comfortable and luxurious place of employment. Further, she wonders why other girls choose to work in disagreeable places like sewing-rooms and shops. F is not borne out by the passage, although later (lines 36–39) Christie daydreams about one day being employed in a more refined household. H overstates Christie's feelings. J may be valid to a point: It's easy to imagine that Christie is proud of herself, but she is definitely not bored—not at the beginning, at any rate.

3. **(B)** Line 6 states outright that Christie "loved luxury," and the Stuarts' home furnishings suggest that Mrs. Stuart loved luxury, too. B accurately describes Mrs. Stuart, but not Christie. Neither C nor D is supported by evidence in passage.

4. **(J)** In line 21, the narrator takes a detour from events in the story, commenting broadly on relationships between servants and employers. The thoughts come from the author, not from any of the story's characters.

5. **(A)** Lines 14–15 state that Mrs. Stuart takes "no personal interest" in her servants. Her indifference keeps her from realizing that Christie is not really a quiet and respectful young woman—except, perhaps, in Mrs. Stuart's presence. B is not accurate because Christie's reticence in Mrs. Stuart's presence comes not from bashfulness but from Christie's keen awareness of the behavior Mrs. Stuart expects of her servants. C is not supported by evidence in the passage. D is contrary to fact: Christie is anything but awed by Mrs. Stuart. In fact, Christie repeatedly reveals to us her scorn for the woman.

6. **(F)** Choice F accurately describes an aspect of Christie's personality. G may be a valid statement, but the passage fails to tell or show us Christie's good manners. Indeed, Christie's comment to Hepsey the cook (lines 32–33) suggests that Christie herself may be a little deficient in the good-breeding department. H is not supported by the passage, and J is probably contrary to fact. Mr. Stuart's cronies are likely to be much like Mr. Stuart himself—in awe of money.

7. **(B)** Christie asserts in lines 36–37 that ". . .sooner or later, I mean to find a place among cultivated people. . . ." Choice A is invalid because there is no evidence that Christie used deception in landing her job with the Stuarts. C is refuted by Christie's ambition to find another position in the future. D cannot be true because Christie finds "pleasure and profit" (lines 1–2) in her employment and expects one day to serve in another household.

8. **(G)** The reasons behind Christie's pleasure, spelled out in lines 44–49, include observing the ladies' "manners, how they carried themselves, and how they bedecked themselves in finery." Choice F describes what Christie wore, but wearing a frilly white apron gives her no particular joy. H fails to identify Christie's ambitions or the source of her pleasure. J is neither stated nor implied by the passage.

9. **(D)** Christie's comment sums up her view of the Stuarts' social circle: Despite their wealth, they are dull people caught in a rut. Choice A describes Christie's state of mind but is unrelated to the view she expresses in lines 51–52. B and C may accurately describe the guests' state of mind, but the passage fails to support either contention.

10. **(F)** Mr. Stuart is "proud of the society" (line 19) he draws about him. The members of his circle, whom the author calls "lions," are likely to be distinguished by their wealth and influence—two attributes that Mr. Stuart himself strives to achieve. Because a lion is regarded as the king of beasts and a symbol of both strength and regal bearing, "lion" is an apt metaphor for Mr. Stuart's guests. Choices G, H, and J, on the other hand, fail to evoke leonine images.

SOCIAL STUDIES

Passages

The ACT reading comprehension test includes a passage from Social Studies. By definition, *Social* Studies focus on people, usually people in groups. A social scientist may be interested in *anthropology,* the study of society's customs and values and the relationships of people to each other and their environment. *Economics,* or how people earn and spend money, is also a social science, as are *sociology,* the study of society's functions and institutions, and *political science,* the study of people's laws and governments. *Psychology* is also considered a social science, even though psychologists study individual behavior as well as the behavior of groups. Passages in this section of the ACT may also be drawn from the worlds of archaeology, business, education, geography, and history.

The task of answering questions about social studies passages becomes more manageable when you understand the main principles of writing followed by social scientists. More often than not, social scientists write to inform others about their observations, to report on their research, and to expound their theories. Their domain is reality, not the world of the imagination.

Therefore, a passage meant to explain the all-too-real phenomenon of poverty reads this way:

Categorizing people as "in poverty" or "not in poverty" is one way to describe their economic situation. The income-to-poverty ratio and the income deficit (surplus) describe other aspects of economic well-being. Where the poverty rate provides a measure of the proportion of people with a family income that is below the established poverty thresholds, the income-to-poverty ratio provides a measure to gauge the depth of poverty and to calculate the size of the population who may be eligible for government-sponsored assistance programs, such as Temporary Assistance to Needy Families (TANF), Medicare, food stamps, and the Low-Income Home Energy Assistance Program (LIHEAP). The income-to-poverty ratio is reported as a percentage that compares a family's or an unrelated individual's (people who do not live with relatives) income with their poverty threshold. For example, a family or individual with an income-to-poverty ratio of 110 percent has income that is 10 percent above their poverty threshold.

The income deficit (surplus) tells how many dollars a family's or an unrelated individual's income is below (above) their poverty threshold. These measures illustrate how the low-income population varies in relation to the poverty thresholds.

U.S. Census Bureau

Analysis

This passage may seem hard to follow at first. Although it contains some specialized terms (*income-to-poverty ratio*, *income deficit*, *poverty thresholds*), the terms aren't so technical that you can't figure them out. Be assured that the passage makes sense and can be understood even by readers not well versed in economics and other social sciences. The author of the passage is attempting to spell out guidelines for an official definition of poverty, a yardstick used in determining who is eligible for certain kinds of government assistance and who is not.

Use the context to determine the meaning of social science terminology.

To deal with a passage such as this on the ACT, you don't need extensive preparation in the social sciences. All the information you need is provided. Your job is simply to read the passage thoroughly and to answer the questions.

Social scientists are concerned about problems ranging from drug addiction to depression, from child abuse to abortion. Social science literature is filled with books and articles about such crucial issues. The passage on the ACT may be an argument for or against a policy or issue. Yet, you can expect it to be relatively free of inflammatory language and controversial opinion. A passage about an issue that usually evokes strong feelings will be written objectively. Yet, some issues really don't have two sides. No one, for instance, favors AIDS or child abuse.

In the following passage, the author discusses the dynamics of social exchange between individuals—in other words, how people talk to each other. The author doesn't intend to provoke an argument or espouse a point of view. Rather, he spells out the observations of a social theorist. Although you should read the passage as though it were fact, be aware that it is mostly opinion. ACT questions on this passage would test whether you understood the author's ideas, not whether you agree with them.

The key task of sociology. . . is to analyze social associations, which are based on the fact that both parties to an exchange can often benefit. But this does not mean that the parties to an exchange benefit equally, that they have complete information about the exchange, or that each exchange occurs in a vacuum isolated from other commitments the parties may have. Often one individual is able to get more from an exchange than the other person does, because he or she has more power of one kind or another.

People are attracted to others if they expect exchanges with them to be rewarding and they need to become attractive to the others in order to develop an enduring association. Often a person wants something from another but has nothing to give in return that the other wants. A person in this uncomfortable situation has three basic alternatives. First, it may be possible to force the other person to give the desired item, perhaps by threat of violence or outright theft. Second, it may be possible to find another person who can provide the item. Third, the person may subordinate himself or herself to the person who has the item, giving that person power. Thus, in the course of a large number of social exchanges, some individuals come to have power over others.

William Sims Bainbridge, *Sociology*
Barron's (1997), pp. 26–27

Analysis

You probably noticed that this passage is impersonal, serious, analytical. It doesn't define terms because the author assumes that readers will understand the ideas it contains. Clearly, it's not meant for readers unaccustomed to abstract concepts about human behavior. It is written in the style of much social science literature and would sound familiar to professionals in the field. To some extent it's "in" talk. Yet, it's not so far "in" that an outsider like you cannot grasp its meaning.

Your reading in social studies classes has most likely given you a taste of historical writing like this:

When the British government began to increase its military presence in the colonies in the mid-eighteenth century, Massachusetts responded by calling upon its citizens to arm themselves in defense. One colonial newspaper argued that it was impossible to complain that his act was illegal since they were "British subjects, to whom the privilege of possessing arms is expressly recognized by the Bill of Rights" while another argued that this "is a natural right which the people have reserved to themselves, confirmed by the Bill of Rights, to keep arms for their own defense." The newspaper cited Blackstone's commentaries on the laws of England, which had listed the "having and using arms for self preservation and defense" among the "absolute rights of individuals." The colonists felt they had an absolute right at common law to own firearms.

Together with freedom of the press, the right to keep and bear arms became one of the individual rights most prized by the colonists. When British troops seized a militia arsenal in September, 1774, and incorrect rumors that colonists had been killed spread through Massachusetts, 60,000 citizens took up arms. A few months later, when Patrick Henry delivered his famed "Give me liberty or give me death" speech, he spoke in support of a proposition "that a well regulated militia, composed of gentlemen and freemen, is the natural strength and only security of a free government. . . ."

Report of the Senate Subcommittee on the Constitution,
"The Right to Keep and Bear Arms"

TIP 

A passage may appear to present just the facts, but stay alert for underlying feelings and opinions that bob to the surface every so often.

Analysis

This passage probably has the familiar ring of a social studies textbook. Authors of textbooks usually cover historical periods and issues in fairly broad terms. They support generalizations with facts and with apt quotations and statistics. On the ACT, you should read the facts, of course, but more important is recognizing the function of those particular facts. In other words, if you know the general idea each fact is meant to support or illustrate, you probably understand the whole passage. For example, it may be interesting to read that 60,000 Massachusetts colonists reached for their guns in September 1774, but it's far more important to understand why the author included that information. In this instance, the author wanted to show that colonists believed in the fundamental right to protect themselves with firearms.

Do you also perceive the point of view implied in the passage? By selecting certain words and details, the author reveals a bias in favor of the rights of U.S. citizens to keep and bear arms, a right that has grown out of a tradition begun centuries ago. Keep in mind that authors have feelings about their subjects. Total objectivity is an ideal rarely achieved.

Sample Questions

Seven of the ten questions that follow the Social Studies passage on the ACT will ask you to reason out the answers. The remaining three questions ask you about material explicitly stated in the passage.

Answer the four sample questions following this passage about terrorism. Techniques for answering these questions are similar to those you used for the sample Prose Fiction passage.

Democracies have always been subject to terrorist attacks. Our constitutional rights, the restrictions set on police power, and our citizens' enjoyment of due process of the law—the very qualities of our society that terrorists despise—are the same qualities that for years made us easy prey. Although many people view this as a cruel irony, we have within our free society the tools with which not only to fight and destroy terrorists but to keep them at bay. Following the attacks of September 11, 2001, America went to war against terrorism. A federal Department of Homeland Security was created. The citizenry was put on alert. Our superbly trained law enforcement people at every level of government began to coordinate their efforts as never before. The courts granted more liberal use of wiretap surveillance and search warrants, and a system of laws was introduced to fight terrorism as both a crime and a military assault instead of merely a political act. Terrorists from foreign lands were put on notice that they faced prosecution in military tribunals, and American citizens who chose to terrorize their own country faced the maximum penalties allowed by criminal law.

In order to preserve our basic freedoms and way of life, we must never cave in to the fear of terrorism. We must depend on the strength of our system to protect us. If we allow dread, as intense as it may be, to control our actions, we will lose our strongest defense against terrorism. The demise of terrorism will be hastened when all freedom-loving countries join us in sending out a strong and clear message to the world's terrorists that terror, like other crime, shall not pay!

Sample Referring Questions:

1. According to the passage, U.S. citizens are popular targets for terrorists because they:

   A. usually don't carry firearms.
   B. represent everything that terrorists hate.
   C. are not accustomed to worrying about their personal safety.
   D. are rich and arrogant.

Before you skim the passage to find the location of the answer, identify what you will look for as your eyes move quickly through the text. Since the question asks why terrorists like to pick on Americans, keep the phrase "popular targets" in mind. Within a few seconds you may pick out "easy prey" (line 4), an idea that may well explain why Americans are "popular targets." Where you found "easy prey," then, is the section of the passage to reread in search of the correct answer.

Choice **A** may be true most of the time, but no such idea is stated in the passage. **B** reiterates a phrase in the passage, "qualities of our society that terrorists despise." Therefore, **B** is correct. **C** and **D** are not mentioned in the passage.

2. According to the passage, the terrorist attacks of September 11, 2001, brought about all of the following changes EXCEPT:

F. an expansion of police powers.
G. an overall restructuring of the federal government.
H. the introduction of military courts to prosecute foreign terrorists.
J. an expanded public awareness of terrorist threats.

Before skimming the passage for the location of the answer, identify the key words in the question, most likely "attacks of September 11, 2001" and "changes." Where you find these or related words and phrases (lines 6–14) is the section to reread. Because this question asks you to identify an idea that is NOT stated in the passage, search for references to each of the four choices.

Choice **F** is covered by the idea that the courts authorized wider use of wiretaps and search warrants. **G** alludes indirectly to the creation of a Department of Homeland Security, but the passage does not indicate that the founding of such an agency is equivalent to an overall restructuring of the federal government. Choice **H** restates the reference to military tribunals for foreign terrorists, and **J** paraphrases the idea that the citizenry was put on alert. **G**, therefore, is the best answer.

Sample Reasoning Questions:

3. The phrase *enjoyment of due process of the law* (second sentence) means that citizens:

A. have a basic right to pursue pleasure and happiness.
B. may protest against distasteful laws.
C. are protected by the laws of our society.
D. can sue the government to redress grievances.

To figure out the answer, find the phrase in the passage and look for contextual clues. The phrase is included as one of three fundamental rights that belong to citizens in a democracy. "*Enjoyment*" is not used in its usual sense, but rather in the sense of *having* or *being in possession of*. Our citizens, the passage says, *have* or *possess* "due process of the law." Review each choice for the best definition.

Choice **A** is the right of every citizen, but it is not the right of "due process." **B** is a right, but our right to protest is not the equivalent of "due process of the law." **C** is a fundamental right that lawbreaking terrorists naturally despise. **C** is the correct answer. **D** is the right of every citizen, but it is not on the same level of importance as the others mentioned in the passage.

4. Which of the following ideas most accurately states the main point of the passage?

F. Terrorists feel a particular hatred for democratic countries.
G. Our system of government serves as the best deterrent to terrorism.
H. Countries must never give in to terrorist demands.
J. Cooperation by the free countries of the world can stop terrorism.

To answer main-idea questions, you need an overview of the whole passage. Each of the four possible answers may be inferred from the passage, but only one of them encompasses more of the passage than the others. Although counting the number of sentences devoted to a particular subject may reveal the main idea, just as often the main idea may be stated briefly or not at all. Therefore, rely on your sense of the entire passage to find the answer.

Choice **F** is too insignificant to be the main idea. **G** summarizes much of the first paragraph. The idea is reiterated in a slightly different form in the second paragraph. **G** is the correct answer. **H** and **J** are too limited to be the main idea.

Now try a full-length Social Studies passage for practice. The text comes from a book review that appeared in a journal published for personnel of the United States Central Intelligence Agency in 2002.

After you answer each of the accompanying questions, compare your approach to the technique described in the analysis following each question.

In a robust democracy like the United States, public channels of information such as newspapers and television are more or less exempt from government restrictions. But during wartime, controlling the public's access to information becomes a difficult and controversial proposition, much more than a simple constitutional or legal issue. Domestic morale and support for wartime policies depend heavily on an informed public. If citizens are denied access to reasonable amounts of information, or, worse, if they are deceived about policies and events, their support can turn to opposition.

In time of war, controlling public information that an enemy might exploit to undermine the conduct of military operations, strategic policy, or homeland defense, becomes as important as managing official secrets. The current war on terrorism is no different. Information once considered innocuous—such as structural data for stadiums, bridges, and public works—is now considered to have intelligence value for terrorists. But how can such information be controlled? Who manages public information? What kinds of information need to be protected? Who enforces restrictions? What is the relationship between censorship, intelligence, security, and propaganda?

During World War II, President Roosevelt had the power to control information given to the media. Legislation had been passed in 1938 that forbade unauthorized photographs, sketches, or maps of military bases, and gave the President the authority to define which types of military information needed security protection. The President was reluctant, however, to exercise these authorities. He recalled the overzealous application of espionage laws during World War I, which resulted in the jailing of hundreds of socialists and pacifists for criticizing President Wilson, war profiteering, and anti-German violence. Believing that it was critical for Americans to receive news about the war, he set two conditions for the media: their stories must be accurate and they could not help the enemy.

To oversee the nation's censorship activity, Roosevelt set up an Office of Censorship and picked Byron Price, the executive news editor of the Associated Press, to run it. Price put the onus for censorship directly on the journalists. His methods were to nudge and talk them into compliance under his motto: "Least said, soonest mended." He also delegated release of information to "appropriate authorities," meaning that those directly involved—from combat commanders to government department heads—decided what information about their activities could be made public. This kept Price's office out of numerous controversies. A case in point was the famous episode in which Gen. George Patton slapped a soldier suffering from battle fatigue. Newsmen filed requests to print the story; Gen. Dwight Eisenhower, the Supreme Allied Commander, gave his approval.

Price worked hard to keep the system voluntary and to solve the problem of finding a proper balance between wartime secrecy and the public's right to know. In general, the system worked. Self-censorship created a supportive culture among reporters and editors. He beat off an attempt by the Military Intelligence Division of the War Department to enforce stronger censorship of information about the military, citing a story in the *Chicago Tribune* alleging a compromise of the secret that America had broken the Japanese war code. The Navy jumped to the conclusion that certain information in a news article came from classified documents; in fact, the Tribune's reporter had seen a copy of a message from Admiral Nimitz [the American fleet's commander] carelessly left out, that listed the Japanese ships that were part of the task force set to attack Midway. The Navy's repeated efforts to punish the Tribune actually increased the chance that the Japanese might discover that we had broken their code.

Censors also restricted photographs of the President and information about his whereabouts. During the 1944 election campaign, these restrictions allowed him to hide the fact that he had polio and was confined to a wheelchair. Censorship also allowed him to cover up his affair with an old friend Lucy Rutherford.

But if there was any mistake by the censorship authorities, it probably came near the end of the war. Military intelligence, with initial agreement from the Office of Censorship, refused to release information to the public about Japanese balloon-born bombs that were carried over the American northwest by prevailing winds. The intention was to keep Tokyo in the dark about the effectiveness of the balloon "attacks." Price subsequently asked for at least a partial release of information on the potential danger of the balloon bombs; however, the Navy refused. The news clampdown may have contributed to some of the (few) casualties that the bombs caused.

Robert J. Hanyok,
Journal of the American Intelligence Professional, 2002

Skim passages for references to specific words or phrases.

1. The author implies that wartime control of information by the government has the potential to do harm because it may:

A. contribute to public distrust of the government.
B. destroy the reputation of government officials.
C. weaken the constitutional rights of a free press.
D. cause innocent people to be unduly victimized.

To answer this question, skim the passage for references to the key words and phrases, namely "wartime control of information" and "harm." Once you discover that "control of information" is the main concern of the first two paragraphs, search for an idea that states or implies a harmful effect of keeping information from the public.

Choices **B** and **D** are not discussed in the passage. Choice **C** is contradicted by the assertion made in the first sentence of the passage. Lines 6–7 say that a public denied access to reasonable amounts of information may turn against its government, implying that secrecy breeds distrust. **A**, therefore, is the best answer.

2. According to the author, it is important in time of war for the government to keep the public well informed in order to:

F. maintain public support.
G. abide by the principles of democracy.
H. keep up the morale of the armed forces.
J. enlist the public's help in gathering intelligence.

The first words in the question ("According to the author") indicate that you are being asked to identify an idea expressly stated, paraphrased, or reiterated in the passage. Look first for a reference to keeping "the public well informed." By skimming the first paragraph, the phrases "public's access to information" and "an informed public" should strike your eye. In fact, that is the section of the passage in which the answer is likely to be found.

Lines 5–6 indicate that support for wartime policies depends on keeping the public informed. **F** is the best answer. Rule out **G** because the author does not say that democracy compels the government to keep the public well informed, however. Eliminate **H** because the passage alludes only to the morale of the public, not the morale of the military. **J** is not discussed.

3. As it is used in line 11, the word *innocuous* most nearly means:

   A. confidential.
   B. innocent.
   C. gentle.
   D. healthy.

Any time you get a vocabulary question like this one ask yourself whether the meaning you seek corresponds to the dictionary definition or to a connotation of the word. More often than not on the ACT, it will be the latter. Perhaps you know right off that *innocuous* means "harmless" and that "innocent" is a virtual synonym. If not, however, look for clues to the meaning of the word in the context of the passage. In this case the word is used to contrast *innocuous* data with information that is "now considered to have intelligence value for terrorists." In other words, it means something nearly the opposite of information valued by terrorists bent on destroying stadiums, bridges, and public works.

Only choice **B** fits. The other definitions don't apply.

4. Based on information in the passage, all of the following are considered legitimate functions of government EXCEPT:

   F. maintaining official secrets.
   G. carrying out military operations.
   H. assuring homeland defense.
   J. censoring the media.

To answer this question, identify the one choice that names a function of government you cannot find mentioned or implied in the passage. To find the answer, skim the passage looking for references to each of the choices. If you understood the passage when you first read it, you may be able to eliminate one or more of the choices right away.

The first sentence of the passage indicates that controlling public channels of information (i.e., censoring the media) is ordinarily not a governmental function. Choice **J**, therefore, is the best answer. **F**, **G**, and **H** are listed in lines 8–11.

5. According to the passage, President Roosevelt was wary of strict censorship laws in World War II because:

   A. such restrictive laws tended to violate the Constitution.
   B. they were extremely difficult to enforce.
   C. they were likely to be challenged in court proceedings.
   D. similar laws had led to abuses of government power in the past.

Any question that begins with the phrase "According to the passage" will refer to an explicitly stated idea. In other words, locate the part of the passage containing words that repeat, paraphrase, or reiterate in some way the key words and phrases in the question. In this case "President Roosevelt" and "wary of strict censorship" are the most obvious choices. In lines 20–21 you will find an allusion to the President's wariness: "The President was reluctant . . . ." Why he was reluctant is detailed later in the same paragraph.

More precisely, lines 20–24 explain the President's reluctance to exercise his authority. Namely, he recalled the "overzealous application" of restrictive espionage laws during World War I, an idea that only choice **D** comes close to expressing.

6. It can reasonably be inferred from the passage that the motto "Least said, soonest mended" (line 29) was meant to:

   F. steer journalists away from investigations of how the war was being conducted.
   G. encourage journalists to advocate a speedy end to the war.
   H. keep journalists from disclosing information that could damage the war effort.
   J. caution journalists that if they said too much they would pay the consequences.

This question asks you not to interpret the meaning of the quotation but to determine its intention. Why, in other words, did Byron Price adopt and promulgate "Least said, soonest mended" as his motto? To find the answer reread the paragraph in which the quotation appears. You'll find that Price gave journalists the responsibility of self-censorship. His motto was meant to "nudge and talk them" into being circumspect about what they reported. It reminded them that irreparable harm could result from thoughtlessly disclosed information.

To interpret the meaning of a specific quotation, read the sentences before and after the quote.

Rule out choice **F** because, as suggested both at the beginning and elsewhere in the passage, censorship of the press is anathema to an open, democratic society. **G** is not discussed in the passage. **J**, in addition to being irrelevant to the passage, is a threat that Price, being a journalist himself, would consider intolerable. **H** is the one choice that approximates the admonition implicit in Price's motto. It's also the only choice that coincides with Price's beliefs and values.

7. The incident involving General Patton and the soldier (lines 33–35) is cited in the passage mainly for the purpose of:

   A. revealing the nature of the relationship between Patton and Eisenhower.
   B. pointing out tensions that exist in the military during time of war.
   C. showing why it was crucial for Price's office to stay out of internal military matters.
   D. illustrating how the policy of "appropriate authorities" (line 30) functioned.

Any time a question asks you to determine the implied or stated purpose of a reference to a specific event, chances are that the author is trying to support, illustrate, or exemplify a general idea. In such cases, reread the material about the event, looking for clues to its function in the overall context. Most often, the best clues will appear in the text just before the event is spelled out.

Just prior to reporting what Patton did, the author says that Price's policy kept the Office of Censorship out of numerous controversies. "A case in point was the famous episode . . ." In other words, the anecdote is meant to show a positive effect of Price's decision to let those directly involved select the information that would be made public. Choice **D**, therefore, is the best answer. Choices **A**, **B**, and **C** are not necessarily wrong, but none of them represents the essential reason that the author included the incident in the passage.

8. As he is portrayed in the passage, Price can most reasonably be characterized as:

   F. willing to go along with the demands of the military for strict censorship during the war.
   G. determined that the public's right to know would not be displaced by government's need to control information.
   H. willing to mediate in disputes that arose on censorship matters between the media and the military.
   J. surprised that he had been chosen to supervise government censorship during World War II, since he himself was a newspaperman.

This question asks you to reason inductively, to draw a general conclusion about Price from evidence in the passage. Basically, inductive thinking works this way:

Fact 1: Sylvie (a hypothetical lass) went outside without a coat when it was below zero.
Fact 2: She caught a cold.

General rule or principle to be drawn from these facts: Wear a coat when you go outside in sub-zero weather, or you'll end up like Sylvie.

Based on information in the passage, Price worked hard to solve the problem of balancing wartime secrecy with the public's right to know (lines 36–37). Choice **G**, therefore, is the best answer. His desire to be fair contradicts **F**. Rule out **H** because Price instituted a system of voluntary censorship in order to keep his office out of such controversies (lines 36–39). It's true that Price was a newspaperman (**J**), but his reaction to being appointed to the censorship job is not discussed in the passage.

9. It may be inferred from the passage that the system of self-censorship instituted in World War II found support among reporters and editors (lines 38–39) because:

A. journalists universally endorsed the war against Japan and Germany.
B. reporters and editors were given the responsibility of making the system work.
C. the news media often found themselves in conflict with the military.
D. rejection of the system would have put journalists' livelihood and reputation at stake.

To answer this question, identify the key words and phrases in the question, in this case "system of self-censorship" and "support among reporters and editors." From your initial reading of the passage, you may remember that these topics are discussed in the second half of the passage. If not, you must skim the entire passage until you come across references to self-censorship. Line 28 mentions the concept first: "the onus for censorship directly on the journalists." Once you have located the place, continue skimming in search of an idea that describes or implies the supportive response of reporters and journalists to the system of self-censorship.

Lines 36–39 suggest that, recognizing the difficulty of balancing wartime secrecy with the public's right to know, reporters and editors appreciated the government's faith in their good judgment. **A** exaggerates historical fact. Choice **C**, although true, does not explain why reporters and editors supported self-censorship. **D** also has merit but is not an issue discussed or implied by the passage. **B**, then, is the best answer. It explains why journalists supported Price's policy.

10. It is most reasonable to infer from the author's assertion in lines 59–60, "the news clampdown may have contributed to some of the (few) casualties that the bombs caused," that he means that:

F. informing the public would have enabled people to defend themselves against attack.
G. it would have been better to publish misleading information about the bombs than to publish nothing at all.
H. the Japanese would have stopped sending the bombs had they been given information about their ineffectiveness.
J. without the clampdown the Japanese might have launched even more bombs.

Because this question asks you for the underlying meaning of a specific quotation, go directly to the passage and read the quoted material in its context. Search for clues just before and after the quotation. If you fail to find a telling clue, determine, if possible, whether the author is saying something generally favorable, generally unfavorable, or neutral. By doing so, you may be able to eliminate one or more of the choices.

According to the passage, Price asked for some information to warn the public about the "potential danger of the balloon bombs." Because the information was not forthcoming, something unfavorable happened—namely, more casualties occurred. Eliminate choice **H** as a choice because it expresses a favorable idea. **G** is not mentioned or implied in the passage. Because **J** contradicts the author's intent, **F** is the correct answer. The author has concluded that fewer casualties might have occurred had the public been forewarned.

Warm-Up Drill

Now that you've seen the tactics used to answer many Social Studies questions, try your skills on the following passage. Answers and explanations follow the questions.

This passage is from a monograph titled "When School's Out and Nobody's Home" by Peter Coolsen et al. The passage discusses studies of children's reactions to coming home to an empty house after school.

How do children feel when they come home from school to an empty house or apartment? Do they feel lonely, deserted, resentful, and angry? Or do they feel proud, trusted, responsible, independent, and grown up? Or doesn't it matter very much one way or the other?

One of the most revealing portraits, albeit unscientific, came about as an accidental outcome of a survey by Sprint, a language arts magazine published for fourth- to sixth-grade children by Scholastic, Inc. Readers were invited to respond in writing to this theme: "Think of a situation that is scary to you. How do you handle your fear?" The editors got an overwhelming response—probably more than 7,000 letters all told, and 5,000 of them dealt with the fear of being home alone, mostly after school while parents were working.

There are other studies, carefully constructed, that bear out the findings suggested in the responses to Sprint. Long and Long report that many children in self-care fear attack from intruders and from other children, particularly siblings. Zill's national survey of children is consistent with these findings. Some 32% of the males and 41% of the females reported that they worried when they had to stay at home without an adult; 20% of both boys and girls admitted being afraid to go outside to play. Rodman and his colleagues, however, report no significant difference between children in self-care and children under the care of adults in a study conducted in a medium-sized city. Rodman contends that studies reporting more fear among children in self-care lack appropriate comparison groups and are subject to interviewer bias. Long and Long respond that their studies have probed more deeply, and that they have done a better job of establishing a relationship with children in which they can express their fear. Another explanation for the discrepancies is that the level of fear for children in self-care varies from setting to setting, being greatest for children in urban apartments (the focus of the Longs' research) and least for children whose homes are in safer small towns, rural areas, or close-knit neighborhoods.

Steinberg studied 865 children in grades five, six, eight, and nine in a small midwestern city. He classified their after-school experience on a continuum from "home with parent, other adult, or older sibling" to "unsupervised, hanging out." He found that the less directly supervised the children, the more likely they were to be susceptible to peer pressure (to conform to peer influence rather than make decisions for themselves). What is more, parents who use an "authoritative" approach rather than "authoritarian" or "permissive" ones have children who are less susceptible to peer influence. *Authoritative* here means parents who ask children for their opinions but maintain ultimate control.

Analyses of the calls children in self-care make to telephone support services provide additional clues to the child's experience. In State College, Pennsylvania, "PhoneFriend" provides a case in point. Of the 1,370 calls received during the first year of operation, 60% were classified as "just want to talk" or "bored," while 19% were classified as "lonely" and 15% as "scared," "worried," or "sad or crying." Relatively few dealt with practical emergencies such as cuts and scrapes (4%) or home maintenance problems (3%). (The system allowed multiple classification of each call, which is why those numbers add up to more than 100%.) Who did the calling? Children seven or younger made up 33% of the calls; another 33% were from eight- to nine-year-olds; 17% from ten- to eleven-year-olds; and 17% from children twelve and older. Most (82%) of the PhoneFriend volunteer responses were "affective," i.e., listening and reflecting feelings. Clearly one of the significant issues facing children in self-care is morale and peace of mind.

Peter Coolsen, Michelle Seligson, and James Garbarino,
"When School's Out and Nobody's Home"

1. As used in the passage, the term *self-care* is applied to children who:

   A. function well without adult supervision.
   B. participate in experiments of independent living.
   C. return to empty apartments and houses after school.
   D. are legally "neglected" and no longer live with their parents.

2. Steinberg (lines 28–34) found that children often left on their own:

   F. frequently make friends with older people.
   G. rapidly develop independence and self-sufficiency.
   H. spend an excessive amount of time "hanging out."
   J. are more than likely to be followers instead of leaders.

3. An analysis of calls to "PhoneFriend" shows that children phoned for all of the following reasons EXCEPT:

   A. a practical joke or prank.
   B. a feeling of isolation.
   C. boredom.
   D. an emergency situation.

4. Studies of children's feelings about self-care take into account all of the following reasons EXCEPT:

   F. the number of children in the family.
   G. age.
   H. where the children live.
   J. gender.

5. The research studies described in the passage indicate that the GREATEST need of children in self-care is:

   A. help in keeping unwanted intruders away from their homes.
   B. safe places to play.
   C. training in how to deal with emergencies.
   D. help in coping with their fears.

6. On the basis of the passage, which group of words most accurately describes how children feel about self-care?

   F. Disinterested, apathetic, unconcerned
   G. Embittered, resentful, upset
   H. Content, resigned, stoic
   J. Uncertain, fearful, sad

7. The passage states that peer influence is strongest on children whose parents:

   A. are permissive.
   B. fail to communicate with their children.
   C. are strict.
   D. involve them in family decisions.

8. Based on the passage, research findings about self-care are often contradictory for all of the following reasons EXCEPT that:

   F. some researchers use better methods than others.
   G. children are often unreliable sources of information.
   H. some researchers are better able to elicit valid information from children.
   J. researchers often study groups of children with different socioeconomic backgrounds.

9. The authors of the passage believe that the findings of the *Sprint* survey (line 6):

   A. should not be taken seriously.
   B. are interesting but not conclusive.
   C. contain information about children's fears too important to ignore.
   D. are enlightening but cannot be supported by evidence from more scientific studies.

10. Which of the following statements would NOT be a valid conclusion to draw from the *Sprint* survey (lines 5–11)?

    F. Children 9 to 11 years old often feel fearful and insecure.
    G. The parents of many fourth, fifth, and sixth graders work outside the home.
    H. Being left home alone is a cause of anxiety among children from 9 to 11 years old.
    J. Children in grades 4 to 6 enjoy writing letters about what scares them.

ANSWERS AND EXPLANATIONS

1. **(C)** The author's concern is children returning to empty homes after school. Choice A includes such children, but the term self-care also applies to children who fail to function well on their own. Neither B nor D is discussed in the passage.

2. **(J)** The passage states explicitly (lines 30–32) that children with little supervision are highly susceptible to peer pressure. F, G, and H describe situations that could develop among children left to fend for themselves, but Steinberg's findings do not include them.

3. **(A)** The phone calls cited in lines 36–41 were made because the children needed to talk with someone; no calls were made for frivolous reasons.

4. **(F)** Researchers did not include the number of children in the family as a variable in their studies. The passage indicates that the factors indicated in G, H, and J were taken into account.

5. **(D)** The passage refers to all the problems listed in A, B, C, and D, but the subject of children's fears receives the most attention.

6. **(J)** The adjectives that make up choices F, G, and H may accurately describe some of the children, but the passage emphasizes the fact that many children are unhappy and scared when they have to take care of themselves.

7. **(A)** Steinberg's study (lines 28–34) shows that children of permissive parents are most likely to be influenced by peers.

8. **(F)** The validity of social research is always beset with problems of uncertainty because of countless variables that researchers cannot take into account. Choices G, H, and J list typical variables associated with doing research on children. Omit F as a problem, however, because the passage does not discuss the inclination of many researchers to criticize their associates' methods of collecting data.

9. **(B)** The authors found the conclusions revealing but inconclusive because the research method was insufficiently scientific.

10. **(J)** Choices F, G, and H express valid findings of the *Sprint* survey. J is inaccurate, however. Although 7,000 children wrote letters, the paragraph provides no evidence that they enjoyed writing them.

HUMANITIES

Passages

The humanities passage on the ACT relates to such creative and cultural disciplines as art, music, architecture, theater, and dance, and even history. The passage may discuss Impressionist painting or the origins of jazz. It could be a portrait of Lady Gaga, an analysis of current sci-fi films, or a critique of modern dance—almost any sort of passage on a multitude of topics.

A passage about a cultural matter will sometimes consist only of *facts*. Consider this brief history of ballet costumes:

> Early in the history of ballet, dancers wore bulky but elaborate costumes on the stage. As dancers' technique improved, however, costumes were redesigned. They became lighter and revealed the movement and steps of the performers. By the start of the 18th century, ballet skirts had risen above the ankles, and heels had been removed from dancing slippers. Over time, as dancers developed spectacular movements and jumps, costumes continued to grow simpler, less cumbersome, and more revealing. Today, most ballet costumes weigh but a few ounces and cling tightly to the body of the dancers.

This passage is a factual chronology, sweeping across centuries in just a few sentences. As often as including a totally factual passage, the ACT will include a passage of interpretation dressed up as fact. A passage that after a quick reading may seem factual and objective may actually be full of opinions. Take this one, for instance, about Johann Strauss, the nineteenth-century composer known as the "Waltz King":

> Perhaps the Vienna that Johann Strauss immortalized in his waltzes never did exist, but the Viennese waltz as he perfected it became the symbol for millions at a time when the world was young and gay—a symbol of romance projected through the magic of three-four time.
>
> The great waltzes—Blue Danube, Wine, Women and Song, Artist's Life and the rest—are more than mere ballroom dances. They are an idealization of the spirit of the dance. Their flowing measures—by turn capricious, nostalgic, gay—capture the poetry of the waltz. . . .
>
> Joseph Machlis, *Johann Strauss*

TIP

Frequently on the ACT you are asked to distinguish between fact and opinion.

Everyone who reads this excerpt may agree fully with the author's statements about Strauss's music. Yet, the content is mostly interpretive. The only hard fact in the text is that Strauss wrote waltzes entitled "Blue Danube," "Wine, Women and Song," and "Artist's Life."

If the ACT humanities passage is not about present-day art and culture, it may be historical—about theater in the Middle Ages, ancient Greek architecture, or songs of World War II. Or you might find a piece of literary history, something like the following passage about the origins of the modern novel.

> The telling of tales is one of the earliest forms of human pastime, and its origins are lost in the mists of antiquity. From the primitive form of the fable, or example, as it was sometimes called, designed to teach some principle, it grew and took on a multitude of expressions which reflected the taste of successive epochs. Before Cervantes's day there existed all the derivations of the epic, the novels of extraordinary adventures, the romances of chivalry, the pastoral novels, the earliest of the Moorish and picaresque novels, these latter both of Spanish invention. But the novel as we know it today came into being with *Don Quixote.* All these preceding forms meet and fuse in a new and glorious synthesis. Cervantes was so in advance of his day that, despite the instant popularity of *Don Quixote*, it had no immediate successors; and it was not until the nineteenth century, when the novel came to be the prevailing literary mode, that his invention was fully understood and utilized. The realistic novel, what Thackeray called "the novel without a hero," dealing with ordinary people seen against their commonplace background, had its origins in Cervantes. And its finest cultivators, forerunners like Fielding, Stern, Smollett in the eighteenth century, Flaubert, Dickens, Dostoievsky, Pérez Galdós, our own Mark Twain, who was never without a copy of *Don Quixote* in his pocket, William Faulkner, who is quoted as saying that he has two passions, his daughter and *Don Quixote*—in short, all novelists deserving of the name have acquired the basic canons of their art directly or indirectly from Cervantes.
>
> Harriet de Onis, Introduction to Miguel de Cervantes, *Six Exemplary Novels*

Even if you've never heard of Miguel de Cervantes, you ought to remember his name after reading this passage. He is an outstanding figure in the history of literature. The central idea of the passage is that Cervantes's *Don Quixote* is the father of all modern novels. If you missed that point, the introductory material in the passage may have misled you. The lengthy account of storytelling before *Don Quixote* takes up almost half the passage. But then the author states the main idea plainly: "... the novel as we know it today came into being with *Don Quixote*."

On the ACT, in addition to recognizing the basic intent of the passage, you should also expect to locate some of its secondary ideas. For example, the author of the excerpt believes that literature reflects the values of the era in which it is written. Can you locate the place where that idea is stated or implied?

Another of the secondary ideas in the passage is that novelists influence each other's work. If you reread the passage now, you may well derive several more implications. Have you noticed that you're never told precisely why *Don Quixote* inspired Fielding, Flaubert, Faulkner, and the others? Perhaps that information is implied by the assertion that Cervantes fused several literary forms into a "glorious synthesis." Still another question to ponder is why *Don Quixote* was not fully appreciated until the nineteenth century.

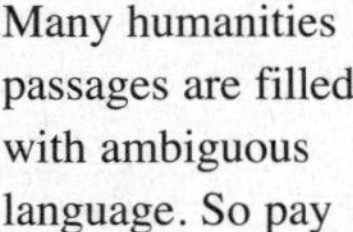

TIP

Many humanities passages are filled with ambiguous language. So pay attention.

Perhaps you've observed that the subject matter of the humanities doesn't always lend itself to exact answers. Unlike chemists or engineers, writers about art or literature must often rely on words rich in connotation but imprecise in meaning. Sometimes you encounter prose that can make you dizzy—take this sentence, for example, from the pen of an art critic: "With regard to the apprehension articulated by the nouveau minimalists, I consider the yearning for a new kind of harmony and new esthetic clarity as the cornerstone on which modern art will achieve unexpected rationality."

At the same time, though, many writers in the humanities express themselves with absolute grace and clarity. They pride themselves in expressing hard-to-grasp ideas in lucid and intelligible writing. In the following passage, listening to music is compared to traveling on a train. The author renders a highly individual and largely emotional experience in understandable, visual terms. As you read this passage, notice that it contains virtually no facts. Based solely on the author's perceptions, it describes what generally happens when a person listens to music.

When we listen to a musical work we are somewhat in the position of the traveler in a train who watches the landscape speed by his window. He carries away only a general impression. With each additional trip through the same territory, the details emerge from the mass and engrave themselves upon his mind—a house here, a clump of trees there—until the terrain has become a clear and familiar pattern.

So too our first hearing of a work is apt to leave us at best with a hazy image. As we become familiar with the piece, we grow increasingly aware of what is in it. First to engage our attention, of course, is the melody. For melody is the most directly appealing element of music. The melody is, what we sing and hum and whistle, what we associate most with inspiration. "It is the melody which is the charm of music," said Haydn a century and a half ago, "and it is that which is most difficult to produce. The invention of a fine melody is a work of genius."

The melody is the musical line that guides our ear throughout the composition. It is the basic idea of the piece, the theme—in much the same way that war or passion is the theme of a novel. It will be stated either at the outset or fairly early in a composition. It may disappear from view for a time; but sooner or later it will return, either in its original guise or in some altered form. The melody is the thread upon which hangs the tale, to which everything in the work is related; the link that binds the musical action into a unity. As Aaron Copland puts it, "the melody is generally what the piece is about."

In painting, the line is set off against a background that gives us perspective—the illusion of depth. Similarly in music the melody line does not exist alone. We hear melody against a background of harmony that supports and shades it, lending it richness, color, weight. Harmony is the element of depth in music. The third dimension.

Joseph Machlis, *How to Listen to Music*

If you found this passage on the ACT, you'd probably need to know that the writer's intent is to analyze the experience of listening to music, that melody moves a listener in several different ways, and that harmony supports melody. Moreover, you might need to grasp several other ideas not explicitly stated but strongly suggested, such as the idea implied by the whole passage that composers follow a number of complex principles as they write a piece of music.

Sample Questions

Of the ten questions that follow the humanities passage on the ACT, seven will be reasoning questions and the remainder, referring questions.

After reading the following passage about the American poet Robert Frost, answer the sample questions.

Louis Untermeyer in his introduction to a book of Frost's poems wrote that the character as well as the career of Robert Frost gives the lie to the usual misconceptions of the poet. Frost has been no less the ordinary man for being an extraordinary creator. The creator, the artist, the extraordinary man, is merely the ordinary man intensified; a person whose life is sometimes lifted to a high pitch of feeling and who has the gift of making others share his excitement.

There are curious contradictions in the life of Robert Frost. Though his ancestry was New England he was born in California; the most American of poets, he was first recognized in England and not in the U.S.; not believing in competitions he never entered them, yet he won the Pulitzer Prize four times; the "rough conversational tones" of his blank verse are remarkable for their lyrical music. Though he has chosen one part of the country on which to focus his poetry, no poetry so regional has ever been so universal.

Ruth Levin, *Ordinary Heroes: The Story of Shaftsbury*

Sample Referring Questions:

1. According to the passage, a distinctive quality of Frost's poetry is its:
   A. obvious symbolism.
   B. spirituality.
   C. unusual rhymes.
   D. association with one section of the country.

To answer this referring question, you must find words, phrases, and ideas in the passage that are similar in meaning to each of the choices. Skim the passage and notice that most of the first paragraph is about poets, while most of the second paragraph pertains to Frost's life and poetry. Therefore, look for the answer in the second paragraph.

Choice **A** refers to a quality not mentioned in the passage. **B** brings up an idea not discussed in the passage. **C** contradicts the passage, which states that Frost wrote blank verse, or poetry without rhyme. **D** paraphrases part of line 14. **D**, therefore, is correct.

2. According to the passage, Robert Frost could be considered "the most American of poets" for all of the following reasons EXCEPT that:
   F. his verses are often patriotic.
   G. his poetry often sounds like everyday American speech.
   H. his background is American.
   J. he focused his poetry on a specific section of America.

To answer this question, you must reread the passage and locate references to the four choices. The one you *don't* find is the correct answer. This variation in ACT questions calls for close reading and takes longer than single-choice answers, especially when you have to find material scattered throughout a full-length passage. In this question, though, all the references to "the most American of poets" are concentrated in the second paragraph.

Choice **F** refers to an idea *not* mentioned in the passage. **F** is correct. **G** is a reference to the "rough conversational tones" of Frost's poetry. **H** refers to the fact that his family came from New England. **J** alludes to the regionalism of Frost's poetry, mentioned in line 12 of the passage.

Sample Reasoning Questions:

3. The author of the passage believes that Robert Frost's life was:
   A. typical of a poet's life.
   B. extraordinary.
   C. rather ordinary.
   D. no different from that of farmers in Vermont.

Material that discusses the quality of Frost's life is found in lines 3–6. Look there to figure out which of the four choices most accurately describes the author's intent. Draw your conclusion only after you've carefully reread the entire paragraph and considered each choice separately.

Choice **A** is contradicted by lines 1–3 of the paragraph. Frost's life "gives the lie" to stereotypical images of poets. **B** seems to correspond with the author's intent. Frost is called both "an extraordinary creator" and an "extraordinary man." **B** is correct. **C** seems like a possible answer, but since Frost is called an "ordinary man intensified," he must be considered extraordinary. **D** is not related to material in the passage.

4. The passage suggests that a successful poet must:

   F. be misunderstood by society.
   G. avoid acting like an ordinary man.
   H. endow ordinary matters with excitement.
   J. invent new forms and styles of expression.

The correct answer to this reasoning question must be inferred from the first paragraph of the passage, where the author generalizes about successful poets.

Choice **F** may accurately describe many poets, but it brings up an idea not discussed in the passage. **G** may describe the behavior of some poets, but it is a generalization outside the scope of the passage. **H** closely resembles the description of a creative artist found in lines 4–6. **H** is correct. **J** raises a matter not discussed in the passage.

Now read the following humanities passage. It is about a trendy art movement called Pop Art that was all the rage back in the 1960s. Compare your technique for answering the questions to the approach explained in the analyses that follow.

American Pop art was created and developed in New York, but found rapid and early acceptance and a particular individual character on the West Coast, where activity was focused on the two centers of Los Angeles in the south and San Francisco in the north. Los Angeles emerged as the more important center, and was the first to recognize the genius of Andy Warhol, giving him his first one-man show as a fully fledged Pop artist in 1962. The city of Los Angeles itself, perhaps the most extraordinary urban environment in the world, was an important influence on West Coast Pop, and it is also, of course, the home of Hollywood, itself an important influence on Pop art everywhere. Equally significant are the various exotic subcultures that flourish in the area: those of the surfers, the hot-rodders, the drag-racers, the car customizers and the outlaw motor cycle clubs like Satan's Slaves and, most famous of all, Hell's Angels.

Commemorated in the title of Tom Wolfe's essay *The Kandy Kolored Tangerine Flake Streamline Baby*, the amazing paint jobs and baroque body-work created by the car customizers and the elaborate decorations of the California surfboards are examples of an industrial folk art of great impact and brilliance which has set the tone for much West Coast Pop art. So too are the bizarre drag-racing cars and hot rods, and so is the Hell's Angels' "chopped hog," a Harley-Davidson 74 which in the hands of the Angels is stripped down and rebuilt to become virtually a mobile piece of sculpture. The Angels' uniform is also a rich item of folk art, particularly the sleeveless denim jacket bearing the "colors": a winged skull wearing a motor cycle helmet with the name Hell's Angels above with, below, the letters MC and the local chapter name, e.g. San Bernardino. These jackets may be further decorated with chains, swastikas and other signs, slogans and emblems: such as the number 13 (indicating use of marijuana), the notorious red wings, or the Angels' motto "Born to lose."

The world of customizing and of the big bikes is strongly reflected in the work of one of the two major Los Angeles Pop artists. Billy Al Bengston has worked since 1960 on a series of paintings of chevrons and motor-bike badges and parts treated as heraldic devices, the images placed centrally on the canvas and painted in glowing colors with immaculate precision and a high degree of finish. About 1962 his painting took on an even greater richness and gloss, when he began to use sprayed cellulose paint on hardboard and later actually on sheets of metal, thus getting even closer to the technique and medium of his sources. Some of these metal sheet works are artfully crumpled, thus adding a suggestion of accident and death to the glamorous perfection of the painted emblem.

The other major Los Angeles Pop artist is Ed Ruscha (pronounced, the artist insists, as Ruschay). He began using Pop imagery (packaging) in 1960 in paintings like *Box Smashed Flat*, where presentation of commercial imagery and what looks like Edwardian commercial lettering is still combined with a painterly style. But his painting quickly took on an almost inhuman exquisiteness, precision and perfection of finish, as in *Noise* . . . of 1963.

Like [Robert] Indiana, Ruscha is fascinated by words, and these have always formed the principal subject matter of his paintings and graphics. In some works the words appear in isolation floating against backgrounds of beautifully graded color that give a feeling of infinite colored space. Sometimes associated images are introduced, such as the cocktail olive in *Sin*, and sometimes the word is given a specific context, as with the company names (e.g. "Standard") for which the architecture becomes a setting in Ruscha's garage paintings (*Standard Station, Amarillo, Texas*). One lithograph, where the word Hollywood streams unforgettably out of the sunset in the steep zooming perspective and giant lettering of wide-screen title sequences, exemplifies the manner in which Ruscha depicts his words in such a way that their meaning is conveyed pictorially as well as verbally.

Garages in themselves are one of Ruscha's most important motifs after words. They first appear in his work in 1962, not in painting or graphic work, but in a book: *Twenty-six Gasoline Stations*, consisting of 26 absolutely deadpan, factual, non-arty photographs of Western garages. The attitude behind these photographs comes very close to that of the New York Pop artists, and especially Warhol: the acceptance of aspects of the world which no one had considered in an art context before.

Simon Wilson, *Pop*

1. Based on the passage, it seems that California is uniquely qualified to host the Pop art movement because:

   A. California is the home of many unconventional people and trends.
   B. Andy Warhol lived there.
   C. New York art critics rejected certain styles of Pop art.
   D. as a big state, California has more open space for displaying Pop.

Concentrate your search for the answer on the first paragraph of the passage, which describes California lifestyles and subcultures. Infer from the description why California was receptive to Pop art. Or, conversely, what is there about Pop art that appealed to people in California?

Choice **A** supports what line 9 implies, that the unconventional quality of California life has provided this unconventional art form a hospitable place to take root and grow. **A** is correct. **B** is wrong because, according to line 56, Andy Warhol was a New York Pop artist. **C** is not supported by the passage. **D** may be a valid observation, but it is not mentioned in the passage.

2. The term *folk art*, as used in the passage, can best be defined as:

   F. a form of primitive, crudely executed art.
   G. art that emphasizes bizarre and fantastic themes.
   H. art that is created by amateur artists and artisans.
   J. the design and decoration of everyday objects.

To interpret the term, skim the passage to find where folk art is discussed. In line 10, the author calls surfboards, drag-racing cars, a Harley-Davidson, and Hell's Angels' uniforms examples of folk art. All are objects that are not commonly thought to be art. After being decorated and redesigned, however, they qualify as examples of folk art.

Choice **F** is not a good one, because folk art is not necessarily primitive or crudely done. **G** is wrong, because folk art gets its identity not from its themes, but from the objects themselves. **H** is wrong, because some folk artists are professionals. **J** is implied by the second paragraph, which lists everyday objects as examples of folk art. **J** is correct.

3. All of the following are cited in the passage as examples of California folk art EXCEPT:

A. the uniforms of the Hell's Angels.
B. decorated surfboards.
C. Ruscha's photographs of gasoline stations.
D. hot rods with unusual and bizarre paint jobs.

To answer this question, skim the passage for references to folk art. Look for the specific examples listed in the four choices. Before you decide on the correct answer, however, you must infer the author's definition of folk art from the examples given in lines 9–24. The choice that *doesn't* fit the definition is the answer to the question.

Choices **A**, **B**, and **D** qualify as folk art. **C** does *not* fall into the category of folk art. **C** is correct.

4. West Coast Pop was influenced by all of the following EXCEPT:

F. the surfboard subculture.
G. the movie industry.
H. motorcycle clubs.
J. Los Angeles freeways.

Skim the first half of the passage (lines 1 to 34), where influences on West Coast Pop are discussed. The influence *not* specifically stated is the answer to the question.

Choices **F** and **H** are named as an influence in lines 9–24. **G** is named as an influence in lines 7–8. **J** is *not* mentioned in the passage. **J** is correct.

5. Based on information in the passage, whose creative work is least likely to be shown in a museum of Pop art?

A. Robert Indiana
B. Tom Wolfe
C. Billy Al Bengston
D. Andy Warhol

To answer this question, find references in the passage to the work of each person. Which of them is not a Pop artist?

Choice **A** is an artist whose work is discussed in lines 41–42. **B** is a writer, not a Pop artist, according to line 12. **B** is correct. **C** is "one of the two major Los Angeles Pop artists" (lines 26–34). **D** is a major figure in Pop art, according to lines 5 and 6.

6. Which of the following statements about Pop art is supported by information in the passage?

F. Pop is a form of artistic expression that flouts conventionality.
G. Pop is an influential movement in the history of American art.
H. Pop is a short-lived, but powerful, artistic fad.
J. Pop is an eccentric movement that should not be taken seriously.

This question asks you to draw a conclusion from information in the passage. Try to locate material in the passage that supports each choice.

Choice **F** is an excellent one, because much of the passage discusses the odd creations of Pop artists. **F** is correct. Although **G** may be true at some time in the future, it is not now, however. Also, the passage does not mention Pop's influence on American art. **H** may be true, but the passage does not mention the duration of the Pop art movement. **J** expresses an opinion not in the passage.

7. Based on information in the passage, one might infer that the creations of both Bengston and Ruscha have been influenced by:

   A. life on and along the highways.
   B. the Los Angeles scene.
   C. the drug culture.
   D. Hollywood movies.

To answer this question, reread the accounts of Bengston and Ruscha in lines 25 through 51. Then, reason out the best answer.

Choice **A** is a good one, because car customizing and motorcycles are reflected in Bengston's work. Lines 46 and 52 indicate that Ruscha painted garages. Both artists apparently have been influenced by things of the highway. **A** is correct. **B** alludes to the fact that both artists come from Los Angeles, but the city has not been influential on their art. **C** is not mentioned as an influence on their art. **D** is not mentioned as a factor in their art.

8. The author implies that the freshest and most original works of Pop art are:

   F. Bengston's crumpled sheets of metal.
   G. Ruscha's photographs of garages.
   H. customized cars.
   J. paintings of boxes and packages.

To answer this question, infer what the author thought about each of the works listed. Which opinion includes a description similar in meaning to the phrase "freshest and most original?"

Choices **F** and **H** are not described as fresh and original. **G** is compared to Andy Warhol's works, which portray "aspects of the world which no one had considered in an art context before" (lines 56–57). Thus, Ruscha, like Warhol, is an original! **G** is correct. **J** is called many things but not fresh or original.

9. Based on the passage, the most important distinguishing feature of West Coast Pop is its:

   A. slick superficiality.
   B. derivation from local industrial folk art.
   C. wild colors and designs.
   D. use of symbolism.

TIP 

Look for main ideas in general paragraphs instead of detailed, narrowly focused paragraphs.

This question asks you to pick the single most important idea about West Coast Pop from a passage containing dozens of ideas on the topic. To find the answer, either skim or carefully read the whole passage. Focus on opening and closing paragraphs, paying particular attention to the first and last sentences of each. In one of those places you're likely to find the main idea or at least a clue that will lead you to the main idea. To answer this question, don't bother to look at the second half of the passage, which focuses narrowly on the work of individual artists. Main ideas show up more frequently in more general paragraphs. Another popular location for main ideas is the start of a passage's second paragraph. After writing an introductory paragraph, authors usually present their main ideas. If you can't find a main idea stated anywhere, you must infer it from your impression of the whole passage.

Choices **A** and **D** are not mentioned as essential elements of West Coast Pop. **B** is stated outright in lines 14–16. **B** is correct. **C** is mentioned, but not sufficiently to be the main idea.

10. Which of the following statements about New York Pop is implied in the passage?

   F. Symbolism is an important ingredient of New York Pop art.
   G. New York Pop artists create more sensational works than West Coast Pop artists.
   H. New York Pop contains more humor than West Coast Pop.
   J. New York Pop art portrays fewer fantasy and dreamlike images than West Coast Pop.

To answer this question, look through the passage for references to New York Pop (line 56). Draw an inference based on information you find.

Choice **F** is not mentioned in the passage. **G** is wrong. All the evidence suggests the opposite. **H** is wrong. The passage suggests the opposite. **J** is supported by the final paragraph, which says that Ruscha's photos of 26 gas stations resemble New York Pop: "deadpan, factual, non-arty." New York Pop artists, it seems, are not given to dreamlike, fantastic subjects. **J** is correct.

Warm-Up Drill

Try your hand at the following humanities passage and questions. Use question-answering tactics that you learned while working on the preceding sample questions. Answers and explanations follow the questions.

Historically the journey that jazz has taken can be traced with reasonable accuracy. That it ripened most fully in New Orleans seems beyond dispute although there are a few deviationists who support other theories of its origin. Around 1895 the almost legendary Buddy Bolden and Bunk Johnson were blowing their cornets in the street and in the funeral parades which have always enlivened the flamboyant social life of that uncommonly vital city. At the same time, it must be remembered, Scott Joplin was producing ragtime on his piano at the Maple Leaf Club in Sedalia, Missouri; and in Memphis, W.C. Handy was evolving his own spectacular conception of the blues.

Exactly why jazz developed the way it did on the streets of New Orleans is difficult to determine even though a spate of explanations has poured forth from the scholars of the subject. Obviously the need for it there was coupled with the talent to produce it and a favorable audience to receive it. During those early years the local urge for musical expression was so powerful that anything that could be twanged, strummed, beaten, blown, or stroked was likely to be exploited for its musical usefulness. For a long time the washboard was a highly respected percussion instrument, and the nimble, thimbled fingers of Baby Dodds showed sheer genius on that workaday, washday utensil.

The story of the twenties in Chicago is almost too familiar to need repeating here. What seems pertinent is to observe that jazz gravitated toward a particular kind of environment in which its existence was not only possible but, seen in retrospect, probable. On the South Side of Chicago during the twenties the New Orleans music continued an unbroken development.

The most sensationally successful of all jazz derivatives was swing, which thrived in the late thirties. Here was a music that could be danced to with zest and listened to with pleasure. (That it provided its younger auditors with heroes such as Shaw, Sinatra, and Goodman is more of a sociological enigma than a musical phenomenon.) But swing lost its strength and vitality by allowing itself to become a captive of forces concerned only with how it could be sold; not how it could be enriched. Over and over it becomes apparent that jazz cannot be sold even when its practitioners can be bought. Like a truth, it is a spiritual force, not a material commodity.

During the closing years of World War II, jazz, groping for a fresh expression, erupted into bop. Bop was a wildly introverted style developed out of a certain intellectualism and not a little neuroticism. By now the younger men coming into jazz carried with them a GI subsidized education and they were breezily familiar with the atonalities of Schönberg, Bartók, Berg, and the contemporary schools of music. The challenge of riding out into the wide blue yonder on a twelve-tone row was more than they could resist. Some of them have never returned. Just as the early men in New Orleans didn't know what the established range of their instruments was, so these new musicians struck out in directions which might have been untouched had they observed the academic dicta adhering even to so free a form as jazz.

The shelf on jazz in the music room of the New York Public Library fairly bulges with volumes in French, German, and Italian. It seems strange to read in German a book called the *Jazzlexikon* in which you will find scholarly résumés of such eminent jazzmen as Dizzy Gillespie and Cozy Cole. And there are currently in the releases of several record companies examples of jazz as played in Denmark, Sweden, and Australia. Obviously the form and style are no longer limited to our own country. And jazz, as a youthful form of art, is listened to as avidly in London as in Palo Alto or Ann Arbor.

Arnold Sungaard, "Jazz, Hot and Cold"

1. Based on the passage, one can infer that the origin of modern jazz is:

A. traceable to the streets of New Orleans.
B. too obscure to be precisely identified.
C. the blues songs of the early twentieth century.
D. the music of slaves in the South.

2. According to the passage, early jazz was primarily a form of:

F. funeral music.
G. piano music rearranged for other instruments.
H. music arranged by bandleaders.
J. songs performed by street musicians and vocalists.

3. The passage indicates that swing declined in popularity because:

A. bop replaced it.
B. swing is not a true derivative of jazz.
C. swing became too commercialized.
D. musical tastes changed as a result of World War II.

4. According to the passage, the appeal of swing music lies primarily in its:

F. beautiful melodies.
G. brassy sound.
H. catchy lyrics.
J. rhythms.

5. The author's main purpose in the passage is to:

   A. explain why jazz is played all over the world.
   B. trace the origins of jazz.
   C. show the influence of jazz on popular music.
   D. describe the main characteristics of jazz.

6. It can be inferred from the passage that New Orleans was a hospitable place for jazz to develop because of the city's:

   F. flamboyant social life.
   G. proximity to the Mississippi River.
   H. acceptance of Baby Dodds.
   J. musical tradition.

7. That the author finds it "strange" (line 41) to read foreign books about jazz and to hear recordings of jazz from abroad implies that:

   A. non-Americans lack the spirit and soul for jazz.
   B. jazz played abroad is an imitation of the real thing.
   C. future developments in jazz may come from unexpected places.
   D. jazz is a uniquely American art form.

8. All of the following descriptions of bop also apply to jazz EXCEPT:

   F. bop arose out of a need for a new form of music.
   G. bop was improvised and spontaneously performed.
   H. bop began as a reaction to existing schools of musical thought.
   J. bop was influenced by earlier forms of music.

9. By calling the rise of Shaw, Sinatra, and Goodman a "sociological enigma" (line 25), the author implies that the three musicians:

   A. were not appreciated solely for their musical talent.
   B. do not seem like typical heroes for young people.
   C. took a long time to become popular.
   D. enjoyed enormous popularity in their day.

10. The author's assertion in lines 31–32 that bop "developed out of a certain intellectualism and not a little neuroticism" means that bop musicians:

    F. knew that jazz could benefit from musical techniques invented by classical composers.
    G. understood modern music and needed to experiment with newer musical techniques.
    H. made a thoughtful effort to push jazz to its limits.
    J. tried out new musical forms to show their dissatisfaction with the state of contemporary music.

ANSWERS AND EXPLANATIONS

1. **(B)** The correct choice, B, is suggested by the first paragraph, which cites several different theories about the origin of jazz. A is just one of the theories given in the first paragraph. C is not mentioned as an origin of jazz. D is not discussed in the passage.

2. **(F)** This correct answer is supported by line 5, which shows the link between early jazz and funeral parades in New Orleans. G suggests the music of Scott Joplin, but, in the early days of jazz, Joplin's music was performed only on the piano. H contrasts with the spontaneity associated with early jazz. J is not discussed in the passage.

3. **(C)** This answer is correct, because it affirms the statement in lines 25–27 about swing's loss of strength and vitality. A is true, but, according to the passage, swing was already in decline when bop became popular. B contradicts information given in line 22 about swing music. D is not discussed in the passage.

4. **(J)** Rhythm gives swing its appeal, particularly to dancers. The passage states that swing "could be danced to with zest" (line 23). F is not a quality of swing music. G is a part of swing music's appeal, but not its most appealing quality. H is not a characteristic of swing music.

5. **(C)** This answer reveals the primary concern of most of the passage. A is discussed in lines 40–46, but it is too limited to be the passage's main purpose. B is discussed early in the passage, but is also too limited to be the main purpose of the passage. D is mentioned throughout the passage, but does not receive the emphasis it needs to be the main purpose.

6. **(J)** This correct choice is supported by the statement in lines 9–12 that New Orleans had a need for jazz, the talent to produce it, and a favorable audience to receive it. F exemplified the lifestyle of New Orleans, but did not cause jazz to develop. G is not mentioned in the passage. H is an example of one musician, but it took more than one person to provide jazz with a home.

7. **(D)** This answer is suggested by the contents of the final paragraph. A contains a criticism of foreign musicians that the passage does not imply. B is not implied by the passage. C may be a valid observation, but it is not implied in the passage.

8. **(H)** The correct choice, H, applies only to bop. F is common to both jazz and bop, according to line 11. G is common to both jazz and bop, although jazz is probably freer than bop. J applies to jazz as well as to bop.

9. **(B)** This is a reference to the unusual excitement that these three unlikely heroes evoked among young fans in the late 30's and the 40's. A is not implied by the phrase or by the passage itself. C is not implied by the passage. D is true, but in the context of the passage the enigma refers more specifically to popularity among young people.

10. **(G)** Choice G is supported by the passage: Many bop composers were educated and could not resist "riding out . . . on a twelve-tone row." F implies that bop musicians wanted to make jazz better, but jazz did not need help, only "fresh expression." H may have been what some bop musicians had in mind, but the idea is not stated or implied in the passage. J is only half right. Bop musicians sought new forms, but they were not dissatisfied with the music of their day.

NATURAL SCIENCE

Passages

Out of a flood of publications by biologists, ecologists, chemists, physicists, geologists, and other natural scientists, the ACT questioners pick one passage. It comes from a textbook or an article, a research or lab report—from almost any scientific writing. The only certainty is that it pertains to the natural world.

TIP 

There is no science fiction on the Science Test of the ACT.

A passage of scientific writing can be a wide-ranging story about the world's endangered species. Or it can be an excerpt from a report on hypothermia, or the greenhouse effect, or volcanoes, or brain waves. Whatever the topic, the passage will probably contain many factual statements, along with statistics and other data, all intended to give an accurate account of reality.

Science writers usually adopt a serious tone. They write dispassionately, because personal feelings have little place in scientific reporting. Yet, in the following passage, the writer seems almost unable to suppress his admiration for the methods that science has devised for collecting and storing huge amounts of gene- and genome-related data.

For most of its history, biology managed to amass its data mostly with the help of plain old arithmetic. By contrast, today's genetic research creates too much data for one person, or even a scientific team, to understand. New technologies are needed to manage this huge amount of data.

Consider this: Gene-sequencing machines can read hundreds of thousands of nucleotides a day. Gene chips are even faster. The information in GenBank, a widely used database of all known DNA sequences, now doubles in just three years. A single laboratory doing cutting-edge research can generate hundreds of gigabytes of data a day, every day. For comparison, 100 gigabytes could hold an entire floor of journals in an academic library.

How can anyone make sense of all this information? The only way is to enlist the aid of computers and software that can store the data and make it possible for researchers to organize, search, and analyze it. In fact, many of today's challenges in biology, from gene analysis to drug discovery, are really challenges in information technology. This is not surprising when you remember that DNA is itself a form of information storage.

Where are genetic and genomic data stored? One of the first biological databases was created to store the huge volume of data from experiments with the fruit fly *Drosophila melanogaster.*

Called Flybase, it has grown into a huge, comprehensive, international electronic repository for information on *Drosophila* genetics and molecular biology, run by scientists for scientists. The information spans a century's worth of published scientific literature on *Drosophila melanogaster* and its relatives, including their complete genome sequence.

Several other communities of researchers have created their own databases, including those dedicated to investigation of the roundworm *Caenorhabditis elegans* (Wormbase), the soil-dwelling amoeba *Dictyostelium discoideum* (*DictyBase*) and the strain of yeast used for many laboratory studies (*Saccharomyces* Genome Database).

A key goal is to make sure that all these databases can "talk" to each other. For database communication to work, researchers in different fields must use the same terms to describe biological processes. The development and use of such universal "ontology"—a common language—is helping scientists analyze the complex network of biology that underlies our health.

The New Genetics, published by the
National Institute of General Medical Sciences,
National Institutes of Health, 2010

Analysis

If the preceding excerpt appeared on the ACT, it would have been introduced, like all reading passages on the exam, by a short description of its origin. Knowing that it came from the National Institutes of Health, you may have anticipated that its tone would be serious and its information, dated 2010, mostly up to date. You may also have expected that the National Institutes of Health, an institution that depends on federal funds, would be cast in a favorable light. Such a slant needn't undermine the credibility of the passage, however.

Remember: You're being tested only on the content of the passage, not on what you may have learned about the subject elsewhere.

Chances are that on the ACT you'd be asked about the main idea of the passage. If you picked an answer that alluded to the necessity of researchers to employ information technology (in the third paragraph), you'd be 100% right. Other questions could pertain to the history, usefulness, and distribution of genetic data as well as recent changes in the way data is gathered, stored, and shared among scientists.

Perhaps you studied genetics in your high school biology class. If so, this passage may not have told you anything new. But don't rely totally on what you learned in school. Although prior knowledge may convince you that you know all the answers, don't pick them unless they're supported by evidence in the passage.

Another type of writing from the natural sciences is meant to alert readers to a problem. Few published works about the deteriorating environment, for example, are strictly informative. Lethal air and filthy water are not subjects to be unemotional about. Notice that the following passage, while informative, also holds a warning about contaminating one of the earth's major sources of clean water:

Most groundwater originates as precipitation, percolates into the soil much as water fills a sponge, and moves from place to place along fractures in rock, through sand and gravel, or through channels in formations such as cavernous limestone. Constantly encountering resistance from the surrounding material, groundwater moves in a manner considerably different from that of surface water. Varying with the type of formation, its flow ranges from a fraction of an inch to a few feet per day. These movement characteristics are important to an understanding of groundwater contamination, since concentrations of pollutants called plumes will also move very slowly, with little dilution or dispersion.

"Unconfined" aquifers are the most susceptible to contamination. These aquifers are not protected by an overlying layer of impermeable material and may occur fairly close to the land surface. The volume of water available in unconfined aquifers will fluctuate with usage and with seasonal replenishment or "recharging" of the source of precipitation.

In contrast to this type of aquifer is the "confined" aquifer which is bounded on top and below by layers of relatively impermeable material. Confined aquifers generally occur at greater depths and their impermeable layers may offer a certain measure of protection from contamination. Some confined aquifers have no recharge zone at all and must be recognized as a finite resource which cannot be replenished.

Concern, Inc. *Groundwater*

Unlike the author who wrote about genetics, this one doesn't hand you the main point of the passage. Rather, the idea that groundwater must be understood in order to keep it pure is dispersed throughout the discussion. In addition to being aware of the writer's point of view about groundwater, you may be required to know the differences between confined and unconfined aquifers, to have a general idea of how water moves underground, and to recognize how aquifers become polluted.

Your aim is to discover the general message of the passage. No passage on the ACT will be beyond reach.

The passage contains some specialized language. The word *aquifer* is used several times, so often in fact, that it's hard not to know what it means by the end of the passage. The word *plumes* appears in the first paragraph, but the writer defines it. *Percolates* is also defined. *Impermeable,* while not a technical word, can give you trouble. Since *impermeable* material is contrasted with spongy material, the meaning becomes apparent.

Required reading in most school science courses is often far more exacting than the science passage on the ACT. While taking chemistry or earth science in school, you are immersed in the subject, and your teachers and texts take you deep into its contents. The natural science passage on the ACT, on the other hand, is accessible to the general reader. The two samples of science writing you've seen so far offer no insurmountable challenges to an alert college-bound student. But you must also be ready for more difficult reading, a passage taken from the literature of scientific research, for example. Researchers often fill their reports with the technical terms of their disciplines. Don't get stuck on these specialized words and phrases.

The following passage reports on the cytoskeleton of cells—that is, on the internal structure that keeps a cell from collapsing or changing its shape.

Many cells in a multicellular organism must combine the seemingly contradictory traits of stability and mobility. With few exceptions, multicellular organisms begin to develop when a motile sperm meets an egg. Many cell divisions occur, and then cells migrate to their final positions. During life, individual cells divide frequently, and certain specialized cells move through the body to accomplish various tasks. In addition, every cell must have a mechanism for moving materials within itself. Balancing the need for movement is the requirement for cell stability. A cell must maintain its shape against the pressure of surrounding cells. Keeping a cell firm while enabling it to move are the twin roles played by the cytoskeleton.

For a long time, microscopists believed that the cytoplasm surrounding the cell's organelles was completely unstructured. But as scientists began to use newer and gentler fixitives to prepare cells for electron microscopy, a lacy network of fibers was revealed. These structures crisscross the cell like girders and it was hypothesized (and later shown experimentally) that, like an animal's bony skeleton, these structures play a role in giving the cell its shape. For this reason, they are known collectively as the cytoskeleton.

There are three main kinds of cytoskeletal fibers—microfilaments, microtubules, and intermediate filaments—which are distinguishable both by their structure and by their protein composition. All three support and stiffen the cell. In addition to their structural roles, microtubules and microfilaments are essential for a variety of dynamic whole-cell activities, including division, contraction, and crawling, as well as for the movement of vesicles within the cell.

"The Cytoskeleton, the Cell's Physical Props"

The passage contains some technical concepts and language from the field of microbiology, but don't let the terminology discourage you. On the ACT you will not be asked details that involve knowledge of highly specialized language, so if you've never even heard of *cytoskeletons*, *microtubules*, and *vesicles*, it's still possible to make sense of the passage.

Sample Questions

Six reasoning questions and four referring questions follow the Natural Science passage on the ACT. Answer the two samples of each after you read this passage on whales.

No animal in prehistoric or historic times has ever exceeded the whale, in either size or strength, which explains perhaps its survival from ancient times. Few people have any idea of the relative size of the whale compared with other animals. A large specimen weighs about ninety tons, or thirty times as much as an elephant, which beside a whale appears about as large as a dog compared to an elephant. It is equivalent in bulk to one hundred oxen, and outweighs a village of one thousand people. If cut into steaks and eaten, as in Japan, it would supply a meal to an army of one hundred and twenty thousand men.

Whales have often exceeded one hundred feet in length, and George Brown Goode, in his report on the United States Fisheries, mentions a finback having been killed that was one hundred and twenty feet long. A whale's head is sometimes thirty-five feet in circumference, weighs thirty tons, and has jaws twenty feet long, which open thirty feet wide to a mouth that is as large as a room twenty feet long, fifteen feet high, nine feet wide at the bottom, and two feet wide at the top. A score of Jonahs standing upright would not have been unduly crowded in such a chamber.

The heart of a whale is the size of a hogshead. The main blood artery is a foot in diameter, and ten to fifteen gallons of blood pour out at every pulsation. The tongue of a right whale is equal in weight to ten oxen, while the eye of all whales is hardly as large as a cow's, and is placed so far back that it has in direction but a limited range of vision. The ear is so small that it is difficult to insert a knitting needle, and the brain is only about ten inches square. The head, or "case" contains about five hundred barrels, of ten gallons each, of the richest kind of oil, called spermaceti.

Whale Fishery of New England

Sample Referring Questions:

1. According to the passage, whales, in addition to being unusually large creatures, are also distinctively:

A. fast swimmers.
B. powerful.
C. adaptable to their environment.
D. intelligent.

As suggested for previous referring questions, skim the passage for thoughts and ideas that refer specifically to each choice.

Choice **A** is not mentioned in the passage. **B** corresponds to information about the strength of whales in the first sentence of the passage. **B** is correct. **C** is not discussed in the passage. **D** contradicts the information in lines 20–21 about the very small size of a whale's brain.

2. According to the passage, all parts of a whale are physically huge EXCEPT its:

F. heart.
G. mouth.
H. eyes.
J. tongue.

To answer this question, find a reference to each body part of the whale. If the passage doesn't mention that part or if it fails to say how big it is, you have probably found the answer.

Choice **F** is described in line 16. The heart is the "size of a hogshead." If you don't know the dimension of a hogshead, you can infer it from the next sentence, which tells you about the one-foot diameter of a whale's main artery. **G** is described in lines 12–15. The mouth is the size of a large room. **H** is discussed in lines 18 and 19. The whale's eye is "hardly as large as a cow's." **H** is the correct answer. **J** is described in lines 17 and 18. The tongue of a right whale weighs as much as ten oxen.

Sample Reasoning Questions:

3. It can reasonably be inferred from the passage that whales often grow as long as:

A. 35 feet.
B. 100 feet.
C. 120 feet.
D. 185 feet

Answer this question as you did previous reasoning questions. From information in the passage, draw a reasonable conclusion about the usual size of whales.

Choice **A** is smaller than any whale mentioned in the passage. **B** is a reasonable answer based on the fact that whales "have often exceeded one hundred feet in length" (line 9). **B** is correct. **C** describes the size of a whale cited as an exceptionally long one. **D** is larger than any whale mentioned in the passage.

4. The passage suggests that people have used whales in all of the following ways EXCEPT:

F. as a source of oil.
G. for sport fishing.
H. as food.
J. as a subject for stories.

Notice that the question uses the word "suggests." That means you probably won't find specific material in the passage about people's use of whales. Look for implications. The correct answer will be the implication that is *not* in the passage.

Choice **F** refers to material at the end of the passage. People use the "richest kind of oil, called spermaceti." **G** is *not* in the passage. **G** is the correct answer. **H** refers to a statement in lines 6–7 that whalesteak is eaten in Japan. **J** alludes to the biblical story of Jonah and the whale, mentioned in lines 14–15.

Here is a Natural Science passage about hibernation. After you have read it, answer the ten sample questions. Compare your approach to the analysis following each question.

Have you ever wondered what it is that tells groundhogs when to begin hibernating in winter and when to awaken in spring? Biologists have, for if they could tap that enzyme, chemical, gene or whatever, they might be able to apply it to other species, including man.

Line

Hibernation, unlike sleep, is a process in which all unnecessary bodily functions are discontinued, for example, growth. The animal's body temperature remains about 1° above the temperature of its environment. During this period, animals appear to be immune to disease and if subjected to a lethal dose of radiation, the animal will not die until the hibernation period is over. (As a point of interest, bears do not hibernate, they only sleep more deeply in winter.)

Early in the 20th century, Dr. Max Rubner proposed that aging was a result of the amount of energy expended in tissues. "Rubner found that the total lifetime energy expenditure per gram of tissue during the adult stage is roughly constant for several species of domestic animals. 'The higher the metabolism, the shorter the life span and vice versa.'"

In this vein, scientists found that the storage of body fat was vital to a hibernating animal's survival: it loses 20–40 percent of its body weight while dormant. The body fat involved here is called "brown fat" and differs structurally from normal, white fat cells which gives it a greater heat producing potential. A low temperature signals the brown fat to increase in temperature, which warms the animal's blood and spreads the warmth to other parts of the body. Newborn human babies have an unusually high percentage of brown fat which diminishes as they grow older. Adults do have some brown fat, and those with underproductive thyroid glands have more than normal:

> Rats subjected to cold temperatures show an increased ratio of brown fat to white fat. It seems reasonable to expect that cold acclimation in man, through a carefully controlled program of cyclic hypothermia . . ., will increase brown fat deposits. After these deposits reach a certain body level, they might perform the same regulatory functions in human hibernation that brown fat performs in natural hibernators.

About ten years after Rubner's experiments, Drs. Jacques Loeb and John Northrop discovered that reduced temperatures extended the life span of fruit flies. In applying this to animals, however, those that were not natural hibernators or who had not been prepared for hibernation, developed ventricular fibrillations (where the heart muscle quivers and stops pumping blood). When a person "freezes to death" this is the cause, not ice crystals forming in the veins.

The process involved in artificially cooling an animal's body temperature is called induced hypothermia. Research in this field led space biologist Dale L. Carpenter (McDonnell Douglas—Long Beach) to determine that both hibernating and non-hibernating animals have the same basic temperature control and he believes that "were a non-hibernating mammal to be artificially biochemically prepared with proper enzymes and energy producing chemicals, it could hibernate." He found that if an animal was cooled just until its heart began quivering and then rewarmed, it could survive. If cooled a second time, a slightly lower temperature could be achieved before ventricular fibrillations occurred, and so on. Each exposure to the cold seemed to condition the heart to accept lower temperatures. This is cyclic hypothermia.

Even with this kind of progress, however, the search goes on for the chemical or enzyme that triggers the hibernation process, that tells the animals it is winter or spring. Scientists hope to gain some insight into this mystery from human infants, who besides having more brown fat than adults, seem less susceptible to ventricular fibrillations. They have different forms of hemoglobin and myoglobin in their tissues which are more efficient in attracting and releasing oxygen. This may hold the clue.

If hibernation could be induced in humans, this could solve the problem of interstellar travel. One would not have to worry about travelling near the speed of light, for the crew would not age as fast and would have more time to reach their destination. Maxwell Hunter suggests that this "biological time dilation" be applied not only to the crews, but to those that remain on Earth.

> We are thus faced with the prospect of a whole society dilated in time. This would form the basis for a Galactic Club which was based on travel rather than communication. . . .
>
> We are not talking about timefaring in the classic science fiction sense where people are able to go both backward and forward in time at will . . . We are postulating, rather, dilating the time experienced by people in one direction in the future . . . which would permit a society to expand throughout the galaxy. If, when one went to bed at night, he actually went into hibernation during which many months passed, it would not seem any different to him than a standard eight-hour sleep . . . When a ship returned home, its crew would be greeted by friends, business colleagues, etc. who had aged no more than the crew.

Report of the Committee on Science and Technology,
"The Possibility of Intelligent Life in the Universe"

1. The information in lines 34–35 that freezing to death is not caused by ice crystals in the veins implies that:

   A. the research findings of Drs. Loeb and Northrop cannot be trusted.
   B. death by freezing results from several complex causes.
   C. readers should not believe the old wives' tales about ice crystals in the veins.
   D. freezing is altogether different from ordinary frostbite.

Because the sentence in lines 34–35 is worded like a fact, its implications, if any, seem well hidden. But note the quotation marks around "freezes to death," an indication that the phrase shouldn't be taken literally. In effect, the author has signaled that the phrase is not scientifically accurate, that contrary to popular belief, a death brought on by extreme cold cannot be attributed to the actual freezing of blood or by the freezing of any other part of the body.

Choice **A** is irrelevant. **B** may sound right, but notice the ambiguous word "several." The passage states the death is caused by ventricular fibrillation, which is a single cause, not "several" causes. **C** implies that many people believe that "freezing to death" occurs when ice crystals form in the veins. Here, the author is setting the record straight. **C** is correct. **D** is a poor choice. The passage does not mention frostbite.

2. A conclusion that may be drawn from research described in the passage is that:

   F. in severe cold a human infant is likely to survive longer than an adult.
   G. a person with many brown fat cells will live longer than someone with many white fat cells.
   H. animals living in cold places live longer than animals in warm places.
   J. metabolic rates in animals remain constant throughout life.

To answer a question using inductive reasoning, you need to think logically and to find the evidence in the passage for drawing a valid conclusion. Guard against overgeneralization. A conclusion may sound right, but if you can't find material in the passage to back it up, consider it wrong! Similarly, on its face a conclusion may seem invalid, but if it can be supported with facts in the passage, you have to consider it correct.

Question writers take great pains to avoid arguments over answers to test questions. In their phrasing of questions and answers they often include such hedging words as *may, often, almost, mostly, usually, generally, rarely, sometimes*—words that forestall controversy.

In answering ACT questions, be wary of conclusions stated as absolutes. They are *often* invalid precisely because they leave no room for exceptions. On the other hand, correct answers will *often* contain a hedging word that renders the statement valid.

Correct answers must always be supported by evidence found in the passage.

Choice **F** seems to correspond with the statement that newborn human babies have an "unusually high percentage of brown fat which diminishes as they grow older" (lines 21 and 22). Since brown fat, according to the passage, serves as a warming agent, it stands to reason that a baby can tolerate severe cold longer than an adult. Notice also that this choice contains the hedging phrase "is likely." **F** is correct. **G** implies that the focus of the passage is longevity rather than hibernation. Since longevity is not the real issue in the passage, however, this is not a good choice. **H** is wrong, because the passage does not discuss animals living in warm places. Notice also that this choice is stated as an absolute, which makes it immediately suspect. **J** is wrong. Since the passage alludes to metabolism in "the adult stage" of life, you may assume that other stages are characterized by different rates of metabolism.

3. Which of the following is NOT a valid conclusion to be drawn from the passage?

   A. Human beings may some day have the ability to hibernate.
   B. Long-term space exploration will be given a big boost when the process of hibernation is fully understood.
   C. It remains unclear why certain creatures have the capacity to hibernate.
   D. By means of hibernation the life span of human beings can be extended indefinitely.

To find the answer, identify the one conclusion that *cannot* legitimately be drawn from the facts in the passage. The discussion after question 2 may give you some hints on how to think out the answer.

Choice **A** is valid. It is the premise in the passage on which the discussion of interstellar travel is based. **B** is valid. The last part of the passage points out that long-term space travel depends on learning the secrets of hibernation. **C** is valid. Much of the passage is about past and present efforts to understand hibernation. **D** is *not* valid. According to line 54, aging slows down during hibernation but doesn't stop altogether. Hibernation may lengthen life but not extend it indefinitely. **D** is correct.

4. As used in the passage, the meaning of *metabolism* is the:

   F. rate at which food is digested.
   G. speed at which an organism uses up energy.
   H. rate at which blood replenishes its supply of oxygen.
   J. rate at which the bodily functions of a hibernating animal slow down.

Even if you know the word, don't depend on your prior knowledge of what it means. Because "metabolism" is a common word, it's likely that the question is asking for an uncommon definition. Don't be fooled into choosing the most popular definition. Determine the meaning of the word only from the way it is used on the passage.

Choice **F** corresponds to the everyday definition of metabolism. The passage, however, does not link metabolism to the digestion of food. **G** resembles the explanation of metabolism given in the passage: "energy expenditure per gram of tissue." **G** is correct. **H** is discussed in the passage but not in connection with metabolism. **J** has nothing to do with metabolism.

5. As used in the passage, the word *dilated* (line 57) means all of the following EXCEPT:

   A. causing years to seem like no more than a moment.
   B. programming space travelers to hibernate during stellar voyages.
   C. having the earth's people hibernate for the same span of time as stellar travelers.
   D. assuring that people remain young by means of hibernation.

The word "dilated" is not unusual, but the idea of a "dilated" society (line 57) is. The word may be defined right in the text or implied by the general meaning of the passage. You'll see the consequences of "dilating" a society by rereading lines 52 through 67.

Choice **A** is a consequence of a dilated society. **B** is a feature of a dilated society. **C** describes what happens in a dilated society. Space travelers return to friends, business colleagues, etc., who had aged no more than they had during flights to the stars. **D** is *not* a consequence of a dilated society. Therefore, **D** is correct.

6. It can most reasonably be inferred from the passage that animals in deep sleep resemble animals in hibernation in which of the following ways?

   F. Identical body temperature.
   G. Similar resistance to disease.
   H. Comparable slowing down of bodily functions.
   J. Equal rate of growth.

To answer this comparison question, draw your inference out of the parts of the passage where you find references to hibernation and sleep.

Choice **F** is wrong. Only hibernating animals experience changes in body temperature as the environment warms and cools (lines 5–7). **G** is wrong. Line 8 says that hibernating animals appear to have a natural immunity to disease. Sleep, on the other hand, is no defense against disease. **H** is supported by lines 5–9. The bodily functions of all animals, whether in hibernation (like the groundhog) or in deep sleep (like the bear), slow down during extended periods of rest. **H** is correct. **J** is wrong. Growth continues during sleep, but during hibernation, according to lines 5–6, it stops.

7. Hibernating animals differ from nonhibernating animals in all of the following ways EXCEPT in the:

   A. number of brown fat cells.
   B. presence of a certain enzyme in the body.
   C. tolerance to extremely cold temperatures.
   D. metabolic rate.

Because characteristics of hibernating animals are discussed throughout the passage, deal with the choices one at a time.

Choice **A** is wrong. Lines 16–18 indicate that hibernating animals have a higher percentage of brown fat cells than other animals. **B** is wrong. Lines 3 and 47 refer to scientists' quest to find the enzyme that sets off hibernation. Presumably, nonhibernating animals lack such an enzyme. **C** is wrong. Experiments described in lines 30 to 34 found that natural hibernators withstand cold temperatures more readily than nonhibernators. **D** is a good choice, because the passage discusses metabolism as a function of the life span of *all* animals, hibernators and nonhibernators alike. **D** is correct.

8. Based on the passage, which of the following procedures holds the greatest promise for inducing human hibernation?

   F. Promoting the growth of brown fat cells in the body
   G. Changing the activity of the thyroid gland
   H. Conditioning the heart to adapt to lower temperatures
   J. Increasing the amount of oxygen in body tissue

Solving a problem from facts is not far different from drawing a conclusion, but, to answer this question, use deductive, instead of inductive, reasoning—that is, consider a number of pieces of information to determine the only reasonable solution to the problem. For example:

FACT 1: Arthur lies dead on the floor with a bullet hole in his chest.

FACT 2: Harold stands over Arthur with a smoking gun in his hand.

PROBLEM: Figure out who killed Arthur.

You can assume that the ACT will present problems somewhat harder to solve than Arthur's murder. The point is to use every available scrap of evidence to solve the problem.

Choice **F** is discussed in lines 16–29. At one time, brown fat cells seemed like a key to human hibernation, but years of research have been unsuccessful. **G** is discussed in line 23. People with underproductive thyroids have a more than normal amount of brown fat cells. To induce the formation of more brown fat cells by slowing the thyroid, however, is hazardous to health. **H** is fully discussed in the passage, but in spite of some progress, the search for a better answer goes on. **J** is discussed in lines 50–51, which says this procedure "may hold the clue" and is correct.

9. Based on information in the passage, scientists can predict which of two kittens from the same litter is likely to live longer by:

   A. studying the brown fat cell/white fat cell ratio in each kitten.
   B. analyzing the kittens' enzyme secretions.
   C. measuring the kittens' metabolic rates.
   D. comparing the amounts of hemoglobin and myoglobin in each kitten's blood.

To answer this question, search the passage for references to longevity. Since life span is discussed in the second paragraph, focus your attention there.

Choice **A** is wrong, because the passage discusses brown and white fat cells with regard to heat production in the body, not to life span. **B** is wrong. According to the passage, enzymes are thought to bring about hibernation and have nothing to do with length of life. **C** coincides with Rubner's finding that the "higher the metabolism, the shorter the life span and vice versa" (lines 14–15). **C** is correct. **D** is wrong, because the composition of blood, while important to hibernation, has nothing to do with longevity.

10. In which of the following sequences (from earliest to latest) were these discoveries made?

    I. In extreme cold, nonhibernating animals develop ventricular fibrillations.
    II. The heart can be conditioned to adapt to low temperatures.
    III. An organism's energy expenditure is related to its life span.
    IV. Fruit flies live longer when their body temperature is lowered.

    F. I, III, IV, II
    G. III, II, IV, I
    H. III, IV, I, II
    J. IV, I, III, II

Sequence questions such as this consume a good deal of time on the ACT. Consider saving them for last. By then you'll know how much test time remains, and you won't neglect other, less time-consuming questions.

First skim the passage to locate the four sequenced items. Mark them I, II, III, and IV. Begin by finding either the first or the last item in the sequence. Nonfiction passages often cue the reader with such words and phrases as *first, to begin, initially, in the first place, to start, early on, finally, in conclusion, last, in the end, most recently*. Intermediate steps are often cued with *then, next, also, soon after, in the meantime, secondly, in addition*, and many other similar transitional words.

Once you've identified either the first or last item, go directly to the question choices and start eliminating those that can't be right. If you know the first item in a sequence, start looking for the last item, and vice versa. Once you've located both the first and the last items, you may have the answer. If you haven't, of course, you'll also need to identify either the second or third item.

Choice **F** is wrong. The paragraph in which ventricular fibrillations (lines 33 and 34) are discussed begins with the phrase "About ten years after Rubner's experiments, . . ." Discovery number I, therefore, could not have occurred first. **G** seems like a possibility. According to line 12, discovery number III was made by Rubner early in this century. Therefore, the proper sequence must begin with III. The last number in this choice refers to a discovery made ten years after Rubner's. Since more recent discoveries are discussed later in the passage, discovery I cannot be last in the sequence. **H** is a possibility. Aside from choice **G,** it is the only one that starts with discovery number III. Indeed, this sequence corresponds with the order of discoveries described in the passage. **H** is correct. **J** is wrong, because it begins with discovery number IV, which took place after Rubner's work.

Warm-Up Drill

In this practice exercise you will have a chance to demonstrate your mastery of the tactics for answering questions about Natural Science reading passages. Answers and explanations follow the questions.

The history of science is composed of three periods: antiquity; classical science, starting with the Renaissance; and modern science, which started at the turn of the twentieth century.

What characterizes the *science of antiquity* is the naive faith in the perfection of our senses and reasoning. What man sees is the ultimate reality. Everybody, being by necessity the center of his universe, knew there was no doubt that ours is a flat earth and man is the center, as expressed in the *cosmology* of Ptolemy. If we touch something, we find it either hard or soft, wet or dry, cold or warm; so these qualities had to be the ultimate building stones of the universe, as taught by Aristotle. There is an "up" and "down," an absolute space, as expressed in Euclidean geometry. Human reasoning was thought to lead to more reliable results than crude trial and experiment, as reflected by the *dictum* of Aristotle that a big stone falls faster than a small one. What is remarkable about this statement is not that it is wrong, but that it never occurred to Aristotle to try it. He probably would have regarded such a proposal as an insult.

Two thousand years later, in that great awakening of the Western mind called the Renaissance, something new must have happened to the human mind. A boisterous young man, Galileo by name, went up a leaning tower with two stones, one big and one small, and dropped them simultaneously, having asked his companions to observe which of the two arrived first on the pavement below. They arrived simultaneously. This same man doubted the perfection of his senses, built a telescope to improve the range of his eyes, and thus discovered the rings of Saturn and the satellites of Jupiter. This was a dramatic discovery because nobody had seen these before. So it now seemed scarcely credible that the whole universe could have been created solely for man's pleasure or temptation.

Galileo was but one of the first swallows of an approaching spring. Somewhat earlier, Copernicus had already concluded that it was not absolutely necessary to suppose that the sun rotates around the earth; it could be the other way around. Johannes Kepler replaced simple observation and reasoning with careful measurement. Somewhat later, Antony van Leeuwenhoek, a greengrocer at Delft, in Holland, improved the range of his senses by building a microscope. With it he discovered a new world of living creatures too small to be seen by the naked eye. Thus began the science which I will call "classical," which reached its peak with Sir Isaac Newton, who, with the concept of gravitation, made a coherent system of the universe.

This *classical science* replaced divine whims by natural laws, corrected many previous errors, and extended man's world into both the bigger and smaller dimensions, but it introduced nothing new that man could not "understand." By the word "understand" we simply mean that we can correlate the *phenomenon* in question with some earlier experience of ours. If I tell you that it is gravitation which holds our globe to the sun, you will say "I understand," though nobody knows what gravitation is. All the same, you "understand" because you know that it is gravitation which makes apples fall, and you all have seen apples fall before.

For several centuries, this classical science had little influence on everyday life or human relations and was merely the intellectual playground of the selected few who wanted to look deeper into Nature's cooking pot.

Around the end of the nineteenth century (1896), two mysterious discoveries signified the arrival of a new period, the period of *modern science*. The one was that of Wilhelm Röntgen, who discovered new rays which could penetrate through solid matter. The other was the discovery of radioactivity by Antoine Henri Becquerel, a discovery which shook the solid foundation of our universe, built of indestructible matter.

Albert Szent-Györgyi, "Horizons of Life Sciences," in *Ideas in Science*, ed. Oscar H. Fidell, Washington Square Press, (N.Y., 1966), pp. 167–169.

1. Based on information in the passage, all of the following sciences were practiced in antiquity EXCEPT:

   A. medicine.
   B. physics.
   C. astronomy.
   D. mathematics.

2. According to the passage, scientists of ancient times believed that:

   F. the gods had created the universe for the happiness of man.
   G. man's intuition led to an understanding of the physical principles that governed the universe.
   H. rational thought could unlock all the secrets of science.
   J. answers to the mystery of life were found within each person.

3. The author of the passage implies that scientists of antiquity were:

   A. well-meaning.
   B. lazy.
   C. short-sighted.
   D. proud of their achievements.

4. Ptolemy was known for his "cosmology," a term that may best be compared to modern-day:

   F. geography.
   G. astrology.
   H. geology.
   J. astronomy.

5. Galileo's astronomical discoveries led to the belief that:

   A. the earth was not the center of the universe.
   B. extraterrestrial life could exist somewhere in the universe.
   C. the universe was not created for the benefit of mankind.
   D. the universe was much larger than anyone had imagined.

6. Based on information in the passage, Galileo's greatest achievement was to:

   F. correct Aristotle's mistakes.
   G. initiate a new age of science.
   H. invent the telescope.
   J. make science more understandable to the general public.

7. All of the following occurred during the age of classical science EXCEPT:

   A. universal scientific rules began to be recognized.
   B. technological inventions extended man's horizons.
   C. the law of gravity was finally explained and understood.
   D. reason became less important than measurement and observation.

8. The passage implies that science had virtually no effect on the daily life of most people until the:

   F. Renaissance.
   G. work of Sir Isaac Newton.
   H. twentieth century.
   J. discoveries of Wilhelm Röntgen.

9. The word "understand" appears in quotation marks (line 39) to suggest that:

   A. gravity cannot be understood; the best we can do is observe its effect.
   B. it signifies the mastery of highly specialized scientific knowledge.
   C. the author is being sarcastic, since it takes years of study to understand gravity.
   D. you have to take gravity on faith; there is no rational explanation for it.

10. The modern age of science seems to have come about when:

   F. scientists began to discover mysterious phenomena that could not be understood by ordinary people.
   G. the nature of matter began to be understood.
   H. X-rays were invented.
   J. the effects of radiation began to be explored.

ANSWERS AND EXPLANATIONS

1. **(A)** Medicine is the only science not mentioned in the passage. Lines 7–9 indicate that Aristotle practiced physics (choice B), Ptolemy was an astronomer (C), and Euclid worked in mathematics (D).

2. **(H)** This answer is supported by the ideas expressed in the second paragraph, which says that the application of human reasoning was the preferred method of scientific research during the age of antiquity. G is wrong because the passage does not refer to intuition. F is partly true, but the passage doesn't discuss the creator of the universe. J is not mentioned in the passage.

3. **(C)** This response is suggested by the description of the ancients' disregard of scientific experimentation. Choice A is not at issue in the passage. B is an incorrect inference. D is not discussed.

4. **(J)** Ptolemy's concern was the shape and place of the earth in the universe; hence, he was an astronomer. F relates to the arrangement of the earth's features. G examines the placement of the stars, and H is the study of the composition and internal structure of the earth.

5. **(C)** This answer is stated in lines 22–24. As a result of Galileo's work, it became clear that the universe had not, after all, been created solely for man's pleasure. Choice A refers to the work of Copernicus. Neither B nor D is discussed in the passage.

6. **(G)** This answer is strongly suggested by lines 15–16. F, H, and J refer to Galileo's work, but they are not considered his *greatest* achievements.

7. **(C)** This is the best answer because, according to lines 38–41, gravity cannot really be understood. Choice A is discussed in lines 34–36. B refers to the invention of both the telescope and the microscope. D refers to methods of research conducted by Kepler.

8. **(H)** Lines 42–44 state that until the age of modern science, only an elite group of intellectuals were interested in scientific study.

9. **(A)** In lines 38 to 41 the law of gravity is described as an acknowledged but inexplicable force in the universe.

10. **(G)** The passage refers to scientists who began to understand the nature of solid matter. F seems to refer to supernatural events not discussed in the passage. H and J are valid, but neither marks the birth of the modern age of science.

SAMPLE READING TEST

Now that you are acquainted with the various types of reading passages and questions on the ACT, see whether you can apply what you have learned. This exercise consists of four passages, each accompanied by ten questions. Because the passages in this Sample Test vary in length from those on the ACT Reading Test, you may wish to allow yourself about forty-five minutes, rather than the thirty-five minutes allotted on the ACT, to complete the exercise. Don't let yourself be distracted by the time limit, however. For the moment, devote yourself to recalling and using the test-taking tactics suggested throughout this chapter.

Directions: This test consists of four passages, each followed by ten multiple-choice questions. Read each passage and then pick the best answer for each question. Refer to the passage as often as you wish while answering the questions.

Passage 1—Prose Fiction

This passage is from "An Old Oregonian in the Snow," a short story by Joachim Miller. The passage describes Joe Meek, a legendary character in the Old West.

I was once, when riding express, "snowed under" with a famous old pioneer in the great cañon that splits Camas Prairie in two and breaks the monotony of its vast levels.

A wild unpeopled and unknown land it was then, but it has since been made immortal by the unavailing battles of Chief Joseph for the graves of his fathers.

Joe Meek! The many books about him tell you he was a savage, buckskinned delegate to Congress from the unorganized territory of Oregon, who lived with the Indians. These statements are almost all untrue. His was a plain, pastoral nature, and he shunned strife and notoriety. He had none of Kit Carson's dash about him, none of Davy Crockett's daring, nor had he Fremont's culture and capacity for putting himself well before the world; he ranked all these men both in the priority and peril of his enterprises.

Indeed, before the chiefest of them was really heard of he had called the people of the far Northwest together under the great pines by the sounding Oregon,* and made solemn protest against the pretensions of England to that region. These settlers sent this man over the plains alone, a journey of more than half a year, to beg the President that they might be made or remain a portion of the United States while most of the now famous mountaineers were yet at their mother's knee. I know of no figure in our history that approaches his in grandeur except that of President Houston, of the Lone Star Republic. And yet you search in vain for his name among those who sat in our Capitol in those early days. Some say he arrived at Washington when Congress was not in session, and so did not present his credentials. Others say that he lost his papers on the way in one of his perilous passages of a stream. And then again I am told that he never had any credentials to present; that the territory had no official existence at that time, and as Congress had not then become as adept in coining States and Territories, the pioneers of the Oregon River gave him no authority to appear in Congress, but that his mission was entirely with the President.

But the spectacle of this man setting out in mid-winter to ride alone over an untracked distance of three thousand miles, the loyalty of this people, their peril from savages, as well as the cupidity of Great Britain, I count one of the finest on the page of pioneer history.

I suspect that his mission was fruitful of little, for he was, as new people came pouring in, quietly relegated to the background, and never afterward came conspicuously forward, save as an occasional leader in the wars against the Indians. But the undertaking and the accomplishment of this terrible journey alone ought to keep his memory green forever. And, indeed, had fate placed him in any other spot than isolated Oregon, he surely now would not be so nearly forgotten.

When gold was discovered in Idaho—or Ida*h*ho, an Indian word meaning, in a broad sense, mountain of light—Joe Meek, now an old man, could not resist the temptation to leave his home in the woods of Oregon and again brave the plains.

But he was no longer in any great sense a conspicuous figure. He, so far from being a leader, was even laughed at by his own people, the Oregonians, the new, young people who had journeyed into the country after his work had been done—the old story of the ingratitude of republics. And if he was laughed at by the long-haired, lank and blanketed Oregonian, he was despised by the quick, trim, sharp and energetic Californian who had now over-run Oregon on his way to the new Eldorado.

I wonder if the world would believe the half that could be written of the coarseness, the lawlessness of these unorganized armies that surged up and down the

*Early name for the Columbia River

Pacific coast in search of gold a quarter of a century ago? I know of nothing like these invasions in history since the days of the Goths and Vandals.

Two wild and strong streams of humanity, one from Oregon and the other from California, had glowed inharmoniously, tumultuously, together on and there, down in the deep cañon that cleft the wide and wintry valley through the middle, this stream of life stopped, as a river that is frozen.

A hundred men, trying to escape the "blizzard," tumbled headlong into the cañon together, and took shelter there as best they could beside the great basalt that had tumbled from the high, steep cliffs of the cañon. They crept under the crags, anywhere to escape the bitter cold.

And how the Californian did despise the Oregonian! He named him the "webfoot" because his feet were moccasined and he came from the land of clouds and rain. The bitter enmity and bad blood of Germany and France were here displayed in epitome and in the worst form. A wonder, indeed, if there would not be some sort of tragedy played here before the storm was over.

Joachim Miller, "An Old Oregonian in the Snow"

1. When the narrator of the passage meets Joe Meek, Joe:

   A. has news to deliver from Washington, D.C.
   B. is past his prime.
   C. is on a mission to see the President of the United States.
   D. is about to get into another fight.

2. The narrator meets Joe Meek in person during:

   F. a rodeo.
   G. the Gold Rush.
   H. an Indian war.
   J. a battle between Californians and Oregonians.

3. Joe Meek travels to Washington, D.C. in order to:

   A. represent the people of Oregon in Congress.
   B. seek government aid in fighting Chief Joseph.
   C. prevent Oregon from being annexed by Great Britain.
   D. demonstrate his courage and daring nature.

4. According to the passage, Joe Meek is a forgotten hero because:

   F. he grew old and senile before his time.
   G. he was too eccentric to become a classical American hero.
   H. his mission to Washington failed.
   J. the Oregon territory was too remote to produce enduring heroes.

5. The cañon referred to in the passage (lines 2, 82):

   A. marks the boundary between California and Oregon.
   B. contained a wooden shelter to protect the travelers.
   C. divides a huge, flat valley.
   D. was shaped by the Oregon (now the Columbia) River.

6. Many rumors persist about Joe Meek, but the one certainty is that:

   F. he lost his papers enroute from Oregon to Washington, D.C.
   G. he once lived with the Indians.
   H. he traveled across the continent by himself.
   J. he met the President of the United States.

7. The narrator believes that Joe Meek deserves greater recognition for his exploits because Joe:

   A. undertook important and dangerous missions.
   B. outlived other heroes like John Fremont and Kit Carson.
   C. was more daring than Davy Crockett.
   D. set a standard for heroism that others followed.

8. After he returned from Washington, Joe Meek did all of the following EXCEPT:

   F. fight Indians.
   G. search for gold.
   H. settle in the woods.
   J. run for public office.

9. In the passage, the traditional antipathy between Californians and Oregonians is exemplified by their:

   A. behavior during the Idaho gold rush.
   B. attitude toward Joe Meek.
   C. ability to deal with cold and snow.
   D. disrespect for the law.

10. According to the passage, many people of Oregon failed to appreciate Joe Meek's work in their behalf because:

    F. he refused to take credit for his success.
    G. so many rumors circulated about Joe that they didn't know what to believe.
    H. his work didn't affect them directly.
    J. it wasn't fashionable to honor such men.

Passage 2—Social Studies

This passage on America's mentally ill homeless people is adapted from an essay written by Henry G. Cisneros, former Secretary of the Department of Housing and Urban Development during the Clinton administration.

On any given night in the United States, an estimated 600,000 people are homeless. Of those, approximately 200,000 suffer from serious mental illness. Unfortunately, these are facts that no longer hold surprise for most Americans. We have grown accustomed to the sight of the wild eyed, dirt-covered man on the corner. We have become used to averting our gaze from the toothless old woman who mutters to herself at the bus stop and wears many layers of clothes even in warm weather. We are no longer as shocked as we once were at the sight of small children crouched beside their parents, panhandling on some of our busiest streets.

A Gallup poll recently reported that although most Americans feel compassion for homeless men and women they encounter on the street, many are puzzled, not knowing how to react to this growing problem that seemed to emerge out of nowhere. Some cities have dealt with their homeless populations by jailing individuals for sitting on the streets or sleeping in parks. Other cities, citing public health concerns, have bulldozed encampments and shantytowns built under city bridges. Unable to find a simple, inexpensive solution to the problem, many individuals and communities prefer to pretend that it does not exist. While there is no single solution for this problem, some responses have been more successful than others. When combined, these responses have, in the past decade, made a tremendous difference in the lives of homeless Americans.

Because homeless men and women are still so visible in our communities, few people realize that over the past decade the number of homeless people helped by the government has increased by more than 1,000 percent. Few seem to know that a major shift in thinking about and creating programs to address homelessness has occurred on the national and local levels, resulting in unprecedented success in dealing with the problems faced by this population. Few people realize that this approach, which we call the *Continuum of Care*, has resulted in a major shift of national priorities away from emergency shelter services toward long-term solutions such as transitional and permanent housing, job training, and medical and mental health services.

It is difficult to imagine a more dangerous or more distressing combination of problems to befall any one person than to be homeless and to suffer from a severe mental illness. Yet those who are homeless and mentally ill are often diagnosed with many accompanying disabilities—such as drug addiction, alcoholism, HIV/AIDS, diabetes, and tuberculosis. Mentally ill homeless people tend to be the sickest, the most ragged, and the most difficult people for society to accept. In addition, because rationality itself is compromised by mental illness, they are often the least able to help themselves, either economically or medically, and thus they slide more deeply into danger.

Who are mentally ill homeless persons, and how do they survive? They are among the poorest people in our nation, earning or receiving in Supplemental Security Income (SSI) and other benefits an average annual income of $4,200. While most would like to work, this population faces some of the highest barriers to employment. It is estimated that one-half of the mentally ill homeless people suffer from drug and alcohol abuse, and many use substances as a method of self-medication. An estimated 4 percent to 14 percent of adults in family shelters have spent time in mental hospitals.

Because mentally ill homeless men and women are vulnerable to attack, they are often victims of violent crime. Some of the crimes against them are examples of the worst behavior imaginable. But many mentally ill homeless also come into contact with the criminal justice system as offenders, arrested as they engage in such illegal activities as trespassing, petty theft, shoplifting, and prostitution—often crimes of survival under the most desperate of conditions, and a direct result of their mental illness.

These individuals suffer from severe mental illness such as schizophrenia, mood disorders, severe depression, and personality disorders. Given consistent medical and psychosocial treatment along with stable housing, many of them could again function at a high level. But such stability and consistent care are impossible to achieve when one is homeless. Thus homelessness and mental illness become a vicious cycle, one compounding the other in a vortex of suffering for the individual. Unfortunately, without mental health treatment and related support services, it is difficult for mentally ill homeless persons to gain access to, and remain in, permanent housing. Often they face stigma associated with their illness and discrimination by potential landlords or neighbors. All of these factors make individuals with serious mental illness extremely vulnerable to homelessness and difficult to help once they become homeless.

11. According to the passage, Americans' attitude toward the homeless has changed from:

    A. surprise to familiarity.
    B. horror to regret.
    C. discomfort to understanding.
    D. awareness to irritation.

12. It is reasonable to infer from the passage that homelessness in America is a problem that occurs mostly in:

F. specific neighborhoods of various cities.
G. urban areas.
H. communities containing homeless shelters.
J. streets and parks near mental hospitals.

13. The author states that homelessness came about:

A. as an aftereffect of an economic downturn.
B. because of changes in the laws related to mental illness.
C. in conditions that took America by surprise.
D. as a consequence of crowding in America's cities.

14. Which of the following community efforts has made a "tremendous difference" (line 27) in the lives of the homeless?

F. Removing homeless people from the streets and parks
G. Passing anti-vagrancy laws
H. Expanding the powers of social agencies
J. Implementing a variety of different strategies

15. The claim that "the number of homeless people helped by the government has increased" (lines 31–32) means that:

A. better education has managed to shrink the homeless population.
B. many new homeless shelters have been built.
C. the government has expanded its welfare programs.
D. forward-looking policies to solve the homeless problem have been successfully put into practice.

16. In lines 48–49, "drug addiction, alcoholism, HIV/AIDS, diabetes, and tuberculosis" are mentioned as examples of:

F. disabilities that strike people who cannot afford to take care of themselves medically.
G. the dangers that many mentally ill people are subject to.
H. the fate of people whose homelessness has been caused by mental illness.
J. disabilities that often grow out of homelessness and mental illness.

17. The passage suggests that homelessness and mental illness are linked because:

A. most homeless people tend to be mentally ill.
B. homeless mentally ill people are usually rejected by society.
C. many mentally ill people, unable to take care of their basic needs, become homeless.
D. homelessness has been known to cause mental illness.

18. By asserting that many mentally ill homeless people have "contact with the criminal justice system" (lines 71–72), the author is pointing out that many mentally ill homeless men and women:

F. have been treated like criminals by the police and the courts.
G. tend to report to the police when victimized by criminals.
H. have been driven to commit crimes in order to survive.
J. look to the police and courts to save them from abuse by society.

19. As it is used in line 85, the word *vortex* most nearly means:

A. inescapable trap.
B. ambush.
C. overabundance.
D. struggle.

20. Which of the following statements best describes the author's method and purpose?

F. Conveying a series of observations and facts in an attempt to inform readers how mental illness makes solving the problem of homelessness more difficult
G. Presenting a series of facts and personal opinions designed to persuade readers to support increased funding for social services for the homeless and mentally ill people
H. Collecting a series of research findings meant to show the positive effects of government programs regarding the homeless
J. Constructing an argument based on emotion meant to move readers to take steps to help the homeless

Passage 3—Humanities

This passage is adapted from an essay about the origins of one of the world's most enduring pieces of literature, the Decameron *by Giovanni Boccaccio.*

In 1334, a mysterious epidemic swept through Hopei, a northeastern province of China, claiming the lives of five-million people—a full 90 percent of the population. The Black Death would eventually kill two-thirds of China's inhabitants and come to be known simply as the plague. It traveled westward from the Orient along the trade route, arriving in Italy in early 1348, blazing its infectious way through country and city and causing chaos and panic everywhere it landed. By the time it was over, half of Italy's population had died.

One of the Florentine survivors was Giovanni Boccaccio, author of the *Decameron*. In the introduction to his work, he announces that the aim of his collection of short stories is to ease the hearts of unhappy women in love and bring them pleasure. He gives an eyewitness account of the plague:

"Its first sign here in both men and women was a swelling in the groin or beneath the armpit, growing sometimes in the shape of a simple apple, sometimes in that of an egg, more or less; a bubo was the name commonly given to such a swelling. Before long this deadly bubo would begin to spread indifferently from these points to crop up all over; the symptoms would develop then into dark or livid patches that many people found appearing on their arms or thighs or elsewhere." The infected person often died within three days of the first appearance of the bubo.

Hysteria and chaos followed the contagion as neither medical science nor the church could explain its source or heal its effects. Out of fear, communal and familial bonds broke down. Many deserted their homes, families, and the city, bringing the plague to the countryside. "Men and women alike were possessed by such visceral terror of this scourge that a man would desert his own brother, uncle would forsake his nephew, sister her brother, and often a wife her husband. What is more, believe it or not, mothers and fathers would avoid visiting and tending their children; they would virtually disown them."

The sight every morning of bodies thrown into the street drove Florentines to react in various ways. Some became monastic and shut themselves away to tend their souls since it seemed that the end of the world was upon them. Still others went about as best they could, keeping from extreme behavior and hoping to ride out the crisis. Fortunes were made by avaricious priests and pallbearers who charged high prices for tending the sick, and lost when they themselves fell ill. All work stopped; houses were deserted, courts and jails emptied, fields left to rot. According to Boccaccio, in four months 100,000 people died in Florence.

Boccaccio uses the plague as a framing device in the *Decameron*, which is composed of one hundred stories narrated by ten storytellers. Meeting by chance in the church of Santa Maria Novella, the seven noblewomen and three noblemen decide to adjourn to a country estate where they can forget the plague for a time and engage in more pleasurable activities—singing, dancing, and especially storytelling.

The stories in the *Decameron* present a microcosm of medieval life in fictional form. Many are about love. Boccaccio dedicates the book to unhappy women in love, writing that when men are heartbroken or depressed, they can turn to outside distractions such as hunting, fishing, gambling, or pursuing business. In contrast women had little freedom to move outside the family circle.

On "Day Two" of the tales, Dioneo narrates the story of Ricciardo and Bartolomea, an old man who marries a young bride whom he cannot satisfy sexually. Trying not to lose face, he brings his bride a religious calendar and points out the inappropriateness of sharing a bed on holy days, fast days, feast days, "as well as Fridays, Saturdays, the Lord's Day and the whole of Lent, as well as certain phases of the moon, and on many another exceptional occasion."

During a fishing excursion, the pirate Paganino captures Bartolomea and whisks her away. Ricciardo eventually discovers the identity of the pirate and finds Paganino and Bartolomea living happily as husband and wife. Bewildered and angry, he asks, "Would you live here as this man's concubine, and in a state of mortal sin, rather than as my wife in Pisa? When he tires of you he'll throw you out, and what a humiliation for you that will be. Are you going to forsake your honor and desert me, who love you more than my life, all on account of this dissolute and disgraceful appetite of yours?"

Bartolomea cares little for his moral attitude. She says, "I'm a hale and hearty young woman. Here I feel like Paganino's wife. To think that we depended on phases of the moon and geometrical calculations for the conjunction of our planets. Here Paganino clasps me all night long in his arms and cuddles me and nibbles me; his particular attentions I'll leave to the Good Lord to describe."

Caroline Kim, "Tales of Beggars and Nuns, Pirates and Kings"

21. It can be inferred from the passage that the Black Death was probably carried from China to Italy by:

A. immigrants.
B. merchants.
C. gypsies.
D. refugees.

22. The passage suggests that the chaos and panic referred to in line 9 came about for all of the following reasons EXCEPT:

F. people were dying at an alarming rate.
G. no one knew the source of the plague.
H. the plague was incurable.
J. churches closed their doors to the public.

23. The passage indicates that Boccaccio's main purpose in writing the *Decameron* was to:

A. arouse women's ardor for men.
B. show women that they had more power than they thought.
C. comfort women aggrieved by love.
D. cheer up women who had lost loved ones in the plague.

24. Based on the passage, the *Decameron* can best be described as:

F. a chronicle of the plague in Florence.
G. ten entertaining memoirs by three noblemen and seven noblewomen.
H. a collection of short fictional pieces.
J. the author's observations of the plague.

25. It is reasonable to infer from the passage that the plague caused healthy people in Italy to look out for:

A. high fevers and headaches.
B. dark growths on their skin.
C. swollen areas on their bodies.
D. rashes on their limbs.

26. Among the severest social consequences of the plague was:

F. a sharp decline in the birthrate.
G. a breakdown of traditional family values.
H. the broadening of the gap between the rich and the poor.
J. an increase in violent crime.

27. As used in line 46 the word *avaricious* most likely means:

A. jealous.
B. greedy.
C. miserly.
D. hungry.

28. By saying that Boccaccio "uses the plague as a framing device" (line 52) the author means that:

F. the plague created a context in which the stories are told.
G. allusions to the plague unify the contents of the *Decameron*.
H. the storytellers have escaped the effects of the plague.
J. all the stories take place in a plague-ridden setting.

29. Dioneo's tale fits the overall pattern of the *Decameron* in that:

A. Bartolomea rebels against the restrictions placed on females.
B. it deals with an old man outsmarted by a young girl.
C. its protagonist is a bride dissatisfied by her love life.
D. its moral is instructive for both men and women.

30. In Dioneo's story, Ricciardo tries to convince Bartolomea to come back to him mainly by:

F. flattering her.
G. threatening her.
H. embarrassing her.
J. pleading with her.

Passage 4—Natural Science

From a U.S. Department of the Interior publication on underground water, this passage describes the aquifer, the area beneath the earth's surface where water flows.

The word *aquifer* comes from two Latin words: *aqua,* or water, and *ferre,* to bring. The aquifer may be a layer of gravel or sand, a layer of sandstone or of cavernous limestone, or even a large body of nonlayered rock that has sizable openings.

An aquifer may be only a few feet thick, or tens or hundreds of feet. It may be just below the surface, or hundreds of feet below. It may underlie a few acres or many square miles. The Dakota Sandstone in the West carries water over great distances, across several states. Many aquifers, however, are only local in extent. Underneath the water-bearing rocks everywhere, at some depth, are rocks that are watertight. This depth may be a few hundred feet, or tens of thousands of feet.

The amount of water that a given rock can contain depends on its porosity—the spaces between the grains or the cracks that can fill with water. If the grains are all about the same size, or well-sorted, as the geologists say, the spaces between them account for a large proportion of the whole volume. This is true of gravel and sand. However, if the grains are poorly sorted, that is, not all the same size, the spaces between the larger grains will fill with small grains instead of water. Poorly sorted rocks do not hold as much water as well-sorted rocks.

If water is to move through the rock, the pores must be connected. If the rock has a great many connected pore spaces, of which a large part are sizable, the rock is permeable. Large amounts of water are available to a well from saturated permeable rocks. But if the pores or cracks are small, poorly connected, or nearly lacking, the aquifer can yield only a small amount of water to a well. The porosity of different kinds of rocks varies widely. In some the porosity is less than 1 percent; in others, mostly unconsolidated rock such as sand and gravel, it may be as high as 30 to 40 percent.

A rock that will be a good source of water must contain either many pore spaces, or many cracks, or both. A compact rock such as granite, almost without pore spaces, may be permeable if it contains enough sizable fractures. Nearly all consolidated rock formations are broken by cracks, called *joints*. The joints are caused by the same kinds of stresses in the earth's crust that cause earthquakes. At first they are just hairline cracks, but they tend to open through the day-to-day action of rain, sun, and frost. The ice crystals formed by water that freezes in rock crevices will cause the rocks to split open. Heating by the sun and cooling at night cause expansion and contraction that produce the same result. Water will enter the joints and gradually dissolve away the rock, enlarging the opening.

If the joints intersect each other, water can move from one to another, much as it flows through the water pipes in a municipal water system. Granite and slate are less porous than sandstone. When water circulates in them, it does so through joint cracks. The water yield of wells drilled in these rocks depends on how many joints are intersected by the well, and how wide they are.

Water will move faster in certain kinds of rocks. A clayey silt having only very tiny pores will not carry water very readily, but a coarse gravel will carry water freely and rapidly. Some rocks, like limestone, are cavernous; they contain hollowed-out openings. Gravel also has numerous open spaces. Water may travel through it at rates of tens or hundreds of feet per day. In silt or fine sand it may move only inches a day. Flow of streams is measured in feet per second; movement of ground water is usually measured in feet per year.

There is no strict correlation between the water-bearing capacity of rocks and the depth at which they are found. A dense granite may be found at the surface, as in New England, while a porous sandstone may lie several thousand feet down, as in the Great Plains. However, on average, porosity and permeability grow less as depth increases. Rocks that yield fresh water have been found at depths of more than 6,000 feet (and salty water has come from oil wells at depths of more than 20,000 feet), but most wells drilled deeper than 2,000 feet find little water. The pores and cracks in the rocks at great depths are closed up because of the weight of overlying rocks.

Helene L. Baldwin and C.L. McGuiness, *A Primer on Ground Water*

31. The passage suggests that most aquifers consist of:

    A. rocks only.
    B. sand and rocks in equal amounts.
    C. sand only.
    D. more rocks than sand.

32. Which of the following determines the porosity of rock?

    F. the temperature of the water
    G. the overall dimensions of the rock
    H. the similarity of the grains that make up the rock
    J. the length of hairline cracks on the rock's surface

33. Which of the following most accurately describes a rock that is *permeable?*

    A. It is likely to be more narrow than wide.
    B. It is generally a few feet thick.
    C. It contains more cracks than pores.
    D. It contains numerous connected pores.

34. All of the following may help to turn watertight rocks into water-bearing rocks EXCEPT:

    F. the sun's heat.
    G. sub-freezing temperatures.
    H. the flow of water.
    J. veins of soft material in the rock.

35. By comparing joints in rock to pipes in a municipal water system (lines 51–53), the author stresses the point that:

    A. water flows through joints at a steady rate.
    B. joints must connect to each other like water pipes.
    C. joints are essential to an aquifer as a water system is essential to a municipality.
    D. a municipal water system is always underground.

36. In which type of rock are productive aquifers most likely to be found?

    F. granite
    G. a blend of slate and granite
    H. limestone
    J. sandstone

37. An aquifer consisting of nonporous consolidated rock formations is a good source of water when:

    A. it contains many wide joints.
    B. an earthquake occurs.
    C. water alternatively freezes and melts.
    D. many hairline cracks run across its surface.

38. An aquifer consisting of gravel will be a better source of water than an aquifer consisting of clay because:

    F. gravel has more well-sorted grains than clay.
    G. clay is more porous than gravel.
    H. gravel pores tend to fill up with sand.
    J. the grains in clay are larger than the grains in gravel.

39. An aquifer is not likely to be found a great distance below the earth's crust because:

    A. water flows very slowly at great depths.
    B. oil far belowground pushes the water toward the surface.
    C. compressed rocks are not porous.
    D. the action of rain, sun, and frost have no effect on rocks far below the surface.

40. Overall, the passage implies that the most promising place to drill a well is:

    F. in a limestone or gravel aquifer less than 2,000 feet underground.
    G. in the Dakota Sandstone aquifer.
    H. in New England granite that is close to the surface.
    J. in a large-jointed slate aquifer more than 2,000 feet below the earth's surface.

Answer Key

1. B	6. H	11. A	16. J	21. B	26. G	31. D	36. H
2. G	7. A	12. G	17. C	22. J	27. B	32. H	37. A
3. C	8. J	13. C	18. H	23. C	28. F	33. D	38. F
4. J	9. A	14. J	19. A	24. H	29. C	34. J	39. C
5. C	10. H	15. D	20. F	25. C	30. G	35. B	40. F

Answer Explanations

1. **(B)** Joe Meek is a "famous old pioneer" (line 2) when the narrator meets him. The events named by choices A, C, and D took place long ago, when Joe was a young man.

2. **(G)** The blizzard that drove the two men together occurred during the Idaho gold rush (lines 54–58). Choice F is not mentioned in the passage. H took place long before. With regard to J, Californians and Oregonians never actually engaged in a specific battle; theirs was a long-standing conflict.

3. **(C)** Line 20 indicates that Joe was sent to "protest against the pretensions of England." Choice A is incorrect because Joe's congressional service is more myth than fact. B is not mentioned in the passage. Although D is true, it was not the main purpose of Joe's trip.

4. **(J)** The narrator says that Joe might have been a famous hero had he been from "any other spot than isolated Oregon" (line 52). Choice F is not discussed in the passage. G may be true but is not discussed. H contradicts information in the passage.

5. **(C)** The first paragraph of the passage sets the scene in a vast prairie divided by the canyon. Choice A is not mentioned in the passage. B is invalid; the people camped under crags to get away from the cold. Choice D is mentioned in the passage but in a different context.

6. **(H)** The narrator says that Joe's solo journey across the continent was his most memorable achievement. The other choices refer to events that may or may not have actually occurred.

7. **(A)** Line 15 says that the "priority and peril" of Joe's enterprises were greater than those of more famous figures in the history of the West. B is incorrect; the passage does not discuss the longevity of heroes. Choice C is contradicted by lines 13–14, and D is incorrect because Joe is an obscure pioneer hero, the opposite of a standard bearer.

8. **(J)** Nothing in the passage suggests that Joe had ambitions for elective office. However, lines 48–49 say that Joe was an "occasional leader in the wars against the Indians." Later, when gold was discovered in Idaho, he left his home in the woods (lines 54–58) to join the rush.

9. **(A)** The last paragraph of the passage is the narrator's comment on the hostilities between the two groups while caught in the snowstorm during the gold rush. With regard to B, C, and D, the choices list characteristics that Oregonians and Californians had in common.

10. **(H)** According to lines 45–48, the "new people" of Oregon took no interest in the work that Joe did for Oregon before they got there. Choice F may be valid, but Joe's modesty is not discussed in the passage. Choice G is true, but unrelated to the question of why Joe received no appreciation. J is not mentioned in the passage.

11. **(A)** Based on the first two paragraphs, homeless people on the street shocked America at first, but now the sight has become distressingly commonplace.

12. **(G)** Details in the second paragraph suggest that the problem of the homeless is most severe in cities. Nothing in the passage implies that it is confined to specific sites.

13. **(C)** In lines 16–17, the author asserts that the growing problem of homelessness seems to have emerged "out of nowhere."

14. **(J)** According to the passage, the homeless have been helped by the combination of responses discussed in lines 21–28. Choices F, G, and H name measures too limited to deal with the complexities of homelessness

15. **(D)** Toward the end of the paragraph, the author explains the *Continuum of Care*, a comprehensive program that emphasizes long-term solutions to the problem of homelessness. Choices A, B, and C describe measures that have failed to help solve the problem of homelessness.

16. **(J)** These disabilities are examples of added woes suffered by mentally ill, homeless people. Choices F, G, and H fail to convey the author's intent.

17. **(C)** Lines 51–55 refer to a common pattern: the mentally ill, handicapped by a loss of rationality, cannot take care of themselves and thus slide into homelessness. Choices A and D are overgeneralized versions of the truth, and B is not relevant to the question.

18. **(H)** The author points out in lines 70–76 that homeless men and women, driven by hopelessness, commit crimes of survival. Choices F and J are not discussed in the passage. G may indeed describe what occurs, but the passage ignores the plight of homeless people who find themselves the victims of crime.

19. **(A)** Ordinarily, *vortex* is a synonym for whirlpool. In the context of the passage, the word reiterates the idea of a "vicious cycle," or trap from which the mentally ill homeless cannot escape.

20. **(F)** Throughout the passage the author explains the severity of the problem of the mentally ill homeless. His observations seem to be based on what he has observed and learned during his years as a government official. Choice G is vaguely suggested by lines 86–89 but cannot be deemed the purpose of the essay. Rule out H because the passage refers to the findings of only one Gallup poll. J is invalid because, if anything, the author presents his views quite objectively.

21. **(B)** The reference to a trade route in line 7 provides the clue needed to answer this question. Nothing in the passage suggests that choice A, C, or D is correct.

22. **(J)** Evidence of choice F is found in several places, especially in the frightful statistic that in Florence alone 100,000 people died in four months (lines 50–51). G and H are supported by lines 28–30. Although J may have occurred, the closing of churches is not discussed in the passage.

23. **(C)** Boccaccio's stated purpose is to "ease the hearts of the unhappy women in love and bring them pleasure" (lines 14–15). Choice B could be a by-product of the stories in the *Decameron,* but it is not Boccaccio's main purpose. A and D, while hypothetically valid, are not discussed in the passage.

24. **(H)** Lines 13–14 refer to the *Decameron* as a "collection of short stories." Line 61 adds the fact that the collection is fiction. Choice F may be suggested by Boccaccio's introduction to the tales, but it is not the main purpose of the *Decameron*. While G correctly identifies the storytellers, the stories are not based on the personal experience. Although Boccaccio describes the plague, his account of its consequences makes up only a fraction of the *Decameron*, ruling out J as the best answer.

25. **(C)** Boccaccio's description of the onset of the plague (lines 17–27) suggests that what men and women must have feared most was the sudden appearance of swelling in the armpit or groin. Such swelling meant that death was imminent. Choice B names a secondary symptom of the plague. A and D are not mentioned.

26. **(G)** The first half of the passage details the plague's effect on Florence. The fourth paragraph (lines 28–39) lists several ways in which familial bonds were destroyed. Choices F, H, and J are not discussed in the passage.

27. **(B)** Even if you didn't know that "greedy" is a common synonym for *avaricious,* the context provides a clue to the meaning of the word. Priests and pallbearers "charged high prices" (lines 47–48) for their services, presumably because the plague gave them a once-in-a-lifetime opportunity to augment their income.

28. **(F)** The author explains the phrase in lines 54–59: Because of the plague, ten people take refuge on a country estate where they entertain each other by telling stories.

29. **(C)** Considering Boccaccio's stated aim (lines 13–16), all the *Decameron's* stories relate to downcast females who manage to overcome their unhappiness in love. Choices A and B accurately describe what happens in Deoneo's tale, but neither coincides with the "overall pattern" of stories in the *Decameron*. D is a dubious, if not downright absurd, description of the story.

30. **(G)** Ricciardo makes a threatening speech (lines 81–87), warning Bartolomea that she is committing a mortal sin and will inevitably be rejected and humiliated.

31. **(D)** The opening paragraph of the passage says what aquifers are made of. Although sand is listed, most of the items on the list are rocks.

32. **(H)** The discussion of porosity (lines 15–24) says that spaces hold more water when grains are all about the same size. F and G are not mentioned as factors in determining porosity. J cannot be a factor because water cannot pass through a surface crack.

33. **(D)** The permeability of rocks is discussed in lines 25–35. According to lines 26–28, the most important factor in permeability is the number of "connected pore spaces." A is not mentioned in the passage. B is wrong because the thickness of an aquifer is not related to permeability. C is also incorrect because the relative merits of cracks and pores are not discussed here.

34. **(J)** In lines 40–50 all the choices except J are mentioned as contributors to the creation of joints. Therefore, J is the correct answer.

35. **(B)** The analogy is made to show that joints intersect each other (line 51), like pipes in a municipal water system. A, C, and D are matters not discussed in the passage.

36. **(H)** The passage describes limestone as "cavernous" (lines 61–62), that is, full of large holes. F and G are named as the least porous rocks. J holds more water than slate and granite, according to lines 53–54, but not as much as limestone.

37. **(A)** Lines 40–41 indicate that wide joints often make consolidated rocks permeable. B is not a good answer because lines 41–42 say that joints are caused by "the kinds of stresses" that cause earthquakes, not by earthquakes themselves. C alone will not cause consolidated rock to become a good source of water. D is only the first step in making nonporous consolidated rock permeable.

38. **(F)** Lines 15–20 indicate that rocks with well-sorted grains hold more water than rocks with poorly sorted grains. Gravel is cited as an example of rock with well-sorted grains. G is contradicted by lines 59–60, which say that clay will not carry water very readily. H is not correct because the passage says small grains tend to fill up rock with only poorly sorted grains. J is not a proper conclusion to be drawn from information in the passage.

39. **(C)** According to lines 78–79, water-bearing rocks are rare at great depths because of the "weight of overlying rocks." A and B are not discussed in the passage. D is an accurate statement but does not explain why aquifers rarely occur far below the surface of the earth.

40. **(F)** Aquifers of limestone and gravel are identified in the passage as the most permeable rocks. The passage also says that little water is found farther below ground than 2,000 feet. G is cited in the passage as an example of an aquifer that is far-reaching, not one that is especially productive. H is mentioned in the passage but not in the context of a promising site to drill wells. J is not mentioned in the passage.

Science Reasoning Review and Practice

CHAPTER 4

- Data Representation Questions
- Research Summaries Questions
- Conflicting Viewpoints Questions

Be prepared for a science test that is probably different from any you have ever taken. It will draw on your general background in science, but will not ask you to make use of your knowledge of scientific facts. Everything you need to know in order to answer the questions will be given to you.

TIP

The ACT tests science reasoning, not knowledge of subject matter.

All questions are multiple choice. Your choice of answer will be in the form of key letters (either A-B-C-D or F-G-H-J in alternate questions). There are 40 questions altogether, and you have 35 minutes in which to answer them by filling in the appropriate spaces on the answer sheet.

The questions are in seven groups, each group containing five or six questions. Each group starts with a passage of information in the form of graphs, diagrams, paragraphs, or tables. The questions in each group can be answered from the information in the passage.

Testing Reasoning Skills

In the Science Reasoning Test, there are three distinctly different kinds of passages, each testing a different kind of reasoning skill.

- Data Representation. Two or three of the seven passages will present you with some sort of graph or chart. The questions that follow will ask you to interpret the information given and to draw conclusions from it.
- Research Summaries. Three or four passages will each present you with a description of a scientific experiment and the results of the investigation. You will be asked to evaluate the experimental method, to interpret the results, and to appreciate some of the implications of the experimental findings.
- Conflicting Viewpoints. One passage will give you two statements to read. The statements will deal with some controversial scientific question. The scientists who wrote the statements disagree with each other. You will be asked to evaluate the arguments of each, identify the points of disagreement, and recognize the evidence that each scientist cites in favor of his viewpoint. You will not be asked to decide who is right.

Cognitive Levels

Within each group of questions, the level of difficulty is graded. The first questions in the group are the easiest; as you go further into the group, the questions will call for deeper levels of understanding. Three cognitive levels are tested in each group:

- Understanding. These questions, about two in each group, test only your ability to know what the passage is saying. If it is a graph, do you know what the variables are and what values of them are presented? If it is an experiment, can you identify the nature of the experimental problem and the kind of data that were taken? If it is a controversy, do you know what are the points at issue?
- Analysis. About three questions will ask you to find the deeper meanings in the passage. If it is a graph, can you tell how the variables relate to each other and what is implied by the relationship? If it is an experiment, were controls adequate, and what conclusions logically flow from the data? If it is a controversy, how well do the arguments flow from the facts presented by each scientist?
- Generalization. What further study might be suggested by the graph, experiment, or controversy? How do the results impact society at large? What does the study imply for systems that were not part of the study itself?

TACTICS

There is a special skill to taking a multiple-choice test. In some cases, there is even a danger of getting the "wrong" answer by knowing too much. This is because it may be possible to read into the question some subtle idea that did not occur to the person who wrote the question. Good item-writers try to avoid this pitfall, but they do make mistakes. In this test, the candidate who gets the right answer is not necessarily the one who knows most about the subject. It is the one who understands the passage thoroughly and *bases the choice of answer strictly on the contents of the passage*. Extraneous information can lead you to confusion and misinterpretation of the question.

A multiple-choice test is highly structured and formalized. To do well in such a test, you must be thoroughly familiar with the mechanics of the test. This is one reason why you should take the Model Examinations in this book under precisely the same conditions that you will meet in the testing room. Time yourself; take no more than 35 minutes for the whole test. Do not use a calculator, nor any writing instrument other than a soft lead pencil with an eraser on it.

Reduce test anxiety by becoming familiar with the exam format in advance.

When you go into the testing room, you should expect to find that in some questions the choices are labelled **A**, **B**, **C**, and **D**, while in others your choices will be **F**, **G**, **H**, and **J**. You should know what the answer sheet will look like, and that you must mark it with a soft lead pencil. And you must expect to find a group of five to seven questions relating to each passage. With all these mechanical details out of the way, you can go into the testing room ready to work.

TEST STRATEGIES

- **Start by scanning the passage.** Read the passage or look at the data presentation quickly, just to get a rough idea of what it is all about. This should take no more than 20 seconds. Do not stop to study in detail any part that you do not understand. With this background, you are ready to move into a more careful study of the passage.
- **Read the passage again.** Now you can take as much as a minute or even more to understand the passage thoroughly. Feel free to mark up the test booklet with notes. Underline key words.
- **Answer the first question in the group.** In most tests, it is a good policy to skip questions you cannot answer immediately, but there is an exception in this test. The first question in each group will probably be a simple test of understanding. If you cannot answer it, you may well get the others wrong also. If necessary, go back to the passage to find the answer. If you cannot answer the first question, skip the whole passage and come back to it later.
- **Skip the hard questions.** After you have answered the first question, do not initially spend more than 30 seconds or so on any question. If you have time at the end, you can come back and reread the questions you could not get the first time around.
- **Read all the choices.** If you think you have found the right answer at once, do not stop reading. You may discover that there is some idea that has not appeared in the one you think is right. Think of the process as one of eliminating the incorrect answers, rather than selecting the right one. You may find that you can throw out three of the four choices quite easily.
- **If the answers are numerical, estimate.** Calculation takes time, and you should avoid it whenever possible. You can usually eliminate three obviously wrong choices quite easily. For example, suppose a graph shows that an object has traveled 32 meters in seven seconds, and you are asked to find its speed. You are given these choices:

  A. 220 m/s
  B. 40 m/s
  C. 4.6 m/s
  D. 1.4 m/s

  You know that 32 divided by 7 will be a little over 4, so you can pick out **C** as the answer without doing the calculation.
- **Pace yourself.** With 35 minutes to answer the questions for seven passages, you have just five minutes for each passage. If you find yourself spending more than that on one passage, skip it and come back to it later. On average, you should spend about two minutes reading each passage and 30 seconds answering each question.
- **Answer every question.** When you have finished doing the easy questions, go back and try again on some that you skipped. If you have only 30 seconds left at the end, turn to the answer sheet, find those questions you have not answered, and mark them at random. However, be careful not to give more than one answer to any question. There is no penalty for guessing, but an item will be marked wrong if you have given two answers.

DATA REPRESENTATION QUESTIONS

Every experiment and many kinds of theoretical studies present results in some kind of numerical matrix. This can be a data table, the familiar line graph, a bar graph, or any other kind that the author can think up. Three of the passages in the Science Reasoning Test will be some kind of data presentation, and about 15 of the questions will ask you to interpret those passages. You may find that the passage presents you with data in a form that you have never seen before.

Here is a sample Data Representation question. It is a graph showing how the population density of two organisms changes with time, under two different conditions of cultivation. Data always consists of variables. In the graphs below, for example, the variables are species, condition of growth, relative population density, and age. The only numerical variable is age; its unit of measure (days) is marked on the horizontal axis.

Two species of the microorganism *Paramecium* are grown in cultures, and the population density is measured daily. The upper graph shows the results if the two species are raised in separate cultures. The lower graph shows the results if the two species are grown together in a single culture.

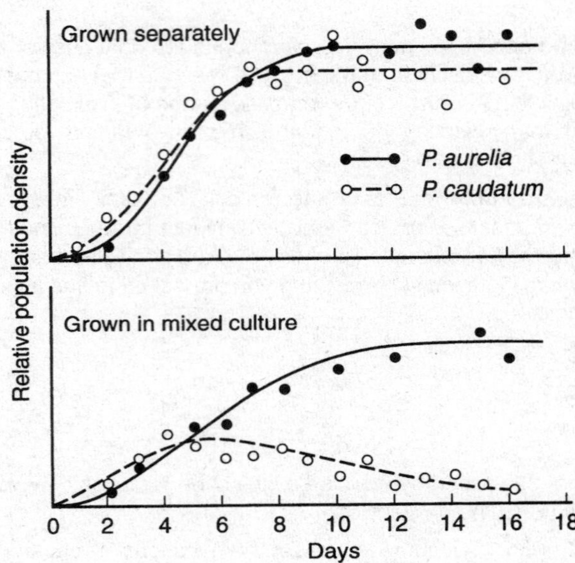

1. When the two species are grown separately,

   A. both species reach maximum population density in 18 days.
   B. both species stop reproducing after 12 days.
   C. populations of both species grow fastest after 3 days.
   D. both species reproduce fastest after 2 days.

This question is at the *understanding* level of cognition. Both **B** and **D** are wrong because the graphs do not indicate rate of reproduction; the population density depends on other factors in addition to reproduction rate. **A** is wrong because the graph levels off at a maximum at 10 days, not 18. The slope of the graph indicates the rate of increase of the population density, and is greatest just after 3 days; the answer is **C.**

2. When the two species are cultured together,

   F. *P. aurelia* is unaffected, but it inhibits the population of *P. caudatum*.
   G. *P. aurelia* reproduces more rapidly than *P. caudatum*.
   H. it takes about a week for the populations to begin to interfere with each other.
   J. each species inhibits the population growth of the other.

   This is an *analysis* question. **G** is wrong because other factors than reproduction rate may affect the population size. **F** is wrong because the population of *P. aurelia* grows more slowly in the presence of *P. caudata* than without it. **H** is wrong because the growth of the *P. caudatum* population starts to diminish in less than 5 days. The answer is **J**.

3. Comparison of the two graphs seems to imply that

   A. the two species of *Paramecium* are competing for the same resources.
   B. no two microorganisms can live successfully in the same culture.
   C. *P. caudatum* could not survive in the wild.
   D. *P. aurelia* is a more common species than *P. caudatum*.

   This question calls on you to decide what general conclusion can reasonably be reached from the information given. **B** is wrong because the experiment deals with only two organisms, and says nothing about any other combinations. **C** and **D** are both wrong because conditions in the wild are nothing at all like those in a culture dish. It seems reasonable that *P. caudatum* is losing out in competition with *P. aurelia;* the answer is **A**.

In interpreting any data representation, you must first be sure you understand what the variables are. If they are not numerical, they will simply be named. There will always be numerical variables as well, and you must be able to find their values. These are the things to look for when you come to a Data Representation question:

What are the units of measure? These will usually be given along with the name of the variable. In a data chart, they will be at the top of the column. In a graph, they will be stated at the bottom and sides of the graph, along with the name of the variable.

What are the values of the variables? In a data chart, the values are entries in the table. In a graph, the values are read off the scales at the bottom and sides of the graph.

Are there any trends? Check to see whether there is an obvious consistent increase or decrease of any values as you move through the chart or graph.

Are there any correlations? If there are trends in any of the variables, how do they relate to trends in other variables? As one variable increases, does another increase or decrease?

These questions are not always applicable, but if they are, it will help you try to find answers to them.

Try these passages for practice. Since they are data representation questions, you must be able to answer certain questions, if they apply. What are the variables? What are the units of measure? How are values read from the data? Are there trends? Are there correlations?

Warm-Up Drill

Passage 1

A growing plant builds its tissues in four regions: the root, the stem, the leaves, and the seeds (grains). The way in which the resources are divided among these four areas is measured by drying the tissues and weighing the four parts separately. As the plant grows, the apportionment of the new tissue among these four regions changes. It also depends on the amount of fertilizer given to them, and on the presence or absence of parasites.

The charts below show the allocation of material into the four regions of wheat plants grown in a square meter of soil under controlled conditions. Separate test plots were given 5 different concentrations of fertilizer, ranging from 0.5 to 4.0 mols per cubic meter. Half of the plots, indicated by [+], were infected with the parasitic plant Striga, and the other half, marked [–], were left uninfected.

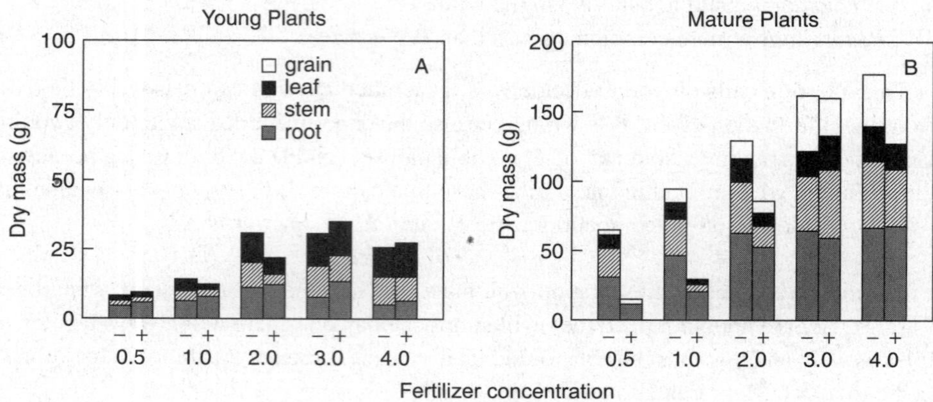

Chart A represents the distribution of mass among the four plant parts 50 days after planting; Chart B gives the same information for wheat 140 days after planting.

1. In the absence of Striga, increasing the concentration of fertilizer from 0.5 to 4.0 raises the dry mass of mature plants by about:

   A. 80 grams.
   B. 110 grams.
   C. 155 grams.
   D. 180 grams.

2. With high fertilizer concentration, the existing parts of a plant that grow most after the first 50 days are the:

   F. roots and leaves.
   G. leaves and grains.
   H. roots and stems.
   J. stems and leaves.

3. When the concentration of the fertilizer is low,

   A. Striga severely restricts the growth of the plants.
   B. no seed is formed in the first 50 days.
   C. Striga does not grow well.
   D. there is little growth after the first 50 days.

4. The parasite does little damage provided that

   F. it attacks only the roots.
   G. it does not attack while the plants are young.
   H. the plants are otherwise healthy.
   J. high doses of fertilizer are used.

5. To a wheat farmer, the main benefit from applying high concentrations of fertilizer is:

   A. more resilient root structure.
   B. suppression of the parasite.
   C. increase in grain mass.
   D. increase in overall size of the plants.

ANSWERS AND EXPLANATIONS

1. **(B)** In the 140-day chart, the bar for 0.5 fertilizer and [–] is about 60 grams; at 4.0 fertilizer, it is 170, so the difference is 110 grams.
2. **(H)** Between the A and the B charts, the roots quadruple and the stems more than double, with or without the parasite. The leaf mass does not change much, and there are no grains present at 50 days.
3. **(A)** With 0.5 level of fertilizer, the [–] bar grows from 10 to 70 grams, while the [+] bar is unchanged between the two charts. No data are given for the growth of Striga.
4. **(J)** In the graph for the mature plants, the bars for the 3.0 and 4.0 units of fertilizer are equal whether or not the parasite is present. No information is provided about where the parasite attacks or in what stage of development, or about the health status of the plants.
5. **(C)** The wheat farmer is in the business of producing grains.

Passage 2

The graphs below show the variation of salt concentration (salinity), temperature, and oxygen concentration at various depths in the Bering Sea. (Note: 0/00 means parts per thousand.)

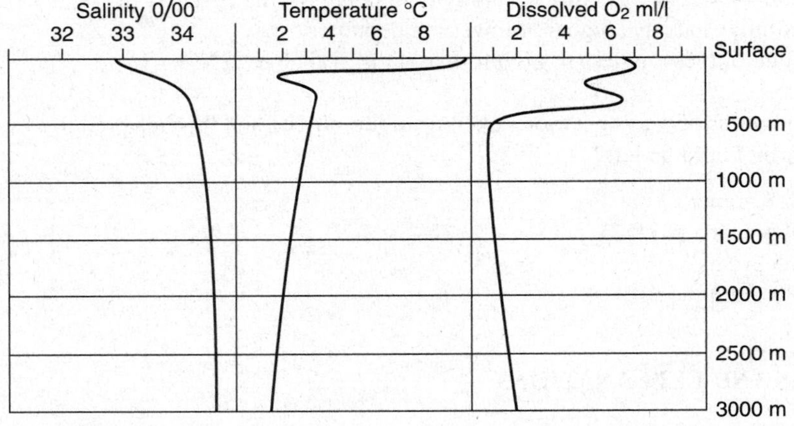

1. According to the graphs, how does salinity vary with depth?

   A. Salt concentration is greatest at or near the surface.
   B. Salt concentration increases uniformly with depth.
   C. Salt concentration is lowest near the surface, and changes only slightly below 1000 m.
   D. Salt concentration is twice as great near the bottom as at the surface.

2. If a diver were rising from a depth of 3000 m, what changes would be registered for most of the trip?

   F. The water would be getting warmer, saltier, and richer in oxygen.
   G. The water would be getting colder, less salty, and richer in oxygen.
   H. The water would be getting colder, less salty, and poorer in oxygen.
   J. The water would be getting warmer, less salty, and poorer in oxygen.

3. Which of the following hypotheses would account for some of the information in the graphs?

   A. Oxygen enters the water through the surface from the air, but little is carried to great depths.
   B. Higher temperatures allow more salt to be held in solution.
   C. Direct heating of the water by the sun has very little effect on the ocean.
   D. Large amounts of salt in solution prevent oxygen from dissolving.

4. A certain kind of fish thrives best at a temperature of 3° C, but needs over 34.2 parts per thousand of salt in its water. According to the graphs, under what conditions would it be most likely to survive?

   F. It would have to live within 100 m of the surface.
   G. It would have to tolerate low oxygen concentration.
   H. Its favored habitat would be below 2000 m.
   J. If the oxygen concentration were high enough, it could thrive in any part of the sea.

5. From these graphs, what general statement could be made about one or more variables in all parts of the ocean?

   A. Salinity and oxygen concentration always increase at depths below 1000 m.
   B. Temperature always drops sharply with depth for the first 100 m.
   C. Salinity is always higher at lower temperatures.
   D. None of these, unless more information is available.

6. If 5 kilograms of sea water were taken from the surface and then allowed to evaporate, how much salt would be left?

   F. 16.5 grams
   G. 33 grams
   H. 165 grams
   J. 330 grams

ANSWERS AND EXPLANATIONS

The independent variable in this graph, depth, is placed on the vertical axis instead of its more usual position on the abscissa. There are three graphs, each with its own dependent variable: salinity, temperature, and dissolved oxygen. Depth is measured in meters, salinity in parts per thousand, temperature in °C, and dissolved oxygen in milliliters per liter. Values of all variables are read off the scales on top and at the right side. The trends are complex. Salinity increases sharply with depth at first, and then only a little at greater depth. Temperature drops abruptly to

100 m, then increases a little, and decreases gradually to greater depths. Oxygen concentration drops, increases, drops substantially, and then increases slightly with greater depths. Below 500 m, there are definite correlations: salinity and oxygen concentration increase while temperature decreases.

1. **(C)** An *understanding* question. While concentration does increase with depth, it surely does not double; it goes from about 32.9 to 34.4. The increase is not uniform; it increases drastically in the first 500 m, and then only a little from there on down.

2. **(J)** Again, a simple test of your *understanding* of the graph. Starting at the bottom and going up, the graphs move to the left (lower) for salinity and oxygen, and to the right (higher) for temperature.

3. **(A)** Now you are required to *analyze* the meanings in the graph. In the first 500 m of the water, the oxygen level is highest at the surface and drops from 6.3 to 1.4 mL/L, so it surely seems that the oxygen enters from the air and little of it penetrates deeply. B is wrong because below 500 m, temperature drops and salinity actually rises. C is wrong because the water is warmest at the surface, where the sun strikes it. D is wrong because both salt concentration and dissolved oxygen increase together below 500 m.

4. **(G)** This is a *generalization* question, requiring you to take several factors into account. Let's eliminate the wrong answers. J is wrong because the fish has to have certain temperatures regardless of the oxygen supply. H is wrong because the temperature is too low below 2000 m. F is wrong because the salinity is too low in the first 100 m. The salinity and temperature are about right at about 500 m but the oxygen concentration is lowest there.

5. **(D)** This question is a warning not to *generalize* from insufficient data. The graphs were made from data taken in the Bering Sea, and there is no particular reason to believe that the same patterns are universal.

6. **(H)** *Analysis*. Salinity at the surface is about 33 parts per thousand, or 33 grams per kilogram. In 5 kg of sea water, there would be 5 × 33 g of salt. You should be able to select the right answer without bothering to do the arithmetic.

RESEARCH SUMMARIES QUESTIONS

The passage for these questions consists of a description of two or more experiments, followed by a statement of the results of the experiments. Your task is to answer five or six questions based on the results. You will succeed if you know what to look for. For purposes of discussing tactics, one experiment will be exemplified.

Here is a sample of a typical Research Summaries passage, along with a typical question at each of the three cognitive levels:

A series of experiments was done to test the hypothesis that air pollution affects fertility.

Experiment 1

Four groups of female mice, with 40 mice in each group, were mated and then exposed to different diets and concentrations of carbon monoxide in the air. The two diets tested were high protein and low protein. Air was either free of carbon monoxide or contaminated with 65 parts per million of carbon monoxide. This is a pollution level that can be found in cities with heavy traffic. The number of females who became pregnant was then recorded:

High protein, clean air:	38
High protein, polluted air:	36
Low protein, clean air:	19
Low protein, polluted air:	9

Experiment 2

The experiment was repeated, this time using ozone instead of carbon monoxide as the pollutant:

High protein, clean air:	35
High protein, polluted air:	22
Low protein, clean air:	20
Low protein, polluted air:	21

1. Since the problem deals with the effects of polluted air, why were groups of mice exposed to clean air?

   A. to keep a healthy strain of mice going
   B. so that they could be compared with mice exposed to polluted air
   C. so that the effects of protein in the diet could be evaluated
   D. to compare the effects of ozone and carbon monoxide

   This is an *understanding* level question. It asks you to apply your knowledge of the meaning of a control. Unless there was a group given clean air, there is no way of telling whether the pollutants really make a difference in the fertility of the mice. The answer is **B**.

2. Which of the following conclusions is justified by the data?

   F. Carbon monoxide pollution by itself reduces the fertility of mice.
   G. A high protein diet promotes good health in mice.
   H. Proteins protect the fertility of mice against the damage caused by carbon monoxide.
   J. Air pollutants reduce the fertility of mice fed on a low protein diet.

   This is an *analysis* question. You must study the data and find in it an implication that supports one of the offered answers. **F** is probably not a good answer because there is very little difference between the mice in good air and air polluted with carbon monoxide if the diet is high in protein. (You must be prepared to make judgment calls in deciding between two answers.) **G** is wrong because nothing in the experiment deals with the general health of the mice. **J** is wrong because there is no justification for extending the results from the carbon monoxide experiment to pollutants in general; indeed, ozone seems to make very little difference, if the protein level is low. The answer is **H**; fertility is little affected by carbon monoxide if there is plenty of protein, but mice produce very few offspring in air polluted with carbon monoxide if the protein level in the diet is low.

3. Which of the following would be an appropriate response to the results of this experiment?

   A. Start a program to inform women who want to become pregnant that they should move to regions with lower air pollution.
   B. Do a similar experiment on women, to see if their ability to become pregnant is affected by air pollutants.
   C. Start a massive campaign to reduce air pollution, particularly in cities.
   D. Start a research program to find out more about how air pollutants affect the fertility rate in animals.

   This *generalization* question requires you to apply the results of the experiment in a broader area. **A** is wrong because mice are not women; there is no evidence that women would react the same way. **B** is wrong; it is good theoretical science, but where would you find women who would volunteer for the experiment? **C** is wrong; while reducing air pollution would probably be a good idea, this experiment does not provide enough evidence to justify such a massive program. **D** is a good idea; with more data in hand, it might be possible to get a better idea of how women might be affected.

Tactics

Here are some hints for attacking questions regarding research summaries, along with a sample passage to show you how these hints apply.

TIP

Approach the Research Summaries questions in a systematic way.

Understand the problem

Each description of an experiment starts with a statement of what the experiment is designed to find out. Read this statement carefully; do not go any further until you are quite sure that you understand exactly what the experimental problem is.

Here is a sample of such a problem statement:

A horticulturist investigated the effects of using a high-nitrogen fertilizer on the growth of privet plants.

Understand the design

Next, study the description of the experimental method. It may be accompanied by a diagram. Try to relate the design of the experiment to the problem that the experiment is designed to solve.

For the sample problem we are considering, the experimental design is as follows:

Fifty 1-year-old privet plants were divided into 10 lots of 5 plants each. All were watered every third day with equal amounts of water. In 9 of the lots, different amounts of high-nitrogen fertilizer were added to the water once every 2 weeks for a year. The heights of the plants were measured at the end of the year.

Identify the variables

Research problems can fall into two general categories. In some problems, the investigator studies some aspect of the natural world, often making measurements of some kind. By comparing measurements, the scientist hopes to come to some understanding of the nature of the process under study. Generally, there will be two or more variables, and what is being sought is a relationship between the variables. If the research problem you are given is of this kind, your first job is to identify the variables.

The second category of research is the experiment. Here, the investigator plays a more active part, varying some condition to see what will happen. The *independent variable* is the quantity that the experimenter adjusts or controls in some way. Presumably, this will make something else change. The something else is the *dependent variable*. Just as in the other kind of problem, you must first be sure that you understand what the variables are.

In the sample we are using, the independent variable is the amount of fertilizer, and the dependent variable is the heights of the plants at the end of the year.

Identify the controls

In an experiment, and sometimes in a strictly observational problem, there is always the danger that some unsuspected variable is affecting the outcome. The experimenter must make sure that whatever outcome is observed is due to changes in the independent variable, not in something else. The way to be sure is to include controls in the experiment. Controls are precautions taken to eliminate all variables except the independent variable.

In our sample experiment, all plants must have identical soil, air, light, and so on. All the plants must be genetically identical. Further, to make sure that the minimum amount of fertilizer has an effect, a special control sample must be included. This is a group of plants that are given no fertilizer. Unless this control group turns out to be different from the experimental groups, there is no way to be sure that the minimum amount of fertilizer is affecting the growth of the plants.

Study the results

The outcome of the experiment may be presented in words, in a diagram, or (most often) in the form of a data table. In such a table, the independent variable appears on the left, and the dependent variable on the right.

For our experiment, a table of experimental results might look like this:

Fertilizer concentration (g/L)	Average height of plant (cm)
0	22.2
5	25.3
10	29.0
15	28.7
20	29.2
25	29.0
30	28.6
35	20.9
40	16.3
45	13.0

An important control in this experiment is the first data point, when no fertilizer was used. Without this, there would be no way to tell whether 5 g/L of fertilizer had any effect at all.

What trend do you notice in these data? You should see that the fertilizer helps, but that over a wide range the amount is not important. There is no significant difference in plant height between 10 g/L and 30 g/L. However, it is also clear that, if too much fertilizer is used, growth is retarded.

Look for flaws in the experiment

Are the controls adequate? Is the conclusion justified by the data? Are the experimental errors so great as to invalidate the results?

In the sample experiment, for example, the experimenter did not specify that all the plants be genetically identical. Another flaw is the failure to describe exactly how the height of the plants was measured.

Once you thoroughly understand the nature of the experiment and the meaning of the results, you should be able to deal with the multiple-choice questions based on the experiment.

Sample Questions

There will be five to seven Research Summaries questions based on a single passage. Look at the following questions, based on the sample experiment described above. Note the reasoning on which your choice of answer might be based.

1. What is the most efficient rate for a commercial grower to apply fertilizer to the privet plants?

   A. 5 g/L
   B. 10 g/L
   C. 20 g/L
   D. 40 g/L

   The answer is B. Higher concentrations cost more, but will not produce any further improvement. Furthermore, too much will actually do damage.

2. If a horticulturist is growing chrysanthemums to produce flowers, how would she know how much fertilizer to use?

   F. Perform an identical experiment with chyrsanthemums.
   G. Use 10 g/L of fertilizer.
   H. Perform a similar experiment with chrysanthemums, but use a different dependent variable.
   J. Grow the plants in sunlight because it is known that sunlight stimulates the formation of flowers.

   The answer is H. The best fertilizer for privet may not be best for chrysanthemums, so G is wrong. The experiment described deals only with growth, not flower formation, so F is wrong. J tells the horticulturist nothing about how much fertilizer is best. She needs a similar experiment, but with flower formation as the dependent variable.

3. In order for the results of this experiment to be meaningful, which of the following would NOT have to be the same for all the experiment samples?

   A. The soil in which the specimens were planted.
   B. The amount of time it took for the plants to flower.
   C. The particular variety of privet used.
   D. The number of hours of daylight to which the plants were exposed.

   The answer is B, since the experimental design proposes only to evaluate rate of growth, not flowering. If none of the other variables were controlled, the experimenter could never be sure whether the differences in growth were due to the fertilizer, or to the soil, the plant variety, or the exposure to daylight.

4. What part of the experimental design was included for the purpose of determining the smallest concentration of fertilizer that has any effect on growth?

   F. Giving one group water only
   G. Using an interval of 5 g/L between fertilizer concentrations
   H. Including a 10-g/L sample
   J. Using plants from a single genetic stock

   The answer is F. This is an important control. Unless there is a different outcome between no fertilizer and 5 g/L, there is no evidence that the 5 g/L of fertilizer did anything.

5. Which of the following situations would NOT invalidate the results of the experiment?

A. Accidental destruction of the sample given 20 g/L of fertilizer
B. The discovery that half of the plants had been potted in a different soil
C. The discovery that the water used already contained substantial amounts of nitrogen
D. The discovery that some of the plants had been taken from a different variety of privet

The answer is A; results of the experiment are quite clear even without this sample. B and D are wrong because a different soil or a different variety might cause differences in the outcome. C is wrong because the nitrogen in the water has not been taken into account in the effort to find the optimum amount.

6. Which of the following hypotheses is suggested by the data?

F. High concentrations of fertilizer damage the roots of plants.
G. Privet plants cannot grow unless there is nitrogen in the soil.
H. If all other conditions are equal, the amount of fertilizer used does not affect plant growth.
J. Any addition of fertilizer to the soil slows photosynthesis.

The answer is F. G is wrong because we have no idea whether there was any nitrogen in the soil of the control, where the plants did grow. H is wrong because the experiment did not test a variety of conditions. J is wrong because we would expect slowing down of photosynthesis to retard growth, while the experiment shows that moderate amounts of fertilizer increase growth. F is right because it offers a reasonable explanation for the growth retardation produced by 35 g/L of fertilizer.

Warm-Up Drill

The Research Summaries questions in the test are likely to be more complex than the example given above. Try the following questions.

Passage 1

A physicist is investigating the effect that different conditions have on the force of friction. The material used is an ordinary brick, with a mass of 1.8 kg. It is pulled across the surface of a wooden table. Friction is measured by pulling the brick with a string attached to a spring scale, calibrated in newtons (N). When the brick is pulled at constant speed, the reading on the scale is equal to the force of friction between the brick and the table top.

Experiment 1

The brick is placed on the table in three different positions. First, it is allowed to rest on its broad face (area = 180 cm^2), then on its side (area = 130 cm^2), and finally on its end (area = 56 cm^2).

Table 1

Area (cm^2)	Friction (N)
180	7.1
130	7.3
56	7.2

Experiment 2

A wooden block of mass 0.6 kg is made to the same dimensions as the brick, and the experiment is repeated.

Table 2

Area (cm^2)	Friction (N)
180	1.2
130	1.1
56	1.2

Experiment 3

This time, the wooden block is loaded by adding 1.2 kg of extra mass on top of it, to give it the same weight as the brick.

Table 3

Area (cm^2)	Friction (N)
180	3.5
130	3.6
56	3.7

1. From Experiment 1, it would be reasonable to hypothesize that:

   A. the surface area of contact does not affect the amount of friction.
   B. friction is large in a brick-to-wood contact.
   C. the amount of friction depends on the way the weight of the object is distributed.
   D. heavy objects have more friction than light ones.

2. Which combination of experiments shows that the amount of friction depends on the weight of the object?

   F. Experiment 1 and Experiment 2
   G. Experiment 1 and Experiment 3
   H. Experiment 2 and Experiment 3
   J. Experiment 1, Experiment 2, and Experiment 3

3. In doing Experiment 3, what was the purpose of adding enough weight to the wooden block to make its weight equal to that of the brick?

   A. To test the hypothesis that adding weight increases friction
   B. To find the relationship between surface area of contact and friction
   C. To find out whether the density of the material influences the amount of friction
   D. To control other factors and test the effect of the nature of the materials in contact

4. The experimenter repeated the experiment with the unloaded wooden block mounted on three tiny wooden points, which were the only contact with the table top. If the results of all these experiments hold good for extreme values of the experimental variables, about how much would the friction be?

   F. About 0.4 N
   G. Substantially less than 1.2 N
   H. About 1.2 N
   J. Substantially more than 1.2 N

5. Common experience indicates that it is much harder to slide some boxes across a floor than others. Which of the following reasons why this is true is demonstrated in these experiments?

   A. Friction is greater if there is more surface in contact.
   B. A heavy box will have more friction against the floor than a light one.
   C. Objects of irregular shape have more friction because they dig into the floor.
   D. The amount of friction depends on how the weight of the object is distributed.

6. The results of these experiments suggest that, if three bricks were piled up and pulled along as before, the amount of friction would be about:

   F. 3.6 N.
   G. 7.2 N.
   H. 14.4 N.
   J. 22.6 N.

ANSWERS AND EXPLANATIONS

1. (A) In spite of the fact that one surface is almost three times as great as another, there is no substantial difference in the amount of friction. The small differences are surely due to experimental variation. This is obvious when it is noted that the value obtained for the 56-cm^2 surface is a little larger than that for the 180-cm^2 surface. B is wrong because there is no comparison with other readings to decide what constitutes large friction. C is wrong because the experiment did not vary weight distribution. D is wrong because in this experiment the same object was used throughout.

2. (H) In these two experiments, both the surface area of contact and the kind of materials in contact are the same, and the only difference is in the weight. The other three choices all include Experiment 1, in which a different kind of material is in contact with the surface, and this might be the reason for the difference in results.

3. (D) With the weight added, all other variables are controlled and the only difference between the brick and the wooden block, as far as contact with the table top is concerned, is in the nature of the material. The other choices are wrong because the experiment makes no comparison of different weights, surface areas, or densities.

4. (H) The data indicate that friction does not depend on surface area of contact. This is tested to extreme limits by repeating the experiment with a very small surface area. If the relationships hold up for extreme values, the friction should be the same for a very small area as for a large one.

5. (B) Comparing Experiment 2 with Experiment 3 shows that, even if the materials and the surface area in contact are the same, friction is greater when the weight of the object is greater. There is no evidence in these experiments that shape or weight distribution affects friction. Choice A is wrong because the experiments do not show any difference due to surface area.

6. **(J)** Experiments 2 and 3 show that, when the effective weight of the wooden block is increased by raising the mass from 0.6 kg to 1.8 kg, the friction triples. This suggests that friction is proportional to the weight of the object. Since three bricks weigh three times as much as one, the friction with three bricks ought to be three times as great as with a single brick.

Passage 2

The alkaloid neotrix seems to have some effect on the higher functions of the brain. To test its possibilities, an experiment was done, using the maze-running capacity of laboratory rats as a measure of mental function. Two properties were tested: intelligence and memory.

The experiment used 3 groups of 10 white rats each. After several runs, each rat eventually learned to go through the entire maze to reach a food pellet without making a wrong turn. The experimental datum was the number of times the rat had to run the maze until it could do it without a mistake.

For each rat, intelligence was measured by counting the number of runs the rat needed to learn the maze (i) at the start of the experiment. A measure of memory (m) was made by putting the rat into the maze again three days later, and again counting the number of runs it required to go through without error. In the data chart, below, data for each rat is entered as i,m. Thus, for example, 6,2 means that at the start, the rat ran the maze without error on the 6th run; three days later, it reached the food without making a wrong turn on the second try.

The experiment was done three times, once with untreated rats, once with rats that had been fed 20 milligrams of neotrix a day before the test began, and once with rats that had been given 20 milligrams of neotrix every day for two weeks before the test began.

Experiment 1. Untreated rats

A	B	C	D	E	F	G	H	I	J	average
7,4	5,3	7,4	8,3	5,4	6,2	4,4	4,5	7,4	5,5	5.7, 4.3

Experiment 2. Rats medicated for one day

K	L	M	N	O	P	Q	R	S	T	average
5,2	5,1	7,4	6,4	4,2	6,2	6,2	6,2	5,2	4,3	5.5, 2.4

Experiment 3. Rats medicated for 2 weeks

U	V	W	X	Y	Z	A'	B'	C'	D'	average
7,4	6,5	5,1	6,3	7,1	6,3	4,3	6,1	8,4	6,1	6.1, 2.5

1. The data seem to indicate that neotrix improves the rats':

   A. memory only.
   B. memory and intelligence.
   C. intelligence only.
   D. neither memory nor intelligence.

2. One notable feature of the unmedicated rats is that:

   F. they lost their memory more quickly than the medicated rats.
   G. they were able to run the maze more rapidly than the medicated rats.
   H. some of them demonstrated no memory of the maze.
   J. none of them performed worse after three days than in their first trials.

3. What accounts for the unusually poor intelligence of rat D?

   A. It is just an accident of sampling.
   B. It was probably chosen as an example of how a less intelligent rat will react.
   C. It responded unusually well to the medication.
   D. It may have had previous experience in maze running.

4. An appropriate measure of the memory of each rat would be:

   F. i/m
   G. i – m
   H. i + m
   J. m/i

5. The most notable effect of medicating the rats for 2 weeks instead of just once is that:

   A. on the average, memory was substantially improved.
   B. on the average, intelligence was substantially improved.
   C. some of the rats retained their memory for a longer period of time.
   D. some of the rats showed perfect memory.

6. It would seem that a valuable control would be to test each rat's intelligence before the medication was given. Why was this not done?

   F. The rat had to be kept unfamiliar with the maze before the experiment began.
   G. It would have taken too much time for a very trivial improvement in the experiment.
   H. It was unnecessary because the rat intelligence was controlled and well known from Experiment 1.
   J. Too much maze-running might tire the rats and invalidate the results.

ANSWERS AND EXPLANATIONS

1. **(A)** Comparing the averages, there is little change in i, the figure before the comma, which represents intelligence. The second figure, m, indicating memory, shows that the rats, on the average, required fewer runs on the second try if they had been treated with neotrix.

2. **(H)** Three of the untreated rats took at least as many runs after the rest as at the beginning. Rat H was actually worse after the rest. No tests for speed or rate of memory loss were made.

3. **(A)** There is some variation in the intelligence of the rats, and this one is not that far out. It was not medicated. Good experimental design would require that rats have no previous experience in mazes, so there would be no way to measure its intelligence in advance.

4. **(G)** A small value of m indicates that the maze is well-remembered after 3 days; if i = m, there was no memory.

5. **(D)** Rats W, Y, B', and D' ran the maze perfectly on the first try after the rest period; none of the rats in the second group did. The higher intelligence is only an accident of sampling; it cannot be the result of medication because i was measured before any medication was given. There is little difference in average m. Since rats of both groups rested for just 3 days, there was no test of the memory duration.

6. **(F)** Since there is considerable variation in the maze-learning ability of the rats, an initial measure of intelligence of each rat would indeed be better than just a measure of the average intelligence of all the rats. This cannot be done, however, because this would familiarize the rats with the maze before the experiment began. There is no reason to suspect exhaustion.

CONFLICTING VIEWPOINTS QUESTIONS

Scientific information is never complete. While ideas and theories are developing, scientists will continue to disagree with each other. It is these disagreements that provide the spur for research. Experiments and other forms of investigation are specifically designed to resolve points at issue. It is through this dialogue of scientists with each other and with nature that consensus is eventually reached.

In the Conflicting Viewpoints questions, you will be given short statements representing the ideas of two scientists. They will disagree with each other. Your job is to analyze the arguments and information in the two statements. You will be asked to identify the nature of the disagreement, to tell why each of the scientists has arrived at the opinion expressed, and to identify forms of evidence that might resolve the conflict.

In this type of question, you will not be asked to decide which of the two scientists is correct. You will be required to identify points of agreement and disagreement. You may be asked to identify kinds of evidence that would tend to support or to deny either of the two viewpoints.

Here is a sample Conflicting Viewpoints passage, with a sample of possible questions at each of the three cognitive levels.

Passage

There has been a steady increase in the average temperature of the earth for the last 150 years. Since 1861, the average temperature, all over the world, has gone up one degree Fahrenheit. This may not seem like much, but if the trend continues, the result will be disastrous. The polar ice caps would melt, flooding all coastal areas and reducing the total land area of the earth by 30 percent. All climatic zones would change; farmland would turn to desert and forest would turn into prairie.

Scientist 1

It has become increasingly clear that global warming is the result of the accumulation of the "greenhouse gases" in the atmosphere. These gases, chiefly carbon dioxide, act as a kind of blanket, preventing heat from escaping into outer space. As industry has advanced and automobiles fill our highways, the burning of coal, oil, gasoline, and natural gas has more than doubled the amount of carbon dioxide in the atmosphere. It is up to industry to find ways to reduce the amount of carbon dioxide coming out of smokestacks and exhaust pipes. Unless drastic steps are taken to deal with this problem, the world as we know it will disappear.

Scientist 2

Before placing an enormously expensive burden on industry, we must be sure of our ground. While the greenhouse effect may well be a part of the reason for the warming of the earth, it cannot be the whole story. Most of the temperature increase occurred before 1940, but most of the carbon dioxide increase has happened since then. Something else is contributing to the warming of the earth. The temperature of the earth depends strongly on the level of sunspot activity on the sun. The sun heats up during high sunspot years. Solar activity goes through cycles. When activity is high, increased levels of ultraviolet radiation deplete the ozone layer of the upper atmosphere and the increased flow of charged particles from the sun affects the formation of clouds. All of these effects have complex and poorly understood effects on the earth's climate, and could easily result in long-range and cyclic climate changes.

1. The two scientists agree that

   F. sunspot activity affects the climate of the earth.
   G. there is a long-range trend to a warmer earth.
   H. the major cause of warming is carbon dioxide.
   J. something must be done to avert a catastrophe.

   This is an *understanding* question. **F** is wrong because Scientist 1 does not address the question of sunspot activity at all. **H** is wrong because Scientist 2 thinks that sunspot activity may play the major role. **J** is wrong because Scientist 2's theory precludes the possibility of ameliorative action. The answer is **G**; both agree that the earth has gotten warmer.

2. In responding to Scientist 2, Scientist 1 might reply that

   A. the measured value of the increase in sunspot activity is far too small to account for the observed warming.
   B. it is widely known that it is the carbon dioxide in the atmosphere that produces the warming.
   C. the flow of charged particles from the sun actually decreases during periods of high sunspot activity.
   D. it is possible to cut down on the atmospheric carbon dioxide by promoting the growth of plants.

   To answer this *analysis* question, you have to eliminate proffered answers that do not deal with issues discussed by either scientist, such as **D**. Appeals to authority, like **B**, are not acceptable scientific debate. **C** is an insult to Scientist 1, who surely knows the properties of an easily measurable phenomenon. The answer is **A**, because there is a strong element of judgment in making this decision, particularly since Scientist 2 admits that the phenomena are not well understood.

3. What course of action might be suggested by Scientist 2 and opposed by Scientist 1?

   F. Convene a committee of industry and government leaders to determine what steps can be taken to reduce carbon dioxide emission.
   G. Start a long-range research project to explore the possibility of neutralizing the flow of charged particles from the sun.
   H. Investigate the possibility that other greenhouse gases such as methane have an important effect on warming.
   J. Start a long-range research project to evaluate the relative importance of carbon dioxide and sunspot activity.

   Now you must look for an appropriate *generalization*. **F** is wrong because Scientist 2 does not believe that carbon dioxide is at the heart of the problem. **G** is wrong; Scientist 2 has not committed himself to the idea that charged particles are the major culprit. **H** is wrong; neither scientist has suggested that other gases are involved. **J** is right; Scientist 2 feels that more information is needed, but Scientist 1 might object to a long-range project because the problem of carbon dioxide is too urgent.

Tactics

In approaching a question of this type, start by reading it quickly. This may be enough for you to apply the first important tactic: *Identify the basic disagreement*. Consider, for example, this passage:

What effect does crash dieting have on long-term loss of weight? There is some evidence that repeatedly losing and gaining weight makes it more difficult to lose weight and keep it off. Two scientists disagree as to the significance of the evidence.

Scientist 1

People who repeatedly gain and lose weight acquire a permanent, long-term change in their metabolism. Their metabolism slows down, so that they use less food energy than others. The result is that the excess energy in their food becomes stored as fat. This means that crash dieting is self-defeating. Experiments on rats have shown that alternating underfeeding with overfeeding results in a lower metabolic rate. The lower rate enabled the rats to gain weight more easily, with less food than they would ordinarily need. Further, a study of high school wrestlers found that some of them lost and regained weight as much as 10 times during the wrestling season. In the off-season, they were no fatter than those whose weight did not vary, but their metabolic rate was substantially lower. The implication is that people who crash-diet and then regain weight are likely to experience more and more difficulty in losing it.

Scientist 2

There is no real evidence that repeated gain and loss of weight makes it more difficult to lose. The studies on rats are suggestive, but there is no reason to believe that they have any implication for obese human beings. The study involving high school wrestlers was severely flawed. The wrestlers in the study were all in summer camp, after the end of the wrestling season. The dieters may have been artificially holding their weight down by careful control of their diets, and this is known to lower the metabolism. There is no evidence that this lowered metabolism made it more difficult to lose weight. There is another study, in which the subjects were not rats or wrestlers, but obese people who had lost weight and then gained it back. When they regained weight, their metabolism was just the same as it was before they dieted. Furthermore, there was no difference in their ability to lose weight again.

You can analyze this passage, and any other like it, by asking yourself a series of questions about it. Only after you have answered them in your own mind are you in a position to look at the questions you will have to answer.

TIP

Generate questions in your mind about the conflicting viewpoints, and answer them before reading the multiple-choice questions.

What is the basic question at issue? Does repeated gain and loss of weight make it more difficult to lose?

What is the position of each of the scientists on the question? Scientist 1 says yes; Scientist 2 says no.

What evidence does Scientist 1 bring to justify his position? Two studies: one on rats and one on high school wrestlers.

What evidence does Scientist 2 bring to support his position? A study of obese people.

What flaws does Scientist 2 find in the position of Scientist 1? The experiments were done on rats and high school athletes, not on obese people. There was inadequate control because the diets of the high school wrestlers in summer camp were not monitored. No connection was made between lowered metabolism and difficulty in losing weight.

What flaws does Scientist 1 find in the position of Scientist 2? In this particular passage, Scientist 1 does not rebut Scientist 2. You may find that this is often the case.

Sample Questions

Here are some multiple-choice questions that might be asked about this passage:

1. The position taken by Scientist 1 involves the assumption that:

   A. a lower metabolic rate makes it more difficult to lose weight.
   B. the metabolism of a rat is exactly like that of a human being.
   C. high school wrestlers generally have a weight problem.
   D. large amounts of food do not necessarily contain large amounts of energy.

   The answer is **A**. In both of the experiments cited by Scientist 1, the only outcome found was lower metabolism, and he assumed that this resulted in more difficulty in losing weight. **B** is wrong because exact similarity in all respects is not needed; a rough resemblance is enough to suggest a relationship. **C** is wrong because there is no implication that any of the results are relevant to high school wrestlers generally. **D** is wrong because neither scientist addressed the question of the energy content of different foods.

2. Scientist 2 could claim that the study he cites is more meaningful because:

   F. it was done with a higher degree of accuracy.
   G. it had better controls.
   H. it was done with the subjects to which the problem applies.
   J. it did not use metabolism as a measure of weight loss.

   The answer is **H**. Weight loss is a problem for obese people, not high school athletes or rats. **F** and **G** are wrong because Scientist 2 said nothing about either accuracy or controls. **J** is wrong because Scientist 1 used metabolism as a measure of *ability* to lose weight, not as a measure of weight loss.

3. What is a point on which both scientists agree implicitly?

   A. Repeated gain and loss of weight is undesirable.
   B. Science must be concerned with finding ways to help people control their weight.
   C. Ways should be found to help people to lower their metabolism.
   D. Experiments with rats are of no use in making decisions about people.

   The answer is **B**. Both scientists are discussing the theory behind the problems of helping people to lose weight; they disagree on the means. Choice **A** is wrong because Scientist 2 could find no evidence for this statement. **C** is wrong because Scientist 2 claims there is no proof that a lower metabolism makes it more difficult to lose weight. **D** is wrong; Scientist 1 quoted experiments with rats, and even Scientist 2 did not deny that they may have some value.

4. What serious flaw did Scientist 2 find in one of the experiments cited by Scientist 1?

   F. The rats were not given the same diet as the wrestlers.
   G. There was inadequate control of the diet of the wrestlers.
   H. The wrestlers were not tested during the wrestling season.
   J. The metabolism of the rats was not tested before the experiment.

   The answer is **G**. Apparently, there was some suspicion that the wrestlers who dieted were still dieting in camp. **F** is wrong because no experiment was made, or could be made, comparing the reaction of the rats with that of the wrestlers. **H** is wrong because the experiment specifically called for measuring metabolism after the period of varying weight. **J** is wrong because Scientist 2 did not bring this question up. He had no reason to suspect Scientist 1 of complete incompetence.

5. When other studies of this problem are made, which of the following outcomes would tend to strengthen the position of Scientist 1?

   A. The discovery that monkeys fed an inadequate diet develop unusually low metabolism.
   B. An experiment showing that rats with artificially lowered metabolism eat less than other rats.
   C. A study showing that obese people eat more than thin people.
   D. A study of people with unusually low metabolism, showing that they can maintain body weight with smaller amounts of food.

   The answer is **D**. Scientist 2 had cast doubt on the proposition that a lower metabolism indicates the need for smaller amounts of food. **A** is wrong because neither scientist raised the question of adequacy of diet. **B** is wrong because this experiment does not address the question of the relationship between amount of food consumed and weight gain. **C** is wrong because it says nothing about the problem of alternate weight gain and loss.

6. Which of the following questions about proper diet would be answered, at least in part, by the resolution of this disagreement?

   F. Is it better to lose weight, at the risk of regaining it, or just to stay obese?
   G. Is it important to control the amount of fat in the diet?
   H. In dieting to lose weight, is it important to be under the care of a doctor?
   J. Are overweight persons at an exceptionally great risk of still further increase in weight as they grow older?

   The answer is **F**. If Scientist 1 is right, repeated loss and regain of weight predisposes to still greater weight gain. The study says nothing about the amount of fat in the diet (**G**), the need for a doctor's supervision (**H**), or aging (**J**).

Warm-Up Drill

Passage 1

Frogs all over the world are in trouble. Populations are diminishing or disappearing, and many frogs are being born with deformities such as extra legs or limbs missing completely. Scientists are trying to find out why this is happening.

Scientist 1

Frogs are a sentinel species, like the canary that tells miners when their air is poisoned. The death and deformity of so many frogs is telling us that our environment is polluted.

A likely cause of the damage to frogs is that the growing tadpoles are being subjected to unusually high levels of ultraviolet radiation. Air pollution has significantly damaged the ozone layer of the atmosphere, allowing more of the damaging ultraviolet rays to reach the earth. In one experiment, when salamander eggs were subjected to normal levels of ultraviolet radiation, 85 percent died before hatching. It seems likely that this radiation is also damaging frogs.

Chemical pollution is another suspect. One pond in Minnesota was found to produce many deformed frogs. When frog embryos were laboratory-raised in water taken from that pond, three quarters of them grew with developmental deformities. One possible cause is methoprene in the water, a chemical that is widely used to control mosquitoes and fleas.

Meanwhile, we must surely take note of the fact that these deformed and dying frogs are giving us the message that pollutants produced by human activity are placing our worldwide biological system in jeopardy.

Scientist 2

There are serious flaws in the experiments that have attributed the frog crisis to pollution. The ultraviolet experiment was done with salamanders, not frogs. Frogs are different; they have an enzyme that repairs the damage caused by ultraviolet radiation. Methoprene is not a serious candidate, since it can do its damage only in concentrations hundreds of times greater than has ever been found in a pond.

It is probable that there is more than one frog problem. A dead embryo is not the same as a frog with a missing arm or with too many legs. A missing arm or leg might be the work of a heron or predatory fish that made a grab for the frog and managed to get only part of it. This surely happens, but no one knows how frequently; no studies have been done.

While there may be many reasons why frogs are deformed, only one reason has been thoroughly substantiated. The main, and perhaps the only, thing that makes a frog grow extra hind legs, is a parasitic worm, a type of trematode. These worms lay their eggs in tadpoles. Field studies on five different species of frogs in different parts of the country have found trematode parasites at the bases of the limbs of deformed frogs.

While the case for pollutants has not been ruled out, parasitism is the only cause of developmental anomalies for which the detailed mechanism of the process is known. It is quite possible that parasites are responsible for other kinds of malformations.

1. The two scientists agree that:

   A. pollution is the main cause of abnormal development in frogs.
   B. there is a worldwide epidemic of death and malformation in frogs.
   C. the main cause of developmental anomaly is ultraviolet radiation.
   D. trematode parasitism causes a frog to form extra legs.

2. Scientist 2 challenges the evidence for methoprene as a cause because:

   F. the required dosages are not found in nature.
   G. methoprene has been shown to be safe.
   H. the necessary experiments were done on salamanders, not frogs.
   J. it has been shown that the cause of the deformities is parasites.

3. According to Scientist 2, an important error in Scientist 1's position is that he overlooked the fact that:

   A. it has been shown that ultraviolet radiation has no effect on salamanders.
   B. wherever frogs are dying, parasites are in the water.
   C. there has been no increase in the amount of ultraviolet radiation reaching the earth as the ozone layer becomes depleted.
   D. methoprene levels in ponds are too low to have an effect.

4. The position taken by Scientist 1 would be greatly strengthened by the discovery that:

   F. there are no parasites in certain ponds that produce deformed frogs.
   G. deformed frogs are not found in certain parts of the world.
   H. there is a common polluting chemical that causes deformation of frog embryos.
   J. parasites can be found in frogs that have not become deformed.

5. A serious limitation of the position of Scientist 2 is that:

   A. it accounts for only one kind of damage to frogs.
   B. it fails to explore the details of the process by which the damage is produced.
   C. it overlooks the damage produced by ultraviolet radiation.
   D. it overlooks the possibility that there may be many causes of deformity.

6. What is a likely response that Scientist 1 might make to the statement of Scientist 2?

   F. Scientist 2 is wrong because it is known that the developmental errors in frogs are the result of environmental pollution.
   G. Scientist 2 is damaging the international effort to deal with chemical pollution of the environment.
   H. Even if Scientist 2 is right, the world must still deal with the problem of chemical pollution.
   J. In the face of a worldwide pollution problem, it is a waste of time and money to investigate frog parasites.

ANSWERS AND EXPLANATIONS

1. **(B)** Both scientists are addressing the problem of the epidemic of deformed embryos in frogs. Scientist 2 challenges the evidence showing that ultraviolet radiation and chemical pollution are the cause, so A and C are wrong. D is wrong because Scientist 1 does not discuss the parasite problem.

2. **(F)** Scientist 2 points out that it would take an enormous dose of methoprene to produce the observed deformities. There is no evidence as to the safety of methoprene, so G is wrong. H is wrong; that evidence applies to the ultraviolet problem, not methoprene. Scientist 2 agrees that there may be many causes in addition to parasites, so J is wrong.

3. **(D)** This known fact was overlooked by Scientist 1. A is wrong because the effect of ultraviolet radiation on salamanders is not an issue. Scientist 1 does not address the problem of the level of ultraviolet radiation, so C is wrong. B is wrong because parasites cause deformities, not the death of frogs.

4. **(H)** Scientist 1's main thesis is that deformation is caused by environmental pollution, so the discovery of a pollutant that can be shown to cause deformation would greatly strengthen his position. F and J are wrong because Scientist 1 does not challenge the idea that some parasites may cause deformation in some frogs but not others. G is wrong because geographic data of this kind would not support the position of Scientist 1 unless correlation with pollution could be shown.

5. **(A)** The trematode hypothesis accounts only for extra limbs, but not for missing limbs or early death. B is wrong because Scientist 2 specifically states the mechanism that interferes with development has been found. C is wrong; Scientist 2 specifically allows for other causes. D is wrong because Scientist 2 specifically makes the point that many other causes may be involved.

6. **(H)** Scientist 1 sees the frog problem as only a part of the pollution of the earth. F is wrong because Scientist 2 has taken no position on pollution. G is wrong because Scientist 2 has said nothing to disparage the idea that pollution may be at fault. J is wrong; any scientist knows that many investigations are important even though they have no immediate application.

Passage 2

The forests of the high Appalachian Mountains are being destroyed. Millions of dead spruce and fir trees cover the peaks of the mountains, from Maine to Georgia. The new growth is low shrubbery, like blackberries, instead of trees. What is causing the loss of trees in the Appalachians? Two differing opinions are presented below.

Scientist 1

The forests are dying because of a combination of air pollution and unusual weather patterns. Recent years have shown a substantial increase in the concentration of ozone and of nitrogen and sulfur oxides in the air. The oxides come from the burning of fossil fuels. Rain, snow, and fog in the mountains pick up these oxides and turn acid. Ozone is produced by the action of ultraviolet light on hydrocarbons in the air, which are found in automobile exhaust and wastes from certain industrial processes. This pollution has been going on for decades, and the effect is cumulative. The last straw was added by the unusually high temperatures and drought of recent years. Unless serious steps are taken to reduce air pollution, there is a distinct danger that we will lose all our forests.

Scientist 2

While the air has surely become more polluted, there is no evidence that this is what is destroying the Appalachian trees. Trees in the high mountains are living precariously at best and are easily destroyed. The hot, dry summers and cold winters of recent years could easily account for the damage. Also, the spruce budworm and other insect pests are now unusually abundant and have done a great deal of damage to the trees. There have been other instances of massive die-off of trees at high elevations in years past, when the air was purer followed by recovery when more favorable conditions return. If the chief source of damage were air pollution, we would expect that the damage would be worse at lower elevations, where the factories and automobiles that produce pollution are concentrated. Yet there is little evidence of damage to the commercial forests at lower elevations. This does not mean that we should ignore air pollution; it is clearly a threat, and we must learn more about it and develop ways to control it.

1. According to Scientist 2, what would be expected to happen to the forest in future years?

   A. Return of a permanent, self-sustaining forest in the high Appalachians
   B. Permanent conversion of the high mountains to low-growing shrubbery instead of trees
   C. Development of timber-producing commercial forest in the high mountains
   D. Regeneration of the forest, which will again be killed off from time to time

2. Without challenging any facts, what might Scientist 1 say to counter Scientist 2's argument about the effect of insect pests?

   F. Insects do not really do much damage.
   G. The insects have been able to proliferate so well because pollution has weakened the trees.
   H. Insect populations are being well controlled by birds.
   J. Insects are actually helpful because they cross-pollinate the trees.

3. What further development would weaken the case made by Scientist 2?

   A. Destruction of the blackberry bushes that are replacing the forests
   B. Evidence of damage to commercial forests at lower elevations
   C. Insect infestations of low-level forests
   D. Evidence that the mountain-top forests are showing signs of healthy regeneration

4. What is the opinion of Scientist 2 with respect to the problem of the effect of polluted air on the high forests?

    F. Polluted air does not damage forests, and no action is needed.
    G. The evidence is inadequate to prove that the damage in the high Appalachians is due to polluted air, but the problem needs to be studied further.
    H. Polluted air damages trees and may soon present a problem to commercial forests at lower levels.
    J. There is no substantial pollution in the air at high elevations, so it is not damaging the trees.

5. Suppose there were to appear a healthy new crop of spruce and fir trees on the mountain tops. Which of the following studies would NOT contribute to a resolution of the difference of opinion between the two scientists?

    A. A study to determine whether there has been any change in the ozone levels in the air
    B. A study of weather patterns over the preceding few years
    C. A study of changes in automobile exhausts due to new antipollution devices in cars
    D. A study of the conditions under which spruce seeds survive in the soil

6. What is a point on which both scientists agree?

    F. The air is being polluted by waste products of industry and transportation.
    G. The spruce budworm is a major cause of the destruction of forests.
    H. Stressful weather conditions alone can account for the destruction of the Appalachian forests.
    J. Low-elevation commercial forests are in imminent danger of destruction by polluted air.

7. To refute Scientist 2's opinion, Scientist 1 might:

    A. show that there is extensive damage to trees wherever in the world the air pollution levels are high.
    B. show that healthy spruce forests recover easily from damage by the spruce budworm.
    C. claim that spruce trees thrive at lower elevations, but are poorly adapted to the extremes of mountaintop weather.
    D. show that, because of atmospheric circulation patterns, the air at high elevations is not heavily polluted.

ANSWERS AND EXPLANATIONS

1. **(D)** Scientist 2 believes that from time to time unusual weather conditions kill off the high forest, even if there is no air pollution. Choice A is wrong because Scientist 2 does not believe that the forest can ever be permanent. B is wrong because he thinks that the forest can regenerate itself after it has been destroyed. C is wrong because he has never made any such suggestion.

2. **(G)** Scientist 1 believes that pollution has damaged the trees, and might well suggest that this damage makes them subject to attack by insects. The other answers are wrong because they ignore the observable facts that the insects are rife and harmful.

3. **(B)** One of the points that Scientist 2 makes is that pollution at low levels does not seem to be damaging the forests there. Choices A and C are irrelevant. D is wrong because regeneration of the high forest would support Scientist 2's contention that forest destruction occurs naturally from time to time.

4. **(G)** Scientist 2 makes no claim that polluted air is innocent; but only that the evidence for its guilt is not conclusive. That is why F and H are wrong. He makes no claim that mountain air is unpolluted, so J is wrong.

5. **(D)** Choices A and C are wrong because, if such studies showed a substantial decrease in pollution, Scientist 1's claim that pollution destroys the forest would be upheld. B is wrong because a correlation of weather patterns with forest regeneration would tend to support Scientist 2.

6. **(F)** Both scientists recognize the existence of pollution, and both see that it is a problem. G is wrong because Scientist 1 might well think that the insects can damage only unhealthy trees. H is wrong because Scientist 1 thinks that the main cause of damage is pollution, and the weather is just a contributing factor. J is wrong because Scientist 2 has not found any damage to low-elevation trees, although he might agree that this could be a long-range problem.

7. **(A)** This would strongly reinforce Scientist 1's opinion that the major cause of damage to trees is air pollution. B is wrong because Scientist 2 believes that forest destruction and recovery are common events. C is wrong because Scientist 2 thinks that mountaintop trees may be destroyed by extremes of weather alone. D is wrong because any such demonstration would undermine Scientist 1's claim that air pollution is the chief culprit.

SAMPLE SCIENCE REASONING TEST

Now that you have had practice on all three kinds of questions, here is a complete test, much like the one you will have to take. In trying it out, it is important that you time yourself. Allow only 35 minutes to complete the whole test. Remember these rules:

For each passage, study it carefully and answer the first question.

For the other questions, skip any that you cannot answer within a half minute or so.

When you have finished all those questions, go back and work on the ones you skipped. If you are not sure of an answer, make your best guess.

If you still have any unanswered questions and there is only a minute left, enter answers at random.

Look at your clock and start NOW. Good luck!

Directions: This test consists of several distinct passages. Each passage is followed by a number of multiple-choice questions based on the passage. Study the passage, and then select the best answer to each question. You are allowed to reread the passage.

Passage 1

The graph below indicates the numbers of three different kinds of rare plants that were found in a grassy plot over a period of years.

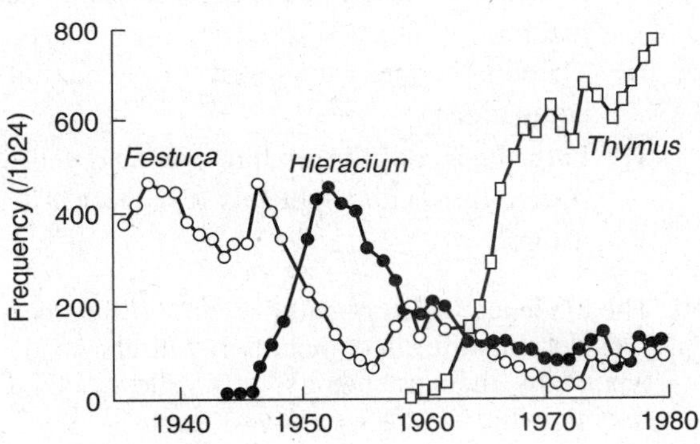

1. Which plants were present in approximately equal numbers in 1950?

   A. *Festuca* and *Thymus*
   B. *Festuca* and *Hieracium*
   C. *Hieracium* and *Thymus*
   D. *Hieracium, Festuca,* and *Thymus*

2. Which of the following statements correctly describes the situation in 1963?

   F. The densities of both *Festuca* and *Hieracium* were rapidly decreasing.
   G. The density of *Thymus* was much greater than that of either of the other two plants.
   H. All three plants had equal and unchanging densities.
   J. All three plants had equal densities, but one was increasing.

3. What was happening to the density of *Hieracium* in 1950?

   A. It was increasing at the rate of 20 units per year.
   B. It was increasing at the rate of 75 units per year.
   C. It did not change at all during that year.
   D. It was increasing at some undetermined rate.

4. Suppose a fourth species were introduced and found conditions there favorable for its growth. Based on experience with the species already there, what pattern might be expected for its density in the next ten years?

   F. It could not survive in competition with those already there.
   G. Its density might be expected to increase slightly for a couple of years and then level off.
   H. It might be expected to remain at low density for a few years and then increase rapidly.
   J. Its density might be expected to increase for a few years and then decrease rapidly.

5. Which of the following is NOT a possible explanation for the changes that took place after 1950?

   A. There was a period of drought.
   B. *Festuca* and *Hieracium* were unable to thrive in competition with *Thymus*.
   C. A newly arrived insect pest fed on some plants, but not others.
   D. A great increase in the shrubbery in the plot made the whole area more shady.

Passage 2

Three experiments are done to test the relative survivability of different mutant strains of fruit fly (*Drosophila*) when different strains are grown together with a limited food supply.

(**Note:** The experimental conditions are highly unnatural.)

Experiment 1

Three pure-bred strains of *Drosophila* are used: wild type, white-eye, and yellow-body. Fifty fertilized eggs of each strain are placed, separately, into standard culture bottles. They go through larval stages, and then form pupae. The adults that hatch out of the pupa cases are counted:

wild type: 42 white-eye: 36 yellow-body: 25

Experiment 2

Pairs of strains are grown together, with their larvae in the same culture bottle. Fifty eggs of each strain are placed in the bottle, and the number of adults of each kind that hatch out of the pupa cases are counted:

Trial 1 wild type: 43, white-eye: 16
Trial 2 wild type: 38, yellow-body: 22
Trial 3 white-eye: 18, yellow-body: 27

Experiment 3

Fifty eggs of each of the three strains are placed in the same culture bottle, with the following numbers of adults produced:

wild type: 33 white-eye: 8 yellow-body: 20

6. In Experiment 2 what was the purpose of growing two different strains of larvae in the same bottle?

   F. To find out how competition between strains affects survivability
   G. To test the effect of crowding of larvae in the culture bottles
   H. To determine the results of crossing two different strains
   J. To see whether the white-eye or yellow-body character can be transferred from one larva to another

7. What important variable was controlled by Experiment 1?

   A. Availability of food supply
   B. Survivability of each strain in the absence of competition
   C. Number of eggs to be used in the experiment
   D. Transformation of larvae to the pupa stage

8. Comparison of the results shows that competition:

   F. increases the survivability of the wild type.
   G. is most detrimental to the yellow-body.
   H. is most favorable to the yellow-body.
   J. is most detrimental to the white-eye.

9. What design factor in the experiments was crucial in establishing the existence of competition between strains?

   A. Keeping all culture bottles under the same conditions.
   B. Supplying only enough food for about 60 larvae
   C. Testing strains in advance to be sure they were pure-bred
   D. Using no more than 3 different strains

10. What do these results imply about the structure of natural populations?

    F. About one fourth of all flies in nature are expected to be yellow-bodied.
    G. One reason why the wild type is most common in nature is that its larvae survive best in competition.
    H. There will be no white-eyed flies in natural populations.
    J. In the course of time, white-eyed and yellow-bodied flies will completely disappear in nature.

11. The evidence seems to show that yellow-bodied flies do not suffer in competition with the wild type. Why, then, are there so few yellow-bodied flies in nature?

    A. The evidence is misleading because the total number of flies in the experiment is so small.
    B. White-eyed flies promote the survivability of the yellow-bodied, and they are rare in nature.
    C. Under natural conditions, many factors other than competition determine survivability.
    D. When yellow-bodied flies mate with wild type, their offspring are wild type.

Passage 3

The cladogram below describes the evolutionary relationships of some vertebrates. Each branching point represents the common ancestor of the branches. The more recent the common ancestor, the closer the relationship is considered to be. Dates, in millions of years, represent the time of transition from each era to the next. Base your answers only on the information in the diagram.

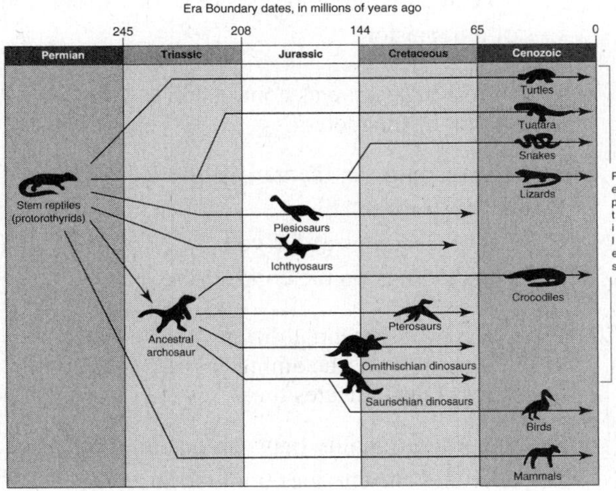

12. The turtles are unique, of this group, in that:

    F. they are the only reptiles with a hard shell formed of ribs.
    G. they are not closely related to any other surviving reptile.
    H. they are not related to any other reptiles.
    J. they have existed unchanged for over 150 million years.

13. Of the following pairs, in which pair are the two forms most closely related?

    A. Ornithischian dinosaurs and lizards
    B. Birds and mammals
    C. Crocodiles and ichthyosaurs
    D. Birds and crocodiles

14. One outstanding feature of the record is that:

    F. there was a mass extinction at the end of the Cretaceous.
    G. there are now far more reptiles than mammals or birds.
    H. about 150 million years ago there was a major radiation of reptiles into a variety of new forms.
    J. the snakes and lizards became distinct about 140 million years ago.

15. Of all the groups shown, only the birds and the mammals are known to be warm-blooded. How can this be interpreted?

    A. It is possible that the ancestral archosaur may also be warm-blooded.
    B. Warm-bloodedness is an ancestral character that has survived in these two lines.
    C. The diagram as given may be wrong, since the fact that these birds and mammals share this character indicates a close relationship.
    D. Warm-bloodedness is a useful property that may arise more than once, independently.

16. If a geologist reports finding a fossil feather in a rock layer 220 million years old, how might his colleagues initially react?

    F. Revise the cladogram to place the origin of the birds at an earlier date.
    G. Suggest a careful reexamination of the evidence for the date of the rock.
    H. Take this as proof that an early Saurischian dinosaur had feathers.
    J. Reject the report because it conflicts with known data of the origin of birds.

Passage 4

To find out how the electric current through various materials is controlled, a physicist applies various potential differences (voltages) to three different objects and measures the current produced in each case.

A milliampere is one thousandth of an ampere.

Experiment 1: 10 meters of #30 copper wire

Potential difference (volts)	Current (milliamperes)
0	0
0.2	60
0.4	120
0.6	180
0.8	240
1.0	300

Experiment 2: 10 meters of #30 aluminum wire

Potential difference (volts)	Current (milliamperes)
0	0
0.2	40
0.4	80
0.6	120
0.8	160
1.0	200

Experiment 3: OC26 transistor

Potential difference (volts)	Current (milliamperes)
0	0
0.2	5
0.4	15
0.6	60
0.8	115
1.0	190

17. What scales on the voltmeter and ammeter would be most appropriate in making these measurements?

    A. 0-20 V, 0-20 A
    B. 0-5 V, 0-5 A
    C. 0-1 V, 0-10 A
    D. 0-1 V, 0-0.5 A

18. Why were wires of identical dimensions used in Experiments 1 and 2?

    F. To increase the variety of readings of the current
    G. To determine how the material of which the wire is made affects the current
    H. To determine how the dimensions of the wire affect the current
    J. To compare the properties of a wire with those of a transistor

19. Which readings serve as controls on the proper adjustment of the meters?

    A. The readings on the transistor
    B. All the zero readings
    C. All the readings at 1.0 volt
    D. The readings on the copper wire

20. When a 10-volt potential difference is applied to the aluminum wire, the ammeter records 1100 milliamperes. This indicates that:

    F. the proportionality between potential difference and current does not hold for large values.
    G. there is no usable rule relating potential difference to current.
    H. large potential differences reduce the current in the wire.
    J. aluminum wire reacts differently from copper wire.

21. Resistance is defined as the ratio of potential difference to current. Which of the following statements holds true over the range of values in the experiments?

    A. All three objects have the same resistance.
    B. The objects have different resistances, but the resistance is constant for each.
    C. None of the objects has constant resistance.
    D. The wires, but not the transistor, have constant resistance.

22. On the basis of these experiments, what hypothesis might be proposed?

    F. Transistors respond to applied potential differences in the same way as metal wires.
    G. In any circuit, a transistor will have more current than a wire.
    H. Transistors are too unreliable to be used in most electronic circuits.
    J. Transistors and wires can be used for different purposes in electronic circuits.

Passage 5

The Papuan aster has two distinct populations. Variety *M* grows in the high mountains, and variety *V* lives in the valleys at midlevel. Experiments are done to test the relative growth patterns of the two varieties under different conditions.

The graphs that follow give you two kinds of information: the height distribution of each variety and the number that survive in each category.

Experiment 1

One hundred seeds of each variety are planted in separate plots in the high mountains. After 3 months, the height of each of the surviving plants is measured and plotted on the bar graph below.

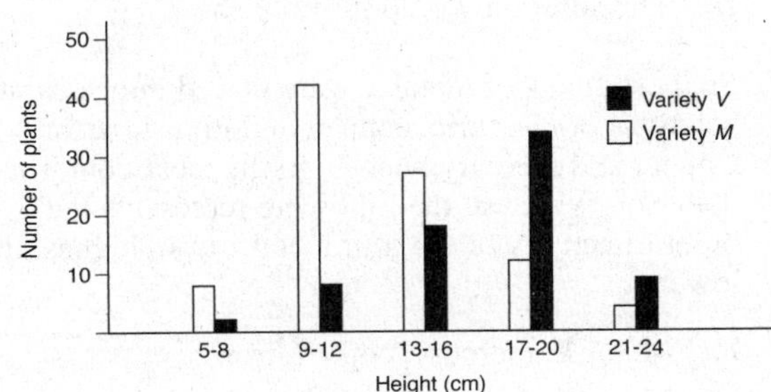

Experiment 2

One hundred seeds of each variety are planted in a midlevel valley, and their height is measured after 3 months and plotted:

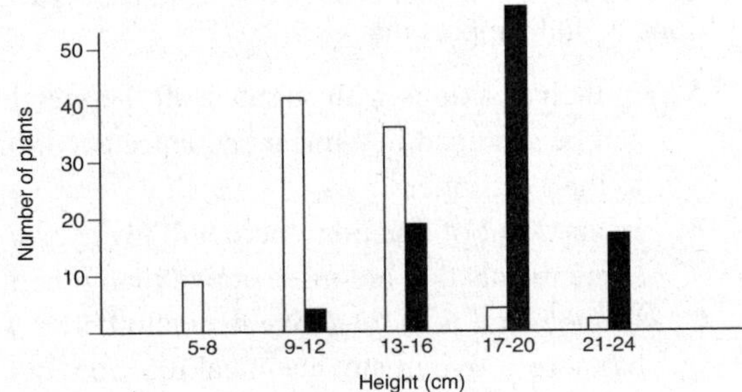

Experiment 3

One hundred seeds of each variety are planted in a dry lowland savannah; after 3 months:

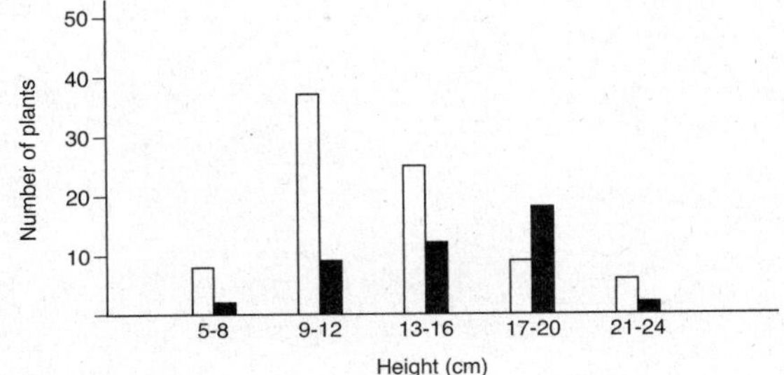

23. How many of the valley variety plants in the high mountains died in the first 3 months?

A. 70
B. 50
C. 30
D. 10

24. Which statement about the plants when in their normal environments is shown by the data?

F. Valley plants are much taller than mountain plants.
G. Valleys are a more favorable environment for this species.
H. Valley plants are healthier than mountain plants.
J. Plants in mountains are generally shorter than the ones that grow under more favorable conditions.

25. Which hypothesis is the most reasonable explanation for the results of Experiments 1 and 2?

A. In the mountains, the *V* plants cannot survive in competition with the *M* plants.
B. The *V* plants shade out the *M* plants, so they cannot grow to their full height.
C. The lack of soil nutrients in the mountaintops keeps all the plants from reaching their full sizes.
D. The *V* plants are programmed to grow tall, but they cannot reach their full height in the mountains.

26. What is the most likely explanation for the fact that the results of Experiment 3 are much like those of Experiment 1?

F. The same kinds of seeds were planted in both places.
G. In both high mountains and dry savannah, the amount of water is limited.
H. In the savannah, the plants were irrigated with plenty of water.
J. In both places, the plants were measured after the same length of growth period.

27. Which variety of the Papuan aster would be most suitable for use as a garden plant?

A. It would depend on the individual taste of the gardener.
B. The *M* variety because it is the hardiest and would be likely to survive best.
C. Either one, depending on where it would be used in the garden.
D. The *V* variety because it is a larger plant and would surely have nicer flowers.

Passage 6

A chemist performs a series of experiments to determine the relative chemical activities of three metals. Metal *A* is considered more active than metal *B* if metal *A* will replace metal *B* in a solution. Metal *B* will plate out on metal *A*.

Experiment 1

A piece of steel wool is placed into a solution of copper sulfate. Copper sulfate is blue because of the copper ions in it. The result of the experiment is that metallic copper forms on the steel wool and the blue solution turns colorless.

Experiment 2

A bundle of fine copper wire is placed into a solution of iron(II) sulfate, which is colorless. No change is observed.

Experiment 3

A fine spray of metallic mercury is inserted into a solution of copper sulfate. No change is observed.

Experiment 4

A bundle of fine copper wire is inserted into a solution of mercuric sulfate, which is colorless. The wire acquires a coating of the silvery color of mercury, and the solution acquires a bluish tint.

28. The results of Experiments 1 and 2 indicate that:

    F. copper is more active than iron.
    G. relative activity depends on how the experiment is done.
    H. iron is more active than copper.
    J. the two metals are probably equally active.

29. In Experiment 4, why did the solution become bluish?

    A. Some of the copper of the wire went into solution.
    B. Removal of the mercury revealed the true color of the solution.
    C. The silvery color of the deposited mercury reflects light and has a bluish cast.
    D. Some of the mercury in the solution changes to copper, which gives the solution a bluish color.

30. Why was there no reaction in Experiment 2?

    F. Copper is not soluble in water.
    G. The metal in the solution is the more active of the two.
    H. Metallic iron and metallic copper cannot mix.
    J. The iron sulfate solution was already saturated.

31. What would probably happen if steel wool were placed into a solution of mercuric sulfate?

    A. It is impossible to predict the result without experiment.
    B. Mercury would plate out on the steel wool.
    C. Nothing would happen.
    D. The solution would turn bluish.

32. Suppose fibers of metal *X* were placed into separate solutions of mercuric, copper, and iron sulfates. Copper and mercury deposit on the metal, but iron does not. Which of the following represents the order of activity of the four metals, from highest to lowest?

    F. Metal *X*, mercury, copper, iron
    G. Mercury, copper, metal *X*, iron
    H. Copper, mercury, iron, metal *X*
    J. Iron, metal *X*, copper, mercury

33. An investigator hypothesizes that the relative activity of any metal depends only on the structure of its own atoms. Which of the following observations would support this view?

    A. In their reactions with sulfates, all the metals can be arranged in a linear sequence according to their activities.
    B. In any kind of reaction, there will always be some metals that are more active than others.
    C. If one metal is more active than another, it will be more active in any chemical reaction, not just with sulfates.
    D. In any reaction, it is always possible to compare two metals and find out which is more active.

Passage 7

Will future human evolution increase the number of twins in the population? Two scientists present opposing views.

Scientist 1

It is an established principle, the rule of Darwinian fitness, that natural selection favors the individuals who leave the largest number of viable and fertile offspring. It is also known that there is a genetic tendency that causes some women to produce more than one ovum at a time. These women will bear twins more often than other women. Since they have more offspring than other women, selection will favor them and the frequency of twin births will increase with time. This did not happen in the past because the conditions of life were so different. A woman in a hunter-gatherer society had to spend much of her time collecting plant food, while carrying her baby with her. She also had to be ready to run or otherwise protect herself from wild animals. Her chance of survival, avoiding both starvation and predation, was much worse if she was carrying two babies instead of only one. Thus, the genes that promote twinning carried an enormous liability, which more than offset the selective advantage of having twins. Under modern conditions, however, these negative features disappear and a woman who bears twins is likely to leave more offspring than one who does not. The frequency of the gene that promotes the release of more than one ovum at a time will increase in the population.

Scientist 2

You cannot think of evolutionary change in terms of a single feature. When many factors affect an outcome, it is necessary to consider how they interact to produce an optimum condition. Twins are often born prematurely, and their average birth weight is only 5.5 pounds. Single babies, on the average, come into the world weighing 7.5 pounds. Premature birth and low birth weight result in many kinds of medical problems. Twins' prospects for survival to a normal, healthy reproductive age are less than those for singly born babies. An evolutionary tendency to overcome this deficiency would call for mothers to produce twins weighing in at 7.5 pounds each. This would be an enormous strain on the mother, since she would have to gain more weight during pregnancy. The only way to neutralize this liability would be for women to be much bigger, weighing more than 200 pounds. This would, however, introduce another liability: strains on the skeleton and musculature. Evolution would have to produce a complete redesign of the body. The gain in selective value produced by twinning would be far outweighed by these disadvantages. Modern civilization has not changed the fact that single births are optimum for human women.

34. What is the basic question on which the two scientists disagree?

    F. Is human evolution a continuing, ongoing process?
    G. Do human twins start life at a disadvantage?
    H. Does natural selection favor genes that produce twins?
    J. Is the tendency to produce twins hereditary?

35. To refute Scientist 2's argument, Scientist 1 might point out that:

    A. modern medical science has greatly improved the survival rate of infants with low birth weights.
    B. many twins result from the division of a single fertilized egg, and this is not genetically controlled.
    C. evolutionary change is extremely slow, and there is no evidence that the human species has changed much in the last 100,000 years.
    D. large women have twins as frequently as small women do.

36. The arguments of both Scientist 1 and Scientist 2 would be invalidated if new evidence indicated that:

    F. the rate of twin births has not changed in the past century.
    G. genetics really makes very little difference in whether or not a woman produces twins.
    H. women in hunter-gatherer societies have twins more often than women in civilization.
    J. the genetic tendency to produce twins passes to women from their fathers, not their mothers.

37. What piece of statistical evidence would greatly strengthen Scientist 2's position?

    A. Twins born at 5.5 pounds have a poorer survival rate than babies born singly at 5.5 pounds.
    B. Twins born at 7 pounds have the same survival rate as babies born singly at 7 pounds.
    C. Twins born to large women have a better survival rate than twins born to small women.
    D. Twins born to small women have a better survival rate than twins born to large women.

38. Underlying the arguments of both scientists is the assumption that:

    F. production of twins is a desirable prospect for the human species.
    G. women who bear twins are healthier, on the average, than women who do not.
    H. the genetic composition of the father is irrelevant to the probability of a woman's bearing twins.
    J. natural selection acts on human beings in the same way as on other animals.

39. Which of the arguments of Scientist 1 was not refuted by Scientist 2?

    A. Modern medicine has no effect on the rate at which twins are born.
    B. In primitive conditions, natural selection will favor single births.
    C. Survival rate is a basic biological factor that is not influenced by external conditions.
    D. Large women are inherently capable of producing twins with large birth weights.

40. Scientist 2 claims that Scientist 1 has overlooked an important general principle of biological science. What is it?

    F. All biological factors interact with each other, and selective value depends on the optimal combination of values of many factors.
    G. Genetic factors must be considered in any long-term prediction.
    H. Genetic factors must be analyzed in terms of their interaction with external conditions.
    J. Evolution is the result of natural selection acting on the genetic composition of individuals.

Answer Key

1. B	6. F	11. C	16. G	21. D	26. G	31. B	36. G
2. J	7. B	12. G	17. D	22. J	27. C	32. J	37. C
3. B	8. J	13. D	18. G	23. C	28. H	33. C	38. J
4. H	9. B	14. F	19. B	24. F	29. A	34. H	39. B
5. B	10. G	15. D	20. F	25. D	30. G	35. A	40. F

Answer Explanations

1. **(B)** The curves for *Festuca* and *Hieracium* cross in 1950, indicating that the density of both plants was the same. *Thymus* did not appear at all until 1960.

2. **(J)** Since the three graphs all cross at this time, all three plants had equal densities; *Thymus* was increasing rapidly. The density of *Hieracium* had dropped, but remained nearly steady from 1963 to 1973. *Festuca* was dropping slowly.

3. **(B)** The density increased from nearly 0 in 1946 to 450 in 1952, an increase of 450 units in six years. This rate of 75 units per year remained steady for the entire six-year period.

4. **(H)** Both *Hieracium* and *Thymus* were newly introduced and followed the same pattern: low density for three or four years and then rapid increase for the next six years. This is the only evidence available.

5. **(B)** *Festuca* began its decline in 1947 and *Hieracium* in 1952, but *Thymus* did not appear until 1959. *Thymus* might well be more tolerant of dry weather, shade, and that particular bug than the other two species.

6. **(F)** With two different strains in competition, one or the other might prove to be better adapted. G is wrong because crowding could be tested, without introducing a different variable, by simply using more eggs of either strain. H is wrong because there is no mating in the larval stage. J is wrong because the experimental design does not allow for the testing of any such transfer, which is most unlikely in any event.

7. **(B)** If the effect of competition is to be established, it is important to know how well each strain survives when there is no competition. None of the other choices represents a variable in the experiment.

8. **(J)** The number of white-eyed adults that hatch is drastically less than the control number (Experiment 1) whenever one of the other strains is present.

9. **(B)** Note that in Experiments 2 and 3 only about 60 larvae produced adults, even though there were 100 or 150 eggs. If there were no restriction on the food supply, it is possible that all the eggs could survive in the same numbers as in Experiment 1.

10. **(G)** Whenever other strains are present with the wild type, it is the others that suffer, while the wild type maintains its predominance. F is wrong because there is no reason to believe that the numbers of eggs laid in nature are like those in the bottle. H and J are wrong because competition does not completely eliminate the white-eyed and yellow-bodied forms.

11. **(C)** Do not confuse a culture bottle with nature. There is no evidence to support any of the other choices.

12. **(G)** The turtles have no ancestor in common with all the other reptiles later than the earliest reptile of all. F is wrong because the cladogram gives no information about shells in reptiles. H is wrong because there is a common ancestor, although it is in the long-distant past. J is wrong because the cladogram gives no information about the way the various reptiles have changed.

13. **(D)** The common ancestor of the birds and crocodiles is an ancestral archosaur, about 220 million years ago. All of the other pairs have no common ancestor later than the stem reptiles, in the Permian.

14. **(F)** Many of the lines in the diagram disappeared at the end of the Cretaceous. G is wrong because no information is given about the relative abundance of the different life forms. H is wrong because the major radiation took place long before 150 million years ago. J is wrong because this event is not a major feature of the whole story.

15. **(D)** A and B are wrong because it would be most unlikely that a character would survive in two distantly related forms and not in any of the others. C is wrong because the cladogram depends on many characters, not just one. Independent evolution of a useful character is the most likely explanation.

16. **(G)** This discovery cannot be rejected out of hand, but it suggests a really drastic revision of current theories, conflicting with much other evidence. It would have to be reviewed by others.

17. **(D)** For best precision, you want the smallest scale that will incorporate the largest reading. The largest potential difference reading is 1 V, so a 1-volt scale will do very well. The largest current reading is 300 mA, or 0.3 A.

18. **(G)** The dimensions are being controlled to eliminate them from consideration, so H is wrong. The only uncontrolled variable is the substance of the wire.

19. **(B)** The meter must be zeroed; that is, it must be adjusted to make sure that it reads zero when there is no current or potential difference.

20. **(F)** For all the readings in the table, the ratio between potential difference and current is constant at 200 mA/V. The ratio for the 10-V setting, however, is only 110 mA/V. G is wrong because there is surely a usable rule below 1 V, and further investigation might turn up a usable rule at higher potentials. H is wrong; the large potential difference increased the current; it was just not as much as might have been expected. J is wrong because there is no evidence about the behavior of copper wire at higher potential differences.

21. **(D)** Checking the ratios at the smallest and largest values gives these results: copper wire, 0.20/60 = 0.0033 and 1.00/300 = 0.0033; aluminum wire, 0.20/40 = 0.0050 and 1.0/200 = 0.0050; transistor, 0.2/5 = 0.040 and 1/190 = 0.0053. The ratios are constant for the wires, but not for the transistor.

22. **(J)** Since transistors and wires have different but reliable properties, they can be used for different purposes. F is wrong because the ratio of potential difference to current (for small currents) is constant for the wires, but not for the transistor. G is wrong because no information is given about the circuits. H is wrong because Experiment 3 gives no information about the reliability of transistors.

23. **(C)** The sizes of the bars for valley plants in the mountains are 2 + 8 + 18 + 33 + 9 = 70. Since only 70 of the 100 survived, 30 died.

24. **(F)** Mountain plants are in their normal environment in Experiment 1, and their height is mainly in the 9 to 12 cm range. G is wrong because the mountain plants do very well in their normal environment. H is wrong because the data give no information about the health of the plants. J is wrong because this generalization (while true) cannot be assumed from data about one species.

25. **(D)** Experiment 2 shows that when the *V* plants are in their normal environment, they grow tall. A and B are wrong because the conditions of the experiment indicate that the two kinds are grown in separate plots, so they cannot interfere with each other. C is wrong because the *M* plants are thriving in their normal environment.

26. **(G)** F and J are wrong because these conditions are true of Experiment 2 also, and the results there were quite different. H is wrong because the purpose of the experiment was to find out how the plants grow under the dry savannah conditions. G is the only alternative.

27. **(C)** Each variety is best suited for a particular environment; the *M* variety might do very well in a rock garden. C is wrong because a gardener must put the plant where it will do best, regardless of personal preference.

28. **(H)** Copper has come out of solution in the form of copper metal. The loss of copper changes the color of the solution. Iron must have replaced copper in the solution, so iron is more active. This follows from the definition of a more active metal, given in the first paragraph of the passage.

29. **(A)** The blue color indicates the presence of copper in solution. B is wrong because we have no reason to believe there is any such thing as the "true color" of the solution. C is wrong because we have no indication that the mercury coating is bluish. D is wrong because mercury cannot change into copper.

30. **(G)** Since iron is more active than copper, copper cannot replace iron in the solution. F is wrong; in the blue solution, copper is dissolved. Nothing in the experiment points to either H or J.

31. **(B)** Since iron is more active than copper (Experiment 1) and copper is more active than mercury (Experiment 4), it is reasonable to assume that iron is more active than mercury. Therefore, iron will replace mercury in solution, and the mercury will deposit on the steel wool.

32. **(J)** We already know from the experiments that iron is more active than copper, and copper than mercury. Since metal *X* replaces copper and mercury from solution, it must be more active than either of them. It does not, however, replace iron.

33. **(C)** The atomic structure of a metal atom is the same as it enters into any reaction. If atomic structure is what determines activity, then the relative activities of two metals do not depend on what the specific chemical reaction is. Choice A is wrong because a ranking with sulfates does not prove that the ranking would hold in other reactions. B and D prove only that there are different levels of activity in different reactions.

34. **(H)** Both scientists agree that evolution continues and might involve changes in the frequency of genes producing twins, so F and J are wrong. Scientist 1 does not challenge the statement that twins have lower survival rates, so G is wrong. The only point at issue is whether the result of selection will be a higher frequency of twinning.

35. **(A)** Scientist 2 argues that twinning has a negative selective value because twins are born small, but gains in medical science might nullify this disadvantage. None of the other choices is germane.

36. **(G)** Both Scientist 1 and Scientist 2 assume that the tendency to produce twins is hereditary; they disagree only on how this will change the evolutionary trend. F is wrong because both might agree that a century is too short a time to show any effect. H is wrong because neither scientist makes any such claim. J is wrong because it would make no difference in the survival value of the gene.

37. **(C)** Scientist 2 claims that large, healthy twins could be produced only by larger women, and statistics to this effect would support his case. B is wrong because this point is not at issue.

38. **(J)** Both scientists base their arguments on natural selection of the most favorable combination of traits; they disagree on what that combination might be. F is wrong because neither scientist makes any value judgment. G is wrong because neither scientist makes any such claim. H is wrong because the arguments of neither scientist require any such assumption.

39. **(B)** This claim is made by Scientist 1, and not addressed by Scientist 2. The others are wrong because Scientist 1 does not make any such claims.

40. **(F)** This is the core of Scientist 2's rebuttal; Scientist 1 has not considered all the genetic interactions involved. G is wrong because both scientists agree that genetic factors are central to the issue. H is wrong because both scientists considered external conditions; they disagreed on which ones were important. J is wrong because they agreed on this point.

ACT Writing Test

CHAPTER 5

• Writing a Convincing Essay in 30 minutes	• Taking a Stand on an Issue
• What ACT Readers Look For	• Using a Writing Style That Works
• Sample Issues and Students' Responses	• Polishing Your Essay for a Top Score

The optional ACT Writing Test, administered after the four multiple-choice sections of the ACT, consists of one essay to be written in 30 minutes.

The Purpose of the Test

The score you earn on the test adds an important dimension to your college admissions profile. It tells admissions officials how well you write, especially how you write under the pressure of time. More specifically, your score provides colleges with practical information about 1) the depth of your thinking, 2) your ability to organize ideas, 3) the way you express yourself, and 4) your mastery of standard written English.

1. You demonstrate your ability to *think* by responding perceptively to the "prompt"—that is, the topic or question about which you are asked to write. Your essay will show whether you understand the prompt and whether you can devise, develop, and focus on a point of view about an issue.
2. You show your ability to *organize ideas* by arranging material purposefully, according to a logical, sensible plan.
3. You reveal your ability to *express yourself* by accurately and succinctly conveying your thoughts to the reader.
4. You demonstrate your use of *correct English* by writing an essay that adheres to the conventions of standard written English.

Why the ACT Writing Test Is Optional

Many colleges use the results of the ACT Writing Test as a criterion for admission. Some of these colleges weigh the scores as heavily as GPAs, class rank, and personal statements. Other colleges merely recommend that applicants take the test. Still others devise alternate means for assessing candidates' writing ability.

TIP

Remember, you cannot take the Writing Test without first taking all four multiple-choice tests.

Who Should Exercise the Option?

Register for the Writing Test if any college to which you plan to apply recommends or requires it. If you must take the test, sign up for it when you register for the ACT.

If you're not yet sure where you'll be applying, it makes sense to take the test. By doing so, you'll save yourself the trouble and expense of later subjecting yourself to the whole ACT just to take the Writing Test. If you're sure that no college to which you are applying recommends or requires the Writing Test, register only for the ACT.

How the Test Is Scored

Your performance on the test is reported with two subscores. The first, called the Writing Test subscore, tells you the grade you earned on the essay. It is determined on a scale of 2 (low) to 12 (high) and is based on two readers' evaluations. The second, an English/Writing subscore, is calculated by combining your Writing Test subscore with your score on the English section of the ACT. (See page 544 for details on how the scores are combined.)

How Test Results Are Used

Precisely how the scores are used depends completely on the college. On some campuses, the scores function solely as criteria for admission. Some may weigh the test results in determining your academic placement. A superb essay may entitle you to waive the freshman basic composition course. A score that reflects deficiencies in writing may steer you into a remedial course to be taken either before the start of classes or during the first semester. To understand just how your test score will affect you, consult the literature of the colleges to which you are applying, or save the question for your interview with an admissions official.

What to Expect on Test Day

After you have finished answering the multiple-choice questions on the ACT and test booklets are collected, you will be given a short break. Then the Writing Test will begin. You will have 30 minutes. Periodically, the proctor will announce how much time remains. Your essay must be written in pencil on the lined paper provided by the ACT. Computers may not be used for the test.

An Essay-Writing Strategy

An essay completed in half an hour is bound to be shorter than most essays required in high school or college courses. Yet, 30 minutes gives you plenty of time to prove that you have what it takes to write a substantial essay. No doubt you've done it before in English, social studies, and other classes. The big difference here, of course, is that you can't study ahead of time. Because you don't know the topic, you must quickly process your thoughts and get them onto paper.

The question, or prompt, to which you must respond describes an issue or set of circumstances on which you must comment. Rest assured that the issue won't require specialized knowledge or training. It will be general and open-ended enough to elicit a response from virtually any high school student.

For example, the prompt may ask you to write an essay that states your views on whether students should be required to attend high school for five years instead of four. In the same vein, a prompt may ask you to express your opinion about the amount of homework assigned in high school. Is the homework load appropriate? Do you instead think it is too heavy or too light?

Although the prompt cannot be predicted, you can always count on the need to abide by the following half-dozen guidelines for ACT essay writing:

1. **Write an essay in response to the given prompt**, which will provide two different points of view on an issue. You may write about either of the two positions, or you may present a different point of view on the question. The choice is yours. Once you have decided on your position, present your case. There is no right or wrong answer. You won't be penalized for taking an unusual or unpopular point of view. Be more concerned about developing your essay's main idea and expressing your thoughts coherently and correctly.

   By using the word "essay," the ACT means *essay*, not a short story, poem, dialogue, one-act play, or any other genre. Therefore, the test calls for an expository piece that focuses on one main idea, or thesis, and consists chiefly of material that explains or supports that idea. At some point in your schooling, you've probably written essays meant to define a term—say, "democracy," "friendship," or "the American dream." Other essays may have been meant to persuade a reader to believe as you do about an issue, and still others may have been intended to explain your opinion about a character in a novel or about a current subject of controversy. In other words, as an experienced writer of essays, you will be entering what should be familiar territory.

TIP

Back up your opinion on an issue with logical and specific reasons.

2. **During the 30 minutes allowed, develop your thoughts clearly and effectively.** Ordinarily, an essay writer has multiple objectives, and therefore, takes a long time to think about ideas and write them down. (The verb *essay*, in fact, means to assess thoughtfully.) Not on the ACT, however. The time limit forces you to plan your essay rather quickly and write a response. If you manage to come up with one or more profound insights, more power to you, but remember, the objective of an ACT essay is more mundane—to show colleges that you can organize your thoughts and express them clearly, interestingly, and correctly.

3. **Try to include relevant examples and specific evidence to support your point of view.** This guideline has three purposes. First, it urges you to plan your essay before you begin writing it. A few minutes spent planning gives you a chance to think about the topic and to come up with compelling ideas to support your point of view. Second, it reminds you to bolster your essay's main argument with specific examples. It's easy to write or speak in generalities, but the heart of an essay is its details. The development of specific supporting evidence reveals more about the depth of your thinking than almost anything else in the essay.

   The third purpose is to encourage coherence, or unity. All parts of an essay should work together to make a single point. If the evidence you provide wanders from the main idea or raises additional issues that you don't have time to discuss, the effect of the essay will be diluted. Above all, you don't want readers to come to the end of your essay puzzling over what point you were trying to make.

TIP

Avoid using inflated words that do little more than make you sound like a show-off.

4. **A plain, natural style is best.** An English teacher may have told you never to use the first-person pronoun "I" in a formal essay. That's a rule that makes sense in many contexts, but not here. After all, this is a personal essay, and to avoid "I" while explaining your opinion may cause the prose to sound stilted or artificial. Moreover, it may keep you from using the plain, natural style that best gives expression to your voice.

   The ACT Writing Test is not a place to show off your vocabulary. Therefore, use a complex word only when it's the only one that says exactly what you mean and will add something to the essay's tone and meaning that would otherwise be lost. Elegant words have their place, of course, but to use them merely to sound elegant is pretentious and, if the meaning is not exactly right, foolish.

5. **The length of your essay is up to you, but quality should take precedence over quantity.** There is no required length. Keep in mind that you are being asked to show your ability to think and to express yourself. A short, well-written essay can produce such evidence. A brief essay allows you to devote more attention to choosing each word and crafting each sentence. Effective development of the main idea matters more than the word count.

   On the other hand, beware of an essay consisting of a single paragraph. It may not give you an opportunity to fully develop your ideas. Expect to write at least two or three paragraphs. Three or more, in fact, may be preferable to two, although that's a generalization that doesn't apply to every essay. (More about that later in this chapter.)

6. **Be sure to write only on the assigned topic.** ACT topics are broad enough to give students of all stripes and abilities an opportunity to express themselves. The prompt won't trick or stump you. Nor is it apt to anger or excite you. In other words, it will be fairly innocuous, and your task is to transform it into an engaging essay.

   Your essay needn't follow a particular format. A straightforward, no-nonsense approach may be best. You won't go wrong, for example, with an essay consisting of a brief introduction that states your main idea, a body of material that supports the main idea, and a brief conclusion. That sort of essay will easily consume the time you are allowed. Variations on this form are possible, of course, but you probably won't have time to be too inventive. Because you will be heavily penalized for an essay that fails to address the topic, read the prompt carefully. Read it twice or three times if necessary, underlining any key words or ideas until you are confident that you know precisely what you are being asked to write about.

As ACT day draws near, review the above guidelines. Knowing exactly what to do when the essay assignment is given out will add to your peace of mind and allow you to set to work immediately, saving you precious time.

Evaluating the Essay

Your essay will be evaluated on a scale of 6 (best) to 1 (worst). ACT readers, most of them experienced high school and college teachers, are trained to read essays quickly, or *holistically*. That is, they don't hunt down every little error but assign a grade based on their overall impression of your writing. Recognizing that ACT essays are written in less than half an hour, they won't hold minor mistakes against you and won't deduct a certain amount for every error. Naturally, an essay overrun with flaws will leave a less favorable impression than one that is mostly correct. Like all readers, they enjoy good writing and delight in lively, neatly phrased ideas. They abhor empty platitudes and know in an instant when a writer is "throwing the bull." Pretentiousness turns them off completely.

TIP 

Readers will not deduct points for every little error.

Readers try to evaluate essays fairly, rewarding students for what they have done well. During the evaluation, your essay won't be competing against some ideal essay written by a professional author. Rather, it will be compared to other students' essays written on the same topic at the same time.

Handwriting is not supposed to count, but think about what can happen if readers have difficulty deciphering yours: Frustration may cause them to be unfavorably disposed toward your essay. When readers are forced to stop regularly to puzzle out the words, your flow of ideas will be interrupted or curtailed—with adverse effects. What is more, readers won't give you the benefit of the doubt about spelling or grammar if the letters are malformed or difficult to read. An essay that is incomprehensible because the handwriting is so bad will be given no credit at all. Granted, at this stage in your life, it's difficult to change your handwriting. But if you know that teachers and others have a problem interpreting your script, try to slow down as you form the letters, or as a last resort, print. Printing takes twice as long as cursive writing, but it is usually easier to read.

Guidelines for Evaluation

Each essay is scored on a scale of 6 to 1.

Performance Categories	Score
Outstanding	6
Very Good	5
Good	4
Fair	3
Poor	2
Very Poor	1

Essays scored 4, 5, and 6 are considered average or above and attest to a level of writing skill appropriate for first-year college students. Essays rated 1, 2, or 3 are below average and suggest the writer's need for remediation.

Each essay is evaluated by two readers. If their evaluations differ by more than a point, the essay is given to a third reader. No list of criteria can cover everything that readers take into account, but the descriptions below include many of the standards that ACT readers use in determining essay scores. No essay is likely to contain all the characteristics below. Readers make every effort to be objective, but being human they must ultimately rely on their judgment. Consequently, an essay that receives a low 5 may not be noticeably better than an essay that earns a high 4. The rating difference is likely to be based on intangibles that cause readers to assign the grade that in their view is most appropriate.

6 **Outstanding**. An *outstanding* essay is a well-conceived, orderly, and insightful treatment of the assigned task. The writer has fashioned a convincing thesis amply supported by appropriate and specific details. Its point of view, syntax, imagery, and diction demonstrate the writer's ability to control a wide range of elements of composition. Any errors that occur are inconsequential. Overall, the work is a model of clarity and sophistication.

5 **Very Good**. A *very good* essay contains a sound thesis and demonstrates the writer's grasp of the task. It develops the main idea with purpose and conviction, but it may be somewhat less thorough and insightful than the best essays. It also may fall short of the mastery, sophistication, and control of composition exemplified by the best essays. Nevertheless, its organization is sensible, its language and usage are appropriate, and its overall intent is clear and consistent.

4 **Good.** A *good* essay deals with the topic competently. It uses conventional language and sentence structure and provides some appropriate specific examples to support a thesis. It gives evidence of the writer's acquaintance with essay organization, coherence, and paragraph development. Some errors in word choice and awkward expression may exist, but no error seriously interferes with meaning.

3 **Fair.** *A fair* essay suggests mediocrity in writing. It may adequately respond to the prompt but gives evidence of an inconsistent control of the elements of composition. Although the essay has a recognizable structure, the organization may be confusing or not fully realized. Inaccuracies or lapses in logic may weaken the essay's overall effect. Occasional mechanical errors may detract from the essay's meaning.

2 **Poor.** A *poor* essay demonstrates a superficial or limited understanding of the prompt. The essay's development is meager and its treatment of the subject imprecise and unconvincing. The point of the essay may be perceptible, but the presentation of ideas is characterized by faulty diction, weak syntax, and incoherent or confused organization.

1 **Very Poor.** A *very poor* essay reveals the writer's inability to make sense of the prompt. It may wander off the topic or substitute an irrelevant or simplistic task. It may also be unacceptably brief or undeveloped. The prose may lack organization, coherence, and meaning. The writer shows little evidence of control of English syntax or the rules of usage and grammar.

SAMPLE STUDENT ESSAYS WITH EVALUATIONS

The essays on the following pages have been written by high school students in a testing situation. Each was composed in half an hour and appears exactly as written.

Prompt: A growing number of educators believe that schools should be in session the year-round. They claim that many students, especially those who struggle to learn, lose important skills and knowledge during extended summer vacations and assert that the education of all students is improved with short summer vacations and several two- or three-week breaks scattered throughout the school year.

Opponents of year-round schooling argue that a lengthy summer break offers students (as well as teachers) the time to pursue individual interests, hold jobs, and develop themselves in nonscholastic ways. Furthermore, a drastic change in the school calendar would create problems for families, upset the routines related to college admissions, and create havoc for businesses that depend on summertime trade, such as travel and tourism.

In your opinion, should year-round schooling be implemented? In an essay, take a position on this question. You may write about either one of the two points of view. You may instead present a different point of view on the issue. Whatever your view, be sure to support your position with specific reasons and examples.

Lucina's Essay:

Some educators believe that a year-round school schedule would contribute to raising the overall quality of our education. They would like to shorten the traditional summer vacation. They say that learning, particularly of low-achieving students, suffers from long breaks and that each year, teachers waste valuable classroom time reviewing the previous year's work before moving ahead to new material. Others feel differently. They think that revising the school calendar can do more harm than good because dropping long vacations deprives students of learning opportunities through travel, special programs, full-time jobs, and even personal self-development over an extended period of time.

It's quite obvious that education does not take place only in school. In school, we learn the basics of writing, reading, and math. With universal mass education, teaching foreign languages, science, and history is far more efficient in a school setting where twenty or thirty students in a class gather to learn the same thing at the same time.

However, much, much more can be learned outside of the school environment. Schools can only simulate reality. They can't give students real, living, first-hand experiences. Since it takes the real world to do that, a year-round school schedule would be detrimental to many students who can learn about the world outside of the traditional classroom.

Speaking personally, I know of many students who have taken advantage of their summer vacation to better themselves and expand their knowledge. Friends of mine have had their first responsible jobs as counselors and coaches at summer camps. One friend participated in an AIDS-related project in Africa under the supervision of doctors. Students have gone on long trips and foreign-exchange programs to France and Spain and have participated in writing workshops at colleges in New England states. My boyfriend spent a summer doing construction work. Last summer, he worked with the Habitat for Humanity, helping to rebuild houses near New Orleans that had been destroyed by Hurricane Katrina. I, myself, have used summers to practice what I love best, playing the piano. During the school year, I hardly have time to play at all. When I have unscheduled days, I make up my mind to master a difficult piece of music and spend the time productively.

These are just some examples of how long vacations can be of benefit to students. Just ask yourself: Is there a better way to learn a foreign language than to go to the country that speaks it? Is it better to read about a historical event or to visit the place where it occurred? Is it preferable to study a culture through textbooks and films or actually to participate in person? The answer to all these questions is obvious. If year-round school were implemented, many students would be deprived of valuable first-hand educational experiences.

Not everyone has the resources or ability to participate in exciting learning experiences. Family situations often keep students close to home. Some students can't or don't want to bother learning from actual experience. They do mindless things, hang out, play video games endlessly, or may look for thrills by smoking pot, seeking sex, or drinking. Three months of summer vacation is three months of wasted time. However, they are not in the majority. The question I ask is should the minority of students control what happens to the majority?

I don't think so. So, a possible solution to the problem may be a flexible school year. How about using a calendar that lets students structure their school year according to their interests and situations? If students need the discipline of regular classes to make the most progress in their education, they should have the opportunity to attend school all year long. For those who can learn outside the classroom, they should have the chance to reserve a stretch of time to do something really worthwhile and get school credit for it.

If educational authorities are truly serious about improving the quality of education, then they ought to rethink what an education consists of. The "one-size fits all" plan of education has not succeeded. Adapting the school year to meet the needs of the variety of students is a more promising way to solve the educational crisis in our country.

Critique: Your response to the prompt consists of a strong argument in defense of the status quo. At the same time, you perceptively recognize the educational problems inherent in the traditional school calendar and offer a reasonable alternative—adapting the school year to meet the needs of the variety of students—that would probably be difficult but not impossible to implement.

In presenting your case, you open with a thoughtful paragraph that fully explains the context of the issue. You also cite several specific examples of students who have made worthwhile use of long breaks from school and take into account that many students do not or cannot take advantage of protracted periods away from the classroom. Your essay's organization is clear and logical. Transitions within and between pararagraphs let readers effortlessly follow the sequence of ideas. You vary your sentences to create interest and employ an especially effective stylistic device in the fourth paragraph—namely, a series of rhetorical questions that support your point of view. The last paragraph puts a final touch on what amounts to a circumspect and thorough argument that can serve as a model of a superior ACT essay. Your essay is rated **6**.

Marshall's Essay:

This is a very interesting question to ask someone like me. The main reason is because I think about it a lot.

My history teacher once told us that we have a long summer vacation because in the old days kids worked on farms. They had to help out with farm chores, so school was let out in the spring and didn't start again until the crops were picked. Also it was too hot to go to school when the temperture was more than 100.

Things are different in the modern world of today. I live about 15 miles from the big city in the suberbs. We only have factories and offices which are air-conditioned. The work is the same threw the four seasons—winter, spring, fall and summer. Who cares if its cold or hot, snowy or rainy and if the sun shines. Nobody cares, they go to work and do the same thing inspite the weather.

Don't get me wrong. I like summer vacations, especially great being away from the pressures of homwork and teachers being on your case day after day, week after week, month after month. I would hate to see summer abolished but if we went to school more, we'd learn more and we'd graduate sooner. If you want to get a job, you could start your job at 16 instead of 18. You have to take the good with the bad.

Critique: You seem to understand the issue stated by the prompt, but you fail to state and clearly develop your position. In fact, you devote most of your essay to background material that explains the history of summer vacations and describes the circumstances of working in your hometown. In the final paragraph, where you finally focus on the issue, your point of view is hard to discern. You cite one advantage of summer vacations—namely, the absence of pressure. Then you allude to one advantage of abolishing summer vacations—the possibility of going to work sooner.

Although your essay contains an introduction and a conclusion of sorts, the last sentence is terribly trite and does little to clarify your position on the issue of year-round schooling. To your credit, each paragraph is generally unified and coherent, suggesting that you know how to group your ideas. In addition, you have made a reasonable attempt to tie your paragraphs to each other with transitions. Overall, however, weak development of a point of view and a number of distracting errors in grammar, spelling, and usage suggest that you have not yet mastered basic essay-writing skills. Your essay is rated **2**.

Edie's Essay:

There are about thirty kids in this room writing an essay on year-round schooling. I'm sure that most of them will opt for the traditional school year consisting of two semesters and a summer vacation starting in June and going until late August or early September, with a week off at Christmas and Easter. That is also my preference because I in my first two years of high school attended a school in southern California that stayed open 12 months a year and my junior year in my school in Kirkwood, Missouri was totally user-friendly in comparrison to the year-round Calif. school.

The program I experienced in my old school was mainly used as a way to prevent overcrowding. The school in California always struggled for money, so they didn't have enough to expand the building for the large number of students. Instead, they put in a complicated schedule that kept about 20 percent of the students out of school at any one time. Even so, classes were bigger than they are here in Missouri. Every eight weeks, we had two or three weeks off, and in the summer we could choose a vacation period of three, four, or five weeks, but there was never a time when all the students were in school at the same time.

This caused all kinds of problems. The problems mostly affected school activities instead of classes. For example, all the players on a sports team had to have the same schedule, for example, because they obviously could not practice or play field hockey or volleyball in shifts. Clubs and other groups had a hard time having meetings and doing their functions when 20 percent of their members were not in school for weeks at a time. However, sometimes students who were on "vacation" would come to school to participate in clubs or performances. In spring of grade 10 I wanted a part in the school's musical and came for rehearsals after school and evenings even though I was supposed to be on vacation. Even though it didn't affect me personally, I heard that juniors and seniors complained about not having time in the summer to get jobs and internships that they could put on college applications. The schedule also sometimes kept boyfriends and girlfriends apart because while one was in school taking classes the other was out of school on vacation.

Teachers and counselors were on staggered schedules, they often were not available and you sometimes had to wait weeks for an appointment with your guidance counselor. Other counselors were substitutes, but I did not like talking with a counselor I didn't know very well.

Some people said they liked the flexibility of a year-round schedule. Some teachers earned extra money by working more weeks than usual. Families took trips when there was less crowding of people than during the peak times. Airfares are cheaper off-season. Savings are a bonus. Believe me, if this school decided to change to a year-round program, I and my parents would look around for a different school for me and my two younger brothers to attend.

Critique: Your opening is catchy. By speculating on what others may write, you make readers curious to know why you claim to know what is happening in the minds of others. Although you may be projecting your strong views about year-round schooling onto your fellow students, the conviction of your views throughout your essay is admirable. In fact, you are in an enviable position, having experienced year-round schooling firsthand.

You use your experience to advantage, especially in citing telling details (particularly in the third paragraph) about the life of students in a year-round program. On the other hand, although you say your present school is "user-friendly" (in the context, a clever metaphorical usage), you neglect to explain precisely how the lives of students are better in a school that uses a traditional calendar.

Perhaps the weakest part of the essay is its abrupt and incoherent ending. The last paragraph begins with a reasonable topic sentence about the flexibility of a year-round schedule. However, the supporting sentences deal with a variety of disconnected topics. Your essay is rated **5**.

Adriana's Essay:

Many schools are discussing whether or not to adopt a year-round schedule. They think that it will improve learning, and I agree. If school was held twelve months a year, it would substantially upgrade the quality of our education. It would give students more time to focus on studies instead of the social aspects of school. Second, it would raise the level of education in the United States. Thirdly, it would prepare students better for going out to work after graduation.

My first reason is that year-round school will expose students in greater depth in all subjects, from English to science. In English class, there's many great pieces of literature to read, but some teachers hesitate to assign long books because they take up too much time in class. If students spend more time in English classes, then the teacher can give them classic books to read that are 750 pages or more instead of short little paperbacks that can be read in a couple of hours such as of Animal Farm and Anthem. Or in chemistry, students can perform various experiments until they have a firm grasp of the concepts instead of rushing from one lab procedure to another with hardly a clue as to what each one is supposed to mean.

Secondly, I think it is awful that the most powerful and richest country in the world ranks so low in comparison to the education given in other countries. It is shocking when teenagers perform at third- or fourth-grade levels, or some even cannot read. Year-long school would give them a chance to bring themselves up to grade level or beyond. The usual school schedule doesn't have enough hours of classroom time to give them a chance to catch up. Without the necessary skills, such people are destined to take unskilled, low-paying jobs. With more time in school, they can avoid a dull life of misery and poverty.

Thirdly, the reason for a longer school year is because it would prepare students for the world of work right after high school or later after college. Most workers get two or three weeks of paid vacation a year if they are lucky. Self-employed people may not get a vacation—ever. Yet school is closed for vacation about a third of the year, with holidays and regular vacations, including two to three months off in the summer. No employer can afford to give so much time off from a job, so schools should not get students accus-

tomed to think that they need to work only part of the year. Similarly, students attending school all year long can work as interns in businesses or agencies as part of their academic program. This is much harder under the traditional calendar which, as stated above, is different from the world of work.

Finally, some members of the school community are opposed to the year-round school on the ground that it would deprive students of time "to pursue individual interests, hold jobs and develop themselves in nonscholastic ways," that point of view is very limited. Just the opposite, keeping the school open all year would raise opportunities to learn. Students can take the usual number of courses in the ordinary amount of time. Since school is open all year, they can take advantage of it and do more learning. Independent study, a rarity during the traditional school year, could even become more common instead of the exception.

To conclude, I think that year-round schooling offers promise in the United States. Not only will it improve education by offering students more opportunities for learning, it will also help our country move up in the educational rankings of the countries of the world, and it will prepare students for jobs they will need to live good and satisfying lives.

Critique: Your essay demonstrates adequate command of writing skills. It responds directly to the prompt. It states your position clearly: *"If school was held twelve months a year, it would substantially upgrade the quality of our education."* In the fifth paragraph it attempts to refute one of the arguments likely to be made by an opponent of year-round schooling. Your refutation, however, lacks specific details that show your opponent's viewpoint is "very limited." On the other hand, your second paragraph might serve as a model of strong development. It uses specific examples that bolster and support the main idea—that year-round school deepens students' knowledge and understanding.

The organization of your essay could hardly be clearer. At the same time, though, it is totally predictable. It follows almost to the letter the conventional five-paragraph essay formula that includes an introduction, conclusion, and three paragraphs of development (plus one of refutation). This format is orderly, of course, but it is also quite dull. Starting each paragraph with such adverbs as "Secondly," "Finally," and so forth does little to catch the reader's interest. By varying paragraph openings as well as sentence structure, you will be more likely to carry along your reader. Your conclusion serves no particular function except to reitereate what you have already said. Thus you missed an opportunity to finish your essay with flair.

In spite of these shortcomings, the overall quality of the essay is above average. The writing is essentially correct, although not flawless. Your essay is rated **4**.

THE CHALLENGE OF WRITING A 30-MINUTE ESSAY

By this time in your education, you've probably written more essays than you could cram into your backpack. When you wrote all those essays, how did you do it? Did you sit down and spill your thoughts onto blank sheets of paper? Or did you write rough drafts on a computer, go back later to cut and paste, and only then print them out? Possibly you thought long and hard ahead of time about what you wanted to say. Perhaps you prepared lists of ideas or an outline showing the structure of your essay and then, while composing, labored over every word. Or maybe you used a combination of methods, varying the process from time to time.

One thing is almost certain about the essay on the ACT Writing Test. You've probably never been given so little time to write an essay that counts so much.

Writing an essay by hand in less than half an hour is a challenge. Even professional journalists, accustomed to working under the pressure of deadlines, would be hard-pressed to produce a good essay in 30 minutes. But take heart! The essay score is but one piece of data on your college application, and no one taking the ACT will have a nanosecond more than you to complete the assignment. Moreover, the grade you earn will be determined not by comparing your work with that of a preeminent writer but with the essays of other students who took the test when you did. If you've been a reasonably proficient essay writer in the past, be confident that you'll perform equally well on the ACT. In fact, you may do even better than usual because you're likely to be pumped up to do your best work.

When writing the ACT essay you must condense into a few minutes all the steps that other writers, enjoying the luxury of time, might stretch into hours or even into days. Chances are you've done it before. An essay test in social studies, for example, may have required you to quickly fill up a blank page with all you knew about the Reign of Terror or causes of the Civil War. The numerous in-class essays you've produced over the years have no doubt trained you for the kind of instant essay asked of you on the ACT. In your classes, of course, success was based partly on how closely your ideas resembled those that the teacher had in mind. That's not true on the ACT. You can't cram for this essay the way you can for a test in physics or English. The answer you write in response to the prompt is not predetermined. What you need to know is already lodged inside you. The task you face on test day is to organize your ideas and put them into readable form on paper. It is a measure of what you can do instead of what you know.

TIP

You will do well if you are pumped up to do your best work.

Making Every Second Count

No book can tell you just how much time to devote to each step in the process. What works for you may be different from what works for others. But the three best ways for anybody to prepare are 1) to practice, 2) to practice, and 3) to practice some more.

Pick sample essay topics found on pages 486–487. Following the instructions for ACT essays, write an essay a day for several days in a row, or until you get the feel of 30 minutes' writing time. Pace yourself. Keep a record of how much time you spend thinking about the topic, how many minutes you devote to composing the essay, and how long it takes you to proofread and edit. As you practice, adjust the following plan until you get the timing that suits you best and produces the results you want:

Prewriting: 5–6 minutes
- Reading and analyzing the prompt
- Picking and narrowing the topic
- Choosing a main idea
- Gathering and arranging supporting ideas

Composing the essay: 15–20 minutes
- Introducing the thesis
- Developing paragraphs
- Choosing the best words for meaning and effect
- Structuring sentences effectively
- Writing a conclusion

Editing and proofreading: 3–5 minutes
- Editing for clarity and coherence
- Editing to create interest
- Checking for standard usage and mechanical errors, including spelling, punctuation, and capitalization

Because readers understand that ACT essays are first drafts, feel free to cross out, insert words using carets (^), and move blocks of text—as though you were cutting and pasting—with neatly drawn arrows. If necessary, number the sentences to make clear the order in which they are to be read. You won't be penalized for a sloppy-looking paper. Just make sure that the essay is readable.

Because of the time limit, don't plan to write a long essay. Essays of more than 400 words are unnecessary. It doesn't take even that many words to demonstrate your writing ability. In fact, less can be more, for a shorter essay of, say, 250 to 300 words can focus sharply on a limited subject. It can also be written more quickly, leaving time for revising and polishing your work. But don't be satisfied with an abbreviated one-paragraph essay. That could suggest a case of airheadedness. Just remember that quantity counts less than quality.

TIP

Don't waste time inventing an essay title (your essay doesn't need one). Don't count words and don't expect to recopy your first draft.

How to Write an Essay in 30 Minutes

Don't be misled by the above heading. It's a come-on, not a promise. For one thing, writing an essay in 30 minutes may be a contradiction in terms. An essay is basically the product of an author's thinking. It expresses a point of view arrived at after reflection, analysis, or interpretation of a subject or issue. When given the topic 30 minutes before the paper is due, you can't expect to pore over the assignment. If you think too deeply, before you know it, you'll have run out of time.

Another reason that the heading is illusory is that you don't learn to write very well by reading about how to do it. You learn to write by writing, by messing around with ideas and words, by experimenting, practicing, and doing what seasoned practitioners do when they face a sheet of blank paper or an empty computer screen: They write!

The Essay-Writing Process

The next several pages won't necessarily transform you into a world-class writer of essays, but you'll become acquainted with what expert writers think about as they practice their craft. In addition, as you learn what works and what to avoid, you'll become more attuned to some of the basic principles of good writing.

Because you won't have time to invent a process when you write the ACT essay, it pays to have one in mind ahead of time. In preparation for the test, try out various processes while writing practice essays. Then develop the one that enables you to work most rapidly and efficiently while producing the best results. In effect, make a plan for what to do during each stage of the writing process.

The first stage, often called *prewriting*, consists of everything that needs to be done before you actually start writing. During the second stage, *composing*, you choose the words and form the sentences that express your thoughts. And during the final stage, *revising and proofreading*, you polish and refine the text of your essay word by word, making it clear, correct, and graceful. The truth is that these three stages are not all discrete. They overlap and blend indiscriminately. For example, writers compose, revise, and proofread simultaneously, they jot down sentences during prewriting, and even late in the process sometimes weave new ideas into their text. In fact, no stage really ends until the final period of the last sentence is put in place—or until time is up and the test booklets are closed.

THIRTEEN PRINCIPLES OF ESSAY WRITING

As you write, keep these principles at your elbow. Refer to them time and again. Soon they'll become habitual, and you'll use them instinctively, not only during the ACT Writing Test, but any time you need to write an essay. They can be *that* useful!

PREWRITING

1. Analyze the topic carefully.
2. Narrow the topic.
3. Choose a main idea that matters.
4. Gather and arrange ideas purposefully.

COMPOSING

5. Write an appealing introduction.
6. Develop paragraphs fully.
7. Include transitions for coherence.
8. Use plain and precise words.
9. Vary the sentence structure.
10. End the essay with a distinct conclusion.

EDITING AND PROOFREADING

11. Edit for clarity.
12. Edit for interest.
13. Check for standard usage and mechanics.

If you've had plenty of writing experience, you probably recognize most, if not all, of these principles. But if any item on the list is new to you, refer to it often and practice it over and over. Let it help you evolve into a better writer.

Prewriting

1. ANALYZE THE TOPIC CAREFULLY

At the risk of stating the obvious, begin by reading the assigned essay topic, or prompt, very carefully. Read it two or three times, or until you are certain what is being asked of you.

An ACT prompt may not turn you on right away, but once you begin to think about it you may begin bursting with ideas. School essay assignments often give you days, or even weeks, to prepare. Before writing a word you can ponder the topic, talk to others, search the Internet, psyche yourself, and do whatever you can to get ready. On the ACT, however, you have only a couple of minutes to prepare.

2. NARROW THE TOPIC

Always favor a well-focused essay on a limited topic to an essay that tries to cover too much ground. The sharper the focus, the better. That is why narrowing the topic is one of the crucial steps in planning any essay.

The good news is that the ACT gives you a gift. The essay prompt narrows the topic for you by asking a direct question something like one of these:

Do schools give too much homework?

Do teachers have the right to charge students in their classes for tutoring in the evening and on weekends?

Should students be allowed to grade their teachers and publish the results in the school newspaper?

Would you approve of an honor code in your school to reduce cheating?

By answering yes or no to any of these questions you narrow the topic in the blink of an eye. Your answer is apt to fit nicely into an essay of roughly 250–300 words written in 30 minutes. (That is about the number of words on a double-spaced typed page using 12-point type.) Even if your answer cannot be reduced to a simple yes or no, a position somewhere in-between is still likely to be narrow enough for you to write a convincing essay.

3. CHOOSE A MAIN IDEA THAT MATTERS

Although the prompt more or less hands you an essay topic for free, you are still obliged to make an important decision—which side of the issue to support. You are free to support either side, of course, or to present an altogether different point of view. Whatever position you take is the essay's *main idea*.

TIP

Your opinion on the issue is your essay's main idea.

Defending that main idea is the purpose, or point, of your essay. An essay may not simply be "about" something—about the school library, about cheating on tests, or about varsity sports. What counts is the statement your essay makes with regard to the library, to cheating, or to varsity sports—in other words, your main idea.

Every piece of the essay, from its opening sentence to the conclusion, should contribute in some way to the development of that main idea.

Any material that wanders from the main idea should be discarded because it not only wastes words but detracts from the impact of your essay.

For example, if the topic happened to relate to required dress codes in high school, a main idea might be any one of the following:

1. Yes, high schools should impose dress codes on students.
2. No, high schools should not impose dress codes on students.
3. High schools should impose dress codes on freshmen and sophomores but not on juniors and seniors.

Using one of these main ideas as your starting point, the essay would then go on to prove the validity of your opinion.

TIP

An essay that is truthful and comes from the heart will serve you best.

If possible, pick a main idea that matters to you personally, one that truly reflects your thinking. ACT readers won't fault you for stating opinions with which they disagree, so there's no good reason for choosing a main idea that makes you sound politically correct or one that you think will please or flatter the reader. If you give your readers only what you think they might want, you're being dishonest, posing as someone you are not. Likewise, because you don't want to sound pompous or pretentious, avoid picking main ideas solely to demonstrate your intellectual superiority.

Chances are that the ACT will give you a topic to which you can respond without much difficulty. Still, brace yourself for the possibility that you don't care a fig for writing about it. What then? Is it possible to write an engaging essay on a topic that makes you yawn? The answer is yes, mainly because you have no choice but to create the illusion that you care deeply about the issue. Doing so may annoy you or grate on your conscience, but raising a stink about it won't get you far.

Instead, accept the challenge. Show your resilience and creativity—two qualities that college admissions officials value and admire. Psyche yourself to write the essay of your life, even if the topic turns you off.

4. GATHER AND ARRANGE IDEAS PURPOSEFULLY

Unless you are blessed with a digital mind that can instantly process an issue and draw insightful conclusions, do yourself a favor: spend a few moments to gather and arrange whatever evidence you can think of to support and develop a main idea.

In fact, you can't go wrong with this tried-and-true technique:

1. Divide a piece of scrap paper into two columns, labeled "Pro" and "Con."
2. In the pro column, jot down arguments, anecdotes, and examples in favor of the issue—just a word or two for each.
3. Now turn to the con column, and do the same with arguments, anecdotes, and examples against the issue.
4. Once the flow of ideas has slowed to a trickle, choose the column that contains the more compelling evidence.
5. Sort through the notes by drawing circles around key words, connecting related ideas with arrows, crossing out the weakest ideas, or just underlining the thoughts you are mostly likely to use in your essay. Your jottings, in effect, will become your essay's working outline.
6. Finally, from the column you did not choose, circle one idea that supports a position contrary to yours. Later, you might strengthen your own essay with a counterargument—that is, with a refutation of that idea.

With materials assembled, put them in some kind of order. Decide what should come first. Second. Third. In most essays, the best order is the clearest, the order your reader can follow with the least effort. But, just as a highway map may show several routes from one place to another, there is no single way to get from the beginning to the end of an essay. The plan that fails is the aimless one, the one in which ideas are presented solely according to how they popped into your head. To guard against aimlessness, rank your ideas in order of importance. Then work toward your best point, not away from it. Giving away your *pièce de résistance* at the start is self-defeating. Therefore, if you have, say, three good ideas in support of your thesis, save the strongest for last. Launch the essay with your second best, and sandwich your least favorite between the other two. A solid opening draws readers into the essay and creates that all-important first impression, but a memorable ending is even more important. Coming last, it is what readers have fresh in their minds when they assign the essay a grade.

TIP

Do not forget to plan a counterargument.

Although the following guideline does not apply to every essay, a body consisting of three sections may be just about right. Why three? Mainly because three is a number that works. When you can support your main idea with three pieces of solid evidence, you appear to know what you are talking about. One is insufficient and two only slightly better. But three indicates thoughtfulness. Psychologically, three also creates a sense of rhetorical wholeness, like "blood, sweat, and tears," and "of the people, by the people, and for the people."

Each of three ideas may not require an equal amount of emphasis, however. You might dispose of the weakest idea in just a couple of sentences, while each of the others gets a whole paragraph. But whatever you emphasize, be sure that each idea is separate and distinct. That is, the third idea mustn't simply rehash the first or second in the guise of something new.

Composing

5. WRITE AN APPEALING INTRODUCTION

Introductions let readers know what they're in for. Don't make a formal announcement of your plan: "This discussion will show the significance of computers as an influence on the learning of children from age 3 to 12. Distinctions will be made between early childhood (age 3–7) and middle childhood (age 8–12)." Such announcements should be reserved for research reports and textbooks. They are out of place in an ACT essay. Readers will recognize your topic soon enough, even without a separate statement of your intention.

Jill B, for example, began an essay on the rights of high school students this way:

On Monday morning, October 20th, I arrived in school to find every locker door in my corridor standing ajar. Over the weekend, school officials had searched through students' lockers for drugs and alcohol. I believe that this illegal action was a violation of both my civil rights and the civil rights of every other student in the school.

This opening sets the essay's boundaries. Jill can't include everything about students' rights or about the duties and responsibilities of school authorities. Instead, she'll concentrate on one issue raised by her personal experience on that Monday morning.

The best essays usually begin with something to draw the reader into the piece. Think of the opening as a hook—a phrase, a sentence, or an idea that will make your audience want to keep reading. Hooks must be very simple and brief because time won't allow you to write a long introduction. Jill's hook is effective because it tells an informative anecdote that leads directly to the main subject of her essay.

To do its job, a hook may not be dull.

Dull hook: Drugs and alcohol are a problem for many young people in today's society.

What dulls this hook is a statement so obvious and general that no one would be moved to continue reading.

Here's a sharper hook on the same subject:

Sharper hook: When sixth-graders get drunk and 13-year-olds smoke pot every Friday night, society's got a problem.

This hook is vivid. It states a problem by using a compelling image of young children out of control. It provokes curiosity. The reader wants to know more about the "problem."

Dull hook: Digital photography is one of the most popular hobbies in the world.

This opening lacks interest because it makes a general statement that cannot possibly be dealt with in a short essay. Besides, no reader indifferent to photography would be driven to read the next sentence.

Sharper hook: I packed my brand-new digital camera when I left for spring break. When I came home, the wrapping was still on the box.

Aha! Here is a hook that leaves the reader wondering what happened during spring break. It implies that the speaker is about to tell a story explaining why he never took the camera out of his suitcase.

Dull hook: Most predictions that George Orwell made in his novel of the future, *1984*, did not happen.

Sharper hook: Why did George Orwell goof?

The first opening, written as an ordinary statement of fact, may interest readers familiar with *1984*, but the second one, consisting of a pithy question, is intriguing. How did Orwell, a brilliant author and thinker, "goof"? The writer is a tease. By hinting that she's going to reveal a secret flaw in Orwell's work, she entices the reader to go on to the next sentence.

Techniques for Hooking Readers

During the 30 minutes allotted for the ACT essay, you probably won't have time to write an elaborate opening. A statement that conveys the topic of your essay may be all you need to lure your readers into the essay. Use any of these five common techniques, each illustrated with an example from an essay by a high school student.

1. Start with a brief account of an incident—real or invented—that leads the reader into the essay:

   By lunch period, Megan, a senior at Brookdale High School, had already traded text messages with her brother in college, with her dad at work, and with a friend who was absent from school that day.

   — Lisa N

   With one sentence, Lisa leaves her readers curious about what comes next. Her list of messages suggests that her essay will be about the effects of staying in touch or about some other aspect of communication. With their interest whetted, readers soon hope to understand the connection between Lisa's opening statement and the point of her essay.

2. State a provocative idea in an ordinary way or an ordinary idea in a provocative way. Either one will ignite reader interest.

   As any football hero will tell you, on the field brains count for more than brawn.

   — Ollie G

   This unconventional idea may cause readers to wonder whether the writer has lost touch with reality. Or it may lead readers to question their own preconceptions and prejudices about football players. Either way, Ollie has aroused his readers' interest with a provocative idea that presumably will be justified and explained as the essay continues.

3. Use a quotation—not necessarily a famous one—from Shakespeare, a rap song, or your grandmother. Whatever the source, its sentiment must relate to the essay's topic.

   "You can take people out of the country but you can't take the country out of the people."

   — Gary F

   With this opening, Gary accomplishes a great deal. He gives a clever new twist to a common adage and with a few words has introduced his main idea, the futility of changing people's basic characteristics or core values.

4. Refute a commonly held assumption or define a word in a new and surprising way.

   Even though she's never written a rhyme or verse, my boss at Safeway is just as much a poet as Shelley or Keats.

   — Rebecca V

   By inviting readers to imagine how someone who has written neither rhymes nor verses can be a *poet*, Rebecca hints at a new and perhaps surprising meaning of the word. That the label "poet" applies to her boss is even more intriguing because you don't often find poets working as supermarket managers. In short, the opening quickens our interest in reading an essay on an unlikely topic.

5. Ask an interesting question or two that you will answer in your essay.

> *Why are stories of crime so fascinating?*
>
> — *Doug T*

Doug's opening question has wide appeal because it pertains to many of us who are riveted to both fictional and real accounts of criminal acts. We read the police blotter in the newspaper, tune to news channels that emphasize crime stories, talk about the latest murder, watch *Law and Order* reruns on the tube. Presumably Doug's essay will explain our fascination with the subject.

When writing your ACT essay, you're not obliged to write an opening for the ages. Remember your purpose: to demonstrate that you can think, organize ideas, and write correctly. Therefore, a direct, clearly worded statement of the essay's main idea should suffice. Work hard to get it right. Be thoughtful. Be clever if that's your style, but not overly cute, coarse, or shocking. And keep it short. An opening that comprises, say, more than a quarter of your essay reflects poorly on your sense of proportion.

6. DEVELOP PARAGRAPHS FULLY

Each paragraph of a well-written essay is, in effect, an essay in miniature. It has a purpose, an organizational plan, and a progression of ideas. You can scrutinize a paragraph just as you would scrutinize a complete essay. You can study its structure and development, identify its main idea and its purpose.

In an essay, most paragraphs play a primary role and one or more secondary roles. An *introductory paragraph*, for instance, launches the essay and makes the intent of the essay clear to the reader. The *concluding paragraph* leaves the reader with a thought to remember and provides a sense of closure. Most paragraphs, however, are *developmental*. That is, they are used to carry forward the main point of the essay. In one way or other, developmental paragraphs perform any number of functions, including

- adding new ideas to the preceding discussion
- continuing or explaining in more detail an idea presented earlier
- reiterating a previously stated idea
- citing an example of a previously stated idea
- evaluating an opinion stated earlier
- refuting previously stated ideas
- turning the essay in a new direction
- providing a new or contrasting point of view
- describing the relationship between ideas presented earlier
- providing background material
- raising a hypothetical or rhetorical question about the topic
- serving as a transition between sections of the essay
- summarizing an argument presented earlier

Whatever its functions, a paragraph should contribute to the essay's overall growth. A paragraph that fails to amplify the main idea of the essay should be revised or deleted. Similarly, any idea within a paragraph that doesn't contribute to the development of the paragraph's topic needs to be changed or eliminated.

Topic Sentences

Whether readers skim your paragraphs or slog doggedly through every word, they need to find sentences now and then that, like landmarks, help them to know where they are. Such guiding sentences differ from others because they define the paragraph's main topic; hence the name *topic sentence*.

TIP 

Most paragraphs contain a topic sentence.

Most, but not all, paragraphs contain topic sentences. The topic of some paragraphs is so obvious that to state it would be redundant. Then, too, groups of paragraphs can be so closely knit that one topic sentence states the most important idea for all of them.

What all topic sentences have in common is their helpfulness. Consider them landmarks that indicate turning points that tell readers the direction they'll be going for a while.

No rule governs every possible use of a topic sentence. A sense of what readers need in order to understand the essay must be your guide. Let topic sentences lead the way.

Most topic sentences come first in a paragraph, but they may be put almost anywhere. Nor are topic sentences always separate and independent grammatical units. Rather, they may be woven into a supporting sentence as a clause or a phrase. (In the paragraph you are now reading, for instance, the topic of the paragraph is stated in the second clause of the first sentence.) Writers frequently vary the location of topic sentences to avoid monotony. A topic sentence saved for the end of a paragraph may stand out boldly as the climax to which the supporting sentences lead.

The key to unlocking a paragraph's purpose usually lies in the topic sentence. If a reader fails to catch the main idea, the meaning of the entire paragraph could be lost. Instead of a coherent unit of meaning, the paragraph may seem like a diffuse collection of unrelated sentences. The overall effectiveness of a paragraph, therefore, is tied to its supporting details. A loose or ambiguous connection erodes the effectiveness of both the paragraph and the entire essay.

Developing Paragraphs

In terms of importance the length of paragraphs takes a back seat to clear and purposeful organization. Like essays, paragraphs should have a discernable plan. Ideas can be arranged from general to specific, or vice versa. Chronological and spatial arrangements make sense in narrative and descriptive paragraphs. Clarity and intent should always govern sequence. Disjointed paragraphs consist of sentences in random order, but in coherent paragraphs every sentence has a place and a function that contributes to its total effect.

7. INCLUDE TRANSITIONS FOR COHERENCE

Picture your readers as naive tourists in a foreign country and your essay as a journey they must take from one place to another. Because you can't expect them to find their own way, you must, in effect, guide them.

In long essays readers need more guidance than in short ones. To keep readers informed, you needn't repeat what you've already written but rather, plant key ideas, slightly rephrased, as milestones along the way. (The sentence you just read contains just such a marker. The phrase *"To keep readers informed"* cues you to keep in mind the topic of this paragraph—helping readers find their way.) By regularly alluding to the main idea of paragraphs, you'll keep readers focused. That is, you'll keep them by your side from start to finish.

You can help readers along, too, by choosing words that set up relationships between one thought and the next. This can be done with such words as *this*, which actually ties the sentence you are now reading to the previous one. The word *too* in the first sentence of this paragraph serves the same function; it acts as a link between this paragraph and the one before. Fortunately, the English language is brimming with transitional words and phrases that tie sentences and ideas together.

Whenever you use a transition, you're doing your readers a favor by ensuring them a smooth trip through your writing. Without transitions readers will find themselves lurching from one idea to another. Although not every sentence requires a transition, three or four sentences in succession without a link of some kind create confusion and incoherence.

Transitions aid writers, too, by helping them stick to the topic and avoid inadvertent detours. While editing your essay, check for ideas that either fail to connect with others around them or are unrelated to the paragraph's main idea. Such ideas should be revised, moved, or discarded.

TIP

To write clearly, use plain words. Never use a complex word because it sounds good or makes you seem more sophisticated.

8. USE PLAIN AND PRECISE WORDS

Plain Language

The ACT Writing Test is not a place to flaunt your vocabulary. Use an elegant word only when it's the only word that will let you add something to the essay that you can't achieve in any other way. Why? Because an elegant word used merely to use an elegant word is bombastic. . . er. . . big-sounding and artificial.

Fortunately, English is loaded with simple words that can express the most profound ideas. A sign that says STOP! conveys its message more clearly than CEASE AND DESIST. When a dentist pokes at your teeth, it *hurts*, even if dentists call it "experiencing discomfort." Descartes, the famous French philosopher, said, "I think, therefore, I am," a statement that forever afterward shaped the way we think about existence. Descartes might have used more exotic words, of course, words more in keeping with the florid writing style of his time, but the very simplicity of his words endows his statement with great power. In fact, a sign of true intelligence is the ability to convey deep meetings with simple words.

Simple doesn't necessarily mean short. It's true that plain words tend to be the short ones, but not always. The word *fid* is short, but it's not plain unless you are a sailor, in which case you'd know that a fid supports the mast on your boat or is an instrument used to pry open a tight knot in your lines. On the other hand, *spontaneously* is five syllables long. Yet it is a plain and simple word because of its frequent use.

Euphemisms

Of course, there are occasions when the plainest words will not do. English, as well as other languages, contains innumerable euphemisms—expressions that soften or mitigate painful, unsavory, or objectionable truths. For example, there are scores of euphemisms for the verb "to die" (*pass away, pass on, be deceased, rest, expire, meet one's maker*, and so on) and for bathroom (*restroom, ladies'/men's room, W.C., lounge*), and for drunk, vomiting, and everything else that might upset a prissy sensibility. Pussyfooting with words has its place. We do it all the time, but in your essay writing, use euphemisms only when you have a valid reason for doing so.

Don't interpret the admonition to use plain words as *carte blanche* to use current, everyday slang or street talk in your ACT essay. Unless you definitely need current lingo to create an effect that you can't produce another way, stick with plain, standard English. Avoid using words, emoticons, and abbreviations that have become common in everyday e-mails, tweets, and text messages—such as LOL, BFF, CU, B4, and GR8. You are free to write as though you are wired, of course, but do not highlight your digital usages with quotation marks. If to make a point you let txt msgs creep in2 your essay, be sure to show your mastery of standard English in at least part of the piece. After all, colleges want to know that you can write good, standard prose.

Be Yourself

For the ACT essay, a plain, conversational style will always be appropriate. The language should sound like you. In formal essays, custom requires you to remove yourself from center stage and focus on the subject matter. But ACT essays encourage more casual responses in which references to yourself are perfectly acceptable. It's not essential to use the first-person singular pronoun, but using *I* is often preferable to using the more impersonal *one*, as in "When *one* is writing an ACT essay, *one* sometimes writes funny," or *you*, as in "Sometimes *you* feel like a dope," or by avoiding pronouns altogether. But an essay that expresses the writer's personal opinion will sound most natural when cast in the first-person singular.

TIP

Don't be phony! ACT essay readers are old hands at spotting pretense in students' writing.

Let your genuine voice ring out, although the way you speak is not necessarily the way you should write. Spoken language is often vague, clumsy, repetitive, confused, wordy. Consider writing as the everyday speech of someone who speaks exceedingly well. It's grammatically correct and free of pop expressions and clichés. Think of it as the kind of speech expected of you in a college interview or in serious conversation with the head of your school. Or maybe even the way this paragraph sounds. You could do a lot worse!

Precise Language

Precise words are memorable, while hazy, hard-to-grasp words fade as quickly as last night's dream. Tell your garage mechanic vaguely, "This car is a lemon," and he'll ask for more information. Say precisely, "My car won't start in freezing weather," and he'll raise the engine hood and go to work. If a patient in the E.R. says, "I feel pain," a surgeon might at least like to know exactly where it hurts before pulling out her scalpels. In other words, precise language is more informative, more functional, and thus, more desirable.

In the first draft of a personal essay about a day he'd like to forget, Jeff wrote this paragraph:

It was an awful day outside. Everything was going wrong. I felt terrible. Things weren't going well in school. I got a below-par grade on a paper, and I was sure that I had failed my science quiz. I also had lots of things to do at home and no time to do them. My mother was in a bad mood, too. She yelled at me for all kinds of things. Then Penny called, and we got into a disagreement. I had trouble watching a movie, and I couldn't pay for repairs. I went to bed early, hoping that tomorrow would be better.

Reviewing the essay a few days later, Jeff realized the paragraph begged for more precise writing. Yes, the day had been dreadful, but his account needed details to prove it. The next draft took care of that:

It had been a cold and rainy November day, and my life was as miserable as the weather. I felt chills all day, and my throat was sore. In school I got a D on a history paper about the Bubonic Plague, and I was sure that I had failed the chemistry quiz. The homework was piling up—two lab reports, over 150 pages to read in Wuthering Heights, a chapter in the history text, and about a hundred new vocabulary words in Spanish. I didn't have time or energy to do it all, especially when my mother started to pick at me about my messy room and the thank-you letters I'm supposed to write to my grandparents. Just as she was reminding me that my registration for the ACT was overdue, Penny called to tell me that she wouldn't be coming over for Thanksgiving after all, and we argued about loyalty and trust and keeping promises. When I tried to watch the last Harry Potter movie again, the player kept skipping scenes. The repairman said he would charge $100 just to look at the damn thing, but I don't have that kind of money. By 9:00 P.M. I was in bed, hoping that tomorrow would be better.

In this version Jeff included many precise details that vividly illustrate the wretchedness of that miserable day. And he's made clear why he picked that day as the subject of his essay.

Of course, not every essay topic calls for such detail. Some topics invite you to write more vaguely, more abstractly, perhaps more philosophically. For example, *loyalty, trust, and keeping promises* as well as *love, freedom, spirit, fairness, conformity, satisfaction*, and countless other words stand for concepts that exist in our hearts and minds. The power to express principles, ideas, and feelings is unique to humans, and such a gift shouldn't go untapped, but an essay consisting solely of abstractions will leave readers at sea. However amorphous the topic, therefore, an essay's success depends on precise, hard-edged, concrete words.

Good writers understand that their words must appeal to the readers' senses. To write precisely is to write with pictures, sounds, and actions that are as vivid on paper as they are in reality. Exact words leave distinct marks; abstract ones, blurry impressions.

Fresh Language and Surprises

Dull language has three main qualities: 1) boring, 2) boring, and 3) boring. When readers know what's coming, they lose interest rapidly. So, do your readers a favor. Instead of relying totally on safe, conventional language, take a chance now and then and give them a verbal surprise. ACT readers, especially after reading hundreds of predictable essays on the same topic, will do cartwheels for something fresh, something new. It takes courage on an essay test to use fresh language, but here's a guarantee: A pleasant verbal surprise will give your readers, not to speak of your essay, a boost.

A verbal surprise is simply a unique and interesting choice of words. That doesn't mean you should use odd words like *twit* for *tease*, *fop* for *fool*. A word or phrase need not be rare to surprise a reader. Most ordinary words, used deftly, will dazzle your readers just as well—maybe even better because they will sound more natural than something forced onto the page just to sound unusual.

Surprise with Comparisons

Of course, it's not always easy to find just the right words. At such times, you can depend on figures of speech such as metaphors and similes to make your meaning clear.

Similes (Tim wrestles *like* a tiger) and metaphors (Tim *is* a tiger) point out likenesses between something familiar (tiger) and something unfamiliar (how Tim wrestles). To convey meaning, one side of a comparison must always be common and recognizable. Therefore, comparing the cry of the Arctic tern to the song of a tree toad won't enlighten a reader familiar with neither water birds nor tree toads. Because you can expect readers to know the sound of a fiddle, however, a more revealing comparison is *The cry of the Arctic tern sounds like a fiddler searching for a C-sharp*.

Make your comparisons fresh and original. Don't rely on old standbys such as "life is like a box of chocolates," or "like a bat out of hell," or "dead as a doornail." Our language is littered with countless comparisons that once may have been vibrant and fresh but have wilted from overuse. The fact is that every familiar combination of words, such as "I could care less" or "you've got to be kidding" or "what a bummer" was once new, cool, even poetic. But repetition has turned them into clichés.

Let clichés rest in the cliché graveyard. Don't drag them out for your ACT essay. That is an admonition easier to say than to follow because clichés crowd our everyday speech. Like the air we breathe (a cliché), we hardly notice them. In an essay, however, especially one that it supposed to demonstrate your unique cast of mind, you must avoid clichés like the plague. "*Like the plague*," in fact, is one you should avoid.

TIP

Clichés are deadly. Let them rest in peace.

Using such trite phrases and expressions declares that you'd rather borrow what someone else has said than think of something on your own. It also signifies an impoverished imagination, for how can people dependent on others' words ever express their unique thoughts and feelings? Take, for example, the many meaningless expressions that are often used to mask life's disappointments and tragedies: *it just goes to show you; that's the way the cookie crumbles; you can't win 'em all; win some, lose some;* and *you've got to take the good with the bad.*

"You can say that again," says the cliché-monger. But don't you believe it. You don't have to put up with bad writing. Expunge clichés that sneak into your prose when *your back is turned, when your defenses are down*, and *when you least expect them*. Be vigilant, and purge them from your prose. Don't use an expression that you have heard or seen before. If you have written a phrase with a familiar ring, drop it, not *like a hot potato*, but just as quickly.

On the ACT Writing Test you won't be penalized for an essay lacking inventive and scintillating expressions, but you'll pay a price if your writing is overrun with clichés. Get into the habit, then, of purging all trite phrases from your writing vocabulary. *Half the battle*, as they say, is knowing a cliché when you meet one. The other half—expelling them—still needs to be fought and won.

9. VARY THE SENTENCE STRUCTURE

Sentence Patterns

Variety for its own sake is hardly preferable to assembly-line writing—writing in which every sentence has been cut from the same pattern. But variety that clarifies meaning or gives emphasis to a particular idea is something else.

As you probably know, most simple declarative sentences start with the subject, followed by the verb, as in:

To avoid boring your readers, serve them a variety of sentences.

Cats (subject) *fall* (verb) asleep in about three seconds.

They (subject) *sleep* (verb) best after eating and cleaning themselves.

I (subject) *wish* (verb) to be a cat in my next life.

A string of sentences with this subject-verb pattern resembles the prose in a grade-school primer. Make your move to a more mature style by analyzing one of your recent essays. Do several sentences begin with grammatical subjects? If so, try shifting the subject elsewhere. Try leading off with a prepositional phrase, or with an adverb, adjective, or some other grammatical unit. By varying sentence openings, you'll write more boldly and vibrantly.

The following pairs of sentences show how a subject can be shifted from its customary position:

Before the shift: Ms. Bennett is one of the most popular teachers in the school.

After the shift: Of all the teachers in the school Ms. Bennett is one of the most popular.

After a prepositional phrase was added (two prepositional phrases, in fact), the subject (*Ms. Bennett*) has been moved further along in the sentence.

Before: She taught *Giants in the Earth* to our eleventh-grade English class with enthusiasm.

After: Enthusiastically, she taught *Giants in the Earth* to our eleventh-grade English class.

Obviously, the revised sentence begins with an adverb.

Before: Students were less excited about the book than she was.

After: Yet, students were less excited about the book than she was.

Well, here the subject (*students*) is stated after an opening connective.

Before: I loved the book, although it turned out to be an intolerable drag for most of my classmates.

After: Although the book turned out to be an intolerable drag for most of my classmates, I loved it.

After introducing the sentence with a dependent clause, the writer names the subject, *I*, and then adds the rest of the sentence.

Before: Ms. Bennett pushed the class to find symbolic meaning in various scenes to make the book more meaningful.

After: To make the book more meaningful, Ms. Bennett pushed the class to find symbolic meaning in various scenes.

To revise this sentence the writer begins with a verbal, in this case "to make," the infinitive form of the verb. (Verbals look and feel much like verbs but serve a different function. Verbals, though, come from verbs. Hence, their name and their resemblance.)

Before: I read the book in two days, hoping that it would never end.

After: Hoping that it would never end, I read the book in two days.

Aiming to diversify sentence openings, the writer starts this sentence with another kind of verbal, known as a *participle*. The *-ing* ending often indicates that a word is a participle.

Before: I was awed by the tenacity of the characters and absorbed by every soul-stirring syllable of the story.

After: Awed by the tenacity of the characters, I was absorbed by every soul-stirring syllable of the story.

Determined to try something different, the writer begins the sentence with an adjective that happens to sound like a verb because of its *-ed* ending.

Still another variation to try now and then is the sentence consisting of paired constructions. Two equally matched ideas are set in juxtaposition, often with a memorable effect, as in John F. Kennedy's famous line:

"Ask not what your country can do for you, ask what you can do for your country."

And also in:

It wasn't that the spirit of the pioneers caught my imagination, it was my imagination that caught the pioneer spirit.

The power of such sentences lies in the balance of parallel clauses. Each clause could stand alone, but together they express the idea more vigorously.

Occasionally, an idea derives strength from a reversal of customary word order. Taken out of context such sentences could sound awkward, but in the right place such sentences leave a mark. "Dull the book is not" packs more wallop than "The book is not dull" or even "The book is exciting." Use inverted sentences sparingly, however. More than once in an essay diminishes the vigor of each occurrence and may even sound foolish.

No rule of thumb governs the proportion of sentences in an essay that should depart from the usual subject-verb word order. It all depends on the purpose and style of the essay. But if you use any sentence pattern repeatedly, be sure you know why. If the repetition is accidental, revise for greater sentence variety.

Sentence Types

Our language offers writers a rich menu of sentence types. Declarative sentences predominate in most essay writing. (Just to refresh your memory, a *declarative* sentence, such as the one you are now reading, simply makes a statement.) But using other types of sentences, you can create all sorts of fascinating effects. Take interrogative sentences, for example. (Do you remember that *interrogative* sentences ask questions?) An interrogative sentence appropriately placed in a passage consisting of declarative sentences changes the pace and rhythm of the prose, can underscore an idea, and promote the reader's involvement in the essay.

Don't forget about *imperative* sentences (keep in mind that they make requests or give commands) and *exclamatory* sentences (What strong emotion they can express!). Furthermore, you can write sentences interrupted at some point by a dash—although some editors and teachers claim that it's not proper to do so in formal prose. And you can use direct and indirect quotations. Once in a while, you may wish to drive home a point with a single emphatic word. Excellent!

There's peril, however, in scrambling up sentence types just to scramble up sentence types, for you may end up with a mess on your hands. Be guided by what expresses your ideas most clearly and also seems varied enough to interest your readers.

Short and Long Sentences

Use a combination of short and long sentences in your essay.

Another technique for fighting monotony in essay writing is to vary the length of sentences. The shortest sentence in the English language is probably the pronoun "I," which stands as a complete sentence when it is used as a response to such questions as, "Should one use 'I' or 'me' as the subject of a sentence?" You could also make a case for any other letter, too, as when someone asks, "Do you spell *xylophone* with an *x* or a *z*?"

The longest English sentence has not yet been written, but rest assured that it will be far longer than your ACT essay. In fact, it will go on infinitely. Long sentences that stretch on and on can still be grammatically correct. (Don't confuse long sentences with "run-ons," which contain structural errors.) But they demand greater effort from readers because, while stepping from one part of the sentence to the next, they must keep track of more words, modifiers, phrases (not to speak of parenthetical asides), and clauses without losing the writer's main thought, which may be buried amid any number of secondary, or less important, thoughts.

Short sentences are easier to grasp—but not always. (Remember Descartes' famous five-word assertion: "I think, therefore, I am"?) But generally, a brief sentence makes its point quickly, sometimes with astonishing intensity, since all the words concentrate on a single point. Take, for example, the last sentence in this passage:

For three days, my parents and I sat in our S.U.V. and drove from college to college to college in search of the perfect place for me to spend the next four years. For seventy-two hours we lived as one person, sharing thoughts and dreams, stating opinions about each campus we visited, taking guided tours, interviewing students and admissions officials, asking directions a hundred times, eating together in town after town, and even sleeping in the same motel rooms. But mostly, we fought.

A terse closing sentence following a windy, 46-word sentence produces a mild jolt. Indeed, it has been planted in that spot deliberately to startle the reader. The technique is easily mastered but should be used sparingly. Overuse dilutes its impact. A balance of long and short sentences works best.

Balancing short and long sentences creates a rhythm. Because readers usually pause, albeit subconsciously, at every period, short sentences slow the tempo. Long sentences speed it up, but the pace depends mostly on the placement of clauses, the amount of parenthetical matter, and word choice. Although essays are usually meant for silent reading, a writer can slow the pace by carefully choosing difficult-to-pronounce words or selecting words containing many hard consonants. *The squad plodded agonizingly across the ugly swamp* is an example. Similarly, speed increases with sentences with softer, more flowing sounds, as in *While shaving and dressing Sam perused his face in the mirror.*

VARYING SENTENCES—A SUMMARY

1. Start sentences with:
   - A prepositional phrase: *From the start, In the first place, At the outset*
   - Adverbs and adverbial phrases: *Originally, At first, Initially*
   - Dependent clauses: *When you start with this, Because the opening is*
   - Conjunctions: *And, But, Not only, Either, So, Yet*
   - Adjectives and adjective phrases: *Fresh from, Introduced with, Headed by*
   - Verbal infinitives: *To launch, To take the first step, To get going*
   - Participles: *Leading off, Starting up, Commencing with*
   - Inversions: *Unique is the writer who embarks . . .*
2. Use a variety of sentence types.
3. Balance long and short sentences.

10. END THE ESSAY WITH A DISTINCT CONCLUSION

At the end of your ACT essay you can lift your pen off the paper and be done with it. Or, if you have the time, you can present your readers with a little gift to remember you by—perhaps a surprising insight, a bit of wisdom, a catchy phrase—something likely to tease their brains, tickle their funny bones, or make them feel smart. Choose the gift carefully. It should fit the content, style, and mood of your essay and spring naturally from its contents.

Because it comes last, the final paragraph leaves an enduring impression. A weak, apologetic, or irrelevant conclusion may dilute or even obliterate the effect that you tried hard to create. Above all, stay away from summary endings. When an essay is short to begin with, it's insulting to review for readers what is evident on the page in front of them. Readers are intelligent people. Trust them to remember what your essay says.

Stay away from summary endings. They insult the reader's intelligence.

A catchy conclusion isn't always necessary, but even a short ending may be preferable to none at all. Effective endings leave readers fulfilled, satisfied that they have arrived somewhere. A judiciously chosen ending may sway readers to judge your essay somewhat more leniently than otherwise. There are no guarantees, of course, but readers are bound to be touched by a memento of your thinking, your sense of humor, or your vision. Even an ordinary thought, uniquely expressed, will leave an agreeable afterglow.

What follows are several techniques for writing conclusions:

1. Have a little fun with your conclusion; try to put a smile on your reader's face.

Topic: Growing Old

Purpose of the essay: To show that old people can still act young. The essay concludes with an anecdote about an elderly gray-haired man of about seventy on a crowded city bus.

Gift: He carried bundles of packages and almost fell down as the bus lurched to a stop. At one point a young, gum-chewing woman stood up and pointed to the unoccupied seat. "Here, Pops, take this."

He looked at her in amazement. "Cool it, girlie," he said, "I still run marathons," and he stood all the way to his stop.

Topic: Extending compulsory education to age 19

Purpose of the essay: To argue against forcing teenagers to attend school until at least age 19. The essay ends with a hypothetical consequence of having a much older classmate.

Gift: When you're assigned to interview an "old person," it shouldn't be the guy who sits behind you.

2. End with an apt quotation drawn from the essay itself, from the ACT prompt, or from another source.

Topic: Survival Training

Purpose of the essay: To describe an incident in which the writer found herself in need of a safe shelter.

Gift: At that point I knew by instinct, "This is the place."

Topic: Computer Glitches

Purpose of the essay: To show that, because many consumers are uninformed, they waste lots of money when purchasing personal computers.

Gift: To paraphrase an old saying, "What you don't know can hurt you."

3. Finish by clearly restating your essay's main point but using new words. If appropriate, add a short tag line, a brief sentence that creates a dramatic effect.

Topic: Sexism

Purpose of the essay: To decry the male chauvinism that exists in the school administration.

Gift: As long as positions of authority are given to sexists, women must be prepared to fight against gender abuse in this institution.

Topic: Twitter

Purpose of the essay: To explain the value and importance of Twitter to teenagers. The writer concludes with a sample of twittering language.

Gift: At the end of the day, I can't go 2 bed B4 tweeting at least 6 of my BFFs.

4. Bring your readers up to date or project them into the future. Say something about the months or years ahead.

TOPIC: Vandalism in School
PURPOSE OF THE ESSAY: To condemn the daily carnage of smashed windows, graffiti, and broken ceiling tiles. The essay ends with a few questions about the future.
GIFT: How long can this go on? How can we turn away meekly? How much longer can we let the vandals make us their victims?

TOPIC: Fighting AIDS
PURPOSE OF THE ESSAY: To explain why it is imperative to rid the world of the scourge of AIDS.
GIFT: When the history of the twenty-first century is written, let us hope that AIDS will have gone the way of the dinosaurs.

Although an effective conclusion will add luster to an essay, don't feel obliged to add an ending just for the sake of form. ACT readers will have developed a fairly accurate sense of your writing ability before reaching your essay's last word. Rest assured that a good but incomplete piece of writing will be graded according to what you have done well instead of what you haven't done at all.

Editing and Proofreading

11. EDIT FOR CLARITY

To understand your essay, a reader needs the kind of help that only you can provide. As you write and revise, therefore, keep asking yourself, "Which words will guarantee that my message will be clear?" If you've written something fuzzy or included an idea expressed in a way that doesn't quite convey what is in your mind, you can't expect readers to understand it. That's why, once you've finished composing your essay, you should use the remaining time to edit it for clarity. Give it a clean sweep, tossing out anything that might interfere with clear communication.

Clear Sentences

Because many words have multiple meanings, check each word for clarity. Ask yourself whether any reader might misconstrue a word or find it ambiguous. Penny O wrote an essay about students who cut classes. One of her sentences read: "The last thing parents should do is talk to their kids." Coming upon that sentence, readers might wonder whether Penny means that parents should talk to their kids only as a last resort, or, that in a list of what parents ought to do, the final step is talking to their kids.

Later in the essay Penny wrote, "Ellen told her friend Debbie that she had made a serious mistake by cutting gym." Penny no doubt understood what she intended to say, but readers can't tell whether Ellen took a dim view of Debbie's actions or whether Ellen herself had second thoughts about her own absence from gym class. Granted, these sentences have been quoted out of context, but the point remains: What may seem like a perfectly clear sentence to the writer may send a puzzling message to the reader.

12. EDIT FOR INTEREST

Your essay will be read by people—real people with feelings, moods, likes and dislikes, and the capacity to laugh, grow restless, and be moved. Most of them are teachers who know that essays can be lively, scintillating, and a joy to read. Like any readers, they will be put off by writing that is dull.

Active Verbs

To an essay writer, it's important to know that *action* verbs differ from *being* verbs. Because active verbs describe or show movement, they create life. They perform, move around, and excel over all other words in pumping vitality into your prose. They add energy and variety to sentences, and as a bonus, promote economy by helping you trim needless words.

TIP 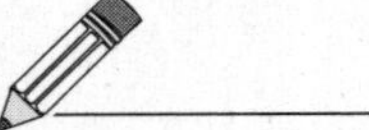

Inject life into your ACT prose by

1. Using *active* instead of *passive* verbs
2. Writing *active* instead of *passive* sentences
3. *Showing* instead of *telling*

Active verbs are full of life; *being* verbs are not. Notice the lifelessness in the most common forms of the verb *to be*:

is	are	was
were	am	has been
had been	have been	will be

When used in sentences, each of these being verbs joins a subject to a predicate—and that's all. In fact, forms of *to be* function much like an equal sign in an equation: "Five minus two *is* three" (5 – 2 = 3), or "Samantha *is* smart" (Samantha = smart), or "Your ACT score is going up" (That = good news!). Because being verbs (and equal signs) show little life, use active verbs whenever you can.

To be sure, it would be hard to get along in speech and writing without being verbs. Be stingy, however. Check over a few of your most recent essays. If more than, say, one-fourth of your sentences use a form of *to be* as the main verb, you may be relying too heavily on being verbs.

Once you habitually clear being verbs out of your prose, you may notice that certain nouns limit the options for using active verbs. For instance, you are almost stuck with a form of *to be* in any sentence that begins with an abstract noun such as *reason*:

"The reason that you should practice writing essays ____ . . ."

What word other than *is* can be used to fill the blank? (A few, perhaps, but not many.)

You have few verb options, too, when the subject of the sentence is *thought, concept, idea, issue, way, cause*, and many other abstract nouns. The same applies to sentences that begin with "There," as in: "*There* is no way for you to do poorly on the ACT essay," and often for sentences that begin with "It," as in "*It* is a foregone conclusion that you'll do well."

In contrast, nouns that stand for specific places, people, events, and objects invite the use of active verbs. When a sentence contains a subject that can do something—a person, for example—you never run out of verb choices.

Being verbs are not the only verbs that sap the life out of sentences. They share that distinction with several other verbs, such as any form of *to have, to come, to go, to make, to move*, and *to get*. Although we use these common verbs all the time, they do little to enliven writing. Each has so many different uses that they creep into sentences virtually unnoticed. According to *Webster's International Dictionary*, the verb *get*, for example, has 16 different meanings, not including those for such phrases as *get up, get along, get around, get together,* and *get away*. Because of constant use, such verbs pale next to more animated verbs. But, like *being* verbs, we can hardly do without them. Of course, you should use them freely, but stick with them only if no other words will do.

Active and Passive Sentences

To write lively prose, also keep in mind the distinction between *active* and *passive* sentences. A passive sentence—that is, a sentence structured in the *passive voice*—is one in which the performer of an action remains unnamed or receives less notice than either the receiver of the action or the action itself. Take the following examples.

1. Six weeks were spent preparing for the spring carnival.

From this sentence it is impossible to tell who performed the action—that is, who prepared for the carnival.

2. A new painting was hung in the gallery.

Similarly, this sentence fails to identify the performer of the action—or who hung the painting. The following revisions clear up the uncertainty:

1. Six weeks were spent preparing for the spring carnival by the cheerleaders.
2. A new painting was hung in the gallery by Carmine.

These versions contain more information than the originals, but each emphasizes the action instead of the performer of the action. Sometimes the writer may want to do that, but more often than not, such passive sentence structure occurs when the writer ignores the advantages of sentences written in the *active voice*. When the performers of action become the grammatical subject, this is what you get:

1. The cheerleaders prepared for the spring carnival for six weeks.
2. Carmine hung a new painting in the gallery.

Cast in the active voice, these sentences give the performers of the action top billing.

Why is the active voice preferable? Mainly because most events in life don't just occur by themselves. Somebody does something; a person or thing *acts*. After all, burgers don't just get eaten; people cook and devour them. Marriages don't just happen; couples deliberately go out and marry each other. Goals don't score, salmon don't get caught, wallets don't get lost all by themselves. People do these things.

Essay writers should take advantage of readers' natural curiosity about others and strive to put the performer of the action into the grammatical subject of sentences. By doing so, they eliminate passive verbs and pep up the prose. Also, passive sentences usually require more words than active sentences, as in:

Passive: The award was presented to Carrie by the town Rotary Club. (11 words)
Active: The town Rotary Club presented an award to Carrie. (9 words)

Passive: West Point was attended by my sister, my cousin, and three of my uncles. (14 words)
Active: My sister, my cousin, and three uncles went to West Point. (11 words)

Although active sentences usually sound more natural, a passive sentence will sometimes work better. When it's irrelevant who performed an action, or when the actor can't be identified, a passive sentence structure makes perfect stylistic sense.

Passive: The curtain was raised at 8:30 sharp.
Active: At 8:30 sharp, a stagehand (or Maryanne, the production assistant) raised the curtain.

In the passive version, curtain time is the important fact. Who flicked the switch is immaterial.

An ACT essay consisting largely of passive sentences will lack energy and life and is bound to bore a reader. Therefore, prepare for the exam by scouring your practice essays for passive sentences. Go with active sentences unless you have a very good reason not to.

Showing vs. Telling

TIP

Showing recreates experience for the reader, ultimately making the prose more interesting.

Remember the principle that a picture is worth a thousand words? Whether it is truly worth a thousand may be arguable, but the point is not. Words can help readers *see*. Therefore, *show* more than you *tell*! Instead of describing your uncle as "absent-minded," *show* him stepping into his morning shower dressed in his p.j.'s. Rather than telling the reader that your room is "a mess," *show* the pile of wrinkled clothes in the corner and the books and Snickers wrappers scattered on the floor next to your unmade futon. The same principle applies to smells: "Her breath was foul with the stench of stale whiskey." To sounds: "the growl of a chain saw in the distance." To touch: "the feel of cool linen bed sheets." And to tastes: "a cold, sweet drink of spring water on a scorching summer day."

Telling: I was happy after my meeting with Mr. Blair.
Showing: I bolted from Mr. Blair's office, bounded down the steps four at a time, and shouted into the wind, "Hurray, I did it."

Telling: My teacher, Mr. Franks, doesn't care to hear that I don't have the time to do math homework after school.
Showing: When I explained to Mr. Franks that I'm kept from math homework by driving my brother Timmy to piano lessons or karate, by yearbook meetings on Tuesdays, by Peer Leaders and Students Against Driving Drunk, by French tutoring, and a part-time job at the florist, he muttered, "That's <u>your</u> problem."

No one expects you to come up with striking images that *show* instead of *tell* whenever you write an essay. Indeed, authors struggle for years to perfect the technique. What's more, too much detail can be as unproductive as too little. A balance is best. No one can tell you exactly how to achieve that balance. You need time to get the feel of it. Like walking a tightrope, riding a bike, or doing a back flip, it becomes instinct after a while. The context, as well as your judgment of the reader's need to know, will have to determine how detailed you need to be. To develop the knack a little more quickly, study a written passage that you admire. Pick out both details and broad statements. Use the passage as a general model for your own writing, but give it your own stamp. After all, it's your voice the reader wants to hear.

13. CHECK FOR STANDARD USAGE AND MECHANICS

Writing correctly and using standard English can take you far in college and beyond. Although potential for error exists with every word you write, familiarity with several common pitfalls could prevent you from stumbling. That's why you should study the material in the English Review and Practice section of this book.

ESSAY-WRITING PRACTICE

At a time when your mind is fresh, set aside 30 minutes to write a practice essay. Do it today, or tomorrow, or next week, but do it, and do it often.

As you write, refer to the essay-writing principles discussed earlier in this chapter. They should help you do your best work. Your essay-writing skills will make great headway with consistent practice in choosing and narrowing topics, pulling ideas together, composing essays, and checking them over. After a few sessions, you'll develop a sense of what you can accomplish in half an hour. If you repeatedly run out of time, analyze the process you are using. Do you waste precious minutes mulling over the topic? Can you speed up the preparation of an outline? Are your goals too ambitious for short essays? On the other hand, if you finish well before time is up, consider how you might use the extra minutes. Can your paragraphs be more fully developed? Should you be editing more rigorously, looking for verbosity and vagueness? Are you proofreading carefully enough?

Three Essays for You to Write

Each of the prompts below is followed by blank lines on which to write an essay. (Add paper if you need to.) Allow yourself 30 minutes from the time you begin reading the topic.

After you have planned, written, edited, and proofread your essay, read the text of five students' responses to the same topic and write your impressions in the space provided. Score each on a scale of 1 (worst) to 6 (best), the scale used for the ACT Writing Test. Then read what an ACT rater has to say about each essay. Finally, reread and score your own essay, or even better, find an impartial and knowledgeable reader to do it for you.

TIP

Nothing can prepare you better for test day than to get into the habit of writing essays.

Essay 1

Prompt: At one time or another, we all do or say things that we regret and would like to do over or take back. Most of the time we must live with our mistakes, but sometimes we get a second chance.

Some people take a dim view of second chances, claiming that second chances not only foster reckless, irresponsible behavior but also weaken our character. Others see value in second chances. They say that second chances help us learn and permit us to take intellectual, creative, and other kinds of risks instead of always playing it safe. In your opinion, are second chances a good thing?

In your essay, take a position on this issue. You may support and defend either of the two points of view about second chances, or you may present a different view. Whatever your position, be sure to support it with specific reasons and examples.

Add paper, if necessary.

What follows are several essays written by students in response to the prompt for Essay 1. All the essays have been typed just as they were written.

Mort's Essay:

We've all laid in our beds at night, staring at the ceiling, wondering why we did the things we did. With tears flowing down our cheeks, we are only able to gasp, "If only I had a second chance."

Let's say that the magical genie came smoking out of my mother's vase with the power to grant me a second chance to repeat any part of my life. I'd rather say, "No, thank you," and be on my way.

My life, with all its ups and downs has been just right. I've learned and gained so much from all my experiences, even the ones that left me hurt, embarrassed, or troubled. The argument which lead to a silent treatment between me and my best friend for two weeks, has taught me not to take a joke too far. The time I vomitted all over the girl who sat in front of me in my third grade class, has taught me not to eat four bowls of raisin bran before going to school. Even when I got caught cheating on a math test, my long-lasting guilt and shame has kept me from repeating such reprimandable action ever again. Repeating or changing any aspect of my past will deprive me of a great knowledge to refer to in my future.

My mistakes have left me stronger and more confident in myself. If the road was not bumpy with many curves and branches in the road, I would not have arrived to the point where I have today. As an individual, hardships are a way of life and a way of growth; a learning skill I will carry with me to the grave.

Your impressions: ____

____

____

____

____

____

Critique: The essay is mechanically flawed. It contains some misused words and awkwardness as well as at least one instance of faulty sentence construction (at the end of the last paragraph). Yet, Mort saves the essay with his sharp focus on the topic, and, in the second paragraph, his terse refusal to accept second chances ("No, thank you") serves as a strongly stated main idea. The next paragraph, the essay's longest and most interesting, is filled with vividly expressed examples that support Mort's assertion that second chances are not for him. The final paragraph contains some general observations about what his no-nonsense approach to life has meant to him. Taken as a whole, then, the essay is unified and logically organized. It leaves a relatively favorable impression of Mort as a writer. Despite its mechanical shortcomings, the essay is rated **4**.

Ilana's Essay:

I have never truly believed in second chances. Although sometimes I would like to have reversed my life and done things differently I know that it is impossible. If I mess up on a test or say something that was mean or stupid, I already did it, I can't change it. I don't have another chance. To believe otherwise is self-delusion or an acute case of wishful thinking.

When I was about 7 or 8 years old, I remember going to my friend Betsy's birthday party. We were playing musical chairs, a game I loved. I got "out" on the third or fourth round and sat down next to my other friends who had lost.

Once again, the contestants ran around the circle of chairs. The music stopped and in all the commotion Betsy was left standing. She was out.

Being an avid fan of musical chairs, I eagerly awaited the next round. Only 4 kids were left to be eliminated. To my surprise, Betsy suddenly erupted into tears, insisting on another chance. Of course her demand was met. It was her birthday, after all, and she deserved a to get her way. The round was played over and this time the birthday girl found a seat when the music stopped. Betsy stayed in the game for the next two rounds and eventually won the game.

Ten years and many birthday parties full of musical chairs later, Betsy's second chance still haunts me. I have always questioned why she got it. Just because it was the anniversay of her birth, she was given the opportunity to do something over. At the same time, though, it taught her a terrible lesson in life. Just because she raised a fuss, she got her way and was able to correct a situation she didn't like. Losing is always hard but if the refrain "Why can't I get a second chance?" echoes through her head everytime she makes a mistake, she would have a distorted view of the way the world works. Second chances then were fun but could have led many birthday girl astray later in life.

I am glad that at my birthday parties I was never given a second chance. Although I may not have realized it or appreciated it at the time, it has made me handle defeat better than some of my friends who, when they did not succeed, were rewarded with another chance to win. When entering a world without party games, defeat is a fact of life. When you lose, you lose. Second chances are rare. Maybe when I was little, I may have been sad when I lost, but in the long run, I am grateful for not being given second chances. I'm glad I haven't been misled, glad that I don't believe in second chances.

Your impressions: ____

____

____

____

____

____

Critique: The essay reveals Ilana's sure grasp of the topic. Her use of the musical chairs anecdote focuses on the issue of second chances and serves as a kind of parable to illustrate her position on the subject. The material is logically and clearly organized. It begins with Ilana's general view of second chances and moves to the anecdote from which she has drawn the conclusions spelled out in the last paragraph. The essay's first sentence and its last sentence are closely related, creating a sense of wholeness to the discussion.

By no means is the essay error-free. It contains a few mechanical errors and an ill-conceived comparison in the second sentence of the final paragraph. Because the essay's unity and depth far outweigh its minor weaknesses, however, the essay has earned a score of **6**.

Cindy's Essay:

Throughout life you lose many things, maybe regain them back or just gain other things. Sometimes you lose a friend or boyfriend—due to yourself. And within time you wonder if that person will give you a second chance. I don't think people realize what they have untill they actual lose it and find themselves without it, him or her.

If and when you do lose that special someone and your thinking constantly about if you will get a second chance, try to let it go for a while and within time, maybe you will get that one last chance. Once you spend a lot of time with a certain someone, you get used to having him around, you grow on him more and more every day and eventually you begin to depend on each other. I had a boyfriend for just about four years, even though it wasn't four straight years it was more or less close to that. We have gone through a lot both together and on our own we've definitely grown on each other and certainly depended on each other for support most of all. We were more than just a typical couple, we were like best friends also, which made it twice as special. We've been through many breakups and stuff, we're giving each other more than a second chance. And like I said before you don't know what you have untill you lose it. I'm upset but happy at the same time—it was like we took advantage of the fact that we both gave each other a second chance all the time. We now are on very bad terms and I don't think there will be any more second chances from my part. Which is a shame but I guess thats the way it goes sometimes.

I think second chances are important. I'm not sure how the saying goes but its something like: everything is good as long as you don't exceed it, or take advantage of it. It makes sense once you think about. And even though you might fail to achieve something once you still have another chance. I feel that if you are determined to achieve something and you don't succeed the first time, there's always that second chance untill you achieve it.

Your impressions: ______________________________

____

____

____

____

____

Critique: Cindy's essay is vaguely related to the topic of second chances, but it often drifts into other matters. Her discussion of a former boyfriend is no doubt meant to illustrate the cliché that people often fail to appreciate what they have until they lose it, but it does little more than review needlessly the history of a tumultuous relationship.

The writing suffers from a general lack of coherence as it jumps from topic to topic. Incoherence is further heightened by several inexplicable shifts of verb tense and by random use of first-, second-, and third-person pronouns.

Some pre-planning of the essay might have rescued it from chaos, as would a serious weeding out of irrelevancies. Cindy's main idea more or less emerges toward the end of the essay, but by that time too much damage has been done to rescue the piece. Score: **2**.

Sarah's Essay:

I would be amazed if everyone in the world at one point or another hasn't thought about what they would do if they had a second chance. Even if they had wished for a salad instead of a burger for lunch, or if they desired another chance to tell a tyrranical teacher what they really thought of him and his grading policies. If the consequences were more serious or even fatal, who could resist the temptation of wishing they had not driven down that road where they totalled the car or wished for a second chance to change their husband's plane ticket from a flight that was crashed into the World Trade Center by terrorists?

Well, any way here I am writing an essay on what I would do if I had a second chance. If I had a chance to start things all over again I guess I would have studied for the ACT, especially the math which I probably failed miserably, and honestly now I wish that I had a second chance to start this miserable essay over again, but fifteen minutes have gone by and it's too late, and my hand is starting to cramp and I don't want to continue with this essay because it is pretty dumb. Not the assignment but what I have written so far, so I better get serious. OK? Here goes:

One thing I would definitely change is my relationship with my grandparents who are now gone. On my father's side of the family, we, that is, my sister and I were never close to them, so I never got to know my grandparents that well. I must have thought I would always have the time in the future. But now I know that I lost my chance and feel really bad about always faking a stomach ache to get out of seeing them. Don't misunderstand, I liked them, but to tell it like it is, they were not as interesting as my friends or a movie, or a television show I wanted to see. Now, if I had a second chance to change things, I would not have faked so many stomach aches. I know they could have told me a lot about my ancestors in Ireland and how they came to the United States and how hard it was to survive for them during the Depression. It's a story that is worth knowing but I'll never hear it because I never gave them the chance to tell it to me and will regret it to my dying day.

Your impressions: ____

____

____

____

____

____

Critique: Sarah's opening paragraph shows promise. By naming both trivial and significant situations in which people might long for second chances, it introduces the main idea and ends with an engaging rhetorical question. The diction, attention to detail, and rhythm of the prose demonstrate Sarah's facility with words.

A switch in tone and voice suddenly takes place in the second paragraph, however. Instead of proceeding with her discussion, Sarah starts to whine about being ill prepared to take the ACT. While the paragraph cleverly serves up a real and immediate example of Sarah's need for a second chance, it also acts as a smoke screen. Sarah, it appears, has suddenly run out of ideas. One might argue that the second paragraph is integral to the essay's development and that it shows Sarah's humanity. But by deviating abruptly from the established tone, it also calls attention to itself and diminishes the essay's unity.

Having talked herself into shaping up, Sarah concludes the essay with a rather poignant account of a strained relationship with her grandparents. The passage says more about Sarah's humanity than the self-deprecating outburst in the preceding paragraph. The essay is scored **4**.

Self-Evaluation of Essay 1

Now reread your own essay. Evaluate it by using the checklist below. Focus on both the strengths and weaknesses of your essay.

	Yes!	Mostly	Hardly	No
Does the essay address the ACT prompt?	____	____	____	____
Is the topic sufficiently narrowed?	____	____	____	____
Is the essay's main idea clear?	____	____	____	____
Have you written an appealing introduction?	____	____	____	____
Does the essay sound natural?	____	____	____	____
Have you used plain words?	____	____	____	____
Have you used precise language?	____	____	____	____
Does your essay have a clear focus?	____	____	____	____
Do all parts fit together coherently?	____	____	____	____
Is each sentence accurately worded?	____	____	____	____
Have you trimmed needless words?	____	____	____	____
Do you show more than tell?	____	____	____	____
Have you used active verbs?	____	____	____	____
Is the language fresh?	____	____	____	____
Do you include verbal surprises?	____	____	____	____
Are the sentences varied?	____	____	____	____
Is sentence length balanced?	____	____	____	____
Does the essay end memorably?	____	____	____	____
Is the essay mostly error-free?	____	____	____	____

Identify the three greatest strengths of your essay:

1. ____

2. ____

3. ____

Name three specific things that you could do to improve your essay:

1. ____

2. ____

3. ____

Circle the score your essay deserves: 6 5 4 3 2 1.

Essay 2

Prompt: It's human nature to plan, dream, and think about the future. In fact, most students go to school and college with the presumption that they are being prepared for what lies ahead. On the other hand, some people think it's foolish to be anything but wary about the future because our vision is limited and unexpected events will inevitably cause us great disappointment. Such people prefer to make the most of what exists here and now. In your opinion, are people better off living for the present?

Write an essay in which you state and explain your view on this issue. Your belief may coincide with either of the two positions described in the prompt, or you may present a different point of view. Whatever your position, however, be sure to support it with specific reasons and examples.

Add paper, if necessary.

What follows are several essays written by students in response to the prompt for Essay 2. All the essays have been typed just as they were written.

Terry's Essay:

If something is resting on the horizon, hovering just above the long straight line where the sky meets the earth, then the object is considered fair game for any poet or philosopher who happens to be passing by.

Ships, birds, great white whales, and even the sun and moon, have fallen prey to this sad fate. The ship glides self-consciously acorss the water as the starry-eyed poet wonders eloquently whether its while sails shall carry it. The ship moves farther away, and thankfully sinks beneath the horizon, a little at a time, until only the tip of the mast can be seen, and then nothing. The philosopher and scientist will now be glad to explain to you that this gradual disappearance is proof that the world is round. One may note, however, that these philosophers were not too eager, a few hundred years ago, to go out and test their theories. They sat comfortably in their homes as explorers set out to find the horizon, hoping fervently that the ship would never reach the edge.

The horizon has long been a source of fascination, of wonder and awe, even to the casual observer. Despite my apparent scorn for poetry dealing with the horizon, I must admit that I have more than a few dusty poems addressing the pressing issue of the sunset (they happen often, have you noticed?) or rambling about sea-gulls sitting comfortably on the edge of the world. And this brings me to the main point of my essay, the question that has been eating at me for years, tormenting me until I am forced to spill all my worries onto this clean white piece of paper. What about my generation? What shall we, the poets and the writers, do when we look to the horizon for guidance and inspiration, and find to our dismay that it doesn't exist? No, do not look at me as if I'm crazy. Listen to me. Walk outside and look around. Houses, high-rises, apartment buildings, and blue and yellow Blockbuster awnings conspire to cut off your view. Do not give up. Walk around the building, down the street. Run, faster and faster until at last you find water—a vast river, a bay, a great lake. Ah, a horizon, at last. But study the horizon. It is crowded with more buildings across the water, or it is obscured in yellow smog, the pollutants pouring from smokestacks and industrial chimneys. We are using up our natural resources, the newspaper warns us. Trees and coal and petroleum won't last forever. And now something else to worry about. Just as the bulldozers carve out portions of the forests, so do the cities and towns gnaw away at the horizon.

I know, I know, there are more important issues in the world. War and poverty and the Academy Awards. Yet I can't help wondering, as a poet and as a person, what will happen when, no matter how fast you run, you can't get around the barricade of buildings to watch the sun sit gently on the horizon. What will happen to the sunsets?

Your impressions: ______________________________

____

____

____

____

____

Critique: The essay cries out for editing. It takes Terry a long time to reach her main idea. In fact, the first third of the essay consists primarily of the author's aimless musings, jotted on paper while she searches for a purpose. Because Terry has an impressive command of words, however, the first paragraphs are not totally inconsequential. For one, they introduce the essay's essential literary conceit—the horizon as a metaphor for the future. Otherwise, they contribute little to the essay's development. Parts of the third paragraph, the core of the essay, also contain more window dressing than substance, suggesting once more that Terry tends to use rhetoric to conceal fuzzy thinking. Toward the end of the essay, Terry undermines her anguish with a witticism about the Academy Awards—as if she suddenly has had second thoughts about her approach and so decides to poke fun at her own efforts.

Despite these shortcomings, Terry's basic image—man-made barriers obscuring the horizon—is a powerful statement about the nature of modern life. As an astute observer and an obviously spirited writer, Terry ends her essay just where it ought to have begun, with the notion that modern life has deprived us of some elemental experiences and that we are diminished as a result. Partly on the strength of Terry's promise as a writer, her essay is rated **4**.

Matt's Essay:

Throughout history, people have speculated about the future. Will it be a utopia, with injustice and want eliminated? Or will technology aid us in creating a trap for ourselves we cannot escape, such as the world of 1984? These are the questions that plague me as I plan the next several years of my life.

Science fiction often has the future portrayed as a technological marvel. However, the problems of the environment and overpopulation seem to point in another direction. Will our society become a world society, with agriculture the norm? Perhaps not, but we could stand to lose some of our sillier inventions such as tablets you put in your toilet tank to make the water blue, or Botox treatments to remove the wrinkles of aging from the skin. My personal version of utopia is a world with very different cultures and peoples, like that of today, but one with a stable population and government by the people. I would imagine the people as free from want and fear. The sad thing is, that we can do this today, but simply have not gotten our priorities straight. In America, we are able to produce enough food to feed the whole country, yet people starve. The world powers could stop defense spending and put the money into aid to developing countries. Perhaps, if everyone had enough to eat and enough material possessions, whatever "enough" is, then people would not have to be ruled by oppressive leaders. The AIDS sickness could disappear from Africa and the world. The idealism that looks good on paper, however, may fail in practice, such as communism. We will just have to wait for tomorrow.

Your impressions: ______________________________

____

____

____

____

____

Critique: To begin a short essay with an overgeneralization ("Throughout history . . ., etc.") often signals the writer's lack of purpose or an inability to choose a main idea. An astute writer would promptly narrow the topic and develop a workable thesis, but Matt does neither. Instead, he records a string of clichés and platitudes vaguely related to the state of the world. His essay contains several impressive-sounding, but virtually meaningless and superficial ideas. A glimmer of substance appears as Matt considers society's technological frills, but overall, the essay, although written by a student who seems far from dull, lacks a coherent discussion of a single topic. The essay is rated **1**.

Jim's Essay

For the first time in my life, or so it feels like, I have things to look forward to. I don't mean little things like a day off from school or a night out with friends, or even my birthday. Rather, I feel like I'm standing on the brink of a new and exciting period of life.

First, I am going away this summer, something I have never done before, at least not for more than a few days, so this is a major event. To start, I am going to a writing course in Vermont (creative writing, not analytical writing), so I will be able to spend three weeks immersed in what I am considering devoting my life to. My parents will be no where in the vicinity, so I will experience true independence for the first time, including taking care of my own laundry. Also this summer I will be going to visit a friend in northern California, and possibly working part-time at a bakery, and reading as much as I possibly can.

Usually at the beginning of summer I am depressed, anticipating over two months of sweltering boredom and monotony with hardly a friend in sight. This year, though I have the pleasant feeling that this summer will be peppered with interesting events. I hope I'm right.

Also on the agenda this summer is getting ready for college, and by extension, getting ready for my adulthood. College is the more immediate event, naturally, but I have also been considering what I will do for the rest of my life. Strange as it may seem, I am not as worried as I could be, being secure in the knowledge that I will be going to a good university less than half an hours drive from home. I will live at home at least at the start, and although that may not be ideal for me (and my parents), I have come to the conclusion that I will manage. I don't know exactly what will happen, but I know that it will be surviving and striving for happiness.

The future does not seem bleak. It appears colorful as I scan the horizon. I feel like a line in Fahrenheit 451 by Ray Bradbury that goes like "And they run together, on out and away to who could possibly guess where."

Your impressions: ______________________________

____

____

____

____

____

Critique: Jim's essay follows the classic five-paragraph format. The introduction includes a concise statement of the essay's main idea and then generates reader interest by discarding topics that he won't discuss in the essay. The second paragraph specifies events that Jim anticipates, and the third serves as a stepping-stone to the climactic fourth paragraph, in which he cites the real impetus behind his enthusiasm for the approaching summer. The apt and upbeat quotation at the end is consistent with the content and spirit of the essay.

The essay falls short of the highest rating, however, because of its fairly pedestrian insights, its wordiness, a relatively plodding style, and its pedantic attention to trivial details. The essay is rated **5**.

Todd's Essay:

In a few months I will graduate from high school, but I will not go to college in the fall; I will wait for that. Instead, I hope to find a job in the adult world.

As I think about journeying forth into the unknown, it is, admittedly, rather frightening. For the past eleven years I have been nestled comfortably in the textbook world that I know. It is a realm of school, day after day, teachers, ruled paper, right and wrong answers. Now, like a baby about to be born, I am being jarred out of the secure place I know and pushed into a whole new dimension.

Functioning in the adult world as a seventeen year old seems, at first, impossible. In the past, it was not uncommon for a young person to find a well-paying full-time job right out of high school. Today it is an oddity. Whenever I tell anyone about my plans, I am greeted by a peculiar smile and a laugh. I cannot tell if they think I am insane or if they admire me for breaking away from the herd.

However, it no longer seems to matter to me what people think. That may sound callous and unfeeling, I admit, but it's true. For a year, I have been quizzed as to the reasons for my decision. I have been asked repeatedly if I know what I'm getting myself into. I have been warned that I may be missing out on something vital by choosing the path I have chosen. For all the doubt that people have expressed, however, I know my decision is a wise one.

By working for a year, I will gain experience and maturity that would otherwise lack. I believe that having responsibilities and duties to perform can make you a better person. When I do finally go to college, I will appreciate it more, because my hard-earned money will have gone to pay for it.

Though I do have mixed feelings about what lies in store for me, I know that my decision will make the future a brighter and clearer one for me.

Your impressions: ____

____

____

____

____

____

Critique: Todd's clearly written, and well-focused essay evidently comes from the pen of a disciplined writer with considerable control of words, ideas, and most importantly, himself. One might snipe at Todd's choppy paragraphing or his self-righteous, even arrogant, tone, but such imperfections aside, the essay is virtually unblemished. As an exemplary ACT essay, it deserves a **6**.

Self-Evaluation of Essay 2

Now reread your own essay. Evaluate it by using the checklist below. Focus on both the strengths and weaknesses of your essay.

	Yes!	Mostly	Hardly	No
Does the essay address the ACT prompt?	___	___	___	___
Is the topic sufficiently narrowed?	___	___	___	___
Is the essay's main idea clear?	___	___	___	___
Have you written an appealing introduction?	___	___	___	___
Does the essay sound natural?	___	___	___	___
Have you used plain words?	___	___	___	___
Have you used precise language?	___	___	___	___
Does your essay have a clear focus?	___	___	___	___
Do all parts fit together coherently?	___	___	___	___
Is each sentence accurately worded?	___	___	___	___
Have you trimmed needless words?	___	___	___	___
Do you show more than tell?	___	___	___	___
Have you used active verbs?	___	___	___	___
Is the language fresh?	___	___	___	___
Do you include verbal surprises?	___	___	___	___
Are the sentences varied?	___	___	___	___
Is sentence length balanced?	___	___	___	___
Does the essay end memorably?	___	___	___	___
Is the essay mostly error-free?	___	___	___	___

Identify the three greatest strengths of your essay:

1. ____

2. ____

3. ____

Name three specific things that you could do to improve your essay:

1. ____

2. ____

3. ____

Circle the score your essay deserves: 6 5 4 3 2 1.

ESSAY 3

Prompt: Some experts in human behavior claim that beliefs and values we acquire at an early age change very little as we grow older. In fact, through experience, our beliefs and values deepen and grow stronger.

Others claim that early beliefs and values are only temporary. As young people mature and gain experience, their beliefs and values are subject to considerable change. As a person on the verge of adulthood, do you think that the basic beliefs and values that you were taught as a child are likely to remain with you in the future?

In your essay, take a position on this issue. Either write an essay that identifies and explains the importance of one of your strong beliefs and values—one that is unlikely to change now or in the forseeable future, or write an essay about a belief or value that you have long held but are beginning to question. You may instead write an essay that presents an altogether different point of view on the issue. Whatever your view, support your position with specific reasons and examples.

Add paper, if necessary.

What follows are several essays written by students in response to the prompt for Essay 3. All the essays have been typed just as they were written.

Jan's Essay:

Free expression is a value that I would die for. Some feel that the right to express whatever you feel can be a desecration of one's country if one speaks out in some way against the policies of the United States, especially in time of war. As an activity protected by the First Amendment it is something that must never be given up.

For a long time flag-burning has been an activity that has angered many people who think that it goes too far in expressing dissatisfaction for your country. They think that you should protest in some other manner. They are fiercely proud of the country and don't want to see others burn what they hold so dear to their hearts. I can understand their point of view. Just because certain groups disagree with flag-burning doesn't mean that it should be restricted from everyone else as a means of free expression. It puts no one in danger and it doesn't violate someone else's rights. It is distasteful to some people and rubs them the wrong way.

I definitely have always had a problem with such people, people who want to restrict others based on their own emotions and beliefs. We live in a multicultural society that has people from every belief and country living in it. For many people, myself included, things such as flag burning are acceptable, and when carried out, make a statement which will be noticed. Politicians need to be spoken to by the people. Burning a flag is not like killing someone. It is a symbol for many people's disgust at what it has come to stand for a government obsessed with going to war, for example, or a government that is made up of dishonest hypocrites who say one thing but act differently.

The First Amendment is meant to cover all forms of expression. When you get moralistic about which forms are proper and which should be banned, you become hypocritical. Take funding for the NEA as another example. If you don't want to give a certain artist a grant because you think his art is sacreligious or demeaning to your values, then you shouldn't be entitled to give anyone a grant, even one who glorifies and praises the country.

What makes this country great is its diversity. Take it away or repress opinion that you don't agree with weakens the principles on which the country was founded. This country would not even be a country if the colonists simply went along with King George III. We became a country only because we protested and fought for the right to express ourselves freely and openly.

Your impressions: ____

____

____

____

____

____

Critique: Using the traditional five-paragraph essay format, the writer presents a heartfelt case in support of freedom of expression. She clearly articulates her main idea in the first paragraph, but whether the essay proves that Jan would "die for" freedom of expression is questionable. The second paragraph contains several of the customary arguments in support of flag burning as a means of expressing dissent. The lengthy discussion, however, leaves little room to cite or fully develop other examples of unfettered expression.

The essay's diction, sentence structure, and tone are appropriate to the topic. Inconsistent use of pronouns, ambiguous pronoun references, considerable repetition, and occasional lapses of coherence weaken the essay's overall effect. The essay is rated **4.**

Greg's Essay:

In response to a belief that I value very much, I would like to express that it is wrong to keep animals in zoos, and anyone who does not agree should be punished. Keeping animals in zoos means taking them out of their natural environment, usually to a very small space. Animals' nature is to be free and wander and not be committed to anything, unlike humans. By placing them in a different enviroment, you are taking away this freedom.

I have been on the National Animal Activist Board for eight years and I have personally seen how animals respond. A few years ago a white tiger, by the name of Dorothy was taken from the hot African sun and placed in a public zoo in North Dakota. Dorothy not only seemed to be sad and lonely, but she became sick from changing lifestyles. No longer was she able to run and catch prey but instead the zookeeper handed it to her. Because I have seen changes in animals like Dorothy, and many others, I know it is wrong to place animals in zoos.

In the United States of America, where we believe in great freedom of people, I find it very hard to believe that many people don't believe in freedoms of animals. They too, are living, breathing creatures that bring life into the world. The possibility that Americans would prefer to cruely torture animals by placing them in a zoo and make money on them, than allow them freedom is very disheartening.

Many people feel uncomfortable not sleeping in their own home for one evening never mind being suddenly moved forever, with no say in the matter. Someone must be the voice for these abused animals and ensure that their rights, their natural rights, are not corrupted. If you have a voice and wish to speak out, you should join the The National Animal Activist Board at www.naab.org or write to

NAAB
111 April Road
Los Angeles, California 93127

Thank you very much.

Your impressions: ____

____

____

____

____

____

Critique: No doubt Greg is a passionate animal rights advocate, but to "punish" those who disagree with him is not only extreme, but incongruous for someone espousing a humane point of view. Regardless of Greg's zeal, he makes a sincere case for giving animals their freedom. The story of the white tiger is compelling. (Whether it's true is another matter.) To argue that animals should be free because humans are free is less persuasive. The ending of the piece turns what should be a rational discussion of a strong belief into a commercial for the NAAB.

Except for the inappropriate conclusion, the essay is competently organized. Stylistically, however, it suffers from, among other things, repetition, wordiness, faulty pronoun reference, and sentence errors. The essay, therefore, is scored **3**.

Samantha's Essay:

I live in an extremely noisy house. My mom is always tapping her pen, talking on the phone, or watching television. My stepfather loves to stream movies on his computer. I also have an aerobics-crazy sister who turns her radio up full blast as she does her floor-shaking exercises and a brother who is a video-game freak. From his room I hear nothing but the rat-tat-tat of guns and motor-like noises punctuated with shrieks of delight from him and his chums. A quiet girl like me, who cherishes time to think peacefully in silence does not belong in this family.

In all of my life, there has been one night that stands out in my memory; I still remember every detail. My mom and stepfather had gone to a party in the next town. My sister and brother had arranged for sleepovers at the homes of friends. My boyfreind was visiting colleges and I had no plans. Realizing this was an opportunity to utilize our empty house, I formulated an ideal plan. Unlike a typical teenage girl, who would instant message a guest list for a party to all her friends, I decided to throw a party for myself, an event to celebrate the silence I value and crave, and so rarely have an opportunity to enjoy.

First, I went to the kitchen and prepared my favorite meal: cheese, tomato, lettuce and mustard on a soft roll, and a can of A & W rootbeer. In my room with my sandwich and drink, I put on a huge sweatshirt and a pair of sweatpants. After putting my hair up in a ponytail on top of my head, I stole all of my sister's pillows from her bedroom, fluffed up my blanket, and arranged the pillows in a perfect cosy nest. I took a sip of my soda and then all of a sudden I heard it. I listened again and then I knew for sure that I had heard correctly. I wrapped my blanket around my toes and pulled the fringy edges up to my neck. After resting my head on six fluffy pillows, I listened again. I really could hear it. For the first time in my life, I heard nothing but beautiful silence. Not a sound intruded into the room. I closed my eyes in order to listen harder. Nothing, absolutely nothing. It was a Zen moment. For an hour or more (I don't know exactly how long because I eventually dozed off) I reveled in the most gorgeous nothing that I had ever heard. In the morning the sandwich was still on my night table.

Your impressions: ____

____

____

____

____

____

Critique: In this well-crafted essay Samantha handles words and ideas with grace and style. Not only does she have a knack for storytelling, she carefully organizes her thoughts and uses expressive, vivid language to convey her ideas. The contrast between the noisy household and the silence of that memorable night is masterfully drawn. Samantha's use of details creates effects that give the essay charm and character. The last sentence, for instance, is particularly rich, for without saying the words, she reiterates the point of the entire essay—that even a favorite meal had less allure than the silence she yearns for. The essay is rated **6.**

Meena's Essay:

On the day that I get married, I hope that my head will grow light and that I will fall away into a dead faint. That is what happened to my mother on her wedding day and also to my grandmother when she married my grandfather. Even though it sounds bizarre, it is a family tradition that is very important to me.

The reason is that I am Indian and proud of it. As I grow to adulthood, I want to maintain my family traditions, even though many other Indian girls I know want to ignore their heritage and become completely Americanized. Nevertheless, I plan to maintain my identity as a Hindu Indian in tact. One way in which I can do this is to have a traditional wedding. I have attended two such weddings when my cousins got married, and my mother has told me how wonderful her own wedding day was. It was a day she will never forget.

In India, a wedding lasts five days. Each day the bride must wear a red sari, a new set of jewelry, and many flowers in her hair. The groom must also wears a new outfit every day. After dressing up, the couple sit before a fire all day while the priest or pandit recites the holy words and marriage vows. After four or five hours, the bride and groom might eat a little snack. Then they will meet with all their friends and family. When they approach the elders in the family, such as parents, grandparents, and uncles and aunts, the bride and groom bend down to touch their feet and be blessed. This blessing ceremony will easily go on for a couple of hours.

Then the married couple will take a bath or clean up, wear new clothes, and go to the temple. Upon returning, they will change clothes again, eat, and then sleep in separate rooms. This procedure will take place on every marriage day (in most of the weddings). Oh, I almost forgot the main thing; all the guests will come about a week before the marriage and stay in hotels, eat, drink at the expense of the bride's father and mother.

After the whole marriage there is a reception ceremony, where the bride and groom dress up again and stand on a stage, or another high place, to welcome all the guests and to receive their gifts. Then everybody eats and drinks. For entertainment there might be a band or a performance of professional dancers. After eight or nine hours the bride and groom finally sit down to eat, which marks the end of the celebration.

When my mother explained the process to me, I asked, "How did you take all the sitting, standing, bending, and starving, Mom? She slowly smiled and said, "I didn't. I couldn't. I fainted almost every day."

Your impressions: ______________________________

____

____

____

____

____

Critique: Meena's delicious opening line sets the tone for the entire essay. Admitting that a desire to faint at her wedding may sound bizarre, Meena goes on to explain why her wish is less odd than it seems. To illustrate her loyalty to Indian traditions, Meena concentrates on the typical Indian wedding. But by dwelling on only one ritual, she is able to describe the event in precise and colorful detail. Her account, however, while often fascinating, includes details that may not be altogether necessary to support her essay's thesis.

The writing in the essay may be a bit repetitious, and the backtracking ("Oh, I almost forgot . . .") while appropriate in conversation, interrupts the flow of ideas. It suggests that Meena might have planned her essay more carefully. Had she been writing on a computer, she might have rearranged her ideas easily. The ending, which recalls the opening line, contributes to the essay's overall unity. The essay is rated **5**.

Self-Evaluation of Essay 3

Now reread your own essay. Evaluate it by using the checklist below. Focus on both the strengths and weaknesses of your essay.

	Yes!	Mostly	Hardly	No
Does the essay address the ACT prompt?	___	___	___	___
Is the topic sufficiently narrowed?	___	___	___	___
Is the essay's main idea clear?	___	___	___	___
Have you written an appealing introduction?	___	___	___	___
Does the essay sound natural?	___	___	___	___
Have you used plain words?	___	___	___	___
Have you used precise language?	___	___	___	___
Does your essay have a clear focus?	___	___	___	___
Do all parts fit together coherently?	___	___	___	___
Is each sentence accurately worded?	___	___	___	___
Have you trimmed needless words?	___	___	___	___
Do you show more than tell?	___	___	___	___
Have you used active verbs?	___	___	___	___
Is the language fresh?	___	___	___	___
Do you include verbal surprises?	___	___	___	___
Are the sentences varied?	___	___	___	___
Is sentence length balanced?	___	___	___	___
Does the essay end memorably?	___	___	___	___
Is the essay mostly error-free?	___	___	___	___

Identify the three greatest strengths of your essay:

1. ______________________________

2. ______________________________

3. ______________________________

Name three specific things that you could do to improve your essay:

1. ______________________________

2. ______________________________

3. ______________________________

Circle the score your essay deserves: 6 5 4 3 2 1.

Prompts for Essay-Writing Practice

1. Increasingly, students are choosing to take time off between high school and college. Some use the year for public service or charity work. Others travel, find internships, or get paying jobs in a variety of fields.

   Advocates of postponing college claim that experiences away from the classroom contribute to personal growth and maturity. Those opposed say that students are bound to lose momentum and often fail to pick up where they left off in their education. In your opinion, should students take time off between high school and college?

   In your essay, you may write about either one of the two points of view. You may instead present a different point of view on the issue. Whatever your view, be sure to support your position with specific reasons and examples.

2. Your local schoolboard is planning to raise high school graduation requirements by adding between 50 and 100 hours of community service for all seniors. Supporters of the change see great educational value in serving others. Those opposed assert that seniors belong in the classroom full time.

   Two related questions have come up: Should students be excused from their classes while performing their service? And should the requirement be waived for seniors already holding part-time jobs?

   In your essay, take a position on these questions. You may write about either one of the two points of view. You may instead present a different point of view on the issue. Whatever your view, be sure to support your position with specific reasons and examples.

3. Concerned about widespread cheating on tests, homework assignments, and research papers, the faculty of your school is promoting a student honor code. At the heart of the code is a provision that requires students to pledge that they will not cheat and will report instances of cheating that they observe. Violators of the pledge will be punished according to the seriousness of the offense.

   Predicting that the code will destroy morale and lead to distrust and animosity among students, the administration does not support the idea. Instead it is seeking other ways to discourage cheating but has no clear plan. In your opinion, should the school put an honor code into effect?

   In your essay, take a position on this question. You may write about either one of the two points of view. You may instead present a different point of view on the issue. Whatever your view, be sure to support your position with specific reasons and examples.

4. Several parents of middle-school students in your district have petitioned the administration to reduce the amount of homework that teachers assign. Hoping to relieve pressure on their kids, they want homework limited to no more than half an hour per subject on weekdays and none on weekends. The teachers argue that homework is essential, not only for learning but to prepare students for standardized state and local examinations.

   As a former student of middle-school age, do you side with the parents?

   In your essay, take a position on this question. You may write about either one of the two points of view. You may instead present a different point of view on the issue. Whatever your view, be sure to support your position with specific reasons and examples.

5. Graffiti is pervasive both inside and outside your school building. The principal has threatened to severely punish perpetrators and has promised a $100 reward for information leading to the apprehension of the guilty students.

   No students have submitted names, and the graffiti problem has grown worse. In response, the principal has cancelled dances and other evening events for the rest of the year, asserting that graffiti detracts from the school climate and interferes with the educational process. In your opinion, are the principal's actions appropriate?

   In your essay, take a position on this question. You may write about either one of the two points of view. You may instead present a different point of view on the issue. Whatever your view, be sure to support your position with specific reasons and examples.

6. Educators have long debated about how students should be grouped in their classes. Some argue that ability grouping makes the most sense because instruction can be geared toward the intellectual level of the students. Bright students will not be held back by slower classmates, and the least-able students will not be left behind by instruction that is too advanced for them. Other educators deplore ability grouping because they believe that slower students benefit from the presence of more-advanced students in mixed classes and are harmed when they are grouped in low-functioning tracks. What's more, bright students are bound to learn regardless of who their classmates are. Those who support mixed, or heterogeneous, groups say that having diverse abilities and interests in a classroom enriches the educational experience for everyone. In your opinion, should students be grouped according to ability?

   In your essay, take a position on this question. You may write about either one of the two points of view. You may instead present a different point of view on the issue. Whatever your view, be sure to support your position with specific reasons and examples.

7. In an effort to improve discipline and the learning environment, your school's administration plans to implement a student dress code that bans among other things, tank tops, ragged jeans, short shorts, and T-shirts with provocative or obscene imprints. Students wearing banned clothing will be sent home for the day; repeated violations will lead to harsher penalties. Also, Wednesdays will be dress-up day, when students must come dressed in a manner appropriate for such occasions as a job or college interview.

   Some parents and students object to the measure, claiming that it will not only create an oppressive atmosphere in the school but that it violates students' rights. In your opinion, should the administration's dress code be implemented?

   In your essay, take a position on this question. You may write about either one of the two points of view. You may instead present a different point of view on the issue. Whatever your view, be sure to support your position with specific reasons and examples.

PART 4

MODEL EXAMS

Answer Sheet

MODEL EXAM A

Directions: Mark one answer only for each question. Make the mark dark. Erase completely any mark made in error. (Additional or stray marks will be counted as mistakes.)

Test 1

1 (A) (B) (C) (D)	21 (A) (B) (C) (D)	41 (A) (B) (C) (D)	61 (A) (B) (C) (D)
2 (F) (G) (H) (J)	22 (F) (G) (H) (J)	42 (F) (G) (H) (J)	62 (F) (G) (H) (J)
3 (A) (B) (C) (D)	23 (A) (B) (C) (D)	43 (A) (B) (C) (D)	63 (A) (B) (C) (D)
4 (F) (G) (H) (J)	24 (F) (G) (H) (J)	44 (F) (G) (H) (J)	64 (F) (G) (H) (J)
5 (A) (B) (C) (D)	25 (A) (B) (C) (D)	45 (A) (B) (C) (D)	65 (A) (B) (C) (D)
6 (F) (G) (H) (J)	26 (F) (G) (H) (J)	46 (F) (G) (H) (J)	66 (F) (G) (H) (J)
7 (A) (B) (C) (D)	27 (A) (B) (C) (D)	47 (A) (B) (C) (D)	67 (A) (B) (C) (D)
8 (F) (G) (H) (J)	28 (F) (G) (H) (J)	48 (F) (G) (H) (J)	68 (F) (G) (H) (J)
9 (A) (B) (C) (D)	29 (A) (B) (C) (D)	49 (A) (B) (C) (D)	69 (A) (B) (C) (D)
10 (F) (G) (H) (J)	30 (F) (G) (H) (J)	50 (F) (G) (H) (J)	70 (F) (G) (H) (J)
11 (A) (B) (C) (D)	31 (A) (B) (C) (D)	51 (A) (B) (C) (D)	71 (A) (B) (C) (D)
12 (F) (G) (H) (J)	32 (F) (G) (H) (J)	52 (F) (G) (H) (J)	72 (F) (G) (H) (J)
13 (A) (B) (C) (D)	33 (A) (B) (C) (D)	53 (A) (B) (C) (D)	73 (A) (B) (C) (D)
14 (F) (G) (H) (J)	34 (F) (G) (H) (J)	54 (F) (G) (H) (J)	74 (F) (G) (H) (J)
15 (A) (B) (C) (D)	35 (A) (B) (C) (D)	55 (A) (B) (C) (D)	75 (A) (B) (C) (D)
16 (F) (G) (H) (J)	36 (F) (G) (H) (J)	56 (F) (G) (H) (J)	
17 (A) (B) (C) (D)	37 (A) (B) (C) (D)	57 (A) (B) (C) (D)	
18 (F) (G) (H) (J)	38 (F) (G) (H) (J)	58 (F) (G) (H) (J)	
19 (A) (B) (C) (D)	39 (A) (B) (C) (D)	59 (A) (B) (C) (D)	
20 (F) (G) (H) (J)	40 (F) (G) (H) (J)	60 (F) (G) (H) (J)	

Test 2

1 (A) (B) (C) (D) (E)	16 (F) (G) (H) (J) (K)	31 (A) (B) (C) (D) (E)	46 (F) (G) (H) (J) (K)
2 (F) (G) (H) (J) (K)	17 (A) (B) (C) (D) (E)	32 (F) (G) (H) (J) (K)	47 (A) (B) (C) (D) (E)
3 (A) (B) (C) (D) (E)	18 (F) (G) (H) (J) (K)	33 (A) (B) (C) (D) (E)	48 (F) (G) (H) (J) (K)
4 (F) (G) (H) (J) (K)	19 (A) (B) (C) (D) (E)	34 (F) (G) (H) (J) (K)	49 (A) (B) (C) (D) (E)
5 (A) (B) (C) (D) (E)	20 (F) (G) (H) (J) (K)	35 (A) (B) (C) (D) (E)	50 (F) (G) (H) (J) (K)
6 (F) (G) (H) (J) (K)	21 (A) (B) (C) (D) (E)	36 (F) (G) (H) (J) (K)	51 (A) (B) (C) (D) (E)
7 (A) (B) (C) (D) (E)	22 (F) (G) (H) (J) (K)	37 (A) (B) (C) (D) (E)	52 (F) (G) (H) (J) (K)
8 (F) (G) (H) (J) (K)	23 (A) (B) (C) (D) (E)	38 (F) (G) (H) (J) (K)	53 (A) (B) (C) (D) (E)
9 (A) (B) (C) (D) (E)	24 (F) (G) (H) (J) (K)	39 (A) (B) (C) (D) (E)	54 (F) (G) (H) (J) (K)
10 (F) (G) (H) (J) (K)	25 (A) (B) (C) (D) (E)	40 (F) (G) (H) (J) (K)	55 (A) (B) (C) (D) (E)
11 (A) (B) (C) (D) (E)	26 (F) (G) (H) (J) (K)	41 (A) (B) (C) (D) (E)	56 (F) (G) (H) (J) (K)
12 (F) (G) (H) (J) (K)	27 (A) (B) (C) (D) (E)	42 (F) (G) (H) (J) (K)	57 (A) (B) (C) (D) (E)
13 (A) (B) (C) (D) (E)	28 (F) (G) (H) (J) (K)	43 (A) (B) (C) (D) (E)	58 (F) (G) (H) (J) (K)
14 (F) (G) (H) (J) (K)	29 (A) (B) (C) (D) (E)	44 (F) (G) (H) (J) (K)	59 (A) (B) (C) (D) (E)
15 (A) (B) (C) (D) (E)	30 (F) (G) (H) (J) (K)	45 (A) (B) (C) (D) (E)	60 (F) (G) (H) (J) (K)

Answer Sheet

MODEL EXAM A

Test 3

1 Ⓐ Ⓑ Ⓒ Ⓓ	11 Ⓐ Ⓑ Ⓒ Ⓓ	21 Ⓐ Ⓑ Ⓒ Ⓓ	31 Ⓐ Ⓑ Ⓒ Ⓓ
2 Ⓕ Ⓖ Ⓗ Ⓙ	12 Ⓕ Ⓖ Ⓗ Ⓙ	22 Ⓕ Ⓖ Ⓗ Ⓙ	32 Ⓕ Ⓖ Ⓗ Ⓙ
3 Ⓐ Ⓑ Ⓒ Ⓓ	13 Ⓐ Ⓑ Ⓒ Ⓓ	23 Ⓐ Ⓑ Ⓒ Ⓓ	33 Ⓐ Ⓑ Ⓒ Ⓓ
4 Ⓕ Ⓖ Ⓗ Ⓙ	14 Ⓕ Ⓖ Ⓗ Ⓙ	24 Ⓕ Ⓖ Ⓗ Ⓙ	34 Ⓕ Ⓖ Ⓗ Ⓙ
5 Ⓐ Ⓑ Ⓒ Ⓓ	15 Ⓐ Ⓑ Ⓒ Ⓓ	25 Ⓐ Ⓑ Ⓒ Ⓓ	35 Ⓐ Ⓑ Ⓒ Ⓓ
6 Ⓕ Ⓖ Ⓗ Ⓙ	16 Ⓕ Ⓖ Ⓗ Ⓙ	26 Ⓕ Ⓖ Ⓗ Ⓙ	36 Ⓕ Ⓖ Ⓗ Ⓙ
7 Ⓐ Ⓑ Ⓒ Ⓓ	17 Ⓐ Ⓑ Ⓒ Ⓓ	27 Ⓐ Ⓑ Ⓒ Ⓓ	37 Ⓐ Ⓑ Ⓒ Ⓓ
8 Ⓕ Ⓖ Ⓗ Ⓙ	18 Ⓕ Ⓖ Ⓗ Ⓙ	28 Ⓕ Ⓖ Ⓗ Ⓙ	38 Ⓕ Ⓖ Ⓗ Ⓙ
9 Ⓐ Ⓑ Ⓒ Ⓓ	19 Ⓐ Ⓑ Ⓒ Ⓓ	29 Ⓐ Ⓑ Ⓒ Ⓓ	39 Ⓐ Ⓑ Ⓒ Ⓓ
10 Ⓕ Ⓖ Ⓗ Ⓙ	20 Ⓕ Ⓖ Ⓗ Ⓙ	30 Ⓕ Ⓖ Ⓗ Ⓙ	40 Ⓕ Ⓖ Ⓗ Ⓙ

Test 4

1 Ⓐ Ⓑ Ⓒ Ⓓ	11 Ⓐ Ⓑ Ⓒ Ⓓ	21 Ⓐ Ⓑ Ⓒ Ⓓ	31 Ⓐ Ⓑ Ⓒ Ⓓ
2 Ⓕ Ⓖ Ⓗ Ⓙ	12 Ⓕ Ⓖ Ⓗ Ⓙ	22 Ⓕ Ⓖ Ⓗ Ⓙ	32 Ⓕ Ⓖ Ⓗ Ⓙ
3 Ⓐ Ⓑ Ⓒ Ⓓ	13 Ⓐ Ⓑ Ⓒ Ⓓ	23 Ⓐ Ⓑ Ⓒ Ⓓ	33 Ⓐ Ⓑ Ⓒ Ⓓ
4 Ⓕ Ⓖ Ⓗ Ⓙ	14 Ⓕ Ⓖ Ⓗ Ⓙ	24 Ⓕ Ⓖ Ⓗ Ⓙ	34 Ⓕ Ⓖ Ⓗ Ⓙ
5 Ⓐ Ⓑ Ⓒ Ⓓ	15 Ⓐ Ⓑ Ⓒ Ⓓ	25 Ⓐ Ⓑ Ⓒ Ⓓ	35 Ⓐ Ⓑ Ⓒ Ⓓ
6 Ⓕ Ⓖ Ⓗ Ⓙ	16 Ⓕ Ⓖ Ⓗ Ⓙ	26 Ⓕ Ⓖ Ⓗ Ⓙ	36 Ⓕ Ⓖ Ⓗ Ⓙ
7 Ⓐ Ⓑ Ⓒ Ⓓ	17 Ⓐ Ⓑ Ⓒ Ⓓ	27 Ⓐ Ⓑ Ⓒ Ⓓ	37 Ⓐ Ⓑ Ⓒ Ⓓ
8 Ⓕ Ⓖ Ⓗ Ⓙ	18 Ⓕ Ⓖ Ⓗ Ⓙ	28 Ⓕ Ⓖ Ⓗ Ⓙ	38 Ⓕ Ⓖ Ⓗ Ⓙ
9 Ⓐ Ⓑ Ⓒ Ⓓ	19 Ⓐ Ⓑ Ⓒ Ⓓ	29 Ⓐ Ⓑ Ⓒ Ⓓ	39 Ⓐ Ⓑ Ⓒ Ⓓ
10 Ⓕ Ⓖ Ⓗ Ⓙ	20 Ⓕ Ⓖ Ⓗ Ⓙ	30 Ⓕ Ⓖ Ⓗ Ⓙ	40 Ⓕ Ⓖ Ⓗ Ⓙ

Model Exam A

ENGLISH TEST

45 MINUTES—75 QUESTIONS

Directions: The following test consists of 75 underlined words and phrases in context, or general questions about the passages. Most of the underlined sections contain errors and inappropriate expressions. You are asked to compare each with the four alternatives in the answer column. If you consider the original version best, choose letter **A** or **F:** NO CHANGE. For each question, blacken on the answer sheet the letter of the alternative you think best. Read each passage through before answering the questions based on it.

Passage 1

(1)

Americans are living longer. The number of citizens sixty years or older totaled more than forty million in 1999, and one out of every nine Americans were [1] sixty-five or older. Because advances in medical science and a more healthful lifestyle have lengthened the life spans of we Americans, [2] more and more of us are finding that the time comes when we either no longer want to—or can— [3] live on our own.

(2)

Unfortunately, in the past the words *retirement home* often brought to mind images of impersonal, lonely places. [4] However, conditions in retirement homes can vary, some homes earning awards for excellence in nursing care, and others earning citations for

1. **A.** NO CHANGE
   B. is
   C. have been
   D. was

2. **F.** NO CHANGE
   G. we, Americans,
   H. us Americans
   J. us, Americans,

3. **A.** NO CHANGE
   B. to or can live
   C. to, or can live
   D. to, or can, live

4. This idea (of "impersonal, lonely places") could best be illustrated in this passage by employing which of the following writing strategies?

   F. Explaining a process
   G. Persuasion
   H. Defining
   J. Description

negligence. [5] Regulations regarding nursing homes are becoming <u>stricter than a research clinic,</u> (6) and it is possible to find retirement conditions that are positive and comfortable. [7]

(3)

But at the same time, the sad fact remains that, although most nursing homes are now licensed by the state, <u>unclean and unhealthy conditions can still be found.</u> (8) Even if the homes follow the licensing procedures perfectly, the law does not guarantee a <u>warm friendly</u> (9) staff or atmosphere. [10]

(4)

When looking at nursing homes, <u>qualities should be placed</u> (11) in priority order. Family members should remember, as they look, that attitude toward patients—the morale and personal contact—can be just as

5. Which of the following writing strategies would permit the writer to present details about both housing extremes?
   - **A.** Classifying and dividing
   - **B.** Narration
   - **C.** Comparison and contrast
   - **D.** Persuasion

6. **F.** NO CHANGE
   - **G.** stricter
   - **H.** stricter than clinics
   - **J.** stricter than they once were

7. Suppose that at this point in the passage the writer wanted to add more information about the impact of government regulations on retirement home conditions. Which of the following additions would be most relevant to the passage as a whole?
   - **A.** A description and brief history of the agencies regulating nursing homes
   - **B.** A bibliography of government reports and summaries published by regulating agencies
   - **C.** A separate paragraph summarizing briefly the recent activity and success of regulating agencies
   - **D.** Inclusion of a typical case report on an existing nursing institution

8. **F.** NO CHANGE
   - **G.** one can still find unclean and unhealthy conditions.
   - **H.** conditions can be found of uncleanliness and unhealthiness.
   - **J.** many of them are unclean and unhealthy.

9. **A.** NO CHANGE
   - **B.** warm - friendly
   - **C.** warm: friendly
   - **D.** warm, friendly

10. The writer could most effectively strengthen this paragraph by adding:
    - **F.** a list of retirement homes found to be substandard in cleanliness.
    - **G.** an anecdote about a woman who has lived in a home for 20 years.
    - **H.** details and examples that typify unclean and unhealthy conditions.
    - **J.** details of the licensing procedure that homes are required to complete.

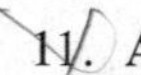

11. **A.** NO CHANGE
    - **B.** interested parties should place qualities
    - **C.** qualities are certainly to be placed
    - **D.** the patient should place qualities

important as new buildings, which, if they do not contain human warmth, can be little better than prisons.

(5)

For these reasons, it behooves us [12] to take the time to carefully check out the nursing homes the family is considering. If members of the family cannot carry out all of the necessary steps, they should have a friend or relative help with the evaluation.

12. **F.** NO CHANGE
G. best suits us
H. is very important
J. is not a bad idea

(6)

Not everyone who is in a nursing home requires the 24-hour skilled care offered there. Many residents are in homes because they can no longer care for themselves at home, and have nowhere else to go. However, alternatives to nursing homes do exist for people who need less care. [13]

13. Which of the following means of discussing alternatives to 24-hour skilled nursing care would be most compatible with the methods employed so far in this passage?
A. Detailed interviews with nursing home inmates who have experienced both forms of care
B. Insertion of medical records of patients who have been moved from occasional care to 24-hour care
C. A short paragraph mentioning several alternatives to 24-hour care
D. Inclusion of a personal diary written by an elderly patient who made the change to permanent care

(7)

Home care services, which [14] allow a patient to stay in a familiar environment rather than being placed in a nursing home, are an option if the elderly person needs only limited help, since home care causes far less disruption to normal life. Such services are provided by a variety of public, voluntary, and private agencies. [15]

14. **F.** NO CHANGE
G. services which
H. services that
J. services

15. Choose the sequence of paragraph numbers that makes the structure of the passage most logical.
A. NO CHANGE
B. 7, 2, 3, 1, 5, 4, 6
C. 1, 2, 3, 5, 4, 6, 7
D. 1, 2, 7, 3, 4, 5, 6

GO ON TO THE NEXT PAGE.

Passage 2

Cultural activities form the loom on which the talents, skills, and dreams of individuals can sprout into [16] something colorful and distinctive—a play, pageant, art [17] center, music festival, museum, library, garden, park—to enrich community life. [18]

Cultural activities are central to Rural Areas Development, a nationwide effort by rural people and those in public service and private endeavors who work with it [19] to enrich the quality of life. [20]

What may not be recognized by area leaders whose primary interest is in economic development is when [21] cultural activities can be part of the steam that supplies the drive.

The first heritage festival of Lawrence County in Arkansas illustrates how a cultural activity may emerge from a ferment of economic development and, in turn, engender still newer ideas for farther [22] social and economic gain, as well as other cultural activities. Lawrence County, a mainly rural area in northeastern Arkansas, had a population of 17,000 in nineteen-sixty. [23] Its eastern half is fertile. The Black River runs beneath the delta, planted to rice, soybeans, and cotton, and the hills, where the farms are in livestock and poultry.

16. **F.** NO CHANGE
    G. can be woven
    H. can be sprouted
    J. can swell

17. **A.** NO CHANGE
    B. distinctive, a play, a pageant
    C. distinctive. A play, a pageant
    D. distinctive; a play, a pageant

18. Which of the following terms needs to be more carefully defined if the first paragraph is to carry substantial meaning?
    F. Pageant
    G. Cultural activities
    H. Loom
    J. Music festival

19. **A.** NO CHANGE
    B. they
    C. him
    D. them

20. Which of the following suggestions would improve the beginning of this passage?
    F. NO CHANGE
    G. OMIT the second paragraph.
    H. Combine the first and second paragraphs.
    J. Move the second paragraph to the end of the passage.

21. **A.** NO CHANGE
    B. is that
    C. is because
    D. is for

22. **F.** NO CHANGE
    G. even farther
    H. further
    J. furthermore

23. **A.** NO CHANGE
    B. nineteen-sixty A.D.
    C. 1960
    D. nineteen hundred and sixty

Family-type farms employ a third of the work force. [25]

Farmers nevertheless made up the largest occupational group in the Lawrence County Development Council when it was organized in 1962. Seventeen members of the Council were farmers—nine in general farming, six livestock and poultry producers, one a dairyman, another a ricegrower. Also on the Council were an industrial worker, two bankers, and several local businessmen and homemakers.

Addressing itself to the economic advancement of the county, the Council spent its first two years of existence. It supported a one-mill tax to guarantee construction of an industrial building in Walnut Ridge, the county seat and the largest town. It was instrumental in getting a comprehensive manpower inventory and economic base study of the area it arranged for workshops in farm management. It helped leaders of Imboden to initiate a housing project for twenty

24. **F.** NO CHANGE
    G. Family type farms
    H. Family type-farms
    J. Family, type farms

25. This paragraph contains a major organizational problem. Which of the following critical statements best describes this problem?
    A. The paragraph does not contain enough specific details to support the main point.
    B. The first sentence of the paragraph presents an idea that is not developed in the body of the paragraph.
    C. No beginning thesis or topic is presented.
    D. There are many ideas in the paragraph, none of them developed.

26. **F.** NO CHANGE
    G. on the contrary
    H. however
    J. thus

27. **A.** NO CHANGE
    B. —nine in general farming, six in livestock and poultry production, one in dairy production, another in rice farming.
    C. —nine are general farmers, six as livestock and poultry producers, one a dairyman, another a ricegrower.
    D. —nine as general farmers, six livestock and poultry producers, one a dairyman, another a ricegrower.

28. **F.** NO CHANGE
    G. During its first two years, the Council addressed the economic advancement of the county.
    H. Addressing itself to the economic advancement of the county, the Council spent its first two years of existence.
    J. The Council spent its first two years of existence while addressing itself to the economic advancement of the county.

29. **A.** NO CHANGE
    B. area, it
    C. area. It
    D. area but it

elderly persons. [30]

30. Which of the following is a major flaw in the structure and sense of this passage?
    - **F.** It omits all mention of children; children are certainly an important part of rural America.
    - **G.** It fails to mention public works projects.
    - **H.** The whole point of the passage is that cultural activities can "supply the drive" for social and economic development, but the passage does not address that issue at all.
    - **J.** The passage does not list enough accomplishments of the Lawrence County Development Council.

Passage 3

Of all the musical instruments produced by human skill, the three <u>of which are the most distinguished</u> [31] are the violin, the piano, and the pipe organ. Of these, the violin still remains the instrument of the virtuoso. No method <u>to play it</u> [32] has yet been <u>discovered</u> [33] except by the slow and tedious process of learning it. It is the instrument of the <u>accomplish</u> [34] musician. [35]

On the other hand, self-playing devices have been employed successfully with both the piano and the organ—but with this difference. Piano music derives some of its <u>essentialness</u> [36] from the personality of the player. The touch of human fingers has never been exactly reproduced by mechanical devices. In some

31. **A.** NO CHANGE
    B. that are most distinguished
    C. of those that are distinguished
    D. most distinguished

32. **F.** NO CHANGE
    G. playing at
    H. in playing it
    J. of playing it

33. **A.** NO CHANGE
    B. invented
    C. divined
    D. developed

34. **F.** NO CHANGE
    G. accomplishing
    H. accomplished
    J. more accomplished

35. Which of the following writing strategies would permit the writer to present details about all three types of instruments?
    A. Classifying and dividing
    B. Narration
    C. Comparison and contrast
    D. Persuasion

36. **F.** NO CHANGE
    G. pith
    H. quality
    J. life-blood

1 1 1 1 1 1 1 1 1 1 1

compositions, however, the mechanical piano player <u>approaches the pianist,</u> (37) although not by any means in all. [38]

37. A. NO CHANGE
    B. approaches the sound of the pianist
    C. comes close to the piano
    D. typifies the piano

38. The writer could most effectively strengthen the passage at this point by adding:
    F. documentation and detail to support opinions delivered as facts.
    G. a review of all the orchestral instruments, including their musical ranges.
    H. a discussion of the great violin makers of the past.
    J. a detailed description of organ structure and mechanism.

The pipe organ <u>consequently</u> (39) is made for automated playing. There is virtually nothing the organist can do with his or her hands or feet that cannot be duplicated by mechanical devices. When an organ manual is touched, the resulting tone is the <u>exact same,</u> (40) whether the touch <u>be</u> (41) hard or <u>soft, slow or quick.</u> (42) The tone continues at the same volume until the key is released. Brilliancy, variety, and other qualities are obtained by other sets of pipes, and these pipes are brought into play by pulling out stops. Such stops can be pulled by mechanical means just as effectively as by human fingers. If the organ music is correctly cut in the music roll, with all the stops, couplers, and swells operated at the proper places, <u>the most acutest ear</u> (43) cannot distinguish between the human organist and

39. A. NO CHANGE
    B. on the contrary
    C. to be sure
    D. similarly

40. F. NO CHANGE
    G. exact identical
    H. same
    J. equal

41. A. NO CHANGE
    B. is
    C. was
    D. has been

42. F. NO CHANGE
    G. soft, slow, or quick.
    H. soft: slow or quick.
    J. soft slow or quick.

43. A. NO CHANGE
    B. the acute ear
    C. the more acute ear
    D. the most acute ear

GO ON TO THE NEXT PAGE.

<u>the organist who is mechanical</u>.[44] [45]

44. **F.** NO CHANGE
G. the organist, who is mechanical.
H. the mechanical organist.
J. the organist who is a nonhuman.

45. The main purpose of this passage is to provide:
A. a discussion of the virtues of the mechanical organ.
B. a history of music.
C. a comparison of the violin, piano, and organ.
D. a general discussion of mechanized musical instruments.

not violin

Passage 4

Until his death, Charles Darwin complained that even many of his scientific critics failed to grasp the meaning of his theory of selection; <u>it is not unlikely</u>[46] that if he were still alive the complaint would be repeated. [47] Even where full comprehension of his theory of the causes of organic evolution has been reached, precise determination of the degree of its <u>adequacy—for</u>[48] adequate in great measure it surely is—has not yet been attained. The generalization that underlies it is so broad, the facts by which it must be verified or limited <u>are always, it seems, accumulating</u>,[49] and the problems interrelated with it are so intricate, that finality with regard to it must be indefinitely postponed. <u>That</u>[50] must be left for the biology of the future.

<u>Moreover</u>,[51] there need be little hesitation in expressing an estimate of the great naturalist and his thought. They are obviously among the greatest

46. **F.** NO CHANGE
G. it is not likely
H. it is likely
J. it is probable

47. When a passage mentions that a famous figure *complained* about a fact or situation, how might the reader be given greater understanding of the personality and character of that subject?
A. By inclusion of a description of the occurrence
B. By quoted examples of what he or she actually said
C. By references to how other persons present at the time reported the conversation
D. By a speculative commentary on what he or she meant

48. **F.** NO CHANGE
G. adequacy; for
H. adequacy, for
J. adequacy for

49. **A.** NO CHANGE
B. are so always accumulating
C. are so constantly accumulating
D. are accumulating

50. **F.** NO CHANGE
G. This
H. Those
J. That judgment

51. **A.** NO CHANGE
B. In addition
C. In other words,
D. However,

intellectual forces of the early twentieth century, as they were of the nineteenth. Notwithstanding certain limitations, which Darwin himself unduly emphasizes,[52] he was one of the greatest of men intellectually, and, without qualification, one of the most attractive of personalities; this[53] must always remain true, whatever may be the ultimate verdict of science in regard to details of his hypotheses. Persons thus grandly molded have nothing to fear from the perspective of time. He was one cool cucumber at one of history's junctures.[54]

Darwin insisted that the principle of natural selection is only one of the causes of evolution of species, "the main but not the exclusive means of modification," and[55] he was also profoundly aware of the evolutionary importance of the underlying problems of variability, heredity, and isolating[56] that has occupied[57] so absorbingly the attention of the post-Darwinians. Naturalists, almost without exception, no longer doubt that natural selection, as expounded by him, is a cause of the evolution of species, and a most important one, and stood[58] as a general law that explains the causation of organic evolution. This view will be supported by the biology of the future, if Darwin's place[59] in the history of science cannot be far below that of Newton. [60]

52. F. NO CHANGE
    G. emphasize
    H. emphasized
    J. had emphasized

53. A. NO CHANGE
    B. this assessment
    C. this alone
    D. this quality

54. F. NO CHANGE
    G. He has been one cool cucumber at one of history's junctures.
    H. He is one cool cucumber at one of history's junctures.
    J. OMIT this sentence.

55. A. NO CHANGE
    B. modification" and
    C. modification." And
    D. modification;" and

56. F. NO CHANGE
    G. isolatability
    H. isolation
    J. isolate

57. A. NO CHANGE
    B. had occupied
    C. has been occupied
    D. have occupied

58. F. NO CHANGE
    G. has stood
    H. stands
    J. will have stood

59. A. NO CHANGE
    B. If this view is supported by the biology of the future, Darwin's place
    C. This view will be supported by the biology of the future, although Darwin's place
    D. Nevertheless, this view is supported by the biology of the future, when Darwin's place

60. Readers are likely to regard the passage as best described by which of the following terms?
    F. Biographical
    G. Confessional
    H. Laudatory
    J. Inspirational

1 1 1 1 1 1 1 1 1 1 1

Passage 5

Almost everywhere spread through the British Isles [61] are to be found antiquities. These are carefully marked on governmental, and many private [62] maps and historians describe them [63] in publicly available guides. Governmental agencies, the National Trust, and private landlords are most accommodating in permitting visits to these unattended sites, most of which are unsupervised yet immaculate. [64] [65]

With interesting exceptions, the rock graphics of the British Isles are a collection of pits, rings, and grooves, as well as carefully-carved [66] symbols of Neolithic power (axheads, fertility symbols, etc.) and roughly sculpted monoliths. The pit, ring, and groove sites usually are found on horizontal surfaces, because [67] many power symbols are found on vertical surfaces of menhirs (upright monoliths) [68] lintels, and the walls of constructions. In the more than five hundred [69] megalithic stone constructions, many have a number of menhirs whose natural shape has been abetted by human enterprise into a variety of shapes. Stonehenge is the

61. A. NO CHANGE
B. widely dispersed through
C. throughout
D. all over, in nook and crook

62. F. NO CHANGE
G. governmental; and many private
H. governmental—and many private
J. governmental and many private

63. A. NO CHANGE
B. and described
C. and describing
D. and descriptively

64. F. NO CHANGE
G. most of which are unsupervised although immaculate.
H. most of which are immaculate.
J. most of which are unsupervised.

65. Suppose this passage were written for an audience that was unfamiliar with antiquities and British history. The writer could most effectively strengthen the passage by:
A. including a brief summary of the biographies of British monarchs.
B. describing with detail and illustration just what an *antiquity* is.
C. supplying a current map of England.
D. defining in great detail the term *National Trust*.

66. F. NO CHANGE
G. carefully, carved
H. carefully carved
J. carefully and carved

67. A. NO CHANGE
B. while
C. although
D. yet

68. F. NO CHANGE
G. monoliths),
H. monoliths,)
J. monoliths,

69. A. NO CHANGE
B. 500
C. 5 hundred
D. five-hundred

1 1 1 1 1 1 1 1 1 1 1

incorporating universal structure by which [70] one can discern many of the features found elsewhere. In Scotland are found [71] a special series of menhirs that depict symbols, both pre-Christian and Christian, as well as human figures, angels, and scenes. [72]

Surely one of the earliest stones to be erected is the one near present-day Edinburgh in an area that came under Britannic control by A.D. 480. [73] Christianity came to this region between the fifth and the seventh centuries: St. Ninian founded the Candida Case monastery near Whithorn on the Solway in A.D. 379–398; St. Oran established holy places in Iona, Mull, and Tiree before A.D. 548. [74] The form of Christianity was the monastic and hermitic type traditionally called Celtic, which demanded poverty and obedience from its clergy, who were all monks. [75]

70. **F.** NO CHANGE
G. with which
H. for which
J. in which

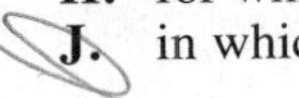

71. **A.** NO CHANGE
B. was found
C. has always been found
D. is found

72. Readers are likely to regard the passage as best described by which of the following terms?
F. Fictional
G. Scholarly
H. Dramatic
J. Persuasive

73. How can this paragraph be changed so that it will be more meaningful and understandable to a young reader?
A. Include a chart of rock types, listing origins, scientific names, and descriptions.
B. Provide a detailed description of many European prehistoric stoneworks.
C. Describe more fully the one stone mentioned in the first sentence.
D. Add a comparison of Easter Island monoliths with the Stonehenge monuments.

74. Look over the structure of this paragraph as it has unfolded so far. With which one of the following characterizations do you agree?
F. It is surely and soundly organized, consisting of a general statement at the beginning that is supported throughout.
G. It is not organized very well. It begins with a statement about monastic orders, but does not develop that idea.
H. It is not organized very well. It begins with a statement about a stone, but then switches to the history of Christianity in the region.
J. It is not organized very well. It begins with a brief history of Britannic rule, and then seems to shift to a history of Pict temples.

75. This paragraph would be strengthened by:
A. supplying more details about the Christian leaders.
B. beginning the paragraph with a general statement that encompasses the details presented in the body.
C. including a short lesson on rock formation.
D. defining the hermitic form of Christianity.

If there is still time remaining, you may review your answers.

MATHEMATICS TEST

60 MINUTES—60 QUESTIONS

Directions: After solving each problem, darken the appropriate space on the answer sheet. Do not spend too much time on any one problem. Make a note of the ones that seem difficult, and return to them when you finish the others. Assume that the word *line* means "straight line," that geometric figures are not necessarily drawn to scale, and that all geometric figures lie in a plane.

DO YOUR FIGURING HERE

1. Which of the following statements about the subsets of real numbers is true?

   A. Every integer is a whole number.
   B. All rational numbers are integers.
   C. 0 is not a real number.
   D. 3.14 is a rational number.
   E. All integers are negative.

2. Jane's score on her first test was 72. On her second test she received a score of 81. What percent increase did she have?

   F. 9%
   G. $11\frac{1}{9}\%$
   H. 12.5%
   J. $88\frac{8}{9}\%$
   K. 112.5%

3. $4^2 - 3 - 5 \cdot 8 - 2[(-3) - (-7)] = ?$

   A. 192
   B. −7
   C. −43
   D. −33
   E. −35

4. Four boxes, each one $2\frac{3}{8}$ feet high, are stacked in a room with a 10-foot ceiling. How much space is there between the top box and the ceiling?

   F. 2 feet
   G. 1 foot
   H. 6 inches
   J. 1 inch
   K. None of these

DO YOUR FIGURING HERE

5. Which of the following inequalities corresponds to the graph?

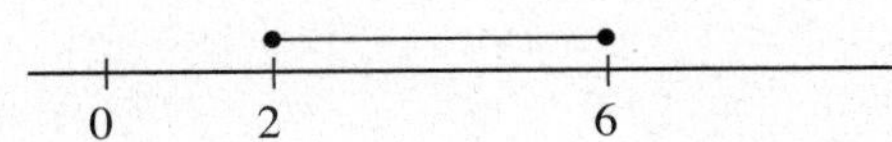

A. $x \leq 6$
B. $x \geq 2$
C. $|x - 2| \leq 6$
D. $|x - 4| \leq 2$
E. $|x - 6| = 2$

6. What is the lowest common denominator of the fractions $\frac{5}{4x^2y}$, $\frac{7}{6xy^2}$, and $\frac{-4}{15xy}$?

F. xy
G. $30xy$
H. $60xy$
J. $360x^2y^2$
K. $60x^2y^2$

7. What is the complete factorization of the polynomial $4x^3 - 24x^2 + 36x$?

A. $4x(x - 3)^2$
B. $x(2x - 6)^2$
C. $x(4x - 12)(x - 3)$
D. $x(4x^2 - 24x + 36)$
E. $4x(x^2 - 6x + 9)$

8. Which of the following numbers is composite?

F. 1
G. 43
H. $\frac{2}{3}$
J. 57
K. 83

9. If $a = -3$ and $b = 4$, then $ab^2 - (a - b) = ?$

A. 151
B. 55
C. −49
D. −47
E. −41

GO ON TO THE NEXT PAGE.

2 2 2 2 2 2 2 2 2 2 2

DO YOUR FIGURING HERE

10. Which of the following is an inscribed angle in the diagram?

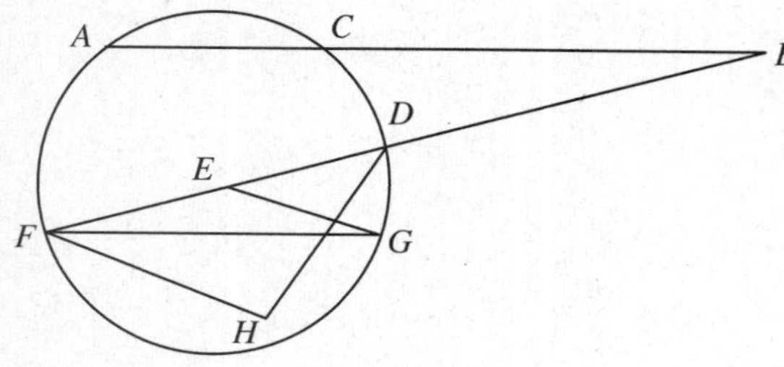

F. $\angle ABF$
G. $\angle DFG$
H. $\angle FEG$
J. $\angle DEG$
K. $\angle FHD$

11. Jon starts out on a trip at 40 mph. If $\frac{1}{2}$ hour later Joel starts out on the same route at 50 mph, which equation may be used to determine how long it will take Joel to overtake Jon?

A. $40\left(x + \frac{1}{2}\right) = 50x$

B. $40x + \frac{1}{2} = 50x$

C. $40x = 50\left(x + \frac{1}{2}\right)$

D. $4(x + 30) = 50x$

E. $40x = 50x + 30$

12. If lines l, m, and n are parallel, and $AB = 2$, $AC = 8$, and $EF = 5$, what is the length of $\overline{DE}$?

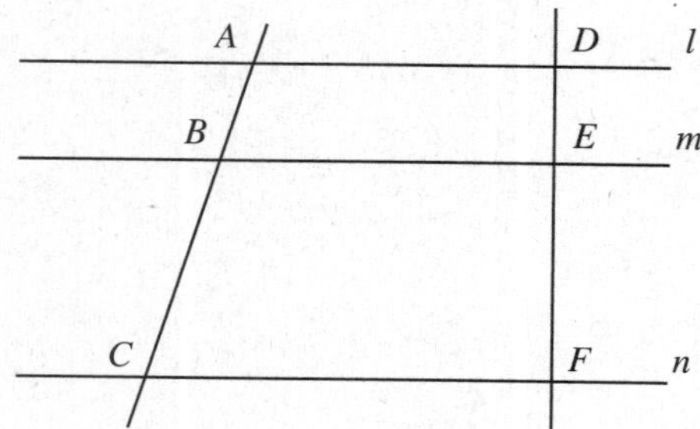

F. 15

G. $3\frac{1}{5}$

H. $1\frac{2}{3}$

J. $1\frac{1}{5}$

K. $\frac{3}{5}$

2 2 2 2 2 2 2 2 2 2 2

DO YOUR FIGURING HERE

13. $5\frac{1}{8} - 3\frac{5}{6} = ?$

A. $1\frac{7}{24}$

B. $2\frac{17}{24}$

C. $1\frac{1}{2}$

D. $1\frac{1}{8}$

E. $2\frac{7}{24}$

14. In the diagram, the right angles are marked and $AB = BC = CD = DE = EF = 1$. What is the length of $\overline{AF}$?

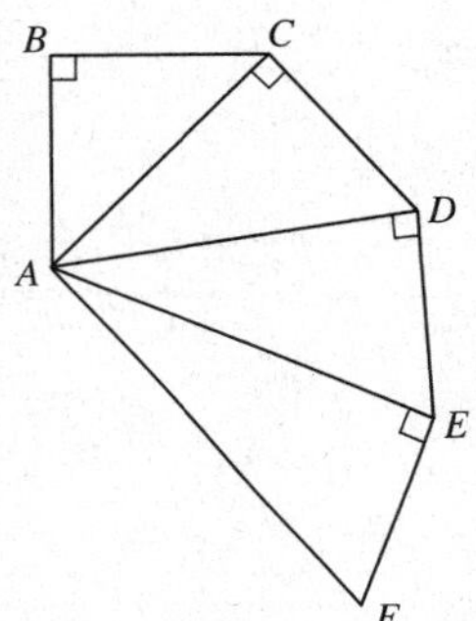

F. 2
G. 3
H. 5
J. $\sqrt{5}$
K. $\sqrt{6}$

15. What is the common decimal numeral for one hundred six and twenty-eight ten thousandths?

A. 106.00028
B. 106.0028
C. 106.028
D. 106.28
E. 106,280,000

16. What is the solution set for $3 - (x - 5) = 2x - 3(4 - x)$?

F. $\left\{-\frac{3}{2}\right\}$

G. $\left\{\frac{3}{10}\right\}$

H. $\left\{\frac{10}{3}\right\}$

J. ø

K. $\{5\}$

GO ON TO THE NEXT PAGE.

2 2 2 2 2 2 2 2 2 2 2

DO YOUR FIGURING HERE

17. Which of the following is an arithmetic sequence?

A. $\frac{1}{2}, \frac{1}{4}, \frac{1}{6}, \frac{1}{8}, \ldots$
B. 2, 4, 8, 16, ...
C. 2, 5, 10, 17, ...
D. 5, 11, 17, 23, ...
E. –1, 3, –9, 27, ...

18. What is the value of i^{53}?

F. 1
G. i
H. –1
J. $-i$
K. 0

19. The Science Club has ten members and wants to form an election committee of four people. If everyone in the club is eligible to be on the committee, how many different committees can be formed?

A. 1
B. 40
C. 210
D. 5040
E. 3,628,800

20. Which of the following trigonometric equations is false for all x?

F. $\sin x = \frac{2}{\sqrt{5}}$

G. $\tan x = -100$

H. $\sec x = \frac{\sqrt{3}}{4}$

J. $\cos^2 x + \sin^2 x = 1$

K. $\cos x = -0.1439$

21. In the diagram, two chords of the circle intersect at point E. If $AE = 3$, $DE = 5$, and $CE = 2$, what is the length of $\overline{BE}$?

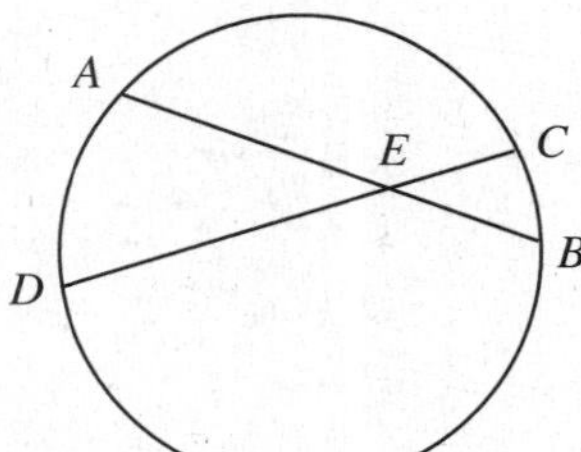

A. $1\frac{1}{5}$
B. $3\frac{1}{3}$
C. 4
D. $7\frac{1}{2}$
E. $8\frac{1}{3}$

2 2 2 2 2 2 2 2 2 2 2

DO YOUR FIGURING HERE

22. What is the probability of drawing a heart from a well-shuffled standard deck of playing cards?

    F. $\frac{1}{4}$
    G. $\frac{1}{52}$
    H. $\frac{1}{13}$
    J. $\frac{4}{13}$
    K. 1

23. Which expression is equal to $x - [3x - (1 - 2x)]$ when completely simplified?

    A. $-3x^2 + 2x - 1$
    B. $-4x + 1$
    C. 1
    D. -1
    E. $-4x - 1$

24. If $f(x) = 2x - 5$ and $g(x) = 1 + x^2$, then what is equal to $f(g(3))$?

    F. $2\sqrt{2} - 5$
    G. 2
    H. 10
    J. 15
    K. 16

25. If the length of a rectangle is 1 foot less than twice its width and its perimeter is 34 feet, what is the length of the rectangle in feet?

    A. 6
    B. 11
    C. $11\frac{2}{3}$
    D. $22\frac{1}{3}$
    E. None of these

26. If $2 \log_3 x - \frac{1}{2} \log_3 y + \log_3 z$ were written as a single logarithm, to what would it be equal?

    F. $\log_3 \frac{x^2z}{\sqrt{y}}$
    G. $\log_3 \frac{x^2}{z\sqrt{y}}$
    H. $\log_3 \frac{xz}{y}$
    J. $\log_3 \frac{4xz}{y}$
    K. $\log_3 (x^2 - \frac{y}{2} + z)$

GO ON TO THE NEXT PAGE.

DO YOUR FIGURING HERE

27. Which expression would be appropriate to complete the following equation in order for the equation to illustrate the commutative property of addition: 5(3 + 0) = ?

A. 5(3)
B. (3 + 0)5
C. 5(0 + 3)
D. 5(3) + 5(0)
E. 5(3) + 0

28. In a class of 27 students, $\frac{2}{3}$ are male. Five-sixths of the males in the class received a grade of C. How many male students received a grade of C?

F. 6
G. 12
H. 15
J. 18
K. 24

29. Which equation corresponds to the graph?

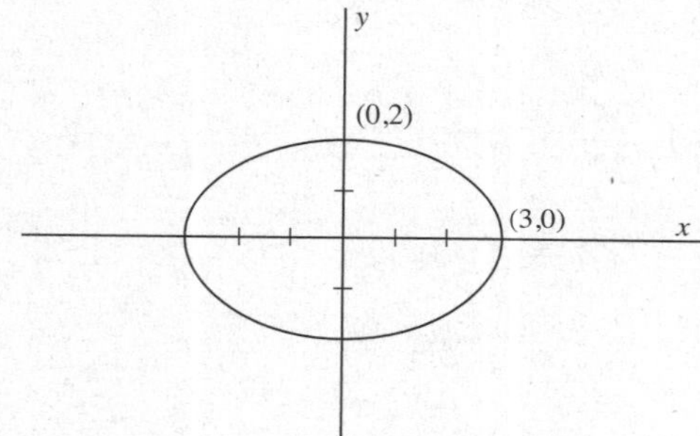

A. $\frac{x^2}{9} + \frac{y^2}{4} = 1$
B. $\frac{x^2}{9} - \frac{y^2}{4} = 1$
C. $\frac{x^2}{3} + \frac{y^2}{2} = 1$
D. $\frac{y^2}{4} - \frac{x^2}{9} = 1$
E. $(x - 3)^2 + (y - 2)^2 = 0$

30. What is the solution set for this system of equations?

$$\begin{aligned} x + z &= 6 \\ y + z &= 1 \\ 2z &= 8 \end{aligned}$$

F. {(2, –3, 8)}
G. {(2, –3, 4)}
H. $\left\{\left(1, \frac{-3}{2}, 4\right)\right\}$
J. {(1, 1, 2)}
K. { }

2 2 2 2 2 2 2 2 2 2 2

DO YOUR FIGURING HERE

31. What is the solution set of $\sqrt{x+1} = x - 1$?

    A. {0, 1}
    B. {3}
    C. {0}
    D. {0, 3}
    E. {–1, 1}

32. Which expression is equivalent to $\sqrt[3]{-12a^4b^2} \cdot \sqrt[3]{-6a^2b^2}$ in simplest radical form?

    F. $\sqrt[3]{72a^6b^4}$
    G. $-2a^2b\sqrt[3]{9b}$
    H. $2a^2b\sqrt[3]{9b}$
    J. $a^2b\sqrt[3]{72b}$
    K. $2\sqrt[3]{9a^6b^4}$

33. Given $\overline{CD}$ is tangent, m $\angle ABD = 62°$ and m $\angle BDC = 28°$, what is the measure of $\angle ADB$?

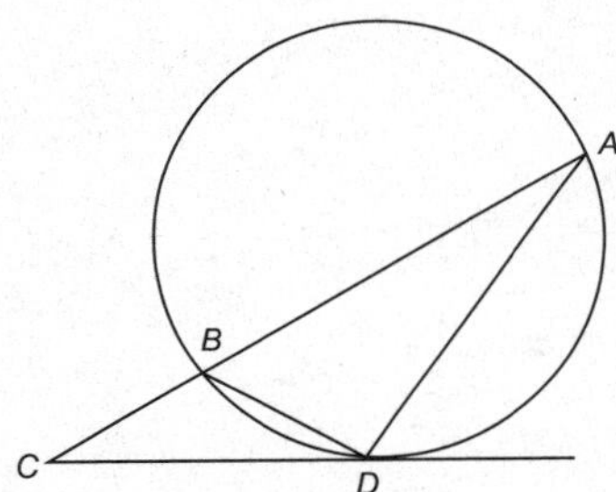

    A. 90°
    B. 100°
    C. 118°
    D. 152°
    E. 180°

34. What is the solution set of the following system of equations?

$$\begin{pmatrix} 2x - 5y = 13 \\ 3x + 2y = 10 \end{pmatrix}$$

    F. $\left\{\left(\frac{4}{19}, \frac{4}{19}\right)\right\}$
    G. {(–3, –1)}
    H. {(4, –1)}
    J. {(–1, –3)}
    K. None of these

GO ON TO THE NEXT PAGE.

DO YOUR FIGURING HERE

35. What is the solution to this system of equations?

$$\begin{pmatrix} 2x + 3y = 12 \\ y = \frac{-2}{3}x + 5 \end{pmatrix}$$

A. {0}
B. {(0, 0)}
C. {(–3, 2)}
D. { }
E. All points on the line.

36. If the measure of arc $ADC = 200°$ and $\overline{AB}$ and $\overline{BC}$ are tangent to circle O, what is the measure of $\angle OCA$?

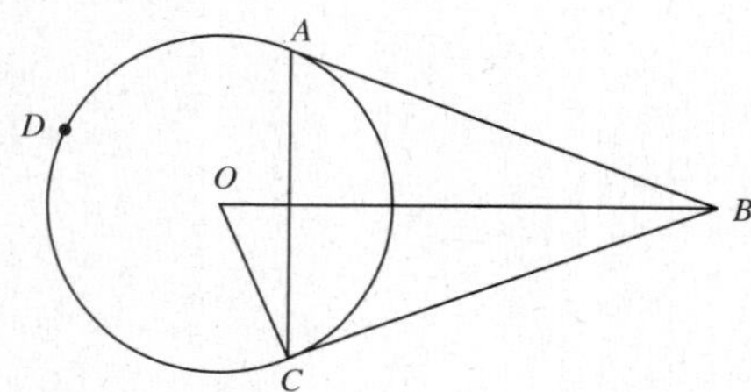

F. 40°
G. 20°
H. 10°
J. 8°
K. 5°

37. Suppose that a circular region (radius 2 cm) is cut from a square with sides 9 cm, leaving the shaded region shown in the diagram. What is the area of the shaded region?

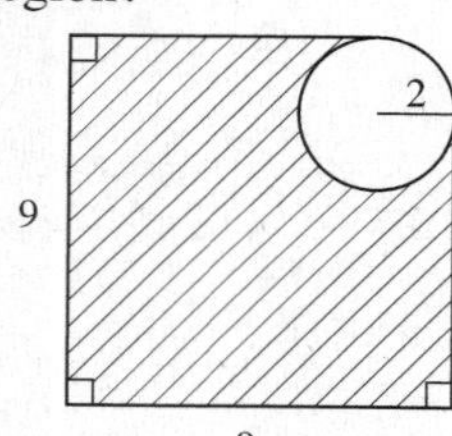

A. $81 - 4\pi$
B. $77 - 3\pi$
C. $78 - 4\pi$
D. $80 - 4\pi$
E. $81 - 3\pi$

38. Which statement is always true concerning an obtuse angle?

F. It measures less than 90°.
G. It measures greater than 180°.
H. It is the supplement of another obtuse angle.
J. There can be only one in a triangle.
K. There cannot be one in a quadrilateral.

DO YOUR FIGURING HERE

39. What is the simplified form of the complex fraction

$$\frac{\frac{x}{y} - \frac{y}{x}}{\frac{1}{x} - \frac{1}{y}}$$

A. $x + y$
B. $x - y$
C. $-x - y$
D. $\frac{x^2 - y^2}{y - x}$
E. $\frac{x^2 - y^2}{x - y}$

40. Which of the following statements is true?

F. All isoceles triangles are similar.
G. If two lines are cut by a transversal, the alternate interior angles are equal.
H. All circles are congruent.
J. The angles of a triangle are supplementary.
K. All four of the above are false.

41. Which of the following is the graph of the solution set of the inequality $|x - 3| > 2$?

A.
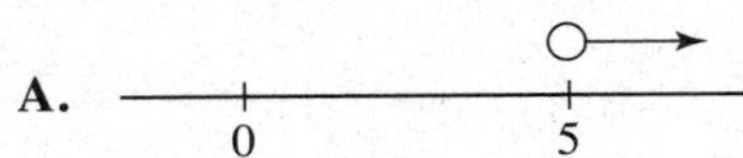

B.

−1 0

C.
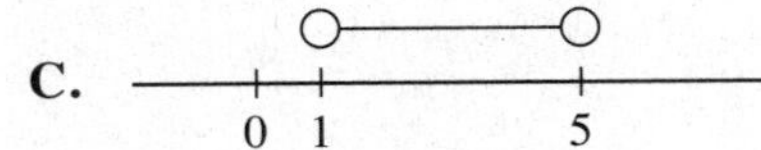

D.

0 1 5

E.

0 1 5

42. If $\overline{AC} \perp \overline{BD}$, $DE = 2$, $BE = 1$, $EC = \frac{1}{2}$, what is the length of $\overline{AB}$?

F. $\sqrt{17}$
G. 4
H. $\sqrt{5}$
J. 3
K. 2

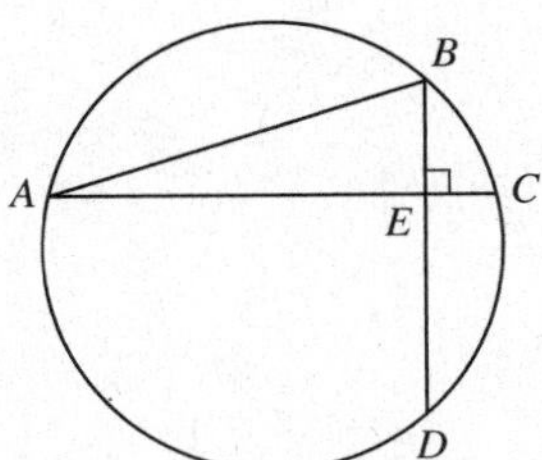

GO ON TO THE NEXT PAGE.

DO YOUR FIGURING HERE

43. In the diagram, lines m and n in a plane are cut by transversal l. Which statement would allow the conclusion that $m \parallel n$?

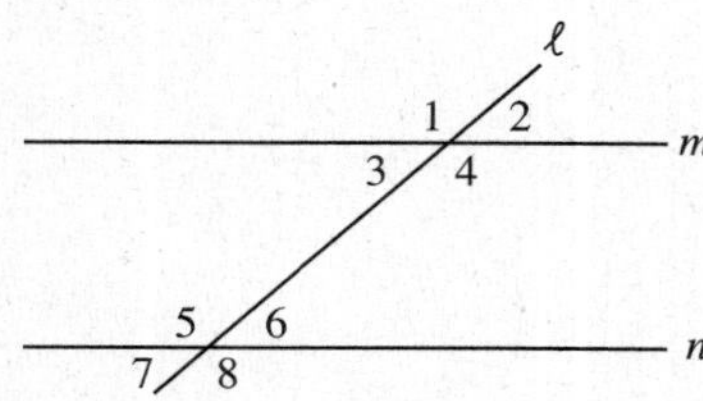

A. $m\angle 1 = m\angle 4$
B. $\angle 3$ and $\angle 4$ are supplementary
C. $m\angle 3 = m\angle 8$
D. $m\angle 3 = m\angle 6$
E. $\angle 1$ and $\angle 6$ are complementary

44. How many terms does the complete expansion of $(x + 2y)^9$ have?

F. 8
G. 9
H. 10
J. 18
K. 81

45. Which of the following is NOT a rational number?

A. 0.5
B. $0.\overline{5}$
C. $\sqrt{48}$
D. $\sqrt{49}$
E. 15%

46. What is the period of the following function: $y = 2\tan\left(3x - \frac{\pi}{2}\right)$?

F. 1
G. π
H. $\frac{\pi}{3}$
J. $\frac{\pi}{2}$
K. $\frac{2\pi}{3}$

47. In a windstorm a tower was bent at a point one fourth of the distance from the bottom. If the top of the tower now rests at a point 60 feet from the base, how tall, in feet, was the tower?

A. 100
B. 80
C. $60\sqrt{2}$
D. $60\sqrt{3}$
E. $240\sqrt{2}$

DO YOUR FIGURING HERE

48. Which of the following is NOT the equation of a conic section?

F. $2x^2 + 5y^2 - 2x + 7y - 8 = 0$
G. $y = 3x^2 + 7x - 3$
H. $y = 2^x + 5$
J. $\frac{x^2}{9} - \frac{(y-3)^2}{16} = 1$
K. $(x - 2)^2 + (y + 3)^2 = 25$

49. If $\cos \theta = \frac{-1}{2}$ and θ is in quadrant III, what is the value of $\sin 2\theta$?

A. $\frac{1}{2}$

B. $\frac{-1}{2}$

C. $\frac{\sqrt{3}}{2}$

D. $\frac{-\sqrt{3}}{2}$

E. -1

50. Given quadrilateral *ABCD*, which statement would allow the conclusion that *ABCD* is a parallelogram?

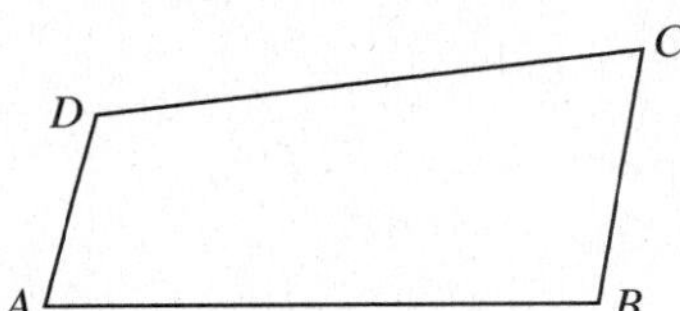

F. $m\angle A = m\angle C$
G. $AD = BC$
H. $m\angle A + m\angle D = 180°$
J. $\overline{AD} \parallel \overline{BC}$
K. None of these

51. What is the standard form of the equation of the line perpendicular to the graph of $2x + 3y = 7$ at point (2, 1)?

A. $x = 2$
B. $2x - 3y = 1$
C. $3x - 2y = 4$
D. $3x + 2y = 8$
E. $y = 1$

52. Which of the following is NOT a real number?

F. $\frac{0}{5}$

G. $3 - 9$
H. $\sqrt{25}$
J. $-\sqrt{7}$
K. $\sqrt{-4}$

GO ON TO THE NEXT PAGE.

2 2 2 2 2 2 2 2 2 2 2

DO YOUR FIGURING HERE

53. What is the degree of the polynomial $2^2x^2yz - 2^3x^3yz - 3$?

A. 0
B. 4
C. 5
D. 6
E. 8

54. Tangent line $\overleftrightarrow{AD}$ and chord $\overline{AC}$ intersect at point A. If the measure of arc $ABC = 220°$, what is the measure of $\angle CAD$?

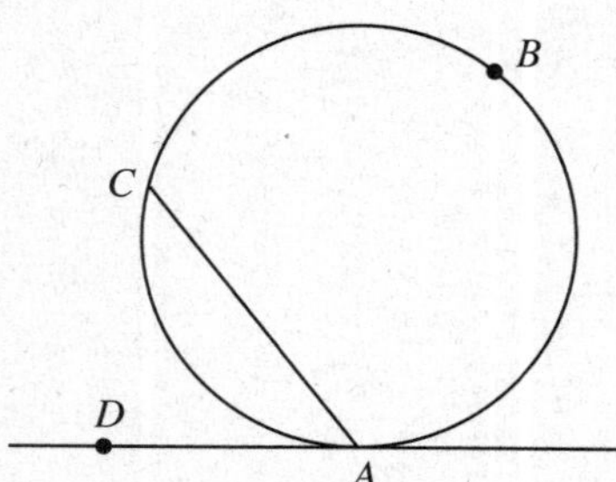

F. 220°
G. 110°
H. 140°
J. 70°
K. 35°

55. Which of the following is NOT equal to the others?

A. 0.015
B. 1.5×10^{-2}
C. 1.5%
D. $\frac{3}{200}$
E. (0.3)(0.005)

56. What is the simplified form of $\frac{6}{4 - \sqrt{2}}$?

F. $12 + 3\sqrt{2}$

G. $\frac{3\sqrt{2}}{2\sqrt{2} - 1}$

H. $\frac{4 + \sqrt{2}}{3}$

J. $\frac{12 + 3\sqrt{2}}{7}$

K. $\frac{24 + 6\sqrt{2}}{14}$

2 2 2 2 2 2 2 2 2 2 2

DO YOUR FIGURING HERE

57. Which of the following is equivalent to $|x - 5| > 2$?

A. $x > 7$
B. $x + 5 > 2$
C. $x < 3$
D. $x > 7$ or $x < 3$
E. $3 < x < 7$

58. In $\triangle ABC$ ($\angle C$ is the right angle), $\overline{CD}$ is drawn perpendicular to $\overline{AB}$. If $AD = 3$ and $BD = 12$, what is the length of $\overline{DC}$?

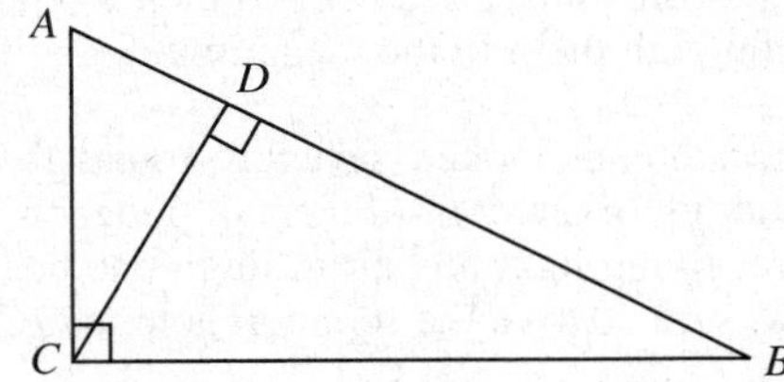

F. 6
G. $3\sqrt{5}$
H. $7\frac{1}{2}$
J. 9
K. $4\frac{1}{2}$

59. Which of the following expressions is NOT equal to cos (–512°) ?

A. cos 208°
B. –cos 28°
C. sin (–62°)
D. sin 152°
E. cos 152°

60. The gravitational attraction between two bodies varies inversely as the square of the distance between them. If the force of attraction is 64 pounds when the distance between the bodies is 9 feet, what is the force, in pounds, when they are 24 feet apart?

F. 5184
G. 729
H. 216
J. 24
K. 9

If there is still time remaining, you may review your answers.

READING TEST

35 MINUTES—40 QUESTIONS

Directions: This test consists of four passages, each followed by ten multiple-choice questions. Read each passage and then pick the best answer for each question. Fill in the spaces on your answer sheet that correspond to your choices. Refer to the passage as often as you wish while answering the questions.

Passage 1—Prose Fiction

This passage, adapted from the short story "Gaspar Ruiz: A Romantic Tale" by Joseph Conrad, takes place after Gaspar, a rebel soldier, has been accused of fighting for the Royalists.

Gaspar Ruiz, condemned to death as a deserter, was not thinking either of his native place or of his parents, to whom he had been a good son on account of the mildness of his character and the great strength of his limbs. The practical advantage of this last was made still more valuable to his father by his obedient disposition. Gaspar Ruiz had an acquiescent soul.

But it was stirred now to a sort of dim revolt by his dislike to die the death of a traitor. He was not a traitor. He said again to the sergeant: "You know I did not desert, Esteban. You know I remained behind amongst the trees with three others to keep the enemy back while the detachment was running away!"

Lieutenant Santierra, little more than a boy at the time, and unused as yet to the sanguinary imbecilities of a state of war, had lingered nearby, as if fascinated by the sight of these men who were to be shot presently—"for an example"—as the *Commandante* had said.

The sergeant, without deigning to look at the prisoner, addressed himself to the young officer with a superior smile.

"Ten Men would not have been enough to make him a prisoner, *mi tenente*. Moreover, the other three rejoined the detachment after dark. Why should he, unwounded and the strongest of them all, have failed to do so?"

"My strength is as nothing against a mounted man with a lasso," Gaspar Ruiz protested eagerly. "He dragged me behind his horse for half a mile."

At this excellent reason the sergeant only laughed contemptuously. The young officer hurried away after the *Commandante*.

Presently the adjutant of the castle came by. The sergeant learned from him that the condemned men would not be shot till sunset. He begged then to know what he was to do with them in the meantime.

The adjutant looked savagely round the courtyard and, pointing to the door of a small dungeon-like guardroom, receiving light and air through one heavily barred window, said: "Drive the scoundrels in there."

The sergeant, tightening his grip upon the stick he carried by virtue of his rank, executed this order with alacrity and zeal. He hit Gaspar Ruiz, whose movements were slow, over his head and shoulders. Gaspar Ruiz stood still for a moment, biting his lip thoughtfully—then followed the others without haste. The door was locked, and the adjutant carried off the key.

By noon the heat of that vaulted place had become unbearable. The prisoners crowded towards the window, begging their guards for a drop of water; but the soldiers remained lying in indolent attitudes wherever there was a little shade under a wall, while the sentry sat with his back against the door smoking a cigarette. Gaspar Ruiz had pushed his way to the window. His capacious chest needed more air than the others; his big face pressed close to the bars seemed to support the other faces crowding up for breath. From moaned entreaties they had passed to desperate cries. The tumultuous howling of those thirsty young men obliged a young officer just then crossing the courtyard to shout, "Why don't you give some water to these prisoners?"

The sergeant, with an air of surprised innocence, excused himself by the remark that all those men were condemned to die in a very few hours.

Lieutenant Santierra stamped his foot. "They are condemned to death, not to torture," he shouted. "Give them some water at once."

Impressed by this appearance of anger, the soldiers bestirred themselves, and the sentry, snatching up his musket, stood to attention.

But when a couple of buckets were found and filled from the well, it was discovered that they could not be passed through the bars, which were set too close. The soldiers were not equipped with canteens. A small tin cup was found, but its approach to the opening caused such a commotion, such yells of rage and pain in the vague mass of limbs behind the straining faces at the window, that Lieutenant Santierra cried out hurriedly, "No, no—you must open the door, sergeant."

The sergeant, shrugging his shoulders, explained that he had no right to open the door even if had the key. But he had not the key. The adjutant of the garrison kept the key. Those men were giving much unnecessary trouble, since they had to die at sunset in any case. Why they had not been shot early in the morning he could not understand.

Lieutenant Santierra kept his back studiously to the window. It was at his earnest solicitations that the *Commandante* had delayed the execution. This favor had been granted to him in consideration of his distinguished family and of his father's high position amongst the chiefs of the Republican party. Lieutenant Santierra believed that the commanding General would visit the fort sometime in the afternoon, and he ingenuously hoped that his naive intercession would induce that severe man to pardon some, at least, of those criminals. In the revulsion of his feeling his interference stood revealed now as guilty and futile meddling.

1. Based on information in the passage, Gaspar Ruiz is alleged to have committed treason because he:

   A. ran away at the height of a battle.
   B. stayed up all night.
   C. got separated from his detachment.
   D. lassoed a soldier riding on a horse.

2. The narrator's assertion that Gaspar had been a "good son" (line 3) is based on which of Gaspar's characteristics?

   F. His willingness to work hard
   G. A strong desire to help others
   H. An agreeable nature
   J. His ambition to be a success in life

3. Considering the events in the entire passage, Sergeant Esteban's attitude toward Lieutenant Santierra can best be described as a combination of:

   A. discretion and prudence.
   B. admiration and respect.
   C. cynicism and contempt.
   D. antagonism and insolence.

4. That Gaspar and the other men are to be shot "for an example" (lines 17–18) suggests which of the following about the *Commandante*?

   F. He wants to raise the morale of his troops.
   G. He is concerned that other soldiers may try to desert.
   H. He is uncertain about Gaspar's guilt.
   J. He thinks that Gaspar and the others need to be taught a lesson.

5. The *Commandante* delays the executions at the behest of Lieutenant Santierra because:

   A. of Santierra's connections.
   B. Santierra made a strong and convincing argument.
   C. he is not convinced that the men are guilty.
   D. he wanted to impress the commanding general.

6. All of the following characters are represented as harsh, brutal military men EXCEPT:

   F. Esteban.
   G. Lieutenant Santierra.
   H. the adjutant.
   J. the *Commandante*.

7. Based on the passage, it is reasonable to infer that the guards assigned to watching the prisoners were:

   A. fearful of the men locked up in the guard-house.
   B. indifferent to the suffering of the men.
   C. confident that Gaspar and the other men were guilty.
   D. anxious to release the men as soon as they were given the order to do so.

8. The details and events in the passage suggest that Lieutenant Santierra:

   F. has quickly grown accustomed to military life.
   G. has won the respect of his commanding officer.
   H. will soon receive a promotion.
   J. has values that differ from those of the other men in his detachment.

9. It can be reasonably be inferred that Santierra feels "guilty" (line 97) because:

   A. his interference in the case caused the prisoners to suffer needlessly.
   B. he has failed to win a pardon for the condemned men.
   C. he lost his temper in ordering water for the men locked inside the guardhouse.
   D. of his inadequacy as an officer and a leader of men.

10. Which of the following events does the passage suggest is the immediate result of Santierra's hurrying away (line 30)?

    F. The sergeant laughs contemptuously.
    G. The adjutant informs the sergeant that the prisoners will die at sunset.
    H. The adjutant utters, "Drive the scoundrels in there."
    J. The sergeant hits Gaspar on the head and shoulders with a stick.

GO ON TO THE NEXT PAGE.

Passage 2—Social Studies

This passage is adapted from an article published by the Naval Historical Center, an agency affiliated with the U.S. Department of the Navy.

Though it now seems merely a folk-memory, the Influenza epidemic of 1918 was the third greatest plague in the history of mankind. The most devastating epidemic since the Middle Ages, it took over 21 million lives and affected over half the world's population. Logically, one would think that an epidemic of this proportion would have left an indelible imprint on the American people. In the United States alone, 550,000 died within the 16-week period from October 1918 to February 1919. Yet, it never inspired awe, not in 1918 and not since.

As one searches for explanation as to why Americans took little notice of the epidemic and then quickly forgot what they did notice, a mystery and a paradox emerge. The mystery was the complacency the American people displayed as a group toward the epidemic. The paradox was the common individual's clear acknowledgment that the epidemic was the most influential experience of his life.

To understand this lack of attention, one must look at the years preceding the outbreak. Lethal epidemics were not as unexpected and therefore not as impressive as they might be in the more technologically advanced surroundings of today. The terror of typhoid, yellow fever, diphtheria, and cholera were well within living memory. Most Americans had lived through the typhoid and small pox epidemics of 1876 and 1890.

Beyond this complacent acceptance of epidemics as a part of life, one must rely almost entirely on speculation in finding further answers.

If the "Spanish Influenza" had settled down as a permanent source of misery in the country, then possibly Americans might have granted this variety of the flu the notoriety it deserved. But the devastation came, scooped up its victims, and all but disappeared within a few short months. If the flu had been a disease that evoked a memory of terror, Americans might have panicked. This complete absence of fear, which until 1918 had inflicted no more than a few uncomfortable days of cold-like symptoms, is reflected in a statement by A.J. McLaughlin of the U.S. Public Health Service: "It is remarkable to see the placidity by which the people have generally taken the almost sudden loss of thousands of lives."

The nature of the disease and its contagiousness encouraged forgetfulness. The swiftness of its spread and its ability to flourish then disappear before it had any real effect on the economy made it easier for people to accept, despite killing 3 percent of the nation's population.

World War I perhaps best explained the relative indifference to the pandemic. The 5 Nov 1918 issue of the *New York Times* suggested that "war had taught the people to think in terms other than individual interest and safety, and death itself had become so familiar as to lose its grimness." Such an explanation may seem quite naive, but most of those who died were young adults of the same age as those lost in combat. The obituary columns of influenza victims became one and the same blur with the war casualty list.

Influenza seemed unimportant compared with the news on the front pages of the city's newspapers. Suffragette agitation was rising as the Senate vote on the rights for women drew near, and Eugene V. Debs was on his way to jail for allegedly violating the Espionage Act. On the last day of August 1918, Babe Ruth made the headlines as he pitched a three-hitter and banged out a long double to win the American League pennant for the Boston Red Sox. It was apparently of no consequence that on the same day the first cases of flu were recognized among Navy personnel in Boston and 26 sailors died.

The interweaving of the war and pandemic seems almost to resemble a pattern of insanity. On 11 Sept 1918 Washington officials disclosed that the Spanish Influenza had arrived in the city. On the next day 13 million men, precisely the age most likely to die of the flu, lined up all over the United States and crammed into city halls, post offices, and schools to register for the draft. It was a gala flag-waving affair everywhere including Boston where 96,000 registered then sneezed and coughed on one another.

The epidemic did not kill the ranks of the famous and powerful. Perhaps if Woodrow Wilson or someone of like stature had died, the world might have remembered. It killed the daughter of General Edwards of the 26th Division of the American Expeditionary Forces, but not the general. It killed the daughter of Samuel Gompers, president of the American Federation of Labor, but left America's most powerful labor leaders alive.

On the level of organizations and institutions, the Spanish Influenza had little impact. It did spur great activity among medical scientists and their institutions, but this was the single great exception. It did not lead to great changes in government, armies, and corporations. It had little influence on the course of political and military events because it affected all sides equally.

Carla R. Morrisey, RN, BSN

11. It can reasonably be inferred that the primary function of the first sentence (lines 1–3) is to:

    A. suggest that folklore is a second-rate medium for recording significant historical events.
    B. emphasize the author's surprise about the place in history of the influenza epidemic of 1918.
    C. suggest that the seriousness of the 1918 epidemic has been overrated.
    D. caution the reader that the account of the influenza epidemic in the rest of the passage is not altogether factual.

12. The phrase "never inspired awe" (lines 9–10), most likely means that:

    F. due to poor communication, specific facts about the epidemic were unavailable.
    G. Americans lacked the ability to grasp the seriousness of the epidemic.
    H. Americans somehow remained relatively insensitive to the gravity of the epidemic.
    J. the death toll in America paled next to the number of deaths abroad.

13. The main function of the second paragraph (lines 11–18) in relation to the passage as a whole is to:

    A. contrast the epidemic's effect on Americans with its effects on citizens of other countries.
    B. shift the passage to a discussion of the mysterious causes of the epidemic.
    C. criticize America's indifference toward the catastrophic epidemic.
    D. provide a framework for comprehending the people's response to the epidemic.

14. Based on the passage, which of the following statements best explains the mystery of America's "complacency" (line 14) toward the epidemic?

    F. In 1918, people were generally accustomed to periods of large-scale sickness and death.
    G. America was spared the worst of the epidemic.
    H. Compared to other epidemics, the 1918 influenza was relatively mild.
    J. Few Americans were personally affected.

15. By using the phrase "technologically advanced" (line 22), the author expresses her belief that:

    A. America is better prepared today to battle a deadly flu epidemic than it was in 1918.
    B. technology played almost no part in the lives of Americans in 1918.
    C. the advent of technology has reduced the likelihood of a deadly flu epidemic today.
    D. advanced technology could have mitigated the effects of the epidemic.

16. Which of the following does NOT reasonably reflect the function of the fourth paragraph (lines 27–29) in relation to the passage as a whole?

    F. To alert the reader that the discussion is about to shift from factual to hypothetical.
    G. To summarize briefly the main point of the previous three paragraphs.
    H. To concede that it is difficult to pinpoint the specific reason for America's reaction to the 1918 epidemic.
    J. To provide evidence that contradicts an important point made earlier in the passage.

17. The tone of the passage suggests that the author's personal view of America's attitude toward the influenza epidemic of 1918 is that of:

    A. admiration that the people did not panic or overreact to the crisis.
    B. astonishment over America's apathy.
    C. puzzlement that the epidemic failed to evoke a more robust response.
    D. disgust over Americans' indifference toward a terrible calamity.

18. Based on the passage, which of the following best describes the spread of influenza across the United States during 1918–1919?

    F. It swept across the land from east to west.
    G. It progressed much like the 19th century epidemics of typhoid, cholera, and other diseases.
    H. The symptoms of infection came and went relatively quickly.
    J. The victims of the disease were mostly children and old people.

19. According to the passage, the single greatest benefit that emerged from the 1918 influenza epidemic was:

    A. a flurry of medical research.
    B. an increase of enlistments into the armed forces.
    C. more enthusiasm for the United States to enter World War I.
    D. the recognition of America's ability to endure great hardship.

20. The primary purpose of the last two paragraphs of the passage (lines 80–94) is to make the point that the influenza epidemic:

    F. had no effect on celebrities or people in power.
    G. took its greatest toll on ordinary people.
    H. victimized people at random.
    J. preyed mostly on people serving in the military.

GO ON TO THE NEXT PAGE.

Passage 3—Humanities

This passage is excerpted from "The Parisian Stage," an essay written for a London newspaper late in the nineteenth century by the American author Henry James.

It is impossible to spend many weeks in Paris without observing that the theater plays a very important part in French civilization; and it is impossible to go much to the theater without finding it a copious source of instruction as to French ideas, manners, and philosophy. I supposed that I had a certain acquaintance with these complex phenomena, but during the last couple of months I have occupied a great many orchestra chairs, and in the merciless glare of the footlights I have read a great many of my old convictions with a new distinctness. I have had at the same time one of the greatest attainable pleasures; for, surely, among the pleasures that one deliberately seeks and pays for, none beguiles the heavy human consciousness so totally as a first-rate evening at the *Théâtre Français*. It was the poet Gray, I believe, who said that his idea of heaven was to lie all day on a sofa and read novels. He, poor man, spoke while *Clarissa Harlowe* was still the fashion, and a novel was synonymous with an eternity. A much better heaven, I think, would be to sit all night on a theater seat (if they were only a little better stuffed) listening to Delaunay, watching Got, or falling in love with Mademoiselle Desclée.

An acted play is a novel intensified; it realizes what the novel suggests, and, by paying a liberal tribute to the senses, anticipates your possible complaint that your entertainment is of the meager sort styled "intellectual." The stage throws into relief the best gifts of the French mind, and the *Théâtre Français* is not only the most amiable but the most characteristic of French institutions. I often think of the inevitable first sensations there of the "cultivated foreigner," let him be as stuffed with hostile prejudices as you please. He leaves the theater crying, Ah, France is the civilized nation *par excellence*. Such art, such finish, such grace, such taste, such a marvelous exhibition of applied science, are the mark of a chosen people, and these delightful talents imply the existence of every virtue. His enthusiasm may be short and make few converts; but certainly during his stay in Paris, whatever may be his mind in the intervals, he never listens to the traditional *toc-toc-toc* which sounds up the curtains in the Rue Richelieu's theaters, without murmuring, as he squares himself in his chair and grasps his opera glasses, that, after all, the French are prodigiously great!

I shall never forget a certain evening in the early summer when, after a busy, dusty, weary day in the streets, staring at charred ruins and finding in all things a vague aftertaste of gunpowder, I repaired to the *Théâtre Français* to listen to Molière's *Mariage Forcé* and Alfred de Musset's *Il ne Faut Jurer de Rien*. The entertainment seemed to my travel-tired brain what a perfumed bath is to one's weary limbs, and I sat in a sort of languid ecstasy of contemplation and wonder—wonder that the tender flower of poetry and art should bloom again so bravely over blood-stained pavements and fresh made-up graves.

Molière is played at the *Théâtre Français* as he deserves to be—one can hardly say more—with the most ungrudging breadth, exuberance and verve, and yet with a kind of academic harmony and solemnity. Molière, if he ever drops a kindly glance on Monsieur Got and Monsieur Coquelin, must be the happiest of immortals. To be read two hundred years after your death is something; but to be acted is better, at least when your name does not happen to be Shakespeare and your interpreter the great American (or, indeed, the great British) tragedian. Such powerful, natural, wholesome comedy as that of Molière certainly never was conceived, and the actors I have just named give it its utmost force. I have often wondered that, in the keen and lucid atmosphere which Molière casts about him, some of the effusions of his modern successors should live for an hour. Alfred de Musset, however, need fear no neighborhood, and his *Il ne Faut Jurer*, after Molière's tremendous farce, was like fine sherry after strong ale. Got plays in it a small part, which he makes a great one, and Delaunay, the silver-tongued, the ever-young, and that plain robust person and admirable artist, Madame Nathalie, and that divinely ingenuous ingénue, Mademoiselle Reichemberg. It would be a poor compliment to the performance to say that it might have been mistaken for real life. If real life were a tithe as charming it would be a merry world.

21. Which of the following descriptions most accurately and completely represents this passage?
    A. The author's fond recollections of his experience in Paris
    B. An evocative and affectionate appreciation of French theater
    C. A detailed and objective critique of the *Théâtre Français*
    D. An abstract and scholarly appraisal of Molière's plays

22. All of the following are clearly identified in the passage as actors EXCEPT:
    F. Delaunay.
    G. Got.
    H. de Musset.
    J. Reichemberg.

23. Which of the following quotations best expresses the main point of the passage?
    A. " . . .in the merciless glare of the footlights I have read a great many of my old convictions with a new distinctness."
    B. "An acted play is a novel intensified."
    C. "The stage throws into relief the best gifts of the French mind."
    D. "Such powerful, natural, wholesome comedy as that of Molière certainly was never conceived."

24. As it is used in line 17, the word *poor* most nearly means:.
    F. deprived.
    G. poverty-stricken.
    H. ill.
    J. lazy.

25. It can be most reasonably concluded from the author's allusions to conditions in Paris (lines 45–56) that:
    A. it was difficult for him to get around in the city.
    B. the city was undergoing a construction boom.
    C. the city suffered from the aftereffects of war.
    D. a major fire had destroyed most of the city.

26. Given the information in the passage, one can infer all of the following about Molière EXCEPT that:
    F. his works serve as a model for other playwrights.
    G. his plays were meant to provoke laughter.
    H. as a playwright, he was not as great as Shakespeare.
    J. he was a founder of the *Théâtre Français*.

27. It can be inferred from the passage that the author most highly valued which of the following about the theater?
    A. Intellectual stimulation
    B. Escaping from the dirty, crowded streets of Paris
    C. Sitting in a comfortable seat
    D. Learning about French culture

28. During his evening at the theater to see a play by Molière and a play by de Musset, which of the following features of the performances does the author observe?
    F. The superiority of Moliere's play
    G. The beauty of the language
    H. The realism of the performances
    J. The audience's appreciation

29. By asserting that Molière "deserves" (line 58) to be played at the *Théâtre Français*, the author implies that:
    A. the best of French plays should be performed in the best of French theaters.
    B. Molière's plays should be performed only in large halls like the *Théâtre Français*.
    C. the tradition of performing Molière at the *Théâtre Français* should continue.
    D. Molière expected his plays to be performed at the *Théâtre Français* after his death.

30. Which of the following best describes the reactions of a hypothetical "cultivated foreigner" (line 32) who sees a play at the *Théâtre Français* for the first time?
    F. France must be envied by cultured people everywhere.
    G. To attend a play in Paris is extraordinarily eye-opening.
    H. France epitomizes refinement in art and culture.
    J. The French theater causes people to lose their prejudices.

GO ON TO THE NEXT PAGE.

Passage 4—Natural Science

This passage, from a publication titled "The Health Effects of Caffeine," discusses the complexities of governing the use of caffeine in food and beverages.

The use of beverages that contain caffeine has been debated for centuries. In almost every part of the world where coffee and tea have been available, religious or government leaders have tried to ban or restrict its use. All such attempts, until the present time, lacked scientific credibility.

New studies linking caffeine use to central nervous system problems and birth defects in test animals have prompted scientists and policy makers in the U.S. to reconsider caffeine's regulatory status. This is a complex task, however, because caffeine is regulated under three different sections of the Federal Food, Drug, and Cosmetic Act. It is a natural ingredient in coffee and tea, a food additive in soft drinks, and an added ingredient in over-the-counter drugs.

Foods containing any poisonous or hazardous substance are defined as adulterated and prohibited by the Food and Drug Act. However, foods which naturally contain harmful substances may be permitted if the amount of the substance does not ordinarily injure health. Thus, foods containing caffeine, like coffee and tea, are approved despite caffeine's adverse health effects at high dose levels.

As a food additive, caffeine is regulated as a "generally recognized as safe" (GRAS) substance. Because of this regulatory status, food processors are not required to prove caffeine's safety before adding it to their products. Instead, caffeine's long and widespread history of use is considered sufficient proof of safety. The Food and Drug Administration (FDA) has published rules which limit the amount of caffeine that can be added to foods.

Caffeine is also an ingredient in many over-the-counter drug preparations. The Food and Drug Act specifies that all drug ingredients must be safe and effective for their intended use. Caffeine is an effective stimulant which is why it is added to pain relievers and cold remedies. When used as directed in these medicines, caffeine is safe and presents no health hazards to the vast majority of consumers.

Recently, a committee of the Federation of American Societies for Experimental Biology reviewed all the scientific evidence on caffeine. Based on caffeine's stimulant properties, this advisory group recommended to the FDA that caffeine be removed from the so-called GRAS list of food chemicals. As a result of this and petitions from other groups, the FDA proposed new regulations for caffeine use. If these proposals are adopted, caffeine will be removed from the GRAS list. The FDA will also amend the current rule which governs the mandatory use of caffeine in certain soft drinks.

Removing caffeine from the GRAS list would have little immediate impact on consumers. This action would require food processors to gather additional scientific evidence to prove caffeine is safe. During the time needed to conduct proper studies, caffeine would still be available for use. However, if food processors fail to provide this required information, or find additional evidence that caffeine is harmful, the FDA could take action to ban the use of caffeine as a food additive.

Current regulations state that caffeine must be an ingredient in "cola" and "pepper" flavored soft drinks. About 10 percent of the caffeine in these products is obtained naturally from cola nuts, the chief flavoring agent. The remaining 90 percent is added caffeine.

Current rules do not require added caffeine other than that naturally present in cola nuts. Added caffeine is an optional ingredient which must be listed on the product label. The caffeine derived from cola nuts does not have to be listed among the product ingredients.

Under the new FDA proposal, both natural and added caffeine would become optional ingredients in cola and pepper soft drinks. Thus, manufacturers could make an essentially caffeine-free product by decaffeinating cola nuts and avoiding added caffeine. The new proposal would also require that any caffeine, whether added or natural, be listed on the ingredient label.

These proposed regulations would not affect the use of caffeine in non-cola soft drinks or in over-the-counter drugs.

American Council on Science and Health

31. Based on information in the passage, the main function of the Food and Drug Administration is to:
    A. make the rules governing the use of caffeine in food products.
    B. force soft-drink manufacturers to keep caffeine in colas and pepper-flavored drinks to a minimum.
    C. make laws that must be followed by food manufacturers.
    D. control caffeine in food products and in over-the-counter drugs.

32. As used in line 17, the word *adulterated* means:
    F. prohibited.
    G. unlawful.
    H. lethal.
    J. dangerous.

33. Despite its apparent hazards, caffeine has not been banned from food products because:
    A. it has a long and honorable history of use.
    B. consumers can avoid caffeine by reading ingredient labels.
    C. small quantities have never been proved harmful.
    D. food manufacturers claim that the caffeine controversy has been exaggerated.

34. "Generally recognized as safe" (lines 24–25) is:
    F. a description of caffeine used by manufacturers of food products.
    G. an official government designation applied to any number of food products.
    H. a phrase called "misleading" by the Federation of American Societies for Experimental Biology.
    J. the FDA's stamp of approval that appears on pain relievers and cold remedies containing caffeine.

35. According to the passage, which of the following is most likely to occur if caffeine is taken off the GRAS list?
    A. All soft drinks will be caffeine-free.
    B. Manufacturers will stop adding caffeine to food products.
    C. All food products containing caffeine will be labeled with a warning to consumers.
    D. Manufacturers of food products will be required to prove that caffeine is harmless.

36. Based on the passage, when changes are planned in federal food and drug laws, the government must consider the interests of all of the following groups EXCEPT:
    F. pharmacists who dispense over-the-counter drugs.
    G. manufacturers of food products.
    H. consumer groups.
    J. scientists and other researchers.

37. Soft drink manufacturers prefer to use the natural caffeine found in cola nuts in their products because:
    A. caffeine makes drinks more flavorful.
    B. consumers enjoy the lift they get from caffeine.
    C. caffeine helps to keep the drink from spoiling.
    D. it is one of the least expensive food additives.

38. According to the passage, past attempts to ban drinks containing caffeine have failed because:
    F. people refused to change their habits.
    G. the tea, coffee, and soft drink industries were too strong.
    H. opponents of caffeine lacked scientific data to back up their objections.
    J. lawmakers could not agree on how to enforce anti-caffeine regulations.

39. Which of the following properties of caffeine is not indicated by information in the passage?
    A. It is addictive.
    B. It has been shown to be hazardous to laboratory animals.
    C. It is found in nature.
    D. It makes sick people feel better.

40. The author of the passage seems primarily concerned with:
    F. procedures for amending the Federal Food, Drug, and Cosmetic Act.
    G. the future of caffeine in foods.
    H. warning readers about the hazards of caffeine.
    J. the need for more scientific investigation of the effects of caffeine.

STOP

If there is still time remaining, you may review your answers.

4 4 4 4 4 4 4 4 4 4 4

SCIENCE REASONING TEST

35 MINUTES—40 QUESTIONS

Directions: This test consists of several distinct passages. Each passage is followed by a number of multiple-choice questions based on the passage. Study the passage, and then select the best answer to each question. You are allowed to reread the passage. Record your answer by blackening the appropriate space on the answer sheet.

Passage 1

The charts below show the composition of the average American diet as it exists (dark bar) and as recommended by the National Research Council (light bar) in 1987. (These recommendations have since been challenged, but their validity has not been decisively disproved.) Chart I gives the total intake in grams per day of each nutrient class. Chart II gives the energy distribution among the nutrients, the fraction of total kilocalories in each nutrient. Chart III gives the fraction of each nutrient by weight.

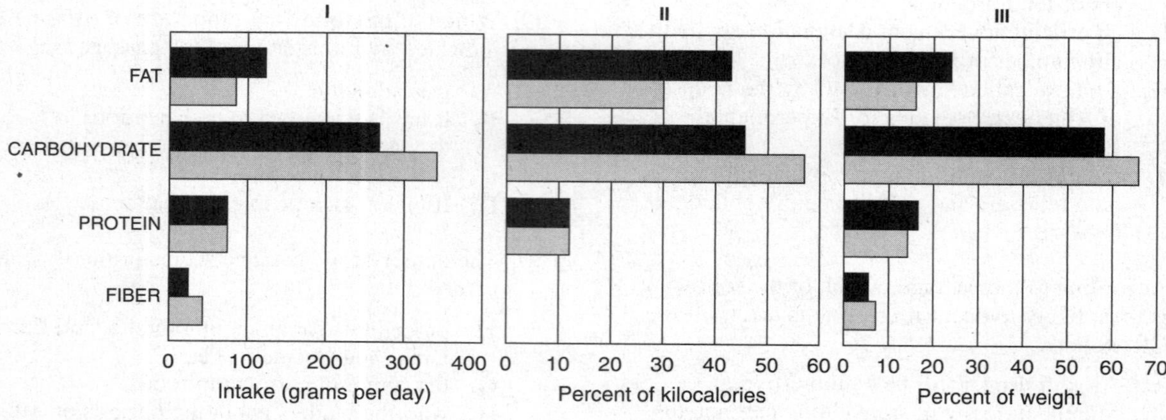

1. If the recommendations of the National Research Council were followed, people would eat:

   A. more protein and less fiber.
   B. more protein and less fat.
   C. more carbohydrate and less fat.
   D. more fiber and less protein.

2. Comparison of the charts shows that:

   F. most of our food energy comes from proteins.
   G. we now get much more of our energy from carbohydrates than from fats.
   H. we cannot increase our energy intake by eating more fiber.
   J. the quantities of fats and carbohydrates in our present diet are approximately equal.

3. According to these recommendations, what comment can be made about the present American diet?

   A. It is overloaded with carbohydrates.
   B. It has too much fiber.
   C. It does not have enough fat.
   D. It contains the proper amounts of proteins.

4. If the recommendations for a changed diet were followed, our diet would have about:

   F. four times as much carbohydrate as fat.
   G. two and a half times as much carbohydrate as fat.
   H. equal amounts of carbohydrate and fat.
   J. nearly twice as much carbohydrate as fat.

5. Comparison of the percent by weight of the different nutrients in the diet and the percent of energy each supplies shows that:

   A. 1 gram of fat supplies more energy than 1 gram of carbohydrate.
   B. 1 gram of carbohydrate supplies more energy than 1 gram of protein.
   C. 1 gram of protein supplies about three times as much energy as 1 gram of fiber.
   D. 1 gram of carbohydrate supplies more energy than 1 gram of fat.

Passage 2

A bacteriologist is investigating the use of glucose by a type of bacterium as a source of energy in spore formation.

Experiment 1

The bacteria are grown in a nutrient solution containing a supply of glucose. When the glucose has been largely depleted, the contents of each cell shrink away from the cell wall and form a spore, which is highly resistant to environmental damage of all kinds.

Experiment 2

A culture of the bacteria is grown in a medium containing little glucose. The bacteria use the glucose as they grow, but do not form spores when the glucose has been depleted.

Experiment 3

A culture is grown in a medium containing ample glucose, but the cells are removed while there is still plenty of glucose in the medium. They are placed in distilled water, and form spores in about 13 hours.

Experiment 4

As in Experiment 3, cells are transferred from a glucose-rich medium to distilled water. If glucose is added to the water 5 hours later, the cells never form spores. If glucose is added 10 hours after the transfer, spores form 3 hours later.

6. Comparison of Experiments 1 and 2 shows that:

   F. glucose is necessary for the bacteria to grow.
   G. the process of spore formation needs a good supply of glucose.
   H. bacteria can protect themselves against unfavorable conditions by forming spores.
   J. spore formation is inhibited by large concentrations of glucose.

7. A reasonable hypothesis from Experiment 3 is that:

   A. distilled water promotes the formation of spores.
   B. distilled water retards the formation of spores, but does not prevent it.
   C. bacterial cells store enough glucose to form spores.
   D. bacterial cells are able to form spores without any source of glucose.

8. Experiment 1 indicates that spore formation is stimulated by deprivation of glucose. Considering the results of Experiment 4, how long must this deprivation continue?

   F. Less than 5 hours
   G. Somewhere between 5 and 10 hours
   H. More than 10 hours
   J. At least 13 hours

9. The results of Experiments 3 and 4 show that withholding glucose for 10 hours:

   A. causes spores to form 3 hours later.
   B. delays the formation of spores for 3 hours.
   C. speeds up the formation of spores by 5 hours.
   D. has no effect at all on the formation of spores.

10. Which of the following experiments would NOT be useful in efforts to learn more about the way bacteria use sugars in spore formation?

    F. Repeat Experiment 4 adding glucose to the water at various times after transferring the bacteria to distilled water.
    G. Repeat Experiments 3 and 4 using bread molds instead of bacteria as the spore-forming organism.
    H. Repeat Experiments 1 and 2 using other kinds of sugar than glucose as energy sources.
    J. Repeat Experiment 2 using different concentrations of glucose.

11. According to these experiments, what condition must be met in order for this type of bacterium to form spores?

    A. A good supply of glucose in the medium, followed by a period in which there is little glucose
    B. A steady supply of glucose in high concentration
    C. A prolonged period of glucose deprivation
    D. A sudden increase in the concentration of glucose in the medium

GO ON TO THE NEXT PAGE.

Passage 3

The graph below represents the number of boys born per thousand girls in the United States for a period of years (♂ = males; ♀ = females).

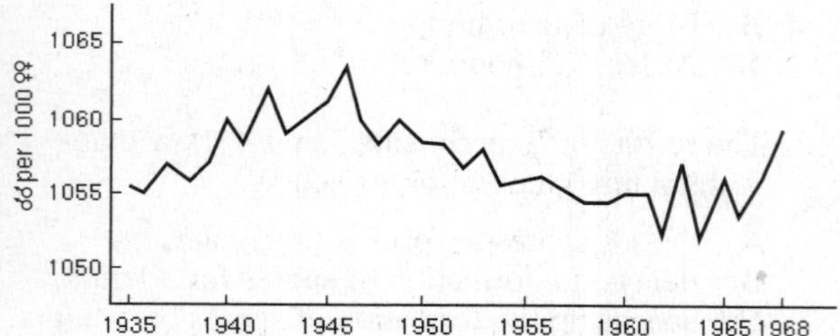

The following graph represents the sex ratio at birth as a function of the ages of the parents. (Sex ratio is the fraction of all newborn babies that are male.)

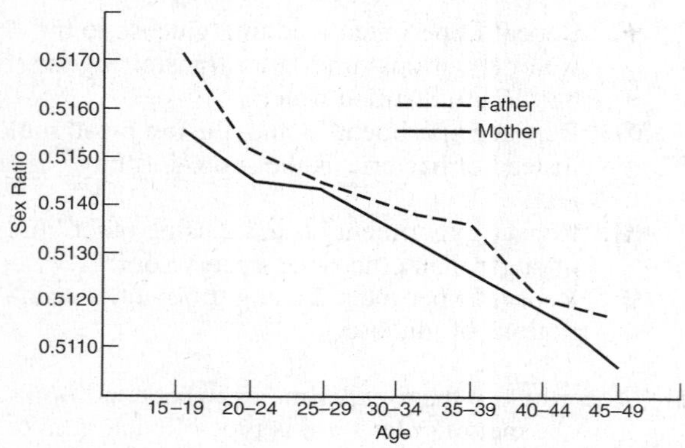

12. The sex ratio in 1946 was:
   - **F.** 1063/2063
   - **G.** 1063/2000
   - **H.** 1063/2
   - **J.** 1063/1052

13. Which general statement is true?
   - **A.** There has been a steady decline in the proportion of male births.
   - **B.** At all times, more boys than girls are born.
   - **C.** The total number of male births decreases with the age of the parents.
   - **D.** Younger parents have more children than older ones.

14. A couple in their early twenties decide that they would like to have a girl. Would it be a good idea for them to wait five years?
   - **F.** No. The probability of having a boy goes up substantially in those years.
   - **G.** Yes. The probability of having a girl goes up substantially during those years.
   - **H.** No. The increased probability of having a girl is too small to make much difference.
   - **J.** Yes. The probability of having a boy goes down substantially during those years.

15. The sex ratio increased during the war years 1940 to 1946, and started to rise again during the Vietnam War in 1967. This increase has been noticed during war years in other countries and during other wars. A possible explanation is that:
   - **A.** many men are killed in wars, so the number of male babies increases to compensate.
   - **B.** as younger men die in the war, more babies are fathered by older men.
   - **C.** prolonged periods of sexual abstinence favor the production of the kinds of sperm that produce male babies.
   - **D.** this may be merely a statistical accident with no real significance.

16. Is it the age of the mother or of the father that is most significant in determining the sex ratio?
   - **F.** The father, since the line for the father lies always above the line for the mother.
   - **G.** The mother, since the line for the mother lies always below that for the father.
   - **H.** They affect the result equally, since both follow the same pattern of decrease with age.
   - **J.** It is impossible to tell from the graphs because people generally tend to marry spouses of about their own age.

Passage 4

The chart below gives the number of diagnosed cases of diabetes in the United States from the years 1958 to 1995, and projections for total cases in 2000 and 2025.

The Diabetes Explosion

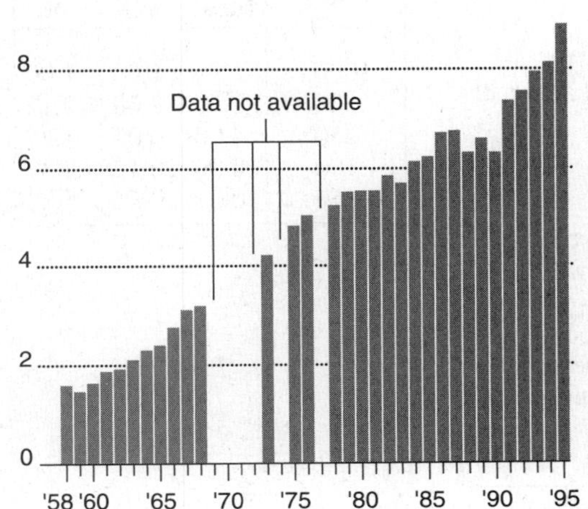

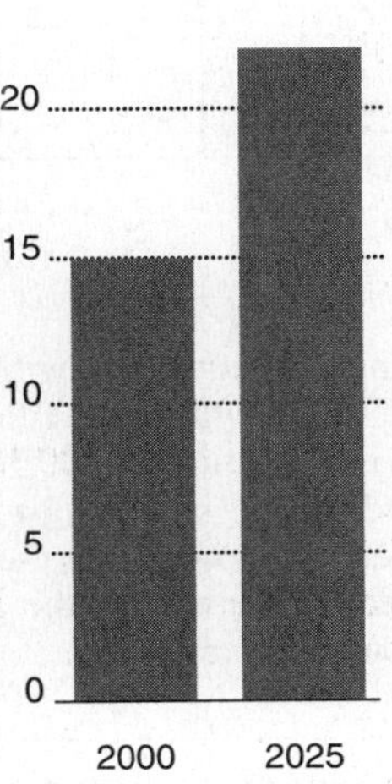

17. Between 1960 and 1980, the number of diagnosed cases of diabetes in the United States increased by:

    A. 1 million.
    B. 2 million.
    C. 4 million.
    D. 6 million.

18. The biggest annual increase in the number of diagnosed cases occurred in:

    F. 1994.
    G. 1991.
    H. 1986.
    J. 1973.

19. The data projected that the number of undiagnosed cases in the year 2000 would be about:

    A. 15 million.
    B. 13 million.
    C. 10 million.
    D. 5 million.

20. An important possible source of error in any conclusion reached from the graphs is that:

    F. data from several years are unavailable.
    G. methods of diagnosis may have improved over the years.
    H. some years show very little increase, while in others, the increase is large.
    J. there is no clue as to the reason for the increase.

21. One assumption made in preparing this chart is that:

    A. there is some increasing factor in the American lifestyle that promotes the development of diabetes.
    B. the trend to increase the incidence of diabetes in the American population will continue for some years.
    C. the health of Americans is increasingly at risk from diabetes.
    D. undiagnosed cases of diabetes are on the increase.

GO ON TO THE NEXT PAGE.

4 4 4 4 4 4 4 4 4 4 4

Passage 5

The ideal gas law is a rule for determining approximately the relationship between volume, pressure, and temperature of a gas. Experiments were done to determine how closely real gases obey this law. These are the gases that were tested, with their respective molecular weights:

Gas	Formula	Molecular weight
helium	He	4
nitrogen	N_2	28
carbon dioxide	CO_2	44
xenon	Xe	54
sulfur dioxide	SO_2	64

Experiment 1

A 1-liter steel cylinder is equipped with a pressure gauge and a thermometer. The cylinder is filled with various gases, in turn, at a temperature of 200 K (–73.2°C). The gases are heated and the pressure is measured at various temperatures. The chart below shows the pressure as calculated from the ideal gas law, and the actual pressures measured at various temperatures.

Temperature (kelvins)	Pressure (atmospheres)					
	Ideal	He	N_2	CO_2	Xe	SO_2
200	1.00	1.00	1.00	1.00	1.00	1.00
500	2.50	2.50	2.51	2.52	2.52	2.54
800	4.00	4.00	4.02	4.04	4.05	4.08
1100	5.50	5.50	5.53	5.56	5.57	5.62
1400	7.00	7.00	7.03	7.07	7.09	7.16
1700	8.50	8.50	8.54	8.59	8.62	8.70
2000	10.00	10.00	10.05	10.11	10.14	10.24

Experiment 2

The same gases are inserted, in turn, into a 1-liter cylinder fitted with a piston that can be pushed in to decrease the volume of the gas, thus increasing the pressure. The cylinder is kept in a water bath that keeps the temperature constant. The pressure is measured at various volumes. As before, the value calculated from the ideal gas law is also listed in the table.

Volume (cm^3)	Pressure (atmospheres)					
	Ideal	He	N_2	CO_2	Xe	SO_2
1000	1.00	1.00	1.00	1.00	1.00	1.00
500	2.00	2.00	2.12	1.98	1.97	1.96
250	4.00	4.02	4.25	3.93	3.85	3.82
100	10.00	10.12	12.32	9.01	8.86	8.55
50	20.00	20.52	25.84	15.87	15.28	13.87

22. If a quantity of gas is heated at constant volume, what might result from using the ideal gas law to predict the pressure?
    - **F.** An incorrect and useless prediction.
    - **G.** A small overestimation.
    - **H.** A small underestimation.
    - **J.** A minor and unpredictable error.

23. Of the gases measured, which behaves LEAST like an ideal gas?
    - **A.** Helium, always
    - **B.** Nitrogen, always
    - **C.** Sulfur dioxide always
    - **D.** It depends on the nature of the experiment

24. What is the most probable explanation of the fact that no deviation from the ideal gas pressure was found when the volume of helium was reduced from 1000 cm^3 to 500 cm^3?
    - **F.** Helium maintains its pressure until its volume is reduced more substantially.
    - **G.** There was an unpredicted drop in the temperature during the experiment.
    - **H.** Measurements were made only to the nearest hundredth of an atmosphere.
    - **J.** Helium is an ideal gas at moderate pressures.

25. As the volume is decreased at constant temperature, what would result from using the ideal gas law to predict the pressure?
    - **A.** Constant minor overestimation.
    - **B.** Either overestimation or underestimation depending on the gas being studied.
    - **C.** Constant underestimation.
    - **D.** Unpredictably, either overestimation or underestimation.

26. Why does the first row of the data for both experiments show a value of 1.00 atmosphere regardless of which gas was used?
    - **F.** Every experiment was started arbitrarily at ordinary atmospheric pressure.
    - **G.** At low pressure, all gases obey the ideal gas law.
    - **H.** Deviations from the ideal gas law are very small at low pressure, and were not detected.
    - **J.** This is pure coincidence; that value might be different if other gases were tried.

27. Which of the following hypotheses is suggested by the data?
    - **A.** The ideal gas law gives the most accurate predictions at high temperatures and pressures.
    - **B.** The ideal gas law always gives a good approximation of pressure.
    - **C.** As a gas is compressed at constant temperature, its pressure is inversely proportional to its volume.
    - **D.** At constant volume, gases with the smallest molecules obey the ideal gas law most closely.

Passage 6

If the highest possible pile is made of a quantity of loose material, the sides of the pile form an angle with the horizontal called the *angle of repose*. This is the largest angle at which the material can remain without having some of it slide down.

The angles of repose of various materials were measured with the apparatus shown in the sketch below. The material, such as sand, is placed in a hopper and then allowed to flow through an opening until it piles up below. The angle of the side of the pile is then measured.

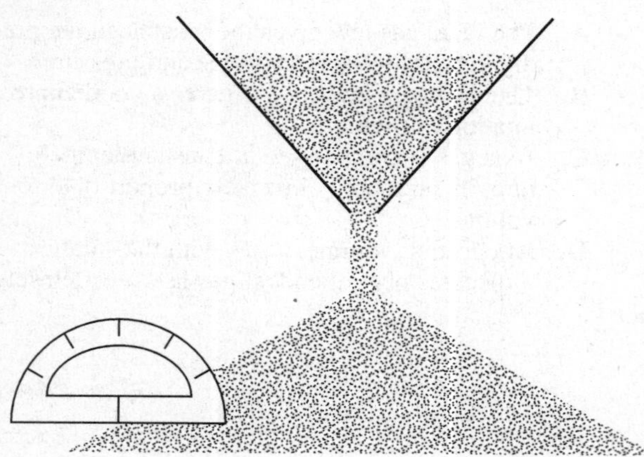

Experiment 1

Smooth, dry, quartz sand, of water-abraded, rounded grains, is sieved and sorted according to size. Each size, separately, is fed into the hopper, and the angle of repose is measured for each.

Grain size (mm)	Angle of repose (degrees)
0.1	18
0.5	20
1.0	23
1.5	25
2.0	28
2.5	30

Experiment 2

Crushed marble, made of dry, sharp-angled fragments of many sizes, is sieved and sorted by size. Each size is then fed separately into the hopper.

Grain size (mm)	Angle of repose (degrees)
1.0	28
1.5	30
2.0	33
2.5	35
3.0	36
3.5	37
4.0	37

Experiment 3

Using the same method, the angles of repose of various other kinds of materials are measured:

Substance	Angle of repose
Crushed marble, unsorted, mixed 1.0–4.0 mm	37
Crushed marble, 3.0 mm, mixed 3 parts to 1 part water	12
Water-abraded sand, 3.0 mm, mixed 3 parts to 1 part water	12
Garden soil, dry	27
Garden soil, slightly moist	46
Garden soil, saturated with water	14

28. The angle of repose depends on:

    F. the size of the particles only.
    G. the particle shape and water content of the material only.
    H. the particle size and shape and the water content of the material.
    J. the particle size and water content of the material only.

29. The experimenter compares the results of Experiments 1 and 2, and concludes that the angle of repose is larger for sharp-angled than for rounded particles. This conclusion might be challenged because:

    A. there was no control of the chemical composition of the material.
    B. no experiments were done with rounded particles larger than 2.5 mm.
    C. no experiments were done with angled particles smaller than 1.0 mm.
    D. all angles of repose were measured as accurate to only the nearest whole degree.

30. What is a reasonable hypothesis based on the trials in Experiments 2 and 3?

    F. Wet sand will pile up in taller piles than an equal quantity of dry sand.
    G. As a pile of water-saturated garden soil dries out, it will slump to form a lower, wider pile.
    H. Natural abrasion of sand, mixed with water, causes its angle of repose to decrease.
    J. In a dry sample of mixed sizes, the angle of repose depends on the size of the largest fragments in the mixture.

31. In hilly or mountainous regions, landslides occur during the rainy season. According to the results of these experiments, why is this so?

    A. Water flowing downhill carries soil along with it.
    B. When materials are mixed with water, the angle of repose becomes smaller.
    C. Water abrades the soil particles and makes them smooth and round.
    D. The slope of the hillsides is less than the angle of repose in the dry season.

32. The results of Experiment 2 suggest a limit to the value of the angle of repose of that material. What additional kind of material might be used to test this hypothesis?

    F. Crushed feldspar, sorted at 3.0 mm
    G. Marble particles 3.0 mm wide, abraded to produce rounding
    H. Sharp-angled marble fragments 5.0 mm wide
    J. Rounded marble particles 3.0 mm wide

33. A company in the business of supplying building and paving materials keeps various kinds of sand and gravel piled up in storage. For equal amounts of material, which of the following materials would use the largest amount of land space?

    A. Beach sand, consisting of rounded grains
    B. Builders' sand, consisting of sharp-angled grains
    C. Crushed stone, consisting of sharp-angled particles
    D. River gravel, consisting of well-rounded particles

Passage 7

It has been found that a chemical called acrylamide is found in many foods and that it is produced when starch is heated to high temperatures, as in baking or especially in frying foods. Two scientists differ as to the appropriate course of action for dealing with this.

Scientist 1

Acrylamide is known to produce cancer in dogs, and is suspected of doing the same in humans. The chemical is widespread in water, and the U.S. Environmental Protection agency has set a standard of tolerance of 0.12 micrograms in a glass of drinking water.

While there is no acrylamide in a boiled potato, a serving of french fries can have over 80 micrograms of it. Breakfast cereals are prepared at high temperatures, and have substantial amounts of acrylamide. Even a slice of bread, baked in the normal way, has more acrylamide than the flour that went into it. Frying uses higher temperatures than baking, and accordingly fried foods have the highest levels.

The danger posed by acrylamide has been brought to the courts. In California, some fast-food outlets are being sued for violation of the state law that requires manufacturers to warn consumers of toxic chemicals in their food. Plaintiffs will argue that most chemical carcinogenics in dogs also promote the formation of cancer in humans. This would put acrylamide into the dangerous chemical category.

Tests are underway to determine what levels of acrylamide pose a serious threat to people, but it is extremely difficult to get reliable data. While these studies are being made it is prudent to eat less fried food, and particularly to eat no foods that are deep fried or burned. Meanwhile, research chemists are studying the production of acrylamide in food, perhaps leading to a method of preventing its formation in the cooking of our favorite foods.

Scientist 2

Acrylamide is a systemic poison, but the lethal dose is thousands of times higher than any that might be gotten in our food. True, it produces cancer in dogs when fed to them in extraordinarily high doses, but it has not been linked to cancer in humans.

Eating is never completely risk-free. Acrylamide is one of many substances in our food that may be detrimental to our health. We are constantly exposed to many kinds of chemicals in our food. Most are natural substances, intrinsic parts of the metabolism of the animals and plants that make up our diet. Plants of the nightshade family, including potatoes, tomatoes, and eggplant, contain solanine, the same deadly poison as in nightshade and loco weed. Other substances have been added to our food by our agricultural and processing practices. Just about any of them could be poisonous, and many carcinogenic, if the dose is high enough.

The crucial question about any of these substances is whether the concentration is high enough to cause concern. In the case of acrylamide, there is no real information about the dosage level in food that might be dangerous. There is really no reason to single it out for special attention; it is just one of a multitude of trace chemicals in our food whose danger level is unknown. The best advice is to eat a balanced, varied diet, with no special concentration on any one food. French fries, in moderation, can be included.

34. Both scientists agree that:

    F. our foods contain many dangerous substances.
    G. many of our foods contain acrylamide.
    H. the standard of the Environmental Protection Agency is too low.
    J. there is too much acrylamide in our food.

35. The chief point of disagreement between the two scientists is whether:

    A. acrylamide is naturally present in the food or is introduced artificially.
    B. acrylamide has been shown to cause cancer in dogs.
    C. acrylamide is present in larger amounts in fried foods.
    D. we should modify our diets to take account of the presence of acrylamide in the food.

36. Scientist 1 might respond to Scientist 2 by saying:

    F. the levels of acrylamide in fried foods are very high.
    G. while the evidence is not in, it is a good idea to err on the side of caution.
    H. since acrylamide is a known carcinogen, it should be kept out of all food we eat.
    J. the amount of acrylamide in our food is too small to present a danger.

37. What additional information would be needed to resolve the differences between the two scientists?

    A. What level of acrylamide in the food constitutes a danger of causing cancer?
    B. What foods contain large amounts of acrylamide?
    C. What other chemicals found in food are carcinogenic?
    D. How much fried food does the average person eat?

38. Scientist 2 points out that tomatoes and potatoes:

    F. naturally contain acrylamide in small quantities.
    G. should be labeled with a warning of their poison content.
    H. are examples of foods containing negligible amounts of poison.
    J. like fried foods, should be eaten in small quantities only.

39. If called as an expert witness in a hearing to determine whether foods should be labeled with acrylamide content, what would Scientist 2 be most likely to say?

    A. The levels of acrylamide in food are too low to constitute a danger.
    B. In the present state of our knowledge, there is no more reason to label acrylamide content than many other chemicals.
    C. To be conservative about the issue, foods should be labeled with acrylamide content.
    D. The issue cannot be decided until more information is available.

40. When this disagreement becomes public knowledge, an important outcome might be:

    F. a ban on the sale of fried foods.
    G. reexamination of the laws requiring labeling of foods containing hazardous substances.
    H. public disgrace of one or the other of the scientists.
    J. a law requiring that foods containing acrylamide be labeled as such.

STOP

If there is still time remaining, you may review your answers.

WRITING TEST

(Optional)

30 MINUTES

Directions: Write an essay in response to the following prompt:

Prompt: The public library in your town has come under criticism for allowing students under the age of 18 to check out R-rated DVDs and books that contain graphic violence, explicit sexual situations, or obscene language. The parents of a high-school sophomore became outraged recently when they found their daughter and some classmates in her bedroom viewing a film from the library containing considerable R-rated material. The parents, joined by many of their friends, complained to the town board, demanding that the board force the library to eliminate questionable books and films from its collection. Other citizens claimed that such action was censorship that violated the rights of the public in a free and open society. In your opinion, should the library be required to remove the controversial material?

In your essay, state your position on the issue. You may take sides with either point of view, or you may present a different point of view altogether. Whatever your view, support your position with specific reasons and examples.

Use the lined paper provided. Add additional sheets if necessary.

STOP

Answer Keys and Analysis Charts

ENGLISH TEST

1. D	16. G	31. D	46. F	61. C
2. H	17. A	32. J	47. B	62. J
3. A	18. G	33. D	48. F	63. B
4. J	19. D	34. H	49. C	64. H
5. C	20. H	35. A	50. J	65. B
6. J	21. B	36. H	51. D	66. H
7. C	22. H	37. B	52. H	67. B
8. J	23. C	38. F	53. B	68. G
9. D	24. F	39. B	54. J	69. A
10. H	25. B	40. H	55. A	70. J
11. B	26. J	41. A	56. H	71. D
12. H	27. B	42. F	57. D	72. G
13. C	28. G	43. D	58. H	73. C
14. F	29. C	44. H	59. B	74. H
15. C	30. H	45. A	60. H	75. B

Analysis Chart

Skills	Questions	Possible Score	Your Score
Usage/Mechanics			
Punctuation	3, 9, 14, 17, 24, 48, 55, 62, 66, 68	10	
Basic Grammar and Usage	1, 2, 6, 19, 21, 23, 34, 50, 53, 69, 70, 71	12	
Sentence Structure	8, 11, 26, 29, 31, 39, 41, 43, 44, 49, 51, 52, 56, 57, 58, 59, 63, 67	18	
Rhetorical Skills			
Strategy	4, 5, 10, 13, 18, 30, 35, 38, 47, 65, 72, 73	12	
Organization	7, 15, 20, 25, 27, 28, 42, 45, 64, 74, 75	11	
Style	12, 16, 22, 32, 33, 36, 37, 40, 46, 54, 60, 61	12	

Number correct: ______

MATHEMATICS TEST

1. D	13. A	25. B	37. B	49. C
2. H	14. J	26. F	38. J	50. K
3. E	15. B	27. C	39. C	51. C
4. H	16. H	28. H	40. K	52. K
5. D	17. D	29. A	41. D	53. C
6. K	18. G	30. G	42. F	54. J
7. A	19. C	31. B	43. D	55. E
8. J	20. H	32. H	44. H	56. J
9. E	21. B	33. A	45. C	57. D
10. G	22. F	34. H	46. H	58. F
11. A	23. B	35. D	47. C	59. D
12. H	24. J	36. H	48. H	60. K

Analysis Chart

Content Area	Skill Level: Basic Skills	Skill Level: Application	Skill Level: Analysis	Possible Score	Your Score
Pre-Algebra Algebra	1, 8, 15, 27, 45, 52, 53, 55	2, 3, 6, 9, 13, 16, 23, 31, 34, 35, 37, 39	4, 11, 25, 28	24	
Intermediate Algebra Coordinate Geometry	17, 29, 30, 44, 48, 51, 56	5, 7, 22, 24, 26, 32, 57	18, 19, 41, 47, 60	19	
Geometry	10, 38, 40, 43, 50	12, 14, 21, 33, 36, 42, 54, 58		13	
Trigonometry	20, 46	49, 59		4	

Number correct: ______

READING TEST

1. C	6. G	11. B	16. J	21. B	26. J	31. C	36. F
2. H	7. B	12. H	17. C	22. H	27. D	32. J	37. A
3. C	8. J	13. D	18. H	23. C	28. G	33. C	38. H
4. G	9. A	14. F	19. A	24. F	29. A	34. G	39. A
5. A	10. G	15. C	20. H	25. C	30. H	35. D	40. G

Analysis Chart

Passage Type	Referring	Reasoning	Possible Score	Your Score
Prose Fiction	1, 2, 5, 6	3, 4, 7, 8, 9, 10	10	
Social Studies	15, 18, 19	11, 12, 13, 14, 16, 17, 20	10	
Humanities	22, 28, 30	21, 23, 24, 25, 26, 27, 29	10	
Natural Science	33, 35, 38, 39	31, 32, 34, 36, 37, 40	10	

Number correct: ______

SCIENCE REASONING TEST

1. C	6. G	11. A	16. J	21. B	26. F	31. B	36. G
2. H	7. C	12. F	17. C	22. H	27. D	32. H	37. A
3. D	8. G	13. B	18. G	23. C	28. H	33. A	38. H
4. F	9. D	14. H	19. D	24. H	29. A	34. G	39. B
5. A	10. G	15. C	20. G	25. B	30. J	35. D	40. G

Analysis Chart

Kind of Questions	Skill Level			Possible Score	Your Score
	Understanding	Analysis	Generalization		
Data Representation	1, 12, 13, 17, 18	2, 3, 16, 19, 20	4, 5, 14, 15, 21	15	
Research Summaries	6, 22, 23, 26, 28	7, 8, 9, 24, 25, 29	10, 11, 27, 30, 31, 32, 33	18	
Conflicting Viewpoints	34, 35, 36	37, 39	38, 40	7	

Number correct: ______

COMPOSITE SCORE

To calculate your composite score (not including the Writing Test) follow these directions:

1. On the form below fill in the first column of blanks with the number of correct answers on each test.
2. Multiply each number by 36 and divide the product by the number of questions on each test. The results are your scale scores.
3. Add up your scale scores and divide by 4. The result should be rounded to the nearest whole number to determine your composite score.

	Number of correct answers				Scale score
English	______	× 36 =	______	÷ 75 =	______
Math	______	× 36 =	______	÷ 60 =	______
Reading	______	× 36 =	______	÷ 40 =	______
Science	______	× 36 =	______	÷ 40 =	______
			Total	______ ÷ 4 =	______ **Composite Score**

No test can give you a totally precise measurement of your academic achievement. Rather, think of your composite score as the mid-point in a range of scores that can vary one or more points in either direction. A composite score of 27, for example, means that you scored somewhere between 25 and 29.

Answer Explanations: English Test

1. **D** The singular subject *one* requires a singular verb, so A and C are wrong. Choice B is incorrect because both the verb *totaled* in the same sentence and the verb in question refer to the year 1999, which is in the past.
2. **H** An objective-case pronoun is required after the preposition *of;* hence choices F and G are wrong. The comma in G and J is unnecessary.
3. **A** The dash is appropriately employed here to dramatize the pathos of *or can.*
4. **J** The first sentence of the paragraph mentions *images,* and therefore calls for description.
5. **C** To present an orderly and economical review of both nursing home extremes, with details characteristic of each type, the best choice of those given is the comparison/contrast strategy.
6. **J** The adverbial clause *than they once were* helps maintain the sequence of tenses in this paragraph.
7. **C** This passage is characterized by quick summaries and sparse detail. It would not be consistent with the rest of the passage to include detailed material.
8. **J** The clause *many of them are unclean and unhealthy* is the best choice because the pronoun *them* refers to the existing *nursing homes;* the other choices introduce a new subject.
9. **D** Parallel adjectives occurring before a noun must be separated by commas.
10. **H** The paragraph is about conditions within nursing homes; the other options touch on related but basically irrelevant subject matter.
11. **B** If the noun *qualities* is used as the subject (A and C), the introductory phrase becomes a dangling participle. *Interested parties* is a better choice of subject than *the patient* (D) because, as the passage makes clear, choosing a home is usually a family undertaking.

12. **H** The phrase *behooves us* (F) is archaic; *best suits us* (G) and *is not a bad idea* (J) depart from the serious tone of the passage.

13. **C** This article is almost journalistic in style, given to quick summary and unembellished detail. Only a sparse summary paragraph would be appropriate in this context.

14. **F** The relative pronoun *which,* preceded by a comma, is needed to introduce a nonrestrictive clause.

15. **C** Paragraph 5 begins with the phrase *For these reasons*. With a quick scanning of the passage, it is clear that the reasons referred to are given at the end of paragraph 3, and that paragraph 5 should follow.

16. **G** The metaphor in this sentence is that of a loom; the verb *can be woven* maintains the metaphor.

17. **A** The dash correctly sets off examples.

18. **G** The term *cultural activities* is the focus of this passage, and yet it is not clearly defined.

19. **D** The antecedent of the pronoun in question is *rural people*.

20. **H** Paragraphs 1 and 2 both deal with the concept *cultural activities* and belong together.

21. **B** The word *that* is needed before the last clause to make it a noun clause. The conjunction *when* (A), *because* (C), or *for* (D) cannot introduce a clause used as a predicate nominative.

22. **H** *Farther* is used to refer to a measurable distance or space. *Further* means "greater in measure, time, and degree."

23. **C** Use digits for dates; years are almost never spelled out.

24. **F** Hyphenate a compound adjective that precedes the noun it modifies.

25. **B** The first sentence suggests that a heritage festival may begin economic development, but the paragraph as it stands does not pick up that idea.

26. **J** The preceding sentence makes the point that farms in this area employ a third of the work force. The conjunction should be *thus* for that reason. The other options suggest contrast, which is meaningless at this point.

27. **B** The repetition of the preposition *in* and the noun *farming* or *production* results in parallelism.

28. **G** The three awkward options employ the phrase *spent its years of existence* in various versions, all of them unnatural sounding. The correct choice is a strong, clear statement.

29. **C** The pattern in this paragraph has been to give each accomplishment of the Council its own sentence. Also, choices A and B are run-on sentences.

30. **H** The paragraph does describe economic development, but does not explain how cultural activities "supplied the drive" for such development.

31. **D** All choices but *most distinguished* are either awkward or unnecessarily wordy.

32. **J** The most familiar idiom using these words is *method of playing*.

33. **D** Fine shades of meaning separate these words, but the only sound one to use here is *developed*.

34. **H** The participle *accomplished* modifies *musician* and is the most sensible choice. *More accomplished* compares *two* musicians.

35. **A** Classifying and dividing is the strategy that permits a writer full scope in exploring three or more subjects in one passage.

36. **H** The only meaningful choice is *quality*.

37. **B** Only the correct phrase conveys meaning that relates to the point being made in the paragraph—the difference in sound between the human and the mechanical piano player.

38. **F** The statements listing the three most distinguished musical instruments and comparing a player piano with a concert pianist are very opinionated; the passage would be more substantial if some hard data accompanied the opinions.

39. **B** The statement about the organ is in contrast to those made about other instruments, so a transitional word that indicates contrast is required.

40. **H** The other options are either redundant (F and G) or inferior (J).

41. **A** The word *whether* signals the need for the subjunctive mood at this point.

42. **F** Two characteristics are being considered in the sentence; *pressure* ("hard or soft") and *speed* ("slow or quick"), so each pair should remain intact, the pairs separated by a comma.

43. **D** *Most acutest* (A) is a double superlative, *more acute* (C) incorrectly suggests that there are only two listeners, and *acute* (B) lacks the force of the superlative and is therefore misleading.

44. **H** All the other options are awkward and wordy, and are not parallel to *the human organist*.

45. **A** The point of the passage is to persuade potential buyers to consider an organ.

46. **F** This phrase, not a common one in popular English, is appropriate to the deliberate, reflective tone of this passage.

47. **B** Quoted material, when available, is one of the most effective means of representing a person's thought and personality.

48. **F** The dash is appropriately used here to punctuate a parenthetical aside.

49. **C** This sentence consists of three clauses ending with predicate adjectives—*broad, (constantly) accumulating,* and *intricate*—each adjective (or adverb) modified by the adverb *so*. The only choice that maintains this parallel structure is C.

50. **J** The pronoun *that* does not have a clear antecedent here, so a noun should be supplied.

51. **D** This sentence is in contrast to the ideas expressed in the preceding paragraph.

52. **H** The past tense is appropriate here. The historical present is usually reserved for discussions of what a writer says or thinks in a particular work of literature.

53. **B** The pronoun *this* almost never is adequate by itself; a noun is required here for clarity.

54. **J** This sentence is incompatible in style and content with the rest of the passage.

55. **A** Coordinate sentences, that is, two independent clauses joined by a coordinate conjunction, must be separated by a comma.

56. **H** Three parallel prepositional phrases modify the noun *problems* in this sentence: problems *of variability, (of) heredity, and (of) isolation*. The object of the preposition is always a noun.

57. **D** The pronoun *that* refers to the plural *problems,* and the verb must agree. The tense must be the present perfect (*have occupied*) since the reference is to the immediate past.

58. **H** The present tense is required because natural selection still stands as a general law today.

59. **B** The statement regarding Darwin's place in history *depends upon* how his theories are regarded in the future—thus the need for the *if* clause at the beginning of the sentence.

60. **H** If nothing else, this passage praises Darwin.

61. **C** The use of *throughout* is clear and direct; the other options are awkward or wordy.

62. **J** There is no need for any punctuation between the parallel adjectives *governmental* and (*many*) *private*.

63. **B** The verb *described* completes the parallel pair of passive verbs *are ... marked* and (*are*) *described*.

64. **H** The word *unattended* in the preceding clause renders the word *unsupervised* redundant.

65. **B** An understanding of the word *antiquities* is essential to an understanding of the passage.

66. **H** Word combinations containing an *-ly* word should not be hyphenated. The adverb *carefully* modifies the adjective *carved,* and there should be no hyphen between them.

67. **B** Instead of a subordinating conjunction indicating *cause,* what is required here is a conjunction signaling *contrast* (*vertical* versus *horizontal*).

68. **G** The comma separating items in a series must come after the parenthesis.

69. **A** Spell out an occasional number that can be expressed in one or two words; with the exception of numbers from twenty-one through ninety-nine, which are always hyphenated, compound numbers are not hyphenated.

70. **J** *In which* is the only prepositional phrase that draws focus to the structure itself.

71. **D** The subject of this sentence is the singular *series*.

72. **G** This passage has all the characteristics of a scholarly paper, including assumption of some sophistication on the part of the reader, close attention to detail, and esoteric language.

73. **C** The paragraph begins with a bare statement about a significant prehistoric stone, one of the earliest erected. A younger reader would require more detail to understand the significance of such early monoliths.

74. **H** This paragraph seems to have two main ideas needing development: the stone first mentioned, and the development of Christianity in the region. With two main ideas, the structure is deeply flawed.

75. **B** The paragraph needs either to be restructured or to be introduced by a general statement that could accommodate both of the ideas present in the paragraph.

Answer Explanations: Mathematics Test

1. **D** Although 3.14 is frequently used as an approximate for π, it is rational since it represents $3\frac{14}{100}$ or $\frac{314}{100}$.

2. **H** Jane's score increased 9 points. The question is "9 is what percent of 72?" $A = 9$, P is unknown, and $B = 72$.

$$\frac{P}{100} = \frac{9}{72}\left(= \frac{1}{8}\right)$$
$$8P = 100$$
$$P = 12.5$$

3. **E** $4^2 - 3 - 5 \cdot 8 - 2[(-3) - (-7)]$
$= 4^2 - 3 - 5 \cdot 8 - 2[(-3) + 7]$
$= 4^2 - 3 - 5 \cdot 8 - 2[4]$
$= 16 - 3 - 5 \cdot 8 - 2[4]$
$= 16 - 3 - 40 - 8$
$= 13 - 40 - 8$
$= -27 - 8$
$= -35$

4. **H** The space at the top is found by multiplying 4 times $2\frac{3}{8}$ and then subtracting the product from 10.

$10 - 4\left(2\frac{3}{8}\right) = 10 - 4\left(\frac{19}{8}\right) = 10 - \frac{19}{2}$

$= 10 - 9\frac{1}{2}$

$= \frac{1}{2}$

(This means $\frac{1}{2}$ of a foot.)

$\frac{1}{2}$(12 inches) = 6 inches

5. **D** The inequality $|x - 4| \leq 2$ is easily translated to

$$-2 \leq x - 4 \leq 2$$
$$2 \leq x \leq 6$$

The solution set of this inequality is the set of numbers between 2 and 6 inclusive. These are the numbers shown on the graph.

6. **K** The lowest common denominator is the least common multiple of the denominators.
$4x^2y = 2 \cdot 2x^2y$,
$6xy^2 = 2 \cdot 3xy^2$,
$15xy = 3 \cdot 5xy$

To find the lowest common denominator, use each factor the greatest number of times it appears in any of the factorizations.

$$\text{LCD} = 2 \cdot 2 \cdot 3 \cdot 5x^2y^2 = 60x^2y^2$$

7. **A** The greatest common factor must be factored out first.
$4x^3 - 24x^2 + 36x$
$= 4x(x^2 - 6x + 9)$
(a perfect square trinomial)
$= 4x(x - 3)^2$

8. **J** Composite numbers are whole numbers, greater than 1, that are not prime. The numbers 1 and $\frac{2}{3}$ are not greater than 1, and 43 and 83 are prime, but 57 = (3)(19).

9. **E** $ab^2 - (a - b) = (-3)4^2 - [(-3) - 4]$
$= (-3)4^2 - [(-3) + (-4)]$
$= (-3)4^2 - (-7)$
$= (-3)\,16 - (-7)$
$= -48 - (-7)$
$= -48 + 7 = -41$

10. **G** Among the choices only $\angle DFG$ has its vertex on the circle.

11. **A**

	$D =$	r	$\cdot\ t$
Jon	$40\left(x + \frac{1}{2}\right)$	40	$x + \frac{1}{2}$
Joel	$50x$	50	x

The distances are equal, so the equation is

$$40\left(x + \frac{1}{2}\right) = 50x$$

12. **H** Three or more parallel lines cut transversals in the same proportion, so

$$\frac{AB}{BC} = \frac{DE}{EF}$$

$$\frac{2}{6} = \frac{DE}{5} \qquad (BC = AC - AB)$$

$$6(DE) = 10$$

$$DE = \frac{5}{3} = 1\frac{2}{3}$$

13. **A**

$$\begin{array}{r} 5\frac{1}{8} \\ -\,3\frac{5}{6} \\ \hline \end{array} \qquad \begin{array}{r} 5\frac{3}{24} \\ -\,3\frac{20}{24} \\ \hline \end{array}$$ The LCD is 24.

$$\begin{array}{r} 4\frac{27}{24} \\ -\,3\frac{20}{24} \\ \hline 1\frac{7}{24} \end{array}$$ Borrow $\frac{24}{24}$ from the 5 and add to $\frac{3}{24}$.

14. **J** Use the Pythagorean Theorem to first find the length of $\overline{AC}$.
$(AC)^2 = 1^2 + 1^2$
$AC = \sqrt{2}$
Then $\overline{AC}$ is a leg of $\triangle ACD$. Another application of the Pythagorean Theorem yields
$(AC)^2 + (CD)^2 = (AD)^2$
$(\sqrt{2})^2 + 1^2 = (AD)^2$
$2 + 1 = (AD)^2$
$AD = \sqrt{3}$
Repeating this process two more times gives $AF = \sqrt{5}$.

15. **B** The last digit must be in the ten thousandths position.

16. **H** $3 - (x - 5) = 2x - 3(4 - x)$
$$3 - x + 5 = 2x - 12 + 3x$$
$$8 - x = 5x - 12$$
$$8 = 6x - 12$$
$$20 = 6x$$
$$x = \frac{20}{6} = \frac{10}{3}$$

17. **D** An arithmetic sequence is one whose successive terms differ by a constant. Only in D is there a constant difference between terms.

18. **G** If the exponent on i is a multiple of 4, the result is 1. But if there is a remainder when the exponent is divided by 4, then it has the following values:

rem	i^n
1	i
2	-1
3	$-i$
0	1

$53 \div 4 = 13$ rem 1, so $i^{53} = i$.

19. **C** This is a combination problem. The number of combinations of n things taken r at a time is given by the formula:
$$_nC_r = \frac{n!}{(n-r)!r!}$$
The number of 4-person committees is
$$_{10}C_4 = \frac{10!}{(10-4)!\,4!}$$
$$= \frac{10!}{6!\,4!}$$
$$= \frac{10 \cdot 9 \cdot 8 \cdot 7 \cdot 6!}{6! \cdot 4 \cdot 3 \cdot 2 \cdot 1}$$
$$= \frac{10 \cdot 3 \cdot 7}{1} = 210$$

20. **H** Since $\frac{\sqrt{3}}{4} < 1$ and the range of the secant function is $\{x/x > 1 \text{ or } x < -1\}$, there are no angles for which $\sec x = \frac{\sqrt{3}}{4}$.

21. **B** If two chords intersect in a circle, the product of the segments of one chord equals the product of the lengths of the segments of the other.
$$3x = (5)(2)$$
$$= 10$$
$$x = 3\tfrac{1}{3}$$

22. **F** The sample space consists of all 52 cards in the deck. The event "drawing a heart" can be satisfied by any one of the 13 hearts.
$$P(\text{Heart}) = \frac{13}{52} = \frac{1}{4}.$$

23. **B** $x - [3x - (1 - 2x)] = x - [3x - 1 + 2x]$
$$= x - 3x + 1 - 2x$$
$$= -4x + 1$$

24. **J** If $g(x) = 1 + x^2$, then
$g(3) = 1 + 3^2 = 1 + 9 = 10$. So
$f(g(3)) = f(10) = 2(10) - 5 = 20 - 5 = 15$

25. **B** Let x = width of the rectangle.
Then $2x - 1$ = length.
The perimeter of a rectangle is found by the formula $P = 2w + 2\ell$. The equation is

$$34 = 2x + 2(2x - 1)$$
$$34 = 2x + 4x - 2$$
$$34 = 6x - 2$$
$$36 = 6x$$
$$x = 6$$

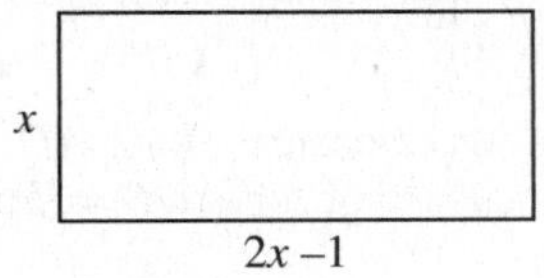

But $x = 6$ is the width. The question is "What is the length?"

$$2x - 1 = 2(6) - 1 = 12 - 1 = 11$$

26. **F** $2 \log_3 x - \frac{1}{2} \log_3 y + \log_3 z$
$= \log_3 x^2 - \log_3 \sqrt{y} + \log_3 z$

$= \log_3 \frac{x^2 z}{\sqrt{y}}$

27. **C** By the commutative property of addition

$$5(3 + 0) = 5(0 + 3)$$

28. **H** The number of male students receiving a grade of
C is $\frac{5}{6}$ of $\frac{2}{3}$ of 27.

$\frac{5}{6} \cdot \frac{2}{3} \cdot 27 = \frac{5}{6} \cdot 18$
$= 15$

29. **A** An equation of an ellipse with center at the origin, x-intercepts 3 and –3, and y-intercepts 2 and –2 is

$$\frac{x^2}{9} + \frac{y^2}{4} = 1$$

30. **G** Solve the bottom equation for z.
$$z = 4$$

Substitute into the top two equations:
$$x + 4 = 6$$
$$x = 2$$

and
$$y + 4 = 1$$
$$y = -3$$

The solution set is $\{(2, -3, 4)\}$.

31. **B** Square both sides of the radical equation.

$$(\sqrt{x + 1})^2 = (x - 1)^2$$
$$x + 1 = x^2 - 2x + 1$$
$$x^2 - 3x = 0$$
$$x(x - 3) = 0$$
$$x = 0 \quad x - 3 = 0$$
$$x = 3$$

Both potential solutions must be checked in the original equation.
Check 0: $\sqrt{0 + 1} \stackrel{?}{=} 0 - 1$
$1 \neq -1$
0 is not in the solution set.
Check 3: $\sqrt{3 + 1} \stackrel{?}{=} 3 - 1$
$\sqrt{4} \stackrel{?}{=} 2$
$2 = 2$ The solution set is $\{3\}$.

32. **H** $\sqrt[3]{-12a^4b^2}\,\sqrt[3]{-6a^2b^2} = \sqrt[3]{72a^6b^4}$

Now separate the radicand into cube and noncube factors.

$$= \sqrt[3]{8a^6b^3 \cdot 9b}$$
$$= 2a^2b\,\sqrt[3]{9b}$$

33. **A** If m $\angle ABD = 62°$, then the measure of arc $AD = 124°$. If m $\angle BDC = 28°$, then the measure of arc $BD = 56°$. So the measure of arc $ADB = (56 + 124)° = 180°$, and the measure of an angle inscribed in a semicircle = 90°.

34. **H** Multiply the top equation by 2 and the bottom equation by 5.

$$2(2x - 5y) = 13$$
$$5(3x + 2y) = 10$$

This gives

$$\begin{aligned} 4x - 10y &= 26 \\ 5x + 10y &= 50 \\ \hline 19x &= 76 \\ x = \frac{76}{19} &= 4 \end{aligned}$$

Substitute $x = 4$ into the top equation:

$$\begin{aligned} 2(4) - 5y &= 13 \\ 8 - 5y &= 13 \\ -5y &= 5 \\ y &= -1 \end{aligned}$$

35. **D** Use the substitution method.

$$\begin{pmatrix} 2x + 3y = 12 \\ y = \dfrac{-2}{3}x + 5 \end{pmatrix}$$ Substitute for y in the first equation.

$$2x + 3\left(\frac{-2}{3}x + 5\right) = 12$$
$$2x - 2x + 15 = 12$$
$$15 = 12$$ False. The solution is empty, { }.

36. **H** The measure of

$$\angle ABC = \frac{1}{2}(200 - 160)° = 20°.$$

$\triangle ABC$ is an isosceles triangle, so $\angle ACB = 80°$. Since a radius is perpendicular to a tangent at the point of tangency, $\angle OCA = (90 - 80)°$.

37. **B** In reality the shaded portion represents the big square minus $\frac{3}{4}$ of the circle minus a small 2×2 square.

$$9^2 - \frac{3}{4}(\pi 2^2) - 2^2 = 81 - 3\pi - 4$$
$$= 77 - 3\pi$$

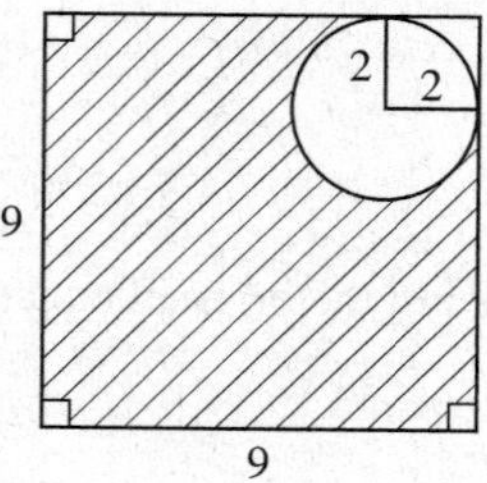

38. **J** There can be only one obtuse angle in a triangle.

39. **C** Multiply the numerator and denominator by xy:

$$\frac{xy\left(\frac{x}{y}-\frac{y}{x}\right)}{xy\left(\frac{1}{x}-\frac{1}{y}\right)} = \frac{x^2-y^2}{y-x}$$

$$= \frac{(x-y)(x+y)}{y-x}$$

$= -(x+y)$ because $y-x$ and $x-y$ are opposites.

40. **K** All four statements are false.

41. **D** $|x-3| > 2$ is equivalent to

$$x-3>2 \text{ or } x-3<-2$$
$$x>5 \text{ or } x<1$$

42. **F** First find AE.

$$(BE)(ED) = (AE)(EC)$$
$$(1)(2) = AE\left(\frac{1}{2}\right)$$
$$AE = 4$$

Then use the Pythagorean Theorem.

$$4^2 + 1^2 = (AB)^2$$
$$16 + 1 = (AB)^2$$
$$AB = \sqrt{17}$$

43. **D** If two lines are cut by a transversal in such a way that a pair of alternate interior angles are equal, the lines are parallel.

44. **H** The binomial expansion of $(a+b)^n$ has $n+1$ terms.

45. **C** The only one of these numbers that cannot be written as a fraction is $\sqrt{48}$. Note that $0.\overline{5} = 0.5555\ldots$ is a nonterminating repeating decimal, which is rational.

46. **H** The period of the function $y = a \tan b(x-c)$ is $\frac{\pi}{|b|}$. So the period of the given function is $\frac{\pi}{3}$ since this function can be rewritten as $y = 2 \tan 3(x - \frac{\pi}{6})$.

47. **C** Let x = height of the tower. Then the distance from the ground to the bend is $\frac{x}{4}$, and the slanted part is $\frac{3x}{4}$.

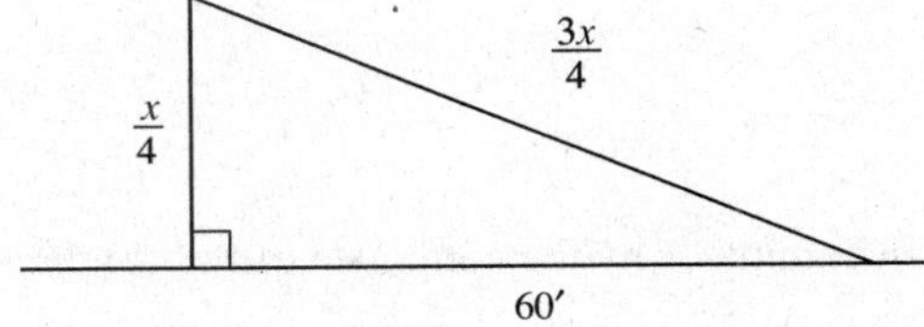

Use the Pythagorean Theorem:

$$\left(\frac{x}{4}\right)^2 + 60^2 = \left(\frac{3x}{4}\right)^2$$
$$\frac{x^2}{16} + 60^2 = \frac{9x^2}{16}$$
$$\frac{8x^2}{16} = \frac{x^2}{2} = 60^2$$
$$x^2 = 2(60^2)$$
$$x = 60\sqrt{2}$$

48. **H** Exponential functions do not represent conic sections.

49. **C** If $\cos\theta = \frac{-1}{2}$ and θ is in quadrant III, then

$$\sin\theta = -\sqrt{1-\cos^2\theta}$$
$$= -\sqrt{1-\left(\frac{-1}{2}\right)^2} = -\sqrt{1-\frac{1}{4}}$$
$$= -\sqrt{\frac{3}{4}} = -\frac{\sqrt{3}}{2}$$
$$\sin 2\theta = 2\sin\theta\cos\theta$$
$$= 2\left(\frac{-\sqrt{3}}{2}\right)\left(\frac{-1}{2}\right)$$
$$= \frac{\sqrt{3}}{2}$$

50. **K** None of these choices is enough to prove that *ABCD* is a parallelogram.

51. **C** The slope of the given line can be found from the slope-intercept form:

$$y = \frac{-2}{3}x + \frac{7}{3}$$

Since the slope is $\frac{-2}{3}$, the slope of the line perpendicular to it is $\frac{3}{2}$. Using the point-slope form of the equation of the line, we have

$$y - 1 = \frac{3}{2}(x-2)$$
$$2y - 2 = 3x - 6$$
$$3x - 2y = 4$$

52. **K** Square roots of negative numbers are imaginary.

53. **C** Degree concerns itself only with the exponents on the *variables*. The degree of a polynomial is the greatest of the degrees of its terms. The degree of the first term is 4; of the second term, 5; and of the third, 0.

54. **J** The measure of arc $AC = (360 - 220)° = 140°$. The angle formed by a chord and a tangent line is measured by half of the intercepted arc. The measure of $\angle CAD = 70°$.

55. **E**

A. 0.015
B. $1.5 \times 10^{-2} = 0.015$
C. $1.5\% = 0.015$
D. $\frac{3}{200} = 0.015$
E. $(0.3)(0.005) = 0.0015$

56. **J** Multiply the numerator and denominator by the conjugate of the denominator.

$$\frac{6(4+\sqrt{2})}{(4-\sqrt{2})(4+\sqrt{2})} = \frac{6(4+\sqrt{2})}{16-2} = \frac{6(4+\sqrt{2})}{14}$$
$$= \frac{3(4+\sqrt{2})}{7} = \frac{12+3\sqrt{2}}{7}$$

57. **D** $|x-5| > 2$ is equivalent to

$$x - 5 > 2 \quad \text{or} \quad x - 5 < -2$$
$$x > 7 \quad \text{or} \quad x < 3$$

58. **F** The altitude to the hypotenuse of a right triangle is the mean proportional between the two segments of the hypotenuse.

$$\frac{AD}{DC} = \frac{DC}{BD}$$
$$\frac{3}{DC} = \frac{DC}{12}$$
$$(DC)^2 = 36$$
$$DC = 6$$

59. **D** cos (– 512°) = cos (208°)
Add 2(360°) to the angle. The reference angle is (208 – 180)°. Cofunctions of complementary angles are equal. –62° is in Quadrant IV, where the sine is negative. 152° is in Quadrant II with the same reference angle (180 – 152°) = 28°, but in Quadrant II the sine is positive.

60. **K** $g = \frac{k}{d^2}$

$64 = \frac{k}{9^2}$

$k = 64(81)$

$g = \frac{64(81)}{24^2}$

$= \frac{8 \cdot 8(9 \cdot 9)}{(8 \cdot 3)(8 \cdot 3)}$

$= 9$ This can be obtained easily by canceling.

Answer Explanations: Reading Test

1. **C** Gaspar explains to the sergeant that he had "remained behind . . . to keep the enemy back while the detachment was running away." The sergeant later alludes to Gaspar's failure to rejoin the detachment after dark (lines 23–24). Nothing in the passage suggests that Gaspar ran away (A) or stayed up all night (B). Choice D states the opposite of what actually occurred; it was Gaspar who was lassoed by a mounted soldier.

2. **H** The first paragraph lists Gaspar's agreeable qualities, including "mildness of character," and an "acquiescent soul." He may well have possessed the traits listed by the other choices, but they are not mentioned.

3. **C** Lines 20–21 find the sergeant addressing Lieutenant Santierra with "a superior smile." Later, given the order to provide water to the prisoners, the sergeant questions the need (lines 61–63). Still later he sneers at the decision to keep the prisoners alive, and D overstates the sergeant's antipathy.

4. **G** It's safe to infer that the *Commandante* orders the soldiers' execution to deter other troops from deserting. Choice F cannot be correct because the troops' morale is likely to suffer as a consequence of an execution of one of their fellow soldiers. H is an equally poor choice. If anything, the Commandante's uncertainty would be more likely to save Gaspar and the others from execution instead of condemning them to death. G is totally illogical. What lesson can you teach men by killing them?

5. **A** According to lines 88–91, the favor had been granted in consideration of the high position of Santierra's father and the lieutenant's distinguished family. If any of the other choices (B, C, or D) influenced the *Commandante*, they are not mentioned in the passage.

6. **G** In line 14, Santierra is described as "little more than a boy." Later, he wishes to give the prisoners a drink of water. We learn at the end of the passage that he tried to gain pardons for some of the condemned men. On the other hand, Esteban, the sergeant, hits Gaspar with a stick and herds the prisoners into the guardhouse "with alacrity and zeal" (lines 41–42). The adjutant looks "savagely" around the courtyard and orders the prisoners, whom he calls "scoundrels," to be locked up in a stifling cell. In condemning the prisoners to death "for an example" (lines 17–18), the *Commandante* shows his lack of human decency.

7. **B** The text of lines 49–51 shows the guards lying around in the shade unconcerned about the welfare of the prisoners. Choice A is not mentioned in the passage. Both C and D may be true but neither is discussed.

8. **J** If anything, Santierra is a misfit. Unlike the other men in his unit, he shows compassion for Gaspar and the other prisoners. Furthermore, he is still not used to "sanguinary imbecilities of a state of war" (lines 15–16). In other words, he has not yet grown accustomed to war's bloody insanity. Rule out F because of Santierra's aversion to the inhumane treatment of the prisoners. Eliminate G because the *Commandante* respects only Santierra's prestigious family, not the lieutenant himself. H is irrelevant to the passage.

9. **A** Realizing that his meddling was "futile" (line 97), Santierra regrets having prolonged the men's agony. Had he not interfered, they would have been shot early in the day and avoided their incarceration in the guardhouse. B may seem like the answer, but Santierra does next to nothing to win a pardon for the prisoners. His loss of temper (C) appears not to bother him, and, if he feels inadequate (D), the passage neither says nor implies it.

10. **G** As we learn only at the end of the passage, Santierra hurried after the *Commandante* in order to ask for the execution to be delayed. Eliminate F because the sergeant laughs out loud *before* Santierra leaves. H and J occur subsequent to Santierra's departure but are not the immediate result of the lieutenant's talk with the *Commandante*.

11. **B** The sentence expresses the author's wonderment that history's third most serious worldwide plague is hardly remembered today. It has been reduced to a "folk-memory."

12. **H** In context, the phrase suggests that Americans took in stride the tragic consequences of the epidemic. Many thousands died, but the country's overall reaction was dispassionate. The remainder of the passage explores the reasons why.

13. **D** In the second paragraph the author begins to analyze America's tepid response to the epidemic. She describes the response as a "mystery" and as a "paradox."

14. **F** Through much of the passage, the author speculates on the reasons for America's complacency: the war, the brevity of the illness that preceded death, the social and political scene at the time of the epidemic, and so forth. Only the "acceptance of epidemics as a part of life" (lines 27–28) is cited as a certainty.

15. **C** The author claims that a lethal epidemic would have a significant impact on contemporary Americans because technological advances have made epidemics a rarity today.

16. **J** The fourth paragraph consists of a single transitional sentence that reinforces the idea that America's ho-hum response can be partially explained by the people's fatalistic acceptance of the epidemic. The sentence further states that additional explanations are speculative rather than factual. Overall, the sentence suggests that the author is groping for answers rather than declaring outright that she knows exactly why America responded as it did. J is the best answer because there is nothing in the sentence that contradicts earlier material.

17. **C** At one point in the passage, the author comments that Americans failed to grant the epidemic "the notoriety it deserved" (lines 32–33), suggesting that America's reaction ought to have been more forceful. In addition, lines 60–69 hint that the author doesn't quite understand how Americans could have been more consumed by daily headlines, including the results of a baseball game, than by the deadly consequences of the flu epidemic. Then, too, the author calls the enlistment of millions of men into the armed forces after the flu arrived in Washington a "pattern of insanity" (line 71).

18. **H** The author makes the point in lines 44–46 that the disease spread and disappeared swiftly—usually within a few days. Choices F and G are not valid because the passage does not discuss the manner in which the disease spread, nor its resemblance to previous epidemics. As for the age of victims, the passage indicates that most deaths occurred in the young adult population, mostly 18–21 year olds.

19. **A** The last paragraph states that the epidemic spurred "great activity among medical scientists and their institutions." Although the epidemic inspired enlistments into the armed forces, the author makes no claim that the increase of military volunteers was beneficial in any way. On the contrary, she describes an event in Boston where 96,000 new registrants "sneezed and coughed on one another" (lines 78–79).

20. **H** In terms of the entire passage, the two final paragraphs argue that the epidemic left a lackluster legacy because it killed almost no famous or powerful people. Also, "it affected all sides equally" (line 94). To put it another way, had well-known people succumbed, or if it had appeared to single out a specific group or nationality, the epidemic might have become more memorable. Its randomness, in short, doomed it to near oblivion.

21. **B** The author devotes virtually the entire passage to an adulation of various aspects of the French theater. Choice A is too broad; the author is fond of Paris but writes only about the theater. Eliminate C; in this passage James is neither detailed nor objective. Reject D; although James is clearly a fan of Molière's plays, he doesn't analyze them.

22. **H** Because the author *listened* to Delauney and *watched* Got (see lines 21–22), both must be performers. Likewise, Reichemberg is described in lines 78–79 as a "divinely ingenuous ingénue." Only de Musset (see lines 72–75) is not an actor but, as the creator of *Il ne Faut Jurer*, a playwright.

23. **C** To one degree or another, all the other choices merely support the idea that French theater exemplifies the best of French thought and culture, but only C conveys the substance of the passage.

24. **F** The epithet "poor man" is applied to the poet Gray because he never had the opportunity to sit in the theater and enjoy performances by Delauney, Got, and others. Instead, he was stuck reading novels such as *Clarissa Harlowe*.

25. **C** The phrase "charred ruins" suggests a recent fire (D), but other phrases such as "aftertaste of gunpowder" and "blood-stained pavements" indicate that the city had been ravaged by war. Neither A nor B is supported by evidence in the passage.

26. **J** There is no indication in the passage that Molière founded the *Théâtre Français*. Choice F is incorrect because de Musset's play is based on Molière's farce (lines 73–74). Because Molière wrote comedies and farces, G is wrong. Nor is H a good answer because lines 63–65 suggest that Molière, although he's very, very good, is not Shakespeare's equal.

27. **D** What attracted James to the theater is "finding it a copious source of instruction as to French ideas, manners, and philosophy" (lines 4–5). It's true that B is appealing, but the theater was a refuge from the busy and dusty streets only one "certain evening in early summer" (lines 45–46). Choice A is wrong because the author enjoys the sensual rewards of a play (lines 24–26), and C is contradicted by the observation that the seats ought to be "better stuffed" (lines 20–21).

28. **G** In line 54, the author admires the "tender flower of poetry." Choice F is contradicted by the author's assertion in line 73 that Musset "need fear no neighborhood," suggesting that his work stacks up quite favorably against that of Moliere. H is also invalid in light of the author's statement in lines 80–82 that the actors' performance could not be "mistaken for real life." J is not a good choice because the author, ignoring the rest of the audience, writes solely about his own reactions.

29. **A** Earlier in the passage (lines 29–30) the author calls the *Théâtre Français* "not only the most amiable but the most characteristic of French institutions." Molière, the premier French playwright, therefore, "deserves" to be performed there. There is no evidence in the passage to support the other choices.

30. **H** The author envisions the foreigner leaving the theater saying "Ah, France is the civilized nation *par excellence*" (line 34). Choice F may be valid to some extent, but there is nothing about international envy in the passage. G describes the foreigner's experience but not his reaction. Likewise, J sums up what happened to the foreigner but fails to describe his reaction.

31. **C** The FDA's legal powers are implied throughout the passage. Choice A states one of the agency's functions, but making rules governing caffeine is by no means its main function. Likewise, B and D fail to identify the FDA's primary function.

32. **J** *Adulterated* usually means impure. In the context of the third paragraph, however, the use of such words as "poisonous" and "hazardous" suggests that a stronger meaning is intended, but not as strong as H, "lethal."

33. **C** According to lines 19–23, caffeine in small amounts poses no threat to health. Adverse effects come only from high doses. A is a weak answer because 21st century food regulations cannot be based on obsolete data from the past. B is wrong because the FDA is supposed to protect consumers, not advise them to read ingredient labels in order to assess the safety of a product. D is not mentioned in the passage.

34. **G** In line 25, the GRAS is identified as a "regulatory" designation. It comes from FDA policy via the Federal Food, Drug, and Cosmetic Act, a measure that regulates the ingredients of all processed food. The other choices—F, H, and J—misrepresent the purpose and meaning of GRAS.

35. **D** Lines 56–59 state that this action "would require food processors to gather additional scientific evidence to prove caffeine is safe." Choices A, B, and C do not name an effect that would follow if caffeine were removed from the GRAS list.

36. **F** The concerns and interests of pharmacists are not mentioned in the passage. Choice G is not a good choice because lines 58–59 and 70–76 deal with the impact of FDA decisions on manufacturers. H is discussed in lines 51–52. J is covered by lines 52–56.

37. **A** Lines 62–64 make the point that caffeine found naturally in cola nuts is the "chief flavoring agent" of soft drinks. Choices B, C, and D are accurate descriptions of caffeine but are not discussed in the passage.

38. **H** Lines 5–6 say that previous attempts to ban or restrict the use of beverages containing caffeine "lacked scientific credibility." The issues raised by the other choices are not discussed in the passage.

39. **A** The addictive quality of caffeine is not stated anywhere in the passage. That caffeine can be harmful to animals is stated in lines 7–9. That it is found in nature is suggested by its presence in coffee and tea (line 13), and its presence in pain killers and cold remedies (lines 36–37) implies its salutary effects.

40. **G** The passage concentrates on what will happen if regulations governing the use of caffeine are changed. The matters mentioned by choices F, H, and J play little or no part in the passage.

Answer Explanations: Science Reasoning Test

1. **C** The intake chart shows that the recommended carbohydrate is more than the carbohydrate consumed, and the recommended fat is less than the fat consumed. The other choices are wrong because there is no recommendation for a change in the protein.

2. **H** The energy chart (II) shows that fiber supplies no energy at all. F is wrong because the energy chart shows much less energy from protein than from carbohydrates or fats. Since the chart shows about equal amounts of energy now obtained from fats and carbohydrates, G is wrong. J deals with quantity, not energy, and the intake chart (I) shows that the quantity of carbohydrates is far greater than the amount of fat.

3. **D** In all these charts the two bars match perfectly for protein intake. A is wrong because the bar for recommended carbohydrate is longer than that for actual intake. Similarly, more, not less, fiber is recommended, so B is wrong. C is wrong because the recommended diet is reduced in fat.
4. **F** The bars for recommended intake (chart I) show about 80 g of fat and 330 g of carbohydrate.
5. **A** When the values for present diet are used, fats are about 23% of our diet by weight, and supply 43% of our energy; carbohydrates constitute 58% of our food, but give us only 45% of our energy. B is wrong because the ratio of percent by weight to energy for carbohydrates (58%/45%) is about the same as the ratio for proteins (16%/13%). C is wrong because fiber supplies no energy at all, and 3 times 0 is 0. D is the opposite of A.
6. **G** In Experiment 2, where there was little glucose, the bacteria were unable to form spores. F is wrong because no data about growth were presented. H is wrong because Experiments 1 and 2 have nothing to do with the usefulness of spores. J is wrong because Experiment 1 shows that glucose actually promotes spore formation.
7. **C** Since Experiment 1 shows that glucose is needed, and there is none in distilled water, it is quite likely that the bacterial cells stored glucose when it was available. A and D are wrong because Experiment 1 shows that the bacteria need glucose to form spores. B is wrong because we have no data indicating how long it took to form spores when there is plenty of glucose.
8. **G** Experiment 4 shows that if glucose is added in less than 5 hours spore formation is prevented, but if it is added after 10 hours spores form anyway.
9. **D** In Experiment 3, spores formed 13 hours after the cells were put into distilled water; in Experiment 4, the same thing happened, even though glucose was added after 10 hours.
10. **G** Bread mold spores are entirely different from bacterial spores, and there is no reason to believe that any similarity exists in the way they are formed.
11. **A** In both Experiment 1 and Experiment 3, spores were formed when a period of growth in an ample supply of glucose was followed by glucose deprivation. B is wrong because no spores are formed as long as there is plenty of glucose in the medium. Experiment 2 shows that no spores can be formed unless there is first an ample supply of glucose, so C is wrong. There is no evidence anywhere to support D.
12. **F** Adding male births (1063) and female births (1000) gives a total of 2063; males are 1063 of this total.
13. **B** Although the sex ratio went down, it then went up, and was always more than 0.5, which would indicate equal numbers of boys and girls. No information was given about total numbers.
14. **H** While parents are in their twenties, the sex ratio decreases by only about 1 or 2 parts per thousand, not enough to take into account.
15. **C** A is wrong because it is not an explanation, since it fails to suggest a mechanism by which the result is brought about. B is wrong because the second graph indicates that older men produce a smaller fraction of boys, not a larger one. D is wrong; you are told that this effect has been noticed in many wars and many countries, so it is unlikely that this result is coincidental. By elimination, C is the only feasible answer of those offered.
16. **J** Since spouses are generally only a little different in age, there is no way that the graphs can distinguish the effect of the mother's age from that of the father's.
17. **C** In 1960 it was about 1.5 million; in 1980, about 5.5 million.
18. **G** The difference between the 1990 bar and the 1991 bar is more than one million, larger than any of the other yearly jumps. The 1973 bar is longer than the 1968 bar by the same amount, but the intervening years are missing.
19. **D** If the present trend continued for another 5 years, the number of diagnosed cases would be about 10 million in the year 2000. Since the total for that year was expected to be 15 million, 5 million will be undiagnosed.
20. **G** It is possible that part, or even all, of the increase is simply because more cases are being found. F is wrong; the steady increase is apparent even without those years. H is wrong because the minor fluctuations do not negate the overall trend. J is wrong because the only function of the graph is to show the trend, without ascribing any cause.
21. **B** The chart predicted 22 million cases by 2025, but only 15 million in 2000. A is wrong because the chart makes no statement as to the cause of the increase. C is a valid conclusion from the chart, not an assumption. D is wrong because there is nothing in the yearly data that gives any indication of the number of undiagnosed cases.
22. **H** On the pressure-temperature chart, the actual pressures are always a little higher than those predicted by the ideal gas law; using this law will give an underestimation, so G is wrong. F is wrong because the error is small and the value calculated would be good enough for many purposes. J is wrong because the error is not unpredictable once the special properties of each gas are known.

23. **C** Of all the gases, sulfur dioxide shows the largest difference from the ideal value in both experiments.

24. **H** It is probable that the pressure rose to, say, 20.001 atmospheres, which would not have been detected at the level of accuracy to which the experiment was done. F is wrong because the pressure actually doubled when the volume dropped to half. Don't insult the experimenter by answering G. It is never safe to conclude that additional accuracy would not reveal something different, so J is wrong.

25. **B** At all volumes, helium and nitrogen had higher pressures than predicted; and carbon dioxide, xenon, and sulfur dioxide had lower pressures. The result can be predicted once you know which gas is being studied.

26. **F** You have to start the experiment with some gas in the cylinder, and the experimenter decides how much and at what pressure and temperature. Why bother to use anything but what is already there?

27. **D** The pressure-temperature chart shows no detectable deviation for the smallest molecules (helium) and successively more for each of the larger molecules. Deviations from the ideal gas law get larger, not smaller, as the pressure goes up. C expresses the ideal gas law; the whole burden of this experiment is to test deviations from this law.

28. **H** Experiments 1 and 2 show that the angle of repose increases with grain size. Comparison of these two experiments shows that sharp-angled fragments have a larger angle of repose than rounded ones. The soil samples of Experiment 3 show that water content is also involved.

29. **A** The two experimental materials differ in both shape and composition of the particles, and no effort was made to distinguish between these two possible causes of the difference found. B and C are wrong because the evidence from particles from 1.0 to 2.5 mm, in both experiments, provides a clear contrast. D is wrong because the differences are of several degrees and are consistent, so accuracy of 1 degree is sufficient to produce an answer.

30. **J** The angle of repose for the mixed sample of crushed marble is the same as for the largest size of the screened samples. F is wrong because the angle of repose is smaller for wet than for dry sand, so the pile of wet sand will be lower than the pile of dry. G is wrong because the angle of repose is smaller for the saturated soil; the pile becomes more stable as it dries out. H is wrong because no information is available to compare sand grains of various sizes if they are mixed with water.

31. **B** The soil is piled up, possibly to its angle of repose when dry. When it gets wet, the angle of repose decreases, so the angle of the hill is larger than the new angle of repose. A is wrong because the experiments do not deal with the effects of running water. C is wrong because the particles are not abraded as they rest during the dry season. D is surely true, but it says nothing about the effect of rain.

32. **H** Since there is no difference between 3.5 mm and 4.0 mm, it could be hypothesized that the angle of repose does not increase for particles beyond 3.5 mm, and this can be tested by trying larger particles.

33. **A** The experiments show that small, rounded particles have the smallest angle of repose. They will form lower, flatter piles and thus will spread out more on the ground.

34. **G** Both scientists agree that there is acrylamide in our food, but J is wrong because they differ on whether the amount represents a danger. F is wrong because Scientist 1 does not discuss the presence of other dangerous substances in our food. H is wrong because neither scientist discusses the EPA standard.

35. **D** Scientist 2 believes that the current state of knowledge does not justify taking any action with our diet. The other points are made by Scientist 1, but Scientist 2 does not dispute any of them.

36. **G** This is the recommendation made by Scientist 1. The other choices are wrong because Scientist 2 says we do not know what constitutes a dangerous level of acrylamide in the diet.

37. **A** This is the main crux of Scientist 1's argument. B is wrong because this information is already available. C is wrong because information about other chemicals is not pertinent. D is wrong because any conclusions must apply to everyone, not just to the average person.

38. **H** Scientist 2 cites these foods as examples of natural poisons in food in negligible quantities. F is wrong because the poison in these foods is not acrylamide. G and J are wrong because Scientist 2 believes that the amount of these substances in food is negligibly small.

39. **B** The other choices are wrong because Scientist 2 believes that there is not enough information to ban acrylamide, any more than many other substances as well.

40. **G** As a result of the hearings, some legislators might feel that the topic deserves further study. F and J are wrong because none of them is likely to take such drastic action until there is more information available. H is wrong; there is no shame for a scientist to hold a contrary opinion.

Essay Self-Assessment

Before evaluating your own essay, read pages 433–434 on the scoring of ACT essays. Then complete the following checklist. Focus on both the strengths and weaknesses of your essay.

	Yes!	Mostly	Hardly	No
Does the essay address the ACT prompt?	___	___	___	___
Is the topic sufficiently narrowed?	___	___	___	___
Is the essay's main idea clear?	___	___	___	___
Have you written an introduction?	___	___	___	___
Does the essay sound natural?	___	___	___	___
Have you used plain words?	___	___	___	___
Have you used precise language?	___	___	___	___
Does your essay have a clear focus?	___	___	___	___
Do all parts fit together coherently?	___	___	___	___
Is each sentence accurately worded?	___	___	___	___
Have you trimmed needless words?	___	___	___	___
Do you show more than tell?	___	___	___	___
Have you used active verbs?	___	___	___	___
Is the language fresh?	___	___	___	___
Do you include verbal surprises?	___	___	___	___
Are the sentences varied?	___	___	___	___
Is sentence length balanced?	___	___	___	___
Does the essay have a conclusion?	___	___	___	___
Is the essay mostly error-free?	___	___	___	___

Identify the three greatest strengths of your essay:

1)____

2)____

3)____

Name three specific things that you could do to improve your essay:

1)____

2)____

3)____

Circle the score your essay deserves: 6 5 4 3 2 1

Table for Calculating the Combined English/Writing Test Score

Instructions:

1. Find your Writing Test subscore (2–12) along the top of the table.
2. Find your English Test score on the left or right side.
3. Your combined score will appear in the table where the two scores intersect. For instance, a 10 on the Writing Test and a 25 on the English Test will yield a Combined English/Writing Test score of 26.

English Test Score	Writing Test Subscore											English Test Score
	2	3	4	5	6	7	8	9	10	11	12	
1	1	2	3	4	5	6	7	8	9	10	11	**1**
2	2	3	4	5	6	6	7	8	9	10	11	**2**
3	2	3	4	5	6	7	8	9	10	11	12	**3**
4	3	4	5	6	7	8	9	10	11	12	13	**4**
5	4	5	6	7	8	9	10	11	12	12	13	**5**
6	5	6	7	8	8	9	10	11	12	13	14	**6**
7	5	6	7	8	9	10	11	12	13	14	15	**7**
8	6	7	8	9	10	11	12	13	14	15	16	**8**
9	7	8	9	10	11	12	13	13	14	15	16	**9**
10	8	9	9	10	11	12	13	14	15	16	17	**10**
11	8	9	10	11	12	13	14	15	16	17	18	**11**
12	9	10	11	12	13	14	15	16	17	18	19	**12**
13	10	11	12	13	14	14	15	16	17	18	19	**13**
14	10	11	12	13	14	15	16	17	18	19	20	**14**
15	11	12	13	14	15	16	17	18	19	20	21	**15**
16	12	13	14	15	16	17	18	19	20	20	21	**16**
17	13	14	15	16	16	17	18	19	20	21	22	**17**
18	13	14	15	16	17	18	19	20	21	22	23	**18**
19	14	15	16	17	18	19	20	21	22	23	24	**19**
20	15	16	17	18	19	20	21	21	22	23	24	**20**
21	16	17	17	18	19	20	21	22	23	24	25	**21**
22	16	17	18	19	20	21	22	23	24	25	26	**22**
23	17	18	19	20	21	22	23	24	25	26	27	**23**
24	18	19	20	21	22	23	23	24	25	26	27	**24**
25	18	19	20	21	22	23	24	25	26	27	28	**25**
26	19	20	21	22	23	24	25	26	27	28	29	**26**
27	20	21	22	23	24	25	26	27	28	28	29	**27**
28	21	22	23	24	24	26	26	27	28	29	30	**28**
29	21	22	23	24	25	26	27	28	29	30	31	**29**

Table for Calculating the Combined English/Writing Test Score (cont.)

English Test Score	Writing Test Subscore 2	3	4	5	6	7	8	9	10	11	12	English Test Score
30	22	23	24	25	26	27	28	29	30	31	32	**30**
31	23	24	25	26	27	28	29	30	30	31	32	**31**
32	24	25	25	26	27	28	29	30	31	32	33	**32**
33	25	25	26	27	28	29	30	31	32	33	34	**33**
34	26	26	27	28	29	30	31	32	33	34	35	**34**
35	26	27	28	28	30	31	31	32	33	34	35	**35**
36	26	27	28	29	30	31	32	33	34	35	36	**36**

Calculating Your Combined English/Writing Test Score

English Test Score _____

Essay Score ___ multiply by 2 = _____

Combined Score (See table): _____

Answer Sheet

MODEL EXAM B

Directions: Mark one answer only for each question. Make the mark dark. Erase completely any mark made in error. (Additional or stray marks will be counted as mistakes.)

Test 1

1 Ⓐ Ⓑ Ⓒ Ⓓ
2 Ⓕ Ⓖ Ⓗ Ⓙ
3 Ⓐ Ⓑ Ⓒ Ⓓ
4 Ⓕ Ⓖ Ⓗ Ⓙ
5 Ⓐ Ⓑ Ⓒ Ⓓ
6 Ⓕ Ⓖ Ⓗ Ⓙ
7 Ⓐ Ⓑ Ⓒ Ⓓ
8 Ⓕ Ⓖ Ⓗ Ⓙ
9 Ⓐ Ⓑ Ⓒ Ⓓ
10 Ⓕ Ⓖ Ⓗ Ⓙ
11 Ⓐ Ⓑ Ⓒ Ⓓ
12 Ⓕ Ⓖ Ⓗ Ⓙ
13 Ⓐ Ⓑ Ⓒ Ⓓ
14 Ⓕ Ⓖ Ⓗ Ⓙ
15 Ⓐ Ⓑ Ⓒ Ⓓ
16 Ⓕ Ⓖ Ⓗ Ⓙ
17 Ⓐ Ⓑ Ⓒ Ⓓ
18 Ⓕ Ⓖ Ⓗ Ⓙ
19 Ⓐ Ⓑ Ⓒ Ⓓ
20 Ⓕ Ⓖ Ⓗ Ⓙ
21 Ⓐ Ⓑ Ⓒ Ⓓ
22 Ⓕ Ⓖ Ⓗ Ⓙ
23 Ⓐ Ⓑ Ⓒ Ⓓ
24 Ⓕ Ⓖ Ⓗ Ⓙ
25 Ⓐ Ⓑ Ⓒ Ⓓ
26 Ⓕ Ⓖ Ⓗ Ⓙ
27 Ⓐ Ⓑ Ⓒ Ⓓ
28 Ⓕ Ⓖ Ⓗ Ⓙ
29 Ⓐ Ⓑ Ⓒ Ⓓ
30 Ⓕ Ⓖ Ⓗ Ⓙ
31 Ⓐ Ⓑ Ⓒ Ⓓ
32 Ⓕ Ⓖ Ⓗ Ⓙ
33 Ⓐ Ⓑ Ⓒ Ⓓ
34 Ⓕ Ⓖ Ⓗ Ⓙ
35 Ⓐ Ⓑ Ⓒ Ⓓ
36 Ⓕ Ⓖ Ⓗ Ⓙ
37 Ⓐ Ⓑ Ⓒ Ⓓ
38 Ⓕ Ⓖ Ⓗ Ⓙ
39 Ⓐ Ⓑ Ⓒ Ⓓ
40 Ⓕ Ⓖ Ⓗ Ⓙ
41 Ⓐ Ⓑ Ⓒ Ⓓ
42 Ⓕ Ⓖ Ⓗ Ⓙ
43 Ⓐ Ⓑ Ⓒ Ⓓ
44 Ⓕ Ⓖ Ⓗ Ⓙ
45 Ⓐ Ⓑ Ⓒ Ⓓ
46 Ⓕ Ⓖ Ⓗ Ⓙ
47 Ⓐ Ⓑ Ⓒ Ⓓ
48 Ⓕ Ⓖ Ⓗ Ⓙ
49 Ⓐ Ⓑ Ⓒ Ⓓ
50 Ⓕ Ⓖ Ⓗ Ⓙ
51 Ⓐ Ⓑ Ⓒ Ⓓ
52 Ⓕ Ⓖ Ⓗ Ⓙ
53 Ⓐ Ⓑ Ⓒ Ⓓ
54 Ⓕ Ⓖ Ⓗ Ⓙ
55 Ⓐ Ⓑ Ⓒ Ⓓ
56 Ⓕ Ⓖ Ⓗ Ⓙ
57 Ⓐ Ⓑ Ⓒ Ⓓ
58 Ⓕ Ⓖ Ⓗ Ⓙ
59 Ⓐ Ⓑ Ⓒ Ⓓ
60 Ⓕ Ⓖ Ⓗ Ⓙ
61 Ⓐ Ⓑ Ⓒ Ⓓ
62 Ⓕ Ⓖ Ⓗ Ⓙ
63 Ⓐ Ⓑ Ⓒ Ⓓ
64 Ⓕ Ⓖ Ⓗ Ⓙ
65 Ⓐ Ⓑ Ⓒ Ⓓ
66 Ⓕ Ⓖ Ⓗ Ⓙ
67 Ⓐ Ⓑ Ⓒ Ⓓ
68 Ⓕ Ⓖ Ⓗ Ⓙ
69 Ⓐ Ⓑ Ⓒ Ⓓ
70 Ⓕ Ⓖ Ⓗ Ⓙ
71 Ⓐ Ⓑ Ⓒ Ⓓ
72 Ⓕ Ⓖ Ⓗ Ⓙ
73 Ⓐ Ⓑ Ⓒ Ⓓ
74 Ⓕ Ⓖ Ⓗ Ⓙ
75 Ⓐ Ⓑ Ⓒ Ⓓ

Test 2

1 Ⓐ Ⓑ Ⓒ Ⓓ Ⓔ
2 Ⓕ Ⓖ Ⓗ Ⓙ Ⓚ
3 Ⓐ Ⓑ Ⓒ Ⓓ Ⓔ
4 Ⓕ Ⓖ Ⓗ Ⓙ Ⓚ
5 Ⓐ Ⓑ Ⓒ Ⓓ Ⓔ
6 Ⓕ Ⓖ Ⓗ Ⓙ Ⓚ
7 Ⓐ Ⓑ Ⓒ Ⓓ Ⓔ
8 Ⓕ Ⓖ Ⓗ Ⓙ Ⓚ
9 Ⓐ Ⓑ Ⓒ Ⓓ Ⓔ
10 Ⓕ Ⓖ Ⓗ Ⓙ Ⓚ
11 Ⓐ Ⓑ Ⓒ Ⓓ Ⓔ
12 Ⓕ Ⓖ Ⓗ Ⓙ Ⓚ
13 Ⓐ Ⓑ Ⓒ Ⓓ Ⓔ
14 Ⓕ Ⓖ Ⓗ Ⓙ Ⓚ
15 Ⓐ Ⓑ Ⓒ Ⓓ Ⓔ
16 Ⓕ Ⓖ Ⓗ Ⓙ Ⓚ
17 Ⓐ Ⓑ Ⓒ Ⓓ Ⓔ
18 Ⓕ Ⓖ Ⓗ Ⓙ Ⓚ
19 Ⓐ Ⓑ Ⓒ Ⓓ Ⓔ
20 Ⓕ Ⓖ Ⓗ Ⓙ Ⓚ
21 Ⓐ Ⓑ Ⓒ Ⓓ Ⓔ
22 Ⓕ Ⓖ Ⓗ Ⓙ Ⓚ
23 Ⓐ Ⓑ Ⓒ Ⓓ Ⓔ
24 Ⓕ Ⓖ Ⓗ Ⓙ Ⓚ
25 Ⓐ Ⓑ Ⓒ Ⓓ Ⓔ
26 Ⓕ Ⓖ Ⓗ Ⓙ Ⓚ
27 Ⓐ Ⓑ Ⓒ Ⓓ Ⓔ
28 Ⓕ Ⓖ Ⓗ Ⓙ Ⓚ
29 Ⓐ Ⓑ Ⓒ Ⓓ Ⓔ
30 Ⓕ Ⓖ Ⓗ Ⓙ Ⓚ
31 Ⓐ Ⓑ Ⓒ Ⓓ Ⓔ
32 Ⓕ Ⓖ Ⓗ Ⓙ Ⓚ
33 Ⓐ Ⓑ Ⓒ Ⓓ Ⓔ
34 Ⓕ Ⓖ Ⓗ Ⓙ Ⓚ
35 Ⓐ Ⓑ Ⓒ Ⓓ Ⓔ
36 Ⓕ Ⓖ Ⓗ Ⓙ Ⓚ
37 Ⓐ Ⓑ Ⓒ Ⓓ Ⓔ
38 Ⓕ Ⓖ Ⓗ Ⓙ Ⓚ
39 Ⓐ Ⓑ Ⓒ Ⓓ Ⓔ
40 Ⓕ Ⓖ Ⓗ Ⓙ Ⓚ
41 Ⓐ Ⓑ Ⓒ Ⓓ Ⓔ
42 Ⓕ Ⓖ Ⓗ Ⓙ Ⓚ
43 Ⓐ Ⓑ Ⓒ Ⓓ Ⓔ
44 Ⓕ Ⓖ Ⓗ Ⓙ Ⓚ
45 Ⓐ Ⓑ Ⓒ Ⓓ Ⓔ
46 Ⓕ Ⓖ Ⓗ Ⓙ Ⓚ
47 Ⓐ Ⓑ Ⓒ Ⓓ Ⓔ
48 Ⓕ Ⓖ Ⓗ Ⓙ Ⓚ
49 Ⓐ Ⓑ Ⓒ Ⓓ Ⓔ
50 Ⓕ Ⓖ Ⓗ Ⓙ Ⓚ
51 Ⓐ Ⓑ Ⓒ Ⓓ Ⓔ
52 Ⓕ Ⓖ Ⓗ Ⓙ Ⓚ
53 Ⓐ Ⓑ Ⓒ Ⓓ Ⓔ
54 Ⓕ Ⓖ Ⓗ Ⓙ Ⓚ
55 Ⓐ Ⓑ Ⓒ Ⓓ Ⓔ
56 Ⓕ Ⓖ Ⓗ Ⓙ Ⓚ
57 Ⓐ Ⓑ Ⓒ Ⓓ Ⓔ
58 Ⓕ Ⓖ Ⓗ Ⓙ Ⓚ
59 Ⓐ Ⓑ Ⓒ Ⓓ Ⓔ
60 Ⓕ Ⓖ Ⓗ Ⓙ Ⓚ

Answer Sheet

MODEL EXAM B

Test 3

1	A	B	C	D	11	A	B	C	D	21	A	B	C	D	31	A	B	C	D
2	F	G	H	J	12	F	G	H	J	22	F	G	H	J	32	F	G	H	J
3	A	B	C	D	13	A	B	C	D	23	A	B	C	D	33	A	B	C	D
4	F	G	H	J	14	F	G	H	J	24	F	G	H	J	34	F	G	H	J
5	A	B	C	D	15	A	B	C	D	25	A	B	C	D	35	A	B	C	D
6	F	G	H	J	16	F	G	H	J	26	F	G	H	J	36	F	G	H	J
7	A	B	C	D	17	A	B	C	D	27	A	B	C	D	37	A	B	C	D
8	F	G	H	J	18	F	G	H	J	28	F	G	H	J	38	F	G	H	J
9	A	B	C	D	19	A	B	C	D	29	A	B	C	D	39	A	B	C	D
10	F	G	H	J	20	F	G	H	J	30	F	G	H	J	40	F	G	H	J

Test 4

1	A	B	C	D	11	A	B	C	D	21	A	B	C	D	31	A	B	C	D
2	F	G	H	J	12	F	G	H	J	22	F	G	H	J	32	F	G	H	J
3	A	B	C	D	13	A	B	C	D	23	A	B	C	D	33	A	B	C	D
4	F	G	H	J	14	F	G	H	J	24	F	G	H	J	34	F	G	H	J
5	A	B	C	D	15	A	B	C	D	25	A	B	C	D	35	A	B	C	D
6	F	G	H	J	16	F	G	H	J	26	F	G	H	J	36	F	G	H	J
7	A	B	C	D	17	A	B	C	D	27	A	B	C	D	37	A	B	C	D
8	F	G	H	J	18	F	G	H	J	28	F	G	H	J	38	F	G	H	J
9	A	B	C	D	19	A	B	C	D	29	A	B	C	D	39	A	B	C	D
10	F	G	H	J	20	F	G	H	J	30	F	G	H	J	40	F	G	H	J

Model Exam B

ENGLISH TEST

45 MINUTES—75 QUESTIONS

Directions: The following test consists of 75 underlined words and phrases in context, or general questions about the passages. Most of the underlined sections contain errors and inappropriate expressions. You are asked to compare each with the four alternatives in the answer column. If you consider the original version best, choose letter **A** or **F:** NO CHANGE. For each question, blacken on the answer sheet the letter of the alternative you think best. Read each passage through before answering the questions based on it.

Passage 1

(1)

Abraham Lincoln has been quoted as advising a new lawyer, "Young man, it's more important to know what cases not to take than it is to know the law." New attorneys soon learn to recognize what cases will probably be unprofitable, or they quickly end up looking for new jobs in the newspaper because of lack of funds.[1] [2]

(2)

During the initial interview with the client, the lawyer discovers whether or not a case is meritorious. Examples of cases without merit include an argument with neighbors over a pesky dog or an accident that results from the victim's own negligence, such as someone falling in a local supermarket because they were drunk.[3] This questionable and dubious[4] type of case can

1. **A.** NO CHANGE
   B. because of lack of funds.
   C. in the newspaper.
   D. OMIT the underlined portion.

2. Is the quotation from Abraham Lincoln an appropriate way to begin this passage?
   F. Yes, because quotations are always better than straight prose as attention-getters.
   G. No, because it misleads the reader, suggesting that Lincoln is the topic of the passage.
   H. No, because it is too short a quotation to add any meaning.
   J. Yes, because Abraham Lincoln is an authority figure, often quoted because of the truth and simplicity of his statements.

3. **A.** NO CHANGE
   B. he or she was drunk.
   C. they had been drinking.
   D. they were considerably under the influence.

4. **F.** NO CHANGE
   G. OMIT the underlined portion.
   H. questionable
   J. dubious

GO ON TO THE NEXT PAGE.

be easily seen as lacking merit, because each of the elements of a tort (a civil wrongdoing) was not present, and thus no law was broken. We must all try to behave as adults as we wend our way through this troubled interval. [5]

(3)

Finally, there is the type of case in which the prospective client has been represented in the matter by another attorney. Accepting such a case can be risky, although [6] multiple lawyers are evidence of a worthless case an [7] uncooperative client, or a client who does not pay his or her bill. Even if the reason for the client's [8] changing attorneys is a good one—let's say [9] a personality clash between the client and the prior attorney—it makes the new lawyer's task of reaching a fair settlement with the other party strategically difficult.

(4)

There are some cases that seem to have merit but are economically unfeasible for a new attorney to handle. Such cases are easy to spot once a full, adequate enough disclosure [10] of the facts has been obtained from the client during the initial interview. One type of unprofitable case is the "hurt feelings" case stemming from an incident where the defendant has been guilty of caddish behavior—but what young man in springtime has been able to resist the pull of the heart?— [11] but where the victim cannot prove he or she

5. A. NO CHANGE
   B. We must all try to be mature.
   C. We must all do our best.
   D. OMIT the underlined portion.

6. F. NO CHANGE
   G. when
   H. because
   J. similarly

7. A. NO CHANGE
   B. case. An
   C. case, an
   D. case: an

8. F. NO CHANGE
   G. clients
   H. client
   J. clients'

9. A. NO CHANGE
   B. one, let's say
   C. one (let's say
   D. one let's say

10. F. NO CHANGE
    G. full, adequate disclosure
    H. full, adequate, complete disclosure
    J. full disclosure

11. A. NO CHANGE
    B. been guilty of caddish behavior—but sometimes that happens to young people—
    C. been guilty of wrongful behavior,
    D. OMIT the underlined portion.

has been specifically damaged, or where damages are nominal. For instance, in an action for slander, not only is it difficult to prove slander but also [12] the monetary damage to the victim resulting from the slanderous action may be small or even nonexistent. In these kinds of cases, a prospective client may be so righteously angered as to say that he or she does not care about the money, that it is the principle that matters, that may [13] be true for the prospective client, but the attorney cannot pay his secretary's salary, his office rent, or his malpractice insurance premium will not be reduced [14] with a client's "principle." [15]

12. **F.** NO CHANGE
G. slander, but also
H. slander. But also
J. slander; but also

13. **A.** NO CHANGE
B. matters that
C. matters. That
D. matters: that

14. **F.** NO CHANGE
G. premium reduction
H. premium reduced
J. premium

15. Choose the sequence of paragraph numbers that makes the structure of the passage most logical.
A. NO CHANGE
B. 1, 4, 2, 3
C. 1, 3, 2, 4
D. 1, 2, 4, 3

Passage 2

(1)

Of all the many differences between people, there is one that goes more deeper [16] than any other or than all combined, and that is whether the person are parents or not. [17] Variations in cultural background, religion, politics, or education do not come close to parent versus nonparent differences. [18]

16. **F.** NO CHANGE
G. deeper
H. deep
J. deepest

17. **A.** NO CHANGE
B. is a parent or not.
C. is parents or not.
D. are a parent or not.

18. This passage was probably written for readers who:
F. are experts in child development.
G. are expecting a child.
H. are general readers.
J. are childless.

1 1 1 1 1 1 1 1 1 1 1

(2)

Conversely, few if any knickknacks remain whole in a home with small children, the only plants left are those hanging, brown and wilted, from a very high ceiling.

19. **A.** NO CHANGE
B. children the only
C. children: the only
D. children. The

Instead, toys strewn carelessly about the living areas. The somewhat disheveled rooms usually look slightly askew, since little ones delight in moving furniture around and are especially prone to do so unless a guest or two are expected. Walls are usually smudged with the prints of tiny hands and feet (yes, feet—don't ask me how) and decorated with children's artwork, which also adorns the refrigerator, kitchen cabinets, message center, and any other available blank space. To a parent, there is no such thing as a sparkling clean mirror or window. A handy way to clean windows and mirrors is by using crushed newsprint. Children simply cannot keep from touching—with their hands, noses, mouths, whatever—clean mirrors and windows. It has something to do with marking one's territory, I believe. [25]

20. **F.** NO CHANGE
G. toys strew
H. toys were strewn
J. toys are strewn

21. **A.** NO CHANGE
B. disheveled rooms
C. rooms
D. somewhat, disheveled rooms

22. **F.** NO CHANGE
G. after
H. as
J. when

23. **A.** NO CHANGE
B. are expecting.
C. is expected.
D. will be expected.

24. **F.** NO CHANGE
G. OMIT the underlined portion.
H. Clean windows with newsprint.
J. A handy way to clean windows is with newsprint.

25. Which of the phrases below demonstrates the intent of the writer to be whimsical and humorous?
A. toys strewn carelessly
B. marking one's territory
C. sparkling clean mirror
D. available blank space

(3)

The very way a house is decorated proclaims the owner's status. My childless friends have plants, expensive accessories, and elegant knickknacks placed strategically about their finely-furnished homes.

26. **F.** NO CHANGE
G. finely furnished
H. finely, furnished
J. furnished

Model Exam B

Framed prints hang on their spotlessly white walls, while their mirrors and windows sparkle. [27]

(4)

Another distinguishing[28] great difference between people without children and people with them is their attitude toward life. Before my daughter came along five years ago, I was a competent legal secretary, a faithful wife, and a person who enjoyed a quiet life-style interspersed with an occasional party or outing. I was well-adjusted but ill-prepared[29] for chaotic living, and, I see now, quite naive. [30]

27. Examination of Paragraphs 2 and 3 reveals that the author of this passage wants to emphasize:
    A. fine art in American homes.
    B. styles and decor in contemporary homes.
    C. the impact of children on a home.
    D. indoor plant styles in contemporary American homes.

28. **F.** NO CHANGE
    G. OMIT this word
    H. discriminating
    J. differentiating

29. **A.** NO CHANGE
    B. well adjusted but ill-prepared
    C. well adjusted but ill prepared
    D. well-adjusted but ill prepared

30. Choose the sequence of paragraph numbers that makes the structure of the passage most logical.
    F. NO CHANGE
    G. 1, 3, 2, 4
    H. 1, 3, 4, 2
    J. 1, 4, 2, 3

Passage 3

(1)

By the late 1900s, the climate were growing[31] slowly better for incarcerated women, and the improvement in their treatment could be directly traced to the women's rights movement. Some changes were significant. Women reformers had argued not only that women should supervised[32] by women but also that reform could not be carried out in a jail cell. By the late 19th century, women prepared for release were

31. **A.** NO CHANGE
    B. are growing
    C. had grown
    D. were growing

32. **F.** NO CHANGE
    G. supervision
    H. be supervision
    J. be supervised

Model Exam B

1 1 1 1 1 1 1 1 1 1 1

placed in programs centered on development of domestic roles some settings were cottages rather than cells. Although these conditions existed in some prisons, the vast majority of women were placed in attics or storage space outside of the regular prison. The effect was that women were deprived of basic (albeit limited) resources that the male prisoners had.

33. **A.** NO CHANGE
B. roles; some
C. roles—some
D. roles. Some

Today, there are many more minority women (along with their male counterparts) in prison. Much of this imbalance can be explained by America's war on drugs. It is not hard to remember the crack epidemic of the mid-1980s to the early 1990s. Media were reporting it, and it was everywhere, on television, in *Time* magazine articles, in the newspapers, and at local high schools. However, when one looks at the New York State Department of Correctional Services Report (written by Clarice Feinman) on new court commitments, one must pause, consider the figures, and realize the awful facts of what is happening to these addicts. Consider the commitments that occurred between 1988 and 1991:

34. **F.** NO CHANGE
G. them
H. many
J. those judged guilty

- There was a 123 percent increase in woman commitments, from 1,014 to 2,264.
- The proportion of females committed for drug offenses had risen from 53 percent to 72 percent.
- Black commitments increased 166 percent, 68 percent drug-related.
- Hispanic commitments increased 1,224 percent, 87 percent drug-related.

35. **A.** NO CHANGE
B. raised
C. rises
D. rose

- White commitments increased 25 percent, 44 percent drug-related. [36]

(2)

Throughout history, if one wished to have a glimpse of the deprived class, a quick trip to a prison <u>is</u> [37] the easiest solution. Today is no different: Prisons still house the poor and uneducated. In books and movies, rarely does one see the face of a woman prisoner. Rather, a person is more likely to see a barbarous and depraved man who, many would agree, belongs where he is. But, truthfully, prisons do not always house the barbarous and depraved: in fact, prisons usually house the weak and unfortunate. And our system of justice does not just incarcerate men: Today, there are tens of thousands of women <u>stuffing</u> [38] into overcrowded prisons.

The city of London established the first workhouse in an abandoned royal palace named Bridewell. The supposed function was to "care for and discipline" the "riffraff," who <u>are considered</u> [39] a danger to the rest of society. England did not always throw its "riffraff" into prison; many times, the royal courts would exile them to places like Australia or the New World.

(3)

The cause of these arrest figures is debatable. While some people suggest that minorities of lower socioeconomic status might use drugs to escape the realities of unemployment and racism, some conclude that the fault is actually in how the police work in minority neighborhoods: <u>It is observed</u> [40] that there is more police surveillance in minority communities, and since black and Hispanic populations are more youth-

36. Is the first sentence of the second paragraph in this section necessary?
    - **F.** No, the author seems to be unfairly referring to minority women.
    - **G.** No. The author is linking drugs with minorities.
    - **H.** No, because the article refers only to those women who are in jail.
    - **J.** Yes, because the facts listed in the bulleted list at the end of the paragraph argue strongly the point that there is imbalance in the numbers of minorities being imprisoned.

37. **A.** NO CHANGE
    - **B.** would be
    - **C.** would have been
    - **D.** will have been

38. **F.** NO CHANGE
    - **G.** being stuffed
    - **H.** are being stuffed
    - **J.** were being stuffed

39. **A.** NO CHANGE
    - **B.** were considered
    - **C.** is considered
    - **D.** had been considered

40. **F.** NO CHANGE
    - **G.** were considered
    - **H.** is considered
    - **J.** They observe

Model Exam B

GO ON TO THE NEXT PAGE.

ful and more likely to be out in the streets for recreation, they are more likely to be picked up for acts that might also occur in private in white, middle-class neighborhoods. Whatever the case, life in minority neighborhoods can be very dangerous and stressful, especially for young black males and females. Consider the statistics: A male black has a 1 in 2 chance of being murdered in his lifetime, and a male white, a 1 in 131 chance. A black female has a 1 in 124 chance of being murdered, while a white female has a 1 in 606 chance. And, regardless of how these young people are arrested, the real hurdles begin in court.

When minority defendants appear in court for the first time, one of the most important issues <u>he faces</u> (41) is whether they will be held for trial or released until their next court date. As history has shown, minorities usually find themselves still in custody or facing a bail amount they cannot afford. Many times, minorities find themselves being represented by young or incompetent court-appointed counsel. Currently, it is estimated that more than 60 percent of accused felons are represented by public defenders. And just imagine what a minority defendant thinks when he or she is not on trial in front of his or her own peers. Minority women, compared with their white counterparts, "are more likely to be single, poor, and responsible for dependent children" (Feinman). Such a profile can be a disaster for a minority defendant on trial in a death penalty case. [42]

41. **A.** NO CHANGE
    B. they face
    C. he is facing
    D. he will be faced

42. Is the reference to jurors meaningful at this place in the passage?
    F. No, because it virtually changes the subject.
    G. No, because the whole passage is about minority defendants.
    H. No, because it is about the problems of jurors, not the defendants.
    J. Yes, because it is a specific example of a "hurdle" minority defendants face in court.

(4)

The death penalty has a long and sordid history in the United States.[43] In the years between 1608 and 1993, 12,438 people were executed in the United States, 287[44] of those were women. The first known woman, Jane Champion of Virginia, was executed in 1632. Throughout the years, many black slave women were lynched and hanged. Many times, a slave woman would be hanged for some crime because her husband had already been lynched or because he was suspected of doing something for which he would have been lynched. Clearly, the United States needs to take a long, hard look at the way we treat minorities in the prison system, as well as the guidelines for the death penalty. [45]

43. How do you regard the supporting material that follows this statement?
   A. It is not effective because it calls up negative images about women.
   B. It is effective because it hammers home the point of the long and sordid history of the death penalty as it pertains to women minorities.
   C. It is not effective or pertinent to the subject at hand.
   D. It is effective because it gives statistics.

44. **F.** NO CHANGE
   G. States; 287
   H. States: 287
   J. States 287

45. Choose the sequence of paragraph numbers that makes the structure of the passage most logical.
   A. NO CHANGE
   B. 2, 1, 3, 4
   C. 1, 4, 3, 2
   D. 4, 1, 3, 2

Passage 4

(1)

My Antonia depicts life on the Nebraska prairie during the early 1900s, mirroring Willa Cather's own experiences as a girl living on the "Great Divide," as that part of Nebraska had been called.[46] The protagonist

46. **F.** NO CHANGE
   G. was called
   H. is called
   J. called

GO ON TO THE NEXT PAGE.

of the novel, Antonia Shimerda was modeled on Annie Sadilek, an actual living Bohemian girl hired by one of Willa Cather's neighbors in the town of Red Cloud. [49]

(2)

A close friend of Willa Cather, the author of *My Antonia,* has written, "Willa forever preferred rural life, although she was never quite so inartistic as to announce that 'the country is preferable to the city'.'' Certainly, *My Antonia,* Willa Cather's third prairie novel, is a joyous song of praise for "the virtues of a settled agricultural existence" as opposed to life in the cities. Her belief that the ideal civilization is to be found in the country, albeit a country tempered with such desirable urban qualities as cultural refinement and order, is developed by the use of multi-level contrasts and comparisons, both obvious and symbolic. [53] [54]

47. **A.** NO CHANGE
    B. , Antonia Shimerda,
    C. Antonia Shimerda
    D. Antonia Shimerda,

48. **F.** NO CHANGE
    G. actual, living
    H. living
    J. actual

49. This paragraph serves as a summary of the novel being discussed in this passage. How might it be strengthened?
    A. NO CHANGE
    B. It should describe the Great Plains setting more fully.
    C. It should give us the entire plot of the story, not part of it.
    D. It should supply more details regarding the family background of the Shimerdas.

50. **F.** NO CHANGE
    G. city' ".
    H. city.' "
    J. city."

51. **A.** NO CHANGE
    B. nevertheless
    C. and
    D. yet

52. **F.** NO CHANGE
    G. multi level
    H. multilevel
    J. many level

53. This paragraph begins with a quotation from a close friend of Willa Cather. Is the use of the quotation relevant to the passage?
    A. No, it is irrelevant and has no bearing on the passage or paragraph.
    B. No, it is misleading, dealing with Willa Cather's life, rather than the substance of the passage.
    C. Yes, it is a valuable insight from a reliable source; in addition, it is relevant to the paragraph and passage.
    D. Yes, it is a humorous touch that does no harm.

54. This passage was probably written for readers who:
    F. are beginning readers in a youngsters' educational program.
    G. are practiced readers who enjoy novels about small-town America and its people.
    H. are Midwesterners who want to learn more about their heritage.
    J. are authors themselves.

1 1 1 1 1 1 1 1 1 1 1

(3)

A richly creative novel, *My Antonia* has been analyzed through a number of critical approaches. John H. Randall's criticism dealt (55) with broad thematic questions regarding Cather's arguments for certain values and ideas, such as the urban versus the bucolic life, using the mythic or archetypal school of criticism to explain many of the symbols employed (56) by the author to show her beliefs. James E. Miller explains the symbolism of the three different cycles used by Cather in the novel: the seasons of the year, the phases of Antonia's life, and, most important to this essay, the people move westward in cycles (57) to America's frontiers. Wallace Stegner, a novelist in his own right, wrote an essay about *My Antonia.* In which (58) he used archetypal criticism in relation to Antonia's identification with the land, and the psychological approach to show how Cather's life and character were crucial to the novel's central theme of country versus city values. [59] [60]

55. **A.** NO CHANGE
    B. had dealt
    C. deals
    D. has been dealing

56. **F.** NO CHANGE
    G. being employed
    H. employing
    J. employ

57. **A.** NO CHANGE
    B. the people moved westward in cycles
    C. the cycles in the movement of people westward
    D. the people were frequently moving westward in cycles

58. **F.** NO CHANGE
    G. *My Antonia* in which
    H. *My Antonia;* in which
    J. *My Antonia*—in which

59. This paragraph begins with the general statement: "... My Antonia has been analyzed through a number of critical approaches." In what ways does the rest of the paragraph support or fail to support this statement?
    A. It supplies the names of several critical approaches and defines them in detail.
    B. It avoids the mention of critical approaches, but names three critics and discusses their ideas.
    C. It names three critics, but says little about critical approaches.
    D. It names three critics and their specific critical approaches to the novel, identifying the critical schools employed by two of them.

60. Choose the sequence of paragraph numbers that makes the structure of the passage most logical.
    F. NO CHANGE
    G. 1, 3, 2
    H. 3, 2, 1
    J. 3, 1, 2

GO ON TO THE NEXT PAGE.

1 1 1 1 1 1 1 1 1 1 1

Passage 5

(1)

Simone de Beauvoir, in *The Second Sex*, makes much of the "antique traditions" that were keeping women tied to the home and marriage. We can still often see the "antique traditions" today in America; for example, there are relatively female firefighters,[61] police officers, or even taxi drivers. Still, in America, men are rapidly becoming almost equal.[62] However, in my country, Japan, even though the situation has been getting a little better because of the change in company policies or laws, we can still see the "antique traditions" operating very often.

Strangely, most Japanese know America's first lady's name and face: Laura Bush is known in Japanese society because she is often featured on television programs or in newspapers. But, the wife of the Japanese Prime Minister is completely unknown. The mass media never pays attention to her, so we do not know her face or even her name. There is a relic notion that women should support their husbands secretly. [63]

In addition, women members of the Diet are still quite rare, especially the Secretaries. This year, the disaster-prevention measures received a lot of media attention because the Secretary of the Ministry of Construction was a woman, because[64] her measures were distinguished. People paid attention, not to the disaster-

61. **A.** NO CHANGE
    B. relatively firefighters,
    C. woefully low numbers of female firefighters,
    D. relatively few firefighters,

62. **F.** NO CHANGE
    G. Still, relatively, men and women are rapidly becoming almost equal.
    H. Still, additionally, men and women are rapidly becoming almost equal.
    J. Still, to me, American men and women are rapidly becoming almost equal.

63. The writer could most effectively strengthen this passage by adding which of the following?
    A. A list of countries that have clearly visible and effective administrators
    B. Mentioning a few other women who are short-changed by the refusal of Japanese society to recognize them and their accomplishments
    C. A list of publications that have reporters so prejudiced
    D. A list of companies and governmental offices that have female workers

64. **F.** NO CHANGE
    G. indeed because
    H. not because
    J. that

prevention measures she did (65) but to how she would perform in front of the world-wide mass media. One of the reporters said ironically, "She is doing a good job, isn't she?" Nobody makes those kinds of statements about men. He implies that she is doing well although she is a woman!

65. **A.** NO CHANGE
B. instituted
C. worked on
D. popularized

(2)

These (66) demonstrate the manner in which women are treated by Japanese society. Let me tell you exactly how women are prevented from growing due to the "antique traditions" that are their heritage. Mainly, in my culture, the traditions are disrupting women's emergence from the ways of the old world. Even now, women are encouraged to stay home and do housework and take care of children, not work in careers outside of the home. When women marry firstborn sons, they usually live in their husband's home with his parents. These women have to take care of the parents. Even though the wives do not want to be so controlled, it is part of their age-old custom and very difficult to avoid. At the same time, the psychological burden of living with another's family is excruciatingly difficult, because, regardless of everything, these women are living in someone else's home: the wives have to keep silent at night, for example, or they may hesitate to go out with their friends or have visitors, or it is simply impossible to know if one can engage in such a simple task as use the kitchen. There is no doubt that this affects their jobs as well as their lives. We Japanese often say, not too jokingly, "I will never marry a first-born son." The situation causes women to have diffi-

66. **F.** NO CHANGE
G. This
H. These things
J. These two examples

GO ON TO THE NEXT PAGE.

culties in their work and families, as a result, there are more and more single women in Japan. They choose their jobs rather than marriage because marriage usually means the end of their careers. I have misgivings about the fact that only women have to suffer from these problems. It is quite unfair.

67. **A.** NO CHANGE
 B. families and
 C. families; as a result,
 D. families, but

(3)

Such problems occur regularly, not only in marriage or the family, and also in the workplace; companies discriminate against women, which prevents women's professional growth. Last spring, my good friend landed a job at a large enterprise. She was happy because she secured a good job in spite of the depression. However, at her entrance ceremony, a man came up to her and said, "I am sorry, but I decided not to employ you." She was so depressed, of course. At the same time, she became very angry. It was not because she was denied the company's offer, or that she was denied the job at the entrance ceremony; it was because she was denied the job due to her gender. That is never understandable or forgivable. [70]

68. **F.** NO CHANGE
 G. but
 H. if
 J. besides

69. **A.** NO CHANGE
 B. "We aren't going to hire you."
 C. "We have decided not to employ any women this year because of the depression."
 D. "We refuse to hire you."

70. Readers are likely to regard the passage thus far as best described by which of the following terms?
 F. Concerned
 G. Conciliatory
 H. Apologetic
 J. Confessional

To be sure, the situation of women in Japan is getting better compared to the past, but still there are many women who are suffering from such "antique traditions." I believe traditions to be very important and valuable, but those traditions that prevent women's growth should be taken away. I believe old people's stultified thoughts and actions about women's rights must not be allowed to prevent the rise of women

71. This sentence alone indicates that the intention of the author is to be:
 A. dominating
 B. understanding
 C. underhanded
 D. superior

72. **F.** NO CHANGE
 G. womens
 H. womens'
 J. Womans

1 1 1 1 1 1 1 1 1 1 1

anywhere. For example, the law guarantees the same employment opportunities; yet, actually, they do not work, as in my friend's case. [73] To improve this situation, we women have to attempt to change this discrimination by never relenting and by being aware of it, just as, for example, women achieving women's suffrage in the past. We cannot accomplish the victory without a lot of effort. I believe we can do it by being ever vigilant. [74] [75]

73. A. NO CHANGE
B. For example, the law guarantees all jobs to men and women; yet, they have no jobs.
C. For example, the law guarantees women the same employment opportunities that men have; yet women are given very few jobs.
D. For example, all women are guaranteed the jobs that men are given; they do not get the jobs.

74. The word "change" in the third sentence from the end takes the position that women have to adopt two stances. What are they?
F. To never relent and to be ever aware of discrimination
G. To improve the situation and attempt to change it
H. To be aware of discrimination and to achieve suffrage as in the past
J. To improve this situation and to achieve suffrage as in the past

75. Choose the sequence of sections that makes the structure of the essay most logical.
A. NO CHANGE
B. 3, 1, 2
C. 3, 2, 1
D. 1, 3, 2

STOP

If there is still time remaining, you may review your answers.

2 2 2 2 2 2 2 2 2 2 . 2

MATHEMATICS TEST

60 MINUTES—60 QUESTIONS

Directions: After solving each problem, darken the appropriate space on the answer sheet. Do not spend too much time on any one problem. Make a note of the ones that seem difficult, and return to them when you finish the others. Assume that the word *line* means "straight line," that geometric figures are not necessarily drawn to scale, and that all geometric figures lie in a plane.

DO YOUR FIGURING HERE

1. The following expression $\frac{a}{b} - \frac{c}{d} = ?$

   A. $\frac{a-b}{cd}$
   B. $\frac{a}{d} - \frac{c}{b}$
   C. $\frac{a-b}{cd}$
   D. $\frac{a-c}{bd}$
   E. $\frac{a-d}{bc}$

2. If $x \neq 0$, which of the following is equal to $\frac{2x^4 + x^3}{x^6}$?

   F. $\frac{3}{x^3}$
   G. $\frac{x+1}{x^2}$
   H. $2x^2 + x^3$
   J. $\frac{2x+1}{x^3}$
   K. $\frac{2x+1}{x}$

3. A certain city has 1600 public telephones. Three-fourths of the phones have dials. If one-third of the dial phones are replaced by push-button phones, how many dial phones remain?

   A. 800
   B. 750
   C. 700
   D. 600
   E. 400

DO YOUR FIGURING HERE

4. If x and y are both positive integers, which of the following is NOT necessarily an integer?

 F. $x + y$
 G. $x - y$
 H. $x\,y$
 J. x^y
 K. $\frac{x}{y}$

5. If a negative number is subtracted from a positive number, which of the following will always be the result?

 A. Zero
 B. A positive number
 C. A negative number
 D. A number having the sign of the number with the larger absolute value
 E. A number having the sign of the number with the smaller absolute value

6. What is the solution set of the equation $\frac{5}{4x - 3} = 5$?

 F. {7}
 G. {4}
 H. {2}
 J. {1.5}
 K. {1}

7. If t represents the tens digit of a two-digit number, and u represents the units digit, which of the following expressions represents the number?

 A. $t + u$
 B. $10t + u$
 C. $10u + t$
 D. $10(t + u)$
 E. tu

8. What is the simplified form of the product of the two polynomials $(x - 1)(x^2 + x + 1)$?

 F. $x^3 + 1$
 G. $x^3 - 1$
 H. $x^3 - x - 1$
 J. $x^3 + x^2 + x$
 K. $x^3 + 2x^2 + 2x + 1$

Model Exam B

GO ON TO THE NEXT PAGE.

DO YOUR FIGURING HERE

9. Find the area of a window in the shape of a rectangle with a semicircle on top.

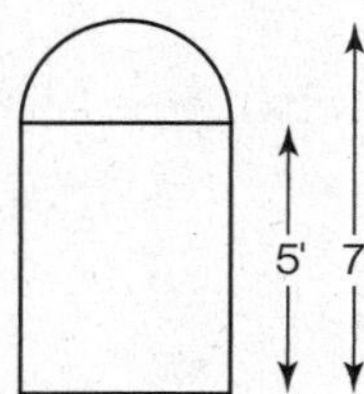

A. 20 square feet
B. $20 + 2\pi$ square feet
C. $20 + 4\pi$ square feet
D. $10 + 2\pi$ square feet
E. $10 + 4\pi$ square feet

10. Which of the following numbers is NOT equal to the others?

F. 2.5%
G. $\frac{1}{40}$
H. $2.5(10^{-2})$
J. $\frac{75}{30}$
K. 0.025

11. If apples are 35 cents or 3 for $1.00, how much is saved on each apple by buying them 3 at a time?

A. 5 cents
B. $1.05
C. $\frac{3}{5}$ cent
D. $1\frac{2}{3}$ cents
E. $11\frac{2}{3}$ cents

12. If Joan can run 1 mile in a minutes, how much of a mile has she run after b minutes if she runs at a constant rate?

F. $\frac{a}{b}$
G. $\frac{b}{a}$
H. $\frac{1}{ab}$
J. ab
K. $\frac{a+b}{a}$

DO YOUR FIGURING HERE

13. Which of the following is NOT a real number?

    A. $\sqrt[5]{0}$
    B. 5^0
    C. 0^5
    D. $0 \cdot 5$
    E. $\frac{5}{0}$

14. $3\frac{3}{5} \times 4\frac{1}{6} = ?$

    F. 15
    G. $7\frac{23}{30}$
    H. $\frac{108}{125}$
    J. $\frac{17}{30}$
    K. $\frac{1}{15}$

15. Yvette has 5 more nickels than dimes. If the value of her money is \$1.30, how many coins of each kind does she have?

    A. 12 dimes and 7 nickels
    B. 5 dimes and 16 nickels
    C. 5 dimes and 10 nickels
    D. 7 dimes and 12 nickels
    E. 3 dimes and 20 nickels

16. What is the tenth term of the arithmetic sequence 3, 8, 13, . . .?

    F. 18
    G. 43
    H. 48
    J. 53
    K. None of these

17. What is the solution set of the equation $0.2(100 - x) + 0.05x = 0.1(100)$?

    A. $\left\{-33\frac{1}{3}\right\}$
    B. $\{10\}$
    C. $\{40\}$
    D. $\left\{66\frac{2}{3}\right\}$
    E. $\left\{95\frac{95}{399}\right\}$

Model Exam B

DO YOUR FIGURING HERE

18. Which of the following statements is false?

    F. A regular triangle is equilateral.
    G. A regular quadrilateral is a square.
    H. An interior angle of a regular pentagon has a measure of 108°.
    J. A regular polygon of seven sides does not exist.
    K. All of these statements are true.

19. What is the simplest form of the radical $\sqrt[3]{54x^4y^6}$?

    A. $3xy^2\sqrt[3]{2x}$
    B. $3x^2y^3\sqrt[3]{6}$
    C. $3y^3\sqrt[3]{2x^4}$
    D. $3x^2\sqrt[3]{6y^6}$
    E. $3xy^2\sqrt[3]{6x}$

20. Which of the following is NOT an equation of a conic section?

    F. $y = 5x^2 - 3x + 2$
    G. $x^2 + y^2 - 5x + 2y - 7 = 0$
    H. $2x^2 - 5y^2 = 7$
    J. $y = x^3$
    K. $\frac{(x+2)^2}{25} + \frac{(y-3)^2}{16} = 1$

21. What is the degree of $-5x^2y + 3xy^3 + 2xy + 6$?

    A. 9
    B. 5
    C. 4
    D. 3
    E. 2

22. What is the solution set of the following system of equations?

$$\begin{pmatrix} 2x - y = 5 \\ x + y = 1 \end{pmatrix}$$

    F. {(2,1)}
    G. {2}
    H. {(3, 1)}
    J. {(4, – 3)}
    K. {(2, – 1)}

Model Exam B

DO YOUR FIGURING HERE

23. A number from the set {1, 2, 3, ..., 20} is selected at random. What is the probability that the number is even and less than 10?

A. $\frac{1}{2}$

B. $\frac{9}{20}$

C. $\frac{1}{5}$

D. $\frac{9}{40}$

E. $\frac{1}{4}$

24. If $x \neq 0$ and $y \neq 0$, what is the simplified form of the complex fraction $\dfrac{x+y}{\frac{1}{x}+\frac{1}{y}}$?

F. $\frac{x+y}{xy}$

G. $\frac{xy}{x+y}$

H. $(x+y)^2$

J. $2+\frac{x}{y}+\frac{y}{x}$

K. xy

25. If m $\angle ABC = 70°$, then m $\angle ADC$ = ?

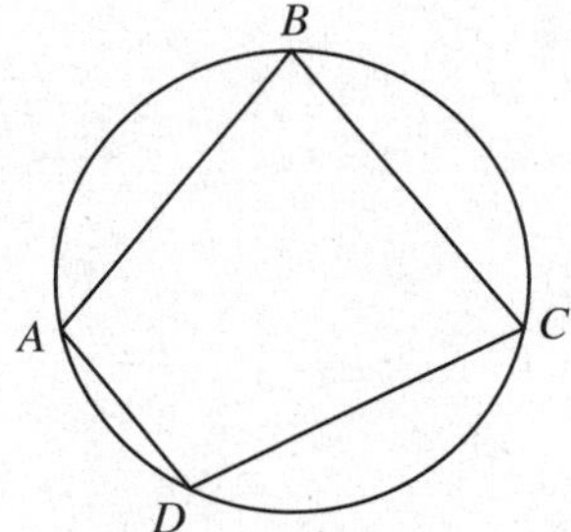

A. 35°
B. 70°
C. 90°
D. 110°
E. 140°

26. If $a > b$, then $|a - b| + |b - a|$ is equal to what expression?

F. 0
G. $2a$
H. $2b$
J. $2a + 2b$
K. $2a - 2b$

Model Exam B

GO ON TO THE NEXT PAGE.

2 2 2 2 2 2 2 2 2 2 2 2

DO YOUR FIGURING HERE

27. What is the value of -3^{-2}?

A. 6
B. 9
C. -9
D. $\frac{-1}{9}$
E. $\frac{1}{9}$

28. What is the center of the ellipse with the equation $x^2 + 4y^2 - 4x + 24y + 36 = 0$?

F. (2, 1)
G. (1, 2)
H. (2, – 3)
J. (– 2, 3)
K. (1, 4)

29. Nick can do a certain job in 2 hours less time than it takes Bonnie to do the same job. If they can complete the job together in 7 hours, what equation could be used to determine how long it would take Bonnie to do the job alone?

A. $7(x - 2) = 7x$
B. $\frac{7}{x-2} = \frac{7}{x}$
C. $7(x - 2) + 7x = 1$
D. $\frac{7}{x-2} + \frac{7}{x} = 1$
E. None of these

30. Which of the following is the graph of a one-to-one function?

F. 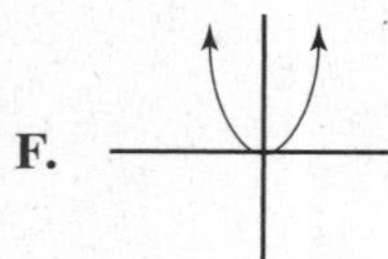

J. 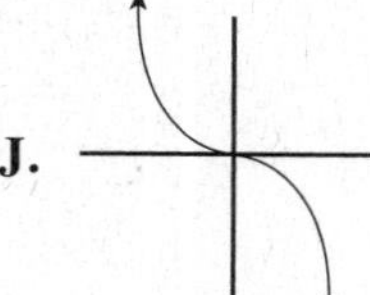

G. 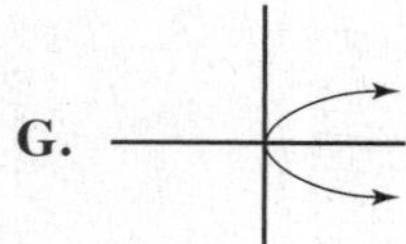

K. 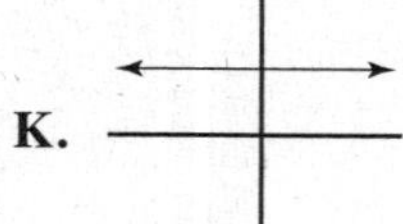

H. 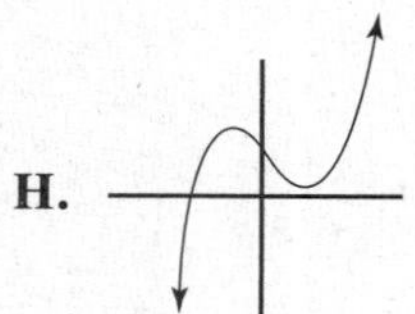

2 2 2 2 2 2 2 2 2 2 2

DO YOUR FIGURING HERE

31. Which of the following numbers could NOT be the base of an exponential function?

    A. $\frac{1}{2}$
    B. 1
    C. 2
    D. 3
    E. $\sqrt{5}$

32. What is the simplified form of the expression $(5x - 3y^2)^2$?

    F. $25x^2 + 9y^4$
    G. $25x^2 - 9y^4$
    H. $25x^2 - 30xy + 9y^2$
    J. $25x^2 - 15xy^2 + 9y^4$
    K. $25x^2 - 30xy^2 + 9y^4$

33. What is the reciprocal of i?

    A. 1
    B. -1
    C. i.
    D. $-i$
    E. None of these

34. What is the simplified form of the expression $\frac{a^{-3}bc^2}{a^{-4}b^2c^{-3}}$? (Assume that the variables are not equal to zero. Write without negative exponents.)

    F. $\frac{c^5}{a^7b}$
    G. $\frac{ac^5}{b}$
    H. $\frac{a^7c^5}{b}$
    J. $\frac{c}{ab}$
    K. $\frac{a^7}{bc^5}$

35. In right triangle ABC, m $\angle A = 30°$, m $\angle B = 60°$, and $AC = 6$. What is the length of $\overline{AB}$?

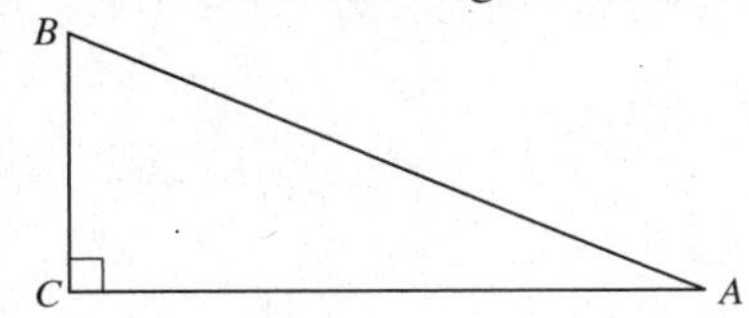

    A. $3\sqrt{2}$
    B. $6\sqrt{3}$
    C. $4\sqrt{2}$
    D. $3\sqrt{3}$
    E. $4\sqrt{3}$

GO ON TO THE NEXT PAGE.

Model Exam B

DO YOUR FIGURING HERE

36. Which of the following is identically equal to sin $2A$?

    F. $1 - \cos^2 2A$
    G. $2 \sin A \cos A$
    H. $\dfrac{1}{\sec 2a}$
    J. $2 \sin A$
    K. None of these

37. What is the solution set of $3x^2 - 4x - 6 = 0$?

    A. $\left\{\frac{-2}{3}, 3\right\}$
    B. $\left\{\frac{2 + 2\sqrt{22}}{3}, \frac{2 - 2\sqrt{22}}{3}\right\}$
    C. $\left\{\frac{4 + \sqrt{22}}{3}, \frac{4 - \sqrt{22}}{3}\right\}$
    D. $\left\{\frac{4 + i\sqrt{66}}{6}, \frac{4 - i\sqrt{66}}{6}\right\}$
    E. $\left\{\frac{2 + \sqrt{22}}{3}, \frac{2 - \sqrt{22}}{3}\right\}$

38. What is the simplified form of the radical expression

    $3\sqrt{3} - \sqrt{48} + 3\sqrt{\frac{1}{3}}$?

    F. 0
    G. $\sqrt{3}$
    H. $4\sqrt{3} - 2\sqrt{12}$
    J. $3\sqrt{3} - 2\sqrt{12} + \sqrt{3}$
    K. It is already in simplest form.

39. Which of the following equations does NOT define a function?

    A. $y = x + 2$
    B. $x = y + 2$
    C. $y = 2^x$
    D. $y = x^2$
    E. $x = y^2$

Model Exam B

2      2 2 2 2 2

DO YOUR FIGURING HERE

40. If tangent $\overline{CD}$ is 6 cm long and $BC = 4$, what is the length of $\overline{AB}$?

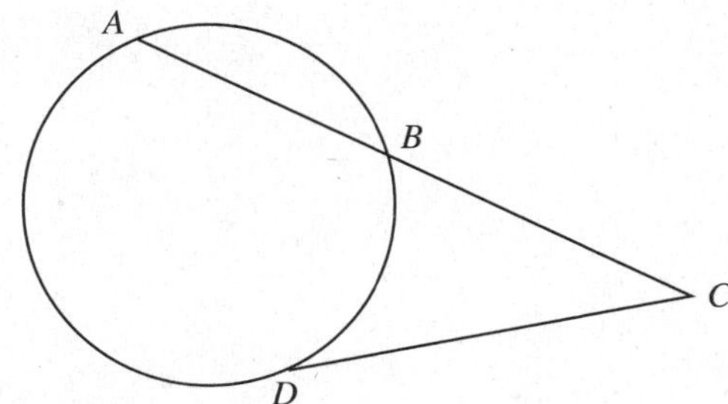

F. $2\frac{2}{3}$
G. 3
H. 4
J. 5
K. 6

41. Diane averages 12 miles per hour riding her bike to work. Averaging 36 miles per hour on the way home by car takes her $\frac{1}{2}$ hour less time. What equation could be used to determine how far she travels to work?

A. $12x + 36x = 30$
B. $\frac{x}{12} = \frac{x}{36} - \frac{1}{2}$
C. $\frac{x}{12} + \frac{x}{36} = 30$
D. $\frac{x}{36} = \frac{x}{12} - \frac{1}{2}$
E. $\frac{36}{x} = \frac{12}{x} + \frac{1}{2}$

42. What are the coordinates of the midpoint of a segment with endpoints $A(3, 7)$ and $B(-5, -6)$?

F. (0, 0)
G. $\left(1, \frac{-1}{2}\right)$
H. $\left(-1, \frac{1}{2}\right)$
J. (– 2, 1)
K. (8, 13)

43. What is the solution set of the radical equation $\sqrt{2x - 3} = -5$?

A. {–1}
B. {4}
C. {7}
D. {14}
E. ∅

DO YOUR FIGURING HERE

44. Which of the following statements is false?

    F. Every whole number is an integer.
    G. Some rational numbers are natural numbers.
    H. The set of integers is a subset of the set of real numbers.
    J. $\sqrt{49}$ is a rational number.
    K. None of these statements is false.

45. If an equilateral triangle is inscribed in a circle of radius 8 cm, what is the perimeter of the triangle?

    A. $24\sqrt{3}$
    B. $8\sqrt{3}$
    C. $4\sqrt{3}$
    D. 12
    E. 24

46. What is the domain of the function $f(x) = \dfrac{x + 3}{x^2 - 2x - 3}$?

    F. All real numbers
    G. $\{x \mid x \text{ is a real number and } x \neq -3\}$
    H. $\{x \mid x \text{ is a real number and } x \neq 3 \text{ and } x \neq -1\}$
    J. $\{x \mid x \text{ is a real number and } x \neq 3, x \neq -1, \text{ and } x \neq -3\}$
    K. $\{x \mid x \neq 0\}$

47. Circles A and B are tangent to each other. $\overline{CD}$ is a common tangent to the two circles. If the radius of circle A is 5 and the radius of circle B is 3, what is the length of $\overline{CD}$?

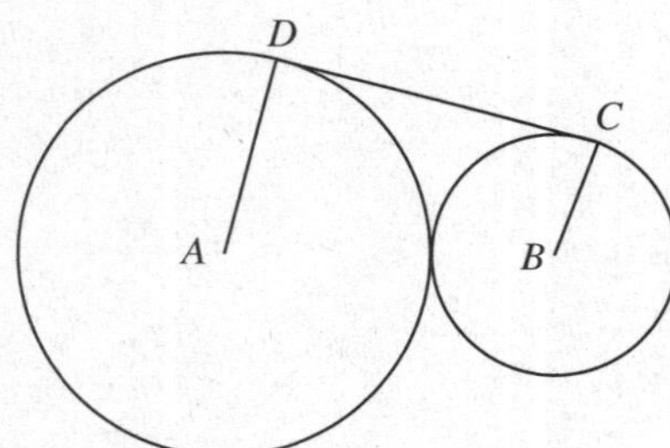

    A. 4
    B. 8
    C. $\sqrt{34}$
    D. $2\sqrt{15}$
    E. $2\sqrt{17}$

Model Exam B

DO YOUR FIGURING HERE

48. If $\overline{AD}$ is a diameter and m $\angle C = 125°$, what is the measure of $\angle A$?

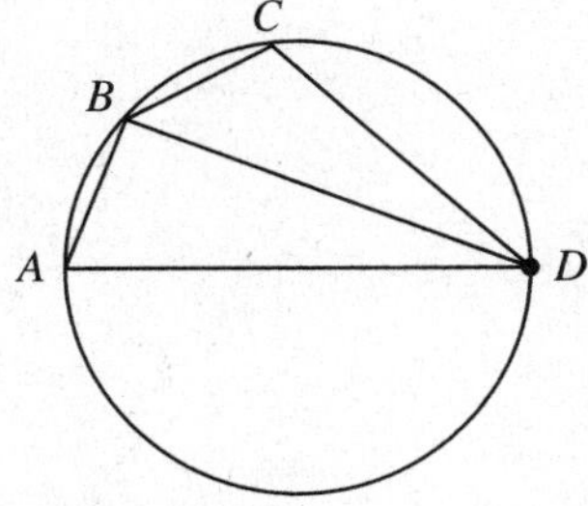

F. 35°
G. 55°
H. 62.5°
J. 90°
K. 125°

49. If $AC = 8$ and $BD = 6$, then what is the length of $\overline{BC}$?

A. 1
B. 5
C. $7\frac{1}{2}$
D. 15
E. There is not enough information.

50. If $A(-3, 4)$ lies on the terminal side of angle θ, what is the value of sec θ?

F. $\frac{-3}{5}$
G. $\frac{4}{5}$
H. $\frac{-3}{5}$
J. $\frac{-4}{3}$
K. $\frac{5}{4}$

51. What is the value of $\sum_{k=1}^{5} 2k^2$?

A. 2
B. 50
C. 52
D. 110
E. None of these.

52. In which quadrant must θ lie if cos θ > 0 and cot θ < 0?

F. I
G. II
H. III
J. IV
K. No such angle exists.

2 2 2 2 2 2 2 2 2 2 2

DO YOUR FIGURING HERE

53. Let A and B be any two sets. Which of the following statements is always true?

A. $(A \cup B) \subseteq A$
B. $(A \cap B) \subseteq B$
C. $(A \cup B) \subseteq (A \cap B)$
D. $B \subseteq (A \cap B)$
E. $(A \cup B) = (A \cap B)$

54. The length of the diagonal of a rectanglar piece of wood is $\sqrt{145}$ feet. If one side is 1 foot longer than the other, what are the lengths of the sides?

F. 8 feet and – 9 feet
G. 8 feet and 9 feet
H. 12 feet and 13 feet
J. 5 feet and 6 feet
K. 2 feet and 36 feet

55. Which is the value of $\sin\left(\cos^{-1}\frac{2}{3}\right)$?

A. $\frac{2}{3}$

B. $\frac{\sqrt{5}}{3}$

C. $\frac{-\sqrt{5}}{3}$

D. $\frac{\pm\sqrt{5}}{3}$

E. $\frac{\sqrt{13}}{3}$

56. Jon scored 75, 84, and 80 on his first three tests. What score must he get on his fourth test so that his average will be at least 80?

F. 81
G. Greater than 81
H. Less than 81
J. Greater than or equal to 81
K. Less than or equal to 81

57. What is the measure of an exterior angle of a regular octagon?

A. 45°
B. 60°
C. 72°
D. 120°
E. 135°

Model Exam B

2 2 2 2 2 2 2 2 2 2 2

DO YOUR FIGURING HERE

58. If the lengths of the diagonals of a rhombus are 6 and 8 meters, what is the perimeter, in meters, of the rhombus?

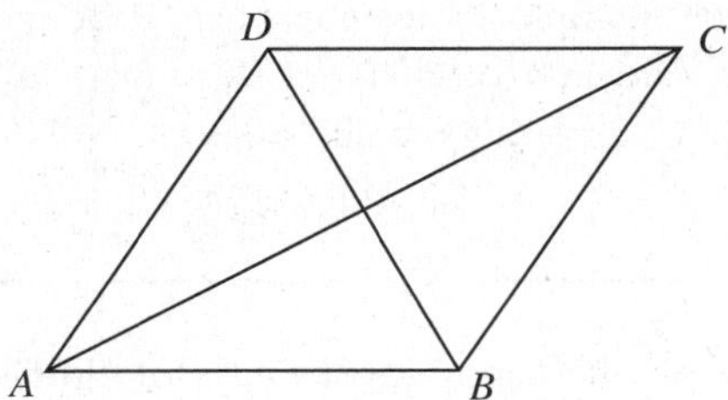

F. 5
G. 14
H. 20
J. 28
K. 40

59. Which of the following statements is true?

A. Complements of complementary angles are equal.
B. A line segment has only one bisector.
C. A line perpendicular to a segment also bisects the segment.
D. An isosceles triangle may also be scalene.
E. None of these statements is true.

60. In $\triangle ABC$, $\overline{AB} \perp \overline{BC}$ and $\overline{BD} \perp \overline{AC}$. If $BD = 4$ and $AC = 10$, what is the length of $\overline{AD}$ (the shorter portion of the hypotenuse)?

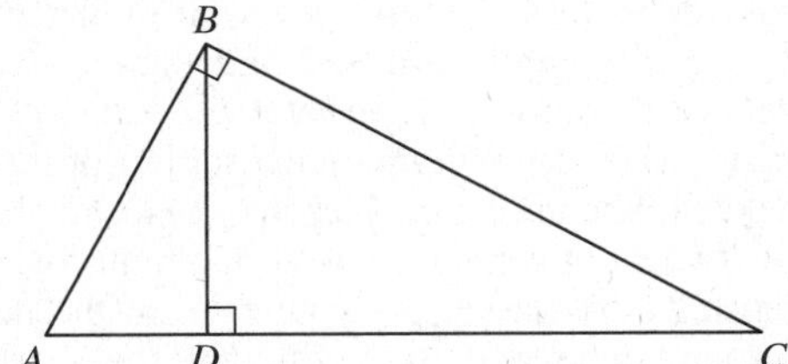

F. 2
G. 3
H. 4
J. 6
K. 8

If there is still time remaining, you may review your answers.

READING TEST

35 MINUTES—40 QUESTIONS

Directions: This test consists of four passages, each followed by ten multiple-choice questions. Read each passage and then pick the best answer for each question. Fill in the spaces on your answer sheet that correspond to your choices. Refer to the passage as often as you wish while answering the questions.

Passage 1—Prose Fiction

This passage is an excerpt from "The Egg," a short story by Sherwood Anderson. In it the narrator recounts his family's vain efforts to run a chicken farm.

My father was, I am sure, intended by nature to be a cheerful, kindly man. Until he was thirty-four years old he worked as a farm hand for a man named Thomas Butterworth whose place lay near the town of Bidwell, Ohio. He had then a horse of his own and on Saturday evenings drove into town to spend a few hours in social intercourse with other farm hands. . . . At ten o'clock Father drove home along a lonely country road, made his horse comfortable for the night and himself went to bed, quite happy in his position in life. He had at that time no notion of trying to rise in the world.

It was in the spring of his thirty-fifth year that Father married my mother, then a country schoolteacher, and in the following spring I came wriggling and crying into the world. Something happened to the two people. They became ambitious. The American passion for getting up in the world took possession of them.

It may have been that Mother was responsible. Being a schoolteacher she had no doubt read books and magazines. She had, I presume, read of how Garfield, Lincoln and other Americans rose from poverty to fame and greatness and as I lay beside her—in the days of her lying-in—she may have dreamed that I would some day rule men and cities. At any rate, she induced Father to give up his place as a farm hand, sell his horse and embark on an independent enterprise of his own. . . .

The first venture into which the two people went turned out badly. They rented ten acres of poor stony land on Grigg's Road, eight miles from Bidwell, and launched into chicken raising. I grew into boyhood on the place and got my first impressions of life there. From the beginning they were impressions of disaster and if, in my turn, I am a gloomy man inclined to see the darker side of life, I attribute it to the fact that what should have been for me the happy joyous days of childhood were spent on a chicken farm.

One unversed in such matters can have no notion of the many and tragic things that can happen to a chicken. It is born out of an egg, lives for a few weeks as a tiny fluffy thing such as you will see pictured on Easter cards, then becomes hideously naked, eats quantities of corn and meal bought by the sweat of your father's brow, gets diseases called pip, cholera and other names, stands looking with stupid eyes at the sun, becomes sick and dies. A few hens and now and then a rooster, intended to serve God's mysterious ends, struggle through to maturity. The hens lay eggs out of which come other chickens and the dreadful cycle is thus made complete. It is all unbelievably complex. Most philosophers must have been raised on chicken farms. One hopes for so much from a chicken and is so dreadfully disillusioned. Small chickens just setting out on the journey of life, look so bright and alert and they are in fact so dreadfully stupid. They are so much like people they mix one up in one's judgments of life. If disease does not kill them they wait until your expectations are thoroughly aroused and then walk under the wheels of a wagon. . . . In later life I have seen how a literature has been built up on the subject of fortunes to be made out of the raising of chickens. . . . Do not be led astray by it. It was not written for you. Go hunt for gold on the frozen hills of Alaska, put your faith in the honesty of a politician, believe if you will that the world is daily growing better and that good will triumph over evil, but do not read and believe the literature that is written concerning the hen. . . .

I, however, digress. My tale does not primarily concern itself with the hen. If correctly told it will center on the egg. For ten years my father and mother struggled to make our chicken farm pay and then they gave up that struggle and began another. They moved into the town of Bidwell, Ohio, and embarked in the restaurant business. After ten years of worry, . . .we threw all aside and packing our belongings on a wagon drove down Grigg's Road toward Bidwell, a tiny caravan of hope looking for a new place from which to start on our upward journey through life.

1. The narrator of the story views life pessimistically because:
   A. he grew up on a chicken farm.
   B. his parents never succeeded at anything they did.
   C. his life has been all work and no play.
   D. he and his family were always in debt.

2. The books and magazines mentioned in lines 19–21:
   F. aided Mother in her work as a schoolteacher.
   G. indicate that Mother was a scholar and an intellect
   H. gave Mother ideas about how one ought to conduct one's life.
   J. were given to Mother in the hospital.

3. When he abandoned chicken farming, Father was about:
   A. 35 years old.
   B. 40 years old.
   C. 45 years old.
   D. 50 years old.

4. Which of these changes did NOT take place after Father got married?
   F. Father gave up his job at Butterworth's.
   G. Father became an ambitious person.
   H. Father stopped his Saturday-night socializing with the boys.
   J. Father wanted to stop working on a farm.

5. According to the narrator, in which way do chickens resemble human beings?
   A. Chickens, like people, appear to be brighter than they really are.
   B. Chickens, like children, are expensive to bring up.
   C. Chickens, as well as humans, are dirty, diseased, and smelly.
   D. Tragedies befall both chickens and humans.

6. According to the narrator, one of the few pleasures in raising chickens is that:
   F. you have the chance to witness the life cycle.
   G. the creatures are cute when they are chicks.
   H. if you are lucky, you can become rich.
   J. you'll never run out of eggs.

7. The narrator's opinion of books and articles written about chicken farming is that they:
   A. are all a pack of lies.
   B. are not written for anyone who is serious about raising chickens.
   C. tend to exaggerate the rewards of chicken farming.
   D. are meant only for people with nothing to lose.

8. Mother's ambition for her family's success led to all EXCEPT which of the following consequences?
   F. Father's cheerful and kindly disposition was changed.
   G. Mother and Father became poverty-stricken.
   H. Mother and Father were forced to work very hard.
   J. Mother and Father thought that they were failures.

9. Which pair of adjectives most accurately conveys the narrator's feelings about his childhood?
   A. resentful/bitter
   B. detached/unemotional
   C. satirical/humorous
   D. sentimental/sad

10. "Most philosophers must have been raised on chicken farms" (lines 49–50) means that chicken farming:
    F. gives you a philosophical outlook on life.
    G. exposes you to profound issues like good and evil, life and death.
    H. allows you time to think.
    J. is so complex that only a philosopher can comprehend it.

Passage 2—Social Studies

This passage is from a governmental report on domestic violence titled "Characteristics of the Abusive Situation." It discusses several problems faced by abused and battered spouses.

Abusive husbands systematically isolate their wives from family and friends. Even women who seek legal, medical or emotional help view themselves as unable to succeed against their all-powerful husbands who, they fear, will "pay witnesses to lie in court," "kill my family if I testify," "get custody of the children," and "refuse to give me a divorce." Physical and emotional abuse of women is an exercise of power and control in which the weight of society has been traditionally on the side of the oppressor. Thus, battered women who feel powerless to alter their circumstances are reacting realistically to what they have experienced. They are trapped, and their descriptions of the responses of police, prosecutors and judges are not paranoid delusions.

Many victims have been beaten repeatedly and their attackers have not been apprehended and punished. Assault is a crime. Legally it makes no difference if the victim and her attacker are strangers or are married to each other. Yet police officers often refuse to arrest husbands (or live-in companions) who beat their wives. Police, prosecutors, judges and society in general share the prejudice that women provoke men by constant nagging, overspending or questioning their virility. Verbal provocation, even assuming it exists, however, is not justification for violence.

The absence of negative sanctions gives the abusive family member license to continue his threats and violence. The lack of societal restraints on the husband's violence, the emphasis on defendant's rights in the courts, the long court delays, the opportunity for intimidation, the husband's promises of reform and the woman's fear of economic privation contribute to the drop out rate of 50 percent by battered-wife complainants in the criminal courts and in the Family Court.

Civil actions for support, separation or divorce are also subject to delays which make it virtually impossible to get emergency relief. Judges frequently refuse to "throw a man out of his home," so it is the woman and children who must leave. Crowded court calendars make the legal process work in favor of the person who controls the family income and assets. Getting temporary alimony or maintenance and child support can take months, sometimes as long as a divorce itself. Unless there is a refuge for battered women, the abused wife may be forced to live with her husband during a divorce action.

Equitable distribution of property may also be problematic for the financially dependent spouse because the litigation to define, evaluate and divide the property can continue for years and is very costly. The ultimate irony is that, even when the battered wife gets an award for alimony and child support, the amount of support is usually inadequate for her to maintain herself and the children. Moreover, often it is not paid at all.

Because the separated or divorced wife cannot rely on payment of court-ordered support, many battered wives stay with their husbands. Professor Richard J. Gelles, a sociologist who studied battered wives, found that the wives who hold a job are better able to obtain assistance and leave the abusive situation . . . Viewing the difficult situation in which legal, economic and social realities place the battered woman, one should ask: where does this woman get the stamina to survive the attacks and the courage to leave? Part of the work of the helping professionals is to convince the battered woman that she must use the enormous strength she has for self-preservation, not just for self-sacrifice.

The legal system requires that an injured adult initiate and follow through with the steps necessary to obtain protection, child custody, financial support, divorce or money damages. Usually the injured person bears the expense of engaging an attorney to represent her in a civil case. The legal process is complex and confusing so that referral to a sympathetic and competent lawyer is important. Other helping professionals must understand the laws concerning family violence if they are to provide effective support. Accompanying a client to court helps develop a first-hand sense of the obstacles that the client faces.

The victim of domestic violence is in the best position to decide if legal action will be the most effective way to stop the violence or psychological abuse. Her decision on this matter must be respected. If just moving away (and getting a divorce if necessary) will work, then there is no reason to get entangled in a complicated legal process in which control is given to an unknown judge. But there are situations in which police assistance and court protection are essential.

Governor's Commission on Domestic Violence

11. According to the first paragraph, the main reason that abused women often feel helpless is that:

A. they don't know where to get help.
B. society customarily takes the man's side.
C. they can't afford to seek assistance.
D. witnesses to incidents of abuse are hard to find.

12. In lines 12–14 the assertion that "their descriptions . . . are not paranoid delusions . . ." implies that battered women:

F. often cannot separate fantasy from reality.
G. tend to exaggerate incidents of abuse.
H. feel maltreated by those whose help they seek.
J. frequently need psychological help.

13. It can be reasonably inferred from the second paragraph that officials often think that incidents of wife abuse:

A. should be settled within the family itself, if possible.
B. are less serious than conflicts between strangers.
C. should be blamed equally on the husband and the wife.
D. have most likely been provoked by the wife.

14. The passage indicates that half the lawsuits brought against abusive husbands remain incomplete because of all the following reasons EXCEPT that the:

F. husband and wife are reconciled.
G. wife feels threatened by loss of financial support.
H. courts take too long to hear cases.
J. husband pledges to stop abusing his wife.

15. The passage suggests that, in an emergency, an abused wife should:

A. call a neighbor.
B. immediately report her husband to the police.
C. try to go to a shelter for battered women.
D. contact a social worker.

16. Which of the following statements most accurately summarizes the author's view on how to solve the problems of abused wives?

F. Change the legal system to give abused wives special consideration.
G. Help abused women overcome feelings of hopelessness.
H. Strictly enforce the laws governing alimony payments.
J. Educate society about the problems of abused wives.

17. A primary purpose of the passage is to:

A. argue for new laws to protect abused women.
B. convince readers that abusive behavior is never justified.
C. point out the injustices faced by abused women.
D. advise abused women of their rights.

18. The passage implies that the severest hardships of abused women pertain to:

F. fears of bodily harm.
G. lack of financial support.
H. psychological trauma.
J. the well-being of their children.

19. According to the passage, an abused wife may invoke all of the following legal remedies EXCEPT:

A. filing for an official separation from her husband.
B. maintaining custody of the children.
C. forcing the husband to continue financial support.
D. requiring the husband to pay her attorney's fees.

20. The passage suggests that, to stop domestic violence, an abused woman should turn to the courts only when:

F. there is no alternative.
G. she suffers psychological trauma.
H. her husband would be charged with criminal behavior.
J. she can get help from an understanding lawyer.

GO ON TO THE NEXT PAGE.

Passage 3—Humanities

This passage is from an essay about the unusual effects that a famous radio program had on its listeners.

On October 30, 1938, the night before Halloween, the Mercury Theater radio program broadcast a dramatization of *The War of the Worlds*, by British writer H. G. Wells. The program began as if it were a musical evening with Ramon Raquello's orchestra in a New York hotel, when news bulletins interrupted to report that a strange meteorite had struck New Jersey. A few minutes later, the music was replaced by eyewitness observations of the object itself, an immense, yellowish-white cylinder that had blasted a crater in a nearby farm. Soon, war machines emerged from it and began annihilating the United States Army. The public was relatively unfamiliar with science fiction stories at that point in history, and many took the realistic drama for actual news reports. Many thousands of people were frightened by the program, and some panicked.

A group of sociologists, including Hadley Cantril, had been working on a major study of the effect of radio, funded by the Rockefeller Foundation. Quickly securing supplementary grants, they were able to launch a sudden research study. Cantril's team interviewed 135 people who had been frightened, collected newspaper stories, administered surveys, and analyzed polls conducted by other organizations. An estimated 6,000,000 people heard the broadcast; 1,700,000 of them thought it was factual news, and 1,200,000 were frightened or disturbed. It did not take many of these people to flood the telephone switchboards of police and radio stations with worried calls.

Among the factors that encouraged listeners to believe that Martians were actually attacking the earth were the realism of the program itself, the fact that radio had become a standard medium for important announcements, the apparent prestige of the speakers who included expert astronomers, the ease of visualizing specific incidents, the realistically baffled behavior of radio characters themselves, and the unified quality of the total experience. Many listeners tuned in late, and others tuned in only because friends who were worried by the broadcast telephoned them. These people missed the beginning of the program when it was clearly labeled fiction drama.

Questionnaires and interviews allowed Cantril to investigate how listeners had tried to verify the impressions they got from the program. Some checked internal evidence from the broadcast against things they already knew. For example, a few had read the first science fiction magazine, *Amazing Stories*, and recognized the style. Or they noticed that events in the story were moving unrealistically fast. Some others checked external evidence, for example, turning to other stations on the radio or checking the program listing in the newspaper. A number of listeners tried to check external evidence but failed for some reason. One person looked out the window and saw a strange greenish glow on the horizon. Failure to reach parents on the telephone was taken as evidence that they had been destroyed. A street full of cars was seen as proof that people were fleeing, and an empty street was seen as evidence the way had been blocked so they could not flee. Other listeners were so confused they didn't even try to check the truth of the invasion report.

People who failed to verify the report tended to be more frightened than those who did so. Listeners with less education and relatively poor people were more likely to panic and less likely to use effective means for testing the veracity of the report. Cantril argued that some people have more critical ability than others, whereas some are especially suggestible or anxious. If two or more people listened to the program together, or if friends called each other on the phone, one person's reaction would be influenced by those of the others. Some listeners perceived themselves to be relatively safe for the time being, for example, those distant from the supposed invasion point in New Jersey.

The Martian invasion panic was greatly stimulated by the fact that the world really was in great danger at that point in history. Hitler had taken Austria and was in the process of seizing Czechoslovakia. Less than a year later, the Second World War would break out in Europe, and most people already sensed it coming. A decade into the Great Depression, many people had good reason to be terrified about their economic futures, and it seemed that the social norms were disintegrating around them. Listeners had become used to hearing alarming news reports on the radio, and it seemed plausible that a new horror could erupt at any moment.

William Sims Bainbridge, *Sociology*, Barron's (1997)

21. The passage suggests that the producers of the Mercury Theater radio program created a sense of realism by:
    A. urging listeners not to call the police or radio stations.
    B. broadcasting realistic sound effects in the background.
    C. canceling commercials for one evening.
    D. employing "experts" to comment on the attack.

22. Which of the following facts was NOT included in the report of the landing of the meteorite?
    F. American soldiers had been killed.
    G. While descending, the meteorite had been brightly illuminated.
    H. It crashed into a rural area of New Jersey.
    J. Its landing had been observed by eyewitnesses.

23. According to the passage, many listeners thought that the report of the landing in New Jersey was true because:
    A. they hadn't realized it was Halloween eve.
    B. they had never before heard a radio program interrupted by a news bulletin.
    C. the report was made to sound authentic.
    D. they had vivid imaginations.

24. It is reasonable to infer that many people were genuinely alarmed by the radio program because:
    F. Hadley Cantril and other sociologists studied their reactions.
    G. phone calls to emergency services increased during the broadcast.
    H. friends quickly gathered to share their fears and worries.
    J. people turned off their radios to keep their families from being frightened.

25. The passage suggests that in October 1938 the genre of science fiction:
    A. was still in its infancy.
    B. had not yet been invented.
    C. was dominated by British writers.
    D. held little interest to Americans.

26. The passage implies that some listeners were convinced of the truth of the attack when they:
    F. discerned similarities between the broadcast and material in *Amazing Stories*.
    G. jumped to conclusions about what they observed.
    H. noticed that the pace of events in the broadcast matched the pace of other crises.
    J. listened to the broadcast alone.

27. Information in lines 42–51 in the fourth paragraph suggests that:
    A. some listeners were skeptical of the program's authenticity.
    B. only very gullible people believed that the attack occurred.
    C. people who had read a certain science fiction magazine immediately recognized the program as a hoax.
    D. most of the radio audience hoped that the attack had not actually occurred.

28. The implications of Cantril's findings on the effect of the broadcast are best summed up by which of the following statements?
    F. All listeners to the program were shaken up to some degree or other.
    G. The program made lasting impressions on poor, uneducated listeners.
    H. Apprehensive, impressionable listeners were more upset by the program than discerning, incisive listeners.
    J. The program left the least impact on listeners located farthest from New Jersey.

29. The "great danger" referred to in line 76 can best be described as:
    A. various political and economic crises.
    B. the threat of mob violence brought about uncontrollable fear.
    C. the daily troubles faced by impoverished Americans.
    D. listeners' lack of self-confidence.

30. The passage states that the public's reaction to the broadcast was influenced by:
    F. the popularity of H. G. Wells' *War of the Worlds*.
    G. the introduction of *Amazing Stories*, a sci-fi periodical.
    H. recent reports of unexplained lights on the horizon.
    J. events taking place overseas.

GO ON TO THE NEXT PAGE.

Passage 4—Natural Science

This passage is adapted from a report prepared by the National Aeronautical and Space Administration (NASA) on the problems associated with establishing settlements in outer space.

Solar sails are a way of moving things around in space, from one orbit to another. They are beginning to look like the best means of transportation in an area as big as space. And space is big! It would take as many Earths to fill the solar system (500,000,000,000,000,000) as elephants to fill the sea (an unpleasant prospect). The Earth's orbit around the Sun is 23,000 times the Earth's circumference. Driving to the Moon (1/400 of the distance to the Sun) would take six months, at 55 mph. Driving to the nearest star would take 50,000,000 years, and so on. Space is Big. To get anywhere you have to go fast.

But, you say, since there is no air resistance in space, perhaps a patient traveler (or load of freight) could start out slowly and simply take whatever time was needed, drifting along. But, alas, gravity is in control. If left to themselves, objects in space don't really go anywhere; they simply go around in orbits. Unless you kick something so hard that it stops completely, in which case it falls into whatever it was orbiting, or kick it so hard in the other direction that it can fly away, despite gravity, never to return, the object will simply grunt at the kick, and shift its orbit somewhat. To get from one orbit to another generally takes two perfectly measured pushes from a rocket.

But rockets have limits because of the weight of fuel they must carry. A rocket can reach the same velocity as its exhaust fairly easily; not much fuel is needed to reach a few kilometers per second. The problem is that fuel has mass, just like a payload. Let's say you have a rocket with enough fuel to reach 1 km/sec, and to take a ton of payload with it. How much fuel would you need to reach 2 km/sec? Enough fuel to take the ton of payload to 1 km/sec, and also enough fuel to take the fuel needed for the second km/sec to 1 km/sec. The total fuel mass needed turns out to increase exponentially with the velocity reached, just as population has been increasing exponentially with time. Both increases can gobble up more resources than you can afford to provide. Using the Saturn V moon rocket as a first stage, and piling up rockets from there, we could have reached 30 km/sec with enough payload to drop one haunch off an elephant into the Sun (an unpleasant prospect).

Rockets burning chemical fuels run out of ability fast when measured against the solar system, although they were decent for getting us as far as the Moon. The exponential curve that gets rockets into trouble can be made less steep, however, if more energy can be put into the exhaust. This is the principle of the electric rocket; by soaking up solar energy in space and using it to throw small amounts of mass away, payloads may be pushed around the solar system in a reasonable way. The main problem is the cost and mass of the solar power plant. To use it efficiently accelerations must be low and trips long. Costs are also low: freight rates from Earth orbit to Mars orbit might be as little as $.20 per pound.

That brings us to solar sails. For decades people have looked at the problem of stuffing about a square mile of folded reflecting surface into the nose of a rocket, of launching it, and of making it unfold and stretch into a reasonably flat surface in space. A design for a kite-like sail, with thin, aluminized plastic film for the reflecting surface, has reached an advanced planning stage at the Jet Propulsion Laboratory in Pasadena, California. Their design can accelerate at about 1/7,000 of gravity, which is actually fairly good: the sail can reach 1 km/sec in about eight days. This lets you get around, and because it needs no fuel, and no fuel to help carry fuel, and so on, it doesn't peter out at high velocities like a rocket. But 1/7,000 of Earth's gravity isn't spectacular, and solar electric rockets, mentioned above, still look good by comparison.

Can solar sails be made better? The answer seems to be yes, if you forget about folding them up and launching them from the ground. Instead, they can be made in space, not as aluminized plastic sheets, but as aluminized nothing, which weighs far less. Designs now worked out on paper use aluminum foil as the reflecting surface, but foil 1/1000 the thickness of the kitchen kind is needed. These sails are over 40 times as light, and therefore over 40 times as fast, as previous designs. This is spectacular.

If I had to draw a sail today, it would be a hexagon about six miles across, and weighing 20 tons. This is somewhere between the size of Manhattan and San Francisco, but the metal of the sail could be wadded up to the size of a Volkswagen bug.

3 3 3 3 3 3 3 3 3 3 3

31. The main point of the first paragraph is that:

    A. compared to the sun, Earth is tiny.
    B. it is impossible to drive to the nearest star.
    C. solar sails are the best means of transportation in space.
    D. high speed is needed to cover the vast distances of space.

32. The passage states that orbiting objects in space:

    F. drift along at a relatively slow rate of speed.
    G. are subject to the force of gravity.
    H. can remain aloft indefinitely.
    J. require occasional adjustments by rockets.

33. According to the passage, one of the main shortcomings of electric rockets is that:

    A. the electricity they need is expensive to generate in space.
    B. they are efficient only on voyages beyond the solar system.
    C. they tend to be too fragile to withstand the rigors of being shot into orbit.
    D. they require larger amounts of chemical fuel than conventional rockets.

34. The passage asserts that solar sails are a promising alternative to rockets for all of the following reasons EXCEPT:

    F. they are cheaper.
    G. they hold more fuel.
    H. their source of power is found in space.
    J. they weigh less.

35. The passage suggests that ordinary rockets have limited use in long-distance space travel because:

    A. their technology is growing increasingly obsolete.
    B. they accelerate too slowly.
    C. they require too much fuel.
    D. their orbits change frequently.

36. The passage states that increasing a rocket's speed from *one* kilometer per second to *two* kilometers per second requires:

    F. multiplying the number of engines on the rocket.
    G. twice the amount of fuel needed to reach one kilometer per second.
    H. reducing the total payload by half.
    J. many times the amount of fuel needed to reach one kilometer per second.

37. In which of the following ways is an electric rocket superior to a chemically fueled rocket of the same size and weight?

    A. It is more resistant to the pull of gravity.
    B. It carries less fuel.
    C. Its thrust exceeds the thrust of a chemical rocket.
    D. It can accelerate faster.

39. It can reasonably be inferred from the third paragraph (lines 26–43) that the velocity of the rocket's exhaust:

    F. increases in proportion to the rocket's altitude.
    G. depends on the distance the rocket is programmed to travel.
    H. is a factor in determining the speed of the vehicle.
    J. can easily be measured.

39. The author suggests that the successful use of solar sails depends on finding solutions to all of the following problems EXCEPT:

    A. reducing the weight of the sails.
    B. determining the best shape for the sails.
    C. speeding up the acceleration rate of the sails.
    D. deploying folded-up sails in space.

40. The phrase "aluminized nothing" (lines 76–77) describes a solar sail that:

    F. can float in the air.
    G. is hypothetical.
    H. can be rolled up like aluminum foil.
    J. is made of plastic.

STOP

If there is still time remaining, you may review your answers.

4 4 4 4 4 4 4 4 4 4 4

SCIENCE REASONING TEST

35 MINUTES—40 QUESTIONS

Directions: This test consists of several distinct passages. Each passage is followed by a number of multiple-choice questions based on the passage. Study the passage, and then select the best answer to each question. You are allowed to reread the passage. Record your answer by blackening the appropriate space on the answer sheet.

Passage 1

Chart I below shows the total areas planted in genetically modified (GM) and unmodified crops in 2002. Chart II breaks down the GM crops into the type of modification: 1) insect resistance to protect the crop against insect damage, and 2) weed-killer tolerance to allow chemical weed-killers to be used without damage to the crop.

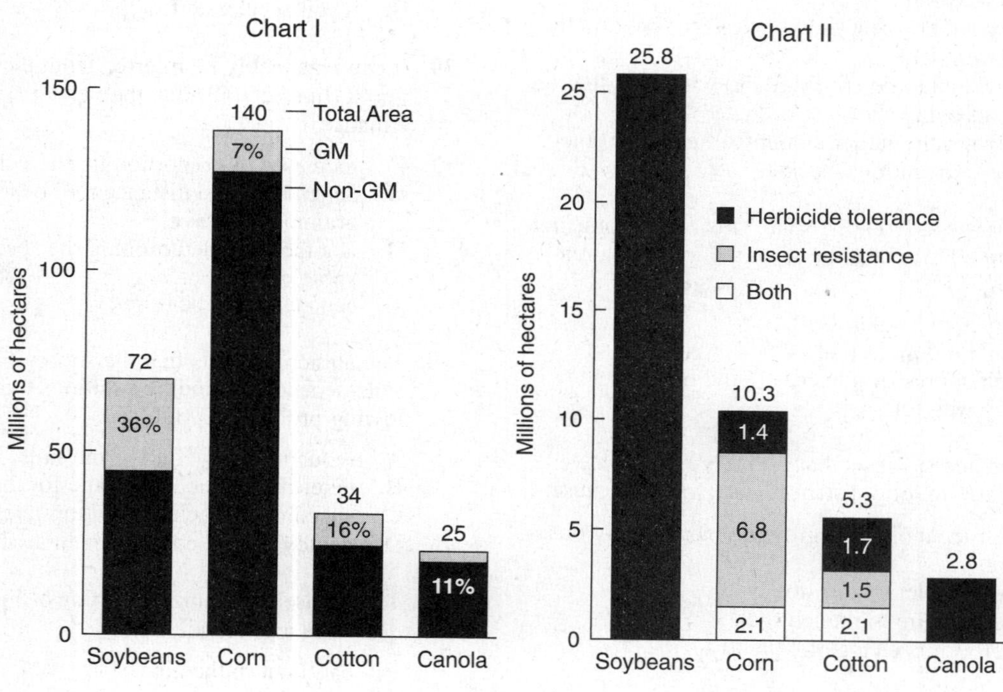

4 4 4 4 4 4 4 4 4 4 4

1. How much area was planted in soybeans that had not been genetically modified?

   A. 12 million hectares
   B. 26 million hectares
   C. 43 million hectares
   D. 70 million hectares

2. Which of the four crops has the largest area using genetically modified plants?

   F. Soybeans
   G. Corn
   H. Cotton
   J. Canola

3. One feature of the use of genetically modified crops is that:

   A. the chief result of the program is protection against insect damage.
   B. most corn in cultivation has been protected against insect damage.
   C. canola is grown less widely than the other three crops.
   D. soybeans have not been protected against insect damage.

4. A major outcome of the genetic modification program is the decreased need for insect killers in:

   F. chiefly, soybean fields.
   G. all four crops.
   H. soybean fields and cornfields.
   J. cornfields and cotton fields

5. An important limitation on the use of GM crops does not apply to:

   A. corn because it is so widely cultivated.
   B. cotton because it is not a food crop.
   C. soybeans because they have not developed GM insect resistance.
   D. canola because it is not widely cultivated.

Passage 2

In the sterilizing process, instruments and cultures are exposed to high temperatures for a definite length of time. The diagram below displays the combinations of temperature and time required to kill various kinds of microorganisms. The six graph areas represent the living stages of bacteria, yeasts, and molds, and the spore stages of these kinds of organisms.

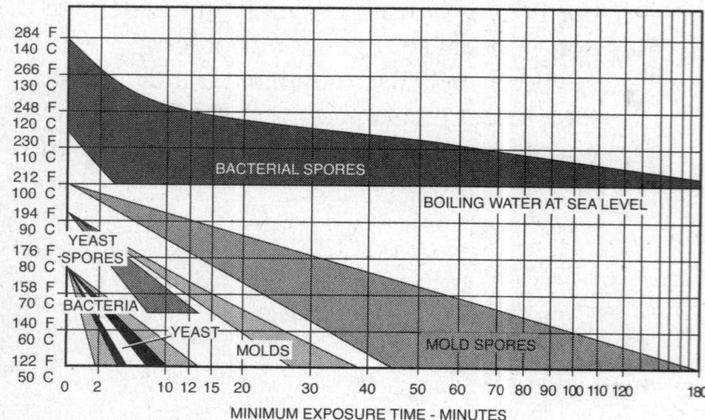

6. The kind of microorganism that is most difficult to kill is:

   F. mold spores.
   G. bacterial spores.
   H. yeasts.
   J. yeast spores.

7. If a laboratory technician keeps instruments in boiling water for 3 hours, the result of the procedure is to kill:

   A. mold spores
   B. bacterial spores.
   C. all spores.
   D. all organisms.

8. What procedure could be used to kill off mold spores in a culture, but leave the yeast spores still viable?

   F. Hold the culture at 80°C for 20 minutes.
   G. Keep the culture at 90°C for 8 minutes and then at 85°C for another 5 minutes.
   H. Keep the culture at 70°C for 10 minutes.
   J. No combination of time and temperature can do this.

9. The chart suggests that, by controlling time and temperature, a technician might be able to:

   A. kill off bacterial spores while leaving live bacteria viable.
   B. kill all bacterial spores without destroying all the mold spores.
   C. kill off certain kinds of bacterial spores and leave other kinds still viable.
   D. destroy all living molds without killing off the living bacteria.

10. What general biological rule might be suggested by the contents of this graph?

    F. Microorganisms form spores to enable them to survive all kinds of unfavorable conditions.
    G. Molds are more sensitive than bacteria to temperature.
    H. Spore formation in microorganisms is a mechanism that protects the species against high temperatures.
    J. Spores are a vital mechanism for the reproduction of certain microorganisms.

4 4 4 4 4 4 4 4 4 4 4

Passage 3

Experiments are done to study some of the factors that determine the rate of a reaction. When sulfuric acid acts on potassium iodate, elemental iodine is released and its concentration increases gradually. Starch is used as an indicator; when the iodine concentration reaches a certain strength, it suddenly turns the starch blue.

Experiment 1

A test solution is made of sulfuric acid and soluble starch. If potassium iodate is added, iodine accumulates at some definite rate. When the iodine reaches a certain concentration, the solution suddenly turns blue. Various concentrations of potassium iodate solution are used, and the time required for the mixture to turn blue is measured.

Potassium iodate concentration (%)	Time (seconds)
10	18
9	20
8	22
7	24
6	26
5	29
4	32

Experiment 2

To determine the effect of temperature on reaction rate, a 5% solution of potassium iodate is added to the test solution at various temperatures.

Temperature (° C)	Time (seconds)
5	36
15	31
25	27
35	24
45	22

11. Starch was added to the solution because:

A. it speeds the reaction that produces iodine.
B. it provides a test for the presence of elemental iodine.
C. it slows down the reaction so that the time becomes easily measurable.
D. it prevents the sulfuric acid from destroying the potassium iodate.

12. Experiment 1 shows that:

F. elemental iodine turns starch blue.
G. at higher iodate concentration, iodine is liberated more quickly.
H. the rate of the reaction depends on the concentration of sulfuric acid used.
J. the release of elemental iodine occurs suddenly.

13. Experiment 2 is an example of a general rule that:

A. higher concentrations speed reactions.
B. higher concentrations slow down reactions.
C. higher temperatures speed reactions.
D. higher temperatures slow down reactions.

14. Experiment 1 was done at a temperature of about:

F. 10° C
G. 20° C
H. 30° C
J. 40° C

15. By studying the results of this experiment, what can be concluded as to the time the reaction would take at a temperature of –15° C?

A. It would take about 48 seconds.
B. It would take longer than 36 seconds, but it is impossible to predict how long.
C. It is not possible to make any prediction because the results of the experiment are too scattered.
D. It might take a long time, or the whole thing might freeze and stop the reaction.

16. About how long would it take for the starch to turn blue if a 10% solution of potassium iodate was used at 45° C?

F. 15 seconds
G. 18 seconds
H. 22 seconds
J. 29 seconds

GO ON TO THE NEXT PAGE.

Passage 4

The graphs below represent the percentages of fat and of water in the human body, by age and sex.

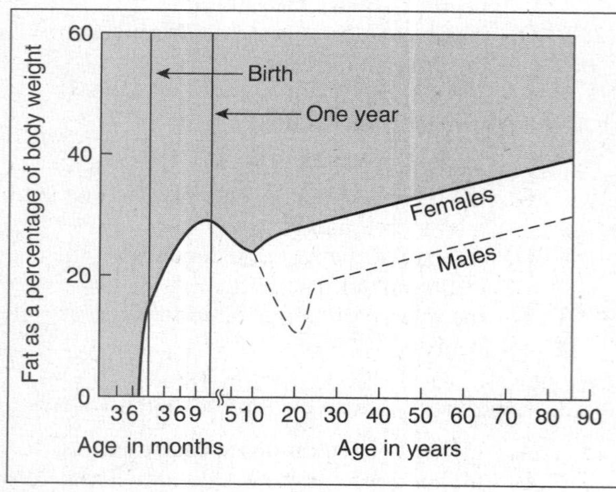

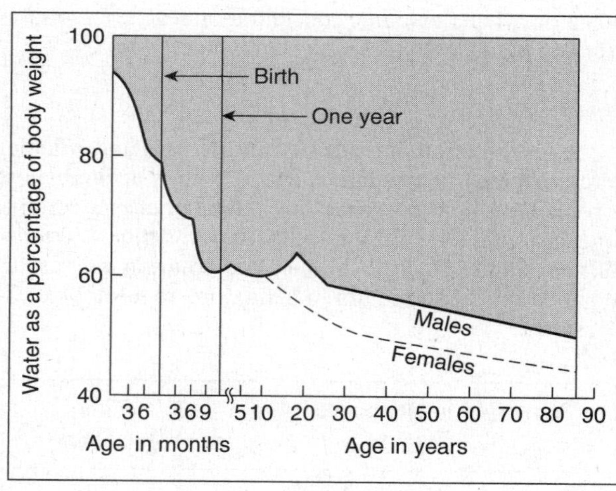

17. During the adolescent years, the most notable change is:
    A. a decrease in fat percentage for boys.
    B. an increase in fat percentage for girls.
    C. a decrease in water percentage for boys.
    D. an increase in water percentage for girls.

18. The percent of fat in the body increases most rapidly during:
    F. middle age.
    G. adolescence.
    H. babyhood.
    J. the prenatal period.

19. At age 60, the amount of water in the body of a 150-pound man is:
    A. the same as that in a 150-pound woman.
    B. twice as much as that in a 150-pound woman.
    C. about the same as that in a 140-pound woman.
    D. about the same as that in a 160-pound woman.

20. As people get older after the age of 40:
    F. men and women become more and more different in the fat content of their bodies.
    G. men and women become more and more different in the water content of their bodies.
    H. both the water and the fat contents of the bodies of men and women become increasingly different.
    J. the difference of both fat and water contents of the bodies of the two genders does not change.

21. What hypothesis about the role of sex hormones during adolescence might be advanced from the graphs?
    A. Both male and female sex hormones cause an increase in the percent of fat in the body.
    B. Male hormones cause a reduction in the percent of fat and an increase in the percent of water.
    C. Female hormones have a much greater influence than male hormones on the percent of water.
    D. Male hormones cause the growth of male secondary sex characteristics.

Passage 5

Seeds are tested for their ability to produce substances that kill microorganisms. Each seed is placed on cultures of two bacteria (*Staphylococcus* and *Es-cherichia*) and two molds. Seeds are classified on a scale of 0 (no effect) to 5 (strong effect), according to the amount of microorganism-free space that develops around the seed.

Experiment 1

Seeds of two members of the Lily family are tested against four different microorganisms:

	Lily Family	
Microorganism	Garlic	Daylily
Staphylococcus	4	0
Escherichia	5	4
Bread mold	2	2
Penicillium mold	3	0

Experiment 2

The same experiment is repeated using seeds of two members of the Composite family:

	Composite Family	
Microorganism	Dandelion	Thistle
Staphylococcus	5	5
Escherichia	4	5
Bread mold	4	3
Penicillium mold	2	2

Experiment 3

The experiment is then done with two members of the Legume family:

	Legume Family	
Microorganism	Soybean	Alfalfa
Staphylococcus	0	0
Escherichia	4	2
Bread mold	2	3
Penicillium mold	3	4

22. Which of the microorganisms is most susceptible to attacks by the chemicals produced by seeds?
    F. *Staphylococcus*
    G. *Escherichia*
    H. Bread mold
    J. *Penicillium* mold

23. Of the following, which kind of seed is more effective against molds than against bacteria?
    A. Alfalfa
    B. Daylily
    C. Thistle
    D. Garlic

24. To find an antibiotic that will protect oranges against *Penicillium* mold, a scientist would concentrate on:
    F. seeds of the thistle and its close relatives.
    G. a variety of members of the Composite family.
    H. members of the Legume family.
    J. seeds of the daylily and its relatives.

25. What hypothesis can be suggested about bread mold?
    A. It can survive by attacking seeds.
    B. It is highly resistant to chemical poisoning.
    C. It cannot be destroyed by seeds of the Composite family.
    D. It is moderately susceptible to attack by many kinds of seeds.

26. What hint might a scientist trying to find an antibiotic to control *Staphylococcus* infections get from these experiments?
    F. Looking for seeds that produce such an antibiotic would be a waste of effort.
    G. It would be inadvisable to concentrate on seeds of the Legume family.
    H. It would be wise to concentrate on *Penicillium* mold and its close relatives.
    J. The scientist should not waste time trying the bread mold and its close relatives.

27. Which of the following ecological hypotheses is supported by the evidence of these experiments?
    A. Molds are better able to survive than bacteria wherever the two kinds of microorganisms compete.
    B. The Legume family produces valuable fodder crops because its seeds have a high survival rate.
    C. The bacteria *Escherichia* and *Staphylococcus* may be highly damaging to leguminous crops.
    D. The Composite family has so many successful sturdy weeds because its seeds destroy microorganisms.

Model Exam B

GO ON TO THE NEXT PAGE.

Passage 6

Experiments are done to test the optical properties of lenses immersed in media having different indices of refraction.

Experiment 1

A lens made of flint glass, index of refraction 1.720, is tested. A beam of parallel light rays is sent into the lens, and the distance from the lens to the point of convergence of the beam is measured. This is the focal length of the lens. This focal length is measured with the lens immersed in media of various indices of refraction.

Medium	Index of refraction	Focal length (cm)
Air	1.00	8
Folinol	1.24	13
Water	1.33	20
11% Sugar solution	1.50	39
Carbon disulfide	1.62	95
Methylene iodide	1.74	*

*Rays do not converge at all.

Experiment 2

Another lens is tested. It is made of the same kind of glass as in Experiment 1, but this lens is thicker, more strongly curved.

Medium	Index of refraction	Focal length (cm)
Air	1.00	5
Folinol	1.24	8
Water	1.33	12
11% Sugar solution	1.50	24
Carbon disulfide	1.62	60
Methylene iodide	1.74	*

Experiment 3

A lens made of a new plastic is then tested. This lens is identical in size and shape to the glass lens in Experiment 2.

Medium	Index of refraction	Focal length (cm)
Air	1.00	13
Folinol	1.24	34
Water	1.33	360
11% Sugar solution	1.50	*
Carbon disulfide	1.62	*
Methylene iodide	1.74	*

28. The index of refraction column is the same in all three experiments because:

   F. all three lenses have the same basic properties.
   G. the same liquids are used in all three experiments.
   H. the temperatures at which the experiments are performed are carefully controlled.
   J. the color of the light source is not allowed to change from one experiment to another.

29. As the index of refraction of the medium increases, what happens to the rays of light emerging from the lens?

   A. They converge more strongly in all cases.
   B. They converge more strongly on leaving the glass lenses, but not the plastic lens.
   C. They converge less strongly in all cases.
   D. They converge less strongly on leaving the plastic lens, but not the glass lens.

30. Making a lens thicker and more strongly curved:

   F. shortens the focal length.
   G. increases the focal length.
   H. increases the index of refraction.
   J. decreases the index of refraction.

31. A reasonable hypothesis that can be derived from Experiments 1 and 2 is that:

   A. a lens will not focus light if its index of refraction is lower than that of the medium it is in.
   B. methylene iodide tends to spread light out so that it does not come to a focus.
   C. the focal length of a lens depends entirely on the index of refraction of the medium it is in.
   D. the thicker a lens, the less the convergence it produces on the light that passes through it.

32. Measurements of the kind made in these experiments would NOT be useful in efforts to find:

   F. the index of refraction of a liquid.
   G. the way a prism in a fluid would bend light rays.
   H. the concentration of a sugar solution.
   J. the transparency of a newly developed plastic.

33. The index of refraction of the plastic lens in Experiment 3 must be:

   A. less than 1.33.
   B. between 1.33 and 1.50.
   C. more than 1.33.
   D. more than 1.50.

Passage 7

Two scientists disagree on the question of the origin of petroleum.

Scientist 1

There have been many theories suggesting a non-organic origin of petroleum, but none of them have been successful. It is now accepted almost universally by geologists that petroleum comes from the decay of living things. Petroleum formation occurs in enclosed oceanic basins, such as the Black Sea. There must be an extremely large and continuous supply of marine organisms, adding their corpses to an accumulation at the bottom of the sea. They are quickly buried in sediment, so quickly that they do not have time to decay. In the enclosed basin, there is little circulation, so there is no supply of fresh, oxygenated water. In the absence of oxygen, there is little decay. The organic matter of the corpses degenerates into hydrocarbons, which accumulate as oil and gas. Since oil is lighter than water, it rises. As the deposits are covered with more sediments, the oil and gas rise into them and accumulate there. Petroleum geologists know that oil is often found in salt domes, formed by the evaporation of seawater.

Scientist 2

The current theory about the origin of petroleum postulates a very unlikely combination of circumstances. It needs an enclosed basin, exceptionally rich in marine life, with sediments pouring rapidly into it from the surrounding countryside. Although this combination might occur occasionally, it is too rare to account for the enormous earth areas underlain by petroleum. In my opinion, oil has been present deep in the earth since its origin. Meteorites, comets, and satellites are rich in hydrocarbons. The earth formed by agglomeration of these kinds of objects. After the earth formed, the hydrocarbons seeped upward, accumulating in porous sedimentary rocks. However, oil and gas are sometimes found seeping out of igneous rocks, which have no fossils at all, if these rocks have been thoroughly fractured by deep earthquakes. Oil wells now drill down to only about 15,000 feet. A recent explorational drilling found an oily sludge at 20,000 feet. If we could get to 30,000 feet, we would find an enormous pool of oil underlying the whole crust of the earth.

34. Both scientists agree that petroleum:
    - **F.** forms at the bottom of the sea.
    - **G.** seeps upward into sedimentary rocks.
    - **H.** is present in great quantities below 30,000 feet.
    - **J.** has always been present on earth.

35. Which of the following discoveries would greatly weaken the argument of Scientist 2?
    - **A.** A vast oil deposit is found in sedimentary strata 20,000 feet deep.
    - **B.** A meteorite is analyzed and found to contain few hydrocarbons.
    - **C.** The sludge discovered at 20,000 feet turns out to be contamination from drilling oil.
    - **D.** A large accumulation of oil is found in highly fractured igneous rock.

36. According to Scientist 2, what strategy would be most likely to increase world supplies of petroleum?
    - **F.** Drill wells to greater depths.
    - **G.** Increase exploration of offshore sedimentary strata.
    - **H.** Drill wells in igneous rocks.
    - **J.** Develop techniques of extraction from meteorites.

37. Exploration of the Persian Gulf reveals that it is an enclosed body of water rich in marine life. According to the hypothesis of Scientist 1, what additional condition would be necessary in order for petroleum deposits to develop?
    - **A.** Vertical circulation to carry oxygen downward
    - **B.** High concentration of salt in the water
    - **C.** An accumulation of meteorites
    - **D.** Rapid deposition of sediments

38. Scientist 2 considers that oil seepage from igneous rocks is damaging to Scientist 1's theory because igneous rocks:
    - **F.** are easily fractured by earthquakes.
    - **G.** never contain fossils.
    - **H.** are always located deep in the crust.
    - **J.** contain many meteorites.

39. What evidence given by Scientist 1 was not refuted by Scientist 2?

 A. There have been many theories of a nonorganic origin of petroleum, and all of them have failed.
 B. Petroleum is very often found associated with salt domes.
 C. All petroleum deposits are in porous sedimentary rock.
 D. Meterorites come to earth in the ocean just as often as on land.

40. The chief objection that Scientist 2 has to the theory of Scientist 1 is that it:

 F. postulates the formation of petroleum in a highly unusual set of conditions.
 G. cannot account for the accumulation of petroleum in sedimentary rocks.
 H. arbitrarily rejects the theory of nonorganic origin.
 J. places a limit on the amount of petroleum that can be extracted from the earth.

STOP

If there is still time remaining, you may review your answers.

5 5 5 5 5 5 5 5 5 5 5

WRITING TEST
(Optional)

30 MINUTES

Directions: Write an essay in response to the following prompt:

Prompt: J. D., a senior, boasts a sterling academic record, is a top athlete, and has the respect of the faculty and her classmates. In the fall, she plans to go to Cornell University on a full scholarship. Mr. M., a new social studies teacher, however, has made a startling discovery: J. D. has regularly been submitting work copied from Internet web sites and from books and periodicals.

After confronting J. D., who insisted on her innocence, Mr. M. reported his findings to the principal. To avoid a scandal and preserve J. D.'s reputation, the principal did nothing except tell J. D. not to do it any more. He also ordered Mr. M. not to penalize J. D. in any way. Mr. M was outraged that J. D. had cheated all year long and gotten away with it. Frustrated, he wrote a letter to Cornell about J. D.'s plagiarism. When the principal found out, he fired Mr. M. on the spot for being insubordinate. Now the school and community are in an uproar, some supporting the principal, some supporting Mr. M., still others offering compromise solutions to the problem. In your opinion, did Mr. M. do the right thing?

In your essay, state your position. Whatever your view, support your position with specific reasons and examples.

Use the lined paper provided. Add additional sheets if necessary.

STOP

Answer Keys and Analysis Charts

ENGLISH TEST

1. D	16. G	31. C	46. H	61. C
2. J	17. B	32. J	47. B	62. J
3. B	18. H	33. B	48. J	63. B
4. G	19. D	34. F	49. C	64. H
5. D	20. J	35. D	50. H	65. B
6. H	21. C	36. J	51. A	66. J
7. C	22. J	37. B	52. H	67. C
8. F	23. A	38. G	53. C	68. G
9. A	24. G	39. B	54. G	69. C
10. J	25. B	40. J	55. C	70. F
11. C	26. G	41. B	56. F	71. B
12. G	27. C	42. J	57. C	72. F
13. C	28. G	43. B	58. G	73. C
14. J	29. C	44. H	59. D	74. F
15. D	30. G	45. B	60. G	75. A

Analysis Chart

Skills	Questions	Possible Score	Your Score
Usage/Mechanics			
Punctuation	7, 9, 12, 26, 29, 33, 44, 47, 50, 72	10	
Basic Grammar and Usage	3, 8, 23, 31, 34, 35, 37, 38, 39, 40, 41, 66	12	
Sentence Structure	6, 13, 14, 16, 17, 19, 20, 22, 32, 46, 55, 56, 57, 58, 62, 64, 67, 68	18	
Rhetorical Skills			
Strategy	2, 18, 25, 27, 36, 42, 43, 49, 53, 54, 70, 71	12	
Organization	5, 15, 24, 30, 45, 59, 60, 63, 73, 74, 75	11	
Style	1, 4, 10, 11, 21, 28, 48, 51, 52, 61, 65, 69	12	

Number correct: ______

MATHEMATICS TEST

1. C	13. E	25. D	37. E	49. E
2. J	14. F	26. K	38. F	50. H
3. A	15. D	27. D	39. E	51. D
4. K	16. H	28. H	40. J	52. J
5. B	17. D	29. D	41. D	53. B
6. K	18. J	30. J	42. H	54. G
7. B	19. A	31. B	43. E	55. B
8. G	20. J	32. K	44. K	56. J
9. B	21. C	33. D	45. A	57. A
10. J	22. K	34. G	46. H	58. H
11. D	23. C	35. E	47. D	59. E
12. G	24. K	36. G	48. G	60. F

Analysis Chart

Content Area	Skill Level: Basic Skills	Skill Level: Application	Skill Level: Analysis	Possible Score	Your Score
Pre-Algebra Algebra	1, 4, 5, 9, 10, 14, 21, 44	2, 6, 7, 17, 22, 24, 27, 32, 34, 37, 38, 43	3, 11, 12, 15	24	
Intermediate Algebra Coordinate Geometry	13, 20, 30, 31, 39, 46, 53	8, 16, 19, 23, 26, 28, 33	29, 41, 54, 56	18	
Geometry	18, 35, 42, 49, 51, 57, 59	25, 40, 45, 47, 48, 58, 60		14	
Trigonometry	36, 50	52, 55		4	

Number correct: ______

READING TEST

1. A	6. G	11. B	16. G	21. D	26. G	31. C	36. J
2. H	7. C	12. H	17. C	22. G	27. A	32. G	37. B
3. C	8. J	13. D	18. G	23. C	28. H	33. A	38. G
4. J	9. C	14. F	19. D	24. G	29. A	34. G	39. B
5. A	10. F	15. C	20. F	25. A	30. J	35. C	40. H

Analysis Chart

Passage Type	Referring	Reasoning	Possible Score	Your Score
Prose Fiction	1, 2, 4, 6	3, 5, 7, 8, 9, 10	10	
Social Studies	11, 14, 19	12, 13, 15, 16, 17, 18, 20	10	
Humanities	22, 23, 30	21, 24, 25, 26, 27, 28, 29	10	
Natural Science	32, 33, 34, 36	31, 35, 37, 38, 39, 40	10	

Number correct: ______

SCIENCE REASONING TEST

1. C	6. G	11. B	16. F	21. B	26. G	31. A	36. F
2. F	7. D	12. G	17. A	22. G	27. D	32. J	37. D
3. D	8. J	13. C	18. J	23. A	28. G	33. B	38. G
4. J	9. C	14. G	19. D	24. H	29. C	34. G	39. B
5. B	10. H	15. D	20. J	25. D	30. F	35. C	40. F

Analysis Chart

Kind of Questions	Skill Level			Possible Score	Your Score
	Understanding	Analysis	Generalization		
Data Representation	1, 2, 3, 6, 17, 18	4, 7, 8, 9, 19, 20	5, 10, 21	15	
Research Summaries	11, 12, 22, 23, 28, 29	14, 24, 25, 30, 31, 33	13, 15, 16, 26, 27, 32	18	
Conflicting Viewpoints	34, 35, 38	36, 37, 39	40	7	

Number correct: ______

COMPOSITE SCORE

To calculate your composite score (not including the Writing Test) follow these directions:

1. On the form below fill in the first column of blanks with the number of correct answers on each test.
2. Multiply each number by 36 and divide the product by the number of questions on each test. The results are your scale scores.
3. Add up your scale scores and divide by 4. The result should be rounded to the nearest whole number to determine your composite score.

	Number of correct answers				Scale score
English	______	× 36 =	______	÷ 75 =	______
Math	______	× 36 =	______	÷ 60 =	______
Reading	______	× 36 =	______	÷ 40 =	______
Science	______	× 36 =	______	÷ 40 =	______

Total ______ ÷ 4 = ______
Composite Score

No test can give you a totally precise measurement of your academic achievement. Rather, think of your composite score as the mid-point in a range of scores that can vary one or more points in either direction. A composite score of 28, for example, means that you scored somewhere between 26 and 30.

Answer Explanations: English Test

1. **D** All meanings carried by the underlined portion are implicit in the words preceding it. The entire portion is redundant.
2. **J** The quotation is pertinent, short, and authoritative. As such, it is a sound way to begin the passage.
3. **B** The antecedent of the pronoun in question is the singular *someone*.
4. **G** The phrase *lacking merit* at the end of the clause is adequate characterization of the type of case under discussion.
5. **D** As idealistic as the thought is, it is off the topic and has no place in this passage.
6. **H** The logic of this sentence requires that a transitional word indicating *cause* be employed in this spot.
7. **C** Three or more items in a series must be set off by commas.
8. **F** The phrase *changing attorneys* is a gerund phrase, that is, a *noun* phrase. Since it is an activity of the noun *client,* that noun requires the possessive apostrophe and final *s*.
9. **A** Dashes are appropriate marks to set off a parenthetical phrase, especially if one intends to emphasize the phrase.
10. **J** All other options are wordy or redundant.
11. **C** Colloquial and whimsical language is not in keeping with the matter-of-fact tone of the passage.
12. **G** Coordinate clauses must be separated by a comma.
13. **C** A new sentence begins at this point.
14. **J** At this spot a third noun—namely, *premium*—should parallel the objects *salary* and *rent*.

15. **D** Paragraph 3 begins with a clear signal that it should follow paragraph 4 rather than precede it, specifically the word *Finally*.

16. **G** The adverb *more* and the comparative adverb ending *-er* are equivalent, and cannot be used together. The result is a double comparison.

17. **B** The subject of this clause is the singular *person*.

18. **H** There is no suggestion or clue to suggest that the passage is intended for any one group.

19. **D** As it stands, the text contains a comma splice at this point; of the options, only the period break is correct.

20. **J** The present-tense, passive-voice verb is appropriate because the focus is on the toys, and the passage is written in the present tense. As it stands, this is a sentence fragment.

21. **C** The fact that the sentence later mentions that the rooms are "slightly askew" is reason enough to avoid the modifiers of the word *rooms*.

22. **J** The logic of this sentence requires that a conjunction indicating time be used at this transition; *when* is the only choice that makes sense.

23. **A** The verb agrees with the nearer subject (two) and is in the present tense.

24. **G** As interesting as the information may be, this sentence is wholly off the topic, and must be removed.

25. **B** The notion of children marking their territory with smudges and smears is humorous and whimsical. The other options do not suggest humor.

26. **G** A compound adjective preceding the noun it modifies is hyphenated, but the two words before *homes* do not comprise a compound adjective; one, *finely,* is an adverb modifying the adjective *furnished*.

27. **C** The enormous difference in the size of these paragraphs, as well as the amount of data they contain, shows the writer's bias.

28. **G** The noun *difference* clearly indicates that two kinds of people are being compared; *distinguishing* is not needed.

29. **C** A compound adjective that *precedes* the noun is hyphenated; one that *follows* the noun usually is not.

30. **G** The word *Conversely* is a clue that paragraph 2 must occur after paragraph 3; the words *another great difference* at the outset of paragraph 4 place it after paragraph 2.

31. **C** The verb *had grown* agrees with the subject *climate* and with the tense of the rest of the sentence and paragraph.

32. **J** The sentence calls for the passive verb *be supervised* (by women). The other choices either are not verbs at all or are verbs that do not make sense in the context.

33. **B** The best choice here is *roles; some* to introduce a new clause. The clause is very close to and a derivative of the first clause of the sentence, so the semicolon is more appropriate than the period.

34. **F** *It* is a pronoun whose antecedent is a substantive in the previous sentence, *crack epidemic*. The other noun choices miss entirely the relationship between the two.

35. **D** *Rose* has as its subject the noun *proportion*; the simple past tense is in agreement with the tense of the upper paragraph as well as all the bulleted sentences at its close.

36. **J** The answer is *yes* because of the facts one garners in the bulleted list at the end of the paragraph.

37. **B** The sentence is cast in the subjunctive mood and is in the simple past tense, while all other choices are written in incompatible tenses.

38. **G** The subject *tens of thousands* calls for the present passive progressive tense *being stuffed*. All other choices are in the wrong tense or voice.

39. **B** The past passive tense *were considered* is the only choice for this verb of the subject "riffraff"; all other choices have incompatible tenses or voices.

40. **J** *Some people*, near the beginning of the paragraph, is the subject of the sentence. It is far enough removed from its original source to require the use of *they* as the subject of the verb *observe*. Other choices present incompatible subjects or sentences left without a subject.

41. **B** The noun *defendants* appears in the introductory clause; the pronoun that is the antecedent to that noun must be plural, as it is in *they face*. No other choices have an appropriate antecedent and or an appropriate verb.

42. **J** This choice is the only correct choice because it has as its purpose delineating the "hurdles" always faced by minority defendants.

43. **B** This choice clearly makes clear many facts about the sordid history of the death penalty in the United States. The other sentences address nonpertinent matters.

44. **H** Between the word *States* and the number *287* occurs a break between sentences. The division using a *colon* is the most appropriate because the second sentence is closely related to and is derived from the first. The other choices either are not signaling the close relationship or are run-on sentences.

45. **B** The second division, [Section (2)], introduces readers to the whole topic of the essay, prisons and prisoners, and its reference to early times of London clearly indicate that it belongs in the first position. Section (1) begins by the late 1900s; in addition, the fact that the number of women have increased as inmates fits nicely in a position just after section (2). Section (3) begins with the point "the cause of these arrest figures is debatable," clearly referring to the data at the end of Section (1). The description of the death penalty history is most understandable here and is a good conclusion to the whole selection.

46. **H** This verb must be in the present tense to express what is still true.

47. **B** The name *Antonia Shimerda* is in apposition with *protagonist* and is properly set off with two commas.

48. **J** The adjective *actual* is the only choice that indicates what is intended, that the girl was a genuine Bohemian girl. The other choices are either redundant or misleading.

49. **C** This "summary" is inconclusive; it should include more information about the story.

50. **H** Commas and periods are *always* placed *inside* quotation marks, even when there are single and double quotation marks because the sentence contains a quote within a quote.

51. **A** The word *albeit* means literally "although it be," a meaning that is required for the sense of the clause to remain intact, and that is not repeated in the other options.

52. **H** The prefix *multi* is most often incorporated with another word as a unit.

53. **C** Since the paragraph deals with Cather's preference in the novel to the country over the city, and since the entire passage is about the novel *My Antonia,* the quotation is clearly meaningful.

54. **G** This passage describes the pastoral life of a young girl in rural America in the early 1900s. It goes on to describe the novel as "a song of praise for agricultural existence as opposed to life in the cities."

55. **C** The passage is written in the present tense, and employs the historical present whenever necessary.

56. **F** *Employed* in this sentence is a participle modifying the noun *symbols.*

57. **C** To be parallel with the phrases naming the first two cycles, this one must begin with the noun *cycle,* rather than a clause describing it.

58. **G** No comma is needed. Choice F results in a sentence fragment beginning with *In which,* and neither the semicolon (H) nor the dash (J) is appropriate.

59. **D** The body of the paragraph does a comprehensive job of developing the beginning generalization.

60. **G** Paragraph 1 begins with broad, general statements about the novel, and prepares the reader for the critical commentary that comes with the next paragraph, paragraph 3. Paragraph 2 is the summary paragraph that effectively ends this passage.

61. **C** This choice is the only complete choice; all other choices leave the sentence without an essential part of the syntax or gender description.

62. **J** The writer makes clear that she is in America with this choice. All other choices present the reader with confusing adverbs or genders.

63. **B** The entire passage is about women in Japan; of the choices, this is the only one to give emphasis to that essential point being made by the author. The other choices are not nearly so specific.

64. **H** This choice is the only one that makes clear the point that the Secretary of the Ministry of Construction received attention from the local press because she was a woman, and not because her work was so distinguished.

65. **B** *Instituted* is the proper verb to represent the Secretary's official actions. All other choices are off in meaning and nuance.

66. **J** The sentence must refer to two specific oblique compliments of faint praise made by a reporter and by people in general to have any point in the present sentence. No other choices come as close to that reference as J.

67. **C** The sentence must be divided by a semicolon in order to set up the following point for the cause-result sentence. None of the other choices provides the cause-effect conclusion.

68. **G** The sentence begins with a well-known phrase, "not only ... but also ... ." F is the only choice that completes this phrase satisfactorily.

69. **C** The whole sentence is about women receiving faint, insincere phrases and polite dismissals. This gentle choice is compatible with the tone of the rest of the essay.

70. **F** The woman who wrote this essay is concerned about the way women are being treated in her native Japan. The other choices miss her intentions by quite a margin.

71. **B** The writer is understanding of the slow progress of women's rights. At the same time, she tacitly admits to a need for recognizing the old world and its traditions. No other choice describes her attitude as well.

72. **F** This choice is the only correct one. All other choices are ungrammatical.

73. **C** This choice states clearly the point of the author. All other choices come close but are slightly maligned or are grammatically incorrect.

74. **F** This choice repeats exactly the two changes that the author set down. The other choices, while close, are not correct.

75. **A** The sequence is correct as it stands. The first section introduces Simon de Beauvoir, her work, *The Second Sex*, and the problems with women's rights in Japan. The second section begins with direct reference to a point made in the first section, namely, the two examples of faint praise made toward the Secretary of the Ministry of Construction. Similarly, the third section makes direct reference to the problems discussed at the end of the second section using the words "such problems...."

Answer Explanations: Mathematics Test

1. **C** $\frac{a}{b} - \frac{c}{d} = \frac{ad}{bd} - \frac{bc}{bd} = \frac{ad - bc}{bd}$

2. **J** First factor the numerator. $\frac{2x^4 + x^3}{x^6} = \frac{x^3(2x + 1)}{x^6}$ Cancel x^3. $= \frac{2x + 1}{x^3}$

3. **A** $\frac{3}{4}(1600) = 1200$ phones have dials.

   $\frac{1}{3}(1200) = 400$ dial phones are replaced by push-button phones.

   $1200 - 400 = 800$ dial phones remain.

4. **K** $\frac{x}{y}$ is not necessarily an integer.

5. **B** For example: $5 - (-7) = 12$, which is positive.

6. **K** Multiply both sides by $4x - 3$.

   ($\frac{3}{4}$ is a restricted value.)

   $\frac{5}{4x - 3}(4x - 3) = 5(4x - 3)$

   $5 = 5(4x - 3) = 20x - 15$

   $20 = 20x$

   $x = 1$

7. **B** Ten times the tens digit plus the unit digit: $10t + u$.

8. **G** Multiply each term of the first polynomial times each term of the second polynominal.

   $(x - 1)(x^2 + x + 1)$

   $= x^3 + x^2 + x - x^2 - x - 1$

   $= x^3 - 1$

9. **B** The radius of the semicircle is 2 feet, so the diameter, also the width of the window, is 4 feet. The area of the rectangular part is 20 square feet, and the area of half a circle with radius 2 feet is $\frac{1}{2}\pi(2^2) = 2\pi$. Therefore, the entire area is $20 + 2\pi$ square feet.

Model Exam B

10. **J** $\frac{75}{30} = 2.5 \neq 0.025$

$$\frac{1}{40} = 0.025$$
$$2.5(10^{-2}) = 0.025$$
$$\frac{75}{30} = 2.5$$

11. **D** Each apple costs $\frac{100}{3} = 33\frac{1}{3}$ in the 3 for \$1.00 deal. The difference between 35 cents and $33\frac{1}{3}$ is $1\frac{2}{3}$ cents.

12. **G** In 1 minute Joan can run $\frac{1}{a}$ part of a mile.

    After b minutes, she has run $b\frac{1}{a} = \frac{b}{a}$.

13. **E** Division by 0 is never allowed.

14. **F** $3\frac{3}{5} \cdot 4\frac{1}{6} = \frac{18}{5} \cdot \frac{25}{6}$

$$= \frac{3}{1} \cdot \frac{5}{1} \quad \text{Cancel.}$$
$$= 15$$

15. **D** Write two equations with two variables, n and d.

$$n = d + 5$$
$$5n + 10d = 130 \quad \text{Then substitute for } n.$$
$$5(d + 5) + 10d = 130$$
$$5d + 25 + 10d = 130$$
$$15d + 25 = 130$$
$$15d = 105$$
$$d = 7$$

Then $n = 12$.

16. **H** In an arithmetic sequence, the nth term is given by

$$a_n = a_1 + (n - 1)d$$

in which a_1 is the first term, n is the number of the term, and d is the common difference between terms. In the given sequence the tenth term is sought and the common difference is 5.

$$a_{10} = 3 + (10 - 1)5 = 3 + 45 = 48$$

17. **D** First multiply by 100 to get rid of the decimals.

$$100[0.2(100 - x) + 0.05x] = 100[0.1(100)]$$
$$20(100 - x) + 5x = 10(100)$$
$$2000 - 20x + 5x = 1000$$
$$-15x = -1000$$
$$x = 66\frac{2}{3}$$

18. **J** There certainly is a regular polygon of seven sides.

19. **A** $\sqrt[3]{54x^4y^6} = \sqrt[3]{27x^3y^6 \cdot 2x}$ Separate the radicand into cube and noncube parts.

$$= 3xy^2\sqrt[3]{2x}$$

20. **J** Conic sections are second-degree (or less) curves only. The equation $y = x^3$ is not of degree 2.

21. **C** The degree of a polynomial is the greatest of the degrees of its terms. The degrees of the terms of the given polynominal are 3, 4, 2, and 0. The greatest degree is 4.

22. **K** Add the two equations.

$$2x - y = 5$$
$$x + y = 1$$
$$\overline{3x = 6}$$
$$x = 2$$

Substitute $x = 2$ into either equation (say the second one).

$$2 + y = 1$$
$$y = -1$$

23. **C** The numbers 2, 4, 6, and 8 satisfy the conditions of being even and less than 10.

$P(A) = \frac{4}{20} = \frac{1}{5}.$

24. **K** Multiply the numerator and denominator by the LCD, which is xy.

$$\frac{xy(x+y)}{xy\left(\frac{1}{x}+\frac{1}{y}\right)} = \frac{xy(x+y)}{y+x}$$

$$= xy$$

25. **D** Inscribed angle ABC intercepts an arc that is twice the measure of the angle, so arc ADC measures 140° and the measure of arc ABC is $(360 - 140)° = 220°$. The measure of inscribed angle ADC is half the measure of its intercepted arc: 110°. (Opposite angles of an inscribed quadrilateral are supplementary.)

26. **K** Since $a > b$, then $a - b > 0$ and $b - a < 0$. The absolute value of a positive number is equal to that number, but the absolute value of a negative number is the opposite of the number.

$|a - b| = a - b$ and $|b - a|$

$= -(b - a) = a - b.$

$|a - b| + |b - a| = (a - b) + (a - b)$

$= 2a - 2b.$

27. **D** The expression -3^{-2} is properly read as "the opposite of 3 to the -2 power." Follow the rules for the order of operations:

$$-3^{-2} = -(3^{-2}) = -\left(\frac{1}{3^2}\right) = -\left(\frac{1}{9}\right)$$

28. **H** To put this equation into standard form, complete the square in both variables.

$$(x^2 - 4x) + 4(y^2 + 6y) = -36$$
$$(x^2 - 4x + 4) + 4(y^2 + 6y + 9) = -36 + 4 + 36$$
$$(x - 2)^2 + 4(y + 3)^2 = 4$$
$$\frac{(x-2)^2}{4} + \frac{(y+3)^2}{1} = 1$$

The center is $(2, -3)$.

29. **D** This is a work-type word problem, for which the formula $w = rt$ applies. Let Bonnie's time to complete the job be x hours, then Nick's time is $x - 2$ hours. Her rate of work is $\frac{1}{x}$ part of the job per hour. His rate is $\frac{1}{x-2}$.

	w =	r	t
Nick	$\frac{7}{x-2}$	$\frac{1}{x-2}$	7
Bonnie	$\frac{7}{x}$	$\frac{1}{x}$	7

The sum of the work column is equal to 1 (one completed job). The equation is

$$\frac{7}{x-2} + \frac{7}{x} = 1.$$

30. **J** A function is one-to-one if all of the ordered pairs in the function not only have different first components but also have different second components. This means that the graph must pass both the vertical line test and the horizontal line test. If a vertical line crosses the graph once at most, then it is a function. If a horizontal line crosses the graph once at most, then the function is one-to-one (and thus it has an inverse). Only J satisfies both tests.

31. **B** An exponential function is any function of the type:

$$f(x) = a^x, \text{ for } a > 0, a \neq 1.$$

32. **K** $(5x - 3y^2)^2 = 25x^2 - 30xy^2 + 9y^4.$

33. **D** The reciprocal of i is $\frac{1}{i}$. Multiply both numerator and denominator by the conjugate of the denominator, $-i$: $\frac{-i(1)}{-i(i)}$.

$$\frac{-i}{1} = -i$$

34. **G** $\frac{a^{-3}bc^2}{a^{-4}b^2c^{-3}} = a^{-3-(-4)}b^{1-2}c^{2-(-3)}$

$$= a^1b^{-1}c^5$$
$$= \frac{ac^5}{b}$$

35. **E** The length of the longer leg of a 30-60-90 triangle is equal to $\sqrt{3}$ times the length of the shorter leg, and the length of the hypotenuse is twice the length of the shorter leg. The length of the longer leg is given, so to find the length of the shorter leg divide by $\sqrt{3}$.

$$BC = \frac{6}{\sqrt{3}} = 2\sqrt{3}$$
$$\text{Therefore } AB = 2(2\sqrt{3}) = 4\sqrt{3}$$

36. **G** The identity is $\sin 2A = 2 \sin A \cos A$.

37. **E** Use the quadratic formula:

$$x = \frac{-b \pm \sqrt{b^2 - 4ac}}{2a}$$

Here

$$x = \frac{4 \pm \sqrt{16 - (-72)}}{6} = \frac{4 \pm \sqrt{88}}{6} = \frac{4 \pm 2\sqrt{22}}{6} = \frac{2 \pm \sqrt{22}}{3}$$

38. **F** $3\sqrt{3} - \sqrt{48} + 3\sqrt{\frac{1}{3}} = 3\sqrt{3} - 4\sqrt{3} + \sqrt{3} = 0$

39. **E** The two ordered pairs (4, 2) and (4, –2) both satisfy the equation $x = y^2$, and so it does not define a function.

40. **J** The length of a tangent is the mean proportional between the length of a secant from a common external point and the length of the secant's external segment.

$$\frac{x+4}{6} = \frac{6}{4}$$
$$4x + 16 = 36$$
$$4x = 20$$
$$x = 5$$

41. **D** This is a uniform motion-type word problem, for which the formula $d = rt$ applies.

	D =	r	t
Bike	x	12	$\frac{x}{12}$
Car	x	36	$\frac{x}{36}$

The time for the car trip is $\frac{1}{2}$ hour less than the time for the bike trip. The equation is:

$$\frac{x}{36} = \frac{x}{12} - \frac{1}{2}$$

42. **H** The midpoint formula is

$$\left(\frac{x_1 + x_2}{2}, \frac{y_1 + y_2}{2}\right)$$

Here

$$\left(\frac{3 + (-5)}{2}, \frac{7 + (-6)}{2}\right) = \left(-1, \frac{1}{2}\right)$$

43. **E** A square root radical by definition is positive. The solution set is empty.

Model Exam B

44. **K** All these statements are true.

45. **A** The diagram shows a 30-60-90 triangle with the hypotenuse equal in length to the radius of the circle, the length of the shorter leg half the length of the hypotenuse, and the length of the longer leg $\sqrt{3}$ times the length of the shorter leg. The perimeter of the triangle is equal to 6 times the length of the longer leg of the triangle.

$$6(4\sqrt{3}) = 24\sqrt{3}$$

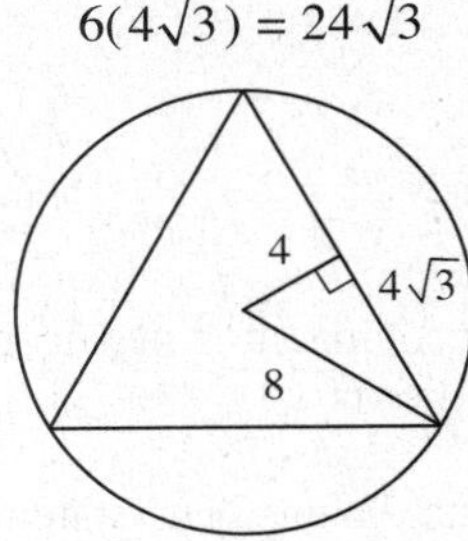

46. **H** The domain contains all real numbers except those for which the denominator is zero. Set the denominator equal to zero and solve.

$$x^2 - 2x - 3 = 0$$
$$(x - 3)(x + 1) = 0$$
$$x - 3 = 0 \qquad x + 1 = 0$$
$$x = 3 \qquad x = -1$$

47. **D** Draw the line of centers and a line parallel to $\overline{CD}$ through B ($\overline{BE} \parallel \overline{CD}$). The length of $\overline{AB}$ is the sum of the lengths of the radii of the circles. A radius of a circle is perpendicular to a tangent at the point of tangency. Therefore $BCDE$ is a rectangle.
$BC = 3$, so $DE = 3$.
$AD = 5$, so $AE = 2$.

Apply the Pythagorean Theorem to right triangle ABE.

$$(BE)^2 + 2^2 = 8^2$$
$$(BE)^2 + 4 = 64$$
$$(BE)^2 = 60$$
$$BE = \sqrt{60} = 2\sqrt{15}$$

And $BE = CD = 2\sqrt{15}$.

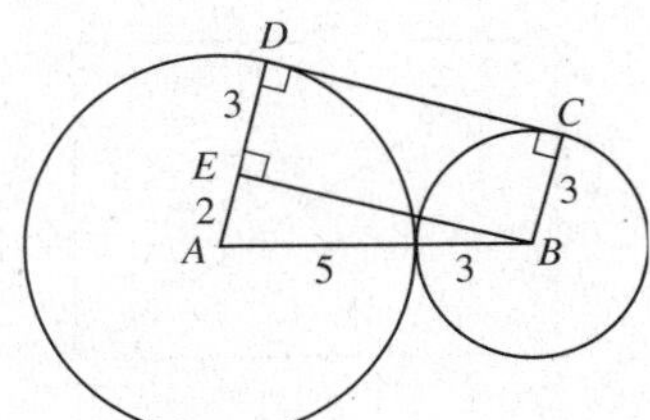

48. **G** The measure of inscribed angle C is half the measure of its intercepted arc BAD.

$$m\angle C = \frac{1}{2}(180 + m\text{ arc }AB)$$

$$125 = \frac{1}{2}(180 + m\text{ arc }AB).$$

$$250 = 180 + m\text{ arc }AB$$
$$m\text{ arc }AB = 70$$

Therefore arc $BCD = 180 - 70 = 110$. The measure of inscribed angle A is half the measure of its intercepted arc.

$m\angle A = \frac{1}{2}(110) = 55$.

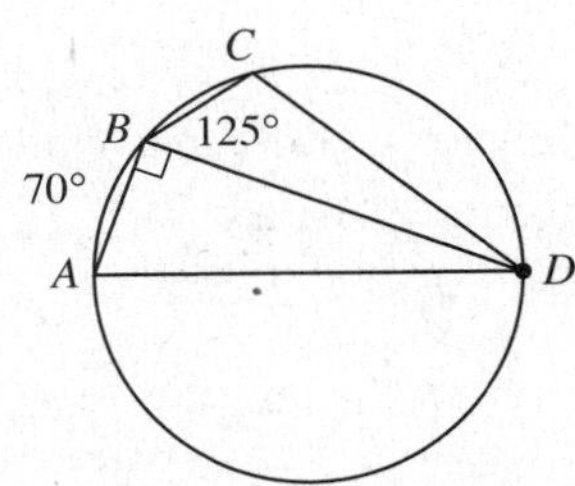

49. **E** There is not enough information to answer this question uniquely.

50. **H** The distance from the origin to A is

$$r = \sqrt{(-3)^2 + 4^2} = 5.$$

The definition of sec θ is $\frac{r}{x}$, so

$$\sec\theta = \frac{5}{-3}$$

51. **D** $\sum_{k=1}^{5} 2k^2 = 2\cdot 1^2 + 2\cdot 2^2 + 2\cdot 3^2 + 2\cdot 4^2 + 2\cdot 5^2 = 2 + 8 + 18 + 32 + 50 = 110$

52. **J** Cosine is positive in quadrants I and IV; cotangent is negative in quadrants II and IV. There is an angle in quandrant IV that satisfies the given conditions.

53. **B** A Venn diagram will help clarify these statements. The statement in B, $(A \cap B) \subseteq B$, is true. Every element in the intersection of sets A and B is contained in B.

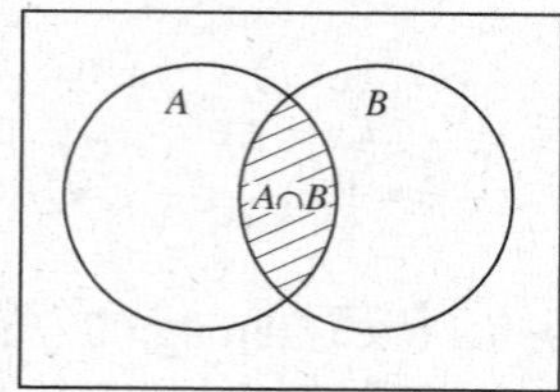

54. **G** Let one side be x; then the other side is $x + 1$. Use the Pythagorean Theorem:

$$x^2 + (x + 1)^2 = (\sqrt{145})^2$$
$$x^2 + x^2 + 2x + 1 = 145$$
$$2x^2 + 2x - 144 = 0$$
$$x^2 + x - 72 = 0$$
$$(x + 9)(x - 8) = 0$$
$$x + 9 = 0 \qquad x - 8 = 0$$
$$x = -9 \text{ (extraneous)} \qquad x = 8$$

Then $x + 1 = 8 + 1 = 9$.

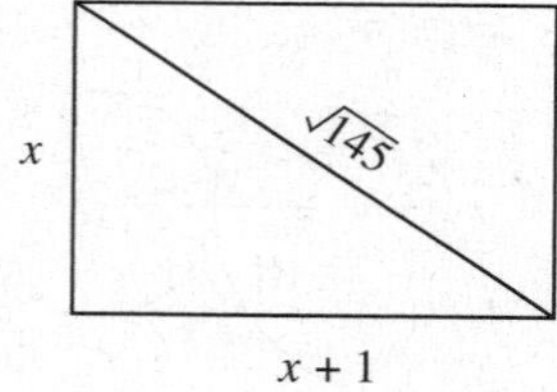

55. **B** Think of $\cos^{-1}\frac{2}{3}$ as an angle, θ. Then the question asks for sin θ, where θ is the angle whose cosine is $\frac{2}{3}$. This angle is in quadrant I.

$$\sin\theta = +\sqrt{1 - \cos^2\theta} = \sqrt{1 - \left(\frac{2}{3}\right)^2} = \sqrt{1 - \frac{4}{9}} = \sqrt{\frac{5}{9}} = \frac{\sqrt{5}}{3}$$

56. **J** Let x be the score on the fourth test. Then

$$\frac{75 + 84 + 80 + x}{4} \geq 80$$
$$239 + x \geq 320$$
$$x \geq 81$$

57. **A** The sum of the exterior angles of any polygon is 360°. In a regular polygon the angles have the same measure, so one exterior angle of a regular octagon is $\frac{360°}{8} = 45°$.

Model Exam B

58. **H** The diagonals of a rhombus are perpendicular bisectors of each other. Therefore in right triangle ABE, $AE = 4$ and $BE = 3$. Use the Pythagorean Theorem.

$$(AB)^2 = 4^2 + 3^2 = 16 + 9 = 25$$
$$AB = 5$$

The perimeter of the rhombus is $4(5) = 20$.

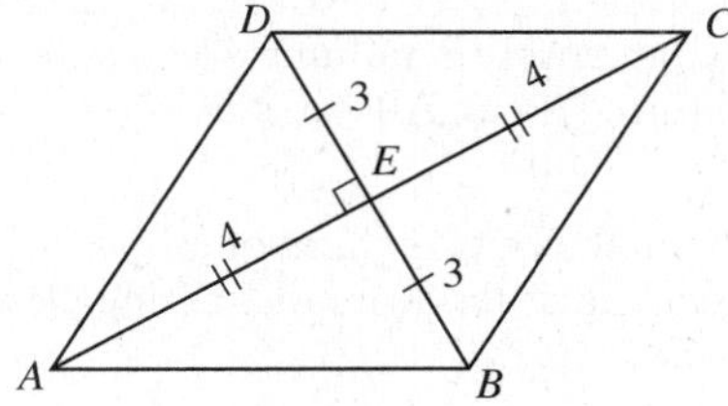

59. **E** All these statements are false.

60. **F** The length of the altitude of a right triangle is the mean proportional between the lengths of the two segments of the hypotenuse.

$$\frac{x}{4} = \frac{4}{10 - x}$$
$$x(10 - x) = 16$$
$$10x - x^2 = 16$$
$$0 = x^2 - 10x + 16$$
$$(x - 8)(x - 2) = 0$$
$$x - 8 = 0 \qquad x - 2 = 0$$
$$x = 8 \text{(extraneous)} \qquad x = 2$$

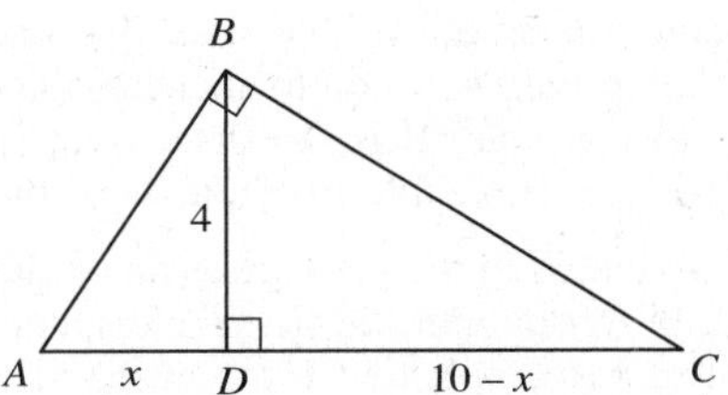

Answer Explanations: Reading Test

1. **A** In lines 31–36, the narrator attributes his gloomy nature to a childhood spent on a chicken farm. B is incorrect because Father, once a happy contented farmhand, and Mother, an ex-schoolteacher, had both experienced success in former years. C sounds as though it could have shaped the narrator's state of mind, but it is not mentioned in the passage. D may border on the truth, but the passage, while mentioning that the family struggled to make the farm pay, doesn't imply that constant debt molded the narrator's view of life.
2. **H** In lines 18–26, the narrator presumes that Mother's reading was responsible for her ambition. F is a tempting answer, but there is no hint that Mother's reading influenced her teaching. G overstates Mother's devotion to reading and studying. J is not mentioned in the passage.
3. **C** Father married at 34 (in "his thirty-fifth year"), according to the third paragraph, and a year later he launched a 10-year period as a chicken farmer.
4. **J** Father continued to work on a farm, not as a hired farmhand, however, but as an owner. Choices F, G, and H are postmarital changes that occurred in Father's life.
5. **A** The narrator comments in lines 53–54 that chickens look so bright and alert but are stupid—much like people. Choices B, C, and D seem like reasonable similarities between people and chickens, but the narrator fails to mention them.
6. **G** In lines 39–40, the narrator describes a chick as "a tiny fluffy thing such as you will see pictured on Easter cards." F is not a good answer because the narrator views the brief life cycle of a chicken as "tragic" (line 38).

H may reflect the experience of some folks who have raised chickens but not the experience of this family, which found few pleasures in chicken farming. J is true but irrelevant to the passage.

7. **C** According to lines 58–60, literature on raising chickens leads unsuspecting people astray by holding out the unrealistic prospects of making a fortune. Choice A overstates the narrator's opinion by saying that everything in these books and articles deliberately misrepresents the truth. B does not apply to the passage. D may be inferred from the circumstances spelled out in the narrative but is not in keeping with the point of the passage.

8. **J** Mother and Father never considered themselves failures. In spite of setbacks they continued on their "upward journey through life," according to lines 72–76. All the other choices—F, G, and H—represent events that took place in the narrative.

9. **C** The narrator gently pokes fun at life on the chicken farm of his youth. Choices A and B are not at all reflected in the tone of the passage. D is only half right; there are distressing elements to the tale, but in dealing with them the narrator adopts a humorous tone.

10. **F** The narrator believes that if chicken farmers were not calm and hopeful (i.e., *philosophical* by nature), they'd grow too frustrated to continue doing their work. Choices G and J express weighty thoughts that don't apply to this relatively light and witty tale. H is not discussed in the passage.

11. **B** Choice A is supported in part by the statement that battered women feel "trapped" (line 12), but choice B is a better answer because the question asks you to identify the *most important* reason behind women's helplessness. The answer is found in lines 9–10, which state outright that the "weight of society has been traditionally on the side of the oppressor," namely, the male. There's no doubt that C also contributes to women's sense of powerlessness, but lack of funds is not discussed until much later in the passage. D is incorrect because the passage ignores the role of witnesses.

12. **H** The assertion clearly implies that police, prosecutors, and sometimes even judges contribute to the victims' feelings of helplessness. Choice F is not discussed or suggested by the passage. G is a generalization not supported by evidence in the passage. J certainly applies to some victims of abuse, but the passage doesn't deal with issues of women's psychology.

13. **D** Lines 20–23 suggest that police and others believe that abused women often provoke violent behavior in men. Choice A seems a reasonable but temporary solution to abuse problems, but later the passage says that without outside intervention abuse is apt to continue. B is not discussed, and C contradicts the assertion that police officers are predisposed to hold wives responsible for their own abuse.

14. **F** Reconciliation is not mentioned anywhere in the passage as an explanation for aborted law suits. The financial implications (G) are discussed fully throughout the passage, especially in paragraphs 3–6. H, the duration of court cases, is discussed in the third paragraph, and J, the husband's vow to shape up, in line 31.

15. **C** Line 44 suggests that, if possible, the wife should seek refuge in a shelter for battered women. Choices A and D seem like reasonable actions, but they are not a quick remedy nor are they suggested by the passage. B may take care of the emergency, but as the first two paragraphs indicate, calling the police won't provide a long-term solution to the problem.

16. **G** Lines 63–66 state that with professional assistance battered women recognize and employ their own enormous powers of self-preservation. The other choices spell out steps that would no doubt help solve abuse problems, but the passage takes the position that women should be helped to take control of their own lives.

17. **C** Most of the passage in one way or other focuses on problems that confront abused women. Choices A, B, and D are details that support the main purpose of the passage.

18. **G** The heart of the passage (paragraphs 3–6) emphasizes the financial hardships faced by abused women. Choices F, H, and J are hardships that the passage briefly alludes to.

19. **D** Because the passage says nothing about requiring husbands to pay for their wives' legal expenses, D is the best answer. Choice A is cited as a course of action—although an ineffective one—in line 35. B and C are discussed in the fifth paragraph (lines 46–54).

20. **F** Lines 81–86 imply that an abused woman should turn to the courts only as a last resort. The passage neither states nor implies that choices G, H, and J are reasons for a woman to go to court.

21. **D** Among the techniques used by the program's producers was the use of prestigious speakers, including astronomers (line 34). A, B, and C may also have been used to create realistic effects, but they are not discussed in the passage.

22. **G** The first paragraph alludes to all the choices except G. There is no indication that the meteorite had been illuminated.

23. **C** The third paragraph contains a list of techniques employed to convince listeners that the reported events were real. A, B, and D may have helped but they are not discussed in the passage.

24. **G** One indication of spreading panic was the "flood" of calls to police and radio stations (lines 26–28). Rule out F because people were alarmed long before Cantril's study. H alludes to something that happened but not necessarily as a consequence of genuine alarm, and J not only seems to go against human nature but is not mentioned in the passage.

25. **A** Taking into account the statement in lines 11–13 that the public was "relatively unfamiliar with science fiction stories at that point in history," it is reasonable to conclude that the genre was new in 1938.

26. **G** Choices F and H raised doubts about the veracity of the report. J is not discussed in the passage. G is the best answer because lines 52–61 give examples of listeners who deluded themselves by giving credence to irrelevant evidence.

27. **A** The lines in question describe the behavior of skeptical people who sought evidence to disprove the veracity of the program. B is not supported by the passage. C overstates the case; perhaps some, but not all, readers of *Amazing Stories* identified the program as a hoax. D is probably true but is not discussed.

28. **H** The passage contains no evidence to support F and J. Choice G might appeal to those who confuse "panic" in line 65 with leaving "lasting impressions." H is supported by the implication in lines 67–68 that people with greater critical ability are likely to react differently from those who are "especially suggestible or anxious."

29. **A** The author links listeners' panic to such great dangers as the rise of Hitler, the threat of a world war, and the Great Depression—crises that kept the world on edge in 1938. C and D may have played an indirect part in the panic that followed the broadcast, but they are not as important as the correct answer, A. Choice B is not stated or implied in the passage.

30. **J** The last paragraph lists several causes of listeners' response to the broadcast, including the turmoil in Europe leading to World War II. None of the other choices are applicable.

31. **C** By emphasizing the size of space, the author shows why solar sails hold promise as the best way to move "things around" out there. While the paragraph refers to the ideas in A, B, and D, each is meant to support the main point.

32. **G** In lines 16–18, the author says that gravity controls orbiting objects. F is incorrect because the passage implies in lines 16–23 that at slow speeds orbiting objects fall into whatever it is they are orbiting. H is not discussed in the passage. J applies only when objects must be moved from one orbit to another.

33. **A** The main problem with electric rockets, says the author in line 53, is "the cost and mass of the solar power plant" used to generate electricity. Rule out B because by definition a solar power plant would not function outside the solar system. Eliminate C because the passage does not discuss the fragility of electric rockets. Nor is D a good answer because electric rockets are powered by electricity not by chemical fuel.

34. **G** According to the passage, solar sails require no fuel at all because they are powered by the sun (H). As a result they are lighter (J) and less costly (F).

35. **C** To achieve the speed required for travel into deep space rockets must carry enormous amounts of fuel—more than they can manage. Choice A may be implied in the passage but it is not stated. Choice B is an effect caused by a rocket's limited fuel supply, and D suggests nonsensically that rockets have a will of their own.

36. **J** In the third paragraph (lines 26–43) the author explains that the total fuel mass needed to double the speed of the rocket increases "exponentially," which implies, in mathematical terms, far more than double the amount of fuel.

37. **B** Two rockets of the same size and weight would behave identically until they reach orbit or beyond. Then, the electric rocket would be powered by the sun. Initially, therefore, it needs to carry less fuel than its chemically-energized counterpart.

38. **H** By stating that a "rocket can reach the same velocity as its exhaust" (lines 27–28), the author implies that the speed of the rocket cannot exceed the velocity of the exhaust. A law of physics may imply F, but a rocket's trajectory is not discussed in the passage. Likewise, the passage largely ignores the matters raised by G and J.

39. **G** The passage discusses problems of weight (lines 77–81), acceleration (64–72), and unfolding of solar sails (57–61). Although the author proposes a hexagonal shape for solar sails (line 82), determining shape is not discussed as a problem that must be solved.

40. **G** According to the passage, solar sails have "reached an advanced planning stage" (line 63). Because they don't exist yet, they are hypothetical. While solar sails might well float in the air A, that feature is irrelevant because such sails would be constructed for use in the vacuum of space. C is a faulty choice because the reference to aluminum foil (line 78) is meant only to describe the thickness of solar sails, not the manner in which they are stored. D contradicts the passage, which states that solar sails are *not* aluminized plastic sheets (line 76).

Answer Explanations: Science Reasoning Test

1. **C** This is the black part of the soybean bar in Chart I.
2. **F** The gray area in the soybean bar of Chart I is larger than the gray area in any of the other three.
3. **D** In Chart II, the only modification is resistance to weed killers. A is wrong because Chart II shows that all four crops have weed killer tolerance but only two of them have insect protection. C is wrong because Chart I shows that about 90 percent of the corn being grown is not genetically modified. The area devoted to canola is irrelevant.
4. **J** F, G, and H are wrong because soybean modification produces only weed killer tolerance, not insect protection.
5. **B** The other crops produce food, which might be affected by genetic modification. Amount of land in cultivation does not affect the usability of the product. Soybeans benefit greatly by weed-killer tolerance.
6. **G** All organisms except bacterial spores can be killed at temperatures below 100°C.
7. **D** This combination of temperature and time will kill bacterial spores; everything else will also be killed, since all other kinds of microorganisms will die at substantially lower temperatures.
8. **J** The chart shows that at every temperature, a longer time of sterilization is needed to kill mold spores than yeast spores.
9. **C** The destruction of bacterial spores is spread out, at 100°C, from 3 minutes to 3 hours, indicating that different kinds of bacterial spores will be killed at different exposure times. Killing bacterial spores also kills everything else, and bacteria are killed more quickly than molds.
10. **H** In every case, the spore stage is more resistant to destruction by heat than the living stage. No information is presented concerning other environmental hazards. In the living form, molds are more resistant than bacteria.
11. **B** The passage informs us that starch turns blue in the presence of elemental iodine, and the gist of the experiments is the determination of the liberation of iodine from the iodate.
12. **G** Looking down the data columns, you can see that, as the concentration of iodate gets smaller, the time delay increases. F is wrong because this is part of the design of the experiment, not a hypothesis to be tested. H is wrong because the concentration of sulfuric acid is kept constant throughout. J is wrong because the passage says that the concentration of iodine increases gradually until it gets strong enough to turn the starch blue.
13. **C** Experiment 2 shows that, as the temperature increases, the time for the reaction decreases. A and B are wrong because the iodate concentration was not changed in Experiment 2.
14. **G** The iodate concentration in Experiment 2 was 5%. In Experiment 1 the time delay at 5% concentration was 29 seconds. Experiment 2 shows that this delay, with 5% iodate, occurs at a temperature between 15°C and 25°C.
15. **D** The temperature given is well below the freezing point of water, and if the whole setup freezes, the whole reaction might stop. All the other answers neglect this probability.
16. **F** Experiment 2 shows that the time for a 5% solution at 45°C is 22 seconds, and we would have to expect that it would be less for a 10% solution. The time would also have to be less than 18 seconds, because that was the time (Experiment 1) for 10% solution at 20°C.
17. **A** The graph for fat content in males (dashed line) shows a strong dip in the years 10 through 20.
18. **J** The rate of increase is represented by the steepness of the graph. The graph for fat content rises very sharply in the last 3 months before birth.
19. **D** The fraction of water is larger in a man's body than in a woman's. For a woman to have as much water as a 150-pound man, she would have to weigh more than the man. B is wrong because the man's body at that age has only about 20 pounds of water more than the woman's.
20. **J** On both the water and fat graphs, the lines for men and women remain parallel after age 40, showing that the differences between them do not change.
21. **B** In adolescence, when sex hormone activity is beginning very strongly, the fat content of boys drops and the water content increases. A is wrong because this sex-hormone effect is not seen in girls. C is wrong because at adolescence there is a marked change in the water content of boys, but only a gradual drop in girls. D is true but irrelevant.
22. **G** The ratings for attack against *Escherichia* are greater in four of the six trials than for any of the other microorganisms.

23. **A** Ratings for alfalfa seeds against molds are 4 and 3, but only 2 and 0 against bacteria. None of the others shows this kind of difference.

24. **H** The strongest attack on *Pennicillium* was made by seeds of the legumes, soybean, and alfalfa.

25. **D** All six seeds attacked the bread mold, at the 2 level or higher. A is wrong because the experiment does not address this question. B is wrong because all 6 of the test seeds had some effect on the bread mold. C is wrong because both the dandelion and the thistle seeds had some effect.

26. **G** Neither of the legumes had any effect on *Staphylococcus,* so this family is not the place to look. F is wrong because some of the other seeds do attack *Staphylococcus.* H and J are wrong because this experiment gives no information about one microorganism attacking another.

27. **D** The dandelion and the thistle seeds attacked all microorganisms, mostly at high levels. A is wrong because the experiment gives no information about microorganisms competing with each other. B is wrong because the two legumes do not show a significantly higher ability to attack than any others. C is wrong because the experiment does not deal with the question of damage to crops.

28. **G** The index of refraction of each liquid is a property of the liquid used. F is wrong because the index of refraction of the liquid has nothing to do with the lens. H and J are wrong because the experimental design says nothing about temperature or color of light.

29. **C** All three data tables show an increase in focal length as the index of refraction of the medium increases. This means that the rays converge further from the lens.

30. **F** Comparing the results of Experiments 1 and 2 shows that the focal length of the thicker lens was always less than that of the thinner one, given the same medium.

31. **A** The index of refraction of the glass is 1.720, which is less than the index for methylene iodide, the only medium in which the light does not focus. B is wrong because light might focus in methylene iodide if a different glass was used. C is wrong because the properties of the glass surely matter, and Experiment 2 shows that the thickness of the lens is also involved. D is wrong; the thicker lens converges the light better, forming a shorter focal length.

32. **J** Transparency is not one of the variables in these experiments. F and G are wrong because they deal with phenomena associated with the bending of light. H is wrong because it is entirely reasonable to suppose that the index of fraction of a sugar solution depends on its concentration.

33. **B** To focus the light, a lens must have an index of refraction greater than that of the medium it is in, so the index of the lens must be at least 1.33. If it were as much as 1.50, it would form a focus in the sugar solution.

34. **G** This is the only way to account for the accumulation of oil in porous sedimentary layers. F is wrong because Scientist 2 thinks that petroleum forms deep under the earth's crust. H is wrong because Scientist 1 does not believe this. J is wrong because Scientist 1 thinks oil has formed from marine organisms, which have not always been there.

35. **C** One of Scientist 2's most important items of evidence is the oil found in igneous rock at great depth. A would tend to strengthen Scientist 2's case. B is wrong because one meteorite would not mean anything, in view of the fact that many of them do contain hydrocarbons. D would greatly strengthen Scientist 2's theory because Scientist 1 has not accounted for oil in igneous rocks.

36. **F** Scientist 2 believes there are vast deposits of petroleum deep in the earth's crust, left there by meteors. G is a strategy that Scientist 1 might suggest, but has nothing to do with Scientist 2's theory. H is wrong because both scientists agree that the oil concentrates in sedimentary rocks. J is wrong because Scientist 2 has not suggested that the oil is still in meteorites.

37. **D** The marine-life corpses must be covered quickly to prevent oxidative decay. A would increase decay, not prevent it. B is irrelevant. Scientist 1's theory does not involve meteorites, so C is wrong.

38. **G** According to the theory of Scientist 1, oil forms from dead bodies, so it should form only in sedimentary rocks, which contain lots of fossils.

39. **B** The fact that oil is found in association with salt seems to imply that oil has its origin in the bottom of the sea. A is wrong because this is a mere appeal to authority, not to evidence. C is wrong because both scientists agree that oil seeps upward into porous sedimentary rocks. D is wrong because Scientist 2's theory postulates that the hydrocarbons came to earth long before there were any oceans.

40. **F** Scientist 2 claims that the particular combination of circumstances suggested by Scientist 1 is so rare that it could not account for all the oil there is. G is wrong because Scientist 1's theory does account for accumulation in sedimentary rocks. H is wrong because Scientist 1 used evidence, not arbitrary authority, in his arguments. J is wrong because the potential usefulness of either theory has nothing to do with its validity.

Essay Self-Assessment

Before evaluating your own essay, 433–434 on the scoring of ACT essays. Then complete the following checklist. Focus on both the strengths and weaknesses of your essay.

	Yes!	Mostly	Hardly	No
Does the essay address the ACT prompt?	___	___	___	___
Is the topic sufficiently narrowed?	___	___	___	___
Is the essay's main idea clear?	___	___	___	___
Have you written an introduction?	___	___	___	___
Does the essay sound natural?	___	___	___	___
Have you used plain words?	___	___	___	___
Have you used precise language?	___	___	___	___
Does your essay have a clear focus?	___	___	___	___
Do all parts fit together coherently?	___	___	___	___
Is each sentence accurately worded?	___	___	___	___
Have you trimmed needless words?	___	___	___	___
Do you show more than tell?	___	___	___	___
Have you used active verbs?	___	___	___	___
Is the language fresh?	___	___	___	___
Do you include verbal surprises?	___	___	___	___
Are the sentences varied?	___	___	___	___
Is sentence length balanced?	___	___	___	___
Does the essay have a conclusion?	___	___	___	___
Is the essay mostly error-free?	___	___	___	___

Identify the three greatest strengths of your essay:

1)____

2)____

3)____

Name three specific things that you could do to improve your essay:

1)____

2)____

3)____

Circle the score your essay deserves: 6 5 4 3 2 1

Table for Calculating the Combined English/Writing Test Score

Instructions:

1. Find your Writing Test subscore (2–12) along the top of the table.
2. Find your English Test score on the left or right side.
3. Your combined score will appear in the table where the two scores intersect. For instance, a 10 on the Writing Test and a 25 on the English Test will yield a Combined English/Writing Test score of 26.

English Test Score	Writing Test Subscore											English Test Score
	2	3	4	5	6	7	8	9	10	11	12	
1	1	2	3	4	5	6	7	8	9	10	11	**1**
2	2	3	4	5	6	6	7	8	9	10	11	**2**
3	2	3	4	5	6	7	8	9	10	11	12	**3**
4	3	4	5	6	7	8	9	10	11	12	13	**4**
5	4	5	6	7	8	9	10	11	12	12	13	**5**
6	5	6	7	7	8	9	10	11	12	13	14	**6**
7	5	6	7	8	9	10	11	12	13	14	15	**7**
8	6	7	8	9	10	11	12	13	14	15	16	**8**
9	7	8	9	10	11	12	13	13	14	15	16	**9**
10	8	9	9	10	11	12	13	14	15	16	17	**10**
11	8	9	10	11	12	13	14	15	16	17	18	**11**
12	9	10	11	12	13	14	15	16	17	18	19	**12**
13	10	11	12	13	14	14	15	16	17	18	19	**13**
14	10	11	12	13	14	15	16	17	18	19	20	**14**
15	11	12	13	14	15	16	17	18	19	20	21	**15**
16	12	13	14	15	16	17	18	19	20	20	21	**16**
17	13	14	15	16	16	17	18	19	20	21	22	**17**
18	13	14	15	16	17	18	19	20	21	22	23	**18**
19	14	15	16	17	18	19	20	21	22	23	24	**19**
20	15	16	17	18	19	20	21	21	22	23	24	**20**
21	16	17	17	18	19	20	21	22	23	24	25	**21**
22	16	17	18	19	20	21	22	23	24	25	26	**22**
23	17	18	19	20	21	22	23	24	25	26	27	**23**
24	18	19	20	21	22	23	23	24	25	26	27	**24**
25	18	19	20	21	22	23	24	25	26	27	28	**25**
26	19	20	21	22	23	24	25	26	27	28	29	**26**
27	20	21	22	23	24	25	26	27	28	28	29	**27**
28	21	22	23	24	24	26	26	27	28	29	30	**28**

Table for Calculating the Combined English/Writing Test Score (cont.)

English Test Score	Writing Test Subscore 2	3	4	5	6	7	8	9	10	11	12	English Test Score
29	21	22	23	24	25	26	27	28	29	30	31	**29**
30	22	23	24	25	26	27	28	29	30	31	32	**30**
31	23	24	25	26	27	28	29	30	30	31	32	**31**
32	24	25	25	26	27	28	29	30	31	32	33	**32**
33	25	25	26	27	28	29	30	31	32	33	34	**33**
34	26	26	27	28	29	30	31	32	33	34	35	**34**
35	26	27	28	28	30	31	31	32	33	34	35	**35**
36	26	27	28	29	30	31	32	33	34	35	36	**36**

Calculating Your Combined English/Writing Test Score

English Test Score _____

Essay Score ___ multiply by 2 = _____

Combined Score (See table): _____

Model Exam B

Answer Sheet

MODEL EXAM C

Directions: Mark one answer only for each question. Make the mark dark. Erase completely any mark made in error. (Additional or stray marks will be counted as mistakes.)

Test 1

1 Ⓐ Ⓑ Ⓒ Ⓓ
2 Ⓕ Ⓖ Ⓗ Ⓙ
3 Ⓐ Ⓑ Ⓒ Ⓓ
4 Ⓕ Ⓖ Ⓗ Ⓙ
5 Ⓐ Ⓑ Ⓒ Ⓓ
6 Ⓕ Ⓖ Ⓗ Ⓙ
7 Ⓐ Ⓑ Ⓒ Ⓓ
8 Ⓕ Ⓖ Ⓗ Ⓙ
9 Ⓐ Ⓑ Ⓒ Ⓓ
10 Ⓕ Ⓖ Ⓗ Ⓙ
11 Ⓐ Ⓑ Ⓒ Ⓓ
12 Ⓕ Ⓖ Ⓗ Ⓙ
13 Ⓐ Ⓑ Ⓒ Ⓓ
14 Ⓕ Ⓖ Ⓗ Ⓙ
15 Ⓐ Ⓑ Ⓒ Ⓓ
16 Ⓕ Ⓖ Ⓗ Ⓙ
17 Ⓐ Ⓑ Ⓒ Ⓓ
18 Ⓕ Ⓖ Ⓗ Ⓙ
19 Ⓐ Ⓑ Ⓒ Ⓓ
20 Ⓕ Ⓖ Ⓗ Ⓙ
21 Ⓐ Ⓑ Ⓒ Ⓓ
22 Ⓕ Ⓖ Ⓗ Ⓙ
23 Ⓐ Ⓑ Ⓒ Ⓓ
24 Ⓕ Ⓖ Ⓗ Ⓙ
25 Ⓐ Ⓑ Ⓒ Ⓓ
26 Ⓕ Ⓖ Ⓗ Ⓙ
27 Ⓐ Ⓑ Ⓒ Ⓓ
28 Ⓕ Ⓖ Ⓗ Ⓙ
29 Ⓐ Ⓑ Ⓒ Ⓓ
30 Ⓕ Ⓖ Ⓗ Ⓙ
31 Ⓐ Ⓑ Ⓒ Ⓓ
32 Ⓕ Ⓖ Ⓗ Ⓙ
33 Ⓐ Ⓑ Ⓒ Ⓓ
34 Ⓕ Ⓖ Ⓗ Ⓙ
35 Ⓐ Ⓑ Ⓒ Ⓓ
36 Ⓕ Ⓖ Ⓗ Ⓙ
37 Ⓐ Ⓑ Ⓒ Ⓓ
38 Ⓕ Ⓖ Ⓗ Ⓙ
39 Ⓐ Ⓑ Ⓒ Ⓓ
40 Ⓕ Ⓖ Ⓗ Ⓙ
41 Ⓐ Ⓑ Ⓒ Ⓓ
42 Ⓕ Ⓖ Ⓗ Ⓙ
43 Ⓐ Ⓑ Ⓒ Ⓓ
44 Ⓕ Ⓖ Ⓗ Ⓙ
45 Ⓐ Ⓑ Ⓒ Ⓓ
46 Ⓕ Ⓖ Ⓗ Ⓙ
47 Ⓐ Ⓑ Ⓒ Ⓓ
48 Ⓕ Ⓖ Ⓗ Ⓙ
49 Ⓐ Ⓑ Ⓒ Ⓓ
50 Ⓕ Ⓖ Ⓗ Ⓙ
51 Ⓐ Ⓑ Ⓒ Ⓓ
52 Ⓕ Ⓖ Ⓗ Ⓙ
53 Ⓐ Ⓑ Ⓒ Ⓓ
54 Ⓕ Ⓖ Ⓗ Ⓙ
55 Ⓐ Ⓑ Ⓒ Ⓓ
56 Ⓕ Ⓖ Ⓗ Ⓙ
57 Ⓐ Ⓑ Ⓒ Ⓓ
58 Ⓕ Ⓖ Ⓗ Ⓙ
59 Ⓐ Ⓑ Ⓒ Ⓓ
60 Ⓕ Ⓖ Ⓗ Ⓙ
61 Ⓐ Ⓑ Ⓒ Ⓓ
62 Ⓕ Ⓖ Ⓗ Ⓙ
63 Ⓐ Ⓑ Ⓒ Ⓓ
64 Ⓕ Ⓖ Ⓗ Ⓙ
65 Ⓐ Ⓑ Ⓒ Ⓓ
66 Ⓕ Ⓖ Ⓗ Ⓙ
67 Ⓐ Ⓑ Ⓒ Ⓓ
68 Ⓕ Ⓖ Ⓗ Ⓙ
69 Ⓐ Ⓑ Ⓒ Ⓓ
70 Ⓕ Ⓖ Ⓗ Ⓙ
71 Ⓐ Ⓑ Ⓒ Ⓓ
72 Ⓕ Ⓖ Ⓗ Ⓙ
73 Ⓐ Ⓑ Ⓒ Ⓓ
74 Ⓕ Ⓖ Ⓗ Ⓙ
75 Ⓐ Ⓑ Ⓒ Ⓓ

Test 2

1 Ⓐ Ⓑ Ⓒ Ⓓ Ⓔ
2 Ⓕ Ⓖ Ⓗ Ⓙ Ⓚ
3 Ⓐ Ⓑ Ⓒ Ⓓ Ⓔ
4 Ⓕ Ⓖ Ⓗ Ⓙ Ⓚ
5 Ⓐ Ⓑ Ⓒ Ⓓ Ⓔ
6 Ⓕ Ⓖ Ⓗ Ⓙ Ⓚ
7 Ⓐ Ⓑ Ⓒ Ⓓ Ⓔ
8 Ⓕ Ⓖ Ⓗ Ⓙ Ⓚ
9 Ⓐ Ⓑ Ⓒ Ⓓ Ⓔ
10 Ⓕ Ⓖ Ⓗ Ⓙ Ⓚ
11 Ⓐ Ⓑ Ⓒ Ⓓ Ⓔ
12 Ⓕ Ⓖ Ⓗ Ⓙ Ⓚ
13 Ⓐ Ⓑ Ⓒ Ⓓ Ⓔ
14 Ⓕ Ⓖ Ⓗ Ⓙ Ⓚ
15 Ⓐ Ⓑ Ⓒ Ⓓ Ⓔ
16 Ⓕ Ⓖ Ⓗ Ⓙ Ⓚ
17 Ⓐ Ⓑ Ⓒ Ⓓ Ⓔ
18 Ⓕ Ⓖ Ⓗ Ⓙ Ⓚ
19 Ⓐ Ⓑ Ⓒ Ⓓ Ⓔ
20 Ⓕ Ⓖ Ⓗ Ⓙ Ⓚ
21 Ⓐ Ⓑ Ⓒ Ⓓ Ⓔ
22 Ⓕ Ⓖ Ⓗ Ⓙ Ⓚ
23 Ⓐ Ⓑ Ⓒ Ⓓ Ⓔ
24 Ⓕ Ⓖ Ⓗ Ⓙ Ⓚ
25 Ⓐ Ⓑ Ⓒ Ⓓ Ⓔ
26 Ⓕ Ⓖ Ⓗ Ⓙ Ⓚ
27 Ⓐ Ⓑ Ⓒ Ⓓ Ⓔ
28 Ⓕ Ⓖ Ⓗ Ⓙ Ⓚ
29 Ⓐ Ⓑ Ⓒ Ⓓ Ⓔ
30 Ⓕ Ⓖ Ⓗ Ⓙ Ⓚ
31 Ⓐ Ⓑ Ⓒ Ⓓ Ⓔ
32 Ⓕ Ⓖ Ⓗ Ⓙ Ⓚ
33 Ⓐ Ⓑ Ⓒ Ⓓ Ⓔ
34 Ⓕ Ⓖ Ⓗ Ⓙ Ⓚ
35 Ⓐ Ⓑ Ⓒ Ⓓ Ⓔ
36 Ⓕ Ⓖ Ⓗ Ⓙ Ⓚ
37 Ⓐ Ⓑ Ⓒ Ⓓ Ⓔ
38 Ⓕ Ⓖ Ⓗ Ⓙ Ⓚ
39 Ⓐ Ⓑ Ⓒ Ⓓ Ⓔ
40 Ⓕ Ⓖ Ⓗ Ⓙ Ⓚ
41 Ⓐ Ⓑ Ⓒ Ⓓ Ⓔ
42 Ⓕ Ⓖ Ⓗ Ⓙ Ⓚ
43 Ⓐ Ⓑ Ⓒ Ⓓ Ⓔ
44 Ⓕ Ⓖ Ⓗ Ⓙ Ⓚ
45 Ⓐ Ⓑ Ⓒ Ⓓ Ⓔ
46 Ⓕ Ⓖ Ⓗ Ⓙ Ⓚ
47 Ⓐ Ⓑ Ⓒ Ⓓ Ⓔ
48 Ⓕ Ⓖ Ⓗ Ⓙ Ⓚ
49 Ⓐ Ⓑ Ⓒ Ⓓ Ⓔ
50 Ⓕ Ⓖ Ⓗ Ⓙ Ⓚ
51 Ⓐ Ⓑ Ⓒ Ⓓ Ⓔ
52 Ⓕ Ⓖ Ⓗ Ⓙ Ⓚ
53 Ⓐ Ⓑ Ⓒ Ⓓ Ⓔ
54 Ⓕ Ⓖ Ⓗ Ⓙ Ⓚ
55 Ⓐ Ⓑ Ⓒ Ⓓ Ⓔ
56 Ⓕ Ⓖ Ⓗ Ⓙ Ⓚ
57 Ⓐ Ⓑ Ⓒ Ⓓ Ⓔ
58 Ⓕ Ⓖ Ⓗ Ⓙ Ⓚ
59 Ⓐ Ⓑ Ⓒ Ⓓ Ⓔ
60 Ⓕ Ⓖ Ⓗ Ⓙ Ⓚ

Answer Sheet

MODEL EXAM C

Test 3

1 Ⓐ Ⓑ Ⓒ Ⓓ	11 Ⓐ Ⓑ Ⓒ Ⓓ	21 Ⓐ Ⓑ Ⓒ Ⓓ	31 Ⓐ Ⓑ Ⓒ Ⓓ
2 Ⓕ Ⓖ Ⓗ Ⓙ	12 Ⓕ Ⓖ Ⓗ Ⓙ	22 Ⓕ Ⓖ Ⓗ Ⓙ	32 Ⓕ Ⓖ Ⓗ Ⓙ
3 Ⓐ Ⓑ Ⓒ Ⓓ	13 Ⓐ Ⓑ Ⓒ Ⓓ	23 Ⓐ Ⓑ Ⓒ Ⓓ	33 Ⓐ Ⓑ Ⓒ Ⓓ
4 Ⓕ Ⓖ Ⓗ Ⓙ	14 Ⓕ Ⓖ Ⓗ Ⓙ	24 Ⓕ Ⓖ Ⓗ Ⓙ	34 Ⓕ Ⓖ Ⓗ Ⓙ
5 Ⓐ Ⓑ Ⓒ Ⓓ	15 Ⓐ Ⓑ Ⓒ Ⓓ	25 Ⓐ Ⓑ Ⓒ Ⓓ	35 Ⓐ Ⓑ Ⓒ Ⓓ
6 Ⓕ Ⓖ Ⓗ Ⓙ	16 Ⓕ Ⓖ Ⓗ Ⓙ	26 Ⓕ Ⓖ Ⓗ Ⓙ	36 Ⓕ Ⓖ Ⓗ Ⓙ
7 Ⓐ Ⓑ Ⓒ Ⓓ	17 Ⓐ Ⓑ Ⓒ Ⓓ	27 Ⓐ Ⓑ Ⓒ Ⓓ	37 Ⓐ Ⓑ Ⓒ Ⓓ
8 Ⓕ Ⓖ Ⓗ Ⓙ	18 Ⓕ Ⓖ Ⓗ Ⓙ	28 Ⓕ Ⓖ Ⓗ Ⓙ	38 Ⓕ Ⓖ Ⓗ Ⓙ
9 Ⓐ Ⓑ Ⓒ Ⓓ	19 Ⓐ Ⓑ Ⓒ Ⓓ	29 Ⓐ Ⓑ Ⓒ Ⓓ	39 Ⓐ Ⓑ Ⓒ Ⓓ
10 Ⓕ Ⓖ Ⓗ Ⓙ	20 Ⓕ Ⓖ Ⓗ Ⓙ	30 Ⓕ Ⓖ Ⓗ Ⓙ	40 Ⓕ Ⓖ Ⓗ Ⓙ

Test 4

1 Ⓐ Ⓑ Ⓒ Ⓓ	11 Ⓐ Ⓑ Ⓒ Ⓓ	21 Ⓐ Ⓑ Ⓒ Ⓓ	31 Ⓐ Ⓑ Ⓒ Ⓓ
2 Ⓕ Ⓖ Ⓗ Ⓙ	12 Ⓕ Ⓖ Ⓗ Ⓙ	22 Ⓕ Ⓖ Ⓗ Ⓙ	32 Ⓕ Ⓖ Ⓗ Ⓙ
3 Ⓐ Ⓑ Ⓒ Ⓓ	13 Ⓐ Ⓑ Ⓒ Ⓓ	23 Ⓐ Ⓑ Ⓒ Ⓓ	33 Ⓐ Ⓑ Ⓒ Ⓓ
4 Ⓕ Ⓖ Ⓗ Ⓙ	14 Ⓕ Ⓖ Ⓗ Ⓙ	24 Ⓕ Ⓖ Ⓗ Ⓙ	34 Ⓕ Ⓖ Ⓗ Ⓙ
5 Ⓐ Ⓑ Ⓒ Ⓓ	15 Ⓐ Ⓑ Ⓒ Ⓓ	25 Ⓐ Ⓑ Ⓒ Ⓓ	35 Ⓐ Ⓑ Ⓒ Ⓓ
6 Ⓕ Ⓖ Ⓗ Ⓙ	16 Ⓕ Ⓖ Ⓗ Ⓙ	26 Ⓕ Ⓖ Ⓗ Ⓙ	36 Ⓕ Ⓖ Ⓗ Ⓙ
7 Ⓐ Ⓑ Ⓒ Ⓓ	17 Ⓐ Ⓑ Ⓒ Ⓓ	27 Ⓐ Ⓑ Ⓒ Ⓓ	37 Ⓐ Ⓑ Ⓒ Ⓓ
8 Ⓕ Ⓖ Ⓗ Ⓙ	18 Ⓕ Ⓖ Ⓗ Ⓙ	28 Ⓕ Ⓖ Ⓗ Ⓙ	38 Ⓕ Ⓖ Ⓗ Ⓙ
9 Ⓐ Ⓑ Ⓒ Ⓓ	19 Ⓐ Ⓑ Ⓒ Ⓓ	29 Ⓐ Ⓑ Ⓒ Ⓓ	39 Ⓐ Ⓑ Ⓒ Ⓓ
10 Ⓕ Ⓖ Ⓗ Ⓙ	20 Ⓕ Ⓖ Ⓗ Ⓙ	30 Ⓕ Ⓖ Ⓗ Ⓙ	40 Ⓕ Ⓖ Ⓗ Ⓙ

Model Exam C

ENGLISH TEST

45 MINUTES—75 QUESTIONS

Directions: The following test consists of 75 underlined words and phrases in context, or general questions about the passages. Most of the underlined sections contain errors and inappropriate expressions. You are asked to compare each with the four alternatives in the answer column. If you consider the original version best, choose letter **A** or **F:** NO CHANGE. For each question, blacken on the answer sheet the letter of the alternative you think best. Read each passage through before answering the questions based on it.

Passage 1

(1)

The knowledge, attitudes, and skill that children acquire concerning money come from a variety of sources. The most important is the family.

(2)

What a child learns at home is reinforced, weakened, or otherwise modified by the influence of his or her friends adults [1] outside the home, and pressures in the social world at large. [2]

1. **A.** NO CHANGE
   B. friends—adults
   C. friends: adults
   D. friends, adults

2. Suppose that at this point in the passage the writer wanted to add more information about pressures in the social world of a child. Which of the following additions would be most relevant to the passage as a whole?
   F. A brief classification of the social strata that may be part of children's lives.
   G. A scientifically accurate definition of *social pressure*.
   H. A simple anecdote about the way a child was influenced by the spending behavior of his or her peers.
   J. A case history of a mentally disturbed teenager with a history of antisocial behavior.

GO ON TO THE NEXT PAGE.

1 1 1 1 1 1 1 1 1 1 1

(3)

There are several important principles involved with sound money management and that[3] children need to learn. The most important is to spend wisely in such a way as to get full enjoyment and satisfaction. Another is to save for future purchases. Still another is understanding[4] credit and how to use it well. Finally, children need to have experience in earning money for their own use. [5]

3. A. NO CHANGE
   B. and which
   C. and whom
   D. that

4. F. NO CHANGE
   G. comprehending
   H. to understand
   J. earning

5. This paragraph is organized according to which of the following schemes?
   A. A series of comparison/contrast sentences.
   B. "Nested" classifications, with several subdivisions of each topic.
   C. A general statement followed by specific examples.
   D. A narrative, with one event after another.

(4)

In other words, he needs[6] to learn that money is valuable as a tool in reaching goals rather than as a goal in itself. The implication for parents is that they need to resist the temptation to regard money only as a restricting, rather than also as a facilitating, element in their lives. Being as how[7] adults overemphasize the importance of money, they should not be surprised when children also do so.

6. F. NO CHANGE
   G. he or she needs
   H. one needs
   J. they need

7. A. NO CHANGE
   B. If
   C. Although
   D. Thus,

(5)

These pressures are strong. Children themselves have become important consumers, having control over more money at earlier ages than ever before. A rise in family incomes, as well as an increase in the number of working adults, have meant[8] that more parents can give children more money for their own use. Business is

8. F. NO CHANGE
   G. has meant
   H. will have meant
   J. meant

1 1 1 1 1 1 1 1 1 1 1

fully aware of this. Modern advertising regards children and teenagers as awesome targets. The cost of clothes is rising at a truly alarming rate. All of these factors emphasize the need to teach children how to manage money.

9. **A.** NO CHANGE
B. that
C. that children are more mature
D. that cash is more available

10. **F.** NO CHANGE
G. massive
H. major
J. herculean

11. **A.** NO CHANGE
B. The cost of children's clothes has remained stable.
C. OMIT the underlined portion.
D. The cost of clothes is just one of the factors that have contributed to inflation.

(6)

On the other hand, unless adults in the company of children can enjoy some of the many fine things in the world that require no expenditure of money and can consistently meet children's needs for affection and companionship, they are well on the way toward teaching these children the proper place that material possessions and worldly goods should have in their lives. [15]

12. **F.** NO CHANGE
G. until
H. when
J. although

13. **A.** NO CHANGE
B. companionship they
C. companionship: they
D. companionship. They

14. **F.** NO CHANGE
G. OMIT the underlined portion.
H. and, thus, more worldly goods
J. and goods

15. Choose the sequence of paragraph numbers that makes the structure of the passage most logical.
A. NO CHANGE
B. 1, 2, 6, 4, 3, 5
C. 1, 2, 5, 3, 4, 6
D. 1, 5, 6, 3, 4, 2

GO ON TO THE NEXT PAGE.

1 1 1 1 1 1 1 1 1 1 1

Passage 2

(1)

Feet and shoes travel many miles. An average, healthy 7-year-old boy may take 30,000 steps every day, an accumulation that adds up to 10 miles per day and more than 300 miles a month. His mother, on a busy shopping day, may walk 10 miles. A police officer, in common with all of his or her fellow officers, <u>walk</u> [16] about 15 miles on the beat.

(2)

The foot is a complicated structure of twenty-six small bones linked by many joints, attached to each other and to the leg bone by numerous ligaments, moved by muscles and tendons, nourished by blood vessels, controlled by nerves, <u>and a covering of skin protects it</u> [17]. In a newborn infant, some of the bones are merely bone-shaped pieces of cartilage, a gristle-like substance. As a child <u>grows, however, real</u> [18] bone appears within, and gradually spreads throughout the cartilage form. The heel, the largest bone, is not completed until the age of about 20 years. [19]

(3)

During all this walking, feet carry the weight of the <u>body, and provide</u> [20] the means to propel a person when he or she walks, climbs, and jumps. As a person steps out, the body weight travels down through the heel, along

16. **F.** NO CHANGE
    G. walked
    H. walks
    J. was walking

17. **A.** NO CHANGE
    B. and a covering of skin has protected it.
    C. and being covered by a covering of skin.
    D. and protected by a covering of skin.

18. **F.** NO CHANGE
    G. grows, however. Real
    H. grows, however real
    J. grows however, real

19. Suppose that at this point in the passage the writer wanted to add more information about foot anatomy. Which of the following additions would be most relevant to the passage as a whole?
    A. A discussion of common foot ailments and their treatment.
    B. An account of foot operations on some well-known athletes.
    C. More specific details about the muscles that control the feet, the bone tissue, the nerves and tendons.
    D. A brief account of some famous myths involving the feet, such as the one about Achilles.

20. **F.** NO CHANGE
    G. body. And provide
    H. body and provide
    J. body, and, provide

1 1 1 1 1 1 1 1 1 1 1

the outside of the foot to the ball, across the heads of the long bones to the first metatarsal, and to the big toe. The big toe launches the walking motion. One after the other, [21] each foot in turn bears the total weight of the body. If your feet ache, try massaging them for 20 minutes. You will be amazed at the results. [22] [23]

21. A. NO CHANGE
B. OMIT the underlined portion.
C. One after the other—
D. One after the other:

22. F. NO CHANGE
G. If your feet ache, massage them!
H. OMIT the underlined portion.
J. If your feet ache, try massaging them, and you will be amazed at the results.

23. Is the description of the physical functioning of the foot appropriate in the passage?
A. Yes, because the passage is actually about sports medicine.
B. Yes, because the passage is about the stresses on the foot and footwear that are brought about by walking.
C. No, there is no relevance to the rest of the passage.
D. No, because it is already well understood that the foot exerts pressure.

(4)

Because [24] a 7-year-old boy weighs 55 pounds, he puts more than 800 tons of weight on his shoes every day (55 pounds times 30,000 steps), or about 24 tons a month. But a boy does more than walk. He jumps, kicks, and often has waded [25] through puddles. His shoes lead a rough life. Estimates of the active life of a pair of shoes ranges [26] from 20 days to 7 or 9 months; the average is about 10 weeks. In fact, no single component or characteristic determine [27] the life of a shoe. Fit is most important, and usually only the wearer can tell

24. F. NO CHANGE
G. If
H. Being that
J. Since

25. A. NO CHANGE
B. wades
C. waded
D. will have waded

26. F. NO CHANGE
G. would range
H. range
J. has ranged

27. A. NO CHANGE
B. determines
C. will determine
D. is determining

whether a shoe fits. Price alone certainly does not guarantee a good fit! [29] [30]
28

28. **F.** NO CHANGE
G. fit."
H. fit?
J. fit.

29. Are the statistics in the first sentence of the paragraph appropriate and meaningful?
A. Yes, because the passage is about the stresses to the feet brought about by walking, jumping, and other physical activities.
B. Yes, because the figures help us understand that everything has a physical consequence.
C. No, because the passage is basically about the anatomy of feet.
D. No, because the physical activity of a 7-year-old boy is irrelevant to the discussion.

30. Choose the sequence of paragraph numbers that makes the structure of the passage most logical.
F. NO CHANGE
G. 1, 2, 4, 3
H. 1, 4, 2, 3
J. 1, 3, 2, 4

Passage 3

(1)

A park in the old part of Philadelphia not only is preeminent among the sites associated with the signers of the Declaration of Independence, but also notably commemorates other major aspects of the nation's founding and initial growth and many momentous national events. These include meetings of the First and Second Continental Congresses, the Declaration was a dopted and signed, which marked the creation of the
31 / 32 / 33

31. **A.** NO CHANGE
B. commemorate
C. will commemorate
D. has commemorated

32. **F.** NO CHANGE
G. Congresses—
H. Congresses;
J. Congresses

33. **A.** NO CHANGE
B. The Declaration was adopted and signed.
C. the Declaration, adopted and signed,
D. the adoption and signing of the Declaration,

1 1 1 1 1 1 1 1 1 1 1

United States; and the labors of the Constitutional Convention of 1787, which perpetuated it. [34]

(2)

Independence Hall was originally the statehouse for the province of Pennsylvania. (35) In 1729 the provincial assembly set aside funds for the building, designed by lawyer Andrew Hamilton. Three years later, construction began under the supervision and overview (36) of master carpenter Edmund Wooley. In 1736 the assembly moved into the statehouse, which was not fully completed until 1756. Thomas Jefferson was in France at the time. (37) As American opposition to British colonial policies mounted, Philadelphia became a center of organized protest. To decide on a unified course of action, in 1774 the First Continental Congress met in newly finished Carpenters' Hall, whose erection the Carpenters' Company of Philadelphia had begun (38) four years earlier. In 1775 the Second Continental Congress, taking over the east room of the ground floor of the statehouse from the Pennsylvania assembly, moved from protest to resistance; Congress had created (39) an army and appointed George Washington as commander

34. Is the reference to the park a meaningful way to begin this passage?
   F. No, because the passage is not about recreational sites, but about the significance of Independence Hall.
   G. No, because everything it signifies is covered elsewhere in the passage.
   H. Yes, because the general reference to scenery is a good way to begin any discussion.
   J. Yes, because the park is the site of fundamental historical events described in the passage.

35. Does the first sentence of the paragraph provide a general basis for the specific supporting details that follow?
   A. Yes, the sentence is a classic topic sentence followed by supporting details about the province of Pennsylvania.
   B. Yes, the sentence suggests a plan, and the rest of the paragraph spells out the plan.
   C. No, the sentence refers to a building that is mentioned again in the paragraph, but it does not adequately prepare the reader for the historical narrative that comprises the main part of the paragraph.
   D. No, the sentence does not relate to any supporting material.

36. **F.** NO CHANGE
   G. supervision
   H. supervision as well as overview
   J. supervision, and overview,

37. **A.** NO CHANGE
   B. Thomas Jefferson had been in France at the time.
   C. OMIT the underlined portion.
   D. Thomas Jefferson would be in France at the time.

38. **F.** NO CHANGE
   G. began
   H. had began
   J. has begun

39. **A.** NO CHANGE
   B. will have created
   C. has created
   D. created

Model Exam C

GO ON TO THE NEXT PAGE.

1 1 1 1 1 1 1 1 1 1 1

in chief. Thus, the final break with the Crown had not come; not until a year later would independence have been declared. [42]

40. F. NO CHANGE
G. Finally,
H. Nevertheless,
J. In addition,

41. A. NO CHANGE
B. be declared.
C. declare itself.
D. been declared.

42. This paragraph is organized according to which of the following schemes?
F. A series of chronological references to Independence Hall, each at an important historical juncture.
G. A general statement about Independence Hall, followed by specific information about the structure.
H. A series of statements comparing and contrasting Independence Hall with other structures.
J. A series of arguments about the historical importance of Independence Hall, followed by answers.

(3)

On July 2, 1776, Congress passed Richard Henry Lee's resolution of June 7 recommending independence. The delegates, then turning their attention to T homas Jefferson's draft of the Declaration, which had been submitted on June 28. After modification, it was adopted on July 4. Four days later, in Independence Square, the document was first read publicly to the citizens of Philadelphia. In a formal ceremony on August 2, about fifty of the fifty-six signers affixed their signatures to the Declaration, the others apparently did so later. [45]

43. A. NO CHANGE
B. Then turning the delegates' attention to Thomas Jefferson's draft of the Declaration, which had been submitted on June 28.
C. The delegates then turned their attention to Thomas Jefferson's draft of the Declaration. Which had been submitted on June 28.
D. The delegates then turned their attention to Thomas Jefferson's draft of the Declaration, which had been submitted on June 28.

44. F. NO CHANGE
G. Declaration the
H. Declaration—the
J. Declaration; the

45. Choose the sequence of paragraph numbers that makes the structure of the passage most logical.
A. NO CHANGE
B. 2, 1, 3
C. 1, 3, 2
D. 2, 3, 1

1 1 1 1 1 1 1 1 1 1 1

Passage 4

(1)

The greatest problem with the abortion issue is that it is far more complex than it first appears. It is a moral issue because it involves what both sides admit is a decision to begin or terminate a life; it is a political issue because many laws encourage or discourage the practice of abortion; finally, [46] social concerns are addressed, [47] because all human beings are affected by the number of people born into the world.

(2)

One of the central issues of the new millennium is abortion. On one side of the question is [48] the pro-lifers, a minority who believe that abortion is the taking of a life and that the government must protect the rights of all its citizens, including the right of an unborn infant to live. On the other side are the pro-choice advocates, comprising a majority of Americans who [49] believe that abortion should be legal under certain circumstances, (particularly those involving the health of the mother) [50] Researchers and pollsters have been surprised at the strength of these convictions and at the extent to which most people have pondered their beliefs.

(3)

However, [51] the majority group that believes [52] in some form of abortion is also willing to describe the medical

46. **F.** NO CHANGE
G. abortion finally,
H. abortion: finally,
J. abortion, finally,

47. **A.** NO CHANGE
B. social concerns have been addressed,
C. it is of social concern,
D. it is a social issue

48. **F.** NO CHANGE
G. have been
H. will be
J. are

49. **A.** NO CHANGE
B. Americans (who
C. Americans, who
D. Americans. Who

50. **F.** NO CHANGE
G. circumstances, particularly those involving the health of the mother.
H. circumstances (particularly those, involving the health of the mother).
J. circumstances particularly those involving the health of the mother.

51. **A.** NO CHANGE
B. Because
C. For example,
D. Although

52. **F.** NO CHANGE
G. believe
H. believed
J. is believing

Model Exam C

process as when a life ends. A woman's decision to abort her pregnancy can be viewed, according to more than half of all the pro-choice people polled, as a choice between two evils and a conscious acceptance of guilt in the necessary termination of life. [54]

53. A. NO CHANGE
B. where a life ends
C. when you end a life.
D. the end of a life.

54. Suppose that at this point in the passage the writer wanted to add more information about the abortion issue. Which of the following additions would be most relevant to the passage as a whole?
F. A brief summary of views on the issue held by significant religious and political leaders.
G. A list of hospitals that perform abortions.
H. An expose of unlicensed or substandard abortion clinics.
J. A case history of an abortion.

(4)

The pro-lifer or anti-abortionist tends to be on the right side of the political spectrum, sometimes believing that social programs are inherently no good and impeding human progress because they tend to discourage initiative. Using the rule of common good, pro-lifers ask what decision made by a woman contemplating abortion would bring about the greatest number of positive consequences that are beneficial for all concerned—one of those concerned, of course, being the unborn fetus. A baby's fine features, such as eyelashes and fingernails, are fully developed by the age of ten weeks. [59] [60]

55. A. NO CHANGE
B. ill advised
C. bad news
D. forbidden

56. F. NO CHANGE
G. impeded
H. impede
J. impedes

57. A. NO CHANGE
B. beneficial
C. also beneficial
D. OMIT the underlined portion.

58. F. NO CHANGE
G. OMIT the underlined portion.
H. A baby's fine features, for example, eyelashes and fingernails, are fully developed by the age of ten weeks.
J. A baby's fine features, such as eyelashes and fingernails, being fully developed by the age of ten weeks.

59. For the most part, this passage is written according to which of the following strategies?
A. Comparison/contrast
B. Argument
C. Description
D. Narration

60. Choose the sequence of paragraph numbers that makes the structure of the passage most logical.
F. NO CHANGE
G. 1, 4, 3, 2
H. 2, 3, 4, 1
J. 2, 1, 3, 4

1 1 1 1 1 1 1 1 1 1 1

Passage 5

(1)

The California Constitution requires that the Governor submit a budget with an explanation to both houses of the Legislature before January 11 of each year. The explanation must contain a complete spending plan, as well as an itemized statement of all expenditures provided by law or proposed by the Governor, <u>and the proposed budget must be compared with last year's.</u>[61] After the Governor has submitted the budget, an appropriation bill, known as the Budget Bill, which reflects the proposed budget, is introduced into each house of the Legislature and referred to the Assembly Ways and Means Committee and the Senate Finance Committee, respectively. The Constitution requires that the Legislature pass the Budget Bill by midnight, June 15. Until the Budget Bill <u>will have been enacted,</u>[62] neither house can send to the Governor any other appropriation bill, other than emergency measures. [63]

(2)

<u>Being</u>[64] a budget approaching 100 billion dollars, the five months allowed by the Constitution for all the item disagreements, resolutions, lobbying by special interest groups, and "dealing" by the legislatures on behalf of their constituents is hardly enough time. Yet, if the budget is not passed, the state of California literally ceases to function. All state employees are asked to stay

61. **A.** NO CHANGE
    B. and it must be compared with last year's budget.
    C. together with a comparison of the proposed budget with last year's.
    D. and it should contain a comparison of last year's and this year's budget.

62. **F.** NO CHANGE
    G. has been enacted,
    H. would have been enacted,
    J. was enacted,

63. Which of the following statements is best supported by the details supplied in this paragraph?
    A. The California Legislature and the Governor are in contention.
    B. The California Constitution punishes lawmakers who violate its rules.
    C. The California Constitution places a high priority on timely passage of the state budget.
    D. The California budget process is hopelessly politicized.

64. **F.** NO CHANGE
    G. Due to its being
    H. Being as how it is
    J. For

Model Exam C

GO ON TO THE NEXT PAGE.

home. Traffic on the freeways is measurably reduced.[65] All state government offices and agencies close and even[66] the Legislature with its heavy responsibilities has to operate with a skeleton staff. When[67] an absolute halt in services and business is so disruptive, and due to the very fact that[68] no other appropriation bill can be sent to the Governor until the budget is passed, both the Assembly and the Senate usually stay in session continuously[69] until the impasse, whatever its genesis, is solved. It is not surprising, under such conditions, that the Legislature and the Governor seem to find solutions rather quickly to disputes and stalemates that have been festering[70] for months. [71]

(3)

The orderly operation of the Government of California depends on the state budget, a document controlling expenditures that are larger than those of any American governmental jurisdiction[72] with the exception of the city of New York and the U.S.

65. **A.** NO CHANGE
    B. Traffic, because it is on the freeway, is measurably reduced.
    C. OMIT the underlined portion.
    D. Traffic is reduced, especially on the freeways.

66. **F.** NO CHANGE
    G. close. And even
    H. close: Even
    J. close, and even

67. **A.** NO CHANGE
    B. If
    C. Because
    D. Until

68. **F.** NO CHANGE
    G. unless
    H. although
    J. because

69. **A.** NO CHANGE
    B. continually
    C. interminably
    D. repeatedly

70. **F.** NO CHANGE
    G. have been solved
    H. have been unresolved
    J. have been unknown

71. This passage was probably written for readers who:
    A. are tax accountants seeking to learn more about their vocation.
    B. are taxpayers and voters interested in how a state government works.
    C. enjoy scientific and quantitative facts.
    D. enjoy works of inspiration and solace.

72. **F.** NO CHANGE
    G. any other American governmental jurisdiction
    H. any, American governmental jurisdiction
    J. any American, governmental jurisdiction

Government. Each year, the process of creating the many parts of the budget (73) begins in January with the Governor's message to the Legislature. 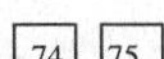

73. **A.** NO CHANGE
    B. so many part of the budget
    C. a budget
    D. the workings of the budget

74. This paragraph emphasizes the importance of:
    F. the Government of California.
    G. the size of the budget.
    H. the budget.
    J. the Governor's message to the Legislature.

75. Choose the sequence of paragraph numbers that makes the structure of the essay most logical.
    A. NO CHANGE
    B. 3, 2, 1
    C. 3, 1, 2
    D. 2, 3, 1

STOP

If there is still time remaining, you may review your answers.

2 2 2 2 2 2 2 2 2 2 2

MATHEMATICS TEST

60 MINUTES—60 QUESTIONS

Directions: After solving each problem, darken the appropriate space on the answer sheet. Do not spend too much time on any one problem. Make a note of the ones that seem difficult, and return to them when you finish the others. Assume that the word *line* means "straight line," that geometric figures are not necessarily drawn to scale, and that all geometric figures lie in a plane.

DO YOUR FIGURING HERE

1. Which of the following is a monomial?

A. $\sqrt{2x}$
B. $\frac{2}{x}$
C. $\frac{x}{2}$
D. $x + 2$
E. 2^x

2. Lisa's salary was raised 8%. If she now receives \$5.67 per hour, what was her hourly salary before her increase?

F. \$0.45
G. \$5.22
H. \$5.25
J. \$5.30
K. \$6.12

3. The expression $5 + 2 \cdot 3^2 =$?

A. 441
B. 121
C. 63
D. 41
E. 23

4. What is the complete factorization of the polynomial $81x^2 - 36y^2$?

F. $(9x - 6y)(9x + 6y)$
G. $9(3x - 2y)^2$
H. $9(3x - 2y)(3x + 2y)$
J. $3(9x - 6y)(3x + 2y)$
K. None of these

5. Which of the following numbers is NOT irrational?

A. π
B. $\sqrt{7}$
C. $\sqrt{49}$
D. 7.313113111311113 . . .
E. $\sqrt{7} - \sqrt{3}$

2 2 2 2 2 2 2 2 2 2 2

DO YOUR FIGURING HERE

6. What is the simplified form of the algebraic fraction $\frac{(x - y)^2}{y^2 - x^2}$?

   F. 1
   G. –1
   H. $2xy$
   J. $\frac{y-x}{y+x}$
   K. $\frac{x-y}{x+y}$

7. Which of the following is a geometric sequence?

   A. 1, 3, 5, 7, . . .
   B. 1, 2, 4, 8, . . .
   C. $1, \frac{1}{2}, \frac{1}{3}, \frac{1}{4}, \ldots$
   D. 1, 4, 9, 16, . . .
   E. 1, 4, 13, 40, . . .

8. Which is the solution set of the equation $4x - 2[3x - (x + 4)] = 5 - 2(x + 1)$?

   F. $\left\{\frac{-5}{2}\right\}$
   G. $\left\{\frac{5}{3}\right\}$
   H. $\left\{\frac{-11}{7}\right\}$
   J. {–2}
   K. Ø

9. If $\overline{AB}$ is a diameter, $\overline{BC}$ is a tangent, and $m\angle ABD = 25°$, what is the measure of $\angle BCD$?

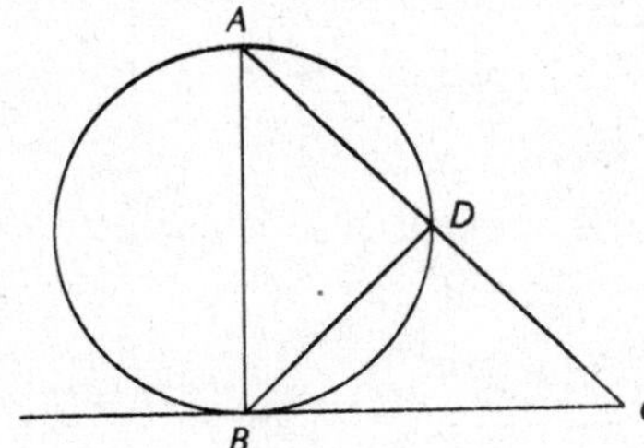

   A. 90°
   B. 65°
   C. $32\frac{1}{2}°$
   D. 25°
   E. $12\frac{1}{2}°$

Model Exam C

2 2 2 2 2 2 2 2 2 2 2

DO YOUR FIGURING HERE

10. Which of the following numbers is smallest?

F. 7.2%
G. $7.2\ (10^{-2})$
H. $\frac{72}{100}$
J. (0.08)9
K. (0.08)(0.09)

11. What is the value of the expression $xy^2(x - y)$ if $x = -3$ and $y = 2$?

A. -180
B. -60
C. -12
D. 12
E. 60

12. If it takes 4 gallons of lemonade for a party of 20 children, how many gallons should one have on hand for a party of 30 children?

F. 5
G. 6
H. 6.5
J. 7.5
K. 8

13. Which expression would be appropriate to complete the following equation in order for the equation to illustrate the associative property of addition: $3 + (-2 + 0) = ?$

A. 1
B. $3 + [0 + (-2)]$
C. $[3 + (-2)] + 0$
D. $3 + (-2)$
E. $(-2 + 0) + 3$

14. Which of the following is a pure imaginary number?

F. $\sqrt{-9}$
G. $-\sqrt{9}$
H. $5 + 2i$
J. -1
K. i^2

15. $7\frac{1}{4} - 2\frac{5}{6} = ?$

A. $4\frac{5}{12}$
B. $4\frac{1}{2}$
C. $5\frac{7}{12}$
D. $10\frac{1}{12}$
E. None of these

2 2 2 2 2 2 2 2 2 2 2 2

DO YOUR FIGURING HERE

16. Stan can do a certain job in 4 hours. If Fred can do the same job in 5 hours, which of the following equations could be used to determine how long it would take them to do the job if they worked together?

 F. $\frac{x}{4}+\frac{x}{5}=1$
 G. $4x+5x=1$
 H. $\frac{x}{4}=\frac{x}{5}$
 J. $\frac{4}{x}+\frac{5}{x}=1$
 K. None of these

17. Which of the following numbers is NOT composite?

 A. 1
 B. 28
 C. 51
 D. 93
 E. 143

18. Which of the following is equivalent to $|x+3| \geq 2$?

 F. $x \geq -1$
 G. $x \leq -5$
 H. $x \geq -5$
 J. $x \geq -1$ or $x \leq -5$
 K. $-5 \leq x \leq -1$

19. What is the solution set of the equation $\frac{2x-1}{3}+\frac{x+2}{4}=\frac{1}{6}$?

 A. $\{0\}$
 B. $\left\{\frac{1}{11}\right\}$
 C. $\left\{\frac{-1}{11}\right\}$
 D. $\left\{\frac{-3}{11}\right\}$
 E. $\left\{\frac{4}{11}\right\}$

Model Exam C

GO ON TO THE NEXT PAGE.

DO YOUR FIGURING HERE

20. If $\overline{CE}$ is a tangent, $\overline{CD}$ is a radius and m $\angle ECB$ = 48°, what is the measure of $\angle BAC$?

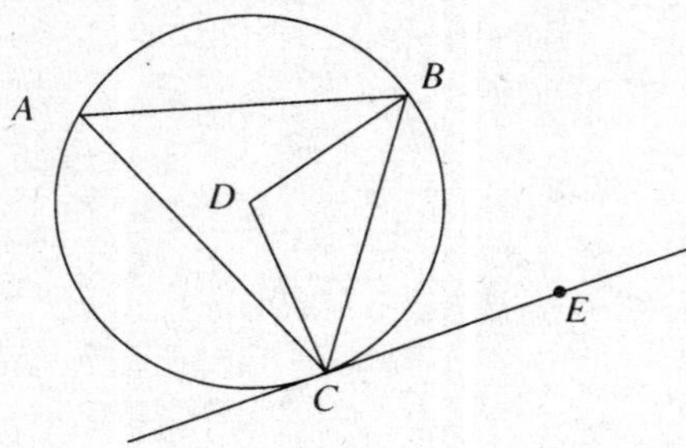

F. 24°
G. 42°
H. 48°
J. 84°
K. 96°

21. What is the degree of the expression $(3x^2 + 5x - 3)^3 + 5$?

A. 2
B. 3
C. 4
D. 5
E. 6

22. What is the simplified form of the expression $(2x - 3y)^2$?

F. $4x^2 + 9y^2$
G. $4x^2 - 9y^2$
H. $4x^2 - 6xy + 9y^2$
J. $4x^2 - 12xy + 9y^2$
K. $4x^2 + 12xy + 9y^2$

23. Which of the following ordered pairs corresponds to a point in quadrant IV?

A. (2, 0)
B. (0, – 4)
C. (– 2, 3)
D. (– 1, – 4)
E. (2, – 8)

DO YOUR FIGURING HERE

24. An ice cream cone is full of ice cream with half a sphere above the cone. Find the volume of ice cream.

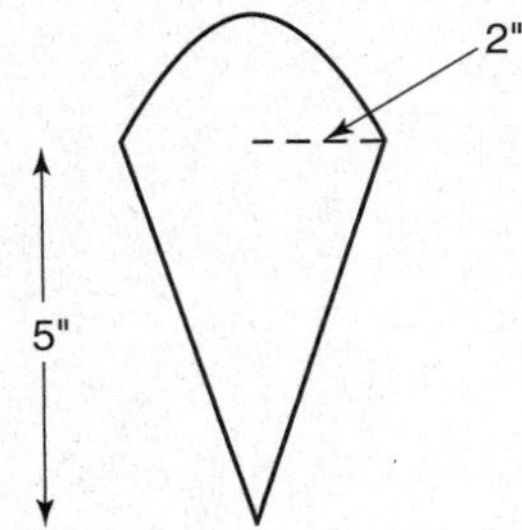

F. $\frac{28}{3}\pi$ cubic inches
G. 12π cubic inches
H. $\frac{56}{3}\pi$ cubic inches
J. 16π cubic inches
K. None of these

25. What is the product of the roots of the equation $5x^2 - 8x + 7 = 0$?

A. $\frac{-7}{5}$
B. $\frac{7}{5}$
C. $\frac{8}{5}$
D. 7
E. 8

26. What is the value of $8^{-(2/3)}$?

F. 16
G. $\frac{-16}{3}$
H. 4
J. $\frac{1}{4}$
K. $\frac{-1}{4}$

27. The expression $3(10^5) + 2(10^3) + 4(10^2) + 7(10^1)$ is the expanded form for what number?

A. 3,247
B. 30,247
C. 32,470
D. 302,470
E. 324,700

Model Exam C

DO YOUR FIGURING HERE

28. What is the lowest common denominator of the fractions $\frac{2}{5a^2b^3}$, $\frac{7}{20ab^4}$, $\frac{8}{15a^3b^2}$?

    F. $5ab^2$
    G. $5a^3b^4$
    H. $60ab^2$
    J. $60a^3b^4$
    K. $1500a^6b^9$

29. What is the average (mean) of the numbers 3, 4, 4, 5, 5, 5, 7, 8, 8, 9?

    A. 5
    B. 6
    C. 5.8
    D. 10
    E. 58

30. Sue is paid $200 per week plus 7% of her total sales, t, for the week. Which of the following equations could she use to determine her salary, S, for a particular week?

    F. $S = 0.07(200 + t)$
    G. $S = 0.07(200) + t$
    H. $S = 200 + 0.07t$
    J. $S = 1.07(200 + t)$
    K. $S = 200t^{0.07}$

31. What is the simplified form of the complex fraction $\dfrac{\frac{1}{x} - \frac{1}{3}}{\frac{1}{x^2} - \frac{1}{9}}$?

    A. 3
    B. $\dfrac{1}{x + 3}$
    C. $\dfrac{3 - x}{3x}$
    D. $\dfrac{3x}{3 + x}$
    E. $\dfrac{9x - 3x^2}{9 - x^2}$

32. Which of the following are the coordinates of the vertex of the parabola whose equation is $y = -2(x + 6)^2 - 9$?

    F. $(2, -9)$
    G. $(6, 9)$
    H. $(-6, 9)$
    J. $(6, -9)$
    K. $(-6, -9)$

DO YOUR FIGURING HERE

33. Which is the solution set of the equation $\frac{x^2+9}{x^2-9} - \frac{3}{x+3} = \frac{-x}{3-x}$?

    A. Ø
    B. {0}
    C. $\left\{\frac{1}{3}\right\}$
    D. {2}
    E. {3}

34. Which of the following is equal to $\frac{2.4(10^{-4})}{6(10^{-2})}$?

    F. $0.4(10^{-6})$
    G. $4(10^{-1})$
    H. $4(10^{-2})$
    J. $4(10^{3})$
    K. $4(10^{-3})$

35. What is the slope of the line that passes through the points with coordinates (– 5, 8) and (– 5, – 3)?

    A. – 11
    B. 5
    C. 0
    D. $\frac{-1}{2}$
    E. The line has no slope.

36. The Smith family has 100 gallons of heating fuel on January 1. During January the Smiths use 20% of their fuel, and in February they use 25% of the remaining fuel. How many gallons of fuel are left on March 1?

    F. 40
    G. 45
    H. 50
    J. 55
    K. 60

37. If lines, l, m, and n are parallel, $\overline{AE} \perp l$, $AC = 10$, $CD = 14$, and $AF = 6$, what is the length of $\overline{DG}$?

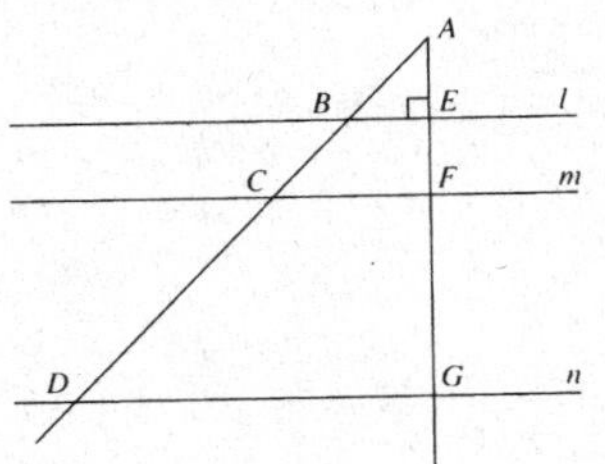

    A. 11.2
    B. 16
    C. 19.2
    D. $23\frac{1}{3}$
    E. 24

GO ON TO THE NEXT PAGE.

Model Exam C

DO YOUR FIGURING HERE

38. Which of the following is always true of an acute angle?

    F. Its measure is greater than 90°.
    G. It is the supplement of another acute angle.
    H. It cannot be equal to its own complement.
    J. Every quadrilateral must have at least one.
    K. All of these statements are false.

39. A triangle is drawn with one side on line $\overleftrightarrow{AE}$. If m∠*ABC* = 140° and m∠*CDE* = 60°, what is the measure of ∠*BCD*?

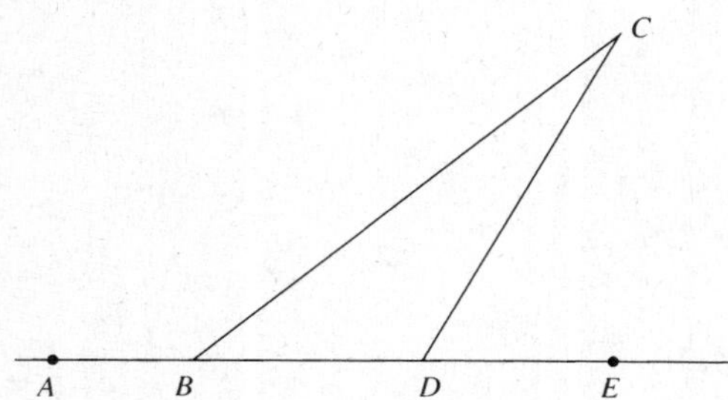

    A. 20°
    B. 30°
    C. 40°
    D. 45°
    E. 50°

40. A car radiator holds 12 liters. How much pure antifreeze, in liters, must be added to a mixture that is 4% antifreeze to make enough of a 20% mixture to fill the radiator?

    F. 0.48
    G. 2
    H. 2.4
    J. 2.88
    K. 3

41. In right triangle *ABC*, m∠*C* = 90°, *AC* = 2, and *AB* = 5. What is the value of sin *A*?

    A. $\frac{2}{5}$
    B. $\frac{5}{2}$
    C. $\frac{\sqrt{21}}{.2}$
    D. $\frac{\sqrt{21}}{5}$
    E. $\frac{5}{\sqrt{21}}$

2 2 2 2 2 2 2 2 2 2 2 2

DO YOUR FIGURING HERE

42. Which equation corresponds to the graph?

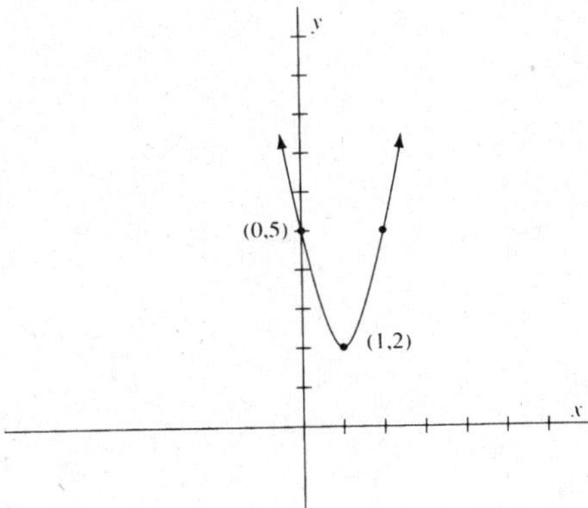

F. $y = 7(x-1)^2 - 2$
G. $y = 3(x-1)^2 + 2$
H. $y = 7(x+1)^2 - 2$
J. $(x-1)^2 + (y-2)^2 = 1$
K. None of these

43. What is the standard form of the quotient of the complex numbers $\frac{3-2i}{2+i}$?

A. $2 - i$

B. $\frac{8-7i}{3}$

C. $\frac{4}{5} - \frac{7}{5}i$

D. $3 + 2i$
E. $4 - 2i$

44. In how many ways can six different books be arranged on a shelf?

F. 6
G. 30
H. 36
J. 64
K. 720

45. What is the value of $\log_2 \frac{1}{8}$?

A. $\frac{1}{3}$

B. $\frac{-1}{3}$

C. $\frac{1}{4}$

D. -3
E. 3

2 2 2 2 2 2 2 2 2 2 2

DO YOUR FIGURING HERE

46. The ratio of the areas of two similar triangles is 9 to 16. What is the ratio of the lengths of the corresponding altitudes of these triangles?

F. 1 to 7
G. 3 to 4
H. 9 to 16
J. 4.5 to 8
K. 27 to 64

47. What is the smallest positive angle that is coterminal with $\frac{75\pi}{4}$ radians?

A. 120°
B. $\frac{\pi}{4}$
C. $\frac{-\pi}{4}$
D. $\frac{-\pi}{4}$
E. $\frac{11\pi}{4}$

48. If $AE = 6$, $AB = 1\frac{2}{3}$, $BC = 1\frac{1}{4}$, and $DE = 1\frac{1}{12}$, what is the length of $\overline{CD}$?

A B C D E

F. $1\frac{1}{2}$
G. 2
H. $2\frac{2}{3}$
J. 4
K. $4\frac{11}{12}$

49. If the height, h, of a thrown object above the ground at any time, t, in seconds is given by the equation $h = -16t^2 + 64t$, in how many seconds will the object reach its maximum height?

A. 8
B. 4
C. 3
D. 2
E. 1

DO YOUR FIGURING HERE

50. What is equal to the product $\sqrt{54x^4y^5} \cdot \sqrt{2x^2y^4}$ of radicals in simplest radical form? (Assume that x and y are nonnegative.)

F. $6x^3y^4\sqrt{3y}$

G. $3x^3y^2\sqrt{12y^5}$

H. $6x^3\sqrt{3y^9}$

J. $2y^3\sqrt{27x^6}$

K. None of these

51. Which of the following statements is always true regarding a parallelogram?

A. The diagonals are perpendicular to each other.
B. The sum of the angles is 180°.
C. Opposite sides are both parallel and congruent.
D. There cannot be a right angle in any parallelogram.
E. Consecutive angles are complementary.

52. A square and a semicircular region have the same perimeter. If the length of the radius of the semicircular region is 8, what is the length of a side of the square?

F. 8π
G. 8
H. 2π
J. $\frac{8}{\pi}$
K. $4 + 2\pi$

53. Which of the following is a pair of vertical angles?

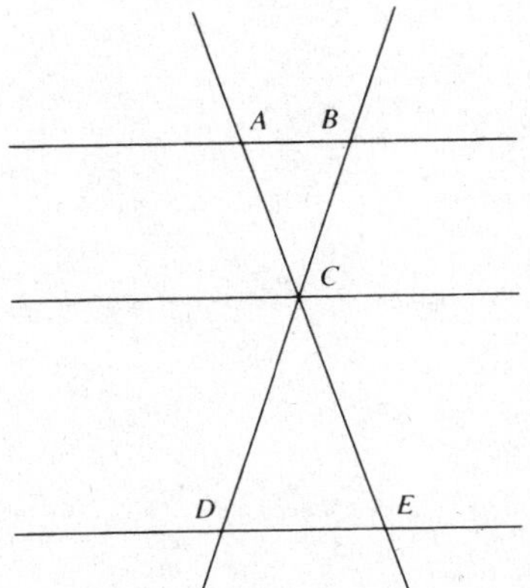

A. $\angle BAC, \angle CED$
B. $\angle ACD, \angle ACB$
C. $\angle CDE, \angle CED$
D. $\angle ACB, \angle DCE$
E. $\angle ACE, \angle BCD$

GO ON TO THE NEXT PAGE.

DO YOUR FIGURING HERE

54. Line $\overleftrightarrow{AD}$ is parallel to line $\overleftrightarrow{CE}$. If $AB = 4$, $BC = 9$, and $CE = 5$, what is the length of $\overline{AD}$?

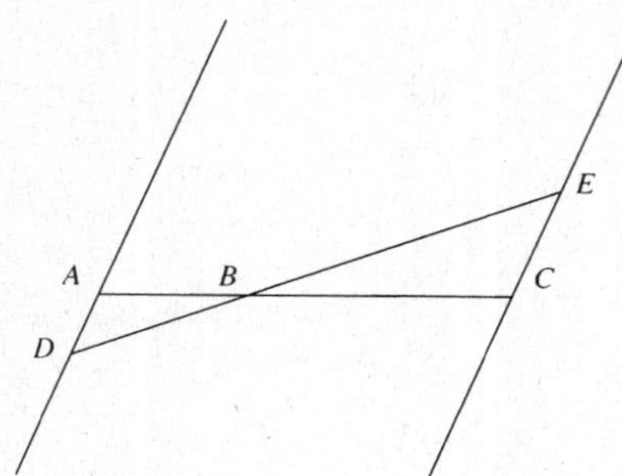

F. 1
G. 2
H. $2\frac{2}{9}$
J. $7\frac{1}{5}$
K. $11\frac{1}{4}$

55. A kite is flying at the end of a taut string that is 50 feet long. The string makes an angle of 25° with the horizontal, and the person flying the kite holds the string 5 feet off the ground. How high is the kite from the ground?

A. $5 + 50 \sin 25°$
B. $5 + 50 \cos 25°$
C. $5 + 50 \tan 25°$
D. $5 + \dfrac{50}{\sin 25°}$
E. $5 + \dfrac{\sin 25°}{50}$

56. Two chords, $\overline{AB}$ and $\overline{CD}$, intersect at E. If $AB = 8$, $CE = 2$, and $DE = 8$, what is the length of $\overline{AE}$?

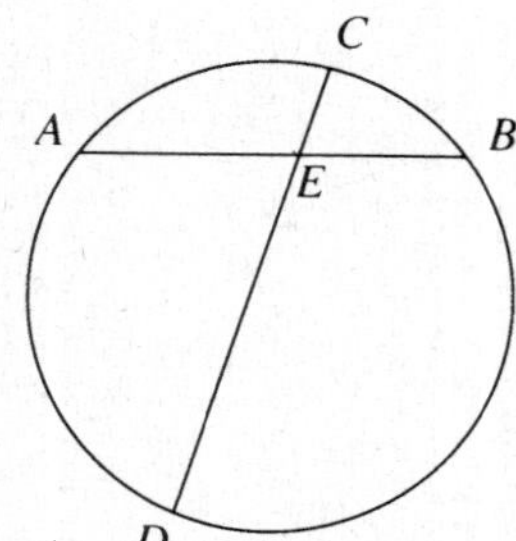

F. 2
G. 3
H. 4
J. 5
K. 6

DO YOUR FIGURING HERE

57. What is the maximum number of common tangents that can be drawn to any two circles?

    A. 1
    B. 2
    C. 3
    D. 4
    E. 5

58. Which of the following statements is true about polygons?

    F. All triangles are convex.
    G. All rectangles are quadrilaterals.
    H. The sum of the angles of a pentagon is 540°.
    J. A square is a rhombus.
    K. All these statements are true.

59. If $AB = BC$ and $m\angle ABC = 24°$, what is the measure of $\angle BDC$?

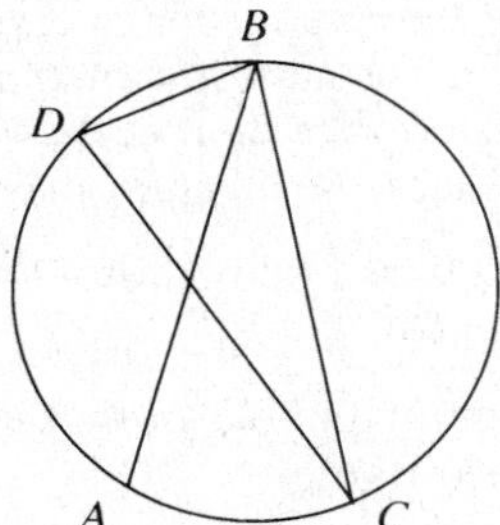

    A. 24°
    B. 48°
    C. 72°
    D. 78°
    E. 90°

60. What is the period of the function $y = -3 \sin (4x + \pi)$?

    F. 3
    G. 4
    H. $\frac{\pi}{4}$
    J. $\frac{\pi}{2}$
    K. $\frac{\pi}{3}$

STOP

If there is still time remaining, you may review your answers.

READING TEST

35 MINUTES—40 QUESTIONS

Directions: This test consists of four passages, each followed by ten multiple-choice questions. Read each passage and then pick the best answer for each question. Fill in the spaces on your answer sheet that correspond to your choices. Refer to the passage as often as you wish while answering the questions.

Passage 1—Prose Fiction

This passage is adapted from William Dean Howells' The Rise of Silas Lapham *(1885). In this excerpt, the protagonist, a newly rich self-made business man, is about to be interviewed by a newspaper reporter.*

When Bartley Hubbard went to interview Silas Lapham for the "Solid Men of Boston" series, Lapham received him in his private office by previous appointment.

"Walk right in!" he called out to the journalist, whom he caught sight of through the door of the counting room.

He did not rise from the desk at which he was writing, but he gave Bartley his left hand for welcome, and he rolled his large head in the direction of a vacant chair. "Sit down! I'll be with you in just half a minute."

"Take your time," said Bartley, with the ease he instantly felt. "I'm in no hurry." He took a note-book from his pocket, laid it on his knee, and began to sharpen a pencil.

"There!" Lapham pounded with his great hairy fist on the envelope he had been addressing. "William!" he called out, and he handed the letter to a boy who came to get it. "I want that to go right away. Well, sir," he continued, wheeling round in his leather-cushioned swivel chair, and facing Bartley, seated so near that their knees almost touched, "so you want my life, death, and Christian sufferings, do you, young man?"

"That's what I'm after," said Bartley. "Your money or your life."

"I guess you wouldn't want my life without the money," said Lapham, as if he were willing to prolong these moments of preparation.

"Take 'em both," Bartley suggested. "Don't want your money without your life, if you come to that. But you're just one million times more interesting to the public than if you hadn't a dollar; and you know that as well as I do, Mr. Lapham. There's no use beating around the bush."

"No," said Lapham, somewhat absently. He put out his huge foot and pushed the ground-glass door shut between his little den and the book-keepers, in their larger den outside.

"In personal appearance," wrote Bartley in the sketch for which he now studied his subject, "Silas Lapham is a fine type of successful American. He has a square, bold chin, only partly concealed by the short reddish-grey beard, growing to the edges of his firmly closing lips. His nose is short and straight; his forehead good, but broad rather than high; his eyes blue, and with a light in them that is kindly or sharp according to his mood. He is of medium height, and fills an average armchair with a solid bulk, which on the day of our interview was unpretentiously clad in a business suit of blue serge. His head droops somewhat from a short neck, which does not trouble itself to rise far from a pair of massive shoulders."

"I don't know as I know just where you want me to begin," said Lapham.

"Might begin with your birth; that's where most of us begin," replied Bartley.

A gleam of humorous appreciation shot into Lapham's blue eyes.

"I didn't know whether you wanted me to go quite so far back as that," he said. "But there's no disgrace in having been born, and I was born in Vermont up near Canada—so well up, in fact I came very near being an adoptive citizen; for I was bound to be an American of *some* sort, from the word Go! That was about—well, let me see!—pretty near sixty years ago: this is '75, and that was '20. Well, say I'm fifty-five years old; and I've *lived* 'em too; not an hour of waste time about *me*, anywheres! I was born on a farm, and—"

"Worked in the fields summers and went to school winters: regulation thing?" Bartley cut in.

"Regulation thing," said Lapham, accepting this irreverent version of his history somewhat dryly.

"Parents poor, of course," suggested the journalist. "Any barefoot business? Early deprivations of any kind, that would encourage the youthful reader to go and do likewise? Orphan myself, you know," said Bartley, with a smile of cynical good-comradery.

Lapham looked at him silently, and then said with quiet self-respect, "I guess if you see these things as a joke, my life won't inter*est* you."

3 3 3 3 3 3 3 3 3 3 3

"Oh yes, it will," returned Bartley, unabashed. "You'll see; it'll come out all right." And in fact it did so, in the interview which Bartley printed.

"Mr. Lapham," he wrote, "passed rapidly over the story of his early life, its poverty and its hardships, sweetened, however, by the recollections of a devoted mother, and a father who, if somewhat her inferior in education, was no less ambitious for the advancement of his children. They were quiet, unpretentious people, religious, after the fashion of that time, and of sterling morality, and they taught their children the simple virtues of the *Old Testament* and *Poor Richard's Almanac*."

Bartley could not deny himself this gibe; but he trusted to Lapham's unliterary habit of mind for his security in making it, and most other people would consider it sincere reporter's rhetoric.

1. Bartley's main interest in writing a newspaper story about Lapham is to:

A. honor one of Boston's most successful businessmen.
B. increase the circulation of his newspaper.
C. prove to his boss that he is a good journalist.
D. attract readers to the "Solid Men of Boston" series.

2. The narrator includes the fact that Lapham met Bartley "in his private office by previous appointment" to suggest that Lapham:

F. managed to squeeze Bartley into a busy schedule of appointments.
G. has hired an office staff to attend to the details of the business.
H. wishes to enhance his image and status.
J. knows that Bartley plans to ask him personal questions.

3. Lapham's reaction to Bartley's arrival in his office (lines 6–10) can best be described as:

A. antagonistic; he takes an instant dislike to Bartley.
B. casual; he wants to appear an easygoing fellow and laid back.
C. cordial; he treats Bartley like a welcome guest.
D. indifferent; he has more pressing matters to attend to.

4. The passage describes Lapham's workplace as:

F. streamlined, up-to-date quarters.
G. a luxurious, comfortable office.
H. a cramped suite of rooms.
J. a shabby space in need of renovation.

5. From the dialogue that takes place in lines 62–86, it is reasonable to infer that Bartley has all of the following characteristics EXCEPT:

A. he has a knack for reading other people's minds.
B. he has heard many other stories like Lapham's.
C. he composes stories mentally before putting words on paper.
D. his main interest is the story he expects to write, not Lapham, the person.

6. Bartley informs Lapham that he is an orphan himself (line 73) for all of the following reasons EXCEPT:

F. to insinuate that Lapham's deprivations were not unique.
G. to win Lapham's sympathy.
H. to establish rapport with Lapham.
J. to lighten up the conversation.

7. The passage indicates that Lapham's physical features include:

A. a ruddy complexion.
B. large hands and feet.
C. cold, steely blue eyes.
D. hair loss.

8. According to Bartley's sketch of Lapham, Silas credits his parents with:

F. bestowing on him an honest and open personality.
G. motivating him to succeed in life.
H. exposing him to the *Old Testament* and *Poor Richard's Almanac*.
J. toughening him up for a career as a businessman.

9. As it is used in the passage (line 69), the word *irreverent* most nearly means:

A. commonplace.
B. unacceptable.
C. disrespectful.
D. destructive.

10. Throughout the passage, Bartley's attitude toward Lapham can best be described as one of:

F. cynicism.
G. resentment.
H. contempt.
J. ingratitude.

GO ON TO THE NEXT PAGE.

Passage 2—Social Studies

This passage is an excerpt adapted from an article that discusses a method that modern anthropologists use to study a Native American tribe of the distant past.

At the end of the eighteenth century the Omaha Indian tribe controlled the fur trade on the upper Missouri River. Without the say-so of Chief Blackbird, French and Spanish fur traders could not do business with tribes farther up the Missouri. Under Blackbird's leadership the Omaha gained wealth, political prestige, and military strength. But in 1800, the tribe was ravaged by smallpox, one of the diseases that accompanied Europeans. The epidemic killed as many as one-third of the Omaha, including Blackbird. By the time Lewis and Clark visited in 1804, the Omaha culture that survived was decidedly different from the one first encountered by Europeans in 1750.

More than ten thousand objects taken from the gravesites of about one hundred members of the tribe have shed light on the life of the tribe in the late 1700s. Within the few decades after the Omaha settled in 1775 at Big Village or Ton won tonga (what is now northeastern Nebraska near the town of Homer), the community changed dramatically—particularly in its economic roles—and the bones of its people offer clues to how and why.

"The most revealing discovery," says Karl J. Reinhard at the University of Nebraska, "is that the Omaha were fully equestrian buffalo hunters by 1770. That makes them the first documented equestrian culture in the Northern Plains. This is nearly one hundred years earlier than the Dakotas." Reinhard documents this by finding similar bone patterns between the Omaha and those of the English cavalry. But a key piece of evidence is unique to the Omaha. "The Omaha used a 'toe stirrup,' which was essentially a thong that went around the big toe," Reinhard explains. "Because riding, mounting, and dismounting puts pressure on the toes, the first toe joints went arthritic prematurely."

Reinhard and his team have been studying the ancestral remains in the context of their cultural and historical significance. "Human skeletons make a kind of record of the life of each person," Reinhard says. "Skeleton study reveals aspects of life such as occupation, disease, age, sex, and sometimes cause of death. By combining the information from skeletons with artifacts from the burials, the role of each person in the society can be seen."

The remains of a fifty-year-old woman tell about the daily life of an Omaha woman before 1800. For instance, the bones reveal severe arthritis in her right elbow, probably caused by repeatedly performing tasks such as wood chopping, farming, and food grinding. "Before the epidemic struck, the women seemed to have had long lives," Reinhard says. "They were having many children and were as healthy as and tended to live as long as the men. But after the epidemic, the women took on more of the responsibility for manufacturing, and this wore them down. We can see that in the bones. There was a constant bending over and scraping the hides that stressed the lower back. And when we look at the teeth of the women, we see that they're very badly worn from chewing hides to prepare them for trade.

"None of them lived past the age of thirty," he says about the women buried after 1800. "They weren't living long enough to regenerate the population. There weren't enough children born to keep the Omaha population viable, so the population was definitely in a decline."

The artifacts show that there were many more roles for men than there were for women, especially before the 1800 smallpox epidemic. Specific bone formations and varied artifacts point to men who were archers, warriors, gunsmiths, and merchants. Ceremonial roles apparently were exclusive to men. The remains of four men between the ages of twenty and fifty were found buried with bundles of animal bone and other items of ceremonial significance. One was buried with a drumstick. "These artifacts indicate that the formal religious system involved men," Reinhard notes. "Because some of these men died as young adults, ceremonial roles could be assigned to individuals early in adult life."

"The death of Chief Blackbird brought an end to the traditional Omaha society in which men had more roles than women," Reinhard says. "After that period, there seems to have been more social mobility. Virtually no silver artifacts were found with women before Lewis and Clark visited in 1804. After Lewis and Clark, most of the expensive silver ornaments were found with women." The change in the Omaha culture resulted not just from disease, which forced the remaining Omaha to take on new roles, Reinhard says, but also a change in economics.

The nature of trade after Chief Blackbird's time was markedly different. "The trade until 1800 was largely in arms and ornaments," Reinhard says. After they began trading under the auspices of the United States "there was an influx in trade in tools and clothing such as scissors, axes, top hats, and buttons.

Paulette W. Campbell, "Ancestral Bones: Reinterpreting the Past of the Omaha, *Humanities*, November/December, 2002.

11. In the history of the Omaha people, the most significant societal changes seem to have occurred:
    A. at the time of Lewis and Clark's visit.
    B. between 1750 and 1775.
    C. between 1775 and 1800.
    D. after 1800.

12. The facts in the passage indicate that Omaha Indians became infected with smallpox as a result of:
    F. an increase in the fur trade.
    G. contact with foreigners.
    H. spreading of the disease throughout the upper Missouri River area.
    J. their dealings with Lewis and Clark.

13. It may be inferred from the passage that Blackbird's leadership of the Omaha is best characterized by a kind of:
    A. conservatism; he labored to keep tribal customs and traditions intact.
    B. democracy; he gave his people a role in governing the tribe.
    C. benevolence; he worked in behalf of his people's well-being.
    D. fearlessness; he refused to be intimidated by neighboring tribes.

14. According to the passage smallpox changed the Omaha society in all of the following ways EXCEPT:
    F. the tribe stopped trading furs with Europeans.
    G. the tribe's population declined.
    H. the tribe lost its chief.
    J. some male roles were taken over by females.

15. As used in line 64, the word *viable* means:
    A. feasible.
    B. employed.
    C. growing.
    D. functioning.

16. In determining that the Omaha hunted buffalo on horseback, Reinhard and his colleagues were aided by:
    F. deformed bones.
    G. unearthed artifacts.
    H. the relation between the Omahas and the Dakotas.
    J. their awareness of the dangers of hunting buffalo on foot.

17. Modern anthropologists have been able to infer details about the lives of long-dead Omaha tribesmen because:
    A. bones reveal the cause of death.
    B. the remains have been well preserved.
    C. the Omaha buried their dead with artifacts.
    D. their bones resemble those of other Indian tribes.

18. It may reasonably be inferred that the smallpox epidemic shortened the lives of Omaha women because:
    F. they assumed the responsibilities of the men who had perished.
    G. they began to die in greater numbers during childbirth.
    H. they were deprived of ceremonial or religious functions.
    J. the reduced population left women unprotected when men went out to hunt or to trade with Europeans.

19. The author's statement that after 1775, "the community changed dramatically—particularly in its economic roles" (lines 19–21) is supported elsewhere in the passage by the discussion of:
    A. Chief Blackbird's relationship with French and Spanish fur traders (first paragraph, lines 1–13).
    B. the use of the "toe stirrup" (third paragraph, lines 31–32).
    C. studying the bones of women (fifth paragraph, lines 45–59).
    D. the ceremonial functions of Omaha males (eighth paragraph, lines 66–78).

20. The passage suggests that the Omaha were introduced to tools and other manufactured goods partly as a result of:
    F. Lewis and Clark's visit.
    G. Chief Blackbird's death.
    H. the signing of a peace treaty with the United States government.
    J. the development of a barter system.

GO ON TO THE NEXT PAGE.

Passage 3—Humanities

This passage is adapted from an essay written by the American author, Jack London, who, about 100 years ago, laid plans to build a new house in California.

Last year I started to build a barn. A man who was a liar undertook to do the stonework and concrete work for me. He could not tell the truth to my face; he could not tell the truth in his work. I was building for posterity. The concrete foundations were four feet wide and sunk three and one-half feet into the earth. The stone walls were two feet thick and nine feet high. Upon them were to rest the great beams that were to carry all the weight of hay and forty tons of roof. The man who was a liar made beautiful stone walls. I used to stand alongside of them and love them. I caressed their massive strength with my hands. I thought about them in bed before I went to sleep. And they were lies.

Came the earthquake. Fortunately the rest of the building of the barn had been postponed. The beautiful stone walls cracked in all directions. I started to repair and discovered the whole enormous lie. The walls were shells. On each face were beautiful, massive stones—on edge. The inside was hollow. This hollow in some places was filled with clay and loose gravel. In other places it was filled with air and emptiness, with here and there a piece of kindling wood or dry-goods box to aid in the making of the shell. The walls were lies. They were beautiful, but they were not useful. Construction and decoration had been divorced. The walls were all decoration. They hadn't any construction in them. "As God lets Satan live," I let that lying man live, but—I have built new walls from the foundation up.

And now to my own house beautiful, which I shall build some seven or ten years from now. I have a few general ideas about it. It must be honest in construction, material, and appearance. If any feature of it, despite my efforts, shall tell lies, I shall remove that feature. Utility and beauty must be indissolubly wedded. Construction and decoration must be one. If the particular details keep true to these general ideas, all will be well.

I have not thought of many details. But here are a few. Take the bathroom, for instance. It shall be as beautiful as any room in the house, just as it will be as useful. The chance is that it will be the most expensive room in the house. No delights of the bath shall be lacking. Also a large part of the expensiveness will be due to the use of material that will make it easy to keep the bathroom clean and in order. Why should a servant toil unduly that my body may be clean? On the other hand, the honesty of my own flesh and the square dealing I give it, are more important than all the admiration of my friends for expensive decorative schemes and magnificent trivialities. More delightful to me is a body that sings than a stately and costly grand staircase built for show. Not that I like grand staircases less, but that I like bathrooms more.

One chief aim in the building of my house beautiful will be to have a house that will require the minimum of trouble and work to keep clean and orderly. I live in California where the days are warm. I'd prefer that the servants had three hours to go swimming (or hammocking) than be compelled to spend those three hours in keeping the house clean. Therefore, I have resolved to build a house that can be kept unsoiled without the need of those three hours.

For countless thousands of years my ancestors have lived and died and drawn all their breaths in the open air. It is only recently that we have begun to live in houses. The change is a hardship, especially on the lungs. I've got only one pair of lungs, and I haven't the address of any repair shop. Therefore, I stick to the open air as much as possible. For this reason my house will have large verandas, and, near to the kitchen, there will be a veranda dining room. Also, there will be a veranda fireplace, where we can breathe fresh air and be comfortable when the evenings are touched with frost.

I have a plan for my own bedroom. I spend long hours in bed, reading, studying, and working. I have tried sleeping in the open, but the lamp attracts all the creeping, crawling, butting, flying, fluttering things to the pages of my book, into my ears and blankets, and down the back of my neck. So my bedroom shall be indoors.

But it will not be of indoors. Three sides of it will be open. The fourth side will divide it from the rest of the house. The three sides will be screened against the creeping, fluttering things, but not against the good fresh air and all the breezes that blow. For protection against storm, to keep out the driving rain, there will be a sliding glass, so made that when not in use it will occupy small space and shut out very little air.

"The House Beautiful," (1906)

21. The mason who did the stonework is called a "liar" because he:
    A. concealed his defective work from view.
    B. used cheap materials.
    C. failed to build what he had promised.
    D. ignored the plans drawn up for the foundation.

22. By saying that he "was building for posterity" in line 4, the author means that he:
    F. had drawn up plans for a beautiful structure.
    G. ordered special concrete for the foundation.
    H. expected the foundation to last a long time.
    J. made plans for an oversize foundation.

23. According to the passage, the author's discovery of defects in the foundation wall took place after:
    A. an earthquake destroyed the wall.
    B. construction of the barn was delayed.
    C. he attempted to repair some cracks.
    D. he stroked the wall with his hands.

24. According to the passage, the foundation wall was flawed in all of the following ways EXCEPT:
    F. its beauty was only skin deep.
    G. the interior contained building debris.
    H. stones had not been laid flat.
    J. it was solid in only a few places.

25. It may reasonably be inferred from the passage that foundation walls should be solid because they must:
    A. withstand damage caused by earthquakes.
    B. carry the weight of structures that rest upon them.
    C. be at least as strong as the earth on which they are built.
    D. resist groundwater from seeping in.

26. In the passage the author discusses the building of the barn before he begins to describe his "house beautiful" mainly to:
    F. illustrate that building can be hazardous and backbreaking work.
    G. warn readers to be wary of dishonest builders.
    H. impress readers with his expertise as a builder.
    J. introduce the design and construction principles he intends to follow.

27. The author states a preference for building a bathroom instead of a constructing a grand staircase (lines 49–52) to suggest that:
    A. an elegant stairway is inappropriate in a modest house.
    B. it's easier to clean a bathroom than a fancy set of stairs.
    C. he values usefulness more than beauty.
    D. his friends will be indifferent to a showy staircase.

28. It may be inferred from the principles of home design espoused by the author that:
    F. he once held a job as a servant.
    G. he is concerned about the cost of building a new house.
    H. he thinks that housecleaning is a waste of time.
    J. his house will have an ocean view.

29. The author states that he sticks "to the open air as much as possible" (lines 67–68) because:
    A. his ancestors lived outside.
    B. inside air is unhealthy.
    C. he dislikes having a roof over his head.
    D. of the warmth of California.

30. By referring to the home he is planning to build as "my own house beautiful," the author suggests all of the following EXCEPT:
    F. the house will contain no decorative features that lack a function.
    G. the house will be built to please him rather than to impress others.
    H. the architect and the builders will share his vision of what a house should be.
    J. in a house, utility is an aspect of its beauty.

GO ON TO THE NEXT PAGE.

Passage 4—Natural Science

This passage is from Mark Twain's Life on the Mississippi *(1883). In this excerpt Twain describes several features of the river he loved.*

The Mississippi is well worth reading about. It is not a commonplace river, but on the contrary is in all ways remarkable. Considering the Missouri its main branch, it is the longest river in the world—four thousand three hundred miles. It seems safe to say that it is also the crookedest river in the world, since in one part of its journey it uses up one thousand three hundred miles to cover the same ground as the crow would fly over in six hundred and seventy-five. It discharges three times as much water as the St. Lawrence, twenty-five times as much as the Rhine, and three hundred and thirty-eight times as much as the Thames. No other river has so vast a drainage-basin; it draws its water supply from twenty-eight states and territories; from Delaware on the Atlantic seaboard, and from all the country between that and Idaho on the Pacific slope—a spread of forty-five degrees of longitude. The Mississippi receives and carries to the Gulf water from fifty-four subordinate rivers that are navigable by steamboats, and from some hundreds that are navigable by flats and keels. The area of its drainage-basin is as great as the combined areas of England, Wales, Scotland, Ireland, France, Spain, Portugal, Germany, Austria, Italy, and Turkey; and almost all this wide region is fertile; the Mississippi valley, proper, is exceptionally so.

It is a remarkable river in this: that instead of widening toward its mouth, it grows narrower; grows narrower and deeper. From the junction of the Ohio to a point halfway down to the sea, the width averages a mile in high water; thence to the sea the width steadily diminishes, until, at the "Passes," above its mouth, it is but a little over half a mile. At the junction of the Ohio, the Mississippi's depth is eighty-seven feet; the depth increases gradually, reaching one hundred and twenty-nine just above its mouth.

The difference in rise and fall is also remarkable—not in the upper, but in the lower river. The rise is tolerably uniform down to Natchez (three hundred and sixty miles above its mouth)—about fifty feet. But at Bayou La Fourche the river rises only twenty-four feet; at New Orleans only fifteen, and just above the mouth only two and one-half.

An article in the New Orleans *Times-Democrat*, based upon reports of able engineers, states that the river annually empties four hundred and six million tons of mud into the Gulf of Mexico—which brings to mind Captain Marryat's rude name for the Mississippi—"the Great Sewer." This mud, solidified, would make a mass a mile square and two hundred and forty-one feet high.

The mud deposit gradually extends the land—but only gradually; it has extended it not quite a third of a mile in the two hundred years which have elapsed since the river took its place in history.

The belief of the scientific people is that the mouth used to be at Baton Rouge, where the hills cease, and the two hundred miles of land between there and the Gulf was built by the river. This gives us the age of that piece of country, without any trouble at all—one hundred and twenty thousand years. Yet it is much the youthfulest batch of country that lies around there anywhere.

The Mississippi is remarkable in still another way—its disposition to make prodigious jumps by cutting through narrow necks of land, and thus straightening and shortening itself. More than once it has shortened itself thirty miles at a single jump!

These cut-offs have had curious effects: they have thrown several river towns out into the rural districts, and built up sand-bars and forests in front of them. The town of Delta used to be three miles below Vicksburg; a recent cut-off has radically changed the position, and Delta is now *two miles above* Vicksburg.

Both of these river towns have been retired to the country by that cut-off. A cut-off plays havoc with boundary lines and jurisdictions: for instance, a man is living in the state of Mississippi today, a cut-off occurs tonight, and tomorrow the man finds himself and his land over on the other side of the river, within the boundaries and subject to the laws of the state of Louisiana! Such a thing, happening in the upper river in the old times, could have transferred a slave from Missouri to Illinois and made a free man of him.

The Mississippi does not alter its locality by cut-offs alone: it is always changing its habitat *bodily*—is always moving bodily *sidewise*. At Hard Times, Louisiana, the river is two miles west of the region it used to occupy. As a result, the original *site* of that settlement is not now in Louisiana at all, but on the other side of the river, in the state of Mississippi. *Nearly the whole of that one thousand three hundred miles of old Mississippi river which La Salle floated down in his canoes, two hundred years ago, is good solid dry ground now.* The river lies to the right of it, in places, and to the left of it in other places.

31. The author's attitude toward the Mississippi River is best characterized as one of:

 A. deliberate indifference.
 B. enthusiastic wonder.
 C. scientific impartiality.
 D. uncontrollable passion.

32. The first paragraph indicates that the Mississippi River is most notable for its:

 F. navigability.
 G. size.
 H. rate of flow.
 J. width.

33. The "subordinate rivers" referred to in line 18 are:

 A. the St. Lawrence, the Rhine, and the Thames.
 B. rivers less navigable than the Mississippi.
 C. tributaries to the Mississippi.
 D. rivers that empty into the Atlantic Ocean.

34. It can reasonably be inferred from the passage that most rivers:

 F. grow wider as they approach the sea.
 G. maintain roughly the same width for most of their length.
 H. flow faster upstream than at their mouth.
 J. are deeper where they intersect with other rivers.

35. The passage suggests that mud deposited in the Gulf of Mexico:

 A. consists mostly of sewage dumped into the river upstream.
 B. adds a square mile to the country's land mass every year.
 C. diminishes the fertile soil of the Mississippi valley.
 D. accounts for shifts in the shape and location of the coastline.

36. The passage indicates that *cut-offs* occur when the river:

 F. slices through a slender piece of land.
 G. temporarily reverses course.
 H. moves sideways.
 J. floods low-lying areas of nearby land.

37. According to the passage, the Mississippi follows a route that:

 A. never varies.
 B. puzzles scientists and engineers.
 C. is unpredictable.
 D. straightens as it approaches the sea.

38. The passage indicates that the Mississippi River's disposition to cut through narrow necks of land may do all of the following EXCEPT:

 F. alter the topography of the land.
 G. change the location of towns relative to the river.
 H. convert river towns into country towns.
 J. reduce the value of riverfront property.

39. That "Delta is now *two miles above* Vicksburg" (lines 69–70) indicates that:

 A. the towns have swapped names.
 B. Delta is two miles higher than Vicksburg.
 C. Vicksburg is located downstream from Delta.
 D. Vicksburg and Delta are closer to each other than they used to be.

40. The passage implies that the Mississippi River has functioned historically as a:

 F. symbolic barrier between Easterners and Westerners.
 G. geographical boundary line.
 H. route between the Eastern seaboard and some Western states.
 J. source of livelihood for many people.

STOP

If there is still time remaining, you may review your answers.

4 4 4 4 4 4 4 4 4 4 4

SCIENCE REASONING TEST

35 MINUTES—40 QUESTIONS

Directions: This test consists of several distinct passages. Each passage is followed by a number of multiple-choice questions based on the passage. Study the passage, and then select the best answer to each question. You are allowed to reread the passage. Record your answer by blackening the appropriate space on the answer sheet.

Passage 1

The diagram below shows the probable evolutionary relationships of the primates.

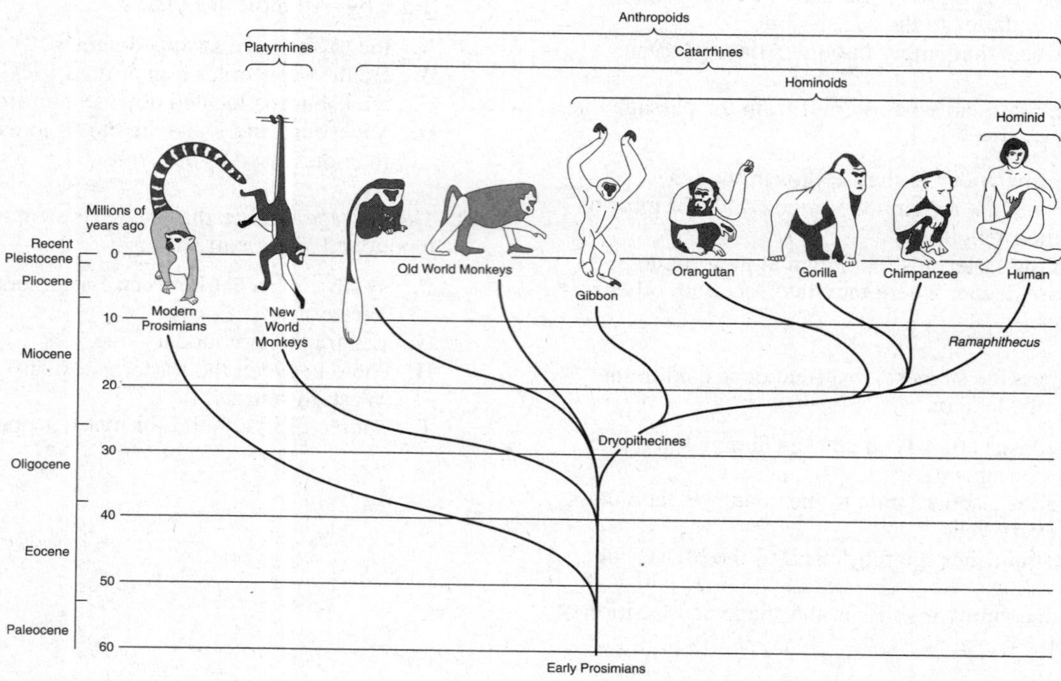

1. The most recent common ancestor of human beings and the gorilla lived about:

   A. 10 million years ago.
   B. 19 million years ago.
   C. 25 million years ago.
   D. 33 million years ago.

2. The diagram proposes that the largest group that descended from Dryopithecines is:

   F. the gibbons.
   G. The Catarrhines.
   H. the Hominoids.
   J. the great apes.

3. Two organisms are sometimes said to be closely related if they have a recent common ancestor. By this criterion, which of the following pairs are most closely related?

   A. Old World and New World monkeys
   B. Modern prosimians and New World monkeys
   C. Human and orangutan
   D. Orangutan and gibbon

4. What does the diagram tell us about the relationships of the lemurs, which are the modern prosimians?

   F. Lemurs have existed unchanged for 60 million years.
   G. Lemurs are the ancestors of all primates.
   H. Of all primates, lemurs are most similar to the ancestors of the whole group.
   J. Lemurs have evolved to a greater extent than any of the other primates.

5. *Australopithecus* is a genus of primates, more recent and humanlike than *Ramapithecus*. Of the taxonomic groups named on the chart, which is the smallest to which *Australopithecus* belongs?

   A. Anthropoids
   B. Hominoids
   C. Catarrhines
   D. Hominids

GO ON TO THE NEXT PAGE.

Passage 2

Experiment 1

An experiment is done to test the survival of Douglas Fir seedlings on a variety of substrates. A stand of seedlings is planted in an open field, where there is full sunlight, on a number of different substrates. The chart below shows the percent of seedlings surviving in each substrate after 1 year, 2 years, and 6 years:

Percent survival in direct sunlight

	1 year	2 years	6 years
charcoal	30	24	23
hard burn	22	20	19
light burn	6	5	4
mineral soil	11	10	9
sawdust	12	9	8

Experiment 2

The same procedure is followed in a field with trees giving light shade:

Percent survival in light shade

	1 year	2 years	6 years
charcoal	34	32	29
hard burn	22	20	19
light burn	12	8	7
mineral soil	17	14	13
sawdust	7	5	4

Experiment 3

The experiment is repeated in the deep shade of a forest.

Percent survival in deep shade

	1 year	2 years	6 years
charcoal	27	18	16
hard burn	12	9	8
light burn	9	7	6
mineral soil	10	6	5
sawdust	5	3	2

6. The experiments show that:

   F. survival improves with the amount of sunlight.
   G. charcoal promotes growth of the seedlings.
   H. seedlings survive best under natural conditions.
   J. most seedlings die in the first year.

7. When seedlings are grown in charcoal, how do they react to the difference in light?

   A. In light shade there is little loss during the second year.
   B. They grow to the largest size in light shade.
   C. Very few survive in heavy shade.
   D. There is substantial loss in the first year.

8. Where survival was poorest on most substrates, the likely cause of loss was:

   F. infections and parasites.
   G. genetic imperfections.
   H. lack of sunlight.
   J. heat damage.

9. One possible reason for the success of plants grown in charcoal is that:

   A. seedlings planted in charcoal are genetically programmed to germinate in the shade of a forest.
   B. charcoal is especially rich in minerals.
   C. rabbits and other herbivores do not move onto patches of charcoal.
   D. areas heavily burned over are rich in charcoal.

10. Which of the following generalizations follows from the data?

    F. Seedlings grown in sawdust have an unusually high need for sunlight.
    G. Growth is most rapid in regions of light shade.
    H. In burned-over areas the heavier the burn, the poorer the seedling survival.
    J. If the soil is rich in minerals, the amount of sunlight is not important.

11. The data seem to indicate that in nature, this species is:

    A. adapted to life in open forests.
    B. adapted to life on charcoal.
    C. unable to survive in deep forests.
    D. severely damaged by forest fires.

4 4 4 4 4 4 4 4 4 4 4

Passage 3

In a research program to find a drug that can be used for weight reduction, strepsin is tried out on 6-month old rats. Twenty in each group are kept for a year under the following conditions:

- a normal rat diet and no treatment
- a normal rat diet with strepsin added to the food
- a reduced fat diet with no treatment
- a reduced fat diet with strepsin added

The results are plotted on the graphs below:

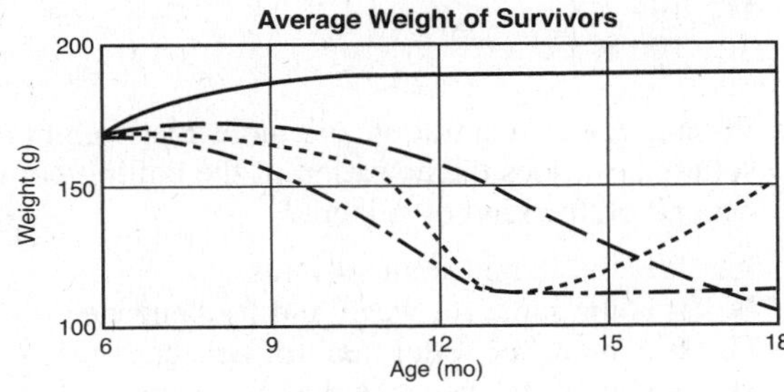

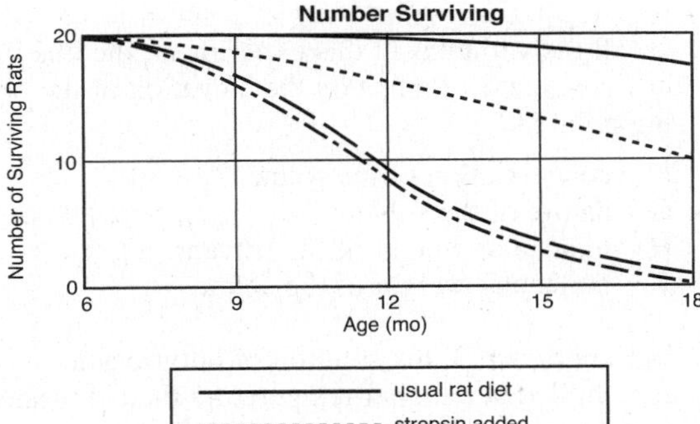

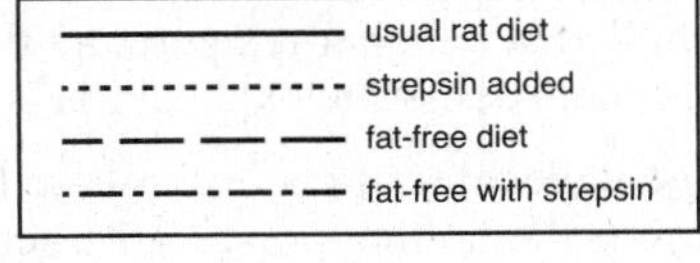

12. Why is the result of a fat-free diet less than satisfactory?

    F. The amount of weight loss is not very great.
    G. The weight loss might not be retained after 18 months.
    H. Most of the rats on this diet died.
    J. Toward the end of the trial, the rats began to gain weight.

13. The administration of strepsin had no noticeable effect on the survival rate:

    A. for the first 12 months.
    B. with a normal diet.
    C. near the end of the trial.
    D. with a fat-free diet.

14. At the end of the trial, what was the total weight of the surviving rats on a normal diet that had been treated with strepsin?

    F. 150 grams
    G. 1,500 grams
    H. 3,000 grams
    J. 4,500 grams

15. A careful experimenter might conclude that the average weight of the rats on a normal diet treated with strepsin increased after the 12th month because:

    A. the surviving rats are those that are least affected by strepsin.
    B. the dosage of strepsin was reduced after the 12th week.
    C. some of the untreated rats got mixed in with the treated ones.
    D. the diet of the rats was changed after the 12th week.

16. The results of this experiment might suggest the following next steps in the research program:

    F. Repeat the experiment using monkeys.
    G. Try strepsin on some overweight people.
    H. Repeat the experiment with different doses of strepsin.
    J. Give up on strepsin and try other drugs.

Passage 4

A chemist is investigating the effect of various kinds and amounts of solutes on the boiling point of a solution.

Experiment 1

Solutions are made of various amounts of glucose dissolved in 1 liter of water, and the boiling point of each solution is measured.

Glucose concentration (g/L)	Boiling point (° C)
0	100.0
100	100.3
200	100.6
300	100.9
400	101.2
500	101.5

Experiment 2

Solutions are made of various solutes (substances dissolved) in water, all with a concentration of 300 g/L. The boiling point of each solution is measured.

Substance	Molecular weight	Boiling point (° C)
Acetaldehyde	44	103.5
Glycerol	92	101.7
Glucose	180	100.9
Sucrose	342	100.5

Experiment 3

Solutions are made of various solutes dissolved in benzene (the solvent), which boils at 80.1° C. All concentrations are 300 g/L.

Solute	Molecular weight	Boiling point (° C)
Butyric acid	88	89.8
Triethylamine	101	88.6
Naphthalene	178	84.8
Cholesterol	387	82.3

17. If 200 g of glucose are dissolved in 500 mL of water, the boiling point of the solution will be:

A. 100.3° C.
B. 100.6° C.
C. 101.2° C.
D. 101.6° C.

18. Three hundred grams of a substance with a molecular weight of 65 are dissolved in 1 liter of water. The boiling point of the solution will be about:

F. 103.5° C.
G. 102.4° C.
H. 101.7° C.
J. 100.3° C.

19. For a given concentration and molecular weight of solute, how does the elevation of the boiling point depend on the kind of solvent?

A. It is the same for all solvents.
B. It is the same for water and for benzene.
C. It is more for water than for benzene.
D. It is more for benzene than for water.

20. Of all the variables in this experiment, the one that has the greatest impact on the elevation of the boiling point is:

F. concentration of the solute.
G. nature of the solvent.
H. molecular weight of the solvent.
J. molecular weight of the solute.

21. In Experiment 3, the solution of butyric acid in benzene boiled at a higher temperature than cholesterol in benzene. A possible explanation is:

A. the molecules of cholesterol are larger, so they lower the boiling point of the benzene.
B. the mass of cholesterol in solution was larger than the mass of butyric acid.
C. cholesterol reacts chemically with benzene, but butyric acid does not.
D. the butyric acid solution contains more molecules of solute than the cholesterol solution.

22. In trying to determine the nature of a newly discovered substance, a chemist might use experiments of this kind to discover its:

F. chemical formula.
G. concentration.
H. molecular weight.
J. boiling point.

Passage 5

The diagram below represents the forms of energy consumption in an old building, in the design for a new building, and in the actual new building after it was built.

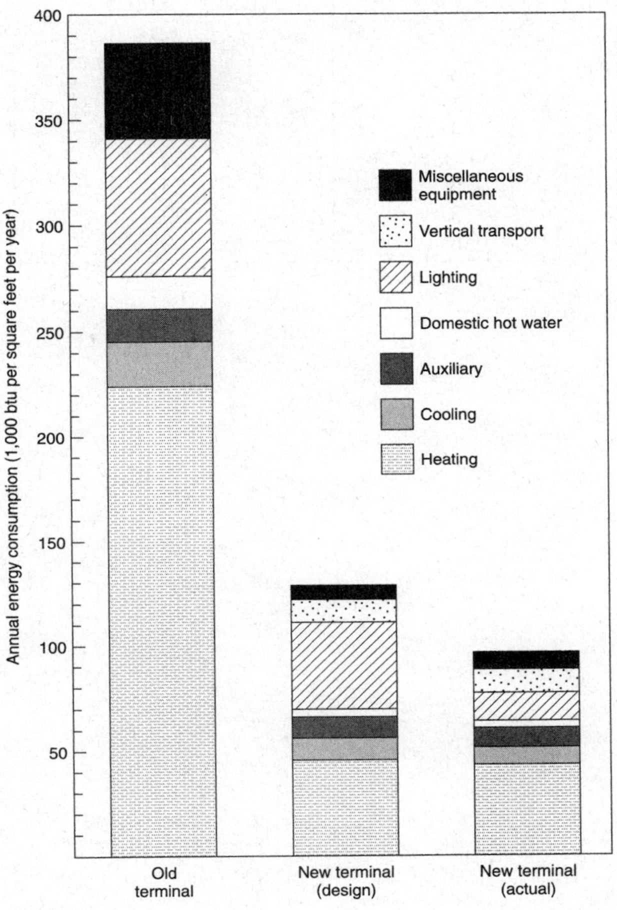

23. How effective was the new design in improving the efficiency of energy use?

    A. It reduced the amount of energy used by about 15%.
    B. It was a great improvement, but did not accomplish all that was expected of it.
    C. It was so good that the new building actually performed better than expected.
    D. It was unnecessary, since the new building was so much better than the old one.

24. What service was provided in the new building that was not available in the old one?

    F. Elevators
    G. Fluorescent lighting
    H. Air conditioning
    J. Electronic energy control

25. The difference between the new design and the performance of the actual building might have been due to miscalculation of the energy saving provided by:

    A. insulation.
    B. fluorescent lighting.
    C. air conditioning.
    D. improved boilers.

26. What approach to future problems of design of energy efficiency is suggested by these results?

    F. Since heating is the largest part of the energy cost even in the new building, this design did little to improve heating efficiency.
    G. Design emphasis should be placed on heating because this is the area where the major savings can be made.
    H. Better designs must be sought because this one did not produce a result better than the one achieved in the actual new building.
    J. Little additional research is needed because this design provided the maximum possible saving of heating fuel.

27. Which of the following questions had to be answered before a decision was made as to whether or not to use the new design in constructing the new building?

    A. Should the new building be equipped with air conditioning?
    B. Will the new design improve the efficiency of hot water heating?
    C. Does the actual new building accurately reflect the gains suggested by the design?
    D. Does the new design cost so much more than the old that the fuel saving would not make up the difference?

Passage 6

The purpose of this experiment is to study the rate at which the eyes of guppies become light-adapted.

Experiment 1

Three guppies are kept in daylight conditions at 24° C. They are fed 50 water fleas (*Daphnia*) once a day. The number of *Daphnia* captured in 5 minutes is counted. In six trials, the following results are obtained:

Number of *Daphnia* captured: 35 32 32 36 34 35

Experiment 2

The guppies are kept in the dark at 24° C for a full day. Then a light is turned on. After a measured time delay, 50 *Daphnia* are added to the tank, and the number captured in 5 minutes is counted. The experiment is repeated with various time delays.

Time delay (minutes)	Number captured in 5 minutes
2	0
4	18
6	24
8	33
10	33
12	32

Experiment 3

A similar experiment is done with the guppies, which have been kept at various temperatures. A uniform time delay of 8 minutes is used before the food is added.

Temperature (° C)	Number captured in 5 minutes
15	12
18	18
21	26
24	35
27	34
30	35
33	22
36	9

28. What assumption underlies the design of these experiments?

    F. Guppies are most active when illumination is high.
    G. The ability of guppies to find food depends on their ability to see it.
    H. Temperature affects the ability of guppies to find food.
    J. The eyes of guppies are just like the eyes of people.

29. What was the purpose of Experiment 1?

    A. To establish a criterion as to when the guppies' eyes are light-adapted
    B. To control any possible effect of temperature
    C. To condition the guppies to respond to the presence of *Daphnia*
    D. To keep the guppies in healthy condition

30. What was the purpose of the time delays in Experiment 2?

    F. To see how long it would take for the guppies to find their food
    G. To allow for differences between guppies in their feeding ability
    H. To find out how long it takes for the eyes of the guppies to become completely light-adapted
    J. To measure the time rate at which guppies find their food under standard conditions

31. What evidence is there that guppies depend solely on their eyesight to find food?

    A. Experiment 3 shows that they cannot see well at low temperatures.
    B. Experiment 2 shows that, in the first 2 minutes after being kept in the dark, they cannot find any.
    C. Experiment 1 shows that they find food very efficiently in daylight.
    D. Experiment 2 shows that the rate at which they find food diminishes as the food supply dwindles.

32. A time delay of 8 minutes was selected for Experiment 3 because this is the amount of time required for:

    F. the guppies to consume most of the food.
    G. the *Daphnia* to become adapted to the tank.
    H. the guppies' eyes to become light-adapted at 24° C.
    J. the water in the tank to reach a steady temperature.

33. Which hypothesis could NOT account for the results of Experiment 3?

    A. Light adaptation is delayed at unusually high temperatures.
    B. Guppies are damaged at very high temperatures, and are thus unable to feed well.
    C. At high temperatures, *Daphnia* become immobile and more difficult to find.
    D. The rate of adaptation to light increases uniformly with temperature.

GO ON TO THE NEXT PAGE.

Passage 7

The peppered moth has two forms, one light and the other dark. In industrial northern England, the dark form increased in frequency during the twentieth century and by 1960 was the most common kind.

Scientist 1

The history of the peppered moth is an outstanding example of natural selection in action. The dark form increased in frequency because, in this industrial region, soot had darkened the tree trunks. As a result, the dark moths were well camouflaged against the bark, while the light forms stood out. The situation has since reversed; the light form is now more common. The reason for the change is apparently the anti-pollution laws that cleaned the air, so the tree trunks are no longer dark. The bark has once again become covered with pale-colored lichens, as they are in remoter areas, and it is now the light form that is well camouflaged.

This hypothesis was tested by an experiment. Captive-bred populations of both forms were released into two forests, one soot-darkened and the other clean. After a period of time, the remaining moths were trapped. In the polluted forest, far more of the dark forms had survived, while more of the pale ones survived in the clean forest. In another test both forms of the moth were placed on soot-darkened tree trunks, and on light, lichen-covered trunks. They were watched as birds came to feed. On the dark background, as expected, the birds ate far more of the light moths than the dark ones, while the reverse was true on the light background. The lesson is clear. Camouflage favored the survival of the dark moths when the polluted air darkened the tree trunks, and the light moths when the lichens returned.

Scientist 2

This often-cited case for natural selection is so flimsy that it is completely unconvincing. The experiment has nothing whatever to do with the actual life of the peppered moth in the wild. This moth is active only at night, and has never been seen resting on a tree trunk in the daytime. It probably lurks out of sight behind leaves until the sun goes down. In the experiment, the moths were placed on tree trunks in the daylight. Though the birds do, in fact, eat them selectively under these conditions, it has nothing to do with what happens in nature. Furthermore, several field studies contradict the hypothesis. In a forest near Detroit the light form of peppered moth increased spectacularly over a period of years, even though there was no change in lichen cover on the trees. In one trial in England, it was found that the dark peppered moths glued to lichen-covred tree trunks, were in fact taken more frequently by birds; however, an actual count of the population showed 80 percent dark. If selection favored the light moths, why were most of them dark? In another part of industrial England, it was found that the proportion of light forms of peppered moth started to increase substantially before the air was cleaned.

These studies show that there is no convincing evidence that change in the frequency of the two forms has anything to do with air quality. Other possible causes were never considered. Is the dark color somehow related to absorption of heat? Does it affect the physical structure of the wing? Is there a difference in the kinds of plants the larvae feed on? These, and many other hypotheses, are possible. Until more is known about the actual life of these moths as they live in the wild, and other possibilities are investigated, the real reason for these shifts in frequency will never be known.

34. The two scientists agree that:
    - **F.** in nature, birds choose one form or the other from tree trunks.
    - **G.** the relative frequency of the two forms in a population sometimes changes drastically.
    - **H.** the dark form tends to be more frequent in the population.
    - **J.** the reason for the shifts in frequency is unknown.

35. The hypothesis in dispute is that:
    - **A.** the change in frequency is commonly the result of changes in air quality.
    - **B.** natural selection controls the relative frequency of the two forms.
    - **C.** the color of a moth is controlled by its heredity.
    - **D.** the ability of birds to find the moths on tree trunks is limited by camouflage.

36. How might Scientist 1 account for the discrepant results of other field studies?
    - **F.** They might have been done with a different species of moth.
    - **G.** Moths with intermediate color might have been misidentified.
    - **H.** The samples taken were too small to be meaningful.
    - **J.** There might be other causes for the frequency shift, but in some cases, the air quality relationship is proven.

37. What discovery would tend to strengthen the position of Scientist 2?
    - **A.** Dark-colored moths tend to mate selectively with other dark moths.
    - **B.** Breeding experiments show that the gene for black color is dominant to the gene for light color.
    - **C.** There is a permanent distribution of patterns such that the black form is more common in the north.
    - **D.** In periods of prolonged drought, more of the light phase die during the larval stage.

38. What evidence in support of the hypothesis given by Scientist 1 was questioned by Scientist 2?
    - **F.** When moths are raised in captivity, their color depends on the color of their cage boxes.
    - **G.** Birds find light peppered moths more easily on tree-blackened tree bark.
    - **H.** The frequency of dark moths generally increases when the trees are dark and decreases when the color is light.
    - **J.** The changes in color frequencies are due to natural selection based on the color of tree bark.

39. The chief objection that Scientist 2 has to the work of Scientist 1 is that:
    - **A.** the observed changes in frequency were not observed in other studies.
    - **B.** the experiment took no account of the behavior of the moths in nature.
    - **C.** only one kind of bird was used in the experiment.
    - **D.** it did not prove that the color is inherited.

40. Scientist 1's position regarding this controversy might be that
    - **F.** Scientist 2 has shown that the hypothesis has been disproved.
    - **G.** in spite of the criticisms, there is enough evidence for the hypothesis that it has some validity.
    - **H.** more work is necessary to test the validity of the hypothesis.
    - **J.** there is no validity to the objections raised by Scientist 2.

STOP

If there is still time remaining, you may review your answers.

5 5 5 5 5 5 5 5 5 5 5

WRITING TEST
(Optional)
30 MINUTES

Directions: Write an essay in response to the following prompt:

Prompt: Several parents have objected to the literature being assigned to children in your school's English classes. They say that the novels, plays, and short stories are mostly about death, crime, violence, illness, unhappy love, and other subjects that depict human suffering. Instead, they insist that teachers select inspiring and uplifting works about courage, love, loyalty, family happiness, patriotism—noble subjects that depict humans at their best.

The English teachers have defended their choices, stating that most worthwhile literature from ancient times until today deals with human conflicts, not with the bright side of life. Furthermore, the books they teach contain provocative ideas that inspire students to think. In your opinion, should the English teachers change the literature they teach to comply with the demands of the parents?

In your essay, take a position on the issue. You may support either one of the points of view, or you may present a different point of view. Whatever your position, support it with specific reasons and examples.

Use the lined paper provided. Add additional sheets if necessary.

Model Exam C

Answer Keys and Analysis Charts

ENGLISH TEST

1. D	16. H	31. A	46. F	61. C
2. H	17. D	32. H	47. D	62. G
3. D	18. F	33. D	48. J	63. C
4. H	19. C	34. J	49. C	64. J
5. C	20. H	35. C	50. G	65. C
6. J	21. B	36. G	51. C	66. J
7. B	22. H	37. C	52. F	67. C
8. G	23. B	38. F	53. D	68. J
9. D	24. G	39. D	54. F	69. A
10. H	25. B	40. H	55. B	70. H
11. C	26. H	41. B	56. H	71. B
12. H	27. B	42. F	57. D	72. G
13. A	28. J	43. D	58. G	73. C
14. G	29. A	44. J	59. A	74. H
15. C	30. J	45. A	60. H	75. C

Analysis Chart

Skills	Questions	Possible Score	Your Score
Usage/Mechanics			
Punctuation	1, 13, 18, 20, 28, 32, 44, 46, 50, 66	10	
Basic Grammar and Usage	8, 9, 16, 17, 25, 26, 27, 31, 33, 38, 52, 53	12	
Sentence Structure	3, 4, 6, 12, 24, 39, 41, 43, 47, 48, 56, 57, 61, 62, 67, 68, 72	17	
Rhetorical Skills			
Strategy	2, 5, 23, 34, 40, 49, 51, 54, 59, 63, 71, 74	12	
Organization	11, 15, 19, 22, 29, 30, 35, 37, 42, 45, 58, 60, 65, 75	14	
Style	7, 10, 14, 21, 36, 55, 64, 69, 70, 73	10	

Number correct: ______

MATHEMATICS TEST

1. C	13. C	25. B	37. C	49. D
2. H	14. F	26. J	38. K	50. F
3. E	15. A	27. D	39. A	51. C
4. H	16. F	28. J	40. G	52. K
5. C	17. A	29. C	41. D	53. D
6. J	18. J	30. H	42. G	54. H
7. B	19. A	31. D	43. C	55. A
8. F	20. H	32. K	44. K	56. H
9. D	21. E	33. A	45. D	57. D
10. K	22. J	34. K	46. G	58. K
11. E	23. E	35. E	47. D	59. D
12. G	24. G	36. K	48. G	60. J

Analysis Chart

Content Area	Skill Level			Possible Score	Your Score
	Basic Skills	Application	Analysis		
Pre-Algebra Algebra	1, 5, 10,13, 17, 23, 27, 29	2, 3, 6, 8, 11, 15, 19, 22, 28, 34, 36, 50	12, 16, 24, 30	24	
Intermediate Algebra Coordinate Geometry	7, 14, 21, 32, 42, 43, 45	4, 18, 25, 26, 31, 33, 35	40, 44, 49, 52	18	
Geometry	38, 48, 51, 53, 56, 57, 58	9, 20, 37, 39, 46, 54, 59		14	
Trigonometry	41, 60	47, 55		4	

Number correct: ______

READING TEST

1. D	11. C	21. A	31. B
2. H	12. G	22. H	32. G
3. D	13. C	23. C	33. C
4. H	14. F	24. J	34. F
5. A	15. D	25. B	35. D
6. G	16. F	26. J	36. F
7. B	17. C	27. C	37. C
8. G	18. F	28. H	38. J
9. C	19. C	29. B	39. C
10. F	20. G	30. H	40. G

Analysis Chart

Passage Type	Referring	Reasoning	Possible Score	Your Score
Prose Fiction	1, 4, 7, 8	2, 3, 5, 6, 9, 10	10	
Social Studies	11, 12, 14	13, 15, 16, 17, 18, 19, 20	10	
Humanities	23, 24, 29	21, 22, 25, 26, 27, 28, 30	10	
Natural Science	32, 36, 37, 38	31, 33, 34, 35, 39, 40	10	

Number correct: ______

SCIENCE REASONING TEST

1. B	6. J	11. A	16. J	21. D	26. G	31. B	36. J
2. H	7. A	12. H	17. C	22. H	27. D	32. H	37. D
3. C	8. H	13. D	18. G	23. C	28. G	33. D	38. G
4. H	9. C	14. G	19. D	24. F	29. A	34. G	39. B
5. D	10. F	15. A	20. G	25. B	30. H	35. A	40. G

Analysis Chart

Kind of Questions	Skill Level			Possible Score	Your Score
	Understanding	Analysis	Generalization		
Data Representation	1, 2, 12, 13, 23, 24	3, 5, 14, 15, 16, 25	4, 26, 27	15	
Research Summaries	6, 17, 28, 29, 30	7, 8, 9, 18, 20, 31, 32	10, 11, 19, 21, 22, 33	18	
Conflicting Viewpoints	34, 35	36, 39	37, 38, 40	7	

Number correct: ______

COMPOSITE SCORE

To calculate your composite score (not including the Writing Test) follow these directions:

1. On the form below fill in the first column of blanks with the number of correct answers on each test.
2. Multiply each number by 36 and divide the product by the number of questions on each test. The results are your scale scores.
3. Add up your scale scores and divide by 4. The result should be rounded to the nearest whole number to determine your composite score.

	Number of correct answers			Scale score
English	_______	× 36 = _______	÷ 75 =	_______
Math	_______	× 36 = _______	÷ 60 =	_______
Reading	_______	× 36 = _______	÷ 40 =	_______
Science	_______	× 36 = _______	÷ 40 =	_______

Total _______ ÷ 4 = _______
Composite Score

No test can give you a totally precise measurement of your academic achievement. Rather, think of your composite score as the mid-point in a range of scores that can vary one or more points in either direction. A composite score of 30, for example, means that you scored somewhere between 28 and 32.

Answer Explanations: English Test

1. **D** Use a comma between the parts of a simple series.
2. **H** It is important to maintain the established subject—the forces that influence the way a child handles money; the other options are all off the topic.
3. **D** There is no need for *and* before the adjective clause *that children need to learn.* Choices B and C repeat the error. Choice C is wrong also because the pronoun *whom* is used to refer to a person, and the antecedent here is *principles.*
4. **H** There is a parallel series of sentences in this paragraph, all employing the infinitive. For this reason, the infinitive *to understand* is correct.
5. **C** The first sentence of the paragraph is a clear topic sentence that prepares the reader for the series of principles that forms the body of the paragraph.
6. **J** The antecedent of the pronoun is the plural noun *children* at the end of the preceding paragraph.
7. **B** The phrase *being as how* is substandard English; the other words create an illogical statement.
8. **G** The subject of the sentence is the singular noun *rise.*
9. **D** The pronoun *this* is almost never adequate by itself; the sentence requires a more complete statement. The point made in the preceding sentences is that money is more available.
10. **H** *Major* is more in keeping with the tone of the passage. The other words do not mean the same as *major* and are less preferable in this context.
11. **C** The underlined statement is off the topic and so must be eliminated.
12. **H** The subordinating conjunction *when* forms a logical link with the rest of the sentence; the other options do not.
13. **A** An introductory adverbial clause, except a very short one, is set off from the main clause by a comma. A stronger mark of punctuation in this place, such as choice D, would create a sentence fragment.

14. **G** The phrase *material possessions* makes a clear point; *worldly goods* is redundant.

15. **C** Paragraph 2 ends with a mention about *pressures,* a train of thought that leads directly to paragraph 5, which begins with the statement *These pressures are strong*. In the same manner, the thought about managing money at the end of paragraph 5 is picked up in the first sentence in paragraph 3; the notion that children need experience in managing money is echoed in paragraph 4, and the emphasis on adults in paragraph 4 is continued in the first words of paragraph 6.

16. **H** A singular subject—in this case, *police officer*—followed by a phrase such as *in common with, accompanied by, in addition to,* or *together with* takes a singular verb.

17. **D** To be parallel with the rest of the sentence, this part must begin with the participle *protected,* which modifies the noun *structure*.

18. **F** A parenthetical expression such as *however* is set off by commas.

19. **C** This choice is the only one that bears on anatomy.

20. **H** Compound verbs are not normally separated by a comma.

21. **B** The words *One after the other* are redundant; the phrase *in turn* means the same.

22. **H** This sentence has no bearing on the topic of the paragraph or passage and must be removed.

23. **B** Because the entire passage deals with the great stress placed on the foot, this description of the physical process of using the foot is meaningful.

24. **G** The word *if* is necessary at this point if the sentence is to be logical. Not all 7-year-old boys weigh 55 pounds.

25. **B** A present-tense verb is necessary to agree with the other verbs in the sentence.

26. **H** The subject of the verb is the plural noun *estimates;* the present tense is correct.

27. **B** When parts of a compound subject are joined by *or* or *nor,* the verb agrees with the nearer part—in this case, *characteristic*. The simple present tense is correct.

28. **J** The sentence is a simple declarative statement that requires a period.

29. **A** The figures provided are quite impressive and clearly dramatize the point of the passage.

30. **J** Paragraph 3 is a more general statement about the foot and should precede the very specific, detailed paragraphs 2 and 4. Note the clue in *During all this walking*.

31. **A** The subject of the verb *commemorates* is the singular noun *park;* the present tense is correct (note *is* in the same sentence).

32. **H** Items in a series are separated by semicolons if they contain commas within themselves. This sentence, when correctly constructed, includes a series of direct objects—*meetings, adoption,* and *labors*—the last two of which introduce clauses set off by commas.

33. **D** To be parallel with the direct objects *meetings* and *labors,* this item must begin with a noun.

34. **J** The park is the site of Independence Hall, around which most of the historical events described in the passage revolve.

35. **C** The topic sentence of this paragraph is flawed; the general point it makes is not broad enough to embrace the historical events described. A better topic sentence would be this: *Independence Hall, originally the statehouse for the province of Pennsylvania, was the site of an important event in early American history.*

36. **G** The word *supervision* is adequate; *overview* is repetitious.

37. **C** Although Thomas Jefferson figures importantly in the events later described in the passage, where he was in 1736 has no bearing on this paragraph.

38. **F** The past perfect tense is required in this sentence because the action described took place *before* the past action that is the subject of the passage.

39. **D** All the actions in the sentence are in the simple past.

40. **H** The word *Nevertheless* provides the contrast that is needed in a sentence describing an unexpected consequence. The other connective words do not provide the contrast, and so make no sense in the context.

41. **B** In combination with the word *would, be declared* signals an event in the future; note "not until a year later."

42. **F** The paragraph, flawed because of a weak topic sentence, presents historical events that occurred in and near Independence Hall. Of the choices given, this is the only one that makes that point.

43. **D** This is the only correct, complete sentence. Choices A and B are sentence fragments. Choice C is a sentence plus a sentence fragment.

44. **J** A semicolon joins two main clauses; there is no conjunction. Anything weaker in this spot results in a run-on sentence.

45. **A** The paragraphs are correct as they stand. Since this passage is in chronological order, the sequence is self-explanatory.

46. **F** Items in a series are separated by semicolons if they contain commas.

47. **D** To be parallel with the other clauses in the sentence, this one must maintain the same pattern, *it is a* . . . .

48. **J** The subject of the verb is the plural noun *pro-lifers;* the present tense is needed.

49. **C** The comma is needed after *Americans* to set off the participial phrase *comprising a majority of Americans.* Otherwise, the sentence can be misread to mean that pro-choice advocates comprise a majority of all Americans who believe that abortion should be legal under certain circumstances, falsely implying that a minority of these Americans are not pro-choice.

50. **G** This phrase is not a digression but rather is information essential to the point being made, and so should not be enclosed in parentheses.

51. **C** This sentence needs to be introduced by a transition that signals the introduction of an example; the other transitions denote contrast *or cause,* and choices B and D result in sentence fragments.

52. **F** The subject of the sentence is the singular noun *group;* the present tense is correct.

53. **D** The word *process* is a noun; it must be described or restated as a noun, not as an adverbial clause.

54. **F** The views of leaders would be useful in this passage about opinions. The information in the other options would be off the topic.

55. **B** The adjective *ill advised* is clear and direct; the other options are colloquial or misleading.

56. **H** The subject of the sentence is the plural noun *programs.* The passage is written in the present tense.

57. **D** The clause *that are beneficial* merely repeats the meaning of the word *positive,* and so should be removed.

58. **G** This sentence has nothing to do with the point of the passage.

59. **A** For the most part, one view of the abortion issue is compared with the other in this passage.

60. **H** Paragraph 2 clearly introduces the topic, and suggests the structure of the passage; paragraph 3 begins with an example of the quality of the thought mentioned at the end of paragraph 2; paragraph 4 presents the other view of the issue, and paragraph 1 sums up the complexity of the issue.

61. **C** The sentence in which this question appears ends with a series of noun objects, in which *comparison of the proposed budget* should be included. Note that the correct choice is the only one that is not a clause.

62. **G** The present perfect tense is required in this sentence because the action referred to extends, at least in its consequences, to the present.

63. **C** The entire passage emphasizes the point that no legislation is more important than the budget.

64. **J** Only the use of the preposition *For* creates a logical, correct sentence; the other choices are substandard English.

65. **C** The statement about traffic on the freeways has no bearing on the point of the passage.

66. **J** Use the comma before a coordinating conjunction linking main clauses.

67. **C** The logic that lies behind each of the options changes the meaning of the sentence dramatically. Only the use of *Because* results in a meaning consistent with the rest of the paragraph.

68. **J** The word *because* creates an adverb clause that is parallel with the adverb clause that begins the sentence. Also, the other choices either are substandard English (F) or alter the meaning (G, H) of the sentence.

69. **A** *Continually* means "occurring in steady, rapid succession," while *continuously* means "occurring in uninterrupted duration," the latter meaning being preferable in this context.

70. **H** The idea of disputes and stalemates festering borders on a mixed metaphor. More sensible in this very business-like passage is the use of the term *unresolved.* The other options make no sense in the sentence.

71. **B** The tone and message of the passage seem to be directed at constituents seeking to be informed.

72. **G** When the comparative (here, *larger*) is used for more than two, it is necessary to exclude from the group the object compared. In the original sentence the expenditures of the government of California would be included in the group *those of any American governmental jurisdiction … U.S. Government.*

73. **C** The word *budget* is what is intended; additional words are distracting.

74. **H** The passage makes clear in several ways the importance of the state budget as an entity.

75. **C** Paragraph 3 is clearly the introductory paragraph for this passage. In addition, it refers to early January and the governor's message, two items mentioned also in the first sentence of paragraph 1. Paragraph 2 continues the chronological narrative, and even ends with a closing statement.

Answer Explanations: Mathematics Test

1. **C** Only $\frac{x}{2}$ satisfies the definition of a monomial.

2. **H** Lisa now receives 108% of her previous salary, so \$5.67 is 108% of what number? $A = 5.67$, $P = 108\%$, B is unknown. The percent proportion is

$$\frac{108}{100} = \frac{5.67}{B}$$

$$108B = 567$$

$$B = 5.25$$

3. **E** $5 + 2 \cdot 3^2 = 5 + 2 \cdot 9$ Exponents first.

$$= 5 + 18$$
$$= 23$$

4. **H** $81x^2 - 36y^2 = 9(9x^2 - 4y^2)$

$$= 9(3x - 2y)(3x + 2y)$$

Always do the greatest common factor first.

5. **C** $\sqrt{49} = 7$, which is rational.

6. **J** $\frac{(x-y)^2}{y^2 - x^2} = \frac{(x-y)(x-y)}{(y-x)(y+x)}$

$$= \frac{(-1)(x-y)}{y+x}$$ Because $x - y$ and $y - x$ are opposites.

$$= \frac{y-x}{y+x}$$

7. **B** Consecutive terms of a geometric sequence have a common ratio. Only in the sequence 1, 2, 4, 8, . . . is there a common ratio, 2.

8. **F** $4x - 2[3x - (x + 4)] = 5 - 2(x + 1)$

$$4x - 2[3x - x - 4] = 5 - 2x - 2$$
$$4x - 6x + 2x + 8 = 5 - 2x - 2$$
$$8 = 3 - 2x$$
$$5 = -2x$$
$$x = \frac{-5}{2}$$

9. **D** Angle *ABC* is a right angle because a diameter is perpendicular to a tangent at the point of tangency. Angle *ADB* is also a right angle because it is inscribed in a semicircle. Therefore $\angle DBC$ is complementary to both $\angle ABD$ and $\angle BCD$. Thus $\angle ABD$ and $\angle BCD$ are equal in measure.

10. **K**

$$7.2\% = 0.072$$
$$7.2(10^{-2}) = 0.072$$
$$\frac{72}{100} = 0.72$$
$$(0.08)9 = 0.72$$
$$(0.08)(0.09) = 0.0072$$

11. **E** $xy^2(x - y) = (-3)(2^2)(-3 - 2)$
$= (-3)(4)(-5)$
$= 60$

12. **G** This is a direct-variation-type problem. The proportion is $\frac{4}{x} = \frac{20}{30}\left(= \frac{2}{3}\right)$ $2x = 12$
$x = 6$

13. **C** The associative property of addition allows regrouping of terms.

14. **F** A pure imaginary number is a complex number with the real part equal to 0. Only $\sqrt{-9} = 3i = 0 + 3i$ is this type.

15. **A**

$$\begin{array}{r} 7\frac{1}{4} \\ -2\frac{5}{6} \\ \hline \end{array} \qquad \begin{array}{r} 7\frac{3}{12} \\ -2\frac{10}{12} \\ \hline \end{array}$$

The LCD is 12.

$$\begin{array}{r} 6\frac{15}{12} \\ -2\frac{10}{12} \\ \hline 4\frac{5}{12} \end{array}$$

Borrow $\frac{12}{12}$ from the 7.

16. **F** This is a work-type problem for which the formula $w = rt$ applies. Since Stan can do the job in 4 hours, his rate of work is $\frac{1}{4}$ of the job per hour. Fred's rate is then $\frac{1}{5}$ of the job per hour. Let x = the number of hours it would take to do the job together.

	w =	r •	t
Stan	$\frac{x}{4}$	$\frac{1}{4}$	x
Fred	$\frac{x}{5}$	$\frac{1}{5}$	x

The equation is $\frac{x}{4} + \frac{x}{5} = 1$ (one job completed).

17. **A** The definition of a composite number includes the phrase "greater than 1."

18. **J** A special rule about absolute value inequalities allows an immediate translation from $|x + 3| \geq 2$ to

$$x + 3 \geq 2 \text{ or } x + 3 \leq -2$$

$$x \geq -1 \text{ or } x \leq -5$$

19. **A** Multiply both sides by the LCD, which is 12.

$$12\left(\frac{2x-1}{3} + \frac{x+2}{4}\right) = 12\left(\frac{1}{6}\right)$$
$$4(2x - 1) + 3(x + 2) = 2$$
$$8x - 4 + 3x + 6 = 2$$
$$11x + 2 = 2$$
$$11x = 0$$
$$x = 0$$

20. **H** The measure of an angle formed by a chord and a tangent at the point of tangency is half of the intercepted arc. An inscribed angle is also measured by half of the intercepted arc. Therefore $m\angle ECB = m\angle BAC$.

21. **E** When completely simplified, the polynomial is

$$27x^6 + \text{(terms of lower degree)}$$

The degree of this polynomial is 6.

22. **J** Follow the rule for squaring a binomial:

$$(a + b)^2 = a^2 + 2ab + b^2$$

Here

$$(2x - 3y)^2 = 4x^2 - 12xy + 9y^2$$

23. **E** In quadrant IV, the first component of the ordered pairs is positive and the second is negative. Only (2, – 8) is of that type.

24. **G** Half of a sphere with radius 2 inches is $\frac{1}{2}\left[\frac{4}{3}\pi(2^3)\right] = \frac{16}{3}\pi$ cubic inches.

The volume of a cone with radius 2 inches and height 5 inches is $\frac{1}{3}\pi(2^2)(5) = \frac{20}{3}\pi$ cubic inches.

The total volume is therefore $\frac{16}{3}\pi + \frac{20}{3}\pi = \frac{36}{3}\pi = 12\pi$ cubic inches.

25. **B** The sum of the roots of the quadratic equation $ax^2 + bx + c = 0$ is $\frac{-b}{a}$ and the product is $\frac{c}{a}$. The product of the roots of $5x^2 - 8x + 7 = 0$ is $\frac{7}{5}$.

26. **J** $8^{-(2/3)} = \frac{1}{8^{2/3}} = \frac{1}{\sqrt[3]{8^2}} = \frac{1}{\sqrt[3]{64}} = \frac{1}{4}$

27. **D** The given expression is the expanded form of 302,470.

28. **J** First factor each denominator, then use each factor the greater number of times it occurs in any factorization.

$5a^2b^3$
$20ab^4 = 2 \cdot 2 \cdot 5 \cdot ab^4$
$15a^3b^2 = 3 \cdot 5 \cdot a^3b^2$

The LCD is $2 \cdot 2 \cdot 3 \cdot 5 \cdot a^3b^4 = 60a^3b^4$.

29. **C** The mean of *n* numbers is found by adding the numbers and dividing by *n*. The sum of the given numbers is 58, so the mean is 5.8.

30. **H** Sue is paid 7% only on her sales. Her salary is $S = 200 + 0.07t$.

31. **D** Multiply the numerator and denominator by the LCD, which is $9x^2$.

$$\frac{9x^2\left(\frac{1}{x} - \frac{1}{3}\right)}{9x^2\left(\frac{1}{x^2} - \frac{1}{9}\right)} = \frac{9x - 3x^2}{9 - x^2} = \frac{3x(3 - x)}{(3 - x)(3 + x)} = \frac{3x}{3 + x}$$

32. **K** The given equation is equivalent to $y + 9 = -2(x + 6)^2$. Compare this to the standard form of such an equation:

$$y - k = a(x - h)^2$$

which has its vertex at (*h*, *k*). The parabola's vertex is at (– 6, – 9).

33. **A** Multiply both sides by the common denominator, $(x - 3)(x + 3)$. There are, therefore, restricted values 3 and – 3.

$$(x - 3)(x + 3)\left(\frac{x^2 + 9}{x^2 - 9} - \frac{3}{x + 3}\right) = (x - 3)(x + 3)\left(\frac{-x}{3 - x}\right)$$
$$x^2 + 9 - 3(x - 3) = x(x + 3)$$
$$x^2 + 9 - 3x + 9 = x^2 + 3x$$
$$18 = 6x$$
$$x = 3$$

But since 3 is a restricted value, the solution set is empty.

34. **K** $\frac{2.4(10^{-4})}{6(10^{-2})} = 0.4(10^{-4-(-2)})$

$= 0.4(10^{-2}) = [4(10^{-1})](10^{-2})$
$= 4(10^{-3})$

Model Exam C

35. **E** Substitute the given coordinates into the slope formula.

$$m = \frac{y_2 - y_1}{x_2 - x_1} = \frac{-3 - 8}{-5 - (-5)} = \frac{-11}{0},$$

which does not exist.

36. **K** During January the Smiths use 0.2(100) = 20 gallons and have 80 gallons left to begin February. In February they use 0.25(80) = 20 gallons, so they have 80 – 20 = 60 gallons left on March 1.

37. **C** Here is one possible approach. Since $\overline{AE} \perp l$, it is perpendicular to each of the parallel lines. Then $\triangle ACF$ is a right triangle, and, by the Pythagorean theorem, $CF = 8$. Then $\triangle ACF$ is similar to $\triangle ADG$, giving the following proportion:

$$\frac{10}{8} = \frac{24}{DG}$$

$$10DG = 192$$

$$DG = 19.2$$

38. **K** All of these statements are false.

39. **A** Angles *CBA* and *CDB* are the supplements of the given angles. Their measures are 40° and 120°. Since the sum of the three angels of a triangle is 180°,

$$m\angle C = 180 - (40 + 120)$$
$$= 180 - 160 = 20°$$

40. **G** Imagine three containers in which the mixtures could be made.

$$\frac{|12 - x|}{4\%} + \frac{|\ x\ |}{100\%} = \frac{|\ 12\ |}{20\%}$$

The equation reflects the fact that the amount of antifreeze does not change as a result of mixing the 4% and 100% solutions.

$$0.04(12 - x) + 1.00(x) = 0.2(12)$$
$$4(12 - x) + 100x = 20(12)$$
$$48 - 4x + 100x = 240$$
$$96x = 192$$
$$x = 2$$

41. **D** The length of side *BC* is $\sqrt{5^2 - 2^2} = \sqrt{21}$.

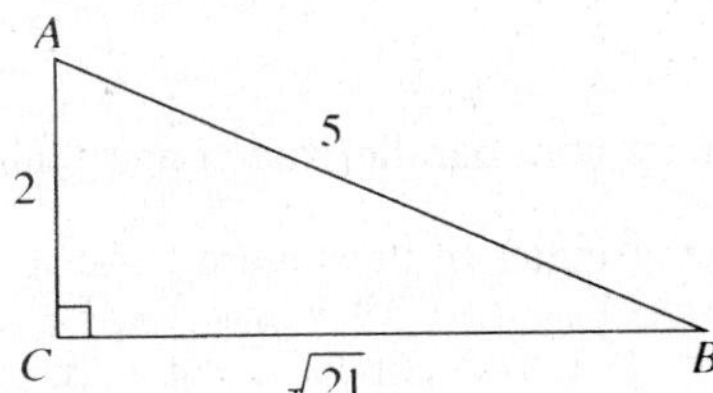

In a right triangle the sine function is

$$\frac{\text{length of opposite side}}{\text{length of hypotenuse}} = \frac{\sqrt{21}}{5}$$

42. **G** This is a parabola that opens upward and its vertex is (1, 2). Therefore the equation in standard form is

$$y = a(x - 1)^2 + 2$$

Substitute the coordinates (0, 5) into the equation to solve for *a*.

$$5 = a(0 - 1)^2 + 2$$
$$5 = a + 2$$
$$a = 3$$

The equation is $y = 3(x - 1)^2 + 2$.

43. **C** Multiply the numerator and denominator by the complex conjugate of the denominator.

$$\frac{(3-i)(2-i)}{(2+i)(2-i)} = \frac{6-3i-4i+2i^2}{4-i^2}$$
$$= \frac{6-7i+2(-1)}{4-(-1)} \qquad (i^2 = -1)$$
$$= \frac{4-7i}{5} = \frac{4}{5} - \frac{7}{5}$$

44. **K** This is a problem of permutations because order is important.

$$_nP_r = \frac{n!}{(n-r)!}$$
$$_6P_6 = \frac{6!}{(6-6)!} = \frac{6!}{0!} = \frac{720}{1} = 720$$

45. **D** Let $x = \log_2 \frac{1}{8}$. Change the equation to its corresponding exponential form.

$2^x = \frac{1}{8} = \frac{1}{2^3} = 2^{-3}$ Therefore $x = -3$.

46. **G** The ratio of the corresponding linear measures of polygons is the ratio of the square roots of the areas. The ratio of the lengths of the corresponding altitudes is $\frac{\sqrt{9}}{\sqrt{16}} = \frac{3}{4}$.

47. **D** Coterminal angles are found by adding or subtracting multiples of 360° or 2π radians.

$$\frac{75\pi}{4} - \frac{9(8\pi)}{4} = \frac{75\pi}{4} - \frac{72\pi}{4} = \frac{3\pi}{4}$$

48. **G** $CD = 6 - \left(1\frac{2}{3} + 1\frac{1}{4} + 1\frac{1}{12}\right) = 6 - 4 = 2$

49. **D** The vertex of the graph of the equation would locate the time (t) and height (h) of the maximum height. Complete the square to put the equation in standard form.

$$h = -16(t^2 - 4t)$$
$$= -16(t^2 - 4t + 4) + 64$$
$$= -16(t-2)^2 + 64$$

The vertex is at (2, 64).

50. **F** $\sqrt{54x^4y^5} \bullet \sqrt{2x^2y^4} = \sqrt{108x^6y^9}$

$$= \sqrt{(36x^6y^8)(3y)}$$
$$= \sqrt{36x^6y^8} \bullet \sqrt{3y}$$
$$= 6x^3y^4\sqrt{3y}$$

51. **C** Opposite sides of a parallelogram are both parallel and congruent.

52. **K** Let x be a side of the square. The perimeter of the square is $4x$, and the perimeter of the semicircular region is $2r + \pi r$.

$$4x = 16 + 8\pi \qquad x = 4 + 2\pi$$

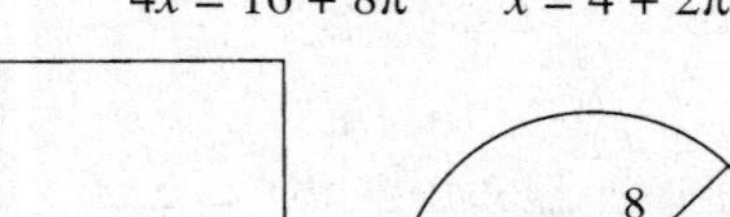
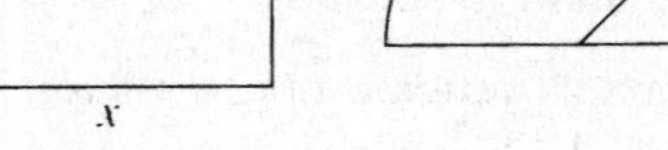

53. **D** Angles *ACB* and *DCE* are vertical angles.

54. **H** Triangles *ABD* and *CBE* are similar, and the corresponding sides have the same ratio.

$$\frac{4}{9} = \frac{x}{5}$$
$$9x = 20$$
$$x = \frac{20}{9} = 2\frac{2}{9}$$

55. **A** Since the sine is $\frac{\text{length of opposite side}}{\text{length of hypotenuse}}$, $\sin 25° = \frac{h}{50}$.

Then $h = 50 \sin 25°$. But the end of the string is 5 feet above the ground, so the total height is $5 + 50 \sin 25°$.

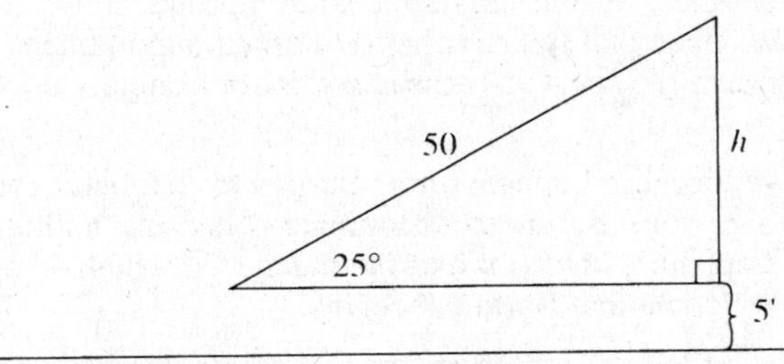

56. **H** Let $AE = x$; then $BE = 8 - x$. The product of the lengths of the segments of one chord equals the product of the lengths of the segments of the other.

$$\begin{aligned} x(8 - x) &= 2 \cdot 8 \\ 8x - x^2 &= 16 \\ x^2 - 8x + 16 &= 0 \\ (x - 4)^2 &= 0 \\ x - 4 &= 0 \\ x &= 4 \end{aligned}$$

57. **D** The maximum number of common tangents is 4.

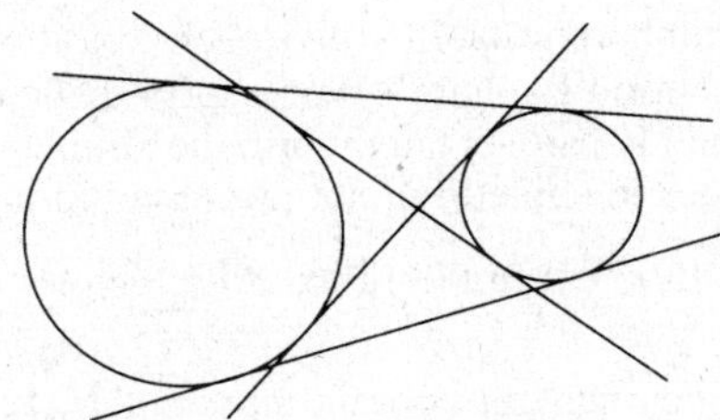

58. **K** All these statements are true.

59. **D** Equal chords intercept equal arcs in a circle. Therefore arc $BC = \frac{1}{2}(360 - 2 \cdot 24)° = \frac{1}{2}(312)° = 156°$

Then

$$\angle BDC = \frac{1}{2}(156)° = 78°$$

60. **J** The period of the sine function

$$y = a \sin b(x - c) \text{ is } \frac{2\pi}{|b|}.$$

The given function can be written in the form

$$y = -3 \sin 4(x + \frac{\pi}{4})$$

so the period is $\frac{2\pi}{4} = \frac{\pi}{2}$.

Answer Explanations: Reading Test

1. **D** The first paragraph of the passage indicates the purpose of the interview. A holds promise as a correct answer, but Bartley's cynicism would keep him from writing a piece that honors a man he barely respects. B and C apply generally to all newspaper reporters, but the passage mentions neither idea.

2. **H** The phrase rings of pretentiousness that might appeal to a proud, self-made man like Lapham. Choice F may be true, but there is no evidence that Lapham has additional appointments. If G had validity, Lapham would not have been addressing an envelope, customarily a clerk or secretary's job. Choice J is unrelated to the point of the question.

3. **D** Choice D is the best answer because Lapham offers Bartley his left hand, remains seated, and nods to the vacant chair with his head—all signs of indifference. Eliminate A because nothing suggests that Lapham dislikes his visitor. The intensity of Lapham's behavior and the manner in which he addresses William contradict B, and C overstates the type of welcome that Bartley receives.

4. **H** In the tiny office, called a "little den" in line 35, the two men's knees almost touch (lines 20–21). A larger den, the "counting room," completes the layout of Lapham's office. No other choice applies.

5. **A** The dialogue reveals that Bartley is accustomed to hearing stories of childhood deprivation and hardship (B). It also suggests that Bartley is searching for compelling words and ideas to attract readers and perhaps inspire poverty-stricken youngsters to succeed in life (C and D). Only A is not an issue in the passage.

6. **G** The best answer is choice G because Bartley has no reason to win Lapham's sympathy. Bartley discloses that he is an orphan as a not-too-subtle hint that Lapham isn't the only man to have suffered through a deprived childhood (choice F). The disclosure helps Bartley to break down the natural barrier between the businessman and the journalist (H). Bartley's words are said with humor (J), but Lapham assumes that Bartley is teasing him and doesn't like it.

7. **B** Lapham has a "great hairy fist" (line 15) and a "huge foot" (line 34). Choices A and D are not mentioned in the passage. C is only partly correct; Lapham's eyes are blue but never cold or steely.

8. **G** Lines 84–86 indicate that both of Lapham's parents had been ambitious for his advancement. F should be discarded because Bartley fails to mention Lapham's personality. Rule out H because Bartley never says that Lapham ever read either book but that his parents taught him the simple virtues espoused by the *Old Testament* and *Poor Richard's Almanac*. J alludes to something not discussed in the passage.

9. **C** Bartley derides Lapham's story. To him, tales of poor boys who make something of themselves are clichés, not worth taking seriously.

10. **F** Bartley is portrayed as a seasoned and cynical reporter unimpressed by Lapham as a person but aware that readers like stories about rich people (lines 28–30). Bartley belittles Lapham's story of childhood deprivation; he's heard it all before and sarcastically asks questions about poor parents and "barefoot business" (line 71) that he might use in his article. Rule out choices G and J because Bartley shows neither resentment nor ingratitude. H may have some appeal as the answer because it is clear that Bartley has no affection or admiration for Lapham. But to call his attitude contemptuous is an overstatement.

11. **C** Researchers found that the most dramatic changes took place in the decades following 1775 (lines 17–22).

12. **G** Choices F and H may have contributed to the epidemic, but lines 7–9 say that Europeans brought smallpox directly to the tribe. J is unrelated to the spread of smallpox.

13. **C** Based on the first paragraph, the Omaha thrived under Blackbird's leadership. He provided "wealth, political prestige, and military strength." Choices A, B, and D may be valid to some extent, but the preponderance of evidence in the passage suggest C as the best answer.

14. **F** Choice G is supported by the statement that smallpox killed "as many as one-third of the Omaha" (lines 9–10). Evidence of H can be found in line 10. The change in roles caused by the smallpox epidemic—choice J—is discussed in lines 66–89. The passage does not discuss the impact of smallpox on the fur trade, making F the best answer.

15. **D** Synonyms for *viable* include "workable," "conceivable," and "practicable." Therefore, D most closely approximates the meaning in the passage. The loss of population prevented the Omahas from functioning as they had before the smallpox epidemic.

16. **F** Evidence that the Omaha hunted buffalo on horseback lay in the arthritic toes of the Omaha's skeletons (lines 31–36). Discussion of G, H, and J are absent from the passage.

17. **C** According to Reinhard, data about the Omaha were derived from both the skeletons and artifacts (lines 39–45). Choice A is only occasionally true, according to line 43. Neither B nor D is discussed in the passage.

18. **F** Based on the discussion of women's bones, stressful manufacturing jobs formerly done by men shortened women's lives. Before 1800, women may have lived fifty years, afterwards only thirty. Choice G may have resulted from women's weakened condition but is not discussed in the passage. Nor do H and J relate to the contents of the passage.

19. **C** From the bones of women, Reinhard and his team realized that before the smallpox epidemic women's work consisted of "wood chopping, farming, and food grinding." Afterward, women "took on more of the responsibility for manufacturing." Choices A, B, and D are unrelated to changing "economic roles."

20. **G** After 1800 an "influx in trade in tools and clothing" occurred that the last two paragraphs attribute to a change in traditional trading practices brought on by the death of Chief Blackbird. Eliminate choice F because Lewis and Clark's visit had nothing to do with this change. Although trade functioned under the auspices of the United States—mentioned in choice H—nothing in the passage refers to a peace treaty. Rule out J because trade had been conducted by barter long before 1800.

21. **A** The mason is a "liar" because "he could not tell the truth in his work." In other words, his work was a deception. Choices B, C, and D are not discussed in the passage.

22. **H** You may know that *posterity* means "generations of the distant future," making H the best answer. J may be suggested by the fact that the "foundations were four feet wide and sunk three and one-half feet into the earth." But wouldn't it be bizarre to build an oversize foundation just to have an oversize foundation? The author must have had another motive. Neither F nor G explain what the author had in mind.

23. **C** In lines 16–17 the author states that he discovered the lie when he started to repair cracks in the wall caused by an earthquake. Choice A overstates the impact of the earthquake on the foundation wall. B and D occurred in the passage but are unrelated to the discovery of the wall's deficiencies.

24. **J** The second paragraph cites all the defects listed by choices F, G, and H. Only J is missing.

25. **B** Lines 4–9 imply that foundation walls need to support not only the walls and roof of the structure but also its contents. Choices A, C, and D name other functions of a foundation wall, but they are not implied or stated in the passage.

26. **J** The author's main purpose is to acquaint readers with principles of design and construction that he favors. Choice F is irrelevant to the passage. Choice G may be slightly implied, but by far the author's purpose is to tell the story of his own experience. Dispensing advice to readers lies outside his concerns and interest. H may be a by-product of the discussion but is by no means its main purpose.

27. **C** To the author choice B may be a valid statement, but in the context of the passage, the author's main concern is utility vs. stateliness, and in his view, utility should win hands down, making C the best answer. A is not discussed, and D alludes to an idea that the author abhors. After all, he's building a house not for friends but for himself.

28. **H** At least twice (in the fourth and fifth paragraphs) the author discusses the irksomeness of housecleaning. The passage lacks evidence to support F. Rule out G because, except for a brief allusion to the cost of building a bathroom, the passage contains no evidence that the author is concerned about paying for the house. Besides, a man with servants is not likely to worry too much about money. J may be true because the author wants his servants to go swimming, but the passage says nothing about where the house will be located other than "in California."

29. **B** The author implies that living inside causes damage to our lungs (lines 65–67). Choice A is incidental to his preference for outside air. C is an obvious inference—not a fact—to be drawn from the author's stated preference for outside air. D is mentioned earlier in the passage but is unrelated to the author's preference for open air.

30. **H** Choices F, G, and J are stated or implied by the second and third paragraphs of the passage. Although H may be desirable, the author doesn't discuss the need for a shared vision.

31. **B** A host of "remarkable" qualities has left the author marveling about this extraordinary waterway. Choice A totally misrepresents the author's feelings. C ignores Twain's affection for the river, and D is hyperbolic; the river may impress Twain, but he shows no signs of uncontrollable passion.

32. **G** The text of the first paragraph emphasizes the river's length, number of tributaries, vastness of its drainage basin, and other size-related features.

33. **C** The phrase refers the hundreds of rivers from which the Mississippi receives its supply of water. Choice C, therefore, is the best answer. B should be ruled out because some rivers that feed the Mississippi carry steamboats (lines 18–20) and are equally navigable. Discard A because such distant rivers could not possibly be tributaries of the Mississippi. Eliminate D because the passage makes no reference to rivers emptying into the Atlantic.

34. **F** Lines 25–27 point out a "remarkable" feature of the river: it narrows as it gets closer to its mouth, suggesting that other rivers widen as they approach the sea. G is contradicted by the variations in width pointed out in lines 26–31. Eliminate H because the rate of flow is not discussed. J is ambiguous at best because the water depth is discussed only as it pertains to the confluence of the Mississippi and Ohio Rivers. Whether water deepens at other intersections is left unclear.

35. **D** Lines 53–56 explain that over many centuries the mud has caused land that once lay by the sea to now be located 200 miles inland. Both choices A and C are wrong because the passage does not discuss the origin of the Mississippi's mud. B describes only a hypothetical mass of mud that if solidified would add to the land mass.

36. **F** This choice coincides with the description of the river's "disposition to make prodigious jumps by cutting through narrow necks of land" (lines 61–62). G may be a tempting answer based on the changes that a cut-off recently brought to Delta and Vicksburg (lines 65–70), but there is no indication that the river suddenly flowed backward. The explanation of the river's sidewise movement (choice H) does not mention cut-offs. Rule out J because the passage does not discuss floods.

37. **C** Choice A is incorrect because the passage describes the Mississippi unexpectedly moving sideways, crossing spits of land and straightening itself. Eliminate B because scientists and engineers, while fascinated by the river, do not seem puzzled by it. As for D, the river does, in fact, straighten itself but not necessarily as it gets closer to the sea. C is the best answer.

38. **J** All choices except J name a consequence of cut-offs. The passage makes no mention of property values along the river.

39. **C** Before a recent cut-off (lines 65–70), the river flowed past Vicksburg before it flowed past Delta. Now it reaches Delta first. There is nothing in the passage to support A or B. Choice D is supported only insofar as distance is measured by river miles; the towns themselves obviously have not moved.

40. **G** Based on the material in the last two paragraphs, the shifting of the river's path altered borders between states. Choice F may be true in reality, but the passage does not discuss it. Neither H nor J is supported in the passage.

Answer Explanations: Science Reasoning Test

1. **B** Trace the *human* line and the *gorilla* line back to the point where they meet in the early Miocene. The time scale shows that this is at 19 million years ago.

2. **H** From the point marked Dryopithecines, move upward on the chart to find all the lines that branch out. They are all included within the group marked *Hominoids*.

3. **C** The *human* and *orangutan* lines diverge from a branching point just over 20 million years ago. For the other pairs, the branching points are as follows: A. 40 million; B 53 million; D 25 million.

4. **H** Lemurs are classified as prosimians, and this can only be because they are the closest relatives of the ancient prosimians that were the ancestors of the whole order. F is wrong because there is no reason to believe that the modern and the ancient prosimians are identical. G is wrong because the ancestral prosimians were not lemurs, but something similar. There is no reason at all to believe J.

5. **D** If *Australopithecus* is more humanlike and more recent than *Ramapithecus,* it must lie somewhere between *Ramapithecus* and human, which puts it squarely in the Hominid group.

6. **J** The best survival at the end of the first year is 34 percent, so in every case, at least 66 percent of the seedlings die during the first year. Dependence of survival on sunlight varies with the substrate, and nothing in the experiment defines "natural conditions." No data are given concerning growth.

7. **A** During the second year, survival drops from 34 percent to 32, a very small loss. Choice B is wrong because size is not a variable. In heavy shade, the loss is greatest, but many do survive. D is wrong because the substantial loss in the first year is true of all cases, not unique to this case.

8. **H** On all substrates, survival is poorest in the deep shade of a forest. There is no data to support any of the other choices.

9. **C** None of the other choices are defensible. All seedlings must be genetically identical, or the experiment is deeply flawed. Charcoal is surely not richer in minerals than mineral soil. While choice D may be true, it has no bearing on the question.

10. **F** On sawdust, survival is much greater in sunlight than in shade. Growth is not a variable in this experiment. Choice C is wrong; survival is actually better where the burn is heavier. In mineral soil, survival is clearly best where there is light shade.

11. **A** On all substrates, survival rates were best in light shade. Choice B is wrong because charcoal is not a natural substrate. C is wrong; survival is poor in deep shade, but not zero. D is wrong; seedlings seem to do quite well in burned over areas.

12. **H** Surely, if the treatment kills most of the subjects, there is little reason to hope that it will be useful. The other choices are comparatively trivial problems.

13. **D** In the survival rate graph, the lines for the fat-free diet, with and without strepsin, are nearly identical.

14. **G** At 18 months of age, the average weight of the rats in this group was 150 grams, but only 10 rats in this group survived, so their total weight was 1,500 grams.

15. **A** In this group, the rats began to die off after the 12th week. All the other choices indicate contamination of the experiment, which would not be found in the work of a careful experimenter.

16. **J** Results using strepsin are not encouraging. Many of the rats died, and it does not seem worthwhile to pursue the studies with strepsin any further.

17. **C** The concentration of 200 g of glucose in 500 mL of water is the same as 400 g/L; the table for Experiment 1 shows that at this concentration the boiling point is 101.2°C.

18. **G** Experiment 2 makes it clear that the boiling point elevation, at constant concentration, depends on the molecular weight of the solute. The new substance is made into a solution with the same concentration as the solutions in Experiment 2. The molecular weight of the new substance is about halfway between that of acetaldehyde and that of glycerol, so the boiling point would also be about halfway.

19. **D** Note that it is the *elevation* of the boiling point that is in question, not the actual boiling point. Naphthalene and glucose have very nearly the same molecular weight. Glucose raised the boiling point of water only 0.9° C from 100.0° C to 100.9° C, while naphthalene, at the same concentration, raised the boiling point of benzene 4.7° C, from 80.1° C to 84.8° C.

20. **G** Glucose in water raises the boiling point only 0.9 degrees; naphthalene in benzene, with equal concentrations and similar molecular weight, raises it 3.7 degrees.

21. **D** With its smaller molecular weight, a given mass of butyric acid has many more molecules than an equal mass of cholesterol. A is wrong because cholesterol does, in fact, raise the boiling point, although to a lesser degree than a substance with smaller molecules will. B is wrong because the experimental design specifies that 300 g was used in both cases. C is wrong because there is no reason to believe there was any chemical reaction; in fact, it is contraindicated because cholesterol follows the pattern of the relationship between molecular weight and boiling point elevation.

22. **H** Since there is a clear relationship between molecular weight and boiling point elevation, measuring this elevation would make it possible to calculate the molecular weight.

23. **C** The design predicted a drop of energy consumption from 385 units to 125, but it actually went down to 95. A is wrong because the actual drop was far greater. B is wrong because the design did more, not less, than was expected of it. D is wrong because the new building was based on the revised design.

24. **F** The item "vertical transport" appears in the new building, but not the old one. G is wrong because the data do not distinguish between different kinds of lighting. H is wrong because the item "cooling" appears in all three bars. J is wrong because no information is given about such an item.

25. **B** Comparing the design with the actual terminal, it is seen that all the items are about the same in both, except for lighting. This item is much smaller in the actual building than in the design.

26. **G** The new design lowered the heating cost from 225 units to 45, an enormous saving. F is wrong because it is the total cost of heating, not its fractional part of the total, that is the important datum. H is wrong because the new design drastically reduced the cost of heating, and the design was accurately reflected in the actual building. J is wrong because there is no indication that further improvement is not possible.

27. **D** If the new design results in a much more expensive building, the difference in cost might not be made up in fuel savings. A is wrong because there are other considerations in the decision. B is wrong because the plan does, in fact, propose improved efficiency in hot water heating. C is wrong because this question cannot be answered until the building is actually built.

28. **G** This is a test of the time it takes for the eyes of the guppies to become light-adapted; using their ability to find food as a test assumes that they use their eyes to find it. F is wrong because no tests of rate of activity were made. H is wrong because the basic experiment (Experiment 2) did not vary temperature. J is wrong because no comparison with people is made.

29. **A** The only way to know when the guppies are fully light-adapted is to find out how well they locate their food when their eyes are known to be light-adapted.

30. **H** This is the basic experiment; when the guppies can find 33 *Daphnia* in 5 minutes, their eyes are light-adapted.

31. **B** In the dark, all other senses function, but the guppies had to wait for their eyes to become light-adapted in order to find food. A is wrong because Experiment 3 shows only that low temperatures interfere somehow. C is wrong because all the senses of the guppies are functioning in daylight, and there is no evidence to indicate which one is used in finding food. D is wrong because, although the statement is true, it would probably hold no matter how the guppies find their food.

32. **H** Experiment 2 established a baseline from which temperature variations could be made. F is wrong because the pertinent question is light adaptation. G is wrong because the adaptation of the *Daphnia* is not dealt with anywhere. J is wrong because the tanks were kept steadily at the prescribed temperatures.

33. **D** The rate of adaptation increased up to a temperature of 24° C, but not above that level. Any of the other choices would be a plausible explanation of the results.

34. **G** Both accept the data showing population changes, but Scientist 1 thinks he knows why it happens. Neither suggests that there is a general tendency for the dark form to dominate; Scientist 2 believes that the birds are not the answer because the experiments did not duplicate what happens in nature.

35. **A** Scientist 2 cites instances in which the frequency change has nothing to do with air quality, but does not rule out natural selection for other causes. Neither raises the question of whether the color is controlled by heredity. Scientist 2 finds that the camouflage against tree trunks is irrelevant.

36. **J** He finds the field study evidence convincing in this case, and this implies that the sample was large enough. No one raises the question of species or intermediate colors.

37. **D** This would provide an alternate explanation for changes in distribution of the color pattern. Dominance, selective mating, or clinal variation would not account for changes in frequency.

38. **G** Scientist 2 agrees that this happens, but contends that this has no significance for natural selection; he cites cases in which frequency shifts have nothing to do with bark color.

39. **B** If moths do not rest on bark in daylight, this part of the study is irrelevant. Scientist 2 did not suggest that other birds should be used, or that the color is not inherited. Other studies might represent different situations, but might not invalidate Scientist 1's position with regard to his study.

40. **G** Scientist 1 feels that the field studies have been convincing enough to validate his hypothesis, rejecting the opposing views of Scientist 2.

Essay Self-Assessment

Before evaluating your own essay, read pages 433–434 on the scoring of ACT essays. Then complete the following checklist. Focus on both the strengths and weaknesses of your essay.

	Yes!	Mostly	Hardly	No
Does the essay address the ACT prompt?	____	____	____	____
Is the topic sufficiently narrowed?	____	____	____	____
Is the essay's main idea clear?	____	____	____	____
Have you written an introduction?	____	____	____	____
Does the essay sound natural?	____	____	____	____
Have you used plain words?	____	____	____	____
Have you used precise language?	____	____	____	____
Does your essay have a clear focus?	____	____	____	____
Do all parts fit together coherently?	____	____	____	____
Is each sentence accurately worded?	____	____	____	____
Have you trimmed needless words?	____	____	____	____
Do you show more than tell?	____	____	____	____
Have you used active verbs?	____	____	____	____
Is the language fresh?	____	____	____	____
Do you include verbal surprises?	____	____	____	____
Are the sentences varied?	____	____	____	____
Is sentence length balanced?	____	____	____	____
Does the essay have a conclusion?	____	____	____	____
Is the essay mostly error-free?	____	____	____	____

Identify the three greatest strengths of your essay:

1)____

2) ____

3) ____

Name three specific things that you could do to improve your essay:

1)____

2) ____

3) ____

Circle the score your essay deserves: 6 5 4 3 2 1

Table for Calculating the Combined English/Writing Test Score

Instructions:

1. Find your Writing Test subscore (2–12) along the top of the table.
2. Find your English Test score on the left or right side.
3. Your combined score will appear in the table where the two scores intersect. For instance, a 10 on the Writing Test and a 25 on the English Test will yield a Combined English/Writing Test score of 26.

English Test Score	Writing Test Subscore											English Test Score
	2	3	4	5	6	7	8	9	10	11	12	
1	1	2	3	4	5	6	7	8	9	10	11	**1**
2	2	3	4	5	6	6	7	8	9	10	11	**2**
3	2	3	4	5	6	7	8	9	10	11	12	**3**
4	3	4	5	6	7	8	9	10	11	12	13	**4**
5	4	5	6	7	8	9	10	11	12	12	13	**5**
6	5	6	7	7	8	9	10	11	12	13	14	**6**
7	5	6	7	8	9	10	11	12	13	14	15	**7**
8	6	7	8	9	10	11	12	13	14	15	16	**8**
9	7	8	9	10	11	12	13	13	14	15	16	**9**
10	8	9	9	10	11	12	13	14	15	16	17	**10**
11	8	9	10	11	12	13	14	15	16	17	18	**11**
12	9	10	11	12	13	14	15	16	17	18	19	**12**
13	10	11	12	13	14	14	15	16	17	18	19	**13**
14	10	11	12	13	14	15	16	17	18	19	20	**14**
15	11	12	13	14	15	16	17	18	19	20	21	**15**
16	12	13	14	15	16	17	18	19	20	20	21	**16**
17	13	14	15	16	16	17	18	19	20	21	22	**17**
18	13	14	15	16	17	18	19	20	21	22	23	**18**
19	14	15	16	17	18	19	20	21	22	23	24	**19**
20	15	16	17	18	19	20	21	21	22	23	24	**20**
21	16	17	17	18	19	20	21	22	23	24	25	**21**
22	16	17	18	19	20	21	22	23	24	25	26	**22**
23	17	18	19	20	21	22	23	24	25	26	27	**23**
24	18	19	20	21	22	23	23	24	25	26	27	**24**
25	18	19	20	21	22	23	24	25	26	27	28	**25**
26	19	20	21	22	23	24	25	26	27	28	29	**26**
27	20	21	22	23	24	25	26	27	28	28	29	**27**
28	21	22	23	24	24	26	26	27	28	29	30	**28**

Table for Calculating the Combined English/Writing Test Score (cont.)

English Test Score	Writing Test Subscore 2	3	4	5	6	7	8	9	10	11	12	English Test Score
29	21	22	23	24	25	26	27	28	29	30	31	**29**
30	22	23	24	25	26	27	28	29	30	31	32	**30**
31	23	24	25	26	27	28	29	30	30	31	32	**31**
32	24	25	25	26	27	28	29	30	31	32	33	**32**
33	25	25	26	27	28	29	30	31	32	33	34	**33**
34	26	26	27	28	29	30	31	32	33	34	35	**34**
35	26	27	28	28	30	31	31	32	33	34	35	**35**
36	26	27	28	29	30	31	32	33	34	35	36	**36**

Calculating Your Combined English/Writing Test Score

English Test Score _____

Essay Score ___ multiply by 2 = _____

Combined Score (See table): _____

Acknowledgments

Passage: Washington Irving, "Buckthorne," *Tales of a Traveller*, reprinted in Library of America, 1991, pp. 500–502.

Passage: *Stuttering: Hope Through Research*, U.S. Department of Health and Human Services, National Institutes of Health Publication 81-2250, GPO, 1981.

Passage: Mario Pei, "Wanted: A World Language," Public Affairs Committee, New York, 1969.

Passage: Rachel Carson, "The Sunless Seas," *The Sea Around Us*, Oxford University Press, 1989.

Passage: Willa Cather, *One of Ours*, Alfred A. Knopf, 1922, reprinted in *Willa Cather: Early Novels and Stories*, Library of America, 1987, pp. 1061–1062.

Passage: Walter Wessels, *Economics*, Barron's Business Review Series, Barron's Educational Series, 1987.

Passage: William Sims Bainbridge, *Sociology*, Barron's Educational Series, 1997, pp. 26–27.

Passage: Robert J. Hanyok, Review of Michael S. Sweeney, *Secrets of Victory*, Study of Intelligence, *Journal of American Intelligence Professional*, 2002.

Passage: Peter Coolsen, *et al,* "When School's Out and Nobody's Home," National Committee for Prevention of Child Abuse, Chicago, 1986.

Passage: Harriet de Onis, "Introduction to Miguel de Cervantes," *Six Exemplary Novels*, Barron's Educational Series.

Passage: Simon Wilson, *Pop*, Barron's Educational Series, 1978.

Passage: Arnold Sungaard, "Jazz, Hot and Cold," *Essays for Modern Youth,* Globe Book Company, 1960.

Passage: "Groundwater: A Community Action Guide," Concern, Inc., Washington, D.C., June 1984.

Passage: "The Cytoskeleton, the Cell's Physical Props," *Inside the Cell,* U.S. Department of Health and Human Services, Public Health Services, National Institutes of Health, NIH Publication No. 90-1050, p. 41.

Passage: *Whale Fishery of New England*, William S. Sullwold Publishing, Taunton, Massachusetts, 1968.

Passage: "The Possibility of Intelligent Life in the Universe," U.S. House of Representatives, Report for the Committee on Science and Technology, GPO, Washington, D.C.

Passage: Albert Szent-Gyorgi, "Horizons of Life Sciences," *Ideas in Science*, Oscar H. Fidell, ed., Washington Square Press, 1966, pp. 167–169.

Passage: Joachim Miller, "An Old Oregonian in the Snow," *The World Begins Here: An Anthology of Oregon Short Fiction*, ed., Oregon State University Press, Corvallis, 1993, pp. 38–40.

Passage: Henry G. Cisneros, "Searching for Home: Mentally Ill Homeless People in America," U.S. Department of Housing and Urban Development, Washington, D.C., 1997.

Passage: Caroline Kim, "Tales of Beggars and Nuns, Pirates and Kings," *Humanities*, May/June 2002, National Endowment for the Humanities.

Passage: Helene L. Baldwin and C. L. McGuiness, *A Primer on Ground Water,* U.S. Department of Interior Geological Ground Survey, Washington, D.C., 1963.

Passage: Joseph Conrad, "Gaspar Ruiz: A Romantic Tale," *The Complete Short Fiction of Joseph Conrad*, Volume I, The Ecco Press (NY, 1991), pp. 239–242.

Passage: Carla R. Morrisey, "The Influenza Epidemic of 1918," United States Department of the Navy, Washington, D.C., 2005.

Passage: "Health Effects of Caffeine." Printed with permission of American Council on Science and Health, *www.acsh.org*.

Passage: "Characteristics of the Abusive Situation," *Guide to Legal Relief*, Governor's Commission on Domestic Violence, New York, October, 1984.

Passage: William Sims Bainbridge, "1940: The Invasion from Mars," *Sociology*, Barron's Educational Series, 1997, pp. 156–158.

Passage: Paulette W. Campbell, "Ancestral Bones: Reinterpreting the Past of the Omaha," *Humanities*, November/December 2002, National Endowment for the Humanities.

Passage: Mark Twain, *Life on the Mississippi* (1883) "The River and Its History," reprinted in *The Family Mark Twain*, Harper and Bros., 1935, pp. 5–6.

Index

NOTES

NOTES

THE FOLLOWING DOCUMENTATION APPLIES IF YOU PURCHASED
ACT, 17th Edition **with CD-ROM.**

How to Use the CD-ROM

The software is not installed on your computer; it runs directly from the CD-ROM. Barron's CD-ROM includes an "autorun" feature that automatically launches the application when the CD is inserted into the CD-ROM drive. In the unlikely event that the autorun feature is disabled, follow the manual launching instructions below.

Windows®

1. Click on the Start button and choose "My Computer" or "Computer."
2. Double-click on the CD-ROM drive, which will be named **ACT.exe**.
3. Double-click **ACT.exe** to launch the program.

MAC®

1. Double-click the CD-ROM icon.
2. Double-click the **ACT** icon to start the program.

SYSTEM REQUIREMENTS

(Flash Player 10.2 is recommended)

Windows®
Intel® Pentium® II 450MHz,
AMD Athlon® 600MHz
or faster processor (or equivalent)
Windows XP, Vista, Windows 7
128 MB of available RAM
CD-ROM drive
1024 × 768 color display

MAC®
Intel Core™ Duo 1.33GHz
or faster processor
MAC OS X 10.4 or higher
CD-ROM drive
1024 × 768 color display